T3-BRK-460

READER IN POLITICAL SOCIOLOGY

Edited by F R A N K L I N D E N F E L D

FUNK & WAGNALLS NEW YORK

·Third Printing

Copyright © 1968 by Frank Lindenfeld
All Rights Reserved.

Library of Congress Catalog Card Number: 67–28159
Published by Funk & Wagnalls, *A Division of*
Reader's Digest Books, Inc.

Printed in the United States of America

ROBERT R. ALFORD, "Stratification and Politics in the Anglo-American Countries." Reprinted from a paper read at an ISA Meeting, Washington, D. C., September 1962, by permission of the author.

DAVID E. APTER, "Ideology and Discontent." Reprinted from David E. Apter, *Ideology and Discontent* (Copyright © 1964, The Free Press of Glencoe, a Division of The Macmillan Company), by permission of The Free Press of Glencoe.

HANNAH ARENDT, "Totalitarianism in Power." Reprinted from *The Origins of Totalitarianism* (Copyright © 1951, 1958, 1966, Hannah Arendt), by permission of Harcourt, Brace & World, Inc., George Allen & Unwin, Ltd., and the author.

DANIEL BELL, "The End of Ideology in the West." Reprinted from Daniel Bell, *The End of Ideology in the West* (Copyright © 1960, The Free Press), by permission of The Macmillan Company.

REINHARD BENDIX AND SEYMOUR MARTIN LIPSET, "The Field of Political Sociology." Reprinted from *Current Sociology* (1957), Vol. 6, No. 2, by permission of *Current Sociology* and the authors.

CRANE BRINTON, "Anatomy of Revolution." Reprinted from Crane Brinton, *Anatomy of Revolution* (Copyright © 1952, Prenctice-Hall, Inc.), by permission of Prentice-Hall, Inc.

RALF DAHRENDORF, "Recent Changes in the Class Structure of European Societies." Reprinted from *Daedalus* (Winter 1964), by permission of *Daedalus* and The American Academy of Arts and Sciences.

JAMES C. DAVIES, "Toward a Theory of Revolution." Reprinted from *American Sociological Review* (February 1962), by permission of The American Sociological Association and the author.

HARRY ECKSTEIN, "A Theory of Stable Democracy." Reprinted from Harry Eckstein, *Division and Cohesion in Democracy; A Study of Norway* (Copyright © 1966, Princeton University Press), by permission of Princeton University Press.

FRANTZ FANON, "The Wretched of the Earth." Reprinted from *The Wretched of the Earth*, translated from the French by Constance-Farrington (Copyright ©

1963, Présence Africaine; Copyright 1961, François Maspera, Editeur S.A.R.L.),
by permission of Grove Press, Inc., and MacGibbon and Kee, Ltd.

PAUL GOODMAN, "Drawing the Line." Reprinted from *Drawing the Line* (Copyright 1946, Paul Goodman), by permission of Random House, Inc.; "On Getting
Into Power." Reprinted from *Liberation* (October 1962) and Paul Goodman
(ed.), *Seeds of Liberation* (Copyright 1964 by *Liberation*), by permission of
Liberation.

ROBERT A. HABER, "The End of Ideology as Ideology." Reprinted from Robert
A. Haber, *Our Generation* (November 1966), by permission of the author.

IRVING LOUIS HOROWITZ, "Three Worlds of Development." Reprinted from *Three
Worlds of Development* (Copyright © 1966, Irving L. Horowitz), by permission
of Oxford University Press, Inc.

SAMUEL P. HUNTINGTON, "Political Development and Decay." Reprinted from
World Politics (April 1965) by permission of Princeton University Press.

PAUL JACOBS AND SAUL LANDAU, "The New Radicals." Reprinted from *The New
Radicals* (© Copyright 1966 by Paul Jacobs and Saul Landau), by permission
of Random House, Inc., Cyrilly Abels, and the authors.

JUAN LINZ, "An Authoritarian Regime: Spain." Reprinted from Erik Allardt and
Yrzo Littunen (eds.), *Cleavages, Ideologies and Party Systems*, by permission of
the author.

SEYMOUR MARTIN LIPSET, "Some Social Requisites of Democracy." Reprinted
from *American Political Science Review* (March 1959), by permission of the
copyright holder, the American Political Science Association, and of the author.

WILLIAM KORNHAUSER, "Mass Society and Democratic Order." Reprinted from
William Kornhauser, *Politics of Mass Society* (Copyright © 1959, The Free
Press), by permission of The Macmillan Company; "Political Vulnerability of
Mass Society." Reprinted from William Kornhauser, *The Politics of Mass Society* (Copyright © 1959, The Free Press), by permission of The Macmillan
Company; "Power Elite or Veto Groups." Reprinted from Seymour Lipset and
Leo Lowenthal (eds.), *Culture and Social Character* (Copyright © 1961, The
Free Press), by permission of The Macmillan Company.

FRANK LINDENFELD, "If Not Now, When?" Reprinted by permission of the
Manas Publishing Company and the author; "Voluntarism and Politics." Reprinted from *Anarchy* (November 1966), by permission of *Anarchy* and the
author.

ERRICO MALATESTA, "Anarchy." Reprinted from the pamphlet "Anarchy" by
Errico Malatesta, by permission of Freedom Press.

HERBERT MARCUSE, "The Closing of the Political Universe." Reprinted from *One-Dimensional Man* (Copyright © 1964, Herbert Marcuse), by permission of The
Beacon Press.

KARL MARX AND FREDERICK ENGELS, "The Communist Manifesto." Reprinted from Karl Marx and Frederick Engels, *The Communist Manifesto* (Copyright 1948, International Publishers Co., Inc.), by permission of International Publishers Co., Inc.

ROBERT MICHELS, "The Iron Law of Oligarchy." Reprinted from *Political Parties* (1959) by permission of Dover Publications, Inc.

C. WRIGHT MILLS, "Liberal Values in the Modern World." Reprinted from I. L. Horowitz (ed.), *Power, Politics and People: The Collected Essays of C. Wright Mills* (Copyright © 1963, the Estate of C. Wright Mills), by permission of Oxford University Press, Inc.; "On Politics." Reprinted from C. Wright Mills, *The Sociological Imagination* (Copyright © 1959 by Oxford University Press, Inc.), by permission of Oxford University Press, Inc.; "The Power Elite." Reprinted from A. Kornhauser (ed.), *Problems of Power in American Democracy* (Copyright © 1957 by Wayne State University Press), by permission of Wayne State University Press.

BARRINGTON MOORE, JR., "Notes on the Process of Acquiring Power." Reprinted from Barrington Moore, Jr., *Political Power and Social Theory* (Copyright © 1958, The President and Fellows of Harvard College), by permission of Harvard University Press; "Sociological Theory and Contemporary Politics." Reprinted from *American Journal of Sociology* (September 1965), by permission of The University of Chicago Press.

FRANZ NEUMANN, "Approaches to the Study of Political Power." Reprinted from *Political Science Quarterly* (June 1950), Vol. LXV, No. 2, by permission of *Political Science Quarterly*.

MARC PILISUK AND THOMAS HAYDEN, "Is There a Military-Industrial Complex Which Prevents Peace?" originally published in *Journal of Social Issues* (July 1965), Vol. XXI, No. 3. Reprinted from M. Pilisuk and R. Perrucci (eds.), *The Triple Revolution: Social Problems in Depth* (Little, Brown, 1968) (Copyright © The Society for the Psychological Study of Social Issues), by permission of Marc Pilisuk.

BERTRAND RUSSELL, "Marx and Socialist Doctrine." Reprinted from *Roads to Freedom* (Copyright © 1965, Bertrand Russell), by permission of George Allen & Unwin, Ltd., Barnes & Noble, Inc., and the author.

KRISHNALAL SHRIDHARANI, "War Without Violence." Reprinted from Krishnalal Shridharani, *War Without Violence* (Copyright 1962 by Mrs. Sundari K. Shridharani), by permission of Bharatiya Vidya Bhavan and Mrs. Sundari K. Shridharani.

ALEXIS DE TOCQUEVILLE, "Despotism in Democratic Nations." Reprinted from *Democracy in America*, Phillips Bradley (trans.) (Copyright 1945 by Alfred A. Knopf, Inc.), by permission of the publisher.

LIBRARY
ALMA COLLEGE
ALMA, MICHIGAN

CONTENTS

PREFACE

We humans are a funny and tragic species. As I write this preface the armed conflict between Arabs and Israelis has temporarily stopped; the American war of intervention in Vietnam continues. By the time of publication, there may well be another war, and nobody knows when one of these will escalate into World War III. Well-fed American college students sit in pleasant lecture halls while in another part of the world Vietnamese peasants are burned alive. We ask why, why, why? Why are some men and nations rich while others are poor? How long will the "wretched of the earth" stand for their misery? And what can we do?

The purpose of this collection of readings is to try to provide for the student some basis for answers to the insistent political questions of our era. It is my hope that with greater understanding people will be able to confront and change the social reality that surrounds them, to make it a better environment for human beings.

The introductory section of this Reader is concerned largely with the value bases of political sociology. Frequently, there is little dispute as to the "facts"; the real controversy lies in the interpretation of the meaning of those "facts." Further, the very theories one begins with determine which facts one is looking for, and which one considers to be important.

Intellectual questions stem from value premises and emotional biases. Thus we must not stop with mere intellect and rationality; we must ask what kind of values they are harnessed to. For armies are rational; napalm, fragmentation, and hydrogen bombs are rational; concentration camps are rational. But intellect must be rejoined to humane emotions and values. We must allow ourselves to *feel* the revulsion against these things, because that is what distinguishes us from computers and robots. And the wholesome fusion of intellect and emotion based on human values can generate the energy with which to build a better society.

The focus of this Reader is on the consequences of the trends toward bureaucratization and rationalization of life within the technologically advanced societies. We are steadily moving toward a world of functional rationality ("I was only obeying orders"), and away from substantial rationality, i.e., modes of thinking that show "intelligent insight into the inter-relations of events."[1] The classical writers of the nineteenth and early twentieth century— men like Marx, Weber, de Tocqueville and Michels—were likewise concerned with these trends. Thus the introductory section of this Reader deals also with the relationship of these classical writers to contemporary political sociology.

The main part of the Reader is organized into four sections. Part One deals with the social bases of political systems. The selections in it relate to the social conditions of democracy, authoritarianism and totalitarianism; a few of the selections deal with anti-democratic tendencies in democracies.

Part Two concerns the relationship between social class and political power in the Anglo-American and western European countries. The selections in Chapter 5 examine the existence of class conflict and its relationship to politics. The next chapter consists of several articles on the question of whether there is an American power elite.

Part Three deals with politics and social change. The selections in Chapter 7 concern political movements; included there is some material on the contemporary American "New Left." Beginning with a selection from Michels, the following chapter traces out the inevitable dilemmas of political parties, their oligarchical tendencies, and the problems of modifying programs and compromising in order to achieve power. Chapter 9 focuses on revolution and the question of the place of violence.

The final part of the Reader is devoted to an examination of

[1] Karl Mannheim, *Man and Society in an Age of Reconstruction* (New York, Harcourt, Brace & Co., 1940), p. 52 *ff.*

the contemporary relevance of political ideology. It begins with a chapter on what has come to be known as the Third World. At least to many of the more educated inhabitants of these countries, socialism and nationalism are very relevant today. Included in this chapter is a selection from Fanon's *Wretched of the Earth,* which shows how things look from the standpoint of the "natives." This is followed by an all too brief chapter on Marxism. Chapter 12 takes up the question of the relevance of liberalism, and the question of whether ideology is "dead" in the West. The final chapter consists of two selections by anarchist writers. Anarchism is one of the strands of ideology found in the contemporary American New Left—it is an ideology that I personally tend to share. The rediscovery of anarchism has developed as one alternative to the warfare-welfare state—the utopian conceptions of the hippies seem increasingly relevant as we move closer to "1984." Such ideals are "impossible" of course, but then the other alternatives seem even more so.

Some areas of contemporary research in political sociology are omitted in this Reader. I have chosen to focus on studies that deal with entire societies, and have therefore not included studies of more limited scope. For example, in the section on power I have left out studies of "local" power structures. The largest omission is of voting and other behavior studies. In part, these studies are not included because I feel that many of them are not addressed to very important questions; also, there are already a number of good collections of behavioral research.[2]

A number of people have made valuable suggestions concerning the contents of this Reader; these include Otto Feinstein, Jim Jacobs, William Kornhauser, Seymour Martin Lipset, and Juan J. Linz. I have not always followed their good advice, partly because of space limitations and partly because of my stubbornness; thus, I must take responsibility for the shortcomings of this collection.

This book would not have been produced without the valuable assistance of my friend Paul Thaxter.

[2] See Heinz Eulau *et al., Political Behavior* (Glencoe, Free Press, 1956); Nelson Polsby *et al., Politics and Social Life* (Boston, Houghton Mifflin, 1963); Sidney Ulmer, *Introductory Readings in Political Behavior* (Chicago, Rand McNally, 1961).

INTRODUCTION

EDITOR'S INTRODUCTION / Some Contemporary Approaches to Political Sociology*

At least three major approaches may be found in the work of contemporary political sociologists: behavioral, correlational, and evolutionary. Obviously, this is an arbitrary classification which overlooks "mixed" strategies, but it should help to place in better perspective a number of the selections in this Reader.

Behaviorists concern themselves with the sentiments and actions of individuals, what makes them vote the way they do, what social backgrounds they come from, etc. Those who use the correlational approach are more concerned with group properties than with those of individuals. Using a sample of nation states, for example, they look for correlations between social and political variables. Evolutionists, in contrast, are more concerned with changes within a given historical political system—how that system undergoes modifications which may result in the emergence of a new type of political system. This is the style in which such writers as Marx and Weber worked.

The different approaches lend themselves to answering somewhat different kinds of questions. The choice of research strategy depends in part on what one is trying to find out. This is one of the themes in the selection from Mills included in this chapter.

The behavioral approach: The behavioral outlook implies a psychological approach to politics, in which individuals are the units of analysis. To a great extent, the work of the students of voting at Columbia University and at the University of Michigan has had this character.[1] Some of the most thoughtful use of be-

---

* Adapted from a chapter in the author's book *Politics and Society*, to be published by the Van Nostrand Co.
[1] Among the books representative of this approach are: Angus Campbell

havioral data can be seen in the work of Lipset.[2] As Bendix and Lipset point out in the selection included below, studies of voting behavior can shed light on such matters as strength of class conciousness and "false" consciousness, and the sources of social support for political movements and parties.

One of the best recent discussions of the behavioral point of view is that of Eulau.[3] The main emphasis of this approach is on why individuals behave as they do. This approach explains social events aggregated in terms of characteristics and actions of individuals.

There are some serious deficiencies in the behavioral approach, however. Perhaps the chief difficulties are that it is a historical and neglects social structure. It focuses on the milieux of individuals and thus leads to explanations of social events in terms of individual psychology or psychopathology. Insofar as it is based on public-opinion polls, the behavioral approach ignores questions of social power. It is important to understand the impact of occupants of certain key institutional positions on public opinion. Political leaders *initiate* policies; the masses *react* one way or another to those policies.

Surely human emotions and personalities play a part in the genesis of such phenomena as war, but to eliminate wars should we concentrate on trying to improve the stereotypes that the masses in one nation hold about those of another? Or should we instead focus on the images held by key political and other leaders, on the relative power of the military within a nation, and on the existence of an international arms race?

Mills puts the matter well in discussing the difference between private troubles and public issues. Private troubles are those things that pertain to an individual's immediate milieu; public issues deal with matters that transcend such individual milieux:

---

et al., The American Voter (New York, Wiley, 1960); the report on the Elmira study by Bernard Berelson *et al., Voting* (Chicago, University of Chicago Press, 1954); and the pioneering book by Paul Lazarsfeld *et al., The People's Choice*, rev. ed. (New York, Columbia University Press, 1948).

[2] See for example, Seymour Martin Lipset, *Political Man* (New York, Doubleday, 1960), Chaps. 6–8.

[3] See Heinz Eulau, *The Behavioral Persuasion in Politics* (New York, Random House, 1963).

> Consider unemployment. When, in a city of 100,000, only one man is unemployed, that is his personal trouble. . . . But when in a nation of 50 million employees, 15 million men are unemployed, that is an issue . . . both the correct statement of the problem and the range of possible solutions require us to consider the economic and political institutions of the society, and not merely the personal situation and character of a scatter of individuals.[4]

Voting and other behavioral studies are omitted from this Reader. In part, this is because I agree that many of them are addressed to questions of secondary importance, and also because there are already a number of good collections of behavioral research.[5]

The correlational approach: In contrast to the behavioral outlook, the correlational approach concerns itself with the characteristics of whole societies. This is a macroscopic approach, which depends on some kind of classification of political systems.

Its general procedure is to collect data on the social correlates of different political systems, on the assumption that the coexistence of certain types of political systems with certain types of social conditions indicates a causal link between the two. Usually, a typology of governments is set up, and the types of social conditions that tend to exist within each type are identified. Alternatively, a typology of social conditions is constructed, and types of political systems found in each are identified.

This approach lends itself to cross national studies. But it has several drawbacks. One is the very real difficulty of trying to compare political systems that may be embedded in very dissimilar cultural contexts. Can one compare a "democratic vote" in a country where both opinion leaders and followers get many ideas about politics from newspapers and television, with the ballot in a country where peasants ask their landlords how to vote? Fur-

---

[4] See C. Wright Mills, *Sociological Imagination* (New York, Grove Press, 1961), pp. 8–9. See also the selection from Mills on the Power Elite in Chapter 6 of this Reader.
[5] See Heinz Eulau *et al., Political Behavior* (Glencoe, Ill., The Free Press, 1956); Nelson Polsby *et al., Politics and Social Life* (Boston, Houghton Mifflin, 1963); Sidney Ulmer, *Introductory Readings in Political Behavior* (Chicago, Rand McNally, 1961).

ther, this strategy focuses attention on the statics of politics, and thus is less suitable for developing an understanding of how one type of political system changes into another.

If there is to be such a thing as a science of politics which cuts across time and space, the correlational method (in spite of its difficulties) is the one most likely to lead to it. In any event, a descriptive, classificatory strategy may advance our understanding of political institutions, since the first step toward understanding often lies in accurate description. Typical of this approach is the work of Kornhauser who analyzes the political implications of the existence of voluntary associations in a society, and examines mass society as a social condition facilitating the rise of totalitarian movements.[6] Another good illustration may be found in the work of Lipset, who traces the correlation between such factors as economic development and democracy.[7]

The evolutionary approach: Essential to the evolutionary point of view is its concern with history. This approach does not necessarily neglect the individual, but studies him in the context of historical social structures. Marx, for example, was concerned with the problems of the evolution of Western societies from feudalism, through capitalism, and into what he hoped was a period of socialism. He tried to point out the specific contradictions within the capitalist order that were making the development of socialism natural and inevitable. Mistaken though he may have been in many of his particular predictions, we have much to learn from his general methods and style.

Contemporary social scientists, both Barrington Moore and the late C. Wright Mills favor the historical concerns of the nineteenth-century writers over the behavioral or correlational methodologies currently in vogue.

Mills criticizes other contemporary social scientists for asking the wrong kinds of questions. In the search for invariant social regularities that cut across time and space, either they focus on high-level theory divorced from social and cultural context, or they get involved in tracing minute empirical facts which gen-

[6] See the selections by Kornhauser in Chapters 4 and 7 of this Reader.
[7] See the selection by Lipset in Chapter 2 of this Reader.

erally do not help us to understand the important social phenomena.[8]

Moore's criticisms of sociology are similar to those of Mills.
Moore points out that not only did nineteenth-century writers
have a strong historical perspective, but their stance often involved a value position which was critical of the existing social
order. The technical virtuosity of social science today has been
gained at the expense of content:

> The fact that we do not yet have any laws in social science
> comparable to those in the natural sciences does not in itself
> prove that such laws will never be discovered. Nevertheless, it
> justifies raising once more the question whether social science is
> on the right track in making the search for such laws its chief
> *raison d'être* ... The logical structure of the kinds of knowledge
> we seek in the social sciences may not be identical with that in the
> advanced natural sciences. ...
>
> Above all, we must not make the mistake of thinking that some
> universal necessity inheres in social relationships that are limited
> to a particular historical epoch, such as capitalism, or for that
> matter, socialism ...[9]

Moore criticizes the correlational approach because it ignores
the reality of historical trends. It merely examines similarities and
differences of various political systems in the hope of formulating
scientific laws. As Moore points out, the use of history as a store-
house of samples starts from the assumption that historical facts
are separate units, instead of being connected with one another
over time. Thus, the investigator who starts out with a set of
categories such as democracy and dictatorship might miss the
manner by which a system may become transformed from one
type to the other.

Is history merely a random process, and are we left with only
unique historical events to consider? Or is there an actual historical process? Moore suggests that the evolutionary perspective may

---

8 See Mills, *op. cit.*, and the article by Mills in this chapter of the Reader.
9 See Barrington Moore, Jr., *Political Power and Social Theory* (New York,
Harper, 1965), pp. 127–131. See also the selection by Moore which is included
in the first part of this Reader.

enable us to understand historical change. We need not assume that all societies must pass through a particular series of stages, but it may be possible to identify a number of alternative chains of evolution.

Thus, to understand the ways in which a given society may develop in the future, Moore suggests that we look at it in the present, and that we examine the straws in the wind, the seeds of change already at work. In many ways, this is precisely Marx's dialectical method which assumes that the future shape of any society is presaged by the contradictions within a given stage of its historical development.

To hold to an evolutionary approach does not necessarily mean that one must also be a historical determinist. The future is *not inevitably* determined by the past. As a matter of fact, it is the task of the social scientist to point out the possible dangers to which certain current trends may lead; timely action may indeed avoid such dangers and change the outcome. By pointing to the range of possible alternatives and to the consequences of present patterns, social scientists can help to widen the range of social choices that are seen as available. In this way they may make it more possible for the members of a society to consciously shape their own future history.

The final two selections in the introductory section of this Reader were included for somewhat different reasons. The piece by Neumann illustrates the vital relationship between sociology and value perspectives. It serves also as a useful introduction to the study of power.

Neumann's discussion of power provides a good explanation of the political consequences of the growing complexity of advanced industrial societies. His generalization that "the significance of persuasion grows with the growing complexity of society" helps us to see why a modern totalitarianism based more on propaganda and conformity than on concentration camps is increasingly possible.

Some of Neumann's other generalizations may help to set the problem of the existence of power elites in better perspective. He maintains that the higher the state of technological development:

the greater the concentration of political power, the greater the significance of political power in the social process, and the greater the independence of political power from social power. The latter seems to me to be especially true in the socialist countries; as applied to capitalist societies such as the United States, it would cast some doubt on the existence of a unified power elite.

Better than any introduction that I could write is the piece by Bendix and Lipset. Their essay presents the major concerns of the classical writers of the nineteenth and early twentieth century and shows how contemporary political sociology has been influenced by and carries on this classical tradition. The concern of political sociology with such matters as class conflict, bureaucracy, anti-democratic tendencies in democratic organizations and societies, etc. can be traced back to de Tocqueville, Marx, Weber, Michels. My own feeling is that it would be a good thing for political sociologists to return even more to the concerns of these classical writers, and to abandon the fads that Mills labeled as "abstracted empiricism" and "grand theory." Hopefully, this Reader can contribute to the process.

1 / POLITICAL SOCIOLOGY, VALUES, AND THE CLASSICAL TRADITION

C. WRIGHT MILLS / On Politics*

There is no necessity for working social scientists to allow the political meaning of their work to be shaped by the "accidents" of its setting, or its use to be determined by the purposes of other men. It is quite within their powers to discuss its meanings and decide upon its uses as matters of their own policy. To a considerable, and largely untested, extent, they can influence or even determine these policies. Such determination requires that they make explicit judgments, as well as decisions upon theory, method, and fact. As matters of policy, these judgments are the proper concern of the individual scholar as well as of the fraternity. Yet is it not evident that implicit moral and political judgments have much more influence than explicit discussions of personal and professional policy? Only by making these influences matters of debated policy can men become fully aware of them, and so try to control their effects upon the work of social science and upon its political meaning.

There is no way in which any social scientist can avoid assum-

* From C. Wright Mills, *The Sociological Imagination* (New York, Oxford University Press, 1959), pp. 177–194. Some of the original footnotes and portions of the original chapter have been omitted.

ing choices of value and implying them in his work as a whole. Problems, like issues and troubles, concern threats to expected values, and cannot be clearly formulated without acknowledgment of those values. Increasingly, research is used, and social scientists are used, for bureaucratic and ideological purposes. This being so, as individuals and as professionals, students of man and society face such questions as: whether they are aware of the uses and values of their work, whether these may be subject to their own control, whether they want to seek to control them. How they answer these questions, or fail to answer them, and how they use or fail to use the answers in their work and in their professional lives determine their answer to the final question: whether in their work as social scientists they are (*a*) morally autonomous, (*b*) subject to the morality of other men, or (*c*) morally adrift. . . .

I

Men are free to make history, but some men are much freer than others. Such freedom requires access to the means of decisions and of power by which history may now be made. It is not always so made; in the following, I am speaking only of the contemporary period in which the means of history-making power have become so enlarged and so centralized. It is with reference to this period that I am contending that if men do not make history, they tend increasingly to become the utensils of history-makers and also the mere objects of history-making.

How large a role any explicit decisions do play in the making of history is itself an historical problem. It depends very much upon the means of power that are available at any given time in any given society. In some societies, the innumerable actions of innumerable men modify their milieux, and so gradually modify the structure itself. These modifications are the course of history; history is drift, although in total "men make it." Thus, innumerable entrepreneurs and innumerable consumers, by ten thousand decisions per minute, may shape and reshape the free-market economy. Perhaps this was the chief kind of limitation Marx had in mind when he wrote, in *The 18th Brumaire:* "Men make their own history, but they do not make it just as they please; they do not make it under circumstances chosen by themselves. . . ."

Fate, or "inevitability," has to do with events in history that are beyond the control of any circle or group of men having three characteristics: (1) compact enough to be identifiable, (2) powerful enough to decide with consequence, and (3) in a position to foresee these consequences and so to be held accountable for them. Events, according to this conception, are the summary and unintended results of innumerable decisions of innumerable men. Each of their decisions is minute in consequence and subject to cancellation or reinforcement by other such decisions. There is no link between any one man's intention and the summary result of the innumerable decisions. Events are beyond human decisions: History is made behind men's backs.

So conceived, fate is not a universal fact; it is not inherent in the nature of history or in the nature of man. Fate is a feature of an historically specific kind of social structure. In a society in which the ultimate weapon is the rifle; in which the typical economic unit is the family-farm and the small shop; in which the national-state does not yet exist or is merely a distant framework; in which communication is by word-of-mouth, handbill, pulpit— in *such a* society, history is indeed fate.

But consider now, the major clue to our condition: Is it not, in a word, the enormous enlargement and the decisive centralization of all the means of power and decision, which is to say—all the means of history-making? In modern industrial society, the facilities of economic production are developed and centralized—as peasants and artisans are replaced by private corporations and government industries. In the modern nation-state, the means of violence and of political administration undergo similar developments—as kings control nobles, and self-equipped knights are replaced by standing armies and now by fearful military machines. The *post-modern* climax of all three developments—in economics, in politics, and in violence—is now occurring most dramatically in the United States and the U.S.S.R. In our time, international as well as national means of history-making are being centralized. Is it not thus clear that the scope and the chance for conscious human agency in history-making is just now uniquely available? Elites of power in charge of these means do now make history—to be sure, "under circumstances not of their own choosing"—but compared to other men and other epochs, these circumstances themselves certainly do not appear to be overwhelming.

Surely this is the paradox of our immediate situation: The facts about the newer means of history-making are a signal that men are not necessarily in the grip of fate, that men *can* now make history. But this fact is made ironic by the further fact that just now those ideologies which offer men the hope of making history have declined and are collapsing in the Western societies. That collapse is also the collapse of the expectations of The Enlightenment, that reason and freedom would come to prevail as paramount forces in human history. And behind it there is also the intellectual and political default of the intellectual community.

Where is the intelligentsia that is carrying on the big discourse of the Western world *and* whose work as intellectuals is influential among parties and publics and relevant to the great decisions of our time? Where are the mass media open to such men? Who among those who are in charge of the two-party state and its ferocious military machines are alert to what goes on in the world of knowledge and reason and sensibility? Why is the free intellect so divorced from decisions of power? Why does there now prevail among men of power such a higher and irresponsible ignorance?

In the United States today, intellectuals, artists, ministers, scholars, and scientists are fighting a cold war in which they echo and elaborate the confusions of officialdoms. They neither raise demands on the powerful for alternative policies, nor set forth such alternatives before publics. They do not try to put responsible content into the politics of the United States; they help to empty politics and to keep it empty. What must be called the Christian default of the clergy is as much a part of this sorry moral condition as is the capture of scientists by nationalist Science-Machines. The journalistic lie, become routine, is part of it too; and so is much of the pretentious triviality that passes for social science.

II

Regardless of the scope of his awareness, the social scientist is usually a professor, and this occupational fact very much determines what he is able to do. As a professor, he addresses students, and on occasion, by speeches and by writings, publics of larger scale and more strategic position. In discussing what his public role may be, let us stick close to these simple facts of power, or if you like, to the facts of his powerlessness.

In so far as he is concerned with liberal, that is to say liberating, education, his public role has two goals: What he ought to do for the individual is to turn personal troubles and concerns into social issues and problems open to reason—his aim is to help the individual become a self-educating man, who only then would be reasonable and free. What he ought to do for the society is to combat all those forces which are destroying genuine publics and creating a mass society—or put as a positive goal, his aim is to help build and to strengthen self-cultivating publics. Only then might society be reasonable and free.

These are very large goals, and I must explain them in a slightly indirect way. We are concerned with skills and with values. Among "skills," however, some are more and some are less relevant to the tasks of liberation. I do not believe that skills and values can be so easily separated as in our search for "neutral skills" we often assume. It is a matter of degree, with skills at one extreme and values at the other. But in the middle ranges of this scale, there are what I shall call sensibilities, and it is these which should interest us most. To train someone to operate a lathe or to read and write is in large part a training of skill; to help someone decide what he really wants out of his life, or to debate with him Stoic, Christian, and Humanist ways of living, is a cultivation or an education of values.

Alongside skill and value, we ought to put sensibility, which includes them both, and more besides: it includes a sort of therapy in the ancient sense of clarifying one's knowledge of self. It includes the cultivation of all those skills of controversy with oneself that we call thinking, and which, when engaged in with others, we call debate. An educator must begin with what interests the individual most deeply, even if it seems altogether trivial and cheap. He must proceed in such a way and with such materials as to enable the student to gain increasingly rational insight into these concerns, and into others he will acquire in the process of his education. And the educator must try to develop men and women who can and who will by themselves continue what he has begun: the end product of any liberating education is simply the self-educating, self-cultivating man and woman; in short, the free and rational individual.

A society in which such individuals are ascendant is, by one major meaning of the word, democratic. Such a society may also be defined as one in which genuine publics rather than masses prevail. By this, I mean the following:

Whether or not they are aware of them, men in a mass society are gripped by personal troubles which they are not able to turn into social issues. They do not understand the interplay of these personal troubles of their milieux with problems of social structure. The knowledgeable man in a genuine public, on the other hand, is able to do just that. He understands that what he thinks and feels to be personal troubles are very often also problems shared by others, and more importantly, not capable of solution by any one individual but only by modifications of the structure of the groups in which he lives and sometimes the structure of the entire society. Men in masses have troubles, but they are not usually aware of their true meaning and source; men in public confront issues, and they usually come to be aware of their public terms.

It is the political task of the social scientist—as of any liberal educator—continually to translate personal troubles into public issues, and public issues into the terms of their human meaning for a variety of individuals. It is his task to display in his work—and, as an educator, in his life as well—this kind of sociological imagination. And it is his purpose to cultivate such habits of mind among the men and women who are publicly exposed to him. To secure these ends is to secure reason and individuality, and to make these the predominant values of a democratic society.

You may now be saying to yourself, "Well, here it comes. He is going to set up an ideal so high that in terms of it everything must seem low." That I might be thought to be doing so testifies to the lack of seriousness with which the word democracy is now taken, and to the indifference of many observers to the drift away from any plain meaning of the word. Democracy is, of course, a complicated idea about which there is much legitimate disagreement. But surely it is not so complicated or ambiguous that it may no longer be used by people who wish to reason together.

What I mean by democracy as an ideal I have already tried to indicate. In essence, democracy implies that those vitally affected by any decision men make have an effective voice in that decision. This, in turn, means that all power to make such decisions be publicly legitimated and that the makers of such decisions be held publicly accountable. None of these three points can prevail, it seems to me, unless there are dominant within a society the kinds of publics and the kinds of individuals I have described. Certain further conditions will presently become evident.

The social structure of the United States is not an altogether democratic one. Let us take that as a point of minimum agreement. I do not know of any society which is altogether democratic —that remains an ideal. The United States today I should say is generally democratic mainly in form and in the rhetoric of expectation. In substance and in practice it is very often non-democratic, and in many institutional areas it is quite clearly so. The corporate economy is run neither as a set of town meetings nor as a set of powers responsible to those whom their activities affect very seriously. The military machines and increasingly the political state are in the same condition. I do not wish to give the impression that I am optimistic about the chances that many social scientists can or will perform a democratic public role, or— even if many of them do so—about the chances that this would

necessarily result in a rehabilitation of publics. I am merely outlining one role that seems to me to be open and is, in fact, practiced by some social scientists. It happens also to be a role that is
in line with both liberal and socialist views of the role of reason
in human affairs.[1]

My point is that the political role of social science—what that
role may be, how it is enacted, and how effectively—this is relevant to the extent to which democracy prevails.

If we take up the third role of reason, the autonomous role, we
are trying to act in a democratic manner in a society that is not
altogether democratic. But we are acting as if we were in a fully
democratic society, and by doing so, we are attempting to remove
the "as if." We are trying to make the society more democratic.
Such a role, I contend, is the only role by which we may as social
scientists attempt to do this. At least I do not know of any other
way by which we might try to help build a democratic polity.

---

[1] In passing, I should like to remind the reader that, quite apart from its
present bureaucratic context and use, the style of abstracted empiricism (and
the methodological inhibition it sustains) is not well suited for the democratic political role I am describing. Those who practice this style as their
sole activity, who conceive of it as the "real work of social science," and who
live in its ethos, cannot perform a liberating educational role. This role
requires that individuals and publics be given confidence in their own capacities to reason, and by individual criticism, study, and practice, to enlarge
its scope and improve its quality. It requires that they be encouraged, in
George Orwell's phrase, to "get outside the whale," or in the wonderful
American phrase, "to become their own men." To tell them that they can
"really" know social reality only by depending upon a necessarily bureaucratic
kind of research is to place a taboo, in the name of Science, upon their efforts
to become independent men and substantive thinkers. It is to undermine the
confidence of the individual craftsman in his own ability to know reality. It
is, in effect, to encourage men to fix their social beliefs by reference to the
authority of an alien apparatus, and it is, of course, in line with, and is
reinforced by, the whole bureaucratization of reason in our time. The industrialization of academic life and the fragmentation of the problems of
social science cannot result in a liberating educational role for social scientists. For what these schools of thought take apart they tend to keep apart,
in very tiny pieces about which they claim to be very certain. But all they
could thus be certain of are abstracted fragments, and it is precisely the job
of liberal education, *and* the political role of social science, *and* its intellectual promise, to enable men to transcend such fragmented and abstracted
milieux: to become aware of historical structures and of their own place
within them.

And because of this, the problem of the social sciences as a prime carrier of reason in human affairs is in fact a major problem of democracy today.

III

What are the chances of success? Given the political structure within which we must now act, I do not believe it is very likely that social scientists will become effective carriers of reason. For men of knowledge to enact this strategic role, certain conditions must be present. Men make their own history, Marx said, but they do not make it under conditions of their own choice. Well then, what are the conditions *we* require to play this role effectively? What are required are parties and movements and publics having two characteristics: (1) within them ideas and alternatives of social life are truly debated, and (2) they have a chance really to influence decisions of structural consequence. Only if such organizations existed, could we become realistic and hopeful about the role of reason in human affairs which I have been trying to outline. Such a situation, by the way, I should consider one major requirement for any fully democratic society.

In such a polity social scientists in their political roles would probably "speak for" and "against" a variety of movements and strata and interests, rather than merely address an often vague, and—I fear—dwindling, public. Their ideas, in short, would compete, and this competition (as a process as well as in its result at any given time)would be politically relevant. If we take the idea of democracy seriously, if we take the democratic role of reason in human affairs seriously, our engagement in such a competition will in no way distress us. Surely we cannot suppose that all definitions of social reality, much less all statements of political ways and means, much less all suggestions of goals, would result in some undebatable, unified doctrine.

In the absence of such parties and movements and publics, we live in a society that is democratic mainly in its legal forms and its formal expectations. We ought not to minimize the enormous value and the considerable opportunity these circumstances make available. We should learn their value from the fact of their absence in the Soviet world, and from the kind of struggle the intellectuals of that world are up against. We should also learn that whereas there many intellectuals are physically crushed, here many morally crush themselves. That democracy in the United States is so largely formal does not mean that we can dodge the conclusion that if reason is to play any free part in a democratic making of history, one of its chief carriers must surely be the social sciences. The absence of democratic parties and movements and publics does not mean that social scientists as educators ought not to try to make their educational institutions a framework within which such a liberating public of individuals might exist, at least in its beginnings, and one in which their discussions might be encouraged and sustained. Nor does it mean that they should not try to cultivate such publics in their less academic roles.

To do so of course, is to risk "trouble"; or what is more serious, to face a quite deadly indifference. It requires that we deliberately present controversial theories and facts, and actively encourage controversy. In the absence of political debate that is wide and open and informed, people can get into touch neither with the effective realities of their world nor with the realities of themselves. Nowadays especially, it seems to me, the role I have been describing requires no less than the presentation of conflicting definitions of reality itself. What is usually termed "propaganda," especially of a nationalist sort, consists not only of opinions on a variety of topics and issues. It is the promulgation, as Paul Kecskemeti once noted, of official definitions of reality.

Our public life now often rests upon such official definitions, as well as upon myths and lies and crackbrained notions. When many policies—debated and undebated—are based on inadequate and misleading definitions of reality, then those who are out to define reality more adequately are bound to be upsetting influences. That is why publics of the sort I have described, as well as men of individuality, are, by their very existence in such a society, radical. Yet such is the role of mind, of study, of intellect, of reason, of ideas: to define reality adequately and in a publicly relevant way. The educational and the political role of social science in a democracy is to help cultivate and sustain publics and individuals that are able to develop, to live with, and to act upon adequate definitions of personal and social realities.

The role of reason I have been outlining neither means nor requires that one hit the pavement, take the next plane to the scene of the current crisis, run for Congress, buy a newspaper plant, go among the poor, set up a soap box. Such actions are often admirable, and I can readily imagine occasions when I should personally find it impossible not to want to do them myself. But for the social scientist to take them to be his normal activities is merely to abdicate his role, and to display by his action a disbelief in the promise of social science and in the role of reason in human affairs. This role requires only that the social scientist get on with the work of social science and that he avoid furthering the bureaucratization of reason and of discourse.

Not every social scientist accepts all the views I happen to hold on these issues, and it is not my wish that he should. My point is that one of his tasks is to determine his own views of the nature of historical change and the place, if any, of free and reasonable men within it. Only then can he come to know his own intellectual and political role within the societies he is studying, and in doing so find out just what he does think of the values of freedom and of reason which are so deeply a part of the tradition and the promise of social science.

If individual men and small groups of men are not free to act with historical consequence, and at the same time are not reasonable enough to see those consequences; if the structure of modern societies, or of any one of them, is now such that history is indeed blind drift and cannot be made otherwise with the means at hand and the knowledge that may be acquired—then the only autonomous role of social science is to chronicle and to understand; the idea of the responsibility of the powerful is foolish; and the values of freedom and of reason are realizable only in the exceptional milieux of certain favored private lives.

But that is a lot of "ifs." And although there is ample room for disagreement over degrees of freedom and scales of consequence, I do not believe that there is sufficient evidence to necessitate abandoning the values of freedom and reason as they might now orient the work of social science.

Attempts to avoid such troublesome issues as I have been discussing are nowadays widely defended by the slogan that social science is "not out to save the world." Sometimes this is the disclaimer of a modest scholar; sometimes it is the cynical contempt of a specialist for all issues of larger concern; sometimes it is the disillusionment of youthful expectations; often it is the pose of men who seek to borrow the prestige of The Scientist, imagined as a pure and disembodied intellect. But sometimes it is based upon a considered judgment of the facts of power.

Because of such facts, I do not believe that social science will "save the world" although I see nothing at all wrong with "trying to save the world"—a phrase which I take here to mean the avoidance of war and the rearrangement of human affairs in accordance with the ideals of human freedom and reason. Such knowledge as I have leads me to embrace rather pessimistic estimates of the chances. But even if that is where we now stand, still we must ask: If there *are* any ways out of the crises of our period by means of intellect, is it not up to the social scientist to state them? What we represent—although this is not always apparent —is man become aware of mankind. It is on the level of human awareness that virtually all solutions to the great problems must now lie.

To *appeal* to the powerful, on the basis of any knowledge we now have, is utopian in the foolish sense of that term. Our relations with them are more likely to be only such relations as they find useful, which is to say that we become technicians accepting their problems and aims, or ideologists promoting their prestige and authority. To be more than that, so far as our political role is concerned, we must first of all reconsider the nature of our collective endeavor as social scientists. It is not at all utopian for one social scientist to appeal to his colleagues to undertake such a reconsideration. Any social scientist who is aware of what he is about must confront the major moral dilemma I have implied in this chapter—the difference between what men are interested in and what is to men's interest.

If we take the simple democratic view that *what men are inter-*

ested in is all that concerns us, then we are accepting the values that have been inculcated, often accidentally and often deliberately, by vested interests. These values are often the only ones men have had any chance to develop. They are unconsciously acquired habits rather than choices.

If we take the dogmatic view that *what is to men's interests,* whether they are interested in it or not, is all that need concern us morally, then we run the risk of violating democratic values. We may become manipulators or coercers, or both, rather than persuaders within a society in which men are trying to reason together and in which the value of reason is held in high esteem.

What I am suggesting is that by addressing ourselves to issues and to troubles, and formulating them as problems of social science, we stand the best chance, I believe the only chance, to make reason democratically relevant to human affairs in a free society, and so realize the classic values that underlie the promise of our studies.

BARRINGTON MOORE, JR. / Sociological Theory and Contemporary Politics*

I

Whenever two sociologists are gathered together, to paraphrase a famous remark by Adam Smith, they are likely to engage in conspiratorial complaints about the low state of the discipline. A major source of our self-criticism is the absence of any sizable core of established theory, any framework of general propositions strong enough to convince a substantial part of the profession.[1] As one of my colleagues is fond of remarking, sociology is the science with the hollow frontier.[2]

Another, though perhaps a less frequent, complaint is that the main stream of contemporary sociological research ignores the central problems of our own epoch and society: the retreat and transformation of the capitalist order, the rise of totalitarianism, or the colonial revolution. Since ideas about appropriate scientific strategy necessarily concern both theory and empirical research, the sources of dissatisfaction are related. Differing assump-

* From *American Journal of Sociology* (September, 1955), pp. 107–115.

[1] But see Franz L. Neumann, "Approaches to the Study of Political Power," *Political Science Quarterly*, LXV, No. 2 (June, 1950), pp. 161–180, which I regard as the most successful attempt thus far at codifying theories on power. (Neumann's article is repeated immediately following this selection in the Reader.)

[2] See George C. Homans, *The Human Group* (New York, Harcourt Brace & Co., 1950), Chap. 1.

tions about strategy lead to quite different diagnoses of the malady and proposals as to a remedy. We should not be unduly disturbed if we discover that full agreement is impossible; a variety of strategies, even if we quarrel among ourselves, may be a healthy sign of potential intellectual growth.

We may distinguish two main lines of thought in the diagnosis of the present state of sociology. The distinction between them corresponds very roughly to that between an emphasis on pure science and one on historical understanding of unique problems or between generalizing and individualizing tendencies in the analysis of human affairs. Lacking any better terms, I call one the "modern" and the other the "old-fashioned" diagnosis. My own sympathies incline rather strongly toward the latter, though both views apparently lead to absurdities if pressed rigorously toward their conclusions. Moreover, no single sociologist necessarily adheres entirely to either viewpoint in the way each is presented here; both are constructs, made to appraise certain intellectual problems.

The modern diagnosis runs somewhat as follows. Science advances insofar as it can find adequate procedures for simplifying and ordering its factual raw materials. In contrast to earlier days the raw world of nature is now often regarded as a chaotic mass on which the scientist to some extent imposes his own order. In part this simplification is achieved through the laboratory, where irrelevant factors are excluded and relevant ones studied until the pattern of their relationship becomes clear. In part it is also achieved by disciplined logical reflection no longer tied to any factual base. By this view theory advances to the extent that it can free itself from the prepossessions of common sense and the observations of facts as they occur in nature. What is called for is the act of creative imagination, best exemplified in the work of the pure mathematician, who explores the pattern of implications in a set of assumptions of his own choosing. Such reasoning lies behind much of the constructing of "ideal types" and mathematical models of portions of social reality. To be sure, as even the most theoretically minded emphasize, it is essential to return from time to time to the world of verifiable observations. But the observations in themselves are not necessarily the source of progress.[3] Newton, it might be argued by a "modernist," came to his conclusions not by carefully observing the fall of an apple but by trying to reach a principle. Furthermore, it is not necessary that the principle conform to known or even possible facts, as witness the concept of motion without friction.

Thus the modernist diagnosis in the social sciences stresses stricter laboratory methods at one end of the intellectual spectrum and imaginative theory at the other, the whole to be tied together somehow by interdisciplinary cooperation, to provide eventually an intellectual synthesis of man's knowledge of man. When this synthesis is achieved, the "modernist" might continue, it will be an extraordinarily powerful tool for the analysis of social problems as they are usually conceived. In the meantime, as progress is made in this direction, by-products may be expected that will yield increased understanding of current problems. But they should definitely and firmly be regarded as mere by-products. Indeed, if we deflect our attention from pure science, we shall merely dissipate our energies in trying to solve problems presented with the headlines and will never achieve our fundamental aims. The more optimistic would add that this failure would be a loss from the standpoint of general welfare, while the more pessimistic are inclined to hold that firmer scientific analysis is likely to reveal many problems to be inherently insoluble and must therefore be a goal in its own right.

In their counterdiagnosis those sympathetic to the old-fashioned standpoint might use the following arguments. Sociologists and other social scientists are persistently frustrating themselves because they set themselves inherently impossible goals. As our critics from Dilthey onward have been fond of remarking, considerable areas of human behavior do not display the regularly recurring uniformities that are the necessary empirical basis of scientific generalization. No amount of intellectual agility, for example, can overcome the differences among the numerous revolutions that have taken place in human history and reduce them

---

3 See the many instances cited by H. Butterfield, *The Origins of Modern Science* (London: G. Bell & Sons, Ltd., 1949). Chaps. 2–4.

to a common pattern. Similarities there may be, but they are of such a broad and general nature as to be unenlightening, and they become less enlightening the more cases one tries to cover with a theory.

Here the old-fashioned sociologist may contrast the fate of Newtonian physics with that of classical economics. Both tried to explain a wide range of phenomena with a minimum number of postulates and in time encountered observations that these postulates could handle only with very great difficulty, if at all. In the case of physics, however, it was not necessary to discard the older views altogether. Instead they were recognized as part of a larger system of valid theory whose applicability was more limited than originally supposed. While some inconsistencies between the old and the new remain, the physicists hope that they will eventually be ironed out. Within their field Newtonian principles still stand.

In the case of classical economics the situation is different. The difference is one of so many degrees as to constitute almost a qualitative distinction. According to many economists, the structure of industrial society has so changed that the major postulates of classical economics no longer apply to any significant extent, particularly those concerned with free competition and the organization of production into units so numerous that no unit by itself can influence price. Though there may be some economic or sociological principles that are just as applicable to Melanesian society as to the United States, we have to work out a new set of postulates for the internal dynamics of each stage of social development. If in the course of less than two hundred years the physicist's postulates no longer serve to predict the movements of the planets, it would be roughly parallel to the position of the classical economist today. Thus, while creative imagination is essential, it is not omnipotent. We have to take nature as it comes, the old-fashioned sociologist might conclude, and cannot impose arbitrary uniformities where none exists.

From there he might press on to the offensive. Since any attempt to construct a grand analytical scheme, a universal mathesis for social science, is doomed from the start to become nothing but an arid formalism, the mere ordering of words or symbols into categories is no achievement, unless it can be shown that these verbal patterns have their counterpart in observable reality. As Santayana has observed, "Without reference to their illustration in things, all consistent propositions would be equally valid and equally trivial. Important truth is truth about something." [4] Modern formal sociology, the old-fashioned scholar might continue, gradually working himself up to a frenzy, represents merely a retreat from the world of real problems. It promotes a trained incapacity to seek any disciplined comprehension of our social and political environment.

To one who accepts any substantial part of this reasoning it follows that the sociologist can expect to make better progress, both scientifically and practically, if he tries to "know something about something" and limits his objectives to a manageable scope. The old-fashioned thinker defines his task in terms of problems to be solved, concrete relationships to be discovered, instead of the erection of a systematic framework of analysis.

II

When pushed as far as it will go, the old-fashioned position breaks down into the absurdity of dogmatic historicism, or the doctrine that all human behavior consists of unique events to be explained by other unique events. The discovery of relationships that hold for more than a single occasion, as in the study of kinship, provides empirical evidence that we are not reduced to historicism for all areas of social life. However, the study of kinship systems, despite its undoubted significance in the demonstration of certain kinds of formal order in human affairs, does not appear to be a strategic point of entry for the understanding of twentieth-century life. This point is of little concern to those who stand on the position of pure science, as do many of the "modernists." But if the possibility of creating any very substantial pure science is doubted, and if it is further believed that most knowledge in the social sciences will always be contingent on a particular, if not

[4] George Santayana, *The Life of Reason: Reason in Science*, 2d ed. (New York, Charles Scribner's Sons, 1948), p. 32.

necessarily altogether unique, set of circumstances, then the point becomes very relevant indeed.

No doubt there is always some conflict between the requirements of understanding the present and those of constructing valid theory for the sake of future knowledge, just as in everyday life there is a conflict between present consumption and saving for future consumption. But in sociology, as in everyday life, I do not believe that the conflict is altogether irreconcilable. From the standpoint offered here, theory can be regarded as a set of tools whose usefulness is tested in their ability to solve concrete problems. There is a division of labor between the tool-makers, or the theorists, and the tool-users, who work on concrete problems, though it is not an absolute one. Indeed, it would be most unfortunate if the two occupations developed into castes.

In more formal terms it may be argued that a major function of sociologists, though by no means the sole one, is the analysis of the grosser structural features of the world in which they live. This would include assessments of possible and probable future developments in particular national states and the likely consequences of various policy alternatives. In turn, concern with these problems involves the analysis of movements and circumstances that will be in many respects unique.

Sociologists need not be frightened off by the dogma that science does not study the unique. In its most sophisticated form, this doctrine holds that whatever understanding we have of a unique event is limited to the more general features that it shares with other events. Thus we understand Caesar's act of crossing the Rubicon in terms of one or more universal categories, such as political ambition, that are common to many men. Undoubtedly we never understand the unique in all its details and all its complexity. But this does not eliminate the possibility of understanding one unique constellation of forces in terms of another and equally unique constellation. Ordinarily such understanding is regarded as historical,[5] but it can equally be labeled "scientific" if the relationship is formulated in a way that can be proved or

5 *Cf.* Heinrich Rickert, *Kulturwissenschaft und Naturwissenschaft,* 7th ed. (Tübingen, J. C. B. Mohr, 1926).

disproved by evidence. Hitherto unknown relations often turn up in this way that later are found to have wider applicability and to gain the respected status of universals. Gaetano Mosca is one of the sociologists who has made many suggestive generalizations on the basis of limited historical illustrations.

In sociology it appears that we frequently face a task of understanding a series of universals that are combined in more or less unique patterns. What forces produced fascism in Germany? To what extent are the same forces at work in the United States? How does their combination, among themselves and with other forces, differ so that we may expect a different result? In comparing one pattern of events against another, we have to be able to discriminate, to assess differences as well as similarities.

In this connection there is no *a priori* reason to adopt a rigidly determinist attitude. To be sure, there may be, in the concrete situation, certain inherent trends that will work themselves out no matter what anyone thinks or does. On the other hand, in most cases we shall be concerned with a range of possible alternative outcomes, some more probable than others. Certain outcomes will mean higher costs for those involved than will others. A depression can be overcome in ways that put a heavy burden on powerful groups, or it can be allowed to continue, different costs being differently distributed. What actually takes place will depend partly on people's understanding of the situation, including elements in their recent experience, as witness the American and British attitudes toward appeasement of dictators in the 1930's and 1950's! To the extent that it enters into people's understanding, social science can nullify its own Cassandra-like predictions. At the moment this happy day seems to be sufficiently far off to eliminate any risk of unemployment among those of us with naturally somber dispositions.

III

What theoretical tools does sociology now possess for a scientific study of unique social phenomena, especially of the major structural characteristics and trends of our own era?

In nineteenth- and twentieth-century theories one may distinguish two types of emphases. I shall designate one "equilibrium theory" and the other "process theory." They are by no means antithetical, but at the same time there are very significant differences in the type of research problems that each suggests.

In equilibrium theory the key assumption is that any social system tends toward a state of rest in which the conflicts and strains among its component parts are reduced to a minimum. In its recent elaboration by the structural functional school, the main line of questioning for empirical investigations concerns the determination of the functional imperatives, or prerequisites, of a society or part of a society. Were this social system to continue, what activities would have to be carried out, what forms of social organization would be necessary, and what limits are there on the ways in which these forms can be combined with one another? [6]

As Parsons makes quite explicit, the equilibrium assumption is not one about empirical facts. Instead it is a theoretical assumption that serves to order a larger body of theory into a consistent whole.[7] Those who work with structural functional theory are for the most part thoroughly aware that social systems do not continue without change. They see history as strewn with the wreckage of social systems that have failed to meet their functional imperatives. Nevertheless, by determining what is necessary for a system to continue, they argue, one may also discover the foci of strain and potential change. Therefore it is not true that structural functional theory is completely unable to cope with problems of social change, as its critics frequently assert.

Reading the literature of this school, one easily gains the impression that it is straining to create a form of process theory but is having great difficulty in so doing. Thus, in a chapter called "The Processes of Change of Social Systems," Parsons writes, in italics, that *a general theory of the processes of change of social systems is not possible in the present state of knowledge.* [8] Elsewhere he speaks of a "moving equilibrium," which he defines in part as an "orderly process of change" in a society which never-

[6] Marion J. Levy, Jr., *The Structure of Society* (Princeton, N. J., Princeton University Press, 1952), pp. 39, 211–226.

[7] Talcott Parsons, *The Social System* (Glencoe, Ill., The Free Press, 1951), p. 481.

[8] *Ibid.,* p. 486.

theless retains the "conditions of distinctiveness ... within its boundaries over against its environment." [9]

No doubt there are several reasons for the difficulties faced by this school in treating historical change. However, a central obstacle may be the concept of equilibrium itself. Without doing violence to its principles, equilibrium theory cannot account for change except in one direction, that is, toward some point of ultimate stability. Hence it cannot cope effectively with some of the most important actual types of change. The elaboration of social institutions beyond the point of any visible utility, for example, finds no place in the theory.[10] Likewise, the theory, at least in its present form, is inadequate for explaining how attempts to meet the functional requirements of a social system can lead to a modification in its structure. For example, in the judgment of some historians, the attempts made by later Roman emperors to strengthen the Empire contributed to the growth of feudalism or to the replacement of one social system by quite a different one. In modern times the New Deal may be plausibly regarded as an attempt to shore up American capitalism, that is, to meet its functional requirements. But this process in turn led to marked modification of American society. Precisely such large-scale movements, generated by internal as well as external conditions in a society, constitute the heart of the problem of understanding our epoch as well as others.

No doubt the structural functional school can find a place in its elaborate scheme of categories for the types of phenomena just mentioned. They might be described as unanticipated and dysfunctional consequences of behavior. However, that amounts to throwing the equilibrium assumption overboard. It says in effect that tendencies toward equilibrium are unexpectedly producing change, a contradiction in terms. Furthermore, this approach conceals causal relations that may exist over time as one social system generates its successor.

At this point it may be illuminating to contrast equilibrium theory with Marxism. As we have seen, under equilibrium theory it is very difficult and perhaps impossible to account for the vi-

[9] *Ibid.*, p. 36.
[10] As noted by Levy, *op. cit.*, p. 46.

cious circle, so common in history, when a progressively deterio-rating state of affairs leads to a revolutionary explosion. Marxism, among other forms of process theory, puts this situation at the center of its intellectual scheme. In this way time is brought in to reveal what is asserted to be a causal relationship. Where equilib-rium theory produces correlations, Marxism tries to produce causal connections. For a Marxist it is almost as difficult to conceive of a situation returning to a state of maximum harmony as it is for an equilibrium theorist to conceive of a self-generating cycle of ever fiercer struggle culminating in destruction. Both equilibrium theory and Marxism, as well as other forms of process theory, if pursued with dogmatic vigor, give rise to elaborate intellectual structures that illuminate important segments of social reality and leave others obscure. Since equilibrium theory fails us at a crucial point, we must look further to process theory for help, aware that it, too, will have its limitations.

Among process theorists one may include, in addition to Marx, such diverse figures as Cooley, Durkheim, Keller, Sorokin, Og-burn, and many others. Within this diversified assembly of ideas it is possible to detect, nevertheless, a common proposition: Any given state of human affairs is likely to contain within it the seeds of its own transformation into a new and different state. This assumption of immanent and continuous change represents, I would suggest, the key assumption and distinguishing feature of process theory. At the same time we should be careful to note that the distinction between the two viewpoints is not watertight. Though fundamental differences appear, there is considerable overlapping.

Even theories emphasizing that every society harbors the seeds of its own destruction share with equilibrium theory the concep-tion of some form of internal social order. Marx stresses the dependence of other social institutions on economic relationships. From a diametrically opposite standpoint Sorokin points out the significance of interrelated institutional forms that express a cul-tural system of meanings,[11] or what some anthropologists call the

[11] See especially Pitirim Sorokin, *Social and Cultural Dynamics* (New York, American Book Co., 1941), IV, pp. 31–40.

basic premises of a culture. Ogburn derives much of the institutional structure of a society from the state of technology. Thus, all theories express some view of the inherent compatibility or incompatibility of two or more social institutions, a fundamental tenet in equilibrium doctrine. The very notion of predictable change is impossible without some idea of the order relation of the parts in whatever is changing. Both a mechanical engine and a living organism display this orderly relation of parts whenever they are capable of movement. However, the difference between equilibrium and process theory lies in the latter's emphasis upon a kind of order that necessarily produces change.

In itself the assumption of ever present change is not particularly enlightening until it is coupled with some theory about the forces that produce change and the direction of the movement. Most comprehensive theories that have been put forth for this purpose have taken either an evolutionary or a cyclical form. It is fashionable just now to reject them as premature attempts at synthesis. Nevertheless, we may also be over-hasty in jettisoning them in their entirety. As already noted, in the development of human thought it has often happened that ideas which were thought universally valid have only a restricted field of application. They are valuable achievements nonetheless. Euclidean geometry is no longer the last work in its field. But its principles have been consciously or unconsciously used by house carpenters for thousands of years.

Cyclical theories are particularly close to equilibrium theory and are sometimes, as in Pareto, combined. They frequently assume, either explicitly or implicitly, that institutional change in a given direction sooner or later sets up counterforces that oppose or modify it. Toynbee's concept of the "nemesis of creativity" provides one of the more suggestive illustrations.[12] Any successful institutional device tends to persist beyond the point at which it is adaptive, becoming a danger to the society in which it has flourished. At the same time cyclical theories run into difficulty precisely because they assume a return to some original state,

12 Arnold J. Toynbee, *A Study of History* (New York, Oxford University Press, 1947), pp. 307–336.

even though they differ from equilibrium theory by assuming that this original state also contains tensions which will renew the cycle. History simply does not repeat itself. There are massive and apparently irreversible changes, such as the industrial revolution, which cyclical theories cannot account for adequately.

Evolutionary theory puts such changes at the center of its scheme. Perhaps in partial combination with some theory of cycles, to give a spiral conception of change, this approach may some day provide the most satisfactory general synthesis. In the meantime it may be the better part of wisdom to avoid integrating theories that are dubious in themselves and to concentrate on finding ways to order smaller portions of reality into meaningful units.

For this purpose the evolutionary theory of stages provides suggestive clues and raises important problems. There is no doubt that the unilinear version of evolutionary theory contained serious mistakes. It posited an inevitable series of stages, in each of which all aspects of social structure (from economic organization to religion and the family) were similar and through which every society would sooner or later pass. Nevertheless, the theory of stages contains a residue of truth. Anthropologists now hold that in some areas, particularly technology, one may observe progressive and cumulative changes where the knowledge gained in one period provides the necessary foundation for further advance. One anthropologist suggests that an essential condition for cumulative change is the possibility of sharing a common core of knowledge and at the same time specializing within it. In the case of marriage, on the other hand, the fact that there are only two sexes limits the number of possible forms to four and precludes cumulative structural change. Since, however, culture changes as a whole, we find the impact of technological change on other parts, such as in the reduction of social functions performed by the modern family.[13] Thus the concept of stages, even of a more or less inevitable "next stage," has at least a limited range of applicability. This concept, however, need not be tied to a form of

[13] Harvey C. Moore, "Cumulation and Cultural Processes," *American Anthropologist*, LVI, No. 3 (June, 1954), pp. 347–357.

technological determinism: the dynamics of change may also be found in other parts of social structure.

However, the most interesting and for our epoch the most significant problems occur in connection with the skipping of stages rather than with their orderly sequence. The transformation of Western liberal and rationalist ideas, together with the alterations in the structure of industrial society as this complex of doctrines and institutions spread eastward to Asia, constitutes perhaps the major example of contemporary stage-skipping. The results certainly cannot be expected to resemble very closely the so-called free capitalist institutions of Victorian England.

In such cases we are observing the interaction of two sets of processes that had been developing independently up to the time of coming in contact. The analysis of such a problem is a great difficulty. Using the illustration of the early impact of the West upon Japan, Sidney Hook argues that such a situation is inherently indeterminate.[14] Certainly one could not have foretold what would have happened solely through an analysis of the processes at work in Japanese society alone nor, for that matter, in the West alone.

One way to a partial solution may be the following: Contact between two or more autonomous processes frequently sets up another and larger process that in turn modifies the original set. The new process may be sufficiently orderly to permit prediction. For example, neither Soviet nor American policy during the second World War and the post-war years can be satisfactorily explained independently of one another. To some it appears that the United States was merely hypocritical in first trying to demilitarize Germany and Japan and then seeking to rearm them as fast as possible. Others explain American behavior by referring to the larger process whereby a coalition, lately victorious against a common enemy, disintegrates when the common threat has disappeared. The next step, as is well known, is for the victors to become suspicious of one another, since the most serious danger now is from the victorious partner. There is therefore an ungraceful

14 See his "Determinism," *Encyclopedia of the Social Sciences* (New York, Macmillan Co., 1937), V, p. 111.

scramble for the assistance of former enemies. Soviet behavior conforms to the same pattern. Certain tendencies, though by no means all, toward the transformation of both societies into garrison states may also be traced to this general process.[15]

It is impossible, however, to reduce the clash of cultures and social systems to a single process. By no means everything, for example, can be explained by the growth and disintegration of international coalitions. Certain processes continue to develop within the state, even though profoundly modified by the latter's position in the international distribution of power. In China and other parts of Asia indigenous revolutionary forces were at work before extended contact with the West and continue down to the present day. Frequently, forces generated in the domestic and the foreign arena come into sharp conflict with one another, as now appears to be the case both in the United States and in France.

From a purely formal point of view there are three possible outcomes when processes that were developing separately come into contact with one another. New processes may be started; old ones may continue in modified form; and still others may persist independently as though nothing had happened. No ready formula exists, however, by which it would be possible to predict in every case where the dividing lines are to be found. The notion that technology, for example, will always spread more rapidly than other cultural traits is probably mistaken. New technology requires new psychological attitudes and new forms of social structure, just as variations in the existing social structure (e.g., in India and Japan) will affect receptivity to new technology.[16] Perhaps a general formula can no more be discovered in the interaction of processes than can a general theory of mixture be given in chemistry without specifying the ingredients.

---

[15] While from the first the Soviet system has displayed many traits of a garrison state, American society, now openly hostile to the Soviet system, has begun to show increasing signs of a totalitarian tendency. Politics may contain a process similar to that expressed by Gresham's law in economics, "the bad" driving out "the good."

[16] For brief but illuminating comments on this point see Kingsley Davis, *The Population of India and Pakistan* (Princeton, N. J., Princeton University Press, 1951), pp. 216–217.

In general, sociological theory tends to be plagued with questions such as this, so broad as to have no specifiable meaning. We ask, for example, what is the role of ideas in social change? Instead, we ought to ask what is the role of certain types of ideas under specified circumstances? Much remains to be learned about the kinds of strain in industrial society that create increased demand for a return to some idealized version of the *status quo ante,* as in extreme right-wing movements here and in Nazi Germany. We should also know about corresponding movements in peasant countries now in the early stages of industrialization. Likewise we want to know about the sources and nature of movements aiming at a new and different type of society. In answering, we must comprehend the interaction of several processes taking place simultaneously.

Where the nature of the processes is properly understood, analysis can proceed toward outlining the range of possibilities for the future and the costs of alternative policies. We need not be deterred by the impossibility of precise prediction for relationships that are not completely determinate. The sociologist has added unnecessarily to his sense of professional inadequacy by feeling compelled to predict the inevitable outcome of any situation.

All that is necessary and all that is useful, in these large-scale instances of interaction among societies and cultures, is a reasonaly accurate assessment of the limits and possibilities of effective human action. In turn, such an assessment makes sense only in terms of some prior set of values. Unless he is content to be a moral eunuch in the service of any bureaucracy that hires him, the student of society will do his best to bring disciplined intelligence to bear on these problems as well.

FRANZ NEUMANN / Approaches to the Study of Political Power*

ATTITUDES TOWARD POWER

Consciously, or unconsciously, every student of politics has a specific attitude toward political power. It is this attitude which determines one's approach to all problems of political science. The valuative premises must be made clear so that objective analyses may be possible. The soul-searching of the political scientist may be facilitated by a classification of the various attitudes exhibited in the history of political theory. The classification presented here is only suggested and is not meant to imply that there are no better and more convincing classifications.

1. For Plato and Aristotle, political power is more than a separate function of the organized community. It *is* the community. Political power is the total power of the community, distinguished from other relationships merely by its techniques. There is, in this view, no distinction between state and society, economics and politics, morals and politics, religion and politics, culture and politics. Man and citizen are equated. Every activity of the community and of its citizens is political. Only through political action can the citizen attain his fulfillment; only through politics does he become man.

2. To this, there is radically opposed what I shall call the Au-

* From *Political Science Quarterly* (June, 1950), pp. 161–180. Portions of the original article have been omitted.

gustinian position. Politics is evil; political power is coercion, evil in origin and purpose. It is "unnatural" that man rule over man. Only at the end of history with the advent of the Kingdom of God can and will coercion be dispensed with. From this philosophy derive two radically different, and yet inherently related, attitudes: that of total conformism and that of total opposition to political power. If politics is evil, withdrawal is mandatory. Forms of government and objectives of political power become irrelevant. Salvation can be attained through faith, and the earthly life should be a mere preparation for it. Monasticism is the first consequence. By the same token, however, the demand for the immediate destruction of politics and the establishment of a Kingdom of God may equally be supported by the Augustinian premise. The Anabaptist movement was perhaps the most striking manifestation of the total rejection of society.

3. The radicalism of St. Augustine is, of course, "impractical." St. Thomas introduces what may be called a common-sense attitude toward political power. Power is not unnatural since hierarchic relationships already existed among the angels. Yet the attitude toward political power is not unambiguously positive. It is not only hedged in by many restraints but also, in some rather unclear way, subordinated to spiritual power operating indirectly through various levels of law.

4. It is this climate which prepared the way for the liberal attitude. Its sole concern is the erection of fences around political power which is, allegedly, distrusted. Its aim is the dissolution of power into legal relationships, the elimination of the element of personal rule and the substitution of the rule of law in which all relationships are to become purposive-rational, that is, predictable and calculable. In reality, of course, this is in large measure an ideology tending (often unintentionally) to prevent the search for the locus of political power and to render more secure its actual holders. Power cannot be dissolved in law.[1]

[1] "Although the laws be never more than mere declarations of anterior rights, nevertheless it is of utmost importance there is always something which cannot be written down, and which must be left in a dark and venerable cloud under pain of overthrowing the state." Joseph de Maistre, *Considérations sur la France*, Chap. 6.

5. Not to be confused with liberalism is the Epicurean attitude toward politics. In contrast to the Platonic-Aristotelian conception, politics is a separate business of society, clearly distinguished and distinguishable from all other activities. But it is a complete matter of indifference how it is organized, who exerts it, for what purposes it is used. Any power is justified which maintains that minimum external order of society which permits the individual to go on with his life.

6. In its psychological consequences, Epicureanism is sometimes closely related to the anarchistic approach. To the anarchist, political power is evil, society good; hence it is possible to organize a society without politics. As in Augustinism, conformism or putschism may follow. Conformism: one should not dirty one's hands by participation in politics; putschism: one can establish an associative society at any time that man wills it.

7. Marxism shares with anarchism and Augustinism the belief that political power is not a natural but an historical phenomenon. In contrast to anarchism, and with Augustinism, however, it believes it to be a necessary historical phenomenon, but the necessity is limited (in contrast to Augustinism) to one historical phase through which mankind must pass before the classless society (a society without politics) can be established. The remedy against political power (again against the anarchists) is more and highly concentrated political power, skillfully used to smash political power (dictatorship of the proletariat). The Marxist thus has a positive approach to political power up to the establishment of a classless society.

8. Marx shares this positive approach with Rousseau. For the latter, political power is at once comprehensive and nonexistent. It is all-encompassing because the organized community (as in Plato and Aristotle) embraces all activities of man, economics, culture, religion; nonexistent because of the alleged identity of rulers and ruled in the general will. It is precisely this dual attitude toward political power which makes Robespierre's theory and actions understandable.

9. The liberal democrat shares with the total democrat a positive attitude toward political power which appears essentially as a

rational instrument to be used for desired and desirable ends. Yet the fear of the liberal prevents him from accepting the total politicizing of life and causes him to insist on the separate character of political power. But the consistent liberal democrat is not, and cannot be, solely concerned with the erection of fences around political power. He is increasingly concerned with the potentialities of a rational use of political power.

This (or any other) typology of the attitudes toward political power enables us to discover contradictory statements often of a hypocritical or demagogic nature and to arrive at a consistent approach to the study of the power phenomenon. If a scholar or politician demands, in the same breath, the exclusion of dissenters from political participation and the inviolability of private property from governmental intrusion, we have before us a mixture of two attitudes: that of Plato-Rousseau, and that of liberalism.

The result is not a "new" attitude toward power but a propagandistic statement. Our typology of attitudes readily reveals that it contains contradictory positions. It is the duty of the critical student to remove such inconsistencies from his own thinking, to expose them when they appear in the statements of others, and to become aware of the premises of his own position.

THE SIGNIFICANCE OF POLITICAL POWER

Once this self-examination is completed, the significance of political power should be squarely faced. No society in recorded history has ever been able to dispense with political power. This is as true of liberalism as of absolutism, as true of *laissez faire* as of an interventionist state. No greater disservice has been rendered to political science than the statement that the liberal state was a "weak" state. It was precisely as strong as it needed to be in the circumstances. It acquired substantial colonial empires, waged wars, held down internal disorders and stabilized itself over long periods of time.

But the methods applied by those who wield power and the scope of its application vary, of course. And it is precisely this problem that is of major significance for the political scientist.

Formally, the methods range from the marginal case of killing to the marginal case of education.[2] Three basic methods are at the disposal of the power group: persuasion, material benefits, violence. Violence is probably most effective as a short-range method, but little effective as the principal method of maintaining power over long periods since it compels the group (particularly under modern conditions) to intensify the methods of violence and to extend it to larger sections of the ruled. The most efficient (that is, cheapest form) is, of course, persuasion. Yet all three, persuasion, benefits, violence, are always present in all forms of government.[3] And it is precisely the mixture of the three elements which constitutes another major problem for the political scientist. I shall attempt to clarify the meaning by the formulation of some sociological generalizations.

SOCIOLOGICAL GENERALIZATION 1

The significance of persuasion grows with the growing complexity of society. It is, perhaps, legitimate to consider persuasion, as a rule, to be merely a form of violence, "violence committed against the soul" as the French historian of Catholic England under Henry VIII formulated it.[4] Through persuasion, the rulers achieve a marked degree of habituation of the ruled so that their reactions assume an almost automatic character. The success of persuasion will, however, depend upon the scope and duration of the propaganda and the skills by which stereotypes are produced. There is little doubt that persuasion is a more efficient and cheaper exercise of political power than the employment of large police forces, armies and militias.

[2] This is not to imply that education is to be considered solely as an instrument of maintaining power; but it must also be considered as a technique in the struggle for power.
[3] Cf. Max Weber, "Politics as a Vocation," Essays in Sociology, edited by H. H. Gerth and C. Wright Mills (New York, 1946), pp. 80–81. Specifically, one may note that the ruling group, even when relying mainly on physical violence, may owe its own cohesion to material benefits and persuasion.
[4] Pierre Janelle, L'Angleterre catholique à la veille du schisme (Paris, 1935), p. 185.

SOCIOLOGICAL GENERALIZATION 2

The increasing complexity of society requires that the rulers increasingly utilize arcana, secret techniques of rule. The struggle for power is a real struggle aiming at the control of the state machine. In any struggle, however, tactical decisions can be effectively made only in secret. Secrecy, in turn, can be preserved only by small numbers. It is this very fact that necessitates the rise of oligarchies within mass movements. Max Weber[5] and Robert Michels[6] (and probably many others) have drawn attention to this phenomenon, and Max Weber, besides, correctly stressed the superiority of small over large numbers because of the significance of secrecy for any rule designed to be more than temporary.[7] It is precisely for this reason that the rule of the few becomes particularly marked in those mass organizations which, more than other movements, are essentially devoted to democracy: the trade unions and the social democratic (labor) parties. The reason is obvious. The opponents of these movements are usually numerically few, but individually powerful, subjects who are thus able to keep their strategic and tactical decisions secret. The mass organization, faced with such opposition, must, in turn, resort to the construction of forms of rule which also permit secrecy. Aristocratic rule thus becomes a sociologically necessary implementation of democratic movements.[8] It is, therefore, no accident that the growth of oligarchies within mass movements was first studied in the example of the German Social Democratic party.

Lenin made a virtue of this necessity. His vanguard theory of leadership frankly replaces the traditional democratic conception of social democracy by an aristocratic one.

SOCIOLOGICAL GENERALIZATION 3

The higher the state of technological development, the greater the concentration of political power. The legal conception of

[5] *Loc. cit.*, pp. 102–103.
[6] *Political Parties* (Glencoe, Ill., 1949).
[7] *Wirtschaft und Gesellschaft*, Part 3, Chap. 1, §3.
[8] That it may become, not its implementation, but its negation should be kept in mind.

ownership is quite irrelevant for an analysis of this phenomenon. It matters not who owns a technical unit: an individual, a corporation, a state, any other organized society. The social organization of large technical units may, of course, be a cooperative one. In every social group which is based on struggle, however, the organization will, of necessity, be hierarchic. The larger the size, the more hierarchic it becomes. Growing hierarchic trends lead to concentration of power at the top. The relation between social and political power will be analyzed at a later place.

SOCIOLOGICAL GENERALIZATION 4

With the growing complexity of society and its increasing industrialization, the significance of political power in the social process grows. Concentration of power (in the economy, in society, in culture) makes for more rigidity. A process of social petrifaction sets in and prevents the system from achieving a semi-automatic balance. The equilibrium, once disturbed, can be restored only through active intervention of the political power. Control of the state then becomes more precious than ever before.[9]

SOCIOLOGICAL GENERALIZATION 5

The same trend also produces a greater separation of political power from social power—a phenomenon that shall concern us later.

Some or all of these generalizations are subject to challenge. They are not meant to be exhaustive, but merely point the direction to a proper study of political power. That they produce uneasiness is to be expected. At first sight it seems difficult to reconcile them with the theory of democracy. If by democracy is understood that mixture of diverse elements, of Locke and Rousseau, St. Augustine and St. Thomas, which is usually called "democratic theory," a reconciliation of those realistic trends with the doctrine is, indeed, impossible. We are not now concerned with the problem of democratic theory. For the present it suffices to say

9 For a more detailed analysis of this phenomenon see *Behemoth: The Structure and Practice of National Socialism* (New York, 1942), pp. 255–361.

that an adequate democratic theory will have to deal with these problems.

ROOTS OF POLITICAL POWER

Three questions have to be faced in the analysis of the roots of political power: the conceptual framework has to be established; the institutional setting to be clarified; and the historical process to be understood which leads to a change in institutions and different attitudes toward power and to a different political behavior. For the ancient historians, this was no problem. Political power derived squarely from economic power, particularly from the control of land. Changes in ownership, the emergence of new modes of production, and so on, created new sources of political power and thus made for conflicts. Modern historians dealing with this period of history have not hesitated to restate the problem in the same way as the ancients stated it.[10]

As we shall directly show, modern capitalist economy has rendered this whole subject problematical. And, despite the fact that the issue is so crucial, analysis has been hindered by senseless taboos. The older insights have been lost or hidden and are rarely brought fully into the open. Thus, the classical approach has been restated in modern times by Marx's interpretation of history (that this did not originate with him—and is not "Marxist"—he himself admitted). Yet since it is fashionable to reject Marxism root and branch—sight unseen so to speak—the student precludes himself from a clear understanding of the relationship between economic power and political power.

The approach is facilitated by the establishment of certain categories of relationships.

1. The ancient conception. Here—and this follows already from what has been said—although the source of political power is economic power, political power permeates all social activities and all spheres of life. The economic power position merely provides the motor of political power which then includes all power relationships.

[10] Models are: Gustave Glotz, *The Greek City* (New York, 1929) and *Ancient Greece at Work* (New York, 1926); Ronald Syme, *The Roman Revolution* (Oxford, 1939); and, of course, Rostovtzeff's works.

2. The feudal conception. In the ideal-typical form, political power does not exist. It is merely a function of an economic-power position: the ownership of land. From it flow judicial, military, religious, legislative and administrative powers.

3. The capitalist conception. It is only in this period that a real problem arises: the independence of political power and yet its interconnection with economic power. Political power (the theoretical construction has been perfected by Hobbes) is a separate activity, carried out in a separate institution: the state. The state has the monopoly of coercive power which it exercises in a separate institutional framework. At the same time, however, this separate institution is intrinsically connected with society in the service of which it operates. It is this conception of political power that unites Locke and Hobbes, and distinguishes both from Rousseau. Both separate political power from social power; both connect them. Hobbes believes it necessary to maximize political power in order to serve society; Locke maintains that only by its minimization can society be served. Both, however, admit of exceptions. In Hobbes's theory, political power will be destroyed if it fails to serve its social function (the social contract lapses); Locke, through the institution of the prerogative and federative power, maximizes political power if it is necessary for the good of the commonwealth. What Hobbes and Locke did not clearly state is that the two are not only functionally but genetically connected; that is, economic power is the root of political power. The first systematic analysis of this relationship stems from Saint-Simon's analysis of the French Revolution and then spreads rapidly into French and English historiography and sociology.

From this general view of Hobbes and Locke it follows that whatever freedom society, and particularly economic activity, is to have, it has for the sake of maintaining a stable political order. There is thus no "pure" economic power and no "pure" political activity. Economics is as much an instrument of politics as politics is a tool of economics. The mythological conception of the *laissez-faire* state ought finally to be destroyed.

If this general view is accepted, the translation of economic power into social power and thence into political power becomes the crucial concern of the political scientist.

THE POLITICAL PARTY

The single most important instrument for the translation of social power into political power is the political party. The reason for the supreme position of the party lies in the very nature of democracy. The party permits the presentation of particularly and, quite frequently, very egoistic interests as national interests. At the same time, however, it prevents the total domination of national interests by particular interests. The function of the political party in democracy is thus ambiguous. The democratic process compels each social group to strive for mass support. Each group, therefore, must present its egoistic interests as universal. Politics in a democracy, the struggle for political power, thus becomes far more ideological than in any previous period in history. What was obvious for the ancients, and clear to the feudal system, becomes hidden in the democratic process. But the valuable side of this process must equally not be forgotten. The very need to appeal to social groups larger than the immediate interest group compels adjustment of various interests. Politics becomes more democratic.[11]

PRIVATE PROPERTY

Social power, in turn, either is derived from private property or is against it. The legal meaning of private property comprises two radically different conceptions: power over an external piece of nature (or an absolute right) and power over other men derived from power over nature.[12] It is only the second meaning of private property with which the political scientist is concerned: with proprietorship in the means of production. This type of property gives power—power in the labor market, in the commodity market, and in the political market of the state.

[11] It is this fact that Marxists usually overlook.
[12] The most significant analysis: Karl Renner, *The Institutions of Private Law and Their Social Functions,* first published in Germany, 1911, edited by O. Kahn-Freund (London, 1949).

The three power functions of property are usually (and particularly in Europe where political and social life is more petrified than in the United States) institutionalized in three types of organization: for the labor market, the employer's association; for the commodity market, the cartel; for the political market, the territorial form of the chambers of commerce and the functional form of the trade associations.

As against property, the trade unions (in Europe) attempt to organize the labor markets and the political markets by the collective power of organized labor, sometimes in one organization, sometimes in several. Consumers' and producers' cooperatives, however, affect only slightly the power of property in the commodity market.

Studies of these organizations and the devices by which their power is translated into political power are vital to the political scientist.[13] Large numbers of individual studies of pressure groups exist, but a really sophisticated, comparative analysis is still lacking. The translation of these economic power positions differs from country to country and from historical situation to historical situation. The relative strength of the competing economic groups is far more important for the analysis of political power than the study of the political institutions proper. There are countries (like Germany and England) where the agents and managers of the economic organizations enter parliaments directly; there are others (like the United States) where the influence is more indirect. There are countries (like Germany and England) where trade unions are political as well as industrial bodies; there are others (like France and the United States in certain situations) where they apparently abstain from politics.

The devices and forms for the translation of economic power into political power thus vary considerably, and yet patterns are discernible which ought to be more sharply defined on a comparative basis. A high degree of knowledge of problems of social

---

13 R. A. Brady, *Business as a System of Power* (New York, 1943), is a first attempt, but a rather crude and mechanistic one. Temporary National Economic Committee Monograph No. 26, *Economic Power and Political Pressures,* should be mentioned here.

stratification and economic organization is thus indispensable for the political scientist.

THE ASCENDANCE OF POLITICS AND OF BUREAUCRACIES

The classical relationship between economics and politics changes. It now appears as if political power has begun to emancipate itself from its economic roots and, indeed, tends to become a base for the acquisition of economic power. In general, bureaucratization is believed to be the manifestation of that trend which culminates in doctrines of managerial rule: private and public managers eliminating property owners and parliaments. The trend toward bureaucratization has unquestionably two roots: the transformation of parliamentary democracy into mass democracy; and the transition of a predominantly competitive enonomy into a predominantly organized economy. While these trends are known and progress under our very eyes, they do not necessarily involve an assumption of political power by bureaucracies. The growth of the scope and number of bureaucratic structures may merely indicate that the social groups which rule now need more and more bureaucracies in order to cope with the exercise of political power. But the equation of a larger number of bureaucrats with increase of their power is due to the inability (or unwillingness) to distinguish sharply three different problems involved in what is called "bureaucratization"; namely, bureaucratic behavior, bureaucratic structure, and bureaucratic power.

Bureaucratic behavior (roughly equated here with routine performance as against initiative or creative performance) is, of course, spreading. No sphere of activity is exempted from it. Whether it is beneficial or not shall not be discussed here. We should merely remember the tremendous extent to which our comforts depend on routine performances. Moreover, it is untrue that the decisions of the bureaucrats (public or private) are exclusively routine decisions. Many, indeed, are creative ones, not derived from precedent or standing rules, but highly discretionary and thus essentially law-making in character. Finally, bureaucratic organization, that is, hierarchies where commands are channeled from above to below and responsibility goes from below to above, is not confined to public life. The facts are obvious.

Though the growth of bureaucratic behavior, with the increase in the number of bureaucratic structures, is a continuous process, it does not thereby follow that power (private or public) has shifted to the bureaucracies. No abstract answer can be given; only empirical investigations can reveal whether shifts in power have taken place. Such investigations are, unfortunately, rare.

The Soviet Union presents a clear-cut marginal case where political power not only has made itself supreme but has become the fount of whatever economic power positions exist. Nazi Germany, on the other hand, exhibited a transitional case. It is undisputed that the Nazi party rose to power with the financial and political assistance of German big-business leaders who doubtless hoped to use the party for the promotion of their own interests. But the party, once having achieved power, emancipated itself from business control, and its political power became autonomous. The party then went further and attempted to create economic power positions for itself. Clearly the new political power was seeking to give itself an economic power base. This, indeed, is the significance of the Goering combine, the expanding enterprises of the Labor Front and the S.S., and the acquisitions resulting from Aryanization and Germanization. The war, which made it inadvisable to carry out sweeping institutional changes, interrupted the process. But it is quite safe to assume that, had there been no war or had the Nazis been victorious, the Soviet pattern would have prevailed.

The reactions to the ascendant role of political power are, as a rule, hostile. Most notable is the attempt to ascribe this phenomenon to democracy. This is, of course, essentially correct. For, as we have indicated, the attitude of democracy toward political power is undoubtedly positive. Yet more is meant by that statement, which by no means is a mere scientific one but has definite political undertones and overtones. It is implied that the growing political power will, by its inner dynamics, be abused and will ultimately lead to a totalitarian system. In this, modern criticism resumes the traditionalist critique not of political power but of democracy. Maistre and Bonald are resurrected. Proceeding from the shaky psychology of the essential evilness of man, they assert the inevitable transformation of democracy into mob rule, which, in conjunction with the modern trend of state interventionism, must culminate in totalitarianism. The remedy is some kind of aristocratic rule. A second reaction believes bureaucracy to be inimical to liberty and attempts to protect democracy by identifying it with individual liberty against the state.

Both reactions base themselves on what they call the tradition of Western civilization, the kernel of which is allegedly hostility to political power as expressed in constitutionalism. This is only a partial truth and, therefore, false. The tradition of Western civilization is more complex. Its richness was hinted at when we attempted to classify the various attitudes toward political power. Certainly, one may say that Rousseauism is a more important element in the political tradition of democracy than the essentially self-contradictory and arbitrary doctrines of Locke and of the natural law. That political power (whether democratic, aristocratic, or monarchic) can be abused is beyond doubt; but is is doubtful that abuses can be effectively checked by constitutionalism.[14] The problem of modern democracy is much less the fencing of political power than its rational utilization and provision for effective mass participation in its exercise.

IDENTIFICATION OF POLITICAL POWER

In the Soviet Union, there is little doubt where political power resides. In Nazi Germany, after June 1934, it was equally clear that the monopolistic party concentrated all political power. In a liberal democracy (and in constitutional systems generally) the identification of political power is extremely difficult. Our contention that political power has its roots in economic power can merely provide a frame within which the analyses have to be made; for we deliberately stated: "Social power . . . is derived from private property or is against it." Since the distribution of the "for" and "against" varies, the empirical sociological analyses of this interrelationship are the crucial concern of the political scientist.

Constitutional law helps but little. The form of government may or may not truly express the distribution of power. The doc-

[14] Edward S. Corwin, *Liberty against Government* (Baton Rouge, 1948).

trine of separate powers may or may not express the fact that social forces are as balanced as are the political institutions. As a rule, they are not.[15] Constitutional law merely supplies the frame for the exercise of political power but does not indicate its holder or its functions. All traditional legal conceptions are negative ones. They limit activities but do not shape them. It is this very character of law which grants to the citizen a minimum of protection. This applies specifically to the conception of external sovereignty, a term which we have so far avoided. It does not indicate the owner of sovereign power nor the use to which this power may or can be put; it merely delimits the power of one territorial unit from any other. The conception of property is fashioned in exactly the same way. It does not reveal the object of property nor its social function; it merely protects man's control of an external piece of nature. Constitutional law, secondly, indicates the form in which political power may be legitimately exercised. While the significance of both aspects of constitutional law may not be underestimated, empirical sociological studies of the locus of political power are indispensable.

There are, however, situations which may reveal in a flash, so to speak, where political power resides. There are emergency situations such as stages of siege, martial law, and so on. It is for this reason that Carl Schmitt, the famous Nazi constitutional lawyer, stated in his pre-Nazi period: "Sovereign is he who decides the emergency situation." [16] While not accepting the implications of Schmitt's doctrine of sovereignty, it is clear that the study of such emergency situations will yield valuable hints as to where political power actually resides in "normal" periods. Such a marginal situation existed in Nazi Germany on June 30, 1934. Up to that date, it could be very doubtful whether political power rested with the party alone, or with a combination of party, army, business, and so on. The liquidation of the Röhm group, of the generals, and of others made it, however, abundantly clear that the party had succeeded in monopolizing political power.

15 See my Introduction to Montesquieu, *The Spirit of the Laws* (New York, 1949).
16 Carl Schmitt, *Politische Theologie* (Leipzig, 1934), p. 11.

Such studies have been neglected. They are carried out mostly in terms of constitutional law, but rarely in political-sociological categories.

POLITICAL POWER AND FREEDOM

I stressed initially that political power is neither comparable to the concept of energy in physics nor the sole conception of political science. Yet the original formulation, power *vs.* idea, is too ideological. If history were a conflict between power groups and ideas, ideas would be invariably defeated. Politics is certainly the conflict between power groups, and the conflicts may be resolved by victory and defeat or by conciliation, that is, compromise. But one group may, in its struggle for power, represent more than a particular interest; it may indeed represent the idea of freedom, the idea crucial to political theory. If, for example, you analyze immigration legislation and come to the conclusion that business groups pressured for its liberalization in order to secure cheaper labor power, you have indeed done part of your task as political scientists, but only part of it. Of equal importance is the analysis of the role of immigration legislation in the historical development of the United States. The task of political theory is thus the determination of the degree to which a power group transcends its particular interest and advocates (in Hegelian terms) universal interests.

This determination is by no means easy. In fact, the distinction between ideology and truth becomes increasingly difficult. Some of the difficulty lies in the ideological character of politics in a democracy (discussed above), but, in the last resort, it results from the tremendous weight of power on what is called public opinion. Every political system impresses the mores of the ruling group upon the population. The greater the tensions, the more stringent the impositions become. The individual then resorts to many forms of dissimulation; and, in certain periods of history, it is the liar who becomes the hero.[17] The lie (in its many forms) becomes the protection of the individual against a universalized system of propaganda. . . .

[17] This is very striking in Stendhal's novels.

REINHARD BENDIX AND
SEYMOUR MARTIN LIPSET / The
Field of Political Sociology*

To bring order into a field of rapidly growing intellectual interest, we think it profitable to pay close attention to the major lines
of inquiry suggested by the classic writers in political sociology.
By relating their preoccupations to the major substantive areas of
empirical research a trial balance may be attempted. A survey of
nineteenth- and twentieth-century historical experience and
intellectual development reveals four problems or issues which
may be designated by the catch-phrases "class conflict," "consensus," "oligarchy," and "bureaucracy." Inquiry into each of these
problems has given rise to a voluminous literature. . . . Yet this
proliferation tends to obscure an underlying intellectual convergence between studies of class conflict and of consensus on the
one hand, and studies of oligarchy and of bureaucracy on the
other. These paired terms may be seen as shorthand designations
of the principal lines of inquiry which characterize political sociology and we will comment on them briefly.

* From *Current Sociology*, Vol. 6, No. 2 (1957), pp. 88–98. Portions of the
original article have been omitted.

CLASS CONFLICT AND CONSENSUS

The idea of class conflict is principally related to Karl Marx's emphasis upon the "material basis" of society.* The plethora of Marx critiques has not diminished the importance of this insight. For our purposes its main point is that the economic organization of every society provides conditions for a unity of interest and action wherever individuals find themselves in the same or similar social and economic positions, and also for diversity of interest and conflict wherever groups thus united face each other in opposition. In its modern, sociological usage this idea is divorced from the Marxian theory of history according to which the organization of production is the long-run or "ultimate" *determinant* of the country's intellectual and political life. Instead of regarding collective actions in some final sense as an inevitable product of common economic interests, political sociology emphasizes the fact that the interaction among individuals occupying the same economic position is also conditioned by cultural, social-psychological, and situational determinants. These conditions intervene between the economic position of individuals and their collective actions, making the latter less predictable than Marx would have us believe. These intervening conditions modify—though they do not nullify—the impact of economic self-interest on conduct.

Throughout the nineteenth century the Marxian position was challenged by conservatives who deplored the emphasis on self-interest as a constructive factor in history and who argued that the intensification of conflict, which Marx saw as the way to the new millennium, was in fact the prelude to social disintegration. These critics were concerned above all with the idea that every society and body politic required a degree of cohesion or consensus without which the values embodied in them could not survive. But the point of interest here is that consensus was idealized as against conflict. Liberal pluralism with its view that the adjustment of conflicts will enhance the wealth and welfare of nations, and Marxism with its view that ultimately a revolution is

* See the selections on class conflict in Chapter 5 and on Marxism in Chapter 11 of this Reader.

needed to resolve the issues which make conflicts under capitalism inevitable, were here opposed by the view that these benign results were impossible without social cohesion and that the conflicts leading to these results undermined that cohesion.

From the vantage point of today this great intellectual controversy of the nineteenth century is perhaps more significant for what each side omitted than for what each made explicit. The Marxian emphasis on the ultimate significance of conflict leads to a neglect of the specific conditions of social cohesion—even where these are relevant for the Marxian theory. Marxism is satisfied rather with broad assertions concerning the material conditions of bourgeois or proletarian class consciousness, and wherever consciousness does not "correspond" to these material conditions it is declared to be "false" and hence subject to change due to long-run historical necessity. All social cohesion arising from factors other than the organization of production (such as local or national traditions, ethnic homogeneity, cultural ideals) is treated as a phenomenon of secondary significance.[1] Exactly the reverse is true of the conservative outlook. Its emphasis on the ultimate significance of cohesion also leads to a neglect of the specific conditions of social cohesion, one of which is that conflicts within societies marked by cohesion are kept within limits. Many nineteenth- and twentieth-century conservatives were satisfied with broad assertions concerning societies as functioning wholes and wherever the lack of cohesion was evident, as in rapidly changing industrial societies, this was accordingly interpreted as indicating a decline of civilization. Thus, all evidence of cohesion within the context of conflict (such as the class-solidarity to which Marx referred, or the agreement on rules of the game characterizing the conflict-ridden relations between labor and management) was treated as a

[1] An amusing illustration of this neglect of inconvenient facts is contained in the 1870 resolution of the General Council of the First International, which was probably written by Marx personally. The resolution begins with the sentence "Although the revolutionary initiative will probably come from France, England alone can serve as the lever of a serious economic revolution. . . ." Apparently, Marx was not even aware of the fact that such a statement implicitly questioned his whole theory of history, which predicated the future political revolution upon antecedent changes in the economic substructure. The resolution is reprinted in Karl Marx, *Letters to Dr. Kugelmann* (New York, International Publishers, 1934, 106 p.).

phenomenon of secondary significance, if indeed it was examined at all.

Clearly, the two perspectives are supplementary, rather than mutually exclusive. They were made to appear irreconcilable during the nineteenth century by being incorporated in theories of history. Every observed fact was "extrapolated" in accordance with certain philosophical assumptions. Thus, the Marxist looked at all collective actions based on common economic interests as merely the preliminaries of an ultimate conflict, just as the conservatives looked at all evidence of conflict as merely the preliminaries of an ultimate decline. Up to a point, both of these perspectives are very useful, and have been used at least implicitly in much of the literature. For it is certainly true that the differential position of people in the economic structure of industrial societies is a major basis for the formulation of common interests and hence for collective political actions. And it is also *possible* that the resulting conflicts may lead to a revolutionary overthrow of the society, though—contrary to Marx—this becomes less probable as industrialization is developed successfully, for Marx was not aware that successful industrialization could lead to increased social cohesion. The class conflict as he envisaged it is therefore only the extreme form which the ordinary conflicts among interest groups may take under very special conditions. Similar statements may be made with regard to the conservative perspective. It is quite true that the materialism of industrial societies has destroyed many cultural values and that the reliance on self-interest and on individualism has jeopardized many ideals and institutions tending to safeguard the unity and solidarity of societies. And it is certainly *possible* that the resulting changes may eventuate in a "decline of civilization," although, contrary to the conservative perspective, that is again less probable as industrialization is developed successfully, because in that case new ideals and institutions arise in place of the old, and different forms of social cohesion may therefore become viable. The decline of civilization envisaged by the conservatives is only the *extreme* form which the transformation of values and institutions may take under very special conditions.

We will indicate briefly how these intellectual perspectives are reflected in the investigations of political sociology. For the political sociologist has taken over from the nineteenth century the analysis of collective actions based either on common economic *interest* or on a cultural and institutionally reinforced *consensus.* Much of the study of political behavior has been concerned with specifying the conditions under which members of social classes support or oppose the movements congruent with their social class. In a sense, if we ignore the normative assumptions inherent in Marx's description of the term, one could say that the analysis of class factors in the political struggle is the problem of true and false consciousness. That is, a considerable part of sociological research actually deals with those factors which increase or decrease the likelihood that a man will support the political movement linked with his class. Under this topic we would include:

1. Voting studies. These specify the elements which are associated with party support. They deal with the effects of factors such as varying status, type of work, property ownership, unemployment or insecurity, community social structure, social mobility, exposure to cross-class experiences, on the propensity of people to identify themselves with or against their class politically.

2. Studies of political participation. These have thrown a great deal of light on the linkage between participation and class position, and have made manifest the ways in which the normal operation of the social structure serves to weaken the political effectiveness of movements based on the lower class by reducing the involvement in politics of their potential followers.

3. Public opinion and attitudes. Analyses in this field have outlined a number of consistent variations in the values and attitudes of different classes, making understandable some of the political behavior of these groups which is not directly tied to interest. For example, the lower classes while liberal (leftist) in their attitudes on economic issues, tend to be less liberal on non-economic issues, e.g. civil liberties, race relations, immigration policy, and so forth.

One difficulty with much of the research which seeks to analyze the determinants of political cleavage is that the researchers too often deal with the relationship of specific variables to a given political event in a single country. Viewed cross-nationally, however, we find a considerable amount of variation in single relationships. For example, upward mobile people in the United States (the middle-class sons of workers) tend to be more conservative than those who have inherited high social status. However, in a number of European countries such as Sweden, Finland, and Germany, the upward mobile are more radical than the stable individuals. Among workers in Germany and Sweden, the better paid and more skilled are more likely to be class-conscious, and vote Social-Democratic or Communist, than those who are less well paid and less skilled. In Britain, the United States and Australia, however, the lower paid and less skilled prove better supporters of left parties than do the upper strata of the working class. Teachers and physicians tend to be on the right in Germany, while as compared with other professionals, they are rather on the left in France and Britain. Workers probably have a lower rate of electoral participation than middle-class people in the United States and Britain, while they have a higher rate in France and in a number of German and Austrian cities. We cite these variations to suggest that a *comparative* analysis of political behavior will be especially helpful in elucidating the effect of different cultural and institutional environments upon groups which—nominally at least—occupy a similar social and economic position in modern industrial societies.

Important as these cultural and structural variations are, they should not be permitted to obscure the pervasive effect of economic interest upon the political process. Every study of the social basis of political movements in the several countries of Western civilization indicates that the parties represent distinctive strata. Despite the great and complex diversity of historical conditions among the "Western" countries, three main political tendencies stand out in all of them: the left, based on the working class; the conservative right, based on the more privileged strata and institutions; and the center, based on the middle classes, especially the self-employed. Each of these three tendencies in the modern world has two expressions, one democratic and the other extremist and authoritarian. On the democratic side are the social democrats on the left, conservatives on the right, and liberals in the center. In crises, and in unstable societies, the social strata backing the democratic movements tend to develop an extremist reaction. The workers turn to communism, the conservative and upper-class strata turn to a traditional authoritarianism of the right, and the middle classes—the classic base of the center—back fascism. It is a real paradox that this evolution of the twentieth century appears to make good Marx's prediction of an ultimate class conflict and the conservatives' prediction of a cultural decline, but that nevertheless this phenomenon is not readily assimilable to either theory. For these movements have occurred in backward as well as in industrialized countries; instead of being the outgrowth of class conflict, they are in effect protests against it; instead of reflecting a decline of social cohesion, they represent a sudden, if perhaps momentary, rebirth of it. But the main point is that any all-embracing political system of whatever label destroys the cohesion which holds modern societies together—contrary to the Marxist who ignores that cohesion, and contrary to the conservatives who deny its existence. It is for this reason that the intellectual legacies of the nineteenth century can no longer suffice as the basis of political sociology. For mass-organization refers to a type of political behavior which cannot be explained adequately either by the coalescence of economic interests or by the consensus based on cultural traditions. The study of totalitarianism must concern itself, therefore, with just those extreme eventualities which the nineteenth-century Marxists *and* conservatives conjured with, but failed to analyze: the breakdown of that cohesion, the politics of the possible, which the class conflict and consensus of industrial societies had always presupposed.

We turn now to the second major theme of political sociology.

BUREAUCRACY AND OLIGARCHY

If the concern with class conflict and consensus arose from nineteenth-century preoccupations, the interest in bureaucracy and oligarchy is a typical twentieth-century phenomenon. The reasons for this shift of emphasis are clear. The problem of "consensus" had arisen from a preoccupation with the disruptive consequences of the Industrial Revolution and of the change from absolutist to democratic regimes; the problem of "class conflict" had arisen from a preoccupation with the dynamics of change in an industrial society. Under these circumstances "bureaucracy" was not a problem to be studied, but an evil to be fought. Conservatives claimed that governments arbitrarily interfered with the organic growth of society, while liberals and radicals maintained that they interfered, equally arbitrarily, with the natural rights and the basic liberties of the people. Similarly, oligarchy was not a problem to be studied—indeed it was not seen as a problem at all. For the conservatives who gloried in the romantic imagery of an estate society, all government was a rule of the few. Their ideal of government was a rule by a superbly endowed aristocracy which represented the traditional estates and was naturally superior to the leveling tendencies of democracy. And for the radicals who gloried in the spontaneity of the people, all existing governments were arbitrary usurpations of power which must be overcome by organizations of the people. In this conflict between usurpation and spontaneity it appeared as if "oligarchy" was always the problem of the government in power, but not the organizations opposing that government.

Several prophetic thinkers of the nineteenth century questioned these naive assumptions. Among them Alexis de Tocqueville stands out today as perhaps the most penetrating analyst of the autocratic tendencies which are implicit in the demand for equality;* and the Swiss historian Jacob Burckhardt is also now well known for his profoundly pessimistic views concerning the dictatorships which would arise from the quest for democratic institutions. But neither de Tocqueville's prophetic insight nor Burckhardt's more personal apprehensions were widely appreciated. Instead, the problems of bureaucracy and oligarchy became of serious intellectual concern in the course of the great socialist debate. In the first volume of *Das Kapital*, Marx dismissed the critics of socialism with the statement that the "enthusiastic apol-

* See the selection from de Tocqueville in Chapter 4 of this Reader.

ogists of the factory system have nothing more damning to urge against a general organization of the labor of society than that it would turn all society into one immense factory." And in his famous pamphlet *State and Revolution,* Lenin suggested that most bureaucratic and oligarchic evils which beset government under capitalism would be eliminated under socialism, because most state functions "have become so simplified and can be reduced to such simple operations . . . that they will be quite within the reach of every literate person." Neither Marx nor Lenin believed that bureaucracy and oligarchy presented a problem in the socialist society of the future.

But other socialists disagreed vehemently. In his famous letter of repudiation Proudhon had challenged Marx's autocratic manner in an eloquent plea against a socialism which would overthrow an old autocracy only to introduce a new dictatorship. And many decades later Rosa Luxemburg wrote her impassioned critique of the Bolshevik revolution in which she accused Lenin of having deserted the cause of freedom. "The whole mass of the people must take part in t[he government]. Otherwise, socialism will be decreed from behind a few official desks by a dozen intellectuals." Clearly, Proudhon and Luxemburg saw the issue and Marx and Lenin did not; but while this debate helped to focus public attention on the problems of bureaucracy and oligarchy in modern society, its polemic emphasis was unfavorable to a systematic consideration.

It is not surprising that such a consideration was initiated on the European continent, with its prevalance of absolutist governments, rather than in England or the United States, where the problems of bureaucracy and oligarchy tended to be considered in a pragmatic rather than a theoretical fashion. In this field political sociologists have taken much of their inspiration from the work of two German scholars, Max Weber and Robert Michels. The two men were well acquainted personally. Weber was principally concerned with bureaucracy in government and in economic enterprises, while Michels was for the most part concerned with oligarchy in voluntary associations. Both were preoccupied with the perennial recurrence of aristocratic or oligarchic tendencies in society. Both had a penchant for a tough-minded appraisal of the contemporary political sence. In their view, class struggles could only occur through the instrumentality of formal organizations, and the great striking power of modern governments and armies made the question of popular consensus a distinctly secondary phenomenon. For them the question was how the instrumentalities of power—governmental bureaucracy and party organizations—affected the distribution and exercise of power. We shall comment briefly on each man's work and on the main lines of inquiry in political sociology which may be related to that work.

Max Weber was in part a disciple of the historical school in economics whose most prominent spokesman, Gustav Schmoller, was well-known for his history of Prussian administration. Politically as well as academically Schmoller represented a scholarly tradition which identified itself closely with the monarchy and its officialdom, and which viewed the latter as an embodiment of morality and efficiency. Perhaps Weber used this perspective when he formulated his ideal type of bureaucratic rule which was characterized by thorough professionalization and a maximum of technical efficiency. On this basis he developed a conceptual framework in which each characteristic of bureaucratic administration was contrasted with its personally arbitrary counterpart under a system of patrimonial administration. Weber then used this framework to interpret the relation between the political structure, the economy, and the major status groups in different civilizations, as for example in his studies of China and India. He also used this typology to interpret the massive process of bureaucratization which had accompanied the rise of absolutism and of democracy as well as the development of modern industry. In his view, modern bureaucratic government was technically superior to other forms of administration, such as those obtaining under charismatic or traditional authority. But he was much concerned lest the preoccupation with administrative efficiency (such as prevailed among German scholars in the late nineteenth century) be permitted to obscure the threat to individual freedom implicit in that efficiency. And he was alarmed by the tendencies of the German bureaucracy which used its privileged position in order to transmute problems of political statesmanship into supposedly routine, administrative questions to the great detriment of constructive political action as well as of administrative impartiality. These comments make it clear that Weber's work in this field had a two-fold emphasis.

He characterized his general analysis of bureaucracy as "purely formal and typological" and he used it principally in a comparative and developmental context. His main thesis concerning the bureaucratization of government and industry has proved very fruitful. Historians, political scientists and sociologists have produced a large number of studies which have examined this process of bureaucratization. Some of these studies have been cast in the framework of a national administrative history such as the great work of T. F. Tout; others have followed Weber's precedent by developing a comparative approach as in the work of C. J. Friedrich or Otto Hintze; still others have examined some part of this process in detail, as in the many studies of civil-service reform or of the changing structure of the modern business corporation. There are many telling examinations of non-bureaucratic governmental structures comparable to Weber's ideal type of patrimonialism, such as Leroy-Beaulieu's classic study of the Tsarist regime or the growing literature on the structure of government under the Chinese dynasties. Also relevant in this general context are the increasing number of studies which focus upon the governmental structures of pre-literate societies (such as the writings of Fortes, Gluckman, Schapera, and others on Africa) or upon the special administrative problems arising from the contact of cultures (as Lord Hailey's African survey or Furnivall's studies of colonial government in Southeast Asia). Naturally, this varied literature is not always directly indebted to Weber's work. But it may be useful to consider it in this context, because these numerous studies have in common an interest in the relations between social structure and the formal organizations of government and economic life, and this emphasis is conspicuously lacking in the literature on public administration and on economic institutions.

The special impact of Weber's work on the study of bureaucracy has been due largely to his clear formulation of an ideal type, which has proved especially useful in developmental studies. Weber himself never confused such "bench-mark devices" with detailed case studies. His own political analysis of the German bureaucracy showed, for example, how its methods of recruitment systematically favored some, and discriminated against other, segments of the population, and thus reinforced the petty conceit of the officials in their dealings with the public. The German officials were in his estimation very far removed from their own vaunted ideal of administrative impartiality, since they constantly dabbled in politics despite their notorious ineptitude for the demands of political life. Indeed, Weber believed that any concrete study of bureaucracy in action must be preeminently the study of a struggle for the power to make decisions, since officials remain outside such struggles only as long as they remain "ideal-typical" as the impartial, technically proficient executors of policies handed down to them. That they do not remain "ideal-typical" in this sense and the reasons why they do not do so, have been important subjects of study since Weber's time.[2]

We should add that studies of large-scale organizations have derived their inspiration also from others than Max Weber, though it is noteworthy that in recent years there is growing evidence of a coalescence of intellectual traditions and interests. In the 1920's the famous Hawthorne studies were initiated by the late Elton Mayo, who was principally indebted to the work of Emile Durkheim. These studies have been followed by a very large number of others which have concerned themselves with the conditions under which the participants in large-scale organizations deviate from the blueprint of their rights and duties as these are formally stipulated. Most of these studies have dealt with the many ways in which primary groups, by informally developing and enforcing a consensus of their own, have helped to further or to obstruct the achievement of managerial goals. And in conse-

[2] For a brief review of some studies which reflect this emphasis see S. M. Lipset, "Political Sociology, 1945–55", in: Hans Zetterberg, ed., *Sociology in the United States,* Paris, Unesco, 1956, pp. 53–55.

quence much attention has been given to the "human relations approach" which would solve the personnel problems of middle management. The managerial orientation of this approach has often been commented on, but it may be that in recent years a slight, but important, shift of emphasis has occurred.

Several studies have appeared which make it clear that the managerial approach to human relations is yet another factor which must be considered in an analysis of modern, large-scale organizations, particularly because there is considerable discrepancy between "human relations practice" and "human relations ideology." Moreover, empirical research has moved on from the examination of factories and government agencies to such other organizations as prisons, hospitals, business offices, churches, and military organizations. As a result, it has had to broaden its perspective to encompass a great variety of managerial goals which are not as readily measurable as productivity. And while it is hazardous to generalize in this field and at this time, it is perhaps fairly close to the mark to say that the study of organizations has become "politicized." Outside of such strictly hierarchical organizations as business, government, and the army, it is perhaps easier for all concerned to admit openly that each organization encompasses not only different levels of authority but also different views of the organization's purpose. Until recently, such differences in outlook were confined to well-known conflicts between labor and management, between privates and officers, and between government administrators, politicians, and the public. But it has become evident that many organizations in fact institutionalize conflicts among their several managerial echelons. Hospitals could not function without administrative and medical staffs; universities must have administrators as well as faculty; department stores must have buyers as well as administrative executives; modern prisons and mental hospitals include among their staff custodians, welfare specialists, teachers, doctors, and psychiatrists. In this view of organization the "trained incapacity" of the specialist and the vested interest of different administrative units become indispensable for the proper functioning of the organization, an asset as well as a liability. For the goals and procedures of organizations are formulated and reformulated by individuals in administrative units, whose ideas frequently clash and who compete with each other for recognition and advancement. Hence, management has the task of properly utilizing conflicts as well as of eliminating them where they become too disruptive. In this perspective, politics in the sense of competition for power does not stop at the door of organizations, and managerial strategies within organizations are properly seen as continuous with the managerial efforts to maximize the advantages of organizations with reference to competitors outside.

But if internal competition and conflict are seen as a necessary concomitant of many hierchical organizations, it should also be stated that internal politics in the democratic sense is conspicuously absent from many voluntary associations. This absence of politics points to the rule of the few, the problem of oligarchy, and that brings us to the work of Robert Michels.* The intellectual antecedents of Michels' concern with the oligarchic tendencies of political parties have again a distinctly Continental origin. Whereas Weber was concerned with the suffocation of German political life under the combined impact of Bismarck and an overweening bureaucracy, Michels was principally interested in exposing the facts behind the sham battles of political controversy. In particular, Michels pointed out that under universal suffrage the interest of all political parties in electoral victories had produced a major hiatus between what party spokesmen believed and what they could say in public. Aristocratic landowners who really regarded themselves as a born ruling class and the people as a dangerous rabble had nevertheless to profess democratic sentiments when they appealed to the voters. The spokesmen of German liberalism had endeavored to reform the monarchy and to reconcile it with democratic principles, but at each step on the road they had recoiled from the dangers of socialism implicit in an extension of the suffrage. And this same contradiction also applied to the revolutionary parties, which professed aloud their opposition to oligarchic rule only to adopt such a rule in fact in their own organizations. "The study of the oligarchical

* See the selection from Michels in Chapter 8 of this Reader.

manifestations in party life is most valuable and most decisive in
its results when undertaken in relation to the revolutionary parties, for the reason that these parties, in respect of their origin
and of their programme, represent the negation of any such tendency, and have actually come into existence out of opposition
thereto." [3] In pursuing this line of inquiry Michels showed that
direct popular control over political parties was technically impossible, especially since parties are fighting organizations which
require internal discipline in order to succeed. The people, moreover, shun the burdens which direct government would impose;
they tend to be apathetic, and they need leadership. The leaders,
on the other hand, seek to perpetuate themselves in office, their
position in the party makes it relatively easy for them to do so,
and attempts to restrict their autocratic use of power and their
continuation in office usually fail.

If we accept Michels' formulation of the problem, we are faced
with the fact that modern democracies do not constitute a government by the people. Instead, this form of government consists
of conflicts of power among oligarchic organizations, with the result that the average citizen exercises his rights of citizenship only
in the sense that he chooses among alternatives presented to him
by these competing oligarchies. It is to be noted, however, that in
this view oligarchic rule in private government means that the
leaders pursue their own interests and do not represent the interests of the members. Although political sociologists have so far
only touched upon the interrelation between the organizational
imperatives and the representativeness of voluntary associations,
there are many theoretical problems and questions of fact which
remain to be dealt with.

Like Michels, a number of other writers have been preoccupied
with the discrepancy between the democratic form and the oligarchic facts of voluntary associations. They have documented in
detail the existence of central administrative control by the leaders, and the absence of political opposition and of membership
control. But by virtue of this preoccupation with the factors responsible for the existence of oligarchic rule, such studies have

[3] Robert Michels, *Political Parties* (Glencoe, Ill., The Free Press, 1949), p. 11.

neglected the possible variations of political life within political parties and other associations. By limiting himself to the European social-democratic movements Michels also limited himself to one specific form of oligarchy. In their various writings, Maurice Duverger, Sigmund Neumann, and others have shown, on the other hand, that there are significant variations in the organizational structure of different political parties. For example, the two major political parties in the United States differ greatly from the social democratic pattern which served Michels as a model, in that they lack central control at the national level and possess comparatively little centralization even at the state level. Moreover, factionalism is replete in America and turn-over in party control is fairly common, presumably because the American parties are parties of "notables" active especially during electoral campaigns rather than mass parties with a permanently functioning organization. But while recent studies have done much to correct Michels' monolithic view of oligarchic tendencies in political parties, studies of private government still continue to stress these tendencies. There are many studies which show that trade unions are controlled by oligarchies, but next to none which concern themselves with the considerable range of variation in the internal government of trade unions within as well as between different countries.

The problem of oligarchy apart, there still remains the question of representativeness. The extent to which leaders are free to deviate from the interests of their members varies considerably. For example, the United Mine Workers of America is probably one of the most oligarchic or dictatorial unions in the world. But although its leader, John L. Lewis, is a Republican politically, he has nevertheless adopted union tactics whose militancy is more marked than that of the miners' unions in some other countries, which are under the leadership of communists or left-wing socialists. Such a discrepancy between political conservatism and tactical militancy—just like the opposite combination, say, between the political radicalism and the tactical conservatism of the German Social Democratic Party—are hardly illuminated by further studies of the "iron law of oligarchy," although in both cases the organizations were ruled by leaders who perpetuated themselves in office. It is clear, therefore, that by itself oligarchy does not determine the actions of the leaders, and this may be related in turn to the considerable variations in the methods of internal control, all of which are compatible with "oligarchy." Thus, organizations representing large masses, such as veterans' organizations, farm groups, trade unions, and certain types of political party will vary among themselves, and they will also differ as a group from the organizations of large business corporations or of the various professions. Does the fact that manufacturers' associations are governed by self-perpetuating oligarchies have the same consequences on their representative character as similar political forms in a trade union or a political party? There is some evidence to indicate that, even with reference to the same type of organization, the official leadership tends to represent the membership in one country, but is unrepresentative of it in another.[4] What is clearly called for in this field is a number of comparative investigations amplifying and extending the theory of organizational government.

COMPARATIVE STUDIES IN POLITICAL SOCIOLOGY

Although comparative studies do not constitute a separate subject matter, their importance is so great that we comment on them separately. Like the other inquiries of political sociology, the comparative study of political systems has a long intellectual history. In that mixture of ethical speculation and empirical observation which is called "political theory" it constitutes in fact one of the oldest fields of study. Yet the antecedents of political sociology are of much more recent date. An empirical approach to comparative political analysis came to the fore during the nine-

[4] According to a study conducted for the British Medical Association (BMA), the rank and file of British doctors has a much more favorable attitude towards state medicine than the officials of the BMA. On the other hand, Oliver Garceau's study of the American Medical Association tends to show that the officials of the organization have changed their policies over the years, on the whole taking a line midway between the more radical and the more reactionary state societies.

teenth century when many European intellectuals raised questions about the success of democracy in the United States, the capacity of England to work out a viable compromise between aristocratic traditions and democratic tendencies, and the failure in these respects of most Continental countries. Many reasons were cited to account for these differences: the United States lacked a feudal tradition, England had a long history of compromises between central and local powers, the American frontier involved large parts of the community in the process of government, the tradition of local autonomy in England and America encouraged voluntary associations to perform many functions which elsewhere required government action, and so forth. The work of Alexis de Tocqueville was perhaps the finest result of this line of inquiry. And it is well to remember that de Tocqueville developed his remarkable insight into the despotic possibilities inherent in democracy by writing about American society in terms of its likenesses and contrasts with France.[5]

In the hands of a genius like de Tocqueville the comparative study of politics tended to become systematic, but most similar studies of the time were merely descriptive and eclectic. During the nineteenth century only Marxism provided a systematic theory of comparative politics and even a century later it is still fruitful to use this theory as a point of departure. Briefly put, Marxism identified democracy with the class interests of the bourgeoisie in a capitalist economy. In a democratic political system these interests could be pursued without much interference by the government. The interest in free trade made also for an interest in a free political system, especially where aristocratic landowners opposed both, for in that case the bourgeoisie could consistently pursue its economic, its social, and its political interests all at the same time. Marxists contended further that the bourgeois interest in democracy necessarily waned wherever the work-

[5] "In my work on America . . . though I seldom mentioned France, I did not write a page without thinking of her, and placing her as it were before me. . . . I believe that this perpetual silent reference to France was a principal cause of the book's success." See the letter to Kergorlay (19 October, 1843) in *Memoir, Letters and Remains of Alexis de Tocqueville* (Boston, Ticknor & Fields, 1862), Vol. I, 342 p.

ing class became organized sufficiently to become a serious rival
for political power. Hence, democracy failed in the countries in
which the bourgeois fear of the workers exceeded the bourgeois
interest in free institutions. In the Marxist scheme of history, the
working class necessarily took over from the bourgeoisie the
struggle for democratic institutions. As an interpretation of the
development of such countries as France, Germany, Italy, and
Russia, this has much to recommend it. But in recent years increasing attention has been devoted to what Marxism failed to
take into account; for it is noteworthy that the theory applied
least to the country on whose historical experience Marx principally relied for his evidence: England. Clearly, the working class
became less radical politically in the country which was farthest
advanced economically. Radicalism, in other words, was a concomitant of economic backwardness; also of a world-wide diffusion of ideologies, the acceptance of which in the receiving countries was not an outgrowth of their class structures, though it
often had a major impact on these class structures. If this be conceded, then it becomes necessary to reconsider the relation between the changing class structure of societies undergoing industrialization and the development of nationalist sentiment, for
which there is obviously more place in history than in Marxism.
We note that today a great deal of thinking and research along
these lines is under way—this topic alone would require a separate report, it being an exceedingly important area of comparative study in political sociology.

Another dimension has been added to that study by the rise in
recent decades of new political mass-movements. In their efforts
to grapple with this phenomenon many scholars have become
concerned once more with the relation between political systems
and the underlying social structure. Recalling the earlier emphasis upon the role of consensus in society, some theorists have suggested that societies are particularly vulnerable to totalitarianism
if their internal social structure fails to provide the citizens with a
widespread network of secondary organizations. In the absence of
such organizations and their countervailing power we get, they
say, a *mass society* in which individuals are not involved in the

political system and consequently helpless before the power of the government and of mass organizations like totalitarian parties.* Accordingly it is suggested that such secondary organizations exist in the Anglo-Saxon countries, but were absent from pre-Hitler German society or nineteenth-century Tsarist Russia. Whatever its merit, this approach is obviously related to the theory of political pluralism which enjoys considerable vogue among British and American political theorists. It is also related to the consideration that democratic institutions are viable only as long as a society is characterized by certain shared values, especially those supporting adherence to the rules of the game in a political democracy. Such consensus is in turn likely to be related to the absence of basic cleavages among the different classes and regions of a country.

The concern with comparative studies in political sociology does not involve theoretical perspectives which differ from those employed in the study of a single political system. Scholars in this field must always ask what are the factors which cause variations in the style and organization of political life in different countries, or in the same country over a period of time. Underlying this question is the assumption that political systems—like family systems, industrial organizations, and others—are interrelated with other aspects of the social structure, so that it should be possible to analyze the co-variation among several such aspects. But it is well to remember also that comparative studies tend to emphasize the varied political possibilities which have been realized in structurally similar situations. These studies therefore help to emphasize that element of leeway for "maximizing and calculating" actions which makes politics an "art" and the study of political sociology a challenging intellectual enterprise.

* See the selections in Chapter 4 of this Reader.

PART I

SOCIAL BASES OF POLITICAL SYSTEMS

EDITOR'S INTRODUCTION

One way of examining the social bases of political systems is to start with an implicit or explicit typology of polities, and then to look for the social variables associated with each type. Another way is to begin with a typology of societies, and then look for the kinds of political systems that spring up in each.

The former is the method that would follow from the well-known classification of Gabriel Almond. He proposed that many polities can be fitted into one of the following categories: Anglo-American; pre-industrial; totalitarian; continental European.[1] This is a very useful classification, but one that may confound social and political variables, and thus make correlational studies invalid. For example, pre-industrial political systems, by definition, are those that are found in societies that have a certain low level of economic development.

My own preference is for a simple division of political systems into democratic, authoritarian, totalitarian. This is the classification system used by Linz, in his discussion of Spain as an authoritarian regime.

An example of how the correlational method works can be seen in the selection by Lipset. Lipset divides countries into two different cultural groups. Within each of these, he further divides countries into "more" and "less" democratic, and then looks for the degree of economic development characteristic of each. In the article included here, Lipset examines development, legitimacy, and "effectiveness" as conditions underlying democracy. (The latter two, however, are social conditions that facilitate the stability of any kind of political regime.)

Eckstein also uses the correlational approach, but he focuses on variables different from those seen by Lipset. Eckstein's thesis is that governmental stability is enhanced when the authority pat-

[1] See Gabriel Almond, "Comparative Political Systems," *Journal of Politics*, Vol. 18 (August, 1956), pp. 391–409.

terns of political institutions are similar to those of social institutions.

He questions Lipset's finding of a correlation between economic development and political democracy. I agree with this criticism, especially because Lipset appears to ignore the question of socialism or communism as a road to economic development. The Soviet Union has made great economic strides, which some observers would link directly to the *absence* of political democracy.

As Horowitz points out in the selection included here, in the "Third World nations" it is more relevant to speak of a *political* basis of economics, rather than an *economic* basis to politics. The decisions of the ruling groups in the Third World countries will largely determine the rate of economic growth; all of which points to a connection between *authoritarianism* and economic development. In this context, democracy would be a "second stage" more likely to result after some level of economic development had been reached.

Perhaps even more difficult than classifying societies by their political structure, is the alternative of classifying them according to their social structure.

Kornhauser's typology of societies is based on the question of the existence of social structures which mediate between the individual and the state, and thus provide insulation for elites as well as the masses.[2] Linking the aristocratic critique of mass society provided by such writers as de Tocqueville and Ortega y Gasset with the democratic critique of people like Hannah Arendt and C. Wright Mills,[3] Kornhauser provides a typology of four societies:

[2] William Kornhauser, *The Politics of Mass Society* (Glencoe, Ill., The Free Press, 1959), Chap. 2.
[3] See Alexis de Tocqueville, *Democracy in America* (New York, Alfred Knopf, 1945), 2 vols.; Jose Ortega y Gasset, *The Revolt of the Masses* (New York, W. W. Norton, 1932); Hannah Arendt, *The Origins of Totalitarianism* (New York, Harcourt Brace, 1951); C. Wright Mills, *The Power Elite* (New York, Oxford U. Press, 1956). One of the best contemporary discussions of the dangers of mass society can be found in the writing of Nisbet. See Robert Nisbet, *Community and Power* (New York, Oxford University Press, 1962).

KORNHAUSER'S TYPOLOGY OF SOCIETIES

Availability of masses for mobilization by elites

		Low	High
Accessibility of elites to influence by the masses	Low	communal (Hopi Indians)	totalitarian (Nazi Germany)
	High	pluralist (contemporary England)	mass (Weimar Republic)

Again, there is some problem as to whether the category "totalitarian" does not combine social and political defining characteristics into one. Kornhauser's main thesis is that the absence of intermediate structures such as voluntary associations makes a mass society vulnerable to the development of totalitarian movements. His theory of mass society attempts to account for the fact that some political democracies have changed into totalitarian systems.[4]

Lower class access via class-district associations

		Prohibited	Enforced or permitted
Individual access from the lower classes	Prohibited	Traditional	Corporatist
	Permitted or encouraged	Plebiscitarian	Pluralist

Reinhard Bendix and Stein Rokkan, "The Extension of National Citizenship to the Lower Classes: A Comparative Perspective," a paper presented to the First World Congress of Sociology, Washington D.C., 1962.

One of the key trends of the twentieth century has been the emergence of totalitarian systems. As Moore points out, there were already totalitarian elements in a number of pre-industrial systems.[5] Contemporary totalitarianism goes further than any

[4] An interesting analysis which parallels Kornhauser's classification in many ways is that of Bendix and Rokkan. Their categories are based on an historical analysis of the access and entry of European lower classes into politics. Their model is as follows:

[5] See Barrington Moore, Jr., *Political Power and Social Theory* (Cambridge, Harvard University Press, 1958), Chap. 2.

previous system. The development of a modern technology of communications and violence provides a more complete system of terrorization and political domination. The selection by Arendt discusses some of the mechanisms of violence by which the Nazi regime was able to maintain its domination.

Perhaps more dangerous than totalitarianism that involves the open use of violence, terror and intimidation is the possibility of a more subtle despotism to which a democratic nation can succumb. This is the theme of the selection by de Tocqueville, and it is carried forward in the analysis by Marcuse. Democratic totalitarianism is more dangerous precisely because it is more subtle, and because it can be even more pervasive than the Nazi or Stalinist models. We have no difficulty in identifying the striped tiger as the enemy. But what if he camouflages his stripes and disguises his claws?

The final problem with which these selections are concerned is the change from one type of political system to another. The work of those who have written about "mass society," like Kornhauser, stems largely from a concern lest certain social characteristics of democratic societies make them vulnerable to being transformed into totalitarian ones. The question of change is alluded to also by Linz in a section of his article not included here. Linz raises the question of whether authoritarian polities have a built-in tendency to move toward totalitarianism or democracy. He concludes that they are not necessarily "transitional," but may constitute stable political regimes.

I have included Huntington's article in this section not only because it is a good discussion of authoritarianism in the developing nations, but also because it takes a less than optimistic view of the effects of economic development on political systems. His main thesis is that there is not necessarily any one unilinear pattern of political development that must be followed: that in terms of democratic values, political "decay" into authoritarian patterns of government is just as likely as political "development" toward an approximation of the American system. However that would not preclude the attainment of some more democratic political system in these countries in the future.

2 / DEMOCRACY

SEYMOUR MARTIN LIPSET / Some Social Requisites of Democracy*

Comparative generalizations dealing with complex social systems must necessarily deal rather summarily with particular historical features of any one society within the scope of the investigation. In order to test these generalizations bearing on the differences between countries which rank high or low in possession of the attributes associated with democracy, it is necessary to establish some empirical measures of the type of political system. Individual deviations from a particular aspect of democracy are not too important, as long as the definitions unambiguously cover the great majority of nations which are located as democratic or undemocratic. The precise dividing line between "more democratic" and "less democratic" is also not a basic problem, since presumably democracy is *not* a quality of a social system which either does or does not exist, but is rather a complex of characteristics which may be ranked in many different ways. For this reason it was decided to divide the countries under consideration into two groups, rather than to attempt to rank them from highest to lowest. Ranking *individual* countries from the most to the least democratic is much more difficult than splitting the countries into two classes, "more" or "less" democratic, although even here borderline cases such as Mexico pose problems.

Efforts to classify all countries raise a number of problems. Most countries which lack an enduring tradition of political democracy lie in the traditionally underdeveloped sections of the

* From *American Political Science Review* (March, 1939), pp. 73–80; 83–95; 97; 102–105. Portions of the original article have been omitted.

world. It is possible that Max Weber was right when he suggested that modern democracy in its clearest forms can only occur under the unique conditions of capitalist industrialization.[1] Some of the complications introduced by the sharp variations in political practices in different parts of the earth can be reduced by dealing with differences among countries within political culture areas. The two best areas for such internal comparison are Latin America as one, and Europe and the English-speaking countries as the other. More limited comparisons may be made among the Asian states, and among the Arab countries.

The main criteria used in this paper to locate European democracies are the uninterrupted continuation of political democracy since World War I *and* the absence over the past twenty-five years of a major political movement opposed to the democratic "rules of the game." [2] The somewhat less stringent criterion employed for Latin Amercia is whether a given country has had a history of more or less free elections for most of the post-World War I period. Where in Europe we look for stable democracies, in South America we look for countries which have not had fairly constant dictatorial rule (See Table I). No detailed analysis of the political history of either Europe or Latin America has been made with an eye toward more specific criteria of differentiation; at this point in the examination of the requisites of democracy, election results are sufficient to locate the European countries, and the judgments of experts and impressionistic assessments based on fairly well-known facts of political history will suffice for Latin America.[3]

1 See Max Weber, "Zur Lage der burgerlichen Demokratie in Russland," *Archiv für Sozialwissenschaft und Sozialpolitik,* Vol. 22 (1906), pp. 346 ff.
2 The latter requirement means that no totalitarian movement, either fascist or communist, received twenty percent of the vote during this time. Actually all the European nations falling on the democratic side of the continuum had totalitarian movements which secured less than seven percent of the vote.
3 The historian Arthur P. Whitaker, for example, has summarized the judgments of experts on Latin America to be that "the countries which have approximated most closely to the democratic ideal have been . . . Argentina, Brazil, Chile, Colombia, Costa Rica, and Uruguay." See "The Pathology of Democracy in Latin America: A Historian's Point of View," *American Political Science Review,* Vol. 44 (1950), pp. 101–118. To this group I have added Mexico. Mexico has allowed freedom of the press, of assembly, and of organization, to opposition parties, although there is good evidence that it does not

TABLE I. CLASSIFICATION OF EUROPEAN, ENGLISH-
SPEAKING AND LATIN AMERICAN NATIONS BY
DEGREE OF STABLE DEMOCRACY

European and English-speaking Nations		Latin American Nations	
Stable Democracies	Unstable Democracies and Dictatorships	Democracies and Unstable Dictatorships	Stable Dictatorships
Australia	Austria	Argentina	Bolivia
Belgium	Bulgaria	Brazil	Cuba
Canada	Czechoslovakia	Chile	Dominican Republic
Denmark	Finland	Colombia	Ecuador
Ireland	France	Costa Rica	El Salvador
Luxemburg	Germany (West)	Mexico	Guatemala
Netherlands	Greece	Uruguay	Haiti
New Zealand	Hungary		Honduras
Norway	Iceland		Nicaragua
Sweden	Italy		Panama
Switzerland	Poland		Paraguay
United Kingdom	Portugal		Peru
United States	Rumania		Venezuela
	Spain		
	Yugoslavia		

ECONOMIC DEVELOPMENT AND DEMOCRACY

Perhaps the most widespread generalization linking political systems to other aspects of society has been that democracy is re-

---

allow them the opportunity to win elections, since ballots are counted by the incumbents. The existence of opposition groups, contested elections, and adjustments among the various factions of the governing *Partido Revolucionario Institucional* does introduce a considerable element of popular influence in the system.

The interesting effort of Russell Fitzgibbon to secure a "statistical evaluation of Latin American democracy" based on the opinion of various experts is not useful for the purposes of this paper. The judges were asked not only to rank countries as democratic on the basis of purely political criteria, but also to consider the "standard of living" and "educational level." These latter factors may be conditions for democracy, but they are not an aspect of democracy as such. See Russell H. Fitzgibbon, "A Statistical Evaluation of Latin American Democracy," *Western Political Quarterly*, Vol. 9 (1956), pp. 607–619.

lated to the state of economic development. Concretely, this means that the more well-to-do a nation, the greater the chances that it will sustain democracy. From Aristotle down to the present, men have argued that only in a wealthy society in which relatively few citizens lived in real poverty could a situation exist in which the mass of the population could intelligently participate in politics and could develop the self-restraint necessary to avoid succumbing to the appeals of irresponsible demagogues. A society divided between a large impoverished mass and a small favored elite would result either in oligarchy (dictatorial rule of the small upper stratum) or in tyranny (popularly based dictatorship). And these two political forms can be given modern labels: tyranny's modern face is communism or Peronism; oligarchy appears today in the form of traditionalist dictatorships such as we find in parts of Latin America, Thailand, Spain, or Portugal.

As a means of concretely testing this hypothesis, various indices of economic development—wealth, industrialization, urbanization, and education—have been defined, and averages (means) have been computed for the countries which have been classified as more or less democratic in the Anglo-Saxon world and Europe and Latin America.

In each case, the average wealth, degree of industrialization and urbanization, and level of education is much higher for the more democratic countries, as the data presented in Table II indicate. If we had combined Latin America and Europe in one table, the differences would have been greater.[4]

4 Lyle W. Shannon has correlated indices of economic development with whether a country is self-governing or not, and his conclusions are substantially the same. Since Shannon does not give details on the countries categorized as self-governing and non-self-governing, there is no direct measure of the relation between "democratic" and "self-governing" countries. All the countries examined in this paper, however, were chosen on the assumption that a characterization as "democratic" is meaningless for a non-self-governing country, and therefore, presumably, all of them, whether democratic or dictatorial, would fall within Shannon's "self-governing" category. Shannon shows that underdevelopment is related to lack of self-government; my data indicate that once self-government is attained, development is still related to the character of the political system. See Shannon (ed.), *Underdeveloped Areas* (New York, Harper, 1957), and also his article, "Is Level of Government Related to Capacity for Self-Government?" *American Journal of Eco-*

The main indices of *wealth* used here are per capita income, number of persons per motor vehicle and per physician, and the number of radios, telephones, and newspapers per thousand persons. The differences are striking on every score, as Table II indicates in detail. In the more democratic European countries, there are 17 persons per motor vehicle compared to 143 for the less democratic countries. In the less dictatorial Latin American countries there are 99 persons per motor vehicle, as against 274 for the more dictatorial ones.[5] Income differences for the groups are also sharp, dropping from an average per capita income of $695 for the more democratic countries of Europe to $308 for the less democratic ones; the corresponding difference for Latin America is from $171 to $119. The ranges are equally consistent, with the lowest per capita income in each group falling in the "less democratic" category, and the highest in the "more democratic" one.

INDUSTRIALIZATION

Indices of wealth are clearly related to this, of course. It is measured by the percentage of employed males in agriculture, and the per capita commercially produced "energy" being used in the country, measured in terms of tons of coal per person per year. Both of these indices show equally consistent results. The average percentage of employed males working in agriculture and related occupations was 21 in the "more democratic" European countries, and 41 in the "less democratic," 52 in the "less dictatorial" Latin American countries, and 67 in the "more dictatorial." The differences in per capita energy employed in the country are equally large.

---

nomics and Sociology, Vol. 17 (1958), pp. 367–382. In the latter paper, Shannon constructs a composite index of development, using some of the same indices, such as inhabitants per physician, and derived from the same United Nations sources, as appear in the tables to follow. Shannon's work did not come to my attention until after this paper was prepared, so that the two papers can be considered as separate tests of comparable hypotheses.

[5] It must be remembered that these figures are means, compiled from census figures for the various countries. The data vary widely in accuracy, and there is no way of measuring the validity of compound calculated figures such as those presented here. The consistent direction of all these differences, and their large magnitude, is the main indication of validity.

TABLE II. A COMPARISON OF EUROPEAN, ENGLISH-SPEAKING AND LATIN AMERICAN COUNTRIES, DIVIDED INTO TWO GROUPS, "MORE DEMOCRATIC" AND "LESS DEMOCRATIC," BY INDICES OF WEALTH, INDUSTRIALIZATION, EDUCATION, AND URBANIZATION*

A. Indices of Wealth

	Per Capita Income in $	Thousands of Persons Per Doctor	Persons Per Motor Vehicle	Telephones Per 1,000 Persons	Radios Per 1,000 Persons	Newspaper Copies Per 1,000 Persons
Means						
European and English-speaking Stable Democracies	695	.86	17	205	350	341
European and English-speaking Unstable Democracies and Dictatorships	308	1.4	143	58	160	167
Latin American Democracies and Unstable Dictatorships	171	2.1	99	25	85	102
Latin American Stable Dictatorships	119	4.4	274	10	43	43
Ranges						
European Stable Democracies	420–1,453	.7– 1.2	3–62	43–400	160–995	242–570
European Dictatorships	128– 482	.6– 4	10–538	7–196	42–307	46–390
Latin American Democracies	112– 346	.8– 3.3	31–174	12– 58	38–148	51–233
Latin American Stable Dictatorships	40– 331	1.0–10.8	38–428	1– 24	4–154	4–111

* A large part of this table has been compiled from data furnished by International Urban Research University of California, Berkeley, California. [Subsequent footnotes to this table omitted.]

LIPSET / *Some Social Requisites of Democracy* 87

B. Indices of Industrialization

Means	Percentage of Males in Agriculture	Per Capita Energy Consumed
European Stable Democracies	21	3.6
European Dictatorships	41	1.4
Latin American Democracies	52	.6
Latin American Stable Dictatorships	67	.25
Ranges		
European Stable Democracies	6–46	1.4 –7.8
European Dictatorships	16–60	.27–3.2
Latin American Democracies	30–63	.30–0.9
Latin American Stable Dictatorships	46–87	.02–1.27

C. Indices of Education

Means	Percentage Literate	Primary Education Enrollment Per 1,000 Persons	Post-Primary Enrollment Per 1,000 Persons	Higher Education Enrollment Per 1,000 Persons
European Stable Democracies	96	134	44	4.2
European Dictatorships	85	121	22	3.5
Latin American Democracies	74	101	13	2.0
Latin American Dictatorships	46	72	8	1.3
Ranges				
European Stable Democracies	95–100	96–179	19–83	1.7–17.83
European Dictatorships	55– 98	61–165	8–37	1.6– 6.1
Latin American Democracies	48– 87	75–137	7–27	.7– 4.6
Latin American Dictatorships	11– 76	11–149	3–24	.2– 3.1

TABLE II. A COMPARISON OF EUROPEAN, ENGLISH-SPEAKING AND LATIN AMERICAN COUNTRIES, DIVIDED INTO TWO GROUPS, "MORE DEMOCRATIC" AND "LESS DEMOCRATIC," BY INDICES OF WEALTH, INDUSTRIALIZATION, EDUCATION, AND URBANIZATION (continued)

D. Indices of Urbanization

	Per Cent in Cities over 20,000	Per Cent in Cities over 100,000	Per Cent in Metropolitan Areas
Means			
European Stable Democracies	43	28	38
European Dictatorships	24	16	23
Latin American Democracies	28	22	26
Latin American Stable Dictatorships	17	12	15
Ranges			
European Stable Democracies	28–54	17–51	22–56
European Dictatorships	12–44	6–33	7–49
Latin American Democracies	11–48	13–37	17–44
Latin American Stable Dictatorships	5–36	4–22	7–26

The degree of *urbanization* is also related to the existence of democracy.[6] Three different indices of urbanization are available from data compiled by International Urban Research (Berkeley, California): the percentage of the population in places of 20,000 and over, the percentage in communities of 100,000 and over, and also the percentage residing in standard metropolitan areas. On all three of these indices of urbanization, the more democratic countries score higher than the less democratic, for both of the political culture areas under investigation.

Many have suggested that the better educated the population of a country, the better the chances for democracy, and the comparative data available support this proposition. The "more democratic" countries of Europe are almost entirely literate: the lowest has a rate of 96 percent, while the "less democratic" nations have an average literacy rate of 85 percent. In Latin America, the difference is between an average rate of 74 per cent for the "less dictatorial" countries and 46 percent for the "more dictatorial." [7] The educational enrollment per thousand total popu-

[6] Urbanization has often been linked to democracy by political theorists. Harold J. Laski asserted that "organized democracy is the product of urban life," and that it was natural therefore that it should have "made its first effective appearance" in the Greek city states, limited as was their definition of "citizen." See his article "Democracy" in the *Encyclopedia of the Social Sciences* (New York, Macmillan, 1937), Vol. V, pp. 76–85. Max Weber held that the city, as a certain type of political community, is a peculiarly Western phenomenon, and traced the emergence of the notion of "citizenship" from social developments closely related to urbanization. For a partial statement of his point of view, see the chapter on "Citizenship," in *General Economic History* (Glencoe, Ill., The Free Press, 1950), pp. 315–338. It is significant to note that before 1933 the Nazi electoral strength was greatest in small communities and rural areas. Berlin, the only German city of over two million, never gave the Nazis over twenty-five percent of the vote in a free election. The modal Nazi, like the modal French Poujadist or Italian neo-Fascist today, was a self-employed resident of a small town or rural district. Though the Communists, as a workers' party, are strongest in the working-class neighborhoods of large cities within countries, they have great electoral strength only in the less urbanized European nations, e.g., Greece, Finland, France, Italy.

[7] The pattern indicated by a comparison of the averages for each group of countries is sustained by the ranges (the high and low extremes) for each index. Most of the ranges overlap: that is, some countries which are in the low category with regard to politics are higher on any given index than some which are high on the scale of democracy. It is noteworthy that in

lation at three different levels, primary, post-primary, and higher educational, is equally consistently related to the degree of democracy. The tremendous disparity is shown by the extreme cases of Haiti and the United States. Haiti has fewer children (eleven per thousand) attending school in the primary grades than the United States has attending colleges (almost eighteen per thousand).

The relationship between education and democracy is worth more extensive treatment since an entire philosophy of democratic government has seen in increased education the spread of the basic requirement of democracy.[8] As Bryce wrote with special reference to Latin America, "education, if it does not make men good citizens, makes it at least easier for them to become so." [9] Education presumably broadens men's outlooks, enables them to understand the need for norms of tolerance, restrains them from adhering to extremist and monistic doctrines, and increases their capacity to make rational electoral choices.

The evidence bearing on the contribution of education to democracy is even more direct and strong in connection with individual behavior *within* countries, than it is in cross-national correlations. Data gathered by public-opinion research agencies which have questioned people in different countries with regard to their belief in various democratic norms of tolerance for opposition, to their attitudes toward ethnic or racial minorities, and with regard to their belief in multi-party as against one-party systems have found that *the most important single factor differentiating those giving democratic responses from others has been education.* The higher one's education, the more likely one is to believe in democratic values and support democratic practices.[10] All

both Europe and Latin America, the nations which are lowest on any of the indices presented in the table are also in the "less democratic" category. Conversely, almost all countries which rank at the top of any of the indices are in the "more democratic" class.

8 See John Dewey, *Democracy and Education* (New York, 1916).

9 Quoted in Arthur P. Whitaker, *op. cit.,* p. 112; see also Karl Mannheim, *Freedom, Power and Democratic Planning* (New York, 1950).

10 See C. H. Smith, "Liberalism and Level of Information," *Journal of Educational Psychology,* Vol. 39 [1948], pp. 65–82; Martin A. Trow, *Right Wing Radicalism and Political Intolerance,* Ph.D. dissertation, Columbia University,

the relevant studies indicate that education is far more significant than income or occupation.

These findings should lead us to anticipate a far higher correlation between national levels of education and political practice than in fact we do find. Germany and France have been among the best educated nations of Europe, but this by itself clearly did not stabilize their democracies. It may be, however, that education has served to inhibit other anti-democratic forces. Post-Nazi data from Germany indicate clearly that higher education is linked to rejection of strong-man and one-party government.[11]

If we cannot say that a "high" level of education is a sufficient condition for democracy, the available evidence does suggest that it comes close to being a necessary condition in the modern world. Thus if we turn to Latin America, where widespread illiteracy still exists in many countries, we find that of all the nations in which more than half the population is illiterate, only one, Brazil, can be included in the "more democratic" group.

A number of processes underlie these correlations, observed in many areas of the world, in addition to the effect, already discussed, of a high level of education and literacy in creating or sustaining belief in democratic norms. Perhaps most important is the relationship between modernization and the form of the

---

1957, p. 17; Samuel Stouffer, *Communism, Conformity and Civil Liberties* (New York, 1955), pp. 138–139; K. Kido and M. Suyi, "Report on Social Stratification and Mobility in Tokyo. . . . Mobility in Tokyo, III: The Structure of Social Consciousness," *Japanese Sociological Review* (January, 1954), pp. 74–100.

11 Dewey has suggested that the character of the educational system will influence its effect on democracy, and this may shed some light on the sources of instability in Germany. The purpose of German education, according to Dewey, writing in 1916, was "disciplinary training rather than . . . personal development." The main aim was to produce "absorption of the aims and meaning of existing institutions," and "thoroughgoing subordination" to them. This point raises issues which cannot be entered into here, but indicates the complex character of the relationship between democracy and closely-related factors, such as education. See Dewey, *Democracy and Education, op. cit.,* pp. 108–110. It suggests caution, too, in drawing optimistic inferences about the prospects of democratic developments in Russia, based on the great expansion of education now taking place there.

"class struggle." For the lower strata, economic development, which means increased income, greater economic security, and higher education, permit those in this status to develop longer time perspectives and more complex and gradualist views of politics. A belief in secular reformist gradualism can only be the ideology of a relatively well-to-do lower class.[12] Increased wealth and education also serve democracy by increasing the extent to which the lower strata are exposed to cross pressures which will reduce the intensity of their commitment to given ideologies and make them less receptive to supporting extremist ones. The operation of this process will be discussed in more detail in the second part of the paper, but essentially it functions through enlarging their involvement in an integrated national culture as distinct from an isolated lower-class one, and hence increasing their exposure to middle-class values. Marx argued that the proletariat were a revolutionary force because they have nothing to lose but their chains and can win the whole world. But de Tocqueville in analyzing the reasons why the lower strata in America supported the system paraphrased and transposed Marx before Marx ever made this analysis by pointing out that "only those who have nothing to lose ever revolt." [13]

Increased wealth is not only related causally to the development of democracy by changing the social conditions of the workers, but it also affects the political role of the middle class through changing the shape of the stratification structure so that it shifts from an elongated pyramid, with a large lower-class base, to a diamond with a growing middle class. A large middle class plays a mitigating role in moderating conflict since it is able to reward moderate and democratic parties and penalize extremist groups.

National income is also related to the political values and style of the upper class. The poorer a country, and the lower the absolute standard of living of the lower classes, the greater the pressure on the upper strata to treat the lower classes as beyond the pale of human society, as vulgar, as innately inferior, as a lower

12 See S. M. Lipset, "Socialism—East and West—Left and Right," *Confluence,* Vol. 7 (Summer, 1958), pp. 173–192.
13 Alexis de Tocqueville, *Democracy in America,* Vol. I (New York, Alfred A. Knopf, Vintage ed., 1945), p. 258.

caste. The sharp difference in the style of living between those at the top and those at the bottom makes this psychologically necessary. Consequently, the upper strata also tend to regard political rights for the lower strata, particularly the right to share in power, as essentially absurd and immoral. The upper strata not only resist democracy themselves, but their often arrogant political behavior serves to intensify extremist reactions on the part of the lower classes.

The general income level of a nation will also affect its receptivity to democratic political tolerance norms. The values which imply that it does not matter greatly which side rules, that error can be tolerated even in the governing party can best develop where (a) the government has little power to affect the crucial life chances of most powerful groups, or (b) there is enough wealth in the country so that it actually does not make too much difference if some redistribution does take place. If loss of office is seen as meaning serious loss for major power groups, then they will be readier to resort to more drastic measures in seeking to retain or secure office. The wealth level will also affect the extent to which given countries can develop "universalistic" norms among its civil servants and politicians (selection based on competence; performance without favoritism). The poorer the country, the greater the emphasis which is placed on nepotism, i.e., support of kin and friends. The weakness of the universalistic norms reduces the opportunity to develop efficient bureaucracy, a condition for a modern democratic state.[14]

Less directly linked but seemingly still associated with greater wealth is the presence of intermediary organizations and institutions which can act as sources of countervailing power, and recruiters of participants in the political process in the manner discussed by de Tocqueville and other exponents of what has come to be known as the theory of the "mass society." [15] They have

[14] For a discussion of this problem in a new state, see David Apter, *The Gold Coast in Transition* (Princeton University Press, 1955), esp. Chaps. 9 and 13. Apter shows the importance of efficient bureaucracy, and the acceptance of bureaucratic values and behavior patterns, for the existence of a democratic political order.

[15] See Emil Lederer, *The State of the Masses* (New York, 1940); Hannah Arendt, *Origins of Totalitarianism* (New York, 1950); Max Horkheimer,

argued that a society without a multitude of organizations relatively independent of the central state power has a high dictatorial as well as a revolutionary potential. Such organizations serve a number of functions necessary to democracy: they are a source of countervailing power, inhibiting the state or any single major source of private power from dominating all political resources; they are a source of new opinions; they can be the means of communicating ideas, particularly opposition ideas, to a large section of the citizenry; they serve to train men in the skills of politics; and they help increase the level of interest and participation in politics. Although there are no reliable data which bear on the relationship between national patterns of voluntary organizations and national political systems, evidence from studies of individual behavior within a number of different countries demonstrates that, independently of other factors, men who belong to associations are more likely to hold democratic opinions on questions concerning tolerance and party systems, and are more likely to participate in the political process—to be active or to vote. Since we also know that, within countries, the more well-to-do and the better educated one is, the more likely he is to belong to voluntary organizations, it seems likely that the propensity to form such groups is a function of level of income and opportunities for leisure within given nations.[16]

Eclipse of Reason (New York, 1947); Karl Mannheim, *Man and Society in an Age of Reconstruction* (New York, 1940); Philip Selznick, *The Organizational Weapon* (New York, 1952); José Ortega y Gasset, *The Revolt of the Masses* (New York, 1932).

16 See Edward Banfield, *The Moral Basis of a Backward Society* (Glencoe, Ill., The Free Press, 1958), for an excellent description of the way in which abysmal poverty serves to reduce community organization in southern Italy. The data which do exist from polling surveys conducted in the United States, Germany, France, Great Britain, and Sweden show that somewhere between forty and fifty percent of the adults in these countries belong to voluntary associations, without lower rates of membership for the less stable democracies, France and Germany, than among the more stable ones, the United States, Great Britain, and Sweden. These results seemingly challenge the general proposition, although no definite conclusion can be made, since most of the studies employed non-comparable categories. This point bears further research in many countries. For the data on these countries see the following studies: for France, Arnold Rose, *Theory and Method in the Social Sciences* (Minneapolis, University of Minnesota Press, 1954), p. 74; and O. R. Gallagher,

It is obvious that democracy and the conditions related to stable democracy discussed here are essentially located in the countries of northwest Europe and their English-speaking off-spring in America and Australasia. It has been argued by Max Weber among others that the factors making for democracy in this area are a historically unique concatenation of elements, part of the complex which also produced capitalism in this area. The basic argument runs that capitalist economic development (facilitated and most developed in Protestant areas) created the burgher class whose existence was both a catalyst and a necessary condition for democracy. The emphasis within Protestantism on individual responsibility furthered the emergence of democratic values. The greater initial strength of the middle classes in these countries resulted in an alignment between burghers and throne, an alignment which preserved the monarchy, and thus facilitated the legitimation of democracy among the conservative strata. Thus we have an interrelated cluster of economic development, Protestantism, monarchy, gradual political change, legitimacy, and democracy.[17] Men may argue as to whether any aspect of this

---

"Voluntary Associations in France," *Social Forces*, Vol. 36 (December, 1957), pp. 154–156; for Germany, Erich Reigrotski, *Soziale Verflechtungen in der Bundesrepublik* (Tübingen, J. C. B. Mohr, 1956), p. 164; for the U. S., Charles R. Wright and Herbert H. Hyman, "Voluntary Association Memberships of American Adults: Evidence from National Sample Surveys," *American Sociological Review*, Vol. 23 (June, 1958), p. 287, and J. C. Scott, Jr., "Membership and Participation in Voluntary Associations," *id.*, Vol. 22 (1957), pp. 315–326; Herbert Maccoby, "The Differential Political Activity of Participants in a Voluntary Association," *id.*, Vol. 23 (1958), pp. 524–533; for Great Britain see Mass Observation, *Puzzled People* (London, Victor Gollanz, 1947), p. 119; and Thomas Bottomore, "Social Stratification in Voluntary Organizations," in David Glass, ed., *Social Mobility in Britain* (Glencoe, Ill., The Free Press, 1954), p. 354; for Sweden see Gunnar Heckscher, "Pluralist Democracy: The Swedish Experience," *Social Research*, Vol. 15 (December, 1948), pp. 417–461.

[17] In introducing historical events as part of the analysis of factors *external* to the political system, which are part of the causal nexus in which democracy is involved, I am following in good sociological and even functionalist tradition. As Radcliffe-Brown has well put it, ". . . one 'explanation' of a social system will be its history, where we know it—the detailed account of how it came to be, what it is and where it is. Another 'explanation' of the same system is obtained by showing . . . that it is a special exemplification of laws of social psychology or social functioning. The two kinds of explanation do not conflict but supplement one another." A. R. Radcliffe-Brown, "On the

cluster is primary, but the cluster of factors and forces hangs together.

LEGITIMACY AND DEMOCRACY

In this section I turn to an examination of some of the requisites of democracy which are derived from specifically historical elements in this complex, particularly those which relate to the need of a democratic political system for legitimacy, and for mechanisms which reduce the intensity of political cleavage. These requisites are correlated with economic development, but are also distinct from it since they are elements in the political system itself.

LEGITIMACY AND EFFECTIVENESS

In the modern world, as the previous section has attempted to document, economic development involving industrialization, urbanization, high educational standards, and a steady increase in the overall wealth of the society, is a basic condition sustaining democracy; it is a mark of the efficiency of the total system.

But the stability of a given democratic system depends not only on the system's efficiency in modernization, but also upon the *effectiveness* and *legitimacy* of the political system. By effectiveness is meant the actual performance of a political system, the extent to which it satisfies the basic functions of government as defined by the expectations of most members of a society, and the expectations of powerful groups within it which might threaten the system, such as the armed forces. The effectiveness of a democratic political system, marked by an efficient bureaucracy and decision-making system, which is able to resolve political problems, can be distinguished from the efficiency of the total system, although breakdown in the functioning of the society as a whole will, of course affect the political sub-system. Legitimacy involves the capacity of a political system to engender and maintain the

Concept of Function in Social Science," *American Anthropologist*, New Series, Vol. 37 (1935), p. 401; see also Max Weber, *The Methodology of the Social Sciences* (Glencoe, Ill., The Free Press, 1949), pp. 164–188, for a detailed discussion of the role of historical analysis in sociological research.

belief that existing political institutions are the most appropriate or proper ones for the society. The extent to which contemporary democratic political systems are legitimate depends in large measure upon the ways in which the key issues which have historically divided the society have been resolved. It is the task of these sections of the paper to show *first,* how the degree of legitimacy of a democratic system may affect its capacity to survive the crises of effectiveness, such as depressions or lost wars and *second,* to indicate the ways in which the different resolutions of basic historical cleavages—which determine the legitimacy of various systems— also strengthen or weaken democracy through their effect on contemporary party struggles.

While effectiveness is primarily an instrumental dimension, legitimacy is more affective and evaluative. Groups will regard a political system as legitimate or illegitimate according to the way in which its values fit in with their primary values. Important segments of the German army, civil service, and aristocratic classes rejected the Weimar Republic not because it was ineffective, but because its symbolism and basic values negated their own. Legitimacy, in and of itself, may be associated with many forms of political organization, including oppressive ones. Feudal societies, before the advent of industrialism, undoubtedly enjoyed the basic loyalty of most of their members. Crises of legitimacy are primarily a recent historical phenomenon, following the rise of sharp cleavages among groups which have been able, because of mass-communication resources, to organize around different values than those previously considered to be the only legitimate ones for the total society.

A crisis of legitimacy is a crisis of change, and therefore its roots, as a factor affecting the stability of democratic systems, must be sought in the character of change in modern society. It may be hypothesized that crises of legitimacy occur during a transition to a new social structure, if (a) all major groups do not secure access to the political system early in the transitional period, or at least as soon as they develop political demands; or, if (b) the *status* of major conservative institutions is threatened during the period of structural change. After a new social structure is established, if the new system is unable to sustain the expectations of major groups (on the grounds of "effectiveness") for a long enough period to develop legitimacy upon the new basis, a new crisis may develop.

Tocqueville gave a graphic description of the first general type of loss of legitimacy, referring mainly to countries which had moved from aristocratic monarchies to democratic republics: ". . . epochs sometimes occur in the life of a nation when the old customs of a people are changed, public morality is destroyed, religious belief shaken, and the spell of tradition broken. . . ." The citizens then have "neither the instinctive patriotism of a monarchy nor the reflecting patriotism of a republic; . . . they have stopped between the two in the midst of confusion and distress." [18]

If, however, the status of major conservative groups and symbols is not threatened during this transitional period even though they lose most of their power, democracy seems to be much more secure. Striking evidence of the link between the preserved legitimacy of conservative institutions and democracy is the relationship between monarchy and democracy. Given the role of the American and French republican revolutions as the initiators of modern democratic political movements, the fact that ten out of twelve of the stable European and English-speaking democracies are monarchies seems a rather ludicrous correlation. Great Britain, Sweden, Norway, Denmark, the Netherlands, Belgium, Luxemburg, Australia, Canada, and New Zealand are kingdoms; while the only republics which meet the twin conditions—of stable democratic procedures since democracy was instituted, and the absence of a major totalitarian movement in the past twenty-five years—are the United States, Switzerland, and Uruguay. Nations which have moved from absolutism and oligarchy (linked to a state church) to a democratic welfare state, while retaining the forms of monarchy, more frequently seem able to make changes while sustaining a continuous thread of legitimacy for their political institutions.[19]

18 *Op. cit.*, pp. 251–252.
19 Walter Lippmann, referring to the seemingly greater capacity of the constitutional monarchies than the republics of Europe to "preserve order with

The preservation of the monarchy has apparently retained for the system the loyalty of the aristocratic, traditionalist, and clerical sectors of the population which resented increased democratization and equalitarianism. And, by more graciously accepting the lower strata, by not resisting to the point that revolution might be necessary, the conservative orders won or retained the loyalty of the new "citizens." Where monarchy was overthrown by revolution, and orderly succession was broken, those forces aligned with monarchy have sometimes continued to refuse legitimacy to republican successors down to the fifth generation or more.

The one constitutional monarchy which became a Fascist dictatorship, Italy, was, like the French Republic, relatively new and still illegitimate for major groups in the society. The House of Savoy alienated the Catholics by destroying the temporal power of the Popes, and was also not a legitimate successor in the old Kingdom of the Two Sicilies. Catholics, in fact, were forbidden by the church to participate in Italian politics until close to World War I, and the church rescinded its original ban only because of its fear of the Socialists. A similar attitude was taken by French Catholics to the Third Republic during the same period. Both Italian and French democracy have had to operate for much of their histories without loyal support from important groups in their society, both on the left and on the right. Thus, one main source of legitimacy lies in the continuity of primary conservative and integrative institutions during a transitional period in which new social institutions are emerging.

The second general type of loss of legitimacy is, as indicated above, related to the way in which societies handle the "entry into politics" problem. The determination of when new social groups shall obtain access to the political process affects the legitimacy of the political system, either for conservative or for emerging groups. In the nineteenth century these new groups were

---

freedom," suggests that this may be because "in a republic the governing power, being wholly secularized, loses much of its prestige; it is stripped, if one prefers, of all the illusions of intrinsic majesty." See his *The Public Philosophy* (New York, Mentor Books, 1956), p. 50.

primarily industrial workers; the "entry into politics" crisis of the twentieth century typically involves colonial elites, and peasant peoples. Whenever new groups become politically active (e.g., when the workers first seek access to economic and political power through economic organization and the suffrage, when the bourgeoisie demanded access to and participation in government, when colonial elites demand control over their own system), comparatively easy access to the *legitimate* political institutions tends to win the loyalty of the new groups to the system, and they in turn can permit the old dominating strata to maintain their own status integrity. In nations such as Germany, where access was denied for prolonged periods, first to the bourgeoisie and later to the workers, and where force was used to restrict access, the lower strata were alienated from the system, and were led to adopt extremist ideologies which, in turn, alienated the more established groups from an acceptance of the workers' political movement as a legitimate alternative.

Political systems which denied new strata access to power except through revolutionary means also inhibited the growth of legitimacy by introducing millennial hopes into the political arena. Groups which feel obliged to push their way into the body politic through forceful means tend to overexaggerate the possibilities which political participation afford. Their hopes are for far more than the inherent limitations of political stability permit. Consequently, democratic regimes born under such stress will not only face the difficulty of being regarded as illegitimate by those groups loyal to the *ancien régime,* but may be also rejected by those whose millennial hopes were not fulfilled by the change. France seems to offer an example of such a phenomenon. Right-wing clericalists have viewed the Republic as illegitimate, while sections of the lower strata still impatiently await millennial fulfillment. Many of the newly independent nations of Asia and Africa face the problem of winning the loyalties of the masses to democratic states which can do little to fulfill the utopian objectives set by nationalist movements during the period of colonialism, and the transitional struggle to independence.

We have discussed several conditions bearing upon the maintenance, or the initial securing of legitimacy by a political system. Assuming reasonable effectiveness, if the status of major conservative groups is threatened, or if access to the political system is denied at crucial periods, the legitimacy of the system will remain in question. Even in legitimate systems, a breakdown of effectiveness, repeatedly or for a long period, will endanger its stability.

A major test of legitimacy is the extent to which given nations have developed a common "secular political culture," national rituals and holidays which serve to maintain the legitimacy of various democratic practices.[20] The United States has developed a common homogeneous secular political culture as reflected in the veneration and consensus surrounding the Founding Fathers, Jefferson, Lincoln, Theodore Roosevelt, and their principles. These common elements to which all American politicians appeal are not present in all democratic societies. In some European countries, the Left and the Right have a different set of symbols, and different historical political heroes. France offers the clearest example of a nation which has not developed such a common heritage. Thus many of the battles involving use of different symbols between the left and the right from 1789 down through much of the nineteenth century are "still in progress, and the issue is still open; everyone of these dates [of major political controversy] still divides left and right, clerical and anti-clerical, progressive and reactionary, in all their historically determined constellations."[21]

As we have seen, nations may vary in the extent to which their political institutions are viewed as legitimate by different strata. And knowledge concerning the relative degree of legitimacy of a nation's political institutions is of key importance in any effort to analyze the stability of these institutions when faced with a crisis of effectiveness. The relationship between different degrees of legitimacy and effectiveness in specific political systems may be more graphically presented in the form of a four-fold table, with

[20] See Gabriel Almond, "Comparative Political Systems," *Journal of Politics,* Vol. 18 (1956), pp. 391–409.
[21] Herbert Luethy, *The State of France* (London, Secker and Warburg, 1955), p. 29.

examples of countries characterized by the various possible combinations.

EFFECTIVENESS

		+	−
LEGITIMACY	+	A	B
	−	C	D

Societies which fall in box A, those which are high on the scales of both legitimacy and effectiveness, will clearly have stable political systems. Nations like the United States, Sweden, and Britain satisfy the basic political needs of their citizens, have efficient bureaucracies and political decision-making systems, possess traditional legitimacy through long-term continuity of the key symbols of sovereignty, the monarchy or constitution, and do not contain any important minorities whose basic values run counter to those of the system.[22] Ineffective and illegitimate regimes, those which would be found in box D, must, of course, by definition be unstable and break down, unless they are dictatorships maintaining themselves by force such as the governments of Hungary and eastern Germany today. The political experiences of different countries in the early 1930's illustrate the effect of varying combinations of legitimacy and effectiveness. In the late 1920's, neither the German nor the Austrian republics was held legitimate by large and powerful segments of their populations, but nevertheless remained reasonably effective.[23] In the four-fold table, they fell in box C.

When the effectiveness of the governments of the various coun-

[22] The race problem in the American South does constitute one basic challenge to the legitimacy of the system, and at one time did cause a breakdown of the national order. The conflict reduces the commitment of many white Southerners to the democratic rules down to the present. Great Britain had a comparable problem as long as Catholic Ireland remained part of the United Kingdom. Effective government could not satisfy Ireland. Political practices by both sides in Northern Ireland, Ulster, also illustrate the problem of a regime which is not legitimate to a large segment of its population.

[23] For an excellent analysis of the permanent crisis of the Austrian republic which flowed from the fact that it was viewed as an illegitimate regime by the Catholics and conservatives, see Charles Gulick, *Austria from Hapsburg to Hitler* (Berkeley, University of California Press, 1948).

tries broke down in the 1930's, those societies which were high on the scale of legitimacy remained democratic, while countries which were low such as Germany, Austria, and Spain, lost their freedom, and France narrowly escaped a similar fate. Or to put the changes in terms of location in the four-fold table, countries which shifted from A to B remained democratic, while the political systems of those which shifted from C to D broke down. It remained for the military defeat in 1940 to prove conclusively the low position of French democracy on the scale of legitimacy. It was the sole defeated democracy which furnished large-scale support for a Quisling regime.[24]

Situations such as those discussed above in which either legitimacy or effectiveness is high while the other is low demonstrate the utility of this type of analysis. From a short-range point of view, a highly effective but illegitimate system, such as a well-governed colony, is more unstable than regimes which are relatively low in effectiveness and high in legitimacy. The social stability of a nation such as Thailand—even with its occasional *coups d'états*—stands out in sharp contrast to the situation in the neighboring former colonial nations of Southeast Asia. The link between the analysis of legitimacy and the earlier discussion of the contribution of economic development to democracy is evident in the processes through which regimes low in legitimacy may gain it, and conversely in those which are related to the collapse of a legitimate system. Prolonged effectiveness which lasts over a number of generations may give legitimacy to a political system; in the modern world, such effectiveness mainly means constant economic development. Thus those nations which

[24] The French legitimacy problem is well described by Katherine Munro: "The Right wing parties never quite forgot the possibility of a counter revolution while the Left wing parties revived the Revolution militant in their Marxism or Communism; each side suspected the other of using the Republic to achieve its own ends and of being loyal only so far as it suited it. This suspicion threatened time and time again to make the Republic unworkable, since it led to obstruction to both the political and the economic sphere, and difficulties of government in turn undermined confidence in the regime and its rulers." Quoted in Charles A. Micaud, "French Political Parties: Ideological Myths and Social Realities," in Sigmund Neumann, ed., *Modern Political Parties* (Chicago, University of Chicago Press, 1956), p. 108.

adapted most successfully to the requirements of an industrial system had the fewest internal political strains, and either preserved their traditional legitimacy, the monarchy, or developed new strong symbols of legitimacy.

The social and economic structure which Latin America inherited from the Iberian peninsula prevented it from following the lead of the former English colonies, and its republics never developed the symbols and aura of legitimacy. In large measure, the survival of the new political democracies of Asia and Africa is related to their ability to sustain a prolonged period of effectiveness, of being able to meet the defined instrumental needs of their populations.

LEGITIMACY AND CLEAVAGE

Prolonged effectiveness of the system as a whole may, as in the case of the United States and Switzerland, eventually legitimate the democratic political system. Inherent, however, in all democratic systems is the constant threat that the conflicts among different groups which are the lifeblood of the system may crystalize to the point where societal disintegration is threatened. Hence, conditions which serve to moderate the intensity of partisan battle, in addition to effectiveness, are among the key requisites for a democratic political system.

Since the existence of a moderate state of conflict is an inherent aspect of a legitimate democratic system, and is in fact another way of defining it, we should not be surprised that the principal factors determining such an optimum state are closely linked to those which produce legitimacy viewed in terms of continuities of symbols and status. Essentially the character and content of the major cleavages affecting the political stability of a society are largely determined by historical factors which have affected the way in which major issues dividing society have been solved or left unresolved over time.

In modern times, three major issues have emerged in western states. The first was the religious issue: the place of the church and/or various religions within the nation. The second has been the problem of the admission of the lower strata, particularly the workers, to "citizenship," the establishment of access to power through universal suffrage, and the legitimate right to bargain collectively in the economic sphere. The third has been the continual struggle over the distribution of the national income.

The significant general question here is this: were these major issues dealt with one by one, and each one more or less solved before the next arose, or did the problems accumulate, so that historical issues and sources of cleavage mixed with newer ones? Resolving tensions one at a time contributes toward a stable political system; carrying over issues from one historical period to another makes for a political atmosphere characterized by bitterness and frustration rather than by tolerance and compromise. Men and parties come to differ with each other, not simply on ways of settling current problems, but rather by fundamental and opposed *weltanschauungen*. They come to see the political victory of their opponents as a major moral threat; and the total system, as a result, lacks effective value-integration.

The religious issue, the place of the church in the society, was fought through and solved in most of the Protestant nations in the eighteenth and nineteenth centuries, and ceased to be a matter for serious political controversy. In some states, such as the United States, the church was disestablished and it accepted this result. In others, such as Britain, Scandinavia, and Switzerland, religion remains state-supported, but the state churches, like constitutional monarchs, have only nominal sway and have ceased to be major sources of controversy. It remains for the Catholic countries of Europe to provide us with examples of situations in which the historic controversy between clerical and anti-clerical forces, sparked by the French Revolution, has continued to divide men politically down to the present day. Thus in countries such as France, Italy, Spain, and Austria, being Catholic has meant being allied with rightist or conservative groups in politics; while being anti-clerical (or a member of a minority religion) has most often meant alliance with the left. In a number of these countries, newer issues, when they emerged, became superimposed on the religious question; and for conservative Catholics, the fight against Socialists was not simply an economic struggle, or a controversy over social institutions, but a deep-rooted conflict between God and Satan, between good and evil.[25] For many secular intellectuals in contemporary Italy, opposition to the church legitimates alliance with the Communists. As long as religious ties reinforce secular political alignments, the chances for democratic give-and-take, and compromise, are weak.

The "citizenship" or "political equality" issue has also been resolved in various ways. Thus the United States and Britain gave citizenship to the workers in the early or mid-nineteenth century. Sweden and a number of European nations resisted through the beginning of the twentieth century, and the struggle for citizenship became combined in these countries with socialism as a *political* movement, thereby producing a revolutionary socialism. Or to put this in other terms, where the workers were denied economic and political citizenship rights, their struggle for redistribution of income and status was superimposed on a revolutionary ideology. Where the economic and status struggle developed outside this context, the ideology with which it was linked tended to be that of gradualist reformism. In Hohenzollern Germany, for example, the workers were denied a free and equal suffrage in Prussia until the revolution of 1918. This denial of "citizenship" facilitated the retention of revolutionary Marxism in those parts of Germany where equal suffrage did not exist.

25 The linkage between democratic instability and Catholicism may also be accounted for by elements inherent in Catholicism as a religious system. Democracy requires a universalistic political belief system in the sense that it legitimates different ideologies. And it might be assumed that religious value systems which are more universalistic in the sense of placing less stress on being the only true church will be more compatible with democracy than those which assume that they have the only truth. The latter belief, held much more strongly by the Catholic than by most other Christian churches, makes it difficult for the religious value system to help legitimate a political system which requires, as part of its basic value system, the belief that "good" is served best through conflict among opposing beliefs.

Kingsley Davis has argued that a Catholic state church tends to be irreconcilable with democracy since "Catholicism attempts to control so many aspects of life, to encourage so much fixity of status and submission to authority, and to remain so independent of secular authority that it invariably clashes with the liberalism, individualism, freedom, mobility and sovereignty of the democratic nation." See his "Political Ambivalence in Latin America," *Journal of Legal and Political Sociology*, Vol. 1 (1943), reprinted in Christensen, *The Evolution of Latin American Government* (New York, 1951), p. 240.

In Southern Germany, where full citizenship rights were granted in the late nineteenth century, reformist, democratic, and non-revolutionary socialism was dominant. The perpetuation of revolutionary dogmas in much of the Social Democratic party served to give ultra-leftists a voice in party leadership, enabled the Communists to win strength after the military defeat and, perhaps even more important historically, served to frighten large sections of the German middle classes. The latter feared that a socialist victory would really mean an end to all their privileges and status.

In France, the workers won the suffrage but were refused basic economic rights until after World War II. Major groups of French employers denied legitimacy to the French trade unions, and sought to weaken or destroy them following every trade-union victory. The instability of the French unions, their constant need to preserve worker militancy to survive, gave access to the workers to the more revolutionary and extremist political groups. Communist domination of the French labor movement can in large part be traced to the tactics of the French business classes.

The examples presented above do not explain why different countries varied in the way they handled basic national cleavages. They should suffice, however, to illustrate the worth of a hypothesis relating the conditions for stable democratic government to the bases of diversity. Where a number of historic cleavages intermix and create the basis for *weltanschauung* politics, the democracy will be unstable and weak, for by definition such political views do not include the concept of tolerance.

Weltanschauung politics have also weakened the possibilities for a stable democracy, since parties characterized by such total ideologies have often attempted to create what Sigmund Neumann has called an "integrated" environment, one in which as much as possible of the lives of their members is encapsulated within ideologically linked activities. These actions are based on the assumption that it is important to isolate their followers from contact with "falsehood" expressed by non-believers. Neumann has suggested the need for a basic analytic distinction between parties of representation, which strengthen democracy, and parties of integration which weaken it.[26] The former are typified by most parties in the English-speaking democracies and in Scandinavia, and by most centrist and conservative parties other than the religious ones. They view the party function as primarily one of securing votes around election time. The parties of integration, on the other hand, are concerned with making the world conform to their basic philosophy or *weltanschauung*. They do not see themselves as contestants in a give-and-take game of pressure politics, in which all parties accept the rules of the game. Rather they view the political or religious struggle as a contest between divine or historic truth on one side and fundamental error on the other. Given this conception of the world, it becomes necessary to prevent their followers from being exposed to the cross-pressures flowing from contact with falsehood, which will reduce their faith.

The two major non-totalitarian groupings which have followed such procedures have been the Catholics and the Socialists. In general, in much of Europe before 1939, the Catholics and Socialists attempted to increase intra-religious or intra-class communications by creating a network of church- and party-linked social and economic organizations within which their followers could live their entire lives. Austria offers perhaps the best example of a situation in which two groups, the Social Catholics and the Social Democrats, divided over all three historic issues and separated the country into two hostile camps, which carried out much of their social activities in party or church-linked organizations.[27]

26 See Sigmund Neumann, *Die Deutschen Parteien: Wesen und Wandel nach dem Kriege* (2nd ed., Berlin, 1932), for exposition of the distinction between parties of integration and parties of representation. Neumann has further distinguished between parties of "democratic integration" (the Catholic, and Social Democratic parties) and those of "total integration" (Fascists and Communist parties) in his more recent chapter, "Toward a Comparative Study of Political Parties," in the volume which he edited: *Modern Political Parties* (Chicago, University of Chicago Press, 1956), pp. 403–405.

27 See Charles Gulick, *op. cit.* For their post-World War II formula for compromising this antagonism, see Herbert P. Secher, "Coalition Government: The Case of the Second Austrian Republic," *American Political Science Review*, Vol. 52 (September, 1958), p. 791.

The evidence available suggests that the chances for stable democracy are enhanced to the extent that social strata, groups, and individuals have a number of cross-cutting politically relevant affiliations. To the degree that a significant proportion of the population is pulled among conflicting forces, such groups and individuals have an interest in reducing the intensity of political conflict.[28] As Robert Dahl and Talcott Parsons have pointed out, such groups and individuals also have an interest in protecting the rights of political minorities.[29]

A stable democracy requires relatively moderate tension among the contending political forces. And political moderation is facilitated by the capacity of a system to resolve key dividing issues before new ones arise. To the extent that the cleavages of religion, citizenship, and "collective bargaining" have been allowed to cumulate and reinforce each other as stimulants of partisan hostility, the system is weakened. The more reinforced and correlated the sources of cleavage, the less the likelihood for political tolerance. Similarly, on the level of group and individual behavior, the greater the isolation from heterogeneous political stimuli,

28 See B. Berelson, P. F. Lazarsfeld, and W. McPhee, *Voting* (Chicago, University of Chicago Press, 1954), for an exposition of the usefulness of cross-pressure as an explanatory concept. Also, see S. M. Lipset, J. Linz, P. F. Lazarsfeld, and A. Barton, "Psychology of Voting," in *Handbook of Social Psychology*, Vol. 2 (Cambridge, Addison-Wesley, 1954), for an attempt to specify the consequences of different group memberships for voting behavior, and a review of the literature.

29 As Dahl puts it, "if most individuals in the society identify with more than one group, then there is some positive probability that any majority contains individuals who identify for certain purposes with the threatened minority. Members of the threatened minority who strongly prefer their alternative will make their feelings known to those members of the tentative majority who also, at some psychological level, identify with the minority. Some of these sympathizers will shift their support away from the majority alternative and the majority will crumble." See Robert A. Dahl, *A Preface to Democratic Theory* (Chicago, University of Chicago Press, 1956), pp. 104–105. Parsons suggests that "pushing the implications of political difference too far activates the solidarities between adherents of the two parties which exist on other, nonpolitical bases so that majorities come to defend minorities of their own kind who differ from them politically." See Parsons' essay "Voting and the Equilibrium of the American Political System," in the volume edited by E. Burdick and A. Brodbeck, *American Voting Behavior* (Glencoe, Ill., The Free Press, forthcoming).

the more that background factors "pile up" in one direction, the greater the chances that the group or individual will have an extremist perspective. These two relationships, one on the level of partisan issues, the other on the nature of party support, are linked together by the fact that parties reflecting accumulated unresolved issues will seek to isolate their followers from conflicting stimuli, to prevent exposure to "error," while isolated individuals and groups will strengthen the intolerant tendencies in the political party system. The conditions maximizing political cosmopolitanism among the electorate are the growth of urbanization, education, communications media, and increased wealth. . . .

The analysis of the social requisites for democracy contained in this paper has sought to identify some, though obviously far from all, of the structural conditions which are linked to this political system. It has been possible in a very limited fashion to attempt some tests of the hypotheses suggested. These preliminary efforts to apply the method of science to comparative political systems can still be considered only as illustrative since we can say so little about actual variations in national social structures. Considerably more research must be done specifying the boundaries of various societies along many dimensions before reliable comparative analysis of the sort attempted here can be carried out. Although the task obviously presents tremendous difficulties, it is only through such methods that we can move beyond the conventional semi-literary methods of giving illustrative examples to support plausible interpretations.

The data available are, however, of a sufficiently consistent character to support strongly the conclusion that a more systematic and up-to-date version of Aristotle's hypothesis concerning the relationship of political forms to social structure is valid. Unfortunately, as has been indicated above, this conclusion does not justify the optimistic liberal's hope that an increase in wealth, in the size of the middle class, in education, and other related factors will necessarily mean the spread of democracy or the stabilizing of democracy. As Max Weber, in discussing the chances for democracy in Russia in the early twentieth century pointed out:

"The spread of Western cultural and capitalist economy did not, *ipso facto,* guarantee that Russia would also acquire the liberties which had accompanied their emergence in European history. . . . European liberty had been born in unique, perhaps unrepeatable, circumstances at a time when the intellectual and material conditions for it were exceptionally propitious." [30]

These suggestions that the peculiar concatenation of factors which gave rise to Western democracy in the nineteenth century may be unique are not meant to be unduly pessimistic. Political democracy exists and has existed in a variety of circumstances, even if it is most commonly sustained by a limited cluster of conditions. To understand more fully the various conditions under which it has existed may make possible the development of democracy elsewhere. Democracy is not achieved by acts of will alone; but men's wills, through action, can shape institutions and events in directions that reduce or increase the chance for the development and survival of democracy. To aid men's actions in furthering democracy was in some measure de Tocqueville's purpose in studying the operation of American democracy, and it remains perhaps the most important substantive intellectual task which students of politics can still set before themselves.

METHODOLOGICAL APPENDIX

The approach of this paper (as has already been indicated) is implicitly different from others which have attempted to handle social phenomena on a total societal level, and it may be useful to make explicit some of the methodological postulates underlying this presentation.

Complex characteristics of a social system, such as democracy, the degree of bureaucratization, the type of stratification system, have usually been handled either by a reductionist approach or by an "ideal-type" approach. The former approach dismisses the possibility of considering those characteristics as system-attributes as such, and maintains that qualities of individual actions are the sum and substance of sociological categories. For this school of thought, the extent of democratic attitudes, or of bureaucratic

[30] Richard Pipes, "Max Weber and Russia," *World Politics,* Vol. 7 (1955), p. 383.

behavior, or the numbers and types of prestige or power rankings, constitute the essence of the meaning of the attributes of democracy, bureaucracy, or class.

The "ideal-type" approach starts from a similar assumption, but reaches an opposite conclusion. The similar assumption is that societies are a complex order of phenomena, exhibiting such a degree of internal contradiction, that generalizations about them as a whole must necessarily constitute a constructed representation of selected elements, stemming from the particular concerns and perspectives of the scientist. The opposite conclusion is that abstractions of the order of "democracy" or "bureaucracy" have no necessary connection with states or qualities of complex social systems which actually exist, but comprise collections of attributes which are logically interrelated, but characteristic in the entirety of no existing society.[31] An example of this type of abstraction is Weber's concept of "bureaucracy," comprising a set of offices, which are not "owned" by the office-holder, continuously maintained files of rcecords, functionally specified duties, etc. Another is the common definition of democracy in political science, which postulates individual political decisions based on rational knowledge of one's own ends and of the factual political situation.

Criticism of categories, or ideal-types, such as this, solely on the basis that they do not correspond to reality is irrelevant, because they are not intended to describe reality, but to provide a basis for comparing different aspects of reality with their deviations from the consistently logical case. Often this approach is quite fruitful, and there is no intention here of substituting another methodological approach in its place, but merely of presenting another possible way of conceptualizing complex characteristics of social systems, stemming from the multi-variate analysis pioneered by Paul Lazarsfeld and his colleagues on a quite different level of analysis.[32]

31 Max Weber's essay on " 'Objectivity' in Social Science and Social Policy," in his *Methodology of the Social Sciences, op. cit.,* pp. 72–93.
32 The methodological presuppositions of this approach on the level of the multi-variate correlations and interactions of individual behavior with various

The point at which this approach differs is on the issue of whether generalized theoretical categories can be considered to have a valid relationship to characteristics of total social systems. The implication of the statistical data presented in this paper concerning democracy, and the relations between democracy, economic development, and political legitimacy, is that there are aspects of total social systems which exist, can be stated in theoretical terms, can be compared with similar aspects of other systems, and, at the same time, are derivable from empirical data which can be checked (or questioned) by other researchers. This does not mean at all that situations contradicting the general relationship may not exist, or that, at lower levels of social organization, quite different characteristics may not be evident. For example, a country like the United States may be characterized as "democratic" on the national level, even though most secondary organizations within the country may not be democratic. On another level, a church may be characterized as a "non-bureaucratic" organization, when compared with a corporation, even though important segments of the church organization may be as bureaucratized as the most bureaucratic parts of the corporation. On yet another level, it may be quite legitimate, for purposes of psychological evaluation of the total personality, to consider a certain individual as "schizophrenic," even though under certain conditions, he may not act schizophrenically. The point is that when comparisons are being made on a certain level of generalization, referring to the functioning of a total system (whether on a personality, group, organization, or society level), generalizations applicable to a total society have the same kind and degree of validity that those applicable to other systems have, and are subject to

social characteristics have been presented in Paul F. Lazarsfeld, "Interpretation of Statistical Relations as a Research Operation," in P. F. Lazarsfeld and M. Rosenberg, eds., *The Language of Social Research* (Glencoe, Ill., The Free Press, 1955), pp. 115–125; and in H. Hyman, *Survey Design and Analysis* (Glencoe, Ill., The Free Press, 1955), Chaps. 6 and 7. See also the methodological appendices to Lipset, *et al., Union Democracy, op. cit.,* pp. 419–432; and S. M. Lipset, "The Political Process in Trade Unions: A Theoretical Statement," in M. Berger, *et al.,* eds., *Freedom and Control in Modern Society* (New York, Van Nostrand, 1954), pp. 122–124.

the same empirical tests. The lack of many systematic and comparative studies of several societies has obscured this point.

This approach also stresses the view that complex characteristics of a total system have multivariate causation, and also multivariate consequences, insofar as the characteristic has some degree of autonomy within the system. Bureaucracy and urbanization, as well as democracy, have many causes and consequences, in this sense.[33]

On this view, it would be difficult to identify any *one* factor crucially associated with, or "causing" any complex social characteristic. Rather, all such characteristics (and this is a methodological assumption to guide research, and not a substantive point) are considered to have multi-variate causation, and multi-variate consequences. The point may be clarified by a diagram of some of the possible connections between democracy, the initial conditions associated with its emergence, and the consequences of an existent democratic system.

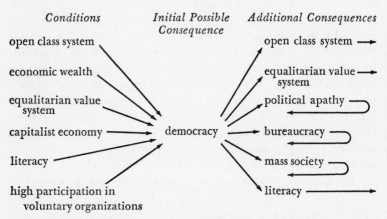

| *Conditions* | *Initial Possible Consequence* | *Additional Consequences* |

open class system

economic wealth

equalitarian value system

capitalist economy → democracy

literacy

high participation in voluntary organizations

open class system →

equalitarian value system →

political apathy

bureaucracy

mass society

literacy →

[33] This approach differs from Weber's attempt to trace the origins of modern capitalism. Weber was concerned to establish that *one* antecedent factor, a certain religious ethic, was crucially significant in the syndrome of economic, political, and cultural conditions leading up to the development of Western capitalism. My concern is not to establish the causal necessity of any one factor, but rather the syndrome of conditions which most frequently distinguish nations which may be empirically categorized as "more democratic" or "less democratic," without implying any absolute qualities to the definition.

The appearance of a factor on both sides of "democracy" implies that it is both an initial condition of democracy, and that democracy, once established, sustains that characteristic of the society, an open class system, for example. On the other hand, some of the initial consequences of democracy, such as bureaucracy, may have the effect of *undermining* democracy, in turn, as the reversing arrows indicate. Appearance of a factor to the right of democracy does not mean that democracy "causes" its appearance, but merely that democracy is an initial condition which favors its development. Similarly, the hypothesis that bureaucracy is one of the consequences of democracy does not imply that democracy is the sole cause, but rather that a democratic system has the effect of encouraging the development of a certain type of bureaucracy, under other additional conditions, which have to be stated if bureaucracy is the focus of the research problem. This diagram is not intended as a complete model of the general social conditions associated with the emergence of democracy, but as a way of clarifying the methodological point concerning the multivariate character of relationships in a total social system.

Thus, in a multi-variate system, the focus may be upon any element, and its conditions and consequences may be stated without the implication that we have arrived at a complete theory of the necessary and sufficient conditions of its emergence. This paper does not attempt a *new* theory of democracy, but only the formalizing, and the empirical testing, of certain sets of relationships implied by traditional theories, on the level of total social systems.

HARRY ECKSTEIN / A Theory of Stable Democracy*

. . . Government will be stable (1) if social authority patterns are identical with the governmental pattern, or (2) if they constitute a graduated pattern in a proper segmentation of society, or (3) if a high degree of resemblance exists in patterns adjacent to government and one finds throughout the more distant segments a marked departure from functionally appropriate patterns for the sake of imitating the governmental pattern or extensive imitation of the governmental pattern in ritual practices. Conditions (2) and (3) are both, of course, looser and less demanding versions of condition (1); all refer to a basic need for considerable resemblance in authority patterns if government is to be stable, particularly in those segments of society which impinge directly on government. Condition (3) may be regarded, in this way, as the minimum required for governmental stability (and the minimum meaning of congruence), but perhaps the most that can be realized in relation to some particular pattern of government. By the same token, *governments will be unstable* (and the authority patterns of a society incongruent) *if the governmental authority pattern is isolated* (that is, substantially different) *from those of other social segments, or if a very abrupt change in authority pattern occurs in any adjacent segments of society, or if several different*

* From Eckstein, *Division and Cohesion in Democracy* (Princeton, N.J., Princeton University Press), pp. 239–280. Portions of original chapter omitted.

authority patterns exist in social strata furnishing a large propor-
tion of the political elite (in the sense of active political participants). In the last case, congruence with the authority patterns
of a particular part of the elite—say, a particular social class—may
be quite possible, but congruence with the overall authority patterns of a society is logically out of the question.

TWO EXAMPLES: GREAT BRITAIN AND GERMANY

To make these propositions less abstract, let us look at two
concrete cases which illustrate them: contemporary Britain and
Weimar Germany.

We have already seen how closely the authority patterns of
government and political parties resemble one another in Great
Britain, and that this resemblance helps to make effective the
processes of cabinet government. One can similarly find great resemblances in authority patterns between British government and
other aspects of British social life. As one moves away from the
governmental segment these resemblances do decline, but never
markedly or in a very abrupt manner.

For example, there is a quite striking resemblance in the authority structures of government and pressure groups, a resemblance also required for effective cabinet government, at least in
this age of the social service state (as I have pointed out in another
work).[1] This resemblance is perhaps greatest in the case of groups
constituted almost exclusively for political purposes (that is, in
"attitude groups"),[2] but it also exists to a surprising extent in
functional organizations, like professional and economic organizations, which go in for politics only as a more or less important
sideline. Among such functional organizations, moreover, the resemblance to government is particularly great in groups most
directly involved in governmental and party affairs, e.g., trade
unions, large-scale employers' organizations, cooperative societies,

---

1 See Harry Eckstein, *Pressure Group Politics, The Case of the British Medical
Association* (London, 1960).
2 Allen Potter, "Attitude Groups," *Political Quarterly* XXIX (January–March
1958), pp. 72–82.

and the like. It is true that, on the whole, involvement by the group in non-political affairs, such as economic bargaining, tends to decrease resemblance to the governmental pattern. Also, certain non-political activities (for example, economic activities as against those of professional associations) act as inhibitions on too great an imitation of the governmental pattern. But throughout the whole universe of British pressure groups, resemblance to the governmental pattern is quite surprisingly great, even in organizations where, for functional reasons, one would least expect this.

Business organizations depart to a rather great extent from the governmental pattern, not only for obvious functional reasons, but also because of a fact just touched upon: they bring into close relation members of the upper and lower social classes. Wherever this occurs in British life, the authoritarian elements of the authority pattern tend to become enlarged and the democratic elements diminished. This is so not only in relations between economic bosses and their workers, but also between domestic servants and masters, enlisted men and officers, and members of the Administrative Class and other classes in the civil service. While all of these relations are governed by a high sense of propriety and functional limitation (by constitutionalist norms), those among members of the higher levels tend to be quite surprisingly democratic, or at least consultative and comradely; here again we might note the ubiquity of committees at every conceivable level in the higher civil service, the unusual use of staff committees in the military services, and the easy relations among officers of all ranks in military regiments, especially in elitist regiments like the Guards. But between members of the Administrative Class and their underlings, officers and their men, managers and their hired help, relations are highly non-consultative and certainly not comradely; the observance of propriety and functional limitations in these cases is complemented by considerable separation of individuals from each other, a general lack of contact among them for purposes other than functional ones.

But all this is quite in keeping with a governmental pattern which is as markedly elitist as the British. . . .

For support from the opposite end of the spectrum, we might look at one of the least stable of all modern governments, the Weimar Republic. How did the authority patterns of interwar Germany differ from modern Britain? Basically, in two ways. On one hand, the German governmental pattern was much more one-sidedly democratic, at any rate if we confine analysis to the level of parliamentary representation and decision making and do not take into account the instrumental adjuncts of government, bureaucracy, the military, and the judiciary. On the other hand, social life, including life in parties and political interest groups, was highly authoritarian and relatively little "constitutionalized" compared with Britain. Not only were society and polity to some degree incongruent; they existed in unprecedented contradiction with one another. And on the basis of the theory of congruence, in consequence, the Weimar Republic could only have been what indeed it was: nasty, brutish, and short-lived—unless, like the Third Republic, it had been more lucky than any political order can expect to be.

Democracy, in interwar Germany, was, for all practical purposes, isolated at the level of parliamentary government, but at that level it was organized in an almost absurdly pure and exaggerated manner. Weimar Germany was governed by a Reichstag chosen on the basis of universal suffrage and by means of one of the purest systems of proportional representation ever devised. The chief of state was a plebiscitary president, and an effort was made, through run-off provisions, to assure that he would have the support of an absolute, not merely a relative, majority. Ministers were easily removable both by the popularly elected Reichstag and popularly elected president, and government was conducted on the basis of a very lengthy and detailed bill of rights. The Weimar constitution was proclaimed in its day as the most perfect of all democratic constitutions, and for good reasons.

This unalleviated democracy was superimposed upon a society pervaded by authoritarian relationships and obsessed with authoritarianism. In his study of interwar German films, *From Caligari to Hitler*,[3] Siegfried Kracauer has pointed out that a morbid concern with despotism, with raw power and arbitrary

3 Princeton, N.J.: Princeton University Press, 1947.

will, was a characteristic alike of reactionary and revolutionary German films, most obviously in films like *Caligari, Waxworks, Dr. Mabuse,* and *Mädchen in Uniform.* That the Germans should have been deeply preoccupied with naked power, large and petty, is hardly very surprising in a society democratized on its parliamentary surface, but shot through with large and petty tyrants in every other segment of life. Compared with their British counterparts, German family life, German schools, and German business firms were all exceedingly authoritarian. . . .

. . . But perhaps a high degree of authoritarianism in these patterns would not matter from the standpoint of democratic government if there were interposed between them and government certain institutions having mixed authority relations—institutions which might mediate between the pervasive despotism of the primary segments and the pure democracy of government, so that individuals would not be tossed abruptly from stark domination in one segment of life to stark liberty in another. But nothing remotely like this was the case in Weimar Germany. Political parties in imperial Germany had served as the principal model for Michels' iron law of oligarchy, and their internal political characteristics persisted in the Weimar period; at a later date, German political parties served as the chief illustration for Hermens' argument that proportional representation with the straight list system inevitably makes for a highly centralized and oligarchical party structure. Associational life in Weimar Germany presents, if anything, an even sharper contrast with Great Britain. Quite apart from the fact that the great interest groups were intimately involved in the party system—every major interest, economic, religious, or sectional, had a party of its own—the main "associations" offering men opportunities for escape from loneliness or from the primary social relations were extraordinarily authoritarian in structure. . . .

We have in the case of the Weimar Republic a government violently contradictory to all non-governmental aspects of life. However, it would not be strictly accurate to say, as so many have said, that the Germans were simply thoroughgoing authoritarians who just had no use for political democracy, that in Germany governmental democracy was imposed upon a country which provided no basis at all for it, so that the first talented and lucky authoritarian to come along could easily demolish the whole structure. There is every reason to think that the great majority of Germans were convinced democrats during the Weimar period and even before—in their attitudes toward government. Imperial Germany was one of the first countries to have universal suffrage, and the fact that pro-democratic, liberal, center, and socialist parties consistently won somewhere between 80 and 90 per cent of the vote in elections before World War I is therefore a matter of some importance. This voting pattern, furthermore, continued under the Weimar Republic right up to the ill-starred elections of the early 1930's; the right-wing Nationalists (the DNVP), the party which best fits the stereotype of the unmitigatedly authoritarian German, rarely polled more than 10 per cent of the vote.[4] Consequently, when one says that there was no basis for democracy in inter-war Germany, one says something much more complicated than that Germans did not really want a governmental democracy. One says that Weimar Germany could provide no proper basis even for a governmental system which the great majority indeed wanted, while imperial Germany, ironically, did furnish a proper basis for a type of government which the great majority did not seem to want. Had the German taste for authoritarianism been absolute, the Germans would probably have constructed after World War I a much more stable, though not a purely democratic, government. The trouble was not that the Germans were so one-sidedly authoritarian; the trouble was rather that they were—and perhaps had always been[5]—so remarkably two-sided (i.e., incongruent) in their political beliefs and social practices. Profound ideological commitment to governmental democracy is not a sufficient basis for stable democracy; in fact,

[4] Herbert J. Spiro, "The German Political System," in (S. H. Beer and A. B. Ulam, eds.), *Patterns of Government* (New York, 1958), pp. 400–401.
[5] K. W. Deutsch and L. D. Edinger, *Germany Rejoins the Powers* (Stanford, Stanford University Press, 1959), pp. 12–14.

it can be worse, in the long run, than a more qualified commitment to democracy.

BALANCED DISPARITIES IN THE GOVERNMENTAL PATTERN

What then are the special conditions that democracies must fulfill if they are to be stable? Undoubtedly one could list here a massive catalog of social characteristics which favor stable democracy, but if we confine ourselves to conditions not merely favorable but indispensable, to necessary conditions, we can deal with this question rather briefly. The most essential special requirement of stable democracy can in fact be deduced from the theory of the congruence of authority patterns—as indeed ought to be the case, since special theories should always be derivable from general theories. If governments tend to be stable when social authority patterns are congruent; if a great many social relations cannot be organized on a purely democratic basis without seriously dysfunctional consequences; and if some of these relations resistant to democratic structure exits in social segments adjacent or close to government; then it follows that *governmental democracy will tend to be stable only if it is to a significant extent impure—if, in short, the governmental authority pattern contains a balance of disparate elements, of which democracy is an important part (but only a part).*

To forestall a tempting, but unjustified, retort to this proposition, it should perhaps be pointed out immediately that I am not now asserting, after arguing that governmental stability requires congruent authority patterns, that stable democracy requires an *incongruent* authority pattern after all. The notion of congruence applies to the relations between governmental and nongovernmental authority patterns, while the present point relates only to governmental patterns. It asserts merely that intolerable strains between governmental and non-governmental patterns are likely to be avoided if the governmental pattern is not extremely, i.e. purely, democratic.

One could even argue that the very minimum definition of congruence cannot be satisfied in a pure governmental democracy. Not only are the primary and occupational relationships of social life inhospitable to democratic organization, but we have every reason to think that associations, parties, and pressure groups also resist democratization after a point—not to mention the still more obvious cases of the civil and military service. Parties, for example, are competitive organizations—Michels called them fighting organizations[6]—which can hardly afford the luxuries of plebiscitary democracy; so are pressure groups. Associations in general are rarely very democratic, if only because of the relatively low rate of participation by members in their affairs, in the great majority of cases[7]—not to mention functional requirements which act as barriers against democratization. The iron law of oligarchy seems to hold pretty well, which is not to say that democracy must always be a chimera in any form. It follows that between a governmental pattern as purely democratic as that of Weimar Germany and any kind of social life, even in the least authoritarian of political cultures, there are bound to be glaring, perhaps insurmountable, disjunctions. Governmental democracy, of course, is never really pure in practice; but, as the case of Weimar shows, it can come very close, certainly in the forms and myths of authority, if not quite so readily in actual practices.

It is certainly curious how often one finds mixtures of heterogeneous characteristics, sometimes even contradictory characteristics, in stable democracies. Take Great Britain once more as the obvious and most essential case in point. British government and British authority beliefs, as already pointed out, are a mixture of all the elements out of which governmental authority can be concocted: popular government, the government of an autonomous elite, and government under an impersonal law; and none of these elements is clearly dominant over the others. British government combines (in a surprisingly easy fit) authority, responsibility, and responsiveness—the dominion of rulers, rules, and the ruled; for this reason there is something in British government to

[6] Robert Michels, *Political Parties* (Glencoe, Ill., The Free Press, 1958), pp. 46–49.

[7] S. M. Lipset, M. A. Trow, and J. S. Coleman, *Union Democracy* (Glencoe, Ill., The Free Press, 1956).

which every aspect of British social life, whether permissive or compulsive, traditional or modern, can have an affinity. . . .

DEMOCRACY AND ECONOMIC DEVELOPMENT

Is there really a close connection between democracy and economic development?

The evidence suggests strongly that there is. Lipset, for example, found a positive correlation of sorts between stable democracy (in *his* sense of the term) and almost every conceivable index of economic development.* . . . [Lipset's] findings are supported by Coleman (in the Conclusion of *The Politics of the Developing Areas*), countries with "competitive" political systems in the "developing areas" coming out much better, on the indices used also by Lipset, than "semi-competitive" and "authoritarian" countries. And Deutsch's work[8] also lends credence to the thesis, since the great majority of the countries located at the highest extreme of economic development in his "country profiles" are also stable democracies—e.g., Switzerland, Australia, New Zealand, Sweden, Norway, Denmark, the United Kingdom, and the United States.

This is a lot of evidence—but far from conclusive. If we look, not at overall averages, but at specific cases and at ranges of economic differences among countries in the same governmental categories, it becomes apparent that we have here a rather weak correlation, not a strong one. A few countries which have been anything but paragons of democratic stability rank quite high in economic development. France, Venezuela, and the U.S.S.R. (not to mention Kuwait) rank high now, and Weimar Germany did in its own day. It is true that the half-dozen countries which are most highly developed are also stable democracies, but difficulties seem to arise only a very little below their level. And the ranges between the most and the least developed stable democracies, as

* See preceding article in this Reader.
8 K. W. Deutsch, "Toward an Inventory of Basic Trends and Patterns in Comparative and International Politics," *American Political Science Review,* LIV (March, 1960), pp. 34–57.

well as the most and the least developed unstable democracies (and non-democracies), are enormous. The least developed stable European democracy had, according to Lipset, an average per capita income of $420, the most developed European dictatorship one of $482. Stable democracies have as many as 62 persons per motor vehicle, dictatorships as few as 10; one has as many as 46 percent of males employed in agriculture, the other as few as 16; in one case as few as 28 percent of the population live in cities, in the other as many as 44 percent. Such overlaps, varying in size, but all large, are found for every index.

It follows that between the great extremes of economic development and economic underdevelopment is a large no-man's-land where apparently any governmental order, from stable democracy to totalitarianism, can exist—and at the great extremes there are not many cases. That stable democracy is not found at the very lowest levels is, of course, not surprising. At that level of underdevelopment the more obvious requisites for any democracy at all, stable or unstable—a certain minimum level of literacy, information, and communications—are not satisfied. But beyond that extreme, in the higher and intermediate ranges of economic development, everything is puzzling and indeterminate, if one assumes a simple correlation between democracy and economic level.

Lipset himself seems well aware of this, for his theory does not stop with economic development, but uses also a large number of other factors to explain the stability or instability of democracies: rapidity (rather than level) of economic development; "legitimacy" (that is, acceptance of a regime as right for a society), with special emphasis on the support of conservative groups; religion; historical development; and governmental structure. By adding all of these conditions to qualify the correlation with economic development, the theory can be made to come out right in every case, but so could any theory whatever; the whole procedure smacks of the familiar methodological fallacy of "saving the hypothesis." Moreover, the theory which finally emerges from all these modifications is extremely complicated, to say the least. It does not blatantly violate the rule of parsimony, for it is not established that a simpler theory with equal explanatory power is available; but it is very cumbersome to use and the significance of any of its variables almost impossible to establish, owing to the number of variables alleged to be independently capable of producing unstable democracy.

For these reasons alone one ought to look for another way to deal with the imperfections of the correlation, and such a way is provided by the present theory. Like religion, we can regard economic development as an aspect of society which correlates with stable (or unstable) democracy only in so far as it has an impact upon the congruence of authority patterns in society and the balancing of disparate patterns in government—as it does frequently (hence the positive correlation) but certainly not always (hence its imperfections).

That this is probably the right way to proceed is suggested by the most important modification Lipset himself makes in his theory. Not only the *level* of economic development seems to him to be associated with the performance of democracies, but also the *rate* of economic development; very rapid economic development, he argues, has consequences inimical to democracy, more gradual economic development supports it. On the evidence, this is a very strong argument—and exactly what one would expect on the basis of the present theory. Rapid industrialization from a traditional base, whatever its long-run effects, obviously introduces into society profound incongruities, particularly if it is imposed by direction, in one form or another. If economic development is relatively slow, strains between the economic and other sectors of life can be kept at tolerable levels by the gradual adaptation of other social institutions to the slowly evolving industrial economy. Nor is this the only reason why rapid economic development has political consequences different from gradual economic development. In the course of rapid economic development, the social order (appearing, as it must, as a barrier to development) is usually attacked in all its aspects, and in that process even aspects of social life which are, if not perfectly, then at least sufficiently, compatible with a modernized economy may be uprooted. Even if social life is not coercively uprooted by those who want to industrialize rapidly, it may nevertheless be uprooted by revolutionary violence resulting from the great strains attendant upon rapid industrialization. In either event, the outcome is the same: society and government will not consist of that mixture of modern and pre-modern patterns, that blending of disparities, which is characteristic of the more stable democracies. Furthermore, rapid industrialization usually occurs, for obvious reasons, at a relatively late stage in the history of industrialism; because of this, the desire for rapid economic modernization is likely for manifest historical reasons to be accompanied by expectations of relatively advanced democracy. Rapid industrialization in non-totalitarian countries will therefore tend to be accompanied by the creation of especially pure democracies, and these are always more tenuous than impure democracies; and if democracy is achieved by revolution, the result is, of course, the same. Worst of all, the sudden creation of an advanced democracy will abruptly liberate men politically, while the exigencies of rapid industrialization will subject them, in the short run, to unprecedented disciplines and compulsions. In this way, rapid industrialization not only unsettles the social order in general, but tends to create particularly great strains between government and other aspects of social life.

The theories of congruence and balanced disparities can thus account comprehensively for the deleterious impact upon democracy of rapid industrialization. But what of the positive correlation between economic development and stable democracy in general? If rapid industrialization is indeed inimical to democracy, and if it leads, as it must, to the attainment of relatively high levels of development in relatively little time, then surely this correlation is rather puzzling—until one remembers that the most advanced industrial societies (at present, or at any rate when Lipset collected his data) are precisely those which developed industry most gradually, but still lead the field because of their early start. In these countries—Great Britain, the United States, Switzerland, Sweden, and Canada—industrialization was associated with the relatively slow growth of populistic democracy and the gradual adaptation, never complete displacement, of pre-industrial patterns, or else the forming of society itself simultaneously with the growth of industry and democracy. When this is realized, it becomes apparent that level of economic development, the moment one goes beyond extreme underdevelopment, matters only because speed of economic development matters; and from this it also follows that the present theory can account for Lipset's general proposition, no less than for the supposed modification of it which he introduces. This is because the modification is, in fact, the really crucial theory.

Economic development thus correlates very imperfectly with stable democracy because certain forms of development produce precisely those incongruities and imbalances which endanger democracy. That is why some very highly developed countries are unstable democracies, or not democracies at all. But economic development need not produce these deleterious consequences, and has not produced them in the (presently) most highly developed countries—that is why there is, nevertheless, a positive correlation between level of economic development and stable democracy. Indirectly, in the ways Lipset mentions, industrialization may even create conditions favorable to democracy, provided it is achieved in the right way. It is even more likely, however, that the two are associated simply because their roots lie in the same historical conditions—that is to say, because the processes of industrialization and democratization coincided, and did not, while both were being achieved gradually, frustrate one another.

If this is so, then it would clearly be unwise to base on the correlation any optimistic predictions about the future impact of industrialization upon the stability of democracies. The only predictions which seem to follow from this analysis are that late industrialization is, in the typical case, likely to have political consequences directly opposite to those of early industrialization, and that rapid industrialization is particularly dangerous to democracy if, paradoxical though it may seem, it is accompanied by rapid democratization.

3 / AUTHORITARIANISM

JUAN J. LINZ / An Authoritarian Regime: Spain*

We prefer for purposes of analysis to reject the idea of a continuum from democracy to totalitarianism and to stress the distinctive nature of authoritarian regimes. Unless we examine the features unique to them, the conditions under which they emerge, the conceptions of power held by those who shape them, regimes which are not clearly either democratic or totalitarian will be treated merely as deviations from these ideal types and will not be studied systematically and comparatively.

Like any ideal type, the notion of the authoritarian regime is an abstraction which underlines certain characteristics and ignores, at least for the time being, the fluidity of reality, differences in degree, and contradictory tendencies present in the real world. In any of the European regimes of the inter-war years that we would call authoritarian, Fascist elements played a role and significant minorities were striving for a totalitarian state; the Hungary of Horthy, the colonels' regime in Poland, the Rumanian and Yugoslav royal dictatorships, the Portuguese Estado Novo, the Austrian corporative Dollfuss regime, Vichy, are examples. Today the model of the Soviet Union operates similarly in many underdeveloped areas. Such regimes exist under many formal garments, and their lack of an elaborate and consistent ideology makes them particularly susceptible to mimicry.[1]

* From Grik Allardt and Yrjo Littunen, eds., *Cleavages, Ideologies and Party Systems* (Helsinki, Academic Bookstore, 1964), pp. 291–341. Some of the original footnotes and portions of the original article have been omitted.

[1] To avoid any misunderstanding let it be said that this "mimicry" or "imitation," while not all the reality, is quite real in its consequences. Particularly

Before defining an authoritarian regime, let us refer briefly to the conceptions of democracy and totalitarianism from which we start in our comparative analysis. This is particularly important since many authoritarian systems claim to be "organic," "basic," "selective," or "guided" democracies, or at least to govern for the people, if not in fact to be "people's" democracies. We consider a government democratic if it supplies regular constitutional opportunities for peaceful competition for political power (and not just a share of it) to different groups without excluding any significant sector of the population by force. This definition is based on those of Schumpeter, Aron, and Lipset,[2] with the addition of the last qualification to include censitary regimes of the nineteenth century, democracies in which the vote has been denied to some groups, but with real competition for support from a limited electorate. As long as new claimants to suffrage were not suppressed forcibly for more than a limited time, we can consider such regimes democratic.

As Schumpeter has stressed, the element of competition for votes makes the whole gamut of civil liberties necessary, since without them there could be no true free competition; this is the link between classical liberalism and democracy. It could be argued that authoritarian regimes, even pre-constitutional monarchies, have or had certain civil liberties, but we would not call them democracies for this reason. To give an example in recent years, legalization of a right to strike—perhaps not under that name—has been discussed in Spain, particularly since de facto strikes are tolerated and government officials participate in the negotiations between workers and employers despite their illegal-

---

so since it provides for some participants a concept of legitimacy which does not respond to reality and thereby creates sources of alienation among those initially attracted by the new system.

[2] Joseph Schumpeter, *Capitalism, Socialism, and Democracy* (New York, Harper & Brothers, 1947), pp. 232–302, esp. 269; Raymond Aron, *Sociologie des Sociétés Industrielles. Esquisse d'une théorie des régimes politiques* (Paris, Le Centre de Documentation Universitaire, "Les Cours de la Sorbonne," Sociologie, 1958), p. 38; Seymour M. Lipset, *Political Man* (Garden City, New York, Doubleday & Co., Inc., 1960), Chap. II, Economic Development and Democracy, p. 46.

ity. Similarly, the courts have assumed quite extensive control over administrative acts through the Law of Administrative Procedure, following the model of continental European administrative law and jurisprudence. Many elements of the Rechtstaat are not incompatible with an authoritarian state and perhaps not even with a "secularized" totalitarian state. However, full civil liberties, including an unlimited right of association and assembly, for example, inevitably create pressures toward political democracy. In this sense, against a strong tradition in continental political theory, we can say that liberalism and democracy are inseparable.

In defining totalitarianism we also want to limit the term somewhat and reserve it for the unique new forms autocratic government has taken since World War I, without denying that similar tendencies existed in the past. Perhaps Kornhauser's characterization is as good as any other, even if it overstresses somewhat the arbitrary aspects, when he writes:

> Totalitarian dictatorship involves total domination, limited neither by received laws or codes (as in traditional authoritarianism) nor even the boundaries of governmental functions (as in classical tyranny), since they obliterate the distinction between State and society. Totalitarianism is limited only by the need to keep large numbers of people in a state of constant activity controlled by the elite.[3]

C. J. Friedrich's well-known definition[4] includes the following

[3] William Kornhauser, *The Politics of Mass Society* (Glencoe, Ill., The Free Press, 1959), p. 123.

[4] There is no point in referring in detail to the extensive literature on totalitarianism since the works of C. J. Friedrich and Z. K. Brzezinski, Sigmund Neumann, Franz Neumann, Emil Lederer, H. Arendt, Barrington Moore, Jr., Adam B. Ulam, Raymond I. Bauer and Alex Inkeles, are well known. A recent review of the problem with references to the non-American literature can be found in the articles by Otto Stammer, G. Schulz, and Peter Christian Ludz, in *Soziale Welt*, Vol. 12, No. 2, 1961, pp. 97–145; Karl D. Bracher, *Die Auflösung der Weimarer Republik* (Stuttgart, Ring-Verlag, 1957); and K. D. Bracher, Wolfgang Sauer, Gerhard Schulz, *Die Nationalsozialistische Machtergreifung* (Köln, Westdeutscher Verlag, 1960) both sponsored by the Berlin Institut für Politische Wissenschaft, incorporate much of recent German scholarship on the breakdown of democracy and the establishment of Nazi totalitarianism. These monumental works should be used to supplement—

five clusters of characteristics: an official ideology, often with chiliastic elements; a single mass party unquestioningly dedicated to the ideology, near complete control of mass media, complete political control of the armed forces, and a system of terroristic police control not directed against demonstrable enemies only. In another version central control and direction of the economy is added. This more descriptive definition provides a clearer yardstick, although in view of recent developments I would not give as much emphasis to the role of the police and terror.[5]

DEFINITION OF AN AUTHORITARIAN REGIME

Authoritarian regimes are political systems with limited, not responsible, political pluralism; without elaborate and guiding ideology (but with distinctive mentalities); without intensive nor extensive political mobilization (except some points in their development); and in which a leader (or occasionally a small group) exercises power within formally ill-defined limits but actually quite predictable ones.

To avoid any confusion we want to make it clear that personal leadership is a frequent characteristic but not a necessary one, since a junta arrangement can exist and the leader's personality might not be the decisive factor. Furthermore, the leader does not need to have charismatic qualities, at least not for large segments of the population nor at all stages of development of the system. In fact he may combine elements of charismatic, legal, and traditional authority in varying degrees, often at different points in time—though the charismatic element often tends to be more important than the legal authority, at least for some sectors of the population.

PLURALISM

We speak of regime, rather than government, to indicate the relatively low specificity of the political institutions: they often

---

and in my opinion modify—much of the dated but classic *Behemoth* of Franz Neumann.

[5] ... C. J. Friedrich and Z. K. Brzezinski, *Totalitarian Dictatorship and Autocracy* (Cambridge, Mass., Harvard University Press, 1956), pp. 9–10.

penetrate the life of the society, preventing, even forcibly, the political expression of certain group interests (as religion in Turkey and Mexico, labor in Spain) or shaping them by interventionist economic policies. But in contrast to some of the analysts of totalitarianism, such as Inkeles, we speak of regimes rather than societies because the distinction between state and society is not obliterated. The pluralistic element is the most distinctive feature of these regimes, but let us emphasize that in contrast to democracies with their almost unlimited pluralism, we deal here with *limited* pluralism. The limitation may be legal or de facto, serious or less so, confined to strictly political groups or extended to interest groups, as long as there remain groups not created by nor dependent on the state which influence the political process one way or another. Some regimes even institutionalize the political participation of a limited number of independently existing groups or institutions, and actually encourage their emergence. To take an example, when Primo de Rivera created his National Assembly he provided for the representation of the church, cultural institutions, the nobility, the army and the business community, as well as the newly created party; at the same time he encouraged the creation of economic-interest groups that have been the pressure groups of Spanish business ever since.[6, 7] An-

6 There is no satisfactory study in Spanish or any other language of the Primo de Rivera Dictatorship. Dillwyn F. Ratcliff's *Prelude to Franco* (New York, Las Americas Publishing Co., 1957) is totally insufficient, even when it gives some useful information and translates some documents. The most important partisan source in favor is José Pemartin, *Los valores historicos en la dictadura española* (Madrid, Publicaciones de la Junta de Propaganda Patriotica y Ciudadana, 1929) and the collected writings of Miguel Primo de Rivera himself, *El Pensamiento de Primo de Rivera*, J. M. Peman, ed. (Madrid, 1929).

7 A work on the economic policy of that time by José Velarde Fuentes is in preparation. For a list of the interest groups created during this period see Roman Perpiña, *De Estructura Economica y Economia Hispana* (Madrid, Rialp, 1952), pp. 317–320.

The interventions of the Dictator in the corporative chamber he created, often in answer to questions from the floor, vividly illustrate the pluralism and autonomy of social forces during that dictatorship. See *Intervenciones en la Asamblea Nacional del General Primo de Rivera* (Madrid, 1930). The comparison with the Cortes of the present regime shows the range of pluralism *vs.* concentration of power in such systems.

other example is the institutionalization of a complex pluralism in the officially dominant Partido Revolucionario Institucional of Mexico, that prompts V. Padgett to write: "An 'official' party need not necessarily be an instrument of imposition. It may be a device for bridging the gap between authoritarianism and representative democracy." [8] With such a limited but relatively autonomous pluralism, there is likely to be some competition for power, more or less informal, despite open declarations of monopoly. . . .

MENTALITY VERSUS IDEOLOGY

Styles of leadership, and different ways of conceiving the relation between state power and society, must be examined if we are to analyze the authoritarian regime in its various forms.

We will purposely use the term mentality rather than "ideology." The German sociologist Theodor Geiger[9] has formulated a useful distinction between *ideologies,* which are systems of thought more or less intellectually elaborated and organized, often in written form, by intellectuals, pseudo-intellectuals, or with their assistance; and *mentalities,* which are ways of thinking and feeling, more emotional than rational, that provide non-codified ways of reacting to situations. Ideologies have a strong utopian element; mentalities are closer to the present or the past. Totalitarian systems have ideologies, a point emphasized by all students of such systems, while authoritarian regimes are based

[8] L. Vincent Padgett, "Mexico's One-Party System: A Re-Evaluation," *American Political Science Review,* Vol. 51 No. 4 (December, 1957); reprinted in Roy C. Macridis and Bernard E. Brown, *Comparative Politics* (Homewood, Ill., The Dorsey Press, 1961), pp. 193–197, see p. 197.

[9] Theodor Geiger, *Die Soziale Schichtung des Deutschen Volkes* (Stuttgart, Ferdinand Enke Verlag, 1932), pp. 77–79.

As he says with a very graphic German expression: "mentality is *subjektiver Geist* (even when collective), ideology is *objektiver Geist.* Mentality is intellectual attitude, ideology is intellectual content. Mentality is psychic predisposition, ideology is reflection, self-interpretation, mentality is previous, ideology later, mentality is formless, fluctuating—ideology however is firmly formed.—Ideology is a concept of the sociology of culture, mentality is a concept of the study of social character." And so on.

more on distinctive mentalities which are difficult to define. The more traditional an authoritarian regime is, the greater the role of the military and civil servants, the more important "mentalities" become in understanding the system, and the more a focus on ideologies, even those loudly proclaimed by the regime, may be misleading.[10]

APATHY VERSUS MOBILIZATION

Stabilized authoritarian regimes are characterized by lack of extensive and intensive political mobilization of the population. Membership participation is low in political and para-political organizations and participation in the single party or similar bodies, whether coerced, manipulated or voluntary, is infrequent and limited. The common citizen expresses little enthusiastic support for the regime in elections, referenda, and rallies. Rather than enthusiasm or support, the regime often expects—even from office holders and civil servants—passive acceptance, or at least that they refrain from public anti-government activity. Let us stress that this depolitization is characteristic of stabilized authoritarian regimes, but would not be necessarily true for their formative stages, particularly since their emergence in a crisis would involve considerable and often very intensive popular participation. We would like to argue that this participation is not likely to be maintained over a long period of time, unless the regime moves into a totalitarian or a more formally democratic direction.

[10] The recent work by Morris Janowitz, *The Military in the Political Development of New Nations* (Chicago, The University of Chicago Press, 1964), shows the difficulty of defining the ideology of the military (often the creators of such regimes) except in some very general terms: nationalism, a certain xenophobia, often anti-communal sentiments, some puritanic tendencies, a proclivity for government intervention as organizational form without much ideological justification and an "antipolitics outlook (particularly divisive party politics and the mixture of making interest cleavages manifest and afterwards bargaining over them so typical of democratic politics). This "ideology" is so closely related to their professional training, experience and role, and so little related to any intellectual elaboration, that we would prefer to call it a "mentality." As Janowitz himself writes: "The 'mentality' of the military officer seems to be a mixture of half-developed but strongly held ideology and a deep sense of pragmatic professionalism." (p. 67).

However, the degrees of mobilization might be the most useful criteria on which to distinguish subtypes of authoritarian regimes.[11]

On the one side we have those that Raymond Aron[12] has characterized as "regimes without parties" which "require a kind of depoliticization of the governed" and others we could call "populistic" in which there is a more continuous effort of mobilization, without reaching the pervasiveness and intensity of the totalitarian model. Recognizing the importance of such a distinction,[13] we would like to suggest that often the difference might be more that of stages in the development of non-democratic regimes than a substantive difference. It would be to misunderstand contemporary Spain to ignore the high level of participation in party activities, youth groups, political oriented welfare activities—not to mention rallies, parades, etc.—during the years of the Civil War in Nationalistic Spain; and the intensity of involvement, ideological and emotional, of people in all sectors of the population must be stressed.[14] No one can deny that this disappeared during the years after the victory. This was not only because, first, the leadership lacked interest in maintaining it, but also because the social structure of a semi-developed country, and the social, institutional, and ideological pluralism, made such levels of participation untenable without either channeling them through organ-

11 Immanuel Wallerstein, *Africa. The Politics of Independence* (New York, Vintage Books, 1961), pp. 96–97. Refers to the differences in mobilization in the different single-party systems in Africa, which "at least in theory" are mass parties.

In theory the Spanish single-party is also a mass party and in recent years José Luis de Arrese has spoken of the need to revitalize the party and even initiated—when he was Secretary General—attempts in that direction. See his collection of writings: *Hacio una Meta Institucional* (Madrid, Ediciones del Movimiento, n.d.), pp. 113–126.

12 Raymond Aron, *op. cit.*, p. 50.

13 The notion of "populist" regimes has been used by Morroe Berger, *The Arab World Today* (Garden City, New York, Doubleday & Co. 1962), pp. 418–423, and in some interpretations of Latin-American dictatorships to distinguish regimes like Vargas' Estado Novo and Peron's Justicialismo from more old-fashioned military dictatorships.

14 This pattern of passive support rather than mobilization has also been noted by Dionisio Ridruejo, *Escrito en España* (Buenos Aires: Losada, S. A., 1962). . . .

ized parties or substituting that pluralism with a hierarchical, disciplined and ideologically committed single party. In the context of the early forties, the first possibility was excluded and the will to impose a truly totalitarian system, destructive of the coalition character of the forces Franco led to victory, was absent from an army (including its leaders) which had no single well-defined ideology. I would like to leave the question open if in the future some of the more "populistic" one-party regimes in Africa and the Moslem countries will not undergo a similar process, transforming the parties and connected organizations into adjuncts of the state apparatus (the bureaucracy) or/and patronage organizations, with little genuine participation, even of a manipulative type.

However, even admitting that the degree of mobilization may depend on the phase in which the system finds itself, we should not ignore that the leaders of such regimes may opt between regarding political mobilization as desirable or preferring to rule without it. The option may reflect ideological predispositions and influences toward social change or arresting such change, but we should not consider this the only or decisive factor. In fact, we could argue that the choice will depend more on the opportunities offered by the social structure, the political context, and the international situation for a mobilization in support of those in power, than on the outlook of the rulers. On the other side, the "outcomes," the capacity to do things, and the power for social change may in part depend on the capacity for sustained mobilization.

Thus on the one side we have regimes coming to power after periods of considerable organized political strife, lack of consensus under democratic governments, and aborted revolutions: all these will tend to use apathy to consolidate their power, at least the apathy of those not likely to be won over to their policies. The depoliticization in these cases would be one way to reduce the tension in the society and achieve a minimum of reintegration, which otherwise could probably be reached only by totalitarian suppression of the dissidents. Privatization under authoritarian regimes has a certain parallel in the "internal migration" of totalitarianism, but differs in that this privatization is consciously or unconsciously encouraged by those in power. Such a politicism would bar people from positions of power and influence in a totalitarian system; in some authoritarian regimes it is even valued as an asset, or so it is publicly claimed by persons appointed to high office who state they have never been actively involved in "politics." Referring to this depolitization some cynics have called the three F's—Fatima, football, and *fados* (folk songs)—the *arcana imperii* of Portugal.

On the other side we have regimes trying to gain control of societies in which the masses have never been mobilized by any political force, particularly if the preceding regime had been one of colonial rule, or a traditional monarchy, or even an oligarchic democracy. These situations are likely to coincide with underdeveloped rather than semi-developed societies, where the underprivileged masses have not given their loyalty to any organized movement, and consequently their manipulation is easy, at least initially. The populistic dictators of Latin America could create a certain mass base among workers that the supporters of Franco, even with socially progressive policies and demagogic appeals, would never have succeeded in creating given the previous history of Spain. The content of the policies might not have been as decisive as the level of political, social and economic development of the country. The degree of mobilization under authoritarian rule may not depend as much on the desires of the rulers as on the opportunities for mobilization, shaped by previous history, economic and social development, and even the degree of pluralism and complexity of the society. Last but not least, the international situation of the country, the possibility to use or not to use a xenophobic appeal, rallying people of all classes and degrees of identification with the system, to a national cause might be decisive. Foreign pressure can maintain participation in an authoritarian system as nothing else can. After all, in Spain the last successful manifestations of mass participation were achieved when the United Nations exercised their pressure or under the cry of Spanish Gibraltar.

... In totalitarian systems membership is either obligatory or necessary for success; in democracies there is generally a free choice among multiple groups.

In authoritarian regimes, intermediate systems are frequent: membership may be obligatory but involve nothing more than paying dues, or strictly voluntary without creating any advantages. Presumably political goals take primacy in totalitarian organizations while specific interests predominate in democratic organizations. . . .

In fact, in countries like Spain we find a rapid and accelerated growth[15] of voluntary associations, necessarily not openly political and generally apolitical, in recent years, particularly in areas where their numbers had been smallest. In this sense some of Lavau's observations would also be applicable to the apoliticism of the masses in Spain.[16]

I would suggest that the closer an authoritarian regime is to pursuing either the totalitarian or democratic model, the greater will its efforts be toward some kind of mobilization. So the Spanish regime made greater efforts to organize mass meetings, parades, public ceremonies, in the Fascist-inspired period than today; while it has become more pluralistic, it has become less participative. Since both pluralism and participation characterize democratic polities, we can say that certain political systems are more or less "democratic" depending on which element we focus on; using participation as a criterion, Nazi Germany was relatively democratic; using pluralism, a regime like Horthy's, which was certainly not participative, could be termed relatively democratic.

The content of the policies being pursued, socially progressive

[15] Data from a study on voluntary associations in Spain, based on a breakdown by province and date of founding of 8329 associations registered until 1960. In provinces with a number of associations above the national average, 50 percent had been founded since 1950, while in a sample of those below the national average it was 73 percent, 50 percent of them between 1955–56.
[16] Georges Lavau, "Les aspects socio-culturels de la dépolitisation" in *La Dépolitisation, Mythe ou Réalité?* ed. by G. Vedel, *Cahiers de la Fondation Nationale des Sciences Politiques,* No. 120 (Paris, Armand Colin, 1962), pp. 167–206.

or conservative, may have something to do with the degree of mobilization a regime encourages, but the social context in which such programs are enacted may have as much importance. I would not be surprised to find quite different degrees of mobilization even where economic development policies, expansion of education or mass media, and welfare-state measures are quite similar. Still, I would agree that without such mobilization the introduction of such measures becomes more difficult and their socially integrative function may not be achieved.

THE AUTHORITARIAN PARTY

According to the legal texts of many authoritarian regimes, their single parties occupy a similarly dominant position: to the totalitarian party monopolizing power, recruiting the elite, transmitting both the aspirations of the people and the directives of the leadership.[17] In fact, however, some regimes that in reality approach the totalitarian model legally have multi-party systems, while in others which are legally single-party monopolies, the party plays a comparatively limited role. Therefore it is imperative to examine the authoritarian party in its sociological reality.

First and foremost, the authoritarian party is not a well-organized ideological organization which monopolizes all access to power. As we will see later, a considerable part of the elite has no connection with the party and does not identify with it. Party membership creates few visible advantages and imposes few, if any, duties. Ideological indoctrination is often minimal, the conformity and loyalty required may be slight, and expulsions and purges are not frequent and do not represent an important mechanism of social control. The party is often ideologically and socially heterogeneous. Far from branching out into many functional organizations, in an effort to control the state apparatus and penetrate other spheres of life as the Nazi party did, it is a

17 On the creation of the unified party, the Falange Española Tradicionalista y de las Juntas de Ofensiva Nacional Sindicalista, see Serrano Suñer, *op. cit.,* pp. 19–39 and Stanley G. Payne, *Falange. A History of Spanish Fascism* (Stanford, Stanford University Press, 1961) Chaps. 13 and 14, pp. 148–198. Payne's book is an indispensable source on the history of the Falange and its place in the regime.

skeleton organization of second-rate bureaucrats. The party becomes only one more element in the power pluralism; one more group pressing for particular interests, one more channel through which divergent interests try to find access to power; one more recruiting ground for elite members. Since tight discipline lacks widespread ideological legitimacy, various functional groups that might have been transmission belts for the leadership's directives, become apolitical interest groups, or autonomous nuclei where a few activists, even those emerging from the grass roots, may follow independent policies.

The importance of the party has many indicators: the number of high officials that were active in the party before entering the elite; the membership figures; the degree of activity indicated by the party budget: agit-prop activity; the prestige or power accorded to party officials; the presence of party cells or representatives in other institutions; the importance of training centers; the attention paid to party organs and publications; the vigor of ideological polemics within the party factions. By all these criteria the Spanish party has never been too strong and today is obviously weak. A look at the party's provincial headquarters, in contrast to other government offices or the Sindicatos (a functional organization theoretically dependent on the party) should convince anyone of the party's second-rate role in Spain.

The different roles of the authoritarian and totalitarian parties may be explained by differences in their origin. Most single parties in authoritarian countries have been created after accession to power rather than before.[18] They have been created by fusing a variety of groups with different ideological traditions and varying social bases, not by completely subordinating some elements to one dominant force. Where politicians of other groupings, including the minor Fascist parties, have been co-opted, no disciplined, integrated organization emerged. In other cases, when the military dictator has tried to create a patriotic national unity organization,

[18] For a description of the slowness and false starts in the creation of the Vaterland Front of Dollfuss, see Gordon Brook Shepherd, *Dollfuss* (London, Macmillan & Co. Ltd., 1961), pp. 103–109. . . . Janowitz, *op. cit.*, also comments on the difficulties found by the military in the creation of mass political organizations, see pp. 84–93. . . .

the effort was carried out by officers and bureaucrats, who typically do not have the demagogic skills needed to create a lively organization. They are further hampered because they continue devoting most of their attention to government or army offices, where real power, and not merely the promise of it, lies. The old politicians, rallying to organizations like the Imperial Rule Assistance Association[19] or the ex-CEDA (conservative-demochristian deputies in the Republic) leaders in the Falange, are not able to adopt the new style that a totalitarian party requires. Since the party is not tested in a struggle for power, it attracts more than its share of office seekers and opportunists, few idealists, true believers, real revolutionaries. Since its ideology is not defined, indoctrination of the numerous newcomers, entering *en masse,* is likely to be scanty, and the facts of life soon disillusion the more utopian. Since the primary need is to staff the state apparatus, the premium will be on recruiting professionals and bureaucrats, and not the armed intellectuals or bohemians, the marginal men that give the totalitarian movement its peculiar style.

FORMS OF SOCIAL CONTROL

Similarities between authoritarian regimes and the totalitarians can perhaps go furthest in the control of mass media, particularly in countries in the process of modernization where the technological and capital requirements for setting up the media make such control very easy. Media may vary greatly in autonomy, even under the same regime, but limited pluralism readily creates some islands of exemption; in Spain, for example, church publications are free from government censorship.

The small size of the elite and the persistence within the regime of ties created prior to it, allow for considerable free communication, unless the regime is willing to use a good deal of coercion. The same may be said of contacts with other countries, particularly by the elite. While the monopoly of mass media may

[19] On the Imperial Rule Assistance Association, see Robert A. Scalapino, *Democracy and the Party Movement in Prewar Japan* (Berkeley, University of California Press, 1953), pp. 388-389.

be as great as that in totalitarian societies, the impact of this monopoly is less because it is not enhanced by intensive personal propagandizing through agitators and other informal leaders. Even when the freedom of the press is curtailed, truly totalitarian control is not present if there is freedom of travel and, at least, freedom of conversation. (As long as one does not make more than five copies of one's opinions, one cannot be prosecuted for illegal propaganda in Spain.) It may well be that the excesses of control to which a Stalin or Hitler went are really unnecessary.

Terror and police control figure prominently among the characteristics of totalitarianism listed by Friedrich, Brzezinski, Arendt and others, as they should in view of the recent Hitlerian and Stalinist experiments. However recent tendencies toward "socialist legality" may reduce this; and the need for political justice or terror in democracies during crisis situations, while not comparable in volume, suggests that this may not be a good distinction between various types of political systems. Undoubtedly there are differences in the ways in which coercion is used. Whatever repressive practices a democracy may resort to, they are more a reflection of public opinion than of government policy, and the importance of civil rights for the functioning of the system puts serious limits to their extension beyond a crisis situation. In authoritarian regimes the existing legal barriers may be weak (though not to be discounted), but the equilibrium of forces on which limited pluralism is based may be a more serious restraint. While repression of the system's open enemies may go far, dissenters within the coalition, or potential members of it, must be handled with more care. While in totalitarian systems members of the elite have often been punished with great harshness, and the setting of examples in show trials has been frequent, in authoritarian regimes exile, kicking upstairs, retirement to private life are more frequent.

While Arendt[20] could perceive no decrease in terror, in fact an

---

[20] H. Arendt in *Origins of Totalitarianism* (New York, 1951), pp. 387 ff. Her analysis may be contrasted with this summary by Herbert Matthews:

"The picture of Franco Spain that is firmly believed by the exiles is distorted and in many respects false. They picture a totalitarian police state increase, after the totalitarian consolidation of power, we may argue that after the birth-pangs of an authoritarian regime are over it may relax. The absence of full ideological self-righteousness is an important restraint. Another is the presence in the elite of men who have held power under states of law, and are themselves lawyers; or, if military, they share at least the military conception of law: legalism may not inhibit repression of the State's enemies, but it does lead to certain procedural rules, to an emphasis on actions rather than intentions. The importance of the armed forces limits the political autonomy and development of the police apparatus; its concern is with actual rather than merely potential opponents. The less dynamic character of such regimes also tends to make the use of force less necessary. The distinction between society and politics, private and public life, means there is less need for the presence of police in many areas of life; limited party membership means information about citizens is also limited, and consequently so is control. Without a "Blockwart"— the Nazi party representative in each dwelling area—gossip available for control purposes is reduced.

THE POSITION OF THE MILITARY

All political systems face the problem of subordinating the military to political authority, and once military dictators start devoting their energies to political problems, they face the same issue. Methods of controlling the military differ in democracies, totalitarian systems, and authoritarian regimes; the equilibrium established between political and military authority will differ as well. In most authoritarian regimes the limited popular consensus, which made such forms of rule necessary or possible in the first place, means there is more need for potential force; this gives the army a privileged position. Normally military affairs are left to military men and not to civilians. The absence of a mass party, and in some countries of a trustworthy and specialized bureauc-

---

that simply does not exist. They have no idea of the degree of tolerance that Franco permits so long as his position and the security of his regime is not threatened," *The Yoke and the Arrows: A Report on Spain* (New York, George Braziller, Inc., 1957), p. 184. See also pp. 178, 183.

racy, often leads to the use of military men in political appointments, patronage positions, and the administration. The technical branches provide experts for public service or nationalized industries. Nationalism as a simple ideology, easily shared by all classes, makes for an emphasis on the army as a bearer of national prestige. If the break with the past was made by a military coup, the position of the army is likely to be even more enhanced.

Nevertheless there is a certain ambivalence toward the army in the authoritarian regime. . . .

In such regimes emerging from a military action, the army may enjoy a privileged position and hold on to key positions, but it soon co-opts politicians, civil servants, and technicians who increasingly make most decisions.[21] The more a regime becomes consolidated, the fewer purely military men staff the government, except when there are no alternative sources of elites. In this sense it may be misleading to speak of a military dictatorship, even when the head of state is an army man. In fact he is likely to carry out a careful policy of depolitization and professionalization of the army, while he maintains close ties with the officer corps to hold its loyalty.[22]

The military background of key men in authoritarian regimes, and their usual lack of ideological sophistication, make it particularly important to understand the military mentality in relation to internal politics, to styles of political life, conceptions of authority, ideas about cost *vs.* results, legitimate forms for expressing grievances, and so on.[23] The few studies on the role of the military

[21] The alternative outcomes of this ambivalence: to turn over quickly power to the old politicians or to hold on to power without giving it any real political content, are well analyzed in José Antonio Primo de Rivera (the founder of the Falangist party and son of the Dictator) in his "Carta a un militar español," pp. 649–651, *Obras Completas* (Madrid, Ediciones de la Vicesecretaria de Educación Popular, 1945), ed. and collected by Agustín del Rio Cisneros and Enrique Conde Gargollo.

[22] A good indicator are the weekly lists of officers received by Franco that are as long as those of civilian officials and personalities.

[23] In an interview with a leading industrialist and banker, after probing about the influence that men of his prestige and influence in the business community could exercise if they acted united and presented their points

in politics have only raised the issue; real data are still to be assembled.

TRADITIONAL AND AUTHORITARIAN REGIMES

One question some of our readers may raise is: Aren't many such regimes really only a form of autocratic and conservative rule like we find in pre-constitutional and traditional monarchies? It would be foolish to deny that the distinctions are fluid, that a number of authoritarian regimes have emerged out of such political forms, and that the formal constitutional framework may still be a monarchical one. However, we want to stress that we would not want to include in our concept any political system which would strictly fit under the concept of traditional authority in Weber's sense and where rule is based on historical continuity, impersonal familial or institutionalized charisma, or various mixtures of patrimonial or feudal rule—using these terms in a somewhat technical sense.[24] To make it clear, neither Abyssinia, nor Yemen before the recent revolution, nor Tibet, Afghanistan, nor some of the other political entities along the Himalayan border, fit our concept, to mention contemporary systems. Nor would the pre-revolutionary European absolute monarchies of the past. Authoritarian regimes are a likely outcome of the breakdown of such traditional forms of legitimacy. This results from a partial social and political mobilization and a questioning of the traditional principles of legitimacy (largely due to their seculari-

---

of view, I received the following comment: "As a Spaniard you should know better, you know very well that in the army collective remonstrances are never tolerated, only individual protests. So we go each separately through different ways, after agreeing, but never collectively."

24 We conceive traditional authority in the sense defined by Weber in his *Wirtschaft und Gesellschaft*. For a summary of this part of his work, only partly translated, see Reinhard Bendix, *Max Weber, an Intellectual Portrait* (Garden City, New York, Doubleday & Co., 1962), pp. 329–384. While we want to stress the conceptual difference between authoritarian regimes and traditional rule, we also want to suggest that they sometimes have elements in common and that the students of such regimes could gain many insights from Weber's analysis of patrimonial rule and bureaucracy as those of totalitarianism have gained from his thinking about charisma.

zation) by significant segments of the society. Authoritarian systems—even those we might call reactionary—are modernizing in the sense that they represent a discontinuity with tradition, introducing criteria of efficiency and rationality, personal achievement and populistic appeals. It should not be forgotten that the regimes we call royal dictatorships in southeastern Europe were created by kings with very limited traditional legitimacy and that those kings who supported dictators, as did Alphonse XIII in Spain, Victor Emmanuel III in Italy, and several mideastern monarchs lost their thrones, giving way to democratic republics or authoritarian regimes without a king. The enormous ambivalences surrounding the legitimacy of the Iranian monarchy[25] that was restored by an authoritarian military leader, Reza Pahlavi, are obvious and certainly would not allow this monarchy to be regarded as a purely traditional regime. The attempts of the present Spanish regime to find its constitutional and legitimacy form as a traditional monarchy certainly suggest the difficulties encountered when moving from an authoritarian regime to a traditional one. There can be no doubt that many of those who are willing to recognize the claims to legitimate rule of Franco would not transfer their allegiance to a traditional monarchy. In our times authoritarian rule almost inevitably leads to questioning traditional authority, if for no other reason than by making the people aware of the importance of the effective head of the government and its secular character. Authoritarian rule might be an intermediate stage in or after the breakdown of traditional authority, but not the route toward its restoration. To specify further the differences would take us at this time too far from the Spanish case.

This might be the place to stress a very important characteristic of many, if not most, authoritarian regimes: the coexistence in them of different legitimizing formulae.[26] The actual pluralism of such regimes and the lack of effective legitimate institutionaliza-

---

[25] See Leonard Binder, *Iran. Political Development in a Changing Society* (Berkeley, University of California Press, 1962), pp. 58–89 *et passim*.

[26] Binder, *op. cit.*, has emphasized the coexistence of different legitimizing formulae and the consequences of this phenomenon, particularly in terms of increased alienation. See pp. 15, 20, and 59–63.

tion of that pluralism within a single legitimate political formula allowing competition of the pluralistic elements for power, almost inevitably lead to the coexistence of competing legitimacy formulae. So in the case of Spain the traditionalist monarchy desired by the Carlists, a restoration of the pre-1931 monarchy, some form of Catholic corporativism like the present regime under monarchical (or even republican) form, a more dynamic totalitarian vision along fascist lines, even a transition to a democratic republic under christian democratic leadership, are all different formulas open to the supporters of the regime. Those supporters give their support in the hope that the regime will satisfy their aspirations and they withdraw their support in so far as they realize that the regime is not doing so, or unable to do so. If we had more space we could develop some of the parallels with Binder's description of the Iranian situation.

Fortunately for many such systems, the great mass of the population in semi- or under-developed societies is not concerned with the legitimizing formulae. Instead the population obeys out of a mixture of habit and self-interest, either characterizing the political culture of passive subjects or the parochial (to use the terminology of Almond and Verba). The confusion concerning the sources of legitimacy inherent in many such regimes contributes much of the confusion and pessimism of those most likely to be politically involved. Because of this, often the more privileged and those close to the centers of power may appear more alienated from the regime than they really are (at least for all practical purposes). This can help to explain the relative stability of many such systems despite the freedom with which criticism is expressed. The identification with such regimes may not be found in their political formulas, but in the identification with the basic values of the society, its stratification system, and many non-political institutions, which are their infra-structure.

SAMUEL P. HUNTINGTON / Political Development and Decay*

MOBILIZATION AND INSTITUTIONALIZATION

Social mobilization and political participation are rapidly increasing in Asia, Africa, and Latin America. These processes, in turn, are directly responsible for the deterioration of political institutions in these areas. As Kornhauser has conclusively demonstrated for the Western world, rapid industrialization and urbanization create discontinuities which give rise to mass society. "The *rapid* influx of large numbers of people into *newly* developing urban areas invites mass movements." [1] In areas and industries with very rapid industrial growth, the creation and institutionalization of unions lag, and mass movements are likely among the workers. As unions are organized, they are highly vulnerable to outside influences in their early stages. "The rapid influx of large numbers of people into a new organization (as well as a new area) provides opportunities for mass-oriented elites to penetrate the organization. This is particularly true during the formative periods of organizations, for at such times external constraints must carry the burden of social control until the new participants have come to internalize the values of the organization." [2]

* From *World Politics* (April, 1965), pp. 405–417. Portions of the original article have been omitted.
[1] William Kornhauser, *The Politics of Mass Society* (Glencoe, Ill., The Free Press, 1959), p. 145.
[2] *Ibid.*, p. 146.

So also in politics. Rapid economic growth breeds political instability.[3] Political mobilization, moreover, does not necessarily require the building of factories or even movement to the cities. It may result simply from increases in communications, which can stimulate major increases in aspirations that may be only partially, if at all, satisfied. The result is a "revolution of rising frustrations." [4] Increases in literacy and education may bring more political instability. By Asian standards, Burma, Ceylon, and the Republic of Korea are all highly literate, but no one of them is a model of political stability. Nor does literacy necessarily stimulate democracy: with roughly seventy-five percent literacy, Cuba was the fifth most literate country in Latin America (ranking behind Argentina, Uruguay, Chile, and Costa Rica), but the first to go Communist; so also Kerala, with one of the highest literacy rates in India, was the first Indian state to elect a Communist government.[5] Literacy, as Daniel Lerner has suggested, "may be dysfunctional—indeed a serious impediment—to modernization in the societies now seeking (all too rapidly) to transform their institutions." [6]

Increased communication may thus generate demands for more "modernity" than can be delivered. It may also stimulate a reaction against modernity and activate traditional forces. Since the political arena is normally dominated by the more modern groups, it can bring into the arena new, anti-modern groups and break whatever consensus exists among the leading political participants. It may also mobilize minority ethnic groups who had been indifferent to politics but who now acquire a self-consciousness and divide the political system along ethnic lines. Nationalism, it has often been assumed, makes for national integration. But in actuality, nationalism and other forms of ethnic conscious-

---

3 See Mancur Olson, Jr., "Rapid Growth as a Destabilizing Force," *Journal of Economic History,* xxvii (December, 1963), pp. 529–52; and Bert F. Hoselitz and Myron Weiner, "Economic Development and Political Stability in India," *Dissent,* viii (Spring, 1961), pp. 172–79.

4 See Daniel Lerner, "Toward a Communication Theory of Modernization," in Pye, ed., *Communications and Political Development,* pp. 330 ff.

5 Cf. Deutsch, *American Political Science Review,* lv, p. 496.

6 Daniel Lerner, "The Transformation of Institutions" (mimeo.), p. 19.

ness often stimulate political disintegration, tearing apart the body politic.

Sharp increases in voting and other forms of political participation can also have deleterious effects on political institutions. In Latin America since the 1930's, increases in voting and increases in political instability have gone hand in hand. "Age requirements were lowered, property and literacy requirements were reduced or discarded, and the unscrubbed, unschooled millions on the farms were enfranchised in the name of democracy. They were swept into the political life of the republics so rapidly that existing parties could not absorb many of them, and they learned little about working within the existing political system." [7] The personal identity crises of the elites, caught between traditional and modern cultures, may create additional problems: "In transitional countries the political process often has to bear to an inordinate degree the stresses and strains of people responding to personal needs and seeking solutions to intensely personal problems." [8] Rapid social and economic change calls into question existing values and behavior patterns. It thus often breeds personal corruption. In some circumstances this corruption may play a positive role in the modernizing process, enabling dynamic new groups to get things done which would have been blocked by the existing value system and social structure. At the same time, however, corruption undermines the autonomy and coherence of political institutions. It is hardly accidental that in the 1870's and 1880's a high rate of American economic development coincided with a low point in American governmental integrity.[9]

Institutional decay has become a common phenomenon of the modernizing countries. *Coups d'état* and military interventions in politics are one index of low levels of political institutionalization: they occur where political institutions lack autonomy and coherence. According to one calculation, eleven of twelve modern-

[7] John J. Johnson, *The Military and Society in Latin America* (Stanford, 1964), pp. 98–99.
[8] Lucian W. Pye, *Politics, Personality and Nation Building* (New Haven, 1962), pp. 4–5.
[9] See, in general, Ronald E. Wraith and Edgar Simpkins, *Corruption in Developing Countries* (London, 1963).

izing states outside Latin America which were independent before World War II experienced *coups d'état* or attempted coups after World War II. Of twenty states which became independent between World War II and 1959, fourteen had coups or coup attempts by 1963. Of twenty-four states which became independent between 1960 and 1963, seven experienced coups or attempted coups before the end of 1963.[10] Instability in Latin America was less frequent early in the twentieth century than it was in the middle of the century. In the decade from 1917 to 1927, military men occupied the presidencies of the twenty Latin American republics 28.7 percent of the time; in the decade from 1947 to 1957, military men were presidents 45.5 percent of the time.[11] In the 1930's and 1940's in countries like Argentina and Colombia, military intervention in politics occurred for the first time in this century. Seventeen of the twenty Latin American states experienced coups or coup attempts between 1945 and 1964, only Chile, Mexico, and Uruguay having clean records of political stability.

In many states the decline of party organizations is reflected in the rise of charismatic leaders who personalize power and weaken institutions which might limit that power. The increasing despotism of Nkrumah, for instance, was accompanied by a marked decline in the institutional strength of the Convention People's Party. In Turkey, Pakistan, and Burma, the Republican People's Party, Muslim League, and AFPFL deteriorated and military intervention eventually ensued. In party organizations and bureaucracies, marked increases in corruption often accompanied significant declines in the effectiveness of governmental services. Particularistic groups—tribal, ethnic, religious—frequently reasserted themselves and further undermined the authority and coherence of political institutions. The legitimacy of post-colonial regimes among their own people was often less than that of the colonial regimes of the Europeans. Economists have argued that the gap between the level of economic well-being of the underde-

10 These figures are calculated from the data in the Appendix of Fred R. von der Mehden, *Politics of the Developing Nations* (Englewood Cliffs, N.J., 1964). 11 Computed from figures in R. W. Fitzgibbon, "Armies and Politics in Latin America," paper, 17th Round Table, International Political Science Association, Opatija, Yugoslavia, September, 1959, pp. 8–9.

veloped countries and that of highly developed countries is widening as the absolute increases and even percentage increases of the latter exceed those of the former. Something comparable and perhaps even more marked is occurring in the political field. The level of political institutionalization of the advanced countries has, with a few exceptions such as France, remained relatively stable. The level of political institutionalization of most other countries has declined. As a result, the political gap between them has broadened. In terms of institutional strength, many if not most of the new states reached their peak of political development at the moment of independence.

The differences which may exist in mobilization and institutionalization suggest four ideal-types of politics (see Table 1). Modern, developed, civic polities (the United States, the Soviet Union) have high levels of both mobilization and institutionalization. Primitive polities (such as Banfield's backward society) have low levels of both. Contained polities are highly institutionalized but have low levels of

Table 1. TYPES OF POLITICAL SYSTEMS

SOCIAL MOBILIZATION	POLITICAL INSTITUTIONALIZATION	
	High	*Low*
High	Civic	Corrupt
Low	Contained	Primitive

mobilization and participation. The dominant political institutions of contained polities may be either traditional (e.g., monarchies) or modern (e.g., political parties). If they are the former, such polities may well confront great difficulties in adjusting to rising levels of social mobilization. The traditional institutions may wither or collapse, and the result would be a corrupt polity with a high rate of participation but a low level of institutionalization. In the corrupt society, politics is, in Macaulay's phrase, "all sail and no anchor." [12] This type of polity characterizes much,

[12] Thomas B. Macaulay, letter to Henry S. Randall, Courtlandt Village, New York, May 23, 1857, printed in "What Did Macaulay Say About America?" *Bulletin of the New York Public Library*, XXIX (July, 1925), pp. 477–479.

if not most, of the modernizing world. Many of the more advanced Latin American countries, for instance, have achieved comparatively high indices of literacy, per capita national income, and urbanization. But their politics remain notably underdeveloped. Distrust and hatred have produced a continuing low level of political institutionalization. "There is no good faith in America, either among men or among nations," Bolivar once lamented. "Treaties are paper, constitutions books, elections battles, liberty anarchy, and life a torment. The only thing one can do in America is emigrate." [13] Over a century later, the same complaint was heard: "We are not, or do not represent a respectable nation . . . not because we are poor, but because we are disorganized," argued an Ecuadorian newspaper. "With a politics of ambush and of permanent mistrust, one for the other, we . . . cannot properly organize a republic . . . and without organization we cannot merit or attain respect from other nations." [14] So long as a country like Argentina retains a politics of coup and counter-coup and a feeble state surrounded by massive social forces, it cannot be considered politically developed, no matter how urbane and prosperous and educated are its citizens.

In reverse fashion, a country may be politically highly developed, with modern political institutions, while still very backward in terms of modernization. India, for instance, is typically held to be the epitome of the underdeveloped society. Judged by the usual criteria of modernization, it was at the bottom of the ladder during the 1950's: per capita G.N.P. of $72, 80 percent illiterate, over 80 percent of the population in rural areas, 70 percent of the work force in agriculture, a dozen major languages, deep caste and religious differences. Yet in terms of political institutionalization, India was far from backward. Indeed, it ranked high not only in comparison with other modernizing countries in Asia, Africa, and Latin America, but also in comparison with many much more modern European countries. A well-developed

[13] Simon Bolivar, quoted in K. H. Silvert, ed., *Expectant Peoples: Nationalism and Development* (New York, 1963), p. 347.
[14] *El Dia*, Quito, November 27, 1943, quoted in Bryce Wood, *The Making of the Good Neighbor Policy* (New York, 1961), p. 318.

political system has strong and distinct institutions to perform both the "input" and the "output" functions of politics. India entered independence with not only two organizations, but two highly developed—adaptable, complex, autonomous, and coherent—institutions ready to assume primary responsibility for these functions. The Congress Party, founded in 1885, was one of the oldest and best-organized political parties in the world; the Indian Civil Service, dating from the early nineteenth century, has been appropriately hailed as "one of the greatest administrative systems of all time." [15] The stable, effective, and democratic government of India during the first fifteen years of independence rested far more on this institutional inheritance than it did on the charisma of Nehru. In addition, the relatively slow pace of modernization and social mobilization in India did not create demands and strains which the Party and the bureaucracy were unable to handle. So long as these two organizations maintain their institutional strength, it is ridiculous to think of India as politically underdeveloped, no matter how low her per capita income or how high her illiteracy rate.

Almost no other country which became independent after World War II was institutionally as well prepared as India for self-government. In countries like Pakistan and the Sudan, institutional evolution was unbalanced; the civil and military bureaucracies were more highly developed than the political parties, and the military had strong incentives to move into the institutional vacuum on the input side of the political system and to attempt to perform interest aggregation functions. This pattern, of course, has also been common in Latin America. In countries like Guatemala, El Salvador, Peru, and Argentina, John J. Johnson has pointed out, the military is "the country's best organized institution and is thus in a better position to give objective expression to the national will" than are parties or interest groups.[16] In a very different category is a country like North Vietnam, which fought its way into independence with a highly disci-

---

[15] Ralph Braibanti, "Public Bureaucracy and Judiciary in Pakistan," in LaPalombara, ed., *Bureaucracy and Political Development*, p. 373.
[16] Johnson, *Military and Society*, p. 143.

plined political organization but which was distinctly weak on the administrative side. The Latin American parallel here would be Mexico, where, as Johnson puts it, "not the armed forces but the PRI is the best organized institution, and the party rather than the armed forces has been the unifying force at the national level." In yet a fourth category are those unfortunate states, such as the Congo, which were born with neither political nor administrative institutions. Many of these new states deficient at independence in one or both types of institutions have also been confronted by high rates of social mobilization and rapidly increasing demands on the political system (see Table 2).

Table 2. INSTITUTIONAL DEVELOPMENT AT
MOMENT OF INDEPENDENCE

INPUT INSTITUTIONS	OUTPUT INSTITUTIONS	
	High	*Low*
High	India	North Vietnam
Low	Sudan	Congo

POLITICAL INSTITUTIONS AND PUBLIC INTERESTS

A society with weak political institutions lacks the ability to curb the excesses of personal and parochial desires. Politics is a Hobbesian world of unrelenting competition among social forces —between man and man, family and family, clan and clan, region and region, class and class—a competition unmediated by more comprehensive political organizations. The "amoral familism" of Banfield's village has its counterparts in amoral clanism, amoral groupism, and amoral classism. Without strong political institutions, society lacks the means of defining and realizing its common interests. The capacity to create political institutions is the capacity to create public interests.

Traditionally the public interest has been approached in three ways.[17] It has been identified either with abstract, substantive

17 See, in general, Glendon Schubert, *The Public Interest* (Glencoe, Ill., 1960); Carl J. Friedrich, ed., *Nomos V: The Public Interest* (New York, 1962); Douglas Price, "Theories of the Public Interest," in Lynton K. Caldwell, ed., *Politics and Public Affairs* (Bloomington, Ind., 1962), pp. 141–160.

ideal values and norms such as natural law, justice, or right reason; or with the specific interest of a particular individual ("L'état, c'est moi"), group, class (Marxism), or majority; or with the result of a competitive process among individuals (classic liberalism) or groups (Bentleyism). The problem in all these approaches is to arrive at a definition which is concrete rather than nebulous and general rather than particular. Unfortunately, in most cases what is concrete lacks generality and what is general lacks concreteness. One partial way out of the problem is to define the public interest in terms of the concrete interests of the governing institutions. A society with highly institutionalized governing organizations and procedures is, in this sense, more able to articulate and achieve its public interests. "Organized (institutionalized) political communities," as Friedrich argues, "are *better adapted* to reaching decisions and developing policies than unorganized communities." [18] The public interest, in this sense, is not something which exists *a priori* in natural law or the will of the people. Nor is it simply whatever results from the political process. Rather it is whatever strengthens governmental institutions. The public interest is the interest of public institutions. It is something which is created and brought into existence by the institutionalization of government organizatons. In a complex polical system, many governmental organizations and procedures represent many different aspects of the public interest. The public interest of a complex society is a complex matter.

We are accustomed to think of our primary governing institutions as having representative functions—that is, as expressing the interests of some other set of groups (their constituency). Hence, we tend to forget that governmental institutions have interests of their own. These interests not only exist; they are also reasonably concrete. The questions, "What is the interest of the Presidency? What is the interest of the Senate? What is the interest of the House of Representatives? What are the interests of the Supreme Court?" are difficult but not completely impossible to answer. The answers would furnish a fairly close approximation

[18] Carl J. Friedrich, *Man and His Government* (New York, 1963), p. 150; italics in original.

of the "public interest" of the United States. Similarly, the public interest of Great Britain might be approximated by the specific institutional interests of the Crown, Cabinet, and Parliament. In the Soviet Union, the answer would involve the specific institutional interests of the Presidium, Secretariat, and Central Committee of the Communist Party.

Institutional interests differ from the interests of individuals who are in the institutions. Keynes's percipient remark that "In the long run, we are all dead" applies to individuals, not institutions. Individual interests are necessarily short-run interests. Institutional interests, however, exist through time: the proponent of the institution has to look to its welfare through an indefinite future. This consideration often means a limiting of immediate goals. The "true policy," Aristotle remarked, "for democracy and oligarchy alike, is not one which ensures the greatest possible amount of either, but one which will ensure the longest possible life for both." [19] The official who attempts to maximize power or other values in the short run often weakens his institution in the long run. Supreme Court justices may, in terms of their immediate individual desires, wish to declare an act of Congress unconstitutional. In deciding whether it is in the public interest to do so, however, presumably one question they should ask themselves is whether it is in the long-term institutional interest of the Supreme Court for them to do so. Judicial statesmen are those who, like John Marshall in *Marbury vs. Madison,* maximize the institutional power of the Court in such a way that it is impossible for either the President or Congress to challenge it. In contrast, the Supreme Court justices of the 1930's came very close to expanding their immediate influence at the expense of the long-term interests of the Court as an institution.

The phrase "What's good for General Motors is good for the country" contains at least a partial truth. "What's good for the Presidency is good for the country," however, contains more truth. Ask any reasonably informed group of Americans to identify the five best Presidents and the five worst Presidents. Then ask them to identify the five strongest Presidents and the five weakest Presidents. If the identification of strength with goodness and

[19] *Politics*, p. 267.

weakness with badness is not one hundred percent, it will almost certainly not be less than eighty percent. Those Presidents— Jefferson, Lincoln, the Roosevelts, Wilson—who expanded the powers of their office are hailed as the beneficent promoters of the public and national interest. Those Presidents, such as Buchanan, Grant, Harding, who failed to defend the power of their institution against other groups are also thought to have done less good for the country. Institutional interest coincides with public interest. The power of the Presidency is identified with the good of the polity.

The public interest of the Soviet Union is approximated by the institutional interests of the top organs of the Communist Party: "What's good for the Presidium is good for the Soviet Union." Viewed in these terms, Stalinism can be defined as a situation in which the personal interests of the ruler take precedence over the institutionalized interests of the Party. Beginning in the late 1930's Stalin consistently weakened the Party. No Party Congress was held between 1939 and 1952. During and after World War II the Central Committee seldom met. The Party secretariat and Party hierarchy were weakened by the creation of competing organs. Conceivably this process could have resulted in the displacement of one set of governing institutions by another, and some American experts and some Soviet leaders did think that governmental organizations rather than Party organizations would become the ruling institutions in Soviet society. Such, however, was neither the intent nor the effect of Stalin's action. He increased his personal power, not the governmental power. When he died, his personal power died with him. The struggle to fill the resulting vacuum was won by Khrushchev, who identified his interests with the interests of the Party organization, rather than by Malenkov, who identified himself with the governmental bureaucracy. Khrushchev's consolidation of power marked the reemergence and revitalization of the principal organs of the Party. While they acted in very different ways and from different motives, Stalin weakened the Party just as Grant weakened the Presidency. Just as a strong Presidency is in the American public interest, so also a strong Party is in the Soviet public interest.

In terms of the theory of natural law, governmental actions are legitimate to the extent that they are in accord with the "public philosophy." [20] According to democratic theory, they derive their legitimacy from the extent to which they embody the will of the people. According to the procedural concept, they are legitimate if they represent the outcome of a process of conflict and compromise in which all interested groups have participated. In another sense, however, the legitimacy of governmental actions can be sought in the extent to which they reflect the interests of governmental institutions. In contrast to the theory of representative government, under this concept governmental institutions derive their legitimacy and authority not from the extent to which they represent the interests of the people or of any other group, but from the extent to which they have distinct interests of their own apart from all other groups. Politicians frequently remark that things "look different" after they obtain office than they did when they were competing for office. This difference is a measure of the institutional demands of office. It is precisely this difference in perspective which legitimizes the demands which the office holder makes on his fellow citizens. The interests of the President, for instance, may coincide partially and temporarily first with those of one group and then with those of another. But the interest of the Presidency, as Neustadt has emphasized,[21] coincides with that of no one else. The President's power derives not from his representation of class, group, regional, or popular interests, but rather from the fact that he represents none of these. The Presidential perspective is unique to the Presidency. Precisely for this reason, it is both a lonely office and a powerful one. Its authority is rooted in its loneliness.

The existence of political institutions (such as the Presidency or Presidium) capable of giving substance to public interests distinguishes politically developed societies from undeveloped ones. The "ultimate test of development," as Lucian Pye has said, "is the capacity of a people to establish and maintain large, complex,

[20] See Walter Lippmann, *The Public Philosophy* (Boston, 1955), esp. p. 42, for his definition of the public interest as "what men would choose if they saw clearly, thought rationally, acted disinterestedly and benevolently."
[21] See Richard E. Neustadt, *Presidential Power* (New York, 1960), *passim*, but esp. pp. 33–37, 150–151.

but flexible organizational forms." [22] The level of organization in much of the world, however, is low. "Except in Europe and America," Banfield notes, "the concerting of behavior in political associations and corporate organizations is a rare and recent thing." [23] The ability to create public organizations and political institutions is in short supply in the world today. It is this ability which, above all else, the Communists offer modernizing countries.

DEGENERATION AND THE CORRUPT POLITY

Most modernizing countries are buying rapid social modernization at the price of political degeneration. This process of decay in political institutions, however, has been neglected or overlooked in much of the literature on modernization. As a result, models and concepts which are hopefully entitled "developing" or "modernizing" are often only partially relevant to the countries to which they are applied. More relevant in many cases would be models of corrupt or degenerating societies, highlighting the decay of political organization and the increasing dominance of disruptive social forces. Who, however, has advanced such a theory of political decay or a model of a corrupt political order which might be useful in analyzing the political processes of the countries that are usually called "developing"? Perhaps the most relevant ideas are the most ancient ones. The evolution of many contemporary new states, once the colonial guardians have departed, has not deviated extensively from the Platonic model. Independence is followed by military coups as the "auxiliaries" take over.[24] Corruption by the oligarchy inflames the envy of rising groups. Conflict between oligarchy and masses erupts into civil strife. Demagogues and street mobs pave the way for the despot. Plato's description of the means by which the despot appeals to

---

[22] Pye, *Politics, Personality and Nation Building,* p. 51.

[23] Edward C. Banfield, *The Moral Basis of a Backward Society* (Glencoe, Ill., 1958), pp. 7–9, 15 ff.

[24] For comments on the short time-lag between independence and the first coup, see Dankwart A. Rustow, "The Military in Middle Eastern Society and Politics," in Sydney N. Fisher, ed., *The Military in the Middle East: Problems in Society and Government* (Columbus, Ohio, 1963), p. 10.

the people, isolates and eliminates his enemies, and builds up his personal strength is a far less misleading guide to what has taken place in Ghana and other new states than many things written yesterday.[25]

Plato is one of the few theorists, ancient or contemporary, with a highly explicit theory of political degeneration.[26] The concept of a "corrupt society," however, is a more familiar one in political theory. Typically it refers to a society which lacks law, authority, cohesion, discipline, and consensus, where private interests dominate public ones, where there is an absence of civic obligation and civic duty, where, in short, political institutions are weak and social forces strong. Plato's degenerate states are dominated by various forms of appetite: by force, wealth, numbers, and charisma. "Those constitutions," says Aristotle, "which consider only the personal interest of the rulers are all wrong constitutions, or perversions of the right forms." [27] So also, Machiavelli's concept of the corrupt state, in the words of one commentator, "includes all sorts of license and violence, great inequalities of wealth and power, the destruction of peace and justice, the growth of disorderly ambition, disunion, lawlessness, dishonesty, and contempt for religion." [28] Modern equivalents of the classical corrupt society are Kornhauser's theory of the mass society (where, in the absence of institutions, elites are accessible to masses and masses are available for mobilization by the elite) and Rapoport's concept of the praetorian state where "private ambitions are rarely re-

---

[25] See, in general, *The Republic,* Book VIII, and especially the description of the despotic regime (Cornford trans., New York, 1945), pp. 291–293.

[26] Perhaps the closest contemporary model comes not from a social scientist but from a novelist: William Golding. The schoolboys (newly independent elites) of *The Lord of the Flies* initially attempt to imitate the behavior patterns of adults (former Western rulers). Discipline and consensus, however, disintegrate. A demagogic military leader and his followers gain or coerce the support of a majority. The symbol of authority (the conch) is broken. The voices of responsibility (Ralph) and reason (Piggy) are deserted and harassed, and reason is destroyed. In the end, the naval officer (British Marine Commandos) arrives just in time to save Ralph (Nyerere) from the "hunters" (mutinous troops).

[27] *Politics,* p. 112.

[28] George H. Sabine, *A History of Political Thought,* rev. ed. (New York, 1950), p. 343.

strained by a sense of public authority; [and] the role of power (i.e., wealth and force) is maximized." [29] Typical of the corrupt, praetorian, or mass societies is the violent oscillation between extreme democracy and tyranny. "Where the pre-established political authority is highly autocratic," says Kornhauser, "rapid and violent displacement of that authority by a democratic regime is highly favorable to the emergence of extremist mass movements that tend to transform the new democracy in anti-democratic directions." [30] Aristotle and Plato saw despotism emerging out of the extremes of mob rule. Rapoport finds in Gibbon an apt summary of the constitutional rhythms of the praetorian state, which "floats between the extremes of absolute monarchy and wild democracy." [31] Such instability is the hallmark of a society where mobilization has outrun institutionalization.

[29] Kornhauser, *Politics of Mass Society, passim;* David C. Rapoport, "Praetorianism: Government Without Consensus," Ph.D. dissertation (University of California, Berkeley, 1959); and Rapoport in Huntington, ed., *Changing Patterns of Military Politics,* p. 72, where the quotation occurs.
[30] Kornhauser, *Politics of Mass Society,* p. 125.
[31] Edward Gibbon, *The Decline and Fall of the Roman Empire* (New York, 1899), pp. 1, and 235, quoted by Rapoport in Huntington, ed., *Changing Patterns of Military Politics,* p. 98.

IRVING LOUIS HOROWITZ / Three Worlds of Development*

At one level, the designation "Third World" is a strategy for economic development rather than a type of economic or social structure. The "mix" in the Third World is ostensibly between *degrees of* (rather than *choices between*) capitalism and socialism at the economic level, and libertarianism and totalitarianism politically. It is not a new synthesis of political economy. One of the typical self-delusions of Third World nations is that they perceive themselves as developing new economic forms, when as a matter of fact this has not been the case thus far. There is little evidence that there will be any real new economic alternatives to either capitalist or socialist development in the immediate future. In the political sphere, however, the Third World seems to have added a new style if not a new structure.

Any sound theory of social change must indicate what development excludes; that is, how it distinguishes itself from such cognate concepts as industrialization, externally induced transformation, growth of population and of the economy.

First, development differs from industrialization in that the latter implies a series of technological, mechanical, and engineering innovations in forms of social production. Social development

* From Horowitz, *Three Worlds of Development* (New York, Oxford University Press, 1966), pp. 21–23; 339–343; 390–397. Portions of the original text have been omitted.

for its part implies transformation in human relations, in the economic and political status in which men relate to each other, irrespective of the level of industrialization. Industrialization does produce stress and strain in human relationships which in turn has a large-scale effect on the overall process of social development. But to identify industrialization with development is to run the grave risk of offering prescriptions for economic growth independent of social inequities.

Second, development differs from change in that the latter implies a continual adaptation through small steps and stages to an existent social condition. Development implies a genuine break with tradition—perceptible disruptions of the "static" equilibrium. Social development requires a new set of conceptual tools to explain "reality" whereas social change may leave intact old conceptual tools adapted to modified situations. Indeed, precisely what is modifiable is subject to change; while that which no longer contains the possibility of elasticity and plasticity is subject to development.

Third, development differs from externally induced transformation in that the latter implies a prime mover which is external to the developmental process. Thus, Caesarism, Stalinism, or simple old-fashioned imperialism may perform important functions with respect to the economic transformation of subject nations, but this is done for the prime, if not the exclusive, benefit of the mother country. Thus the building of a network of roads, communications systems, or the like is designed to expedite the shipment of raw materials to the home country. Similarly, the relationship of the urban complex to the rural regions may undergo similar transformations for the benefit of the city needs, of the needs of "internal colonialism," or of dominant minorities. Here too one cannot speak of development, despite the obvious stimulus such colonial contributions do make to long-run social development.[1]

[1] On this matter of internal colonialism, see the following two brilliant studies: Pablo González Casanova, "Internal Colonialism and National Development," *Studies in Comparative International Development,* Vol. I, No. 4 (1965), pp. 27–37; and Rodolfo Stavenhagen, "Classes, Colonialism and Acculturation," *Studies in Comparative International Development,* Vol. I, No. 6 (1965), pp. 53–77.

Fourth, development differs from growth in population or national wealth since, like the simple process of quantitative change, these do not call forth any new process, but are simply processes of adaptation. Furthermore, it should be noted that growth in "natural events" of a society may actually sap development—thus the rapid rise in population may in fact serve to lower the total financial reserves of a nation. In short, some types of growth may be dysfunctional with respect to the needs of a developing society.

Development thus implies a new technology which makes available consumer goods. New methods of production radically alter the position of labor with respect to management. New markets radically alter the position of empire nations to colonized nations. New sources of raw materials and energy supplies radically alter the balance of world commerce and trade, and new forms of social organization radically alter the position of old strata since they now must reckon with a new "technocratic" stratum in addition to their traditional rivals. It is precisely this revolutionary side of the developmental process that has come to characterize the Third World—and precisely this side which is most conveniently forgotten by developmental theorists in the West.[2]

In the main, the Third World is a low industrial, goods-producing area no less than a high commodity-cost area.[3] This affects the quality as well as the amount of foreign aid that they receive from the First and the Second Worlds. Disregarding the question of whether this aid is harmful or beneficent, with or without strings, the fact is that the Third World *receives* economic assist-

[2] For a serious theoretical appreciation of the developmental process, at the economic level at least, see Joseph A. Schumpeter, *The Theory of Economic Development* (Cambridge, Mass., Harvard University Press, 1934). He was the first social scientist to develop a typology of development which distinguished development from change and from externally induced transformations. For criticisms of the developmental economists, see Chap. 12. In Horowitz, *Three Worlds of Development.*—Ed.

[3] The neglect of this correlation between low industrialization and high commodity costs in the Prebisch thesis has been called attention to by Ramón Gómez. "El Informe Prebisch y la Realidad Latinoamericana," *Cuadernos Americanos,* Vol. CXXXI, No. 6 (November–December, 1963), pp. 7–72.

ance, some kinds of funds, while the First and Second Worlds represent funding agencies for it. Thus national independence does not in itself guarantee an end to foreign domination. This distinction between nations receiving aid and nations rendering aid is central to a definition of the Third World.

The Third World supplies world markets with primary commodities, primary agricultural supplies, nonferrous base metals, etc. The First and Second Worlds basically export not primary commodities but manufactured goods. The Soviet Union has been more sensitive to the international imbalance between raw materials and finished products than has the United States. With the exception of wartime conditions, export of primary commodities is never as financially lucrative as export of manufactured goods. While it is true that without these primary commodities there can be no manufacture of goods, still the source of primary supplies is wider than imagined. Therefore, the First World has tended to maintain the imbalance between the fully advanced and the underdeveloped nations. Contrary to the rhetoric of foreign aid, the extent of First and Second World assistance to Third World development is not so much a question of direct fiscal support but rather of prices paid for raw materials, costs of importing goods, and control of international trade and money markets.

The question of setting market prices is generally allocated to the First and Second Worlds. That is, the Soviet Union can set the price on wool; the United States, along with its western European cotton manufacturers, can set the price on cotton. This ability to set the price is a characteristic of monopolies in general, and this ability to monopolize prices is a characteristic of the First World. Monopolization is therefore a form for preventing price and wage fluctuation in the metropolitan areas. At the same time, by controlling the flow of vital parts, it is a way for preventing mass expropriation in the backward areas. Underdeveloped regions in the Third World suffer heavy price fluctuations and accentuated inflationary spirals, because they cannot control world markets, set or regulate prices, or expropriate property or resources when this is nationally desirable or feasible.

In the Third World the *formal* systems are nearly always and everywhere republican in character, while their *real* systems are nearly always authoritarian. They are neither monarchies nor total dictatorships. They are under the "rule of law"—that is, they have constitutions—but this lawfulness is deposited in the hands of the dynamic leader of the single party. They have an unchecked higher political directorate, a party charisma. There is neither a developed parliamentary system nor the kind of relatively stable multi-party groupings found in western Europe and the United States. Where such parliamentary systems have been allowed to expand, they have been a conservative force which has served to fragment the political power of progressive social groups. Parliamentary rule is often present in older sectors of the Third World which already have achieved formal independence, as in Latin America. Here, for instance, the agricultural proletariat has been systematically excluded from effective participation, either directly through disenfranchisement, or indirectly through electoral frauds of various sorts. In such circumstances the legislative branch becomes the legal front for property ownership. In Africa, nations have avoided this situation by abandoning the multi-party system.[4] Thus, in Ghana, Algeria, Tunisia, Kenya, Egypt, and Guinea there has been the gradual erosion of parliamentary norms in the name of mass participation. The Parliament has become an upper-class forum while the President has become the hope of the masses. This struggle is simply another way of describing the differences between formal and real political systems in emerging nations.

Given the great importance of this element, the revolutionary system is often identified in the minds of the mass with a particular party. Hence, Congress Party, however amorphous its organization may be, retains a virtual monopoly of the political apparatus in India. The same is true of the PRI in Mexico. Thus, even in nations which are traditionally identified with Western values of democracy and libertarianism, parliamentary norms are more

4 See Gwendolen M. Carter (ed.), *African One-Party States* (Ithaca, New York, Cornell University Press, 1962).

formal than real. To achieve even a minimum rate of growth, to enter the "take-off" period, the Third World nations have had to recognize the need for central planning. And such high-level planning is in itself a political act, necessarily under the aegis of the state system. The politics of this system, while often "benevolent" in character, cannot be said to be particularly concerned with the observance of parliamentary norms.

A parliament is a forum of conflicting and contrasting interests and opinions. As such, its ability to serve the "whole people" is subject to ridicule and, ultimately, to disrepute. In the cases of the Congo and Pakistan, parliamentary rifts prevented the normal functioning of society. And only with the passing of such nominally democratic forums was social order maintained.

Parliamentary development can be afforded as a splendid luxury when time and history allow. This was the case for the United States in the nineteenth century. Whether there is a margin for parliamentary developments in the Third World depends on the role that parliaments perform in these nations. The case histories presently available are hardly encouraging. In Latin America they have tended to preserve the status quo and to retard the development of central planning.[5] It is hard to imagine the new African states following such a model. Therefore, there is within the Third World a development of radical political orientations without many basic constitutional safeguards. This is one basic reason why Western social democratic ideology has found it extremely difficult to champion the Third World cause.[6]

The authoritarian nature of the Third World has resulted from the rapid growth and consolidation of the one-party state. Yet, this rarely spills over into totalitarianism, into the control of the total social system. Technological advance and bureaucratic efficiency have not advanced to the point where this is possible. A

[5] See on this Irving Louis Horowitz, *Revolution in Brazil: Politics and Society in a Developing Nation* (New York, E. P. Dutton & Co., 1964), pp. 279–304; and for a more panoramic introduction, R. A. Gómez, *Government and Politics in Latin America*, rev. ed. (New York, Random House, 1963).
[6] For a sound introduction to this subject see Richard Harris, *Independence and After: Revolution in Underdeveloped Countries* (London, Oxford University Press, 1962).

verbal commitment to democratic values is retained. The democratic society remains a goal to be attained, while authoritarian solutions are considered temporary necessities. However, its governmental machinery is feared for its total control and the effect on the social system. Yet, almost every Third World nation has a written constitution and a formal legislative body. Oftentimes, these documents are tailored after those extant in the advanced countries. But generally these documents serve to legitimize bodies which act as rubber stamps. Actual political structures bear a much closer resemblance to the Second World of the Soviet orbit than to the First World.

The Third World is subject to a unique set of political circumstances. Nearly every industrial, highly developed society has emerged in the wake of political, economic, or religious conflicts reaching a point of open armed hostilities, and resolved by the play of internal forces with a minimum of external intervention or interference. This is illustrated by the English Revolution of 1640–88, the American Revolution of 1775–81, the French Revolution of 1789, the Russian Revolutions of 1905 and 1917, and even the Chinese Revolution of 1948–49. At present, however, the costs of development under circumstances of international conflict have become prohibitive. Development must now, more than ever, be a response to both international and national pressures. The fact is also that every one of these past revolutionary events resulted in part from the pressures exerted by a newly created working mass for participation in the political process. As much as anything else, these revolutions democratized politics by bringing about the participation of a vast, previously excluded public. These humanistically inspired revolutions were designed to transform the human species from masses into classes.

The Third World nations, as presently constituted, have attempted to develop military alternatives to the First and Second Worlds—not just political options to military power, but genuine large-scale military force.[7] The most powerful Third World nations are nations that had popular revolutions, which means revo-

[7] See on this Morris Janowitz, *The Military in the Political Development of New Nations* (Chicago, University of Chicago Press, 1964).

lutions which have either crushed or eliminated the old elites rather than just reshuffling power among them. It is no accident that nations such as Ghana, Algeria, Cuba, India, and Yugoslavia are leaders of the Third World; they represent the nations which have had this fully developed "revolution from below." For this reason Mexico can probably be considered a more fully developed member of the Third World than Venezuela, because in the 1910–20 Mexican Revolution the old military caste was crushed. The old military caste was tied up with the feudal aristocracy and the landed nobility. The new military was at the outset a popular peasant militia.

In the Third World, where revolutions have been successful, the traditional military has either been crushed or fully absorbed into revolutionary actions. There has not always been an armed struggle between military groupings. Nevertheless, the national liberation front has been the major stimulus to successful popular reform and revolutionary movements in the Third World nations. The development of these nations in large measure is connected to the outcomes of these internal military conflicts.[8]

Third World nations also cannot really operate with foreign military bases on their soil. Dependent colonial states have in general granted extraterritorial rights to imperialist or colonialist powers. When a nation has a foreign military base, it is almost axiomatic that it is not fully accepted into the Third World. Therefore, one would have to say that East Germany is not a member of the Third World any more than South Vietnam, for both these nations, irrespective of their radically different levels of development, are clear illustrations of regimes buttressed by the presence of foreign military bases, a presence which makes development, as I have defined it, exceedingly difficult.

---

[8] See J. K. Zawodny (ed.), "Unconventional Warfare," *The Annals of the American Academy of Political and Social Science*, Vol. 341, 1962.

NECESSARY COERCION VERSUS INTERNECINE TERRORISM

Although inherited models of development may not be applicable to a developing nation, there remains the question of relevance in these inherited ideologies. One writer has seen the choices as between totalitarian models, in which there is a total appropriation of power by a single group, and authoritarian models, in which the formal apparatus, however repressive, admits of a considerable latitude at the level of informal life. This distinction has the advantage of delineating between public and private spheres, if nothing else. Now while this model has much to recommend it, it does not quite face the issue.[9]

The main issue is not the institutionalization of legal safeguards. Such a legal superstructure is simply a consequence of development without deformities—*in vacuo*. Such restraints may well involve the abandonment of the revolutionary impulse toward development. In any comparison of economic growth rates between China and India, one notices a direct ratio between the rate of industrial growth and the presence of coercive mechanisms. When Baran points out that India's stagnation is due to its being "neither able nor willing to accept that challenge [of breaking the hold of the property-owning strata] and to provide the leadership in breaking the resistance of urban and rural vested interests," he has in mind the willingness and/or the capacity of the Chinese to do just that.[10] It serves no purpose to recoil in horror or employ disparaging slogans about oriental despotism and authoritarianism.

Therefore, legal safeguards are clearly going to be violated whenever a high priority is placed on rapid industrial development. It is a relatively simple matter for a citizen of an advanced country, which has long since "internalized" the necessity for judicial restraints or witnessed no serious repressive parliamentary

[9] Cf. Lewis Coser, "Prospects for the New Nations: Totalitarianism, Authoritarianism or Democracy?" *Dissent*, Vol. 10, No. 1 (1963), pp. 43–58.
[10] Cf. Paul A. Baran, *The Political Economy of Growth* (New York, Monthly Review Press, 1957), pp. 225–226.

forms, to be outraged by authoritarian measures in the nations of Africa and Asia which are now entering the modern world. To be sure, what complicates growth patterns in Latin America is precisely this long history of parliamentary cretinism, the mystical regard for formal restraints to expropriation or land redistribution that suited the interests of the vested classes.

The real issue is to distinguish between necessary coercion— i.e., those forms of coercion which both suppress vested interests and also ensure the normal functioning of the productive classes —and politically inspired terrorism—i.e., that form of coercion which spends itself on the maintenance of state power and the prevention of free criticism and free choice by the citizenry. Whether we start with Lord Acton's formula that power corrupts and absolute power corrupts absolutely, or a more specific sociological variation such as Robert Michels' theory of the oligarchical tendencies of organization, or Max Weber's concept of a rise in the bureaucratic sector as a direct response to the rationalizing agencies of state power, we are still confronted with the problem of distinguishing necessary coercion from internecine terrorism.

The Soviet Union and China represent classic examples of the failure to maintain a distinction between these two factors. Once rapid industrialization was decided upon, it was also decided that to oppose this process in any size or shape was tantamount to betrayal, treason, and "wrecking." Indeed, if any useful definition of Stalinism is to be made, it must emphasize its liquidation of the distinction between "class struggle" and "party struggle." The Stalinist period in Russian industrialization rested not simply on coercion but on terrorism. And the distinction between these two words is not inconsequential—the former may involve persuasion, education, relocation, as well as expropriation, while terrorism as an exclusive principle involves the liquidation of all private existence and the replacement of the private man with the thoroughly "integrated" industrial man.

It is in this sense that a concept of law (what is at times ignorantly called "liberalism") might well prove fundamental. For without rules for the "circulation of elites," without rules for leadership as well as for membership, the impulse for coercion to become terror is almost irresistible. This is particularly so in those newly emerging nations where the "basic industry," and at times the exclusive lucrative industry, is the maintenance of the state as such. This is not to say that terrorism is without pragmatic value for growth. No one has proven that terrorism and development are incompatible. One might argue that from the Communist point of view the two are mutually exclusive; and therefore that the Revolution is "betrayed." But this is an argument which begins with the absolute need for an ideology to deliver "the goods" down to the final prophecy. However distasteful to Western opinion, the position expressed by E. H. Carr and Isaac Deutscher—that Soviet society has indeed satisfied the requirements of a growing society, however deformed its method of doing so—can no longer be doubted.

From the standpoint of development the most dysfunctional feature of coercion turned inward, turned terroristic, is that the revolutionary social process thus unleashed will be aborted.[11] The "great leap forward" in Communist China, the suppression of the "hundred flowers" doctrine, had a profound boomerang effect on the developmental process. Even so sympathetic a reporter of China as Edgar Snow[12] criticizes the bad effects brought on by the extreme pressures to "catch the West" in the shortest possible time. The slipping of coercion into terror demonstrates only the political efficacy of violence, not its value for development. In this connection it is significant that the Chinese have avoided the technique of the general political purge and the internecine factional strife that played such havoc with the evolution of Soviet Russia between 1927 and 1953. Khrushchev's own denunciations of Stalinism, whatever else they signify, are a clear announcement that "inner party struggle" has little to do with "class struggle," and that since the latter has been resolved in favor of the combination of a worker-peasant state, development will be through "consciousness" and "harmony," or what in the West is referred

[11] Cf. John J. Johnson (ed.), *The Role of the Military in Underdeveloped Countries* (Princeton, Princeton University Press, 1962).
[12] Edgar Snow, *The Other Side of the River: Red China Today* (London, Gollancz, 1963).

to as consensus. And it is here that we can see the increasing similarities of the functional prerequisites of growth in Russia and the West—however distinct the goals of these societies may remain.

The "models" for the developing nations remain paradoxical. Western liberal styles do not seem to "deliver the goods." And while the social and political traditions of many new nations remain Western-influenced, their great needs for economic and technological development make them move from Western liberalism in favor of "oriental despotism." In this context the strongest argument against terrorism can be made by an authentic socialism, which fully recognizes the needs for maintenance of a coercive apparatus but at the same time seeks to sharply distinguish class struggle from party struggle and necessary suppression from politically inspired terror.

Coercion is often necessary because private industries either fail to accelerate developmental patterns or are unwilling to alter conventional patterns of development. Even if one were to assume the sufficiency of available resources, the private investor will undertake to make investments which are profitable and directed toward short-run return on the investment rather than costly (such as explorations in the technological uses of nuclear power) and directed toward the long run. The private sector in underdeveloped economies generally has neither the means nor the will to interest itself in those industries that require a large initial investment with the prospect of slow returns for an immediate future. In a private-sector economy, the uncertainties attached to any given combination of factors of industrial production tend to inhibit growth patterns. Thus given the fact that in an underdeveloped country risks are infinite and the task of capital formation complicated by intervening social variables, some form of coercion will undoubtedly be required. Coercion would thus be used to rationalize productivity, avoid excessive expenditures on consumer goods, create the basis of support for unprofitable but necessary lines of scientific industrialization, curb speculative spending, and minimize the exercise of power by the former ruling classes. Coercion in this sense is actually the reverse of naked power—since the former may imply a wide use of persuasive devices, while the latter eschews persuasion in favor of raw power—often used ignorantly and maliciously.

WHICH WAY THE THIRD WORLD?
DEVELOPMENTALISTS AND DEVELOPMENT

Three problems loom large in the decision to accelerate development: First, should the rate of national development be determined by the needs of the sovereign citizens, by other nations' rates of growth, or by general principles of planning? Second, are entrepreneurial or proletariat classes best suited to carry forth the developmental process, or, to state the issue another way, should elites or masses determine the tempo and themes of development? Third, what is the proper proportion of coercion and consensus in the developmental process?

At a more generic level, the solution would seem to hinge upon whether there is an economic basis to politics, as in the First World and Second World, or a political basis to economics, as in most of the Third World. In some measure this is an analytic problem of how the world is "carved up," and not exclusively a pragmatic one of how men shape their world. This combination of analytical, empirical, and practical may be untidy, but it is precisely the intellectual blend which we must ultimately come to terms with.

Putting the master issue in paradigm form, there is an economic continuum between capitalism and socialism and a political continuum extending from elite totalitarianism to mass democracy. The Third World mix is essentially unstable. What is at issue for the immediate future is the proportion of the "mix," that is, the particular combinations involving capitalism, socialism, democracy, and authoritarianism. The unstable mix is often taken to indicate the "transitional" character of the Third World. The problem is no longer traditionalism versus modernism, but rather the different political and economic arrangements covered by the word "modern."

Revolution is now being made in terms of socialism *plus* maximum social control. The alternative is not capitalism plus democracy, but rather capitalism and maximum social control. Third World revolutions have overthrown absolute tyrants, sheikdoms, petty militarists in the service of foreign rulers, and even some of the feudal "remnants." That these revolutions are not at the same time democratic is due to a multitude of factors— from the backwardness of the peoples involved to the political elitism bred by traditionalism. Modernization may be rapid, but development is still a slow and laborious process. The former is defined by industrialism while the latter must locate industrialism in an overall developmental scheme. One has to choose not simply between freedom and slavery, as free enterprise apologists maintain. The choice is really between socialism, with a minimum of conventional democratic safeguards, and colonialism, with little more conventional democracy than now obtains. To expect any more is simply asking for utopia. The Cuban Revolution of 1959 did not "crush" democracy, as there was precious little of it to crush. The Algerian Revolution did not abolish personal freedoms; under the French colonialists there were none to guarantee. The Egyptian Revolution did not deprive the bourgeoisie of the free trade it did not possess.

Second World socialism differs in its political profile from Third World adaptations of it. Socialism in the Afro-Asian nations replaces traditionalism or a semi-colonialism which contains little in the way of political democracy, except in so far as democracy was part of the colonialist rhetoric. In such East European countries as Czechoslovakia and Poland, however, an externally induced socialist economy replaces neo-capitalist systems which had already achieved some measure of formal democracy. It is futile to consider rapid development exclusively in terms of democracy or autocracy, without also examining the specific social systems at the point of "liberation." Astute observers of the developmental processes have indeed avoided such banalities. The difference between socialism in the Second and Third Worlds illustrates the shift from an economy imposed by an outside power as the "spoils of war" to an economy imposed by the internal logic of post-World War II colonialism.

Not every nation needs to go through every phase of the developmental process. Historic backwardness makes possible a "law of combined development," an amalgam of archaic and contemporary forms.[13] This "law" does not mean that such combined development is automatically advantageous to the newly emergent nations. In the process of grafting on new forms of industrial production to a traditional culture, privileged sectors in emerging societies often seek to preserve old social relations. "Backward" classes no less than "established classes"—peasants no less than landlords—may show this instinct. The Third World, lacking as it does a well-defined and well-developed mass, runs the risk of uneven development rather than accelerated development.

Latin America reveals just how far deformities can be carried. In the absence of a mobilized class of urban proletarians, development is continually fragmented. The Argentine middle classes merge with the big oligarchical landholders to forestall national control of basic utilities and mineral wealth. The Peruvian cities preserve their commercial, administrative, and military features and remain centers of consumption instead of bases of production. The Central American "banana republics" become "industrialized" only insofar and to the degree that the processing of crops for export is involved. The simple emergence of industrialism, however decisive a part of the developmental process it may be, can never be equated with development as such. It must always be judged in terms of the character of class relations within a nation and of political relations between nations.

On an international scale, foreign colonialism has been a root factor in the process of holding back economic progress—or, more piquantly, in the devolution of falling expectations. Within the domestic context, a home-grown class of exploiters has managed to develop an economic system based on internal colonialism.[14]

---

13 See on this Leon Trotsky, *The History of the Russian Revolution*, Vol. 1. (New York, Simon & Schuster, Inc., 1932), pp. 4–9.

14 Pablo Casanova, "Société plurale, colonialisme interne et développement," *Tiers-Monde*, Vol. 5, No. 18, April-June, 1964, pp. 291–312; in this same connection, see also Torcuato S. Di Tella, "Los Procesos Políticos y Sociales de la Industrialización," *Desarrollo Económico*, Vol. 2, No. 3, October-December, 1962, pp. 19–48.

The connections between national bourgeoisie and foreign colonial sectors, the economic fusion of the two, have served to define the present situation in Latin America. Latin America offers abundant evidence that the Third World is not underdeveloped because it is historically backward, but that its development was aborted by foreign and native interests which derive great advantages from keeping the nation as a whole politically and economically subordinate.

4 / TOTALITARIANISM

ALEXIS DE TOCQUEVILLE / Despotism in Democratic Nations*

I had remarked during my stay in the United States that a democratic state of society, similar to that of the Americans, might offer singular facilities for the establishment of despotism; and I perceived, upon my return to Europe, how much use had already been made, by most of our rulers, of the notions, the sentiments, and the wants created by this same condition for the purpose of extending the circle of their power. This led me to think that the nations of Christendom would perhaps eventually undergo some oppression like that which hung over several of the nations of the ancient world.

A more accurate examination of the subject, and five years of further meditation, have not diminished my fears, but have changed their object.

No sovereign ever lived in former ages so absolute or so powerful as to undertake to administer by his own agency, and without the assistance of intermediate powers, all the parts of a great empire; none ever attempted to subject all his subjects indiscriminately to strict uniformity of regulation and personally to tutor and direct every member of the community. The notion of such an undertaking never occurred to the human mind; and if any man had conceived it, the want of information, the imperfection of the administrative system, and, above all, the natural obstacles caused by the inequality of conditions would speedily have checked the execution of so vast a design.

* From de Tocqueville, *Democracy in America* (New York, Knopf, 1945), Book II, Chap. 6. First published in 1840.

When the Roman emperors were at the height of their power, the different nations of the empire still preserved usages and customs of great diversity; although they were subject to the same monarch, most of the provinces were separately administered; they abounded in powerful and active municipalities; and although the whole government of the empire was centered in the hands of the Emperor alone and he always remained, in case of need, the supreme arbiter in all matters, yet the details of social life and private occupations lay for the most part beyond his control. The emperors possessed, it is true, an immense and unchecked power, which allowed them to gratify all their whimsical tastes and to employ for that purpose the whole strength of the state. They frequently abused that power arbitrarily to deprive their subjects of property or of life; their tyranny was extremely onerous to the few, but it did not reach the many; it was confined to some few main objects and neglected the rest; it was violent, but its range was limited.

It would seem that if despotism were to be established among the democratic nations of our days, it might assume a different character; it would be more extensive and more mild; it would degrade men without tormenting them. I do not question that, in an age of instruction and equality like our own, sovereigns might more easily succeed in collecting all political power into their own hands and might interfere more habitually and decidedly with the circle of private interests than any sovereign of antiquity could ever do. But this same principle of equality which facilitates despotism tempers its rigor. We have seen how the customs of society become more humane and gentle in proportion as men become more equal and alike. When no member of the community has much power or much wealth, tyranny is, as it were, without opportunities and a field of action. As all fortunes are scanty, the passions of men are naturally circumscribed, their imagination limited, their pleasures simple. This universal moderation moderates the sovereign himself and checks within certain limits the inordinate stretch of his desires.

Independently of these reasons, drawn from the nature of the state of society itself, I might add many others arising from causes beyond my subject; but I shall keep within the limits I have laid down.

Democratic governments may become violent and even cruel at certain periods of extreme effervescence or of great danger, but these crises will be rare and brief. When I consider the petty passions of our contemporaries, the mildness of their manners, the extent of their education, the purity of their religion, the gentleness of their morality, their regular and industrious habits, and the restraint which they almost all observe in their vices no less than in their virtues, I have no fear that they will meet with tyrants in their rulers, but rather with guardians.

I think, then, that the species of oppression by which democratic nations are menaced is unlike anything that ever before existed in the world; our contemporaries will find no prototype of it in their memories. I seek in vain for an expression that will accurately convey the whole of the idea I have formed of it; the old words *despotism* and *tyranny* are inappropriate: the thing itself is new, and since I cannot name, I must attempt to define it.

I seek to trace the novel features under which despotism may appear in the world. The first thing that strikes the observation is an innumerable multitude of men, all equal and alike, incessantly endeavoring to procure the petty and paltry pleasures with which they glut their lives. Each of them, living apart, is as a stranger to the fate of all the rest; his children and his private friends constitute to him the whole of mankind. As for the rest of his fellow citizens, he is close to them, but he does not see them; he touches them, but he does not feel them; he exists only in himself and for himself alone; and if his kindred still remain to him, he may be said at any rate to have lost his country.

Above this race of men stands an immense and tutelary power, which takes upon itself alone to secure their gratifications and to watch over their fate. That power is absolute, minute, regular, provident, and mild. It would be like the authority of a parent if, like that authority, its object was to prepare men for manhood; but it seeks, on the contrary, to keep them in perpetual childhood: it is well content that the people should rejoice, provided they think of nothing but rejoicing. For their happiness such a government willingly labors, but it chooses to be the sole agent and the only arbiter of that happiness; it provides for their security, foresees and supplies their necessities, facilitates their pleasures, manages their principal concerns, directs their industry, regulates the descent of property, and subdivides their inheritances: what remains, but to spare them all the care of thinking and all the trouble of living?

Thus it every day renders the exercise of the free agency of man less useful and less frequent; it circumscribes the will within a narrower range and gradually robs a man of all the uses of himself. The principle of equality has prepared men for these things; it has predisposed men to endure them and often to look on them as benefits.

After having thus successively taken each member of the community in its powerful grasp and fashioned him at will, the supreme power then extends its arm over the whole community. It covers the surface of society with a network of small complicated rules, minute and uniform, through which the most original minds and the most energetic characters cannot penetrate, to rise above the crowd. The will of man is not shattered, but softened, bent, and guided; men are seldom forced by it to act, but they are constantly restrained from acting. Such a power does not destroy, but it prevents existence; it does not tyrannize, but it compresses, enervates, extinguishes, and stupefies a people, till each nation is reduced to nothing better than a flock of timid and industrious animals, of which the government is the shepherd.

I have always thought that servitude of the regular, quiet, and gentle kind which I have just described might be combined more easily than is commonly believed with some of the outward forms of freedom, and that it might even establish itself under the wing of the sovereignty of the people.

Our contemporaries are constantly excited by two conflicting passions: they want to be led, and they wish to remain free. As they cannot destroy either the one or the other of these contrary propensities, they strive to satisfy them both at once. They devise a sole, tutelary, and all-powerful form of government, but elected by the people. They combine the principle of centralization and that of popular sovereignty; this gives them a respite: they console themselves for being in tutelage by the reflection that they have chosen their own guardians. Every man allows himself to be put in leading-strings, because he sees that it is not a person or a class of persons, but the people at large who hold the end of his chain.

By this system the people shake off their state of dependence just long enough to select their master and then relapse into it again. A great many persons at the present day are quite contented with this sort of compromise between administrative despotism and the sovereignty of the people; and they think they have done enough for the protection of individual freedom when they have surrendered it to the power of the nation at large. This does not satisfy me: the nature of him I am to obey signifies less to me than the fact of extorted obedience.

I do not deny, however, that a constitution of this kind appears to me to be infinitely preferable to one which, after having concentrated all the powers of government, should vest them in the hands of an irresponsible person or body of persons. Of all the forms that democratic despotism could assume, the latter would assuredly be the worst.

When the sovereign is elective, or narrowly watched by a legislature which is really elective and independent, the oppression that he exercises over individuals is sometimes greater, but it is always less degrading; because every man, when he is oppressed and disarmed, may still imagine that, while he yields obedience, it is to himself he yields it, and that it is to one of his own inclinations that all the rest give way. In like manner, I can understand that when the sovereign represents the nation and is dependent upon the people, the rights and the power of which every citizen is deprived serve not only the head of the state, but the state itself; and that private persons derive some return from the sacrifice of their independence which they have made to the public. To create a representation of the people in every centralized country is, therefore, to diminish the evil that extreme centralization may produce, but not to get rid of it.

I admit that, by this means, room is left for the intervention of individuals in the more important affairs; but it is not the less suppressed in the smaller and more private ones. It must not be forgotten that it is especially dangerous to enslave men in the minor details of life. For my own part, I should be inclined to think freedom less necessary in great things than in little ones, if it were possible to be secure of the one without possessing the other.

Subjection in minor affairs breaks out every day and is felt by the whole community indiscriminately. It does not drive men to resistance, but it crosses them at every turn, till they are led to surrender the exercise of their own will. Thus their spirit is gradually broken and their character enervated; whereas that obedience which is exacted on a few important but rare occasions only exhibits servitude at certain intervals and throws the burden of it upon a small number of men. It is in vain to summon a people who have been rendered so dependent on the central power to choose from time to time the representatives of that power; this rare and brief exercise of their free choice, however important it may be, will not prevent them from gradually losing the faculties of thinking, feeling, and acting for themselves, and thus gradually falling below the level of humanity.

I add that they will soon become incapable of exercising the great and only privilege which remains to them. The democratic nations that have introduced freedom into their political constitution at the very time when they were augmenting the despotism of their administrative constitution have been led into strange paradoxes. To manage those minor affairs in which good sense is all that is wanted, the people are held to be unequal to the task; but when the government of the country is at stake, the people are invested with immense powers; they are alternately made the playthings of their ruler, and his masters, more than kings and less than men. After having exhausted all the different modes of election without finding one to suit their purpose, they are still amazed and still bent on seeking further; as if the evil they notice did not originate in the constitution of the country far more than in that of the electoral body.

It is indeed difficult to conceive how men who have entirely given up the habit of self-government should succeed in making a proper choice of those by whom they are to be governed; and no one will ever believe that a liberal, wise, and energetic government can spring from the suffrages of a subservient people.

A constitution republican in its head and ultra-monarchical in all its other parts has always appeared to me to be a short-lived monster. The vices of rulers and the ineptitude of the people would speedily bring about its ruin; and the nation, weary of its representatives and of itself, would create freer institutions or soon return to stretch itself at the feet of a single master.

HERBERT MARCUSE / The Closing of the Political Universe*

The society of total mobilization, which takes shape in the most advanced areas of industrial civilization, combines in productive union the features of the Welfare State and the Warfare State. Compared with its predecessors, it is indeed a "new society." Traditional trouble spots are being cleaned out or isolated, disrupting elements taken in hand. The main trends are familiar: concentration of the national economy on the needs of the big corporations, with the government as a stimulating, supporting, and sometimes even controlling force; hitching of this economy to a world-wide system of military alliances, monetary arrangements, technical assistance and development schemes; gradual assimilation of blue-collar and white-collar population, of leadership types in business and labor, of leisure activities and aspirations in different social classes; fostering of a pre-established harmony between scholarship and the national purpose; invasion of the private household by the togetherness of public opinion; opening of the bedroom to the media of mass communication.

In the political sphere, this trend manifests itself in a marked unification or convergence of opposites. Bipartisanship in foreign policy overrides competitive group interests under the threat of international communism, and spreads to domestic policy, where the programs of the big parties become ever more undistinguish-

* From Marcuse, *One Dimensional Man* (Boston, Beacon Press, 1964), pp. 19; 48–55. Portions of the original chapter have been omitted.

able, even in the degree of hypocrisy and in the odor of the clichés. This unification of opposites bears upon the very possibilities of social change where it embraces those strata on whose back the system progresses—that is, the very classes whose existence once embodied the opposition to the system as a whole.

THE WELFARE AND WARFARE STATE

... The prospects of containment of change, offered by the politics of technological rationality, depend on the prospects of the Welfare State. Such a state seems capable of raising the standard of *administered* living, a capability inherent in all advanced industrial societies where the streamlined technical apparatus—set up as a separate power over and above the individuals—depends for its functioning on the intensified development and expansion of productivity. Under such conditions, decline of freedom and opposition is not a matter of moral or intellectual deterioration or corruption. It is rather an objective societal process insofar as the production and distribution of an increasing quantity of goods and services make compliance a rational technological attitude.

However, with all its rationality, the Welfare State is a state of unfreedom because its total administration is systematic restriction of (a) "technically" available free time;[1] (b) the quantity and quality of goods and services "technically" available for vital individual needs; (c) the intelligence (conscious and unconscious) capable of comprehending and realizing the possibilities of self-determination.

Late industrial society has increased rather than reduced the need for parasitical and alienated functions (for the society as a whole, if not for the individual). Advertising, public relations, indoctrination, planned obsolescence are no longer unproductive overhead costs but rather elements of basic production costs. In order to be effective, such production of socially necessary waste requires continuous rationalization—the relentless utilization of

---

[1] "Free" time, not "leisure" time. The latter thrives in advanced industrial society, but it is unfree to the extent to which it is administered by business and politics.

advanced techniques and science. Consequently, a rising standard of living is the almost unavoidable by-product of the politically manipulated industrial society, once a certain level of backwardness has been overcome. The growing productivity of labor creates an increasing surplus-product which, whether privately or centrally appropriated and distributed, allows an increased consumption—notwithstanding the increased diversion of productivity. As long as this constellation prevails, it reduces the use-value of freedom; there is no reason to insist on self-determination if the administered life is the comfortable and even the "good" life. This is the rational and material ground for the unification of opposites, for one-dimensional political behavior. On this ground, the transcending political forces *within* society are arrested, and qualitative change appears possible only as a change from *without*.

Rejection of the Welfare State on behalf of abstract ideas of freedom is hardly convincing. The loss of the economic and political liberties which were the real achievement of the preceding two centuries may seem slight damage in a state capable of making the administered life secure and comfortable. If the individuals are satisfied to the point of happiness with the goods and services handed down to them by the administration, why should they insist on different institutions for a different production of different goods and services? And if the individuals are preconditioned so that the satisfying goods also include thoughts, feelings, aspirations, why should they wish to think, feel, and imagine for themselves? True, the material and mental commodities offered may be bad, wasteful, rubbish—but *Geist* and knowledge are no telling arguments against satisfaction of needs.

The critique of the Welfare State in terms of liberalism and conservatism (with or without the prefix "neo-") rests, for its validity, on the existence of the very conditions which the Welfare State has surpassed—namely, a lower degree of social wealth and technology. The sinister aspects of this critique show forth in the fight against comprehensive social legislation and adequate government expenditures for services other than those of military defense.

Denunciation of the oppressive capabilities of the Welfare

State thus serves to protect the oppressive capabilities of the society *prior* to the Welfare State. At the most advanced stage of capitalism, this society is a system of subdued pluralism, in which the competing institutions concur in solidifying the power of the whole over the individual. Still, for the administered individual, pluralistic administration is far better than total administration. One institution might protect him against the other; one organization might mitigate the impact of the other; possibilities of escape and redress can be calculated. The rule of law, no matter how restricted, is still infinitely safer than rule above or without law.

However, in view of prevailing tendencies, the question must be raised whether this form of pluralism does not accelerate the destruction of pluralism. Advanced industrial society is indeed a system of countervailing powers. But these forces cancel each other out in a higher unification— in the common interest to defend and extend the established position, to combat the historical alternatives, to contain qualitative change. The countervailing powers do not include those which counter the whole.[2] They tend to make the whole immune against negation from within as well as without; the foreign policy of containment appears as an extension of the domestic policy of containment.

The reality of pluralism becomes ideological, deceptive. It seems to extend rather than reduce manipulation and coordination, to promote rather than counteract the fateful integration. Free institutions compete with authoritarian ones in making the Enemy a deadly force *within* the system. And this deadly force stimulates growth and initiative, not by virtue of the magnitude and economic impact of the defense "sector," but by virtue of the fact that the society as a whole becomes a defense society. For the Enemy is permanent. He is not in the emergency situation but in the normal state of affairs. He threatens in peace as much as in

[2] For a critical and realistic appraisal of Galbraith's ideological concept see Earl Latham, "The Body Politic of the Corporation," in: E. S. Mason, *The Corporation in Modern Society* (Cambridge, Harvard University Press, 1959), pp. 223, 235 f.

war (and perhaps more than in war); he is thus being built into the system as a cohesive power.

Neither the growing productivity nor the high standard of living depend on the threat from without, but their use for the containment of social change and perpetuation of servitude does. The Enemy is the common denominator of all doing and undoing. And the Enemy is not identical with actual communism or actual capitalism—he is, in both cases, the real spectre of liberation.

Once again: the insanity of the whole absolves the particular insanities and turns the crimes against humanity into a rational enterprise. When the people, aptly stimulated by the public and private authorities, prepare for lives of total mobilization, they are sensible not only because of the present Enemy, but also because of the investment and employment possibilities in industry and entertainment. (Even the most insane calculations are rational: the annihilation of five million people is preferable to that of ten million, twenty million, and so on.) It is hopeless to argue that a civilization which justifies its defense by such a calculus proclaims its own end.

Under these circumstances, even the existing liberties and escapes fall in place within the organized whole. At this state of the regimented market, is competition alleviating or intensifying the race for bigger and faster turn-over and obsolescence? Are the political parties competing for pacification or for a stronger and more costly armament industry? Is the production of "affluence" promoting or delaying the satisfaction of still unfulfilled vital needs? If the first alternatives are true, the contemporary form of pluralism would strengthen the potential for the containment of qualitative change and thus prevent rather than impel the "catastrophe" of self-determination. Democracy would appear to be the most efficient system of domination.

The image of the Welfare State sketched in the preceding paragraphs is that of a historical freak between organized capitalism and socialism, servitude and freedom, totalitarianism and happiness. Its possibility is sufficiently indicated by prevalent tendencies of technical progress, and sufficiently threatened by explosive forces. The most powerful, of course, is the danger that preparation for total nuclear war may turn into its realization: the deterrent also serves to deter efforts to eliminate the *need* for the deterrent. Other factors are at play which may preclude the pleasant juncture of totalitarianism and happiness, manipulation and democracy, heteronomy and autonomy—in short, the perpetuation of the pre-established harmony between organized and spontaneous behavior, preconditioned and free thought, expediency and conviction.

Even the most highly organized capitalism retains the social need for private appropriation and distribution of profit as the regulator of the economy. That is, it continues to link the realization of the general interest to that of particular vested interests. In doing so, it continues to face the conflict between the growing potential of pacifying the struggle for existence, and the need for intensifying this struggle; between the progressive "abolition of labor" and the need for preserving labor as the source of profit. The conflict perpetuates the inhuman existence of those who form the human base of the social pyramid—the outsiders and the poor, the unemployed and unemployable, the persecuted colored races, the inmates of prisons and mental institutions.

In contemporary communist societies, the enemy without, backwardness, and the legacy of terror perpetuate the oppressive features of "catching up with and surpassing" the achievements of capitalism. The priority of the means over the end is thereby aggravated—a priority which could be broken only if pacification is achieved—and capitalism and communism continue to compete without military force, on a global scale and through global institutions. This pacification would mean the emergence of a genuine world economy—the demise of the nation state, the national interest, national business together with their international alliances. And this is precisely the possibility against which the present world is mobilized:

> L'ignorance et l'inconscience sont telles que les nationalismes demeurent florissants. Ni l'armement ni l'industrie du XXe siècle ne permettent aux *patries* d'assurer leur sécurité et leur vie sinon en

ensembles organisés de poids mondial, dans l'ordre militaire et économique. Mais à l'Ouest non plus qu'à l'Est, les croyances collectives n'assimilent les changements réels. Les Grands forment leurs empires, ou en réparent les architectures sans accepter les changements de régime économique et politique qui donneraient efficacité et sens à l'une et à l'autre coalitions.

and:

Dupes de la nation et dupes de la classe, les masses souffrantes sont partout engagées dans les duretés de conflits où leurs seuls ennemis sont des maîtres qui emploient sciemment les mystifications de l'industrie et du pouvoir.

La collusion de l'industrie moderne et du pouvoir territorialisé est un vice dont la réalité est plus profonde que les institutions et les structures capitalistes et communistes et qu'aucune dialectique nécessaire ne doit nécessairement extirper.[3]

The fateful interdependence of the only two "sovereign" social systems in the contemporary world is expressive of the fact that the conflict between progress and politics, between man and his masters has become total. When capitalism meets the challenge of communism, it meets its own capabilities: spectacular development of all productive forces after the subordination of the private interests in profitability which arrest such development. When communism meets the challenge of capitalism, it too meets

3 "Ignorance and unconsciousness are such that nationalism continues to flourish. Neither twentieth-century armaments nor industry allow 'fatherlands' to insure their security and their existence except through organizations which carry weight on a world-wide scale in military and economic matters. But in the East as well as in the West, collective beliefs don't adapt themselves to real changes. The great powers shape their empires or repair the architecture thereof without accepting changes in the economic and political regime which would give effectiveness and meaning to one or the other of the coalitions."

(and:)

"Duped by the nation and duped by the class, the suffering masses are everywhere involved in the harshness of conflict in which their only enemies are masters who knowingly use the mystifications of industry and power.

The collusion of modern industry and territorial power is a vice which is more profoundly real than capitalist and communist institutions and structures and which no necessary dialectic necessarily eradicates." François Perroux, *La Coexistence Pacifique* (Paris, Presses Universitaires, 1958), Vol. III, pp. 631–632; 633.

its own capabilities: spectacular comforts, liberties, and allevi-
ation of the burden of life. Both systems have these capabilities
distorted beyond recognition and, in both cases, the reason is in
the last analysis the same—the struggle against a form of life
which would dissolve the basis for domination.

WILLIAM KORNHAUSER / Mass Society and Democratic Order*

The present study has examined conditions in Western society that favor mass politics. Mass politics occurs when large numbers of people engage in political activity outside of the procedures and rules instituted by a society to govern political action. Mass politics in democratic society therefore is anti-democratic, since it contravenes the constitutional order. The extreme case of mass politics is the totalitarian movement, notably communism and fascism. Less extreme examples of mass politics are McCarthyism and Poujadism.

Modern democratic systems possess a distinct vulnerability to mass politics because they invite the whole population, most of which has historically been politically quiescent, to engage in politics. However, this does not mean that all or even most democratic systems succumb to mass politics. The problem is to identify those factors that increase the vulnerability of democratic systems to mass politics, and those that decrease it, in order to be able to specify the conditions that may strengthen democratic politics and civil liberty.

The most satisfactory theory of the vulnerability of social systems to mass politics is the theory of mass society. This theory has two major versions. One, which may be called the aristocratic criticism, asserts that the primary cause of mass politics lies in the

* From Kornhauser, *The Politics of Mass Society* (Glencoe, Ill., The Free Press, 1959), pp. 227–238.

loss of exclusiveness of elites as a result of the rise of popular participation in the critical centers of society. According to this version of the theory of mass society, the main danger to political order and civil liberty is the domination of elites by masses. The other version, which may be called the democratic criticism, stresses the vulnerability of masses to domination by elites. This danger to political order and civil liberty is believed to result from the atomization of society and the rise of elites capable of mobilizing isolated and unattached people. A combination of these two versions produces a stronger theory than either one alone. This integrated theory of mass society locates the causes of mass politics in the condition of both elite and non-elites, that is, in the total social structure and especially in the structure of groups intermediate between the state and the family.

"Mass society," then, is treated as an abstract type. It is always a question of the *degree* to which an actual society is a "mass society." A society is a "mass society" to the extent that both elites and non-elites are directly accessible to one another by virtue of the weakness of groups capable of mediating between them. Insofar as these conditions prevail, neither elites nor non-elites are capable of preventing frequent political activity outside of established channels. Other types of society are more capable of minimizing mass politics (and other forms of mass behavior). Since both elites and non-elites are bound by fixed status in communal (e.g., feudal) society, there is little mass behavior in this kind of system. Since non-elites are subject to extensive control by the political elite in totalitarian (e.g., communist and fascist) society, there is little mass politics in this kind of system.

By means of this theory of mass society, a large number of observations on political phenomena in particular organizations, classes, communities, and whole societies can be fitted together to form a coherent picture of the conditions that favor mass behavior in politics. Groups which are particularly vulnerable to mass movements manifest major discontinuities in their structure during periods of change. Thus, communism and fascism have gained strength in social systems undergoing sudden and extensive changes in the structure of authority and community. Sharp tears in the social fabric caused by widespread unemployment or by major military defeat are highly favorable to mass politics. Social classes which provide disproportionate support for mass movements are those that possess the fewest social ties among their members. This means above all the lower social classes. However, since there are sections of all social classes which tend to be socially atomized, members of all social classes are to be found among the participants in mass politics: unattached (especially free-lance) intellectuals, marginal (especially small) businessmen and farmers, and isolated workers have engaged in mass politics in times of crisis.

Elsewhere, we have stated conditions which favor mass movements destructive of political order and civil liberty. We now shall summarize our analysis by assessing what it implies about the conditions favorable to liberal democracy. This should help to dispel fears that a theory of mass society necessarily is antagonistic to liberal democratic values, or that it is a prophecy of doom.

The theory of mass society stresses the need for the autonomy of certain social units if order with freedom is to be secured. The various versions of this theory tend to divide into two camps according to whether primary stress is placed on the autonomy of elites or on the autonomy of non-elites. The aristocratic view stresses the need for the independence of elites on the premise that constitutional liberty above all requires leadership with the capacity to define, exemplify, and defend it. The democratic view stresses the need for the independence of non-elites on the premise that constitutional liberty above all requires safeguards against the accumulation of power by any group, especially elites. In this fundamental matter, the two views are not incompatible; on the contrary, each is strengthened when it is combined with the other. Civil liberty requires considerable social autonomy of *both* elites and non-elites. This means specifically that elites and non-elites must have the following characteristics:

(a) There must be extensive self-government, private as well as public, and individuals must belong to several self-governing units.

(b) There must be extensive opportunities for elites to formulate policies and take action without *ad hoc* interference from the outside.

However, democracy entails a fundamental restriction on the autonomy of elites, especially in politics. This restriction is two-fold: first, elites will be restricted by one another in that they will be constrained to compete with one another for leadership; and secondly, elites will be restricted by non-elites in that they will be constrained to compete for the people's votes. An implication of this conception of democracy also involves a restriction on non-elites: the electorate will accept the leadership that they have se-lected, until the time when it may be rejected according to duly constituted procedure.[1]

In summary, a liberal democracy requires widespread partici-pation in the selection of leaders, and a large amount of self-governing activity on the part of non-elites. It also requires com-petition among leaders and would-be leaders, and considerable autonomy for those who win positions of leadership. The basic question arises, what kind of social structure will meet these con-ditions of liberal democracy? The theory of mass society ex-pounded in the present study implies that social pluralism is a social arrangement which performs this function. A plurality of independent and limited-function groups supports liberal de-mocracy by providing social bases of free and open competition for leadership, widespread participation in the selection of leaders, restraint in the application of pressures on leaders, and self-government in wide areas of social life. Therefore, where so-cial pluralism is strong, liberty and democracy tend to be strong; and conversely, forces which weaken social pluralism also weaken liberty and democracy.

In the transition from medieval to modern society, the extent to which pluralist forms emerged as substitutes for communal forms was one decisive factor which determined the fate of liberal democracy. Social pluralism flourished in northwestern Europe and in North America, and these are the areas where liberty and

[1] See Joseph Schumpeter, *Capitalism, Socialism, and Democracy* (New York, Harper and Bros., 1947), pp. 269–296.

democracy have found their greatest strength. In seventeenth-century England, for example, a plurality of class and religious groups already were developing strong roots. As a consequence, it was possible for new social forms adapted to the requirements of urban-industrial life to emerge from older relations. For a long time, it has been widely feared that urban-industrial conditions would destroy an independent group life. But in the modern world, it is among the highly urbanized and industrialized societies that social pluralism and liberal democracy have achieved their fullest and firmest expression. The Communist movement, for example, has won its widest following within the less industrialized societies of the Western world—in Italy and France,[2] rather than in such nations as Britain or the United States. Liberal democracy is strongest in countries possessing the highest per capita output of industrial energy and personal income (for example, among Western countries, the correlation between size of Communist vote and per capita energy is $-.83$; and the correlation between size of Communist vote and per capita income is $-.93$).

But the fact that countries like the Soviet Union are attaining high levels of economic development without liberty or democracy shows that the extent of industrialization alone is not decisive. More important is the mode of economic development, especially whether that development is accomplished through pluralist as well as bureaucratic agencies. Where economic development takes place by means of a variety of social forms, including private as well as public enterprises, liberty and democracy are more likely to grow than where it occurs under the exclusive aegis of the state.

In any case, Marx was wrong: it is not the most highly developed capitalist systems which reveal the greatest social unrest and revolutionary tendencies. Instead, this has been the fate of the less developed countries of Europe (and, even more, of Asia and Africa).

But if Marx is wrong, will Weber prove to be right? For Weber, bureaucratization, not the class struggle, provides the central dy-

[2] However, France is now undergoing a rapid industrial expansion.

namic of the modern world.[3] It is widely believed that bureauc-racy constitues the strongest threat to social pluralism and liberal democracy in the highly industrialized countries. This view raises important issues about the future development of American soci-ety. Several of these issues are briefly noted in the remaining pages.

One of the most prominent arguments which attribute mass consequences to the rationalization of organization focuses on the transformation of the middle classes: the advent of large corpo-rate organization at the expense of small productive property transforms the bases of middle-class power and undermines the capacity of this class to continue as a major pluralist force in the contemporary social order.[4] If an independent middle class served to support democratic rule prior to the emergence of large-scale urban-industrial organization, it is believed that the ascend-ancy of bureaucratic organization now threatens to atomize the middle classes and as a result weaken the social foundations of liberal democracy. The shift from the old to the new middle classes is fraught with peril, according to this line of reasoning.

The trouble with this argument is that it is based on too nar-row a conception of the bases of social participation and social power. It may be granted that the property basis of social power and participation is weakened by the shift from an entrepreneur-ial to an employee society. But at the same time new forms of organization, such as professional associations and civic groups, have been developing to take its place. As a result, members of the new middle class have high rates of participation in voluntary associations, political affairs, and community life.

A burgeoning literature of social criticism is directed toward the meaning of this heightened participation of the new middle classes, especially in the United States. Some social critics of the new middle class argue that far from being non-participants, members of this class engage in group activity to such an extent

---

[3] Max Weber, *Essays in Sociology*, H. H. Gerth and C. W. Mills, eds. (New York, Oxford University Press, 1946), p. 49.
[4] C. Wright Mills, *The Power Elite* (New York, Oxford University Press, 1956), p. 262.

that they lose their autonomy as individuals. This is the major characteristic imputed to the "organization man," who is absorbed by the organization for which he works and whose family is absorbed by the (suburban) community in which he lives.[5] The threat to individual autonomy is believed to lie not in the lack of organization but in the inclusiveness of relations to the organization: the hold of the modern corporation over its members begins to resemble that of the medieval corporation over its members. A closely related issue concerns the quality of many community[6] religious[7] and other social ties of members of this class: these relations are often alleged to mask an underlying passivity and lack of commitment, and to feed on a widespread disposition to overconform. These issues remain to be settled but, in any case, the evidence does not support the contention that the new middle classes are composed of atomized masses.

A second prominent argument that attributes mass consequences to the ascendancy of large-scale organization focuses on the transformation of the public realm. It is frequently asserted that the expanding scale of bureaucratic organization tends to *centralize* public activities and to substitute administration for politics, and therefore to undermine the basis for political participation. But if many people feel ineffective in public affairs, it is in no small part due to the complexity of public problems and events, rather than the result of the lack of opportunity to engage in political activities. In many ways, national politics are more accessible than they have been in the past (although the secrecy surrounding matters of national security is a major force decreasing access). But the growing scope and complexity of the public realm have made distant decisions and events more decisive for private life and simultaneously less manageable. The local community is less and less the locus of major decisions, so that local self-government cannot have the same significance today that it once did. However, it continues to play an important role in

---

[5] See William H. Whyte, *The Organization Man* (New York, Doubleday, 1957).
[6] See Whyte, *op. cit.*, Part VII.
[7] See Will Herberg, *Protestant, Catholic, Jew* (New York, Doubleday, 1955).

some spheres, for example, in public education in the United States.

Commensurate with the nationalization and even internationalization of the public realm is the comparable shift in the locus of communication. The major media of communication tend to be highly sensitive to their audiences (witness the spread of public-opinion polls, market research, etc.). They seek to reflect as well as shape nation-wide opinion, and thereby increase its influence on national policies. Thus there arises the paradox of high *aggregate* access combined with low *individual* access—so that the individual who is responding as an individual feels isolated, and participates psychologically in the power of the aggregate only to the extent that he (along with his personal associates) is capable of identifying himself with his anonymous fellows.

A feeling of political impotence does not stem from the powerlessness of the individual alone. When, after all, have most individuals *qua* individuals been able to readily affect the outcome of public issues? The sense of ineffectiveness results also from the difficulty for citizens to meet and speak together in a public realm dominated by issues of great complexity and by impersonal means of communication. Political apathy would appear to be in large part a response to the resulting distance between the citizen and the locus of major events. However, there are important differences among subgroups in the degree of political apathy and powerlessness. Certain kinds of people, by virtue of their training and position in society, are in relatively better positions to hear and be heard as individuals. This is especially true for professional leaders in government, in business, and, to a lesser extent, in labor—men who are believed to be and consider themselves qualified to head up major institutions by virtue of their education and training. It is also true for the rapidly increasing proportion of the population that is receiving a higher education and going into professional occupations.

Closely related to the question of the impact of large-scale organization on participation in politics is the issue of its consequences for pluralist authority. There are those who believe that American elites are becoming increasingly responsive, even hypersensitive, to public demands and to one another, so much so that leadership and authority are seriously weakened. Thus Lippmann[8] is concerned that the great complexities and needs of foreign policy in the nuclear age are being denied by virtue of public pressures on foreign-policy makers. There are those, on the other hand, who believe that American elites increasingly constitute a closed and unified group, so much so that liberty and democracy are seriously weakened. Thus Mills[9] is concerned that the great consequences of foreign policy are being suffered by a public which has little hand in their determination.

The present study has sought to show that directly accessible elites make ready targets for mass movements. Constitutions and other appropriate institutional devices are needed to regulate access to elites, and to reduce pressures on them.[10] But this does not mean that the mere insulation of elites protects liberty and democracy. Ultimate control over elites must be lodged in the community, even as elites are needed to set specific standards and to propose and implement detailed policies. If democratic institutions are to remain salient, even the complex and perilous nature of international relations cannot justify the abrogation of free competition for national leadership. But is it true that the main drift is toward a closed and unified elite? Such a view cannot account for the increasing social representativeness of national elites, nor for the myriad of conflicts among them; and still less can it be made consistent with the growth of powerful organizations among previously unorganized segments of the community (for example, among industrial workers and among Negroes in the United States).

Furthermore, the power of government cannot be viewed merely defensively, as a danger to the community which therefore must take all precautions to limit it. Power also is the capacity to achieve goals, and therefore must be granted to and assumed by those who possess special competence to use it. The very concept of elite is distasteful to many democrats, so much so that those

---

[8] Walter Lippmann, *The Public Philosophy* (New York, Mentor Books, 1956)
[9] *Op. cit.*
[10] Schumpeter, *op. cit.,* p. 288.

who are elite often feel illegitimate and those who are not elite feel resentful. Herein lies a fundamental dilemma for democracy, the adaptation to which requires widespread appreciation of *the necessary tension between elites and non-elites*.

The major guarantee against the aggrandizement of power by elites is the existence of a plurality of groups that are equal enough in power to generate genuine competition for leadership on the several levels of political society. A danger of bureaucratization is that it will undermine the bases for a plurality of group interests and organizations. For example, it may undermine class organization, so that people in a similar class situation, who therefore have certain economic interests in common, will despair of improving those interests through joint action, and consequently attach themselves to mass movements subversive of all groups, including classes. The nihilism of masses tends to be a greater threat to liberal democracy than the antagonism between classes. Actions taken for economic interests tend to be moderate; whereas mass actions tend to be extremist. A good part of the response to mass appeals is an expression of social atomization, rather than action oriented toward either self-interest or the public interest. *Differences in receptivity to mass symbols and leaders are due primarily to the strength of social ties, and not to the influence of class, or any other social status, by itself.*

The central problem posed by the theory of mass society is that of *social alienation,* or the distance between the individual and his society. Social alienation may occur on all levels of society. The mark of mass society is the alienation of elites as well as the alienation of non-elites. Social alienation has increased with the dissolution of medieval society. Aristocratic critics of mass tendencies offer no solution when they beckon us back to a society based on status: certain social processes are irreversible, and among them is the growing equality of condition. Democratic critics of mass society also do not consider alternative outcomes of the modernization of the world when they assert that urbanization and industrialization, and the correlative spread of large-scale organization entail alienation; for in this case, too, we are confronted with irreversible social processes. The present study has sought to argue that these conditions of modern life carry with them both the heightened possibility of social alienation *and* enhanced opportunities for the creation of new forms of association. Modern industry destroys the conditions for a society of small enterprises, but it also provides the condition of abundance which frees people to seek new ways of life. Modern urban life atomizes traditional social groups, but it also provides a variety of range of social participation. Modern democracy diminishes the contacts and experiences that broaden social horizons and the legitimacy of elites, but it also encourages a multiplicity of competing elites. By enlarging our understanding of such diverse potentialities in the modern world, concepts of mass society and social pluralism promise to stimulate further studies of the social bases of political integration and autonomy.

HANNAH ARENDT / Totalitarianism in Power*

THE SECRET POLICE

Up to now we know only two authentic forms of totalitarian domination: the dictatorship of National Socialism after 1938, and the dictatorship of Bolshevism since 1930. These forms of domination differ basically from other kinds of dictatorial, despotic or tyrannical rule; and even though they have developed, with a certain continuity, from party dictatorships, their essentially totalitarian features are new and cannot be derived from one-party systems. The goal of one-party systems is not only to seize the government administration but, by filling all offices with party members, to achieve a complete amalgamation of state and party, so that after the seizure of power the party becomes a kind of propaganda organization for the government. This system is "total" only in a negative sense, namely, in that the ruling party will tolerate no other parties, no opposition, and no freedom of political opinion. Once a party dictatorship has come to power, it leaves the original power relationship between state and party intact; the government and the army exercise the same power as before, and the "revolution" consists only in the fact that all government positions are now occupied by party members. In all these cases the power of the party rests on a monopoly guaranteed by the state and the party no longer possesses its own power center.

* From Arendt, *Origins of Totalitarianism,* 3rd ed. (Cleveland, Meridian Books, 1966), pp. 419–443. Portions of the original chapter have been omitted.

The revolution initiated by the totalitarian movements after they have seized power is of a considerably more radical nature. From the start, they consciously strive to maintain the essential differences between state and movement and to prevent the "revolutionary" institutions of the movement from being absorbed by the government.[1] The problem of seizing the state machine without amalgamating with it is solved by permitting only those party members whose importance for the movement is secondary to rise in the state hierarchy. All real power is vested in the institutions of the movement, and outside the state and military apparatuses. It is inside the movement, which remains the center of action of the country, that all decisions are made; the official civil services are often not even informed of what is going on, and party members with the ambition to rise to the rank of ministers have in all cases paid for such "bourgeois" wishes with the loss of their influence on the movement and of the confidence of its leaders.

Totalitarianism in power uses the state as its outward façade, to represent the country in the non-totalitarian world. As such, the totalitarian state is the logical heir of the totalitarian movement from which it borrows its organizational structure. Totalitarian rulers deal with non-totalitarian governments in the same way they dealt with parliamentary parties of intra-party factions before their rise to power and, though on an enlarged international scene, are again faced with the double problem of shielding the fictitious world of the movement (or the totalitarian country) from the impact of factuality, and of presenting a semblance of normality and common sense to the normal outside world.

Above the state and behind the façades of ostensible power, in

[1] Hitler frequently commented on the relationship between state and party, and always emphasized that not the state, but the race, or the "united folk community," was of primary importance (cf. the ... speech, reprinted as annex to the *Tischgespräche*). In this speech at the Nuremberg Parteitag of 1935, he gave this theory its most succinct expression: "It is not the state that commands us, but we who command the state." It is self-evident that, in practice, such powers of command are possible only if the institutions of the party remain independent from those of the state.

a maze of multiplied offices, underlying all shifts of authority and in a chaos of inefficiency, lies the power nucleus of the country, the super-efficient and super-competent services of the secret police.[2] The emphasis on the police as the sole organ of power, and the corresponding neglect of the seemingly greater power arsenal of the army, which is characteristic of all totalitarian regimes, can still be partially explained by the totalitarian aspiration to world rule and its conscious abolition of the distinction between a foreign country and a home country, between foreign and domestic affairs. The military forces, trained to fight a foreign aggressor, have always been a dubious instrument for civil-war purposes; even under totalitarian conditions they find it difficult to regard their own people with the eyes of a foreign conqueror.[3] More important in this respect, however, is that their value becomes dubious even in time of war. Since the totalitarian ruler conducts his policies on the assumption of an eventual world government, he treats the victims of his aggression as though they were rebels, guilty of high treason, and consequently prefers to rule occupied territories with police, and not with military forces.

Even before the movement seizes power, it possesses a secret police and spy service with branches in various countries. Later its agents receive more money and authority than the regular military intelligence service and are frequently the secret chiefs of embassies and consulates abroad.[4] Its main tasks consist in forming fifth columns, directing the branches of the movement, influencing the domestic policies of the respective countries, and generally preparing for the time when the totalitarian ruler—after

2 Otto Gauweiler, *Rechtseinrichtungen und Rechtsaufgaben der Bewegung*, 1939, notes expressly that Himmler's special position as Reichsfuehrer-SS and head of the German police rested on the fact that the police administration had achieved "a genuine unity of party and state" which was not even attempted anywhere else in the government.

3 During the peasant revolts of the twenties in Russia, Voroshilov allegedly refused the support of the Red Army; this led to the introduction of special divisions of the G.P.U. for punitive expeditions. See Ciliga, Anton Ciliga, *The Russian Enigma* (London, 1940), p. 95.

4 In 1935, the Gestapo agents abroad received 20 million marks while the regular espionage service of the Reichswehr had to get along with a budget of 8 million. See Pierre Dehillotte, *Gestapo* (Paris, 1940), p. 11.

overthrow of the government or military victory—can openly feel at home. In other words, the international branches of the secret police are the transmission belts which constantly transform the ostensibly foreign policy of the totalitarian state into the potentially domestic business of the totalitarian movement.

These functions, however, which the secret police fulfill in order to prepare the totalitarian utopia of world rule, are secondary to those required for the present realization of the totalitarian fiction in one country. The dominant role of the secret police in the domestic politics of totalitarian countries has naturally contributed much to the common misconception of totalitarianism. All despotisms rely heavily on secret services and feel more threatened by their own than by any foreign people. However, this analogy between totalitarianism and despotism holds only for the first stages of totalitarian rule, when there is still a political opposition. In this as in other respects totalitarianism takes advantage of, and gives conscious support to, non-totalitarian misconceptions, no matter how uncomplimentary they may be. Himmler, in his famous speech to the Reichswehr staff in 1937, assumed the role of an ordinary tyrant when he explained the constant expansion of the police forces by assuming the existence of a "fourth theater in case of war, internal Germany." [5] Similarly, Stalin at almost the same moment half succeeded in convincing the old Bolshevik guard, whose "confessions" he needed, of a war threat against the Soviet Union and, consequently, an emergency in which the country must remain united even behind a despot. The most striking aspect of these statements was that both were made after all political opposition had been extinguished, that the secret services were expanded when actually no opponents were left to be spied upon. When war came, Himmler neither needed nor used his SS troops in Germany itself, except for the running of concentration camps and policing of foreign slave labor; the bulk of the armed SS served at the Eastern front where they were used for "special assignments"—usually mass murder—and the enforcement of policy which frequently ran counter to the military

[5] See *Nazi Conspiracy and Aggression* (Washington, U. S. Government, 1946), IV, pp. 616 ff.

as well as the Nazi civilian hierarchy. Like the secret police of the Soviet Union, the SS formations usually arrived after the military forces had pacified the conquered territory and had dealt with outright political opposition.

In the first stages of a totalitarian regime, however, the secret police and the party's elite formations still play a role similar to that in other forms of dictatorship and the well-known terror regimes of the past; and the excessive cruelty of their methods is unparalleled only in the history of modern Western countries. The first stage of ferreting out secret enemies and hunting down former opponents is usually combined with drafting the entire population into front organizations and re-educating old party members for voluntary espionage services, so that the rather dubious sympathies of the drafted sympathizers need not worry the specially trained cadres of the police. It is during this stage that a neighbor gradually becomes a more dangerous enemy to one who happens to harbor "dangerous thoughts" than are the officially appointed police agents. The end of the first stage comes with the liquidation of open and secret resistance in any organized form; it can be set at about 1935 in Germany and approximately 1930 in Soviet Russia.

Only after the extermination of real enemies has been completed and the hunt for "objective enemies" begun does terror become the actual content of totalitarian regimes. Under the pretext of building socialism in one country, or using a given territory as a laboratory for a revolutionary experiment, or realizing the *Volksgemeinschaft,* the second claim of totalitarianism, the claim to total domination, is carried out. And although theoretically total domination is possible only under the conditions of world rule, the totalitarian regimes have proved that this part of the totalitarian utopia can be realized almost to perfection, because it is temporarily independent of defeat or victory. Thus Hitler could rejoice even in the midst of military setbacks over the extermination of Jews and the establishment of death factories; no matter what the final outcome, without the war it would never have been possible "to burn the bridges" and to realize some of the goals of the totalitarian movement.

The elite formations of the Nazi movement and the "cadres" of the Bolshevik movement serve the goal of total domination rather than the security of the regime in power. Just as the totalitarian claim to world rule is only in appearance the same as imperialist expansion, so the claim to total domination only *seems* familiar to the student of despotism. If the chief difference between totalitarian and imperialist expansion is that the former recognizes no difference between a home and a foreign country, then the chief difference between a despotic and a totalitarian secret police is that the latter does not hunt secret thoughts and does not use the old method of secret services, the method of provocation.[6]

TOTAL DOMINATION

The concentration and extermination camps of totalitarian regimes serve as the laboratories in which the fundamental belief of totalitarianism that everything is possible is being verified. Compared with this, all other experiments are secondary in importance—including those in the field of medicine whose horrors are recorded in detail in the trials against the physicians of the Third Reich—although it is characteristic that these laboratories were used for experiments of every kind.

Total domination, which strives to organize the infinite plurality and differentiation of human beings as if all of humanity were just one individual, is possible only if each and every person can be reduced to a never-changing identity of reactions, so that each of these bundles of reactions can be exchanged at random for any other. The problem is to fabricate something that does not exist, namely, a kind of human species resembling other animal species whose only "freedom" would consist in "preserving the species." [7]

---

[6] Maurice Laporte, *Histoire de l'Okhrana* (Paris, 1935), rightly called the method of provocation "the foundation stone" of the secret police (p. 19).

In Soviet Russia, provocation, far from being the secret weapon of the secret police, has been used as the widely propagandized public method of the regime to gauge the temper of public opinion. The reluctance of the population to avail itself of the periodically recurring invitations to criticize or react to "liberal" interludes in the terror regime shows that such gestures are understood as provocation on a mass scale. Provocation has indeed become the totalitarian version of public opinion polls.

[7] In the *Tischgespräche*, Hitler mentions several times that he "[strives] for a condition in which each individual knows that he lives and dies for the

Totalitarian domination attempts to achieve this goal both through ideological indoctrination of the elite formations and through absolute terror in the camps; and the atrocities for which the elite formations are ruthlessly used become, as it were, the practical application of the ideological indoctrination—the testing ground in which the latter must prove itself—while the appalling spectacle of the camps themselves is supposed to furnish the "theoretical" verification of the ideology.

The camps are meant not only to exterminate people and degrade human beings, but also serve the ghastly experiment of eliminating, under scientifically controlled conditions, spontaneity itself as an expression of human behavior and of transforming the human personality into a mere thing, into something that even animals are not; for Pavlov's dog, which, as we know, was trained to eat not when it was hungry but when a bell rang, was a perverted animal.

Under normal circumstances this can never be accomplished, because spontaneity can never be entirely eliminated insofar as it is connected not only with human freedom but with life itself, in the sense of simply keeping alive. It is only in the concentration camps that such an experiment is at all possible, and therefore they are not only *"la société la plus totalitaire encore réalisée"* (David Rousset) but the guiding social ideal of total domination in general. Just as the stability of the totalitarian regime depends on the isolation of the fictitious world of the movement from the outside world, so the experiment of total domination in the concentration camps depends on sealing off the latter against the world of all others, the world of the living in general, even against the outside world of a country under totalitarian rule. This isolation explains the peculiar unreality and lack of credibility that characterize all reports from the concentration camps and constitute one of the main difficulties for the true understanding of totalitarian domination, which stands or falls with the existence of these concentration and experimentation camps; for, unlikely as it may sound, these camps are the true central institution of totalitarian organizational power.

---

preservation of his species" (p. 349). See also p. 347: "A fly lays millions of eggs, all of which perish. But the flies remain."

There are numerous reports by survivors.[8] The more authentic they are, the less they attempt to communicate things that evade human understanding and human experience—sufferings, that is, that transform men into "uncomplaining animals."[9] None of these reports inspires those passions of outrage and sympathy through which men have always been mobilized for justice. On the contrary, anyone speaking or writing about concentration camps is still regarded as suspect; and if the speaker has resolutely returned to the world of the living, he himself is often assailed by doubts with regard to his own truthfulness, as though he had mistaken a nightmare for reality.[10]

This doubt of people concerning themselves and the reality of their own experience only reveals what the Nazis have always known: that men determined to commit crimes will find it expedient to organize them on the vastest, most improbable scale. Not only because this renders all punishments provided by the legal system inadequate and absurd; but because the very immensity of the crimes guarantees that the murderers who proclaim their in-

[8] The best reports on Nazi concentration camps are David Rousset, *Les Jours de Notre Mort* (Paris, 1947); Eugen Kogon; Bruno Bettelheim, "On Dachau and Buchenwald" (from May, 1938, to April, 1939), in *Nazi Conspiracy*, VII, pp. 824 ff. For Soviet concentration camps, see the excellent collection of reports by Polish survivors published under the title *The Dark Side of the Moon;* also David J. Dallin; though his reports are sometimes less convincing because they come from "prominent" personalities who are intent on drawing up manifestos and indictments.

[9] *The Dark Side of the Moon;* the introduction also stresses this peculiar lack of communication: "They record but do not communicate."

[10] See especially Bruno Bettelheim, *op. cit.* "It seemed as if I had become convinced that these horrible and degrading experiences somehow did not happen to 'me' as subject but to 'me' as an object. This experience was corroborated by the statements of other prisoners.... It was as if I watched things happening in which I only vaguely participated.... 'This cannot be true, such things just do not happen.' ... The prisoners had to convince themselves that this was real, was really happening and not just a nightmare. They were never wholly successful."

See also Rousset, *op. cit.*, p. 213. "... Those who haven't seen it with their own eyes can't believe it. Did you yourself, before you came here, take the rumors about the gas chambers seriously?"

"No," I said.

"... You see? Well, they're all like you. The lot of them in Paris, London, New York, even at Birkenau, right outside the crematoriums ... still incredulous, five minutes before they were sent down into the cellar of the crematorium...."

nocence with all manner of lies will be more readily believed than the victims who tell the truth. The Nazis did not even consider it necessary to keep this discovery to themselves. Hitler circulated millions of copies of his book in which he stated that to be successful, a lie must be enormous—which did not prevent people from believing him as, similarly, the Nazis' proclamations, repeated *ad nauseam,* that the Jews would be exterminated like bedbugs (i.e., with poison gas), prevented anybody from *not* believing them.

There is a great temptation to explain away the intrinsically incredible by means of liberal rationalizations. In each one of us, there lurks such a liberal, wheedling us with the voice of common sense. The road to totalitarian domination leads through many intermediate stages for which we can find numerous analogies and precedents. The extraordinarily bloody terror during the initial stage to totalitarian rule serves indeed the exclusive purpose of defeating the opponent and rendering all further opposition impossible; but total terror is launched only after this initial stage has been overcome and the regime no longer has anything to fear from the opposition. In this context it has been frequently remarked that in such a case the means have become the end, but this is after all only an admission, in paradoxical disguise, that the category "the end justifies the means" no longer applies, that terror has lost its "purpose," that it is no longer the means to frighten people. Nor does the explanation suffice that the revolution, as in the case of the French Revolution, was devouring its own children, for the terror continues even after everybody who might be described as a child of the revolution in one capacity or another—the Russian factions, the power centers of party, the army, the bureaucracy—has long since been devoured. Many things that nowadays have become the specialty of totalitarian government are only too well-known from the study of history. There have almost always been wars of aggression; the massacre of hostile populations after a victory went unchecked until the Romans mitigated it by introducing the *parcere subjectis;* through centuries the extermination of native peoples went hand-in-hand with the colonization of the Americas, Australia, and Africa; slavery is one of the oldest institutions of mankind and all empires of antiquity were based on the labor of state-owned slaves who erected their public buildings. Not even concentration camps are an invention of totalitarian movements. They emerge for the first time during the Boer War, at the beginning of the century, and continued to be used in South Africa as well as India for "undesirable elements"; here, too, we first find the term "protective custody" which was later adopted by the Third Reich. These camps correspond in many respects to the concentration camps at the beginning of totalitarian rule; they were used for "suspects" whose offenses could not be proved and who could not be sentenced by ordinary process of law. All this clearly points to totalitarian methods of domination; all these are elements they utilize, develop, and crystallize on the basis of the nihilistic principle that "everything is permitted," which they inherited and already take for granted. But wherever these new forms of domination assume their authentically totalitarian structure they transcend this principle, which is still tied to the utilitarian motives and self-interest of the rulers, and try their hand in a realm that up to now has been completely unknown to us: the realm where "everything is possible." And, characteristically enough, this is precisely the realm that cannot be limited by either utilitarian motives or self-interest, regardless of the latter's content.

What runs counter to common sense is not the nihilistic principle that "everything is permitted," which was already contained in the nineteenth-century utilitarian conception of common sense. What common sense and "normal people" refuse to believe is that everything is possible.[11] We attempt to understand elements in present or recollected experience that simply surpass our powers of understanding. We attempt to classify as criminal a thing which, as we all feel, no such category was ever intended to cover. What meaning has the concept of murder when we are confronted with the mass production of corpses? We attempt to understand the behavior of concentration-camp inmates and the SS-men psychologically, when the very thing that must be realized is that the psyche *can* be destroyed even without the destruction

[11] The first to understand this was Rousset in his *Univers Concentrationnaire,* 1947.

of the physical man; that, indeed, psyche, character, and individuality seem under certain circumstances to express themselves only through the rapidity or slowness with which they disintegrate.[12] The end result in any case is inanimate men, i.e., men who can no longer be psychologically understood, whose return to the psychologically or otherwise intelligibly human world closely resembles the resurrection of Lazarus. All statements of common sense, whether of a psychological or sociological nature, serve only to encourage those who think it "superficial" to "dwell on horrors." [13]

If it is true that the concentration camps are the most consequential institution of totalitarian rule, "dwelling on horrors" would seem to be indispensable for the understanding of totalitarianism. But recollection can no more do this than can the uncommunicative eyewitness report. In both these genres there is an inherent tendency to run away from the experience; instinctively or rationally, both types of writer are so much aware of the terrible abyss that separates the world of the living from that of the living dead, that they cannot supply anything more than a series of remembered occurrences that must seem just as incredible to those who relate them as to their audience. Only the fearful imagination of those who have been aroused by such reports but have not actually been smitten in their own flesh, of those who are consequently free from the bestial, desperate terror which, when confronted by real, present horror, inexorably paralyzes everything that is not mere reaction, can afford to keep thinking about horrors. Such thoughts are useful only for the perception of political contexts and the mobilization of political passions. A change of personality of any sort whatever can no more be induced by thinking about horrors than by the real experience of horror. The reduction of a man to a bundle of reactions separates him as radically as mental disease from everything within him that is personality or character. When, like Lazarus, he rises from the dead, he finds his personality or character unchanged, just as he had left it.

12 Rousset, *op. cit.*, p. 587.
13 See Georges Bataille in *Critique*, January, 1948, p. 72.

Just as the horror, or the dwelling on it, cannot affect a change of character in him, cannot make men better or worse, thus it cannot become the basis of a political community or party in a narrower sense. The attempts to build up a European elite with a program of intra-European understanding based on the common European experience of the concentration camps have foundered in much the same manner as the attempts following the first World War to draw political conclusions from the international experience of the front generation. In both cases it turned out that the experiences themselves can communicate no more than nihilistic banalities.[14] Political consequences such as post-war pacifism, for example, derived from the general fear of war, not from the experiences in war. Instead of producing a pacifism devoid of reality, the insight into the structure of modern wars, guided and mobilized by fear, might have led to the realization that the only standard for a necessary war is the fight against conditions under which people no longer wish to live—and our experiences with the tormenting hell of the totalitarian camps have enlightened us only too well about the possibility of such conditions.[15] Thus the fear of concentration camps and the resulting insight into the nature of total domination might serve to invalidate all obsolete political differentiations from right to left and to introduce beside and above them the politically most important yardstick for judging events in our time, namely: whether they serve totalitarian domination or not.

In any event, the fearful imagination has the great advantage to dissolve the sophistic-dialectical interpretations of politics which are all based on the superstition that something good might result from evil. Such dialectical acrobatics had at least a semblance of justification so long as the worst that man could inflict upon man was murder. But, as we know today, murder is

[14] Rousset's book contains many such "insights" into human "nature," based chiefly on the observation that after a while the mentality of the inmates is scarcely distinguishable from that of the camp guards.

[15] In order to avoid misunderstandings it may be appropriate to add that with the invention of the hydrogen bomb the whole war question has undergone another decisive change. A discussion of this question is of course beyond the theme of this book.

only a limited evil. The murderer who kills a man—a man who has to die anyway—still moves within the realm of life and death familiar to us; both have indeed a necessary connection on which the dialectic is founded, even if it is not always conscious of it. The murderer leaves a corpse behind and does not pretend that his victim has never existed; if he wipes out any traces, they are those of his own identity, and not the memory and grief of the persons who loved his victim; he destroys a life, but he does not destroy the fact of existence itself.

The Nazis, with the precision peculiar to them, used to register their operations in the concentration camps under the heading "under cover of the night (*Nacht und Nebel*)." The radicalism of measures to treat people as if they had never existed and to make them disappear in the literal sense of the word is frequently not apparent at first glance, because both the German and the Russian systems are not uniform but consist of a series of categories in which people are treated very differently. In the case of Germany, these different categories used to exist in the same camp, but without coming into contact with each other; frequently, the isolation between the categories was even stricter than the isolation from the outside world. Thus, out of racial considerations, Scandinavian nationals during the war were quite differently treated by the Germans than the members of other peoples, although the former were outspoken enemies of the Nazis. The latter in turn were divided into those whose "extermination" was immediately on the agenda, as in the case of the Jews, or could be expected in the predictable future, as in the case of the Poles, Russians, and Ukrainians, and into those who were not yet covered by instructions about such an overall "final solution," as in the case of the French and Belgians. In Russia, on the other hand, we must distinguish three more or less independent systems. First, there are the authentic forced-labor groups that live in relative freedom and are sentenced for limited periods. Secondly, there are the concentration camps in which the human material is ruthlessly exploited and the mortality rate is extremely high, but which are essentially organized for labor purposes. And, thirdly, there are the annihilation camps in which the inmates are systematically wiped out through starvation and neglect.

The real horror of the concentration and extermination camps lies in the fact that the inmates, even if they happen to keep alive, are more effectively cut off from the world of the living than if they had died, because terror enforces oblivion. Here, murder is as impersonal as the squashing of a gnat. Someone may die as the result of systematic torture or starvation, or because the camp is overcrowded and superfluous human material must be liquidated. Conversely, it may happen that due to a shortage of new human shipments the danger arises that the camps become depopulated and that the order is now given to reduce the death rate at any price.[16] David Rousset called his report on the period in a German concentration camp *"Les Jours de Notre Mort,"* and it is indeed as if there were a possibility to give permanence to the process of dying itself and to enforce a condition in which both death and life are obstructed equally effectively.

It is the appearance of some radical evil, previously unknown to us, that puts an end to the notion of developments and transformations of qualities. Here, there are neither political nor historical nor simply moral standards but, at the most, the realization that something seems to be involved in modern politics that actually should never be involved in politics as we used to understand it, namely all or nothing—all, and that is an undetermined infinity of forms of human living-together, or nothing, for a victory of the concentration-camp system would mean the same inexorable doom for human beings as the use of the hydrogen bomb would mean the doom of the human race.

[16] This happened in Germany toward the end of 1942, whereupon Himmler served notice to all camp commandants "to reduce the death rate at all costs." For it had turned out that of the 136,000 new arrivals, 70,000 were already dead on reaching the camp or died immediately thereafter. See *Nazi Conspiracy*, IV, Annex II.—Later reports from Soviet Russian camps unanimously confirm that after 1949—that is, when Stalin was still alive—the death rate in the concentration camps, which previously had reached up to 60 percent of the inmates, was systematically lowered, presumably due to a general and acute labor shortage in the Soviet Union. This improvement in living conditions should not be confused with the crisis of the regime after Stalin's death which, characteristically enough, first made itself felt in the concentration camps. Cf. Wilhelm Starlinger, *Grenzen der Sowjetmacht* (Würzburg, 1955).

PART II

SOCIAL CLASS
AND POWER
IN THE WEST

EDITOR'S INTRODUCTION

This part of the Reader deals with the perennial themes of class conflict and political power as they relate to the contemporary Anglo-American and European societies.

In many ways, politics in these countries is a continuing expression of the class struggle. Workers have tended to vote for "left" parties such as Communist and Socialist parties, that promise a more just distribution of social products and resources. A good analysis of the social factors in "left" voting may be found in Lipset, who maintains, "More than anything else the party struggle is a conflict among classes, and the most impressive single fact about political party support is that in virtually every economically developed country the lower-income groups vote mainly for parties of the left, while the higher-income groups vote mainly for parties of the right." [1]

While there is a connection between social class and political behavior in contemporary Western societies, this connection is not an invariant one. The comparative study of the United States, England, Canada, and Australia by Alford should serve to make this clear.

Dahrendorf's analysis raises the question of whether class conflict in Europe has not been diminishing rather than increasing, as Marx predicted.[2] He points to the upper middle class, or "service class," as he calls it, as more and more setting the tone and directions for European society. It is from the bureaucratic positions occupied by members of this group that the ruling circles are increasingly drawn. The members of the service class tend

[1] Seymour Martin Lipset, *Political Man* (New York, Doubleday, 1960), pp. 223–224.
[2] Evidence of some decline in the sharpness of contrast between rich and poor in Western societies has helped to provide a basis for the contention of some observers that ideology is no longer relevant; or at least that socialist ideology is no longer relevant. See Part 4 of this Reader.

to see problems of politics as problems of administration; their values tend to make them downplay the existence of social conflict.[3] Nevertheless, so long as there are economic and social inequalities in a society, we must expect the presence of political efforts aimed at change. And so long as there are people who feel they do not have enough of a say in the decisions that affect their lives, there will be conflict between the administrators and the human beings they administer.

Some of the difficulty in obtaining an accurate description of the power situation in a society can be seen in the three selections included in Chapter 6 which relate to the existence of a power elite in the United States. Is there a unified power elite, as Mills maintained,[4] or is there a plurality of competing veto groups? [5] Kornhauser presents a rather concise summary of the differences between the elitist and the pluralist theories of American power. Probably both elitists and pluralists would agree that there are a number of centers of power in American society. In addition to the major corporations, these power centers include the executive branch of the federal government, the semi-autonomous government agencies, and the military establishment. A major point in dispute is whether the men who occupy the top positions in these institutions tend to act in concert or whether they function as veto groups for each other.

Mills's thesis, which he expounds in the selection included below, is that there is a power elite in America consisting of "those who occupy the command posts at the heads of the major institutions of the country." That is, those at the head of our economic, political, and military institutions. Mills maintains that incumbents of key posts in these institutions form an interlocking directorate which works together in a unified fashion. He does not single out one of these as the most important institutional order. Further, he recognizes that there are differences and disagreements among occupants of the "power elite" positions: "The

[3] Cf. John Horton, "Order and Conflict Theories of Social Problems as Competing Ideologies," *American Journal of Sociology* (May, 1966).

[4] See C. Wright Mills, *The Power Elite* (New York, Oxford University Press, 1956).

[5] For an excellent analysis of power from the pluralist viewpoint, see Arnold Rose, *The Power Structure* (New York, Oxford University Press, 1967).

power elite is composed of political, economic, and military men, but these instituted elites are frequently in some tension: they come together only on certain co-inciding points and only on certain occasions of 'crisis.' "

Extending Mills's analysis in an article not included here, Hacker names a dozen institutions that direct the course of contemporary American life:

> General Motors Corporation
> Standard Oil Company of New Jersey
> American Telephone and Telegraph Company
> Atomic Energy Commission
> Central Intelligence Agency
> Ford Foundation
> National Education Association
> Chase Manhattan Bank
> Metropolitan Life Insurance Company
> Columbia Broadcasting System
> *The New York Time*s
> Merrill, Lynch, Pierce, Fenner and Smith[6]

The President of the United States, his key advisors and Cabinet members, the members of the Joint Chiefs of Staff, and the key officials of the above-mentioned agencies constitute the apex of the power elite. It is not necessary to assume that they are *always* in agreement. This is where the argument of the pluralists is strongest. The pluralists assert that there are definite conflicts of interest that exist within the apex of the power pyramid in the United States. And so there are. On some issues that are central and many that are peripheral there is some approximation of the veto group model. But it would be nonsensical to say that the occupants of these positions are rarely in agreement with each other. They *do* tend to see the world in similar fashion—simply because they *are* at the apex of power. And the assumptions and interests they share seem to outweigh their differences. The *denial* of the existence of a power elite serves the ideological function of *protecting* the power position of that elite.

As Pilisuk and Hayden point out, "all that countervailing

6 Andrew Hacker, "Proper to do What," in Irving L. Horowitz, ed., *The New Sociology* (New York, Oxford University Press, 1964), pp. 134–146.

power refers to is the relationship between groups who fundamentally accept the American system but who compete for advantages within it." There is some disagreement among the powerful regarding domestic issues, but little on foreign policy. There seems to be a general agreement that efficacy is preferable to principle in foreign affairs,[7] that capitalism and private property are better than socialism and collective property, and that the American form of limited parliamentary democracy is the best form of government. Pilisuk and Hayden answer their question as to whether there is a military-industrial complex that prevents peace, by saying that American society *itself* is a military-industrial complex. It can accommodate a wide range of disagreement, according to Pilisuk and Hayden, but only within the framework of the consensus on the points mentioned above. They conclude that in the United States "there is no ruling group. Nor is there any easily discernible ruling institutional order, so meshed have the separate sources of elite power become. But there is a social structure which is organized to create and protect power centers with only partial accountability."

[7] Thus American military intervention in revolutions abroad may be regrettable but necessary, the cold war and the arms race are regrettable but necessary, etc.

5 / POLITICS AND CLASS CONFLICT

ROBERT R. ALFORD / Stratification and Politics in the Anglo-American Countries*

This paper briefly summarizes the results of an inquiry into the social bases of political cleavage in four Anglo-American countries, Great Britain, Australia, the United States, and Canada. The data utilized were over fifty surveys of the electorate in these countries, over the period 1936 to 1966. Information on the occupation, political preference, religion, and region of residence of each respondent was available, and from these data, indices of class-voting (the association of social class and voting), religiously based voting, and regionally based voting were constructed. Detailed discussion of the data appears elsewhere.[1]

The main questions guiding the study were: how much do levels of class-voting diverge in four Anglo-American countries—economically developed countries with high levels of consensus upon the form of government? And, to what extent do religious and regionally based loyalties to party affect class-voting? The empirical approach to answers to these questions involved certain assumptions which may briefly be reviewed here before the findings are summarized.

* This is a slightly revised version of a paper read at the International Sociological Association meetings, Washington, D.C., September, 1962.
[1] Robert R. Alford, *Party and Society: The Anglo-American Democracies* (Chicago, Rand-McNally, 1963). More recent data and studies are summarized in Robert R. Alford, "Class Voting in the Anglo-American Political Systems," in S. M. Lipset and Stein Rokkan, eds., *Party Systems and Voter Alignments* (New York, The Free Press, 1967).

The four Anglo-American countries have a common political culture and a limited range of political cleavages. In neither Britain, Australia, the United States, nor Canada is there an important threat to the basic constitutional and parliamentary framework. The focus of political conflict is therefore around the political parties, and upon alternative policies to be pursued by the government dominated by one of the major parties. A contrast of these four societies, remarkably alike in many respects when compared to pre-industrial or totalitarian societies, but remarkably different in their political histories, may clarify the problems of political stability and change in stable two-party systems and also contribute to a more general theory of cleavage and change in democratic political systems.

A certain level of class-voting is to be expected, because of the nature of both the stratification and political orders. Deprived groups seek redress through political action. In a democratic system, political parties provide representation for many different groups. Such representation would not be necessary, however, if the ruling order were not challenged in some respects. Party *systems* (as distinct from "parties") arose and continue partly in order to provide access by less privileged groups to decisions made by authoritative agencies—mainly government. Before the rise of mass parties of the Left in the nineteenth century, there were "parties" of the Right—competing coalitions of ruling groups—but no party systems as such.

An important point of view in modern political thought holds that parties need not be representatives of social classes. Parties in this view can constitute competing bodies of men seeking political power, but need not represent any given set of interests or coalition of such interests. This is the economist Joseph Schumpeter's view of the essence of democracy. Democracy is a political form which need not have any class content.[2] The competing political factions need not represent *any* set of interests consistently, but need only be alternative sets of leaders for the given political unit, be it organization, party, or nation.

[2] See Joseph Schumpeter, *Capitalism, Socialism, and Democracy* (New York, Harpers, 1947), p. 269.

If social classes in the Western democracies become so shifting and blurred that no social interests with a degree of stability can be distinguished, then we might expect that democracy in these countries will come to resemble Schumpeter's model. Support for a party would not be predictable from either an assessment of the legislative behavior of its representatives or an analysis of stratification among the electorate. The United States and Canada, among these four countries, are closest to the state of affairs where neither parties nor electorate can be divided sharply into Left and Right, have-nots and haves.

But an objective basis for class-voting does still exist in the character of the stratification order. The similarities of these four countries suggest that if rational and structural factors were the only ones affecting voting behavior, the social bases of politics in these countries should be coming to be more *similar*. Class-voting may decline ultimately, but there seems to be little reason to suppose that it will disappear as long as these societies remain stratified.

A number of methodological assumptions concerning ways of measuring class position, voting behavior, and the extent of religious and regional political loyalties were made. Since public-opinion surveys were the main source of data for the study, occupational status, divided into manual and non-manual occupations, has been used as the measure of class divisions. Voting intention in a national election as indicated in answers to interviewer's question was the measure of actual voting behavior.

Whether religious allegiances and identifications are the real basis for the differences discovered in the political behavior of Protestants and Catholics is difficult to know for certain. Examination of religious differences within various age-groups, regions, and so forth, has shown that differences in political behavior between religious groups exist, but this is still a major assumption. Wherever religious differences were found in *both* manual and non-manual occupations, it has been assumed that this was actually a religious difference, and not one which could be accounted for by other non-religious factors.

Similarly, it is difficult to know whether the apparent regional differences in political behavior are actually due to specifically regional identifications and loyalties. As with the case of religious differences, it has been assumed that if a regional difference was found within both manual and non-manual occupations (as evidenced by extremely high or low levels of class-voting), that this was due to some special character of the region as a cultural or social entity.

Given these assumptions, which may seriously qualify the generality of the conclusions which can be drawn from the data, the findings of the study may now be briefly summarized.

Great Britain not only has the highest level of class-voting of any of the four Anglo-American countries, but nothing else seems to matter except class-factors, or at least matter in the way they do in the other countries. Voting is highly correlated with occupation, education, income, and subjective class identification, whether considered separately or together. Combinations of class factors almost completely account for variations of voting behavior in Great Britain.

The greatest regional variations in class-voting occur in Wales and Scotland, the areas with the greatest sectional identification and cultural identity. Unlike the regions with similar kinds of identities in the United States and Canada—the South and Quebec—class-voting is generally higher in those regions, indicating that whatever effect the regional loyalties have, they do not produce alignments of both strata behind one party. Similarly, although class-voting was lower among the Catholics in England than among any other religious group, it was not due to a higher level of Labor voting among both manual and non-manual strata, but actually lower Left voting among manual workers. The pattern of religious deviation from class-voting was therefore different in Great Britain from any of the other countries, where the Left party received disproportionate support from both social strata. Catholic identifications in England do not express themselves in allegiances to one party.

Great Britain therefore has a relatively "pure" class-politics. Regional and religious loyalties in such a system tend not to be expressed through political parties, but, in a sense, may become demands upon the whole system. If the Scots want more representation in Parliament, they will demand it of the "system," not of any party. The political parties are no longer mediators of any parochial or sectional interests except class interests (which can also be parochial and sectional, but in a different sense).

Perhaps the most surprising empirical finding was that class-voting has not declined in Great Britain in the period 1943 to 1959, but has actually increased, if anything. Manual workers were no less likely to vote Labor in 1959 than they were in 1943, and a decline in Labor votes occurred among persons in non-manual occupations. If blurring of social class lines has taken place in Great Britain, it has not yet reduced class-voting. One single piece of evidence that a decline of class-voting may occur was found: class-voting was lowest in the London and Southern metropolitan area, where educational opportunities have been more equalized for the classes, and which probably is better-off economically than other areas. If such social changes continue, the lower level of class-voting around London may constitute an omen for the future decline of class-voting in Britain.

The level of class-voting in Australia is somewhat lower than in Great Britain, but the Catholics, regardless of their occupation, are far more likely to be Labor supporters. Regional loyalties are not important in Australian politics, but the older and more ur-banized states—New South Wales and Victoria—exhibit lower levels of class-voting. A special study of the largely Catholic Dem-ocratic Labor party which emerged in 1955 found that the DLP served as a vehicle for the transition of upward mobile Catholics away from the old Labor party in an era in which their ethnic and religious loyalties have become politically less relevant (although as long as the Communist issue remains, the potential for such relevance also remains).

No sharp or regular decline of class-voting occurred in Australia between 1943 and 1958, and actually an increase occurred in four of the six states between 1946 and 1951, despite a drop of the total Labor vote. Overall trends in Australia do not therefore support the hypothesis of a decline of the importance of the class-bases of politics.

In the United States the level of class-voting has vacillated considerably between 1936 and 1960, rising to high points in 1940 and 1948, but remaining higher in the 1956 and 1960 elections than it was in 1936, when both manual and non-manual strata were pulled over to Roosevelt. Class-voting is lowest in the South, where sectional loyalties override social class as a basis for political cleavage. No decline of the Southern deviation was evident from these data.

The importance of religious voting has also vacillated considerably, with Catholics usually being pulled over to the Democratic Party. This was not true in 1952, however, when non-manual Catholics voted Republican almost to the extent of non-manual Protestants. Any decline of the "Catholic vote" through secular assimilation was obscured by the 1960 election, which marked the greatest difference between Protestant and Catholic voting (in both strata) of any election since 1944. Whether the achievement of the Presidency by a Catholic will mark the end of the Catholic sense of minority consciousness and therefore the end of their distinctive political behavior is an open question.

In Canada, non-class factors assume a paramount role. Class-voting in Canada has since 1943 been consistently lower than in any of the other three countries. Economic and cultural heterogeneity, and the political veto-power exercised by the French-Catholic cultural "island" of Quebec are probably the major factors reducing class alignments around the parties, although class interests and struggles are by no means absent from Canadian political history.

Some evidence of an increase of class-voting was found in the 1957–1961 period, despite the swing of all social groups toward the Progressive-Conservative Party and its leader John Diefenbaker. This increase, and signs of a breakdown of the extreme provincialism characteristic of Canadian politics, may indicate that the absence of class-voting in Canada is not a sign of its having reached political and social maturity, but rather a sign that it may yet come to exhibit the forms of political cleavage characteristic of more homogeneous nations.

In sum, where class-factors are paramount in determining national political cleavages, religious and regional loyalties do not significantly affect political behavior. Where social classes do not support the national parties in sharply different degrees, regional and religious loyalties are strong. In addition, there is no evidence that class-voting is decreasing substantially in any of the four countries.

My predictions for the future, which are testable by means of electoral surveys yet to be conducted, are that class-voting will decline in Great Britain, as the society becomes more economically and culturally homogeneous, but traditional class loyalties wither. In Australia, the Catholic deviation will probably dwindle, and class-voting drop slightly. In the United States and Canada, class-voting will probably increase as regional and religious deviations decrease.

Two general points may be made in conclusion. Where both religious and regional voting, and class-voting are high, the conditions for a breakdown of political consensus exist, and therefore a fragmentation of the boundaries of the existing political community. At the other extreme, where none of these cleavages exist, a "mass-society" is approximated. Here, the political parties are mere bureaucratic entities, competing for power. They have no solid base in allegiances to groups intervening between individual and nation, whether these groups are based upon regional, religious, or class loyalties. It is an open question whether such a situation is potentially dangerous for the continuation of a given political structure. In any case, it seems an unlikely possibility for these four countries.[3]

Evidence from this study indicates that systems with relatively "pure" class politics may exist without any apparent loss of political consensus. This suggests that the view, expressed by Lipset, must be modified that the "two-party system works best where it is based on an elaborate, cross-cutting solidarity structure, in which men and groups are pulled in different directions by their diverse roles and interests. Wherever the solidarity structure is

[3] See W. Kornhauser, *The Politics of Mass Society* (Glencoe, Ill., The Free Press, 1959), for the view, ultimately deriving from Alexis de Tocqueville, that the masses in such a political system are easily manipulated by political elites, and the political elites in turn cannot easily isolate themselves from irresponsible influence from the masses. (See Chapter 4 of this Reader.)

polarized by class, race, or religion, and the political lines follow those of social cleavage, a two-party system may intensify internal conflict rather than help integrate the society." [4] Since the politics of Great Britain are almost exclusively based upon class (despite the cross-class voting which does exist), it seems clear that a high level of class-voting without any cross-cutting cleavages such as religion or region need not intensify internal conflict nor disintegrate the society. Politics based on class therefore need not endanger the democratic order.

[4] S. M. Lipset, "Party Systems and the Representation of Social Groups," *European Journal of Sociology*, 1, (1960), p. 76. A similar point is made in Talcott Parsons, "Voting and the Equilibrium of the American Political System," in E. Burdick and A. Brodbeck, eds., *American Voting Behavior* (Glencoe, Ill., The Free Press, 1959), pp. 80–120.

RALF DAHRENDORF / Recent Changes in the Class Structure of European Societies*

INTRODUCTION

If by the class structure of a society we understand the relationship of its members to the exercise of power, there are above all four groups which demand our attention: (1) those who, by virtue of their position in a given country, are able to lay down the law for others in both the literal and the metaphorical sense (*the ruling groups*); (2) those who assist the ruling groups in their legislative task by executing and adjudicating law as well as by advising and generally helping those in power (*the service class*); (3) those who are subject to the power of the rulers as well as their servants, even if their citizenship rights enable them occasionally to make their voice heard (*the ruled or subjected groups*); (4) and finally, those who stand outside this whole structure of leaders and led, the "free-floating intellectuals," "those who"—in Bertrand Russell's words—"withdraw" and who therefore "do not fit readily into the social structure, and in one way or another . . . seek a refuge where they can enjoy a more or less solitary freedom" (*the intellectuals*).[1]

If there is any formula to describe the change in the interrelationships among these groups with which I am above all con-

* From *Daedalus* (Winter, 1964), pp. 225-270. Portions of the original article have been omitted.
[1] Bertrand Russell, *Power: A New Social Analysis* (London, 1960).

cerned in this essay, it would be the enormous expansion of the
service class at the expense of all others and—even more significantly perhaps—the infusion of the values characteristic of this
class into the behavior of all others, including even the ruling
groups.[2] Thus the service class and its properties will be the focus
of our attention in this essay.

I THE DEMISE OF THE OLD ORDER

. . . Of all sociological models, Marx's theory of two antagonistic social and political classes emerging from the economic conditions of industrial production would alone seem applicable.

There is some evidence in political reality as well as in social
research that this kind of division into two classes is still a fact in
most European countries. In the political systems of Europe, the
vis-à-vis of conservative and socialist, that is managerial and
labor, parties has become almost universal, at the expense largely
of the liberal parties of an earlier period of political history.
Moreover, studies in several countries have shown that what the
Polish sociologist S. Ossowski called "la vision dichotomique de la
stratification sociale" is still very widespread in Europe, and more
particularly among those who think of themselves as being placed
"below." [3]

But, of course, parliamentary disputes between conservatives
and socialists are rather unlike a revolutionary class war, and the
dichotomous view of society bears little similarity to the increasingly hostile class consciousness envisaged by Marx, to say noth-

[2] If there is any criticism of this essay which I should find it hard to defend
myself against, it would be that I have left the notion of European societies
as vague as it is in everyday language. Throughout, I am referring to western
Europe. Most of the materials used are German, French, and British; only
occasionally are Scandinavian, Belgian, Dutch, Italian, and Swiss data introduced. Some other countries of western Europe are referred to in passing.
Foolhardy as it may be, I shall nevertheless claim that the conclusions presented in this essay apply to most of the countries of western Europe.
[3] See Ralf Dahrendorf, *Class and Class Conflict in Industrial Society* (Stanford-London, 1959); R. Hoggart, *The Uses of Literacy* (London, 1957); S.
Ossowski, "La Vision dichotomique de la stratification sociale," *Cahiers
Internationaux de Sociologie*, XX (1955); H. Popitz, *et al., Das Gesellschaftsbild
des Arbeiters* (Tübingen, 1957), and "Zum Begriff des Klassengesellschaft,"
Hamburger Jahrbuch für Wirtschafts und Gesellschaftspolitik, Vol. III (1958).

ing of the fact that "conservative" and "socialist" are labels that require much closer inspection, and that by no means all of those interviewed by sociologists displayed a dichotomous image of their social environment. Generally speaking, the Marxian notion of a society split into two antagonistic classes growing out of the property structure of the economy is no longer a correct description of European reality. The European Nightmare has become as old-fashioned as the American Dream. Perhaps the European and American societies have grown closer together; in any case, a new type of class structure is emerging in Europe which differs in many respects from the old.

THE SOCIAL MIRACLE

It is often not realized that in 1913 there was hardly a country in Europe in which suffrage extended to more than twenty-five percent of the population, but many in which (if they had popular elections at all) fewer were entitled to vote, for example, in Great Britain (seventeen percent).[4] Of those who had the right to vote, only a portion actually did, so that the conclusion is borne out by the evidence that, before World War I, only between ten and fifteen percent of the population of Europe had a realistic chance to take part at all in the political life of their countries. Moreover, this state of affairs was a recent achievement at the time. If we go back another thirty years, Italy is by no means untypical, with suffrage extending to two percent of the population, and only half of these actually going to the polls. Even in Britain, often described as the classical instance of modern representative government, barely four percent of the population took part in national elections before the reforms of 1885. Curious as it may seem, in terms of suffrage, the German Empire was among the most progressive countries of Europe at this time.

... While the ideas of the French Revolution and the half-

[4] The main problem of these figures is in the fact that the percentages are calculated on the basis of total populations, that is, including children, so that different demographic structures of countries must necessarily result in different percentages. However, this shortcoming cannot, in my opinion, destroy the interest of this type of analysis.

hearted measures of 1848 may have given to the extension of citizenship rights to all persons their pathos and much of their impetus, it was not until a century later—and, possibly, in large measure due to the effect of the intellectual and political force of socialism—that for the majority of Europeans, these rights acquired reality.

"One man, one vote" has become a powerful slogan for all the underprivileged peoples of the world. But the slogan, as our reference to the development of suffrage and political participation, points to a symptom of the development of equality of citizenship rights rather than to its entire substance. Citizenship is the social institution of the notion that all men are born equal. Its establishment requires changes in virtually every sphere of social structure. Apart from universal suffrage, equality before the law is as much part of this process as is universal education, protection from unemployment, injury and sickness, and care for the old. Representative government, the rule of law, and the welfare state are in fact the three conditions of what I should describe as the social miracle of the emergence of the many to the light of full social and political participation. For it is a startling fact, peculiar to modern societies, that in certain important respects everybody counts for as much as everybody else; and while one hesitates to use the notion of progress in our time not only because of its naive abuse in the late nineteenth century, but above all in the face of Auschwitz and Buchenwald, the conclusion is forced upon us that in recent decades most European societies have experienced tremendous progress in the effective realization of basic equality for all citizens.

This is not to say, of course, that social differences, including differences of class, have ceased to matter. For one thing, the social miracle has not by any means reached every part of Europe yet. Once again we have to remember the great national and regional differences within Europe (which, from this point of view, coincide fairly accurately with the North-South slope). Secondly, one is almost irresponsibly overstating the case if one asserts that the social miracle of generalizing equality of citizenship rights has already occurred. In every country of Europe—indeed, in every country of the world—these rights are still restricted by traditional dependencies, social and even legal barriers, and new differentials of social position. For this is the third and most important comment to be added to the general thesis of this section, that citizenship does not abolish differences of class.[5] There are certainly fundamental differences between the slave, the vassal, the subject, and the citizen, but even the citizen cannot do away with the realities of power. In fact, Orwell's bitter dictum might almost be taken as a serious description of social reality everywhere: in a society of citizens all men are equal; but it remains a stubborn fact that some are more equal than others, that is to say, that some occupy positions which enable them to lay down the law for their "equals." The extension of citizenship in European societies has certainly changed the basis and the ramification of the old dichotomous structure of class; but a new class structure has emerged on their new basis.

THE ECONOMIC MIRACLE

There is one change in the social face of Europe after World War II which cannot escape even the passing traveler from abroad, and which is itself the source of many other transformations: namely, Europe's economic development. More appropriately, this development must be described as an explosion or—with a term originally applied to the Federal Republic of Germany, but often extended to other countries now—a miracle. Once again, I am not using the word "miracle" to indicate that it would be impossible to explain this development; I am using it rather in a figurative sense to emphasize the almost incredible order of magnitude involved. . . .

Through the social miracle people have become citizens with a definite set of rights in which they are equal to all others. But it may be surmised that this development would have remained rather abstract and unreal had it not been followed by the economic miracle. Higher incomes and shorter working hours enable more and more people to make effective use of their citizenship

[5] T. H. Marshall, *Citizenship and Social Class* (Cambridge, Mass., 1950).

rights. More, they place in the reach of many the chance of a life of which their grandfathers would hardly have dared to dream. It is not surprising that under these conditions old ideologies of class are increasingly losing their grip on people, and new and more complicated structures are emerging.

CHANGES IN THE STRUCTURE OF POWER

But class is about power. While social and economic status affect the relations of power, these have their own peculiar characteristics and laws of development. By power, we shall mean what John Locke meant when he said: "Power, then, I take to be a right of making laws with penalties of death, and consequently all less penalties, . . . and of employing the force of the community in the execution of such laws, and in the defense of the commonwealth from foreign injury." [6] To try a somewhat more modern formulation: power is the right to make laws, that is, norms binding upon those subject to them by virtue of the sanctions attached to them, as well as the right to execute these laws and to enforce the sanctions. This "making" of laws thus involves all three of the classical branches of government.

Regarding the structure of classes in contemporary Europe, four trends in the recent history of power require our attention. The first of these is closely related to the advancement of citizenship in the last half-century. It is the transformation (in Max Weber's terms) of *Macht* into *Herrschaft*, that is, of personal power into institutional power.[7] Strictly speaking, personal power does not come under Locke's definition. It is not a right, but simply a capacity to make others do what one wants them to do. The relation of dependence constituted by personal power is tied to the individuals involved; thus, in a sense, it is not a social relation at all. Yet there have been such relations of personal power throughout history. Where they have taken the form of

[6] John Locke, *Second Treatise of Civil Government* (Chicago, 1955, new ed.).
[7] Unfortunately, terminology is not settled here in English. Numerous concepts—power, authority, rule, domination, dominion, imperative coordination, and others—compete, so that it seemed wisest to me to express the trend in question by adjectives.

"charismatic rule" they have involved not two but hundreds and often thousands of people; perhaps there is an element of personal power in the genesis of every form of institutional power. However, there is a general trend in politics as well as in all other social organizations today to reduce the unbounded potentialities of control inherent in personal power to power vested in positions and incumbent on persons only for the duration of their occupancy of such positions. (As a consequence, the claim to charismatic rule becomes increasingly unlikely in modern social organizations.[8] At no time could the powerful really "do what they want"—as many would have it—although this notion is akin to that of personal power; but in modern Europe, their radius of action is much more limited still by the comparative neutrality of power exercised only within well-defined roles associated with social positions.

This domestication of power would of course not be very effective if it were not coupled with the development of mechanisms to control the exercise of power more effectively than can be done by unchanneled expressions of protest or agreement. The generalization of the "rule of law" is the second relevant trend in our context. Hobbes had, if not logic, then at least probability on his side when he claimed that the sovereign is exempted from the laws which, after all, he himself has a right to make. In actual fact, it can still be demonstrated by many instances that the law— that is, those who execute and enforce it—tends to become more lenient with people as they occupy positions closer to the source of the law. Prime ministers are unlikely to get tickets for speeding. At the same time, Laski was right in observing that the very paradox of the sovereign—the legislative, executive, and judicative—who is subject to his own law has come true in modern societies. The courts are open to all; and that means that everybody can find himself on either side of their disputes.[9] Possibly, the rule of law is only part of a syndrome of control to which elec-

[8] Weber himself has often discussed the mutual exclusiveness of charisma and bureaucracy. However, I am here using Weber's so-called "types of power" in a rather different sense than was intended by Weber.
[9] See Th. Hobbes, *Leviathan*, new ed. (London-New York, 1934); and H. Laski, *Grammar of Politics*, rev. ed. (London-New Haven, 1934).

tions, parliaments, a free press, and other institutions of modern representative government also belong. In any case, the extension of these controls to most—though not all—European countries has changed the nature of class and class conflict profoundly.

A third modern development of power, although no less significant, is of a somewhat different kind. There are several reasons why, in the phase of industrialization, economic and political power tend to coincide in the sense of being held by the same group. In nineteenth-century Europe, industrialization created huge instruments of power in a sphere of life where many people had to spend almost the whole of their waking life, and at a time when the influence of the state was largely restricted to the tasks prescribed by Locke, that is, to "the regulating and preserving of property." Thus, the economically powerful tended to be all-powerful by the same token, and of course vice versa. Industrialization in the twentieth century is invariably the result of vigorous and direct action by the state. Thus, the politically powerful tend to be all-powerful, and vice versa. However, insofar as European societies have passed through this first stage of industrialization—whichever of the two forms intimated here it may have taken—neither of these coincidences holds true any more. Instead, everywhere there is a large, relatively independent machinery of political administration; and those who have power in other institutions, whether economic organizations, churches, universities, trade unions or women's clubs, act as influence groups in the penumbra of political decision-making. Clearly, some of these influence groups are able to exert more pressure than others. This is true notably for the military and for the leaders of industry and labor; but none of these is exclusive in a world in which people's lives are no longer confined to one and only one sphere of organization.[10]

I have described the machinery of political administration as being large and relatively independent. In fact, the fourth important trend in the nature of power in European societies today is

[10] Few theses of my book on *Class and Class Conflict in Industrial Society* (Stanford-London, 1959) have been more widely criticized than that of the "institutional isolation of industry and industrial conflict" in the modern world (pp. 267 ff.). Perhaps the preceding formulations can help to clarify this discussion.

the seemingly ever increasing division of labor in the business of making, enforcing, and executing laws. Where a comparatively small—and thus easily identifiable—group of people controlled the classical branches of public and private governments a century or even half a century ago, numerous positions of partial power have since come into being, many of them so apparently subordinate that it is hard to discover their relation to the exercise of power. The analogy to the division of labor is striking: in the exercise of power, too, one process has been subdivided into so many contributing part-processes that it is hard to discover the whole in any one of its individual parts. Just as in a modern shoe factory it is hard to answer the question, "Who makes the shoes?" it is hard to tell who, in the bureaucratic administration of a modern enterprise, church, trade union, or state, holds the reins and in this sense has the power.

This last observation is indeed the main source of an interpretation of society which is today almost equally widespread among sociologists and ordinary citizens. In a word, this interpretation amounts to saying that the peoples of Europe have once again turned into "tribes without rulers." Since it is hard to localize power, power itself has disappeared. There is no longer a ruling class but only a market of veto groups, or the reduction of power to administration, or the transformation of power over men into power over things, or simply the power of the law. This of course is also David Riesman's conclusion with respect to the United States.[11] But, in one form or the other, a number of European scholars have followed Riesman or advanced similar interpretations on different grounds—although it is a striking fact that these are more numerous on the continent than in England, and, again, more numerous in German-speaking countries than in all others.[12] I shall try to show that the alleged disappearance of power is as much of a myth as its opposite, the tightly-knit, conspiratorial "power elite" *à la* Mills.[13] But if there is any conclusion to be drawn already from this cursory analysis of some trends

[11] David Riesman, *The Lonely Crowd* (New Haven, 1950).
[12] H. Schelsky, "Die Bedeutung des Klassenbegriffes für die Analyse unserer Gesellschaft," *Jahrbuch für Sozialwissenschaft,* XII (1961), p. 3.
[13] C. W. Mills, *The Power Elite* (New York, 1956).

which have changed the structure of class in many European societies, it is that this structure has become rather more complicated today than it was as described by Marx and seen by many people throughout much of the last century. Class in Europe is no longer a matter of the antagonism of a small group of all-powerful rulers and a large mass of powerless subjects. Indeed, Europe can no longer be properly described as a "fairly rigid class society."

But these remarks can do little more than set the stage. Let us turn, therefore, to the principal characters in the new drama of class and power.

II THE CLASSES IN PERSPECTIVE

THE RULING GROUPS

Upon closer inspection, even Africa's "tribes without rulers" turn out to recognize some positions of power.[14] It would be very surprising indeed if this were different in contemporary Europe. As a matter of fact, our definition of power makes it quite clear where to look for the rulers; they are evidently those who have a say in the making, carrying out and enforcing of laws. For the purpose of the present analysis, I should like to restrict the definition of the ruling groups even further to those who, above all others, participate in making laws, and in making those laws which concern every citizen as such.[15] Probably no more than about two thousand people in any given European society can be described as belonging to these groups. Among these, the following categories may be distinguished. (It must be understood that these distinctions are introduced purely for purposes of identification and are not meant to indicate lines of cleavage within the power elite.)

a. Incumbents of formal political positions of political power; that is, members of both houses of parliament, cabinet ministers, other ministers, undersecretaries of state (or their equivalent) insofar as their position is regarded as "political" in the sense that they are tied to a given government.

14 D. Middleton and D. Tait, *Tribes Without Rulers* (London, 1958).
15 *Berichte aus dem Soziologischen Seminar der Universität Tübingen* I (1963).

b. Incumbents of formal administrative positions of political power, including the highest civil servants as well as generals, diplomats, and judges of the Supreme Court (or its equivalent).

c. Incumbents of other positions of political power.

d. Incumbents of positions of political influence.

What is the social origin, what is the recruitment of the ruling groups of contemporary European societies? If there is any general answer to this question, one of three first posed by Raymond Aron it would resemble the heading of a section of one of M. Dogan's studies of the French political elite: "from the republic of dukes to the reign of the middle class and lower-middle class." [16] Not all European countries are of course republics, and from the evidence we have there is some doubt as to the importance of the lower middle class as a reservoir of the ruling groups in our restricted sense, but the general trend observed by Dogan is certainly confirmed by studies in many countries. Throughout the last decades, there has been an increasing trend for the upper two thousand to be recruited from fathers in professional and commercial occupations rather than from the older agricultural and often aristocratic groups.[17]

. . . In other words, the recruiting ground for the ruling groups of today is what we shall call the service class.

Which are the qualities that seem to assure success, and what are the modalities of the career? The transition from upper-class to "middle-class" origin—the answer to Aron's second question—would seem to imply a transition from ascribed to achieved status as the basis of personal success. For instance, the proportion of "dukes" with hereditary privileges has declined fairly consistently in the political elites of all European countries. Apart from the occasional "cabinet of barons" (Hitler's first cabinet in 1933),

---

16 M. Dogan, "Political Ascent in a Class Society: French Deputies 1870–1958," in D. Marvick, ed., *Political Decision-Makers* (Glencoe, 1961).

17 Since D. R. Matthews published his little booklet on *The Social Background of Political Decision-Makers* (Garden City, 1954), there has been an ever increasing number of studies of this subject. At the same time, the question has rarely been asked what precisely these studies tell us. Thus we really know very little about the ways in which social background determines political behavior.

and of the permanently renewed peerage of Britain, aristocratic origin does not seem an advantage to speak of in the top power positions of Europe today. Once again, incumbents of formal administrative positions of political power are the most conservative group in these terms.[18]

This also holds for a new type of ascriptive status less easily recognizable but equally effective: self-recruitment. In Germany, seven percent of all judges are the sons of judges, eight percent of all professors the sons of professors, very nearly one third of all higher civil servants are the sons of higher civil servants.[19] Girard's study in France confirms this conclusion, and Guttsman found in Britain that there is a considerable number of what he calls "political families" where political activity is inherited (although their number is apparently rather smaller among non-aristocrats than among aristocrats).[20] Without doubt, the degree of self-recruitment varies from country to country as well as in the different segments of the power elite. It is not likely to be as great among members of parliament as it is among generals or diplomats. But self-recruitment—that is, the invisible hand of the family—certainly plays an even larger part in the careers of top people than it does in society in general.[21]

However, emphasizing this point should not make us overlook the fact that an increasing proportion of the members of Europe's ruling groups acquire their position by their own achievement, and that generally means by education. Nowadays, the road to the top almost invariably leads through a successful university

18 See: G. D. H. Cole, *Studies in Class Structure* (London, 1955); M. Dogan article in D. Marvick, ed., *op. cit.;* and W. Zapf, in *Berichte aus dem Soziologischen Seminar der Universität Tübingen* I (1963).
19 Ralf Dahrendorf, "Deutsche Richter. Ein Betrag zur Soziologie der Oberschicht," *Gesellschaft und Freiheit* (München, 1961).
20 See: A. Girard, *La Réussite sociale en France* (Paris, 1961); D. V. Glass, *Social Mobility in Britain* (London, 1954); and B. Gleitze, *Wirtschafts- und Sozialstatistiches Handbuch* (Köln, 1960). Also see W. L. Guttsman, "The Changing Social Structure of the British Political Elite, 1886–1935," *British Journal of Sociology* LI/2 (1951).
21 All mobility studies since D. V. Glass's *Social Mobility in Britain* confirm the conclusion that throughout society (with the deceptive exception of peasants, in whose case only one son can succeed his father) the most likely status of sons is that of their fathers.

career, or at least a secondary education. Of a sample of 250 members of the ruling groups in Germany in 1955, a mere 14 percent had received primary education only, and 23 percent either primary or secondary education, all others having at least started university studies.[22] Of the much larger sample studied by Girard in France, 5.1 percent had received primary education only, 10.4 percent secondary education, and no less than 84.5 percent a "higher education." [23] In England, a university education is socially regarded as rather less important, but here too "the rise of the meritocracy"—as M. Young, an English sociologist, has called it—is unmistakable.[24] The school is replacing the family as an avenue to the top.

To understand the modalities of the career of top people, reference to the importance of a "good" or higher education is, however, too general to be of real interest. The important question is: is there any particular kind of education which helps the ambitious to make a success of their careers? While there is no type of education which guarantees entry to the upper reaches of the power structure anywhere in Europe, there are two types of institution which—with varying weight in the various countries of Europe—make success very probable, to say the least. One of these consists in especially prestigious schools, of which the English Public Schools are perhaps the outstanding example. . . . But the real continental equivalent to the Public School as an avenue to power is the study of law. . . .

What is the coherence, what is the consciousness of solidarity among the members of this category? Several years ago, the English weekly *Spectator* started a discussion about the question of whether Britain is ruled by a small Establishment—a coherent set of powerful people—or not. If I am not mistaken, most English intellectuals seem inclined to believe in the reality of the Establishment and thus to subscribe to a variant of the conspiracy the-

[22] W. Zapf, *op. cit.*
[23] A. Girard, *op. cit.*; D. V. Glass, *op. cit.*; and B. Gleitze, *op. cit.*
[24] G. D. H. Cole, *op. cit.*; and M. Young, *The Rise of the Meritocracy* (London, 1958).

ory of society according to which a few invisible hands pull all the strings and monopolize the roads to power. The outside observer, on the contrary, is inclined to regard the very discussion of the Establishment as a symptom of the dissolution of the old upper class of British society. Yet it remains probable that the two thousand people with whom we are here concerned are a more coherent and solid social category in Britain than in most other European countries. Many of them have attended the same, or the same kind of, school and university; many of them belong to the same clubs, follow the same pastimes, meet and talk regularly, and feel part of the same "set." In this sense, the ruling groups of Britain do in fact tend to what might be called the "established" type.

Near the other end of the scale, we have the German case. The ruling groups of West Germany today are an almost perfect example of the "abstract" type: their unity exists nowhere except in the minds of some social analysts. In actual fact they are a highly heterogeneous and heteromorphous category. A career characteristic of a member of an established elite which leads him successively to being a university professor, director-owner of an investment trust, brigadier general and cabinet minister, and who may yet become an ambassador or director-general of the BBC, would be unthinkable in Germany, where every one of these "estates" has its own standards, interests and, above all, well-guarded boundaries. It is for this type of elite that the plural "ruling groups" is particularly appropriate, for ruling classes of this kind consist in fact of a plurality of competing and often hostile groups, the members of which are separated by great social distance.

In summarizing the evidence presented in this section, I would contend that the abstract type of elite, in Europe, constitutes the ruling class of the future. There are of course still remnants of the established elites of pre-industrial Europe, especially in countries like Spain or Portugal. There are also new kinds of establishment brought about, for example, by similar educational biographies (the "meritocracy"). But by and large, there is the indication that the ruling groups of the majority of countries in Europe really form coherent classes. They are anxious rulers, divided among themselves, uncertain of their position, and too hard-working to enjoy its rewards. In many ways, they have become indistinguishable from those one or two or three steps below them on the ladder of success, the service class.

THE SERVICE CLASS

To a generation of politically minded social scientists whose image of modern society and its development was almost invariably painted in Marxian colors, the most striking development of this century was the emergence of the "new middle class." This was the name given by E. Lederer and J. Marschak—the first to study this development extensively in the early 1920's—to the new occupations whose names are as numerous as the group involved is many-faceted and hard to describe: clerks, black-coated workers, salary earners, white-collar workers, employees, and their brothers and sisters in many other languages. The emergence of this group was, and continues to be, disturbing to all those who believed that the polarization of classes predicted by Marx was bound to occur. . . .

Let us take a set of occupations usually described as belonging to the "new middle class" say; postman, bank clerk, senior civil servant, shop assistant, secretary general of a football club, waiter, tax official, chauffeur. I suggest that in terms of their relation to the exercise of power these occupations fall easily into two categories. There are, on the one hand, those jobs which might be more properly described as "new working class" (if this term was not generally used in a different context, as later in this essay), that is, the purely subordinate positions in the vastly expanding new industries of the tertiary sector of the economy. In this group belong the shop assistant as well as the waiter, but also the older service occupations of chauffeur and postman; the proportion of women in it is especially large. All these people may receive salaries; they may be insured as *Angestellte* (or, in the case of the postman, even *Beamte*); they may not regard themselves as workers; but they are in fact in no way part of the power structure of their occupational contexts except as subordinates. In terms of power at least, their position is the precise equivalent of that of workers in the secondary sectors of employment.

On the other hand, the bank clerk, the senior civil servant, the secretary general of a football club and the tax official, as well as the army of public and private bureaucrats, may not strike one as a power elite if one compares them with the kings and nobles of the Middle Ages or even the ruling groups of today; but in some peculiar, though definable way they do in fact take part in the exercise of power. This is the group with which we are here concerned, and although these terms do not cover all of them, we may describe its members for the time being as bureaucrats, or, more generally, as administrators. . . .

. . . I should suggest that only about one third of all *Angestellte* in Germany, or roughly eight percent of the employed population, can be described as bureaucrats, so that the group under discussion would comprise about twelve percent of the gainfully employed in the Federal Republic. Considering general similarities in occupational structure, this figure can at least indicate the approximate size of the group elsewhere in Europe as well.[25]

But of course, even this twelve percent is an obviously heterogeneous category. It includes the foreman as well as the managing director, the junior official behind the counter as well as the permanent undersecretary. Is it not rather nonsensical to include in one class the numerous ranks characteristic of every hierarchy? The skeptical question is understandable. Indeed the foreman and the managing director would probably both deny that they are members of the same class. Yet here I should insist that it does make sense to lump them together. The top of the ladder may be far removed from its bottom—this is certainly true for modern bureaucratic hierarchies—but in terms of the exercise of power it is more significant that top and bottom are both steps on the same ladder. More precisely, the hierarchical internal structure of the category under discussion is in itself its primary characteristic. . . .

Despite some claims to the contrary by its members, the economic miracle has of course not bypassed this class, whose members in the past could often be characterized by the combination

[25] [British] General Register Office: *One Per Cent Sample Tables* [1951 Census]; [British] General Register Office: *Classification of Occupations 1950;* and see also G. D. H. Cole, *op. cit.*

of poverty and status ambition.[26] They can no longer be described as a "proletariat"; nor is the clerical worker who foregoes the necessities of life for the sake of the appearances of status a reality any more. This conclusion is clearly borne out by studies of white-collar consumption patterns in several countries.[27]

At the same time, prosperity has not diminished the preoccupation of the service class with matters of prestige and status. . . .

As far as the social origin of the members of the service class is concerned, Bolte has compared a number of (largely German) studies. His main conclusion is that since World War I the proportion of clerical workers recruited from the "old middle class" of independent businessmen and craftsmen has decreased (from over 50 percent to less than 25 percent), that of working-class origin has increased (from 20–25 percent to 30–35 percent), but the bulk of the service class is recruited today from service-class families (40–45 percent).[28] It may be assumed that the latter figure hides a great deal of upward mobility within the ranks of bureaucracy, for the general conclusion seems indicated that social mobility in contemporary Europe often requires in the first place that some member of a family get his foot on a rung of the ladder of service, and that more than half of the members of this group in most countries of Europe today have risen socially. If any class bears witness to the comparative openness of European societies, it is the service class.

At this point, the last and most difficult question about the service class must be raised: what is its political orientation? If our analysis is correct, we should expect its members to be somewhat conservative in orientation, and to support the parties of the moderate right.[29] There are no survey figures of the social strat-

26 Th. Geiger, *Die soziale Schichtung des deutschen Volkes* (Stuttgart, 1932).
27 K. M. Bolte, "Angestellenfrage," in H. Bayer, ed., *Der Angestellte zwischen Arbeiterschaft und Management* (Berlin, 1961); and F. Croner, *Sociologie der Angestellten* (Köln-Berlin, 1962).
28 K. M. Bolte, *op. cit.*
29 See: J. Bonham, *The Middle Class Vote* (London, 1956); Ralf Dahrendorf, "Demokratie und Sozialstruktur in Deutschland," *Gesellschaft und Freiheit* (München, 1961); E. Faul, *Wahlen und Wähler in Westdeutschland* (Villingen, 1961); Th. Geiger, *op. cit.;* W. Hirsch-Weber and K. Schütz, *Wähler und*

ification of the electorate of different parties in the 1920's. But on external evidence it seems likely that the "new middle class" was one of the main sources of support for the Nazis, and possibly for the Italian Fascists too.[30] On the other hand, membership in labor unions, or indeed radicalism of the left, is rare among bureaucrats, if we except their own estatelike organizations and interesting, but isolated, instances like the French teachers. Thus there appears to be a general trend to the right in the political orientation of the service class; but dependent on the national context, this trend takes the form of supporting either moderate conservatives or authoritarian extremists.

Quite a few explanations of the apparent political unreliability of the "new middle class" have been offered in the literature. Some of these are at least implied by our discussion of the role and status of the administrator. But the question to which such explanations invariably return is: is it a class, that category of bureaucrats and administrators, or is it not?

Among the groups discussed in this essay, the one under review in this section is the only one which I have described as a "class" in the title of the section. At the risk of appearing extremely confused as well as confusing, I now wish to offer the conclusion that of our four groups, the service class is in fact the one which is quite clearly not a class in any terminologically strict sense. In terms of social position, this is so since this group must be described as an appendage of the ruling groups. In one possible usage of the term "class," ruling groups plus service "class" might be called the ruling class of a society. In terms of the social characteristics of the service class, there is one further fact to be considered. Class involves a certain amount of class consciousness and political solidarity, if the term is to make any sense at all. The members of the service class, however, are, in Crozier's words, a "classe sans conscience."[31] Instead of feeling cohesive, they all

---

Gewählte [Berlin, 1957]; and S. M. Lipset, "Fascism—Left, Right, and Center," *Political Man* (Garden City, 1960).

[30] By "external evidence" I mean here the analysis of election figures, coupled with plausible assumptions about the social sources of support of various parties.

[31] M. Crozier, "Classes sans conscience," *European Journal of Sociology* I/2 (1960).

stand in a relation of individual competition to each other. Of course, not every bureaucrat competes with every other one. In fact, Bahrdt has shown that even that minimum of communication which is a prerequisite of competition is generally missing along the horizontal line of bureaucratic organizations.[32] But for the bureaucrat, advancing his status is essentially an individual achievement. He has little to hope from collective action which would leave his status exactly where it was in relation to those with whom he compares himself, that is, to all others who have stepped on at least the first rung of the ladder of service. In the service class, individual competition takes the place of collective solidarity. But individual competition is a strenuous and, at times, an ugly type of behavior, especially if it pervades the entire life of a person. Even on general psychological grounds, it may seem likely that a price has to be paid for this kind of life—a price which may be private and make the person mentally or physically ill, but which under certain historical conditions may also become public and lead him to support a romantic movement of "community" (*Gemeinschaft*), of which fascism is a prototype in the modern world.

THE RULED GROUPS

In all society no boundary is probably more cruelly felt by those involved than the one between those who stand just above and those just below the line dividing power from impotence.[33] . . .

But the actualities of class conflict are nowadays determined less by the clear line that divides rulers and ruled than by the blurring of the lines between people of differing social status. In other words, there is many a compensation for those who are excluded from the exercise of power in contemporary European society. While those "below" may still feel the superiority of the policeman and other petty officials who can push them around, there are spheres of life where they are and feel equal to at least many of those in power, or where distinctions of power do not seem to matter at all. The dichotomous image of society is still

[32] H. P. Bahrdt, *Industriebürokratie* (Stuttgart, 1958).
[33] Th. Geiger, *op. cit.*

there, but it is no longer an image of resentment and boundless hostility toward "them." The studies by Popitz and Willener confirm other observations in their finding that even among industrial workers in most European countries, only a dwindling minority adheres to a Marxian view of a revolutionary class struggle.[34] ...

Throughout this survey of social classes in Europe, we found "groups" which have the same relation to the structure of power to be in fact highly heterogeneous aggregates of competing individuals and groups. This is no less true for the ruled groups than for the rulers and their servants. In this section, we are concerned with about eighty-five percent of the people of Europe. Even the crudest of distinctions has to recognize among these three vastly different social categories: (1) the "old middle class" of small independent craftsmen, shopkeepers, and—above all—peasants; (2) those parts of the "new middle class" which we have not included, on account of their power position, in the service class; and (3) the working class. What has been said so far in this section was meant to apply to all these groups, if perhaps in varying degrees. But even if we stick strictly to our main line of argument, some of the striking peculiarities of these groups, and their own subgroups, cannot be left unmentioned.

It was of course the "old middle class" which Marx had in mind when he predicted the polarization of society into two classes. To the present day it has remained a nice topic of argument among Marxists and Marxians, whether this prediction has come true or not. In statistical fact, the proportion of self-employed people is between about fifteen percent and twenty-five percent in all European countries—with the single exception of Britain, the country which provided Marx with most of his data, where only about seven percent are now self-employed. The larg-

---

[34] Ralf Dahrendorf, *Class and Class Conflict in Industrial Society* (Stanford-London, 1959); also see S. Ossowski, *op. cit.*; H. Popitz, *et al.*, *Das Gesellschaftsbild des Arbeiters* (Tübingen, 1957), and "Zum Begriff des Klassengesellschaft," *Hamburger Jahrbuch für Wirtschafts und Gesellschaftspolitik*, Vol. III (1958); A. Willener, *Images de la société et classes sociales* [Bern, 1957).

est single bloc within this census category is in most countries that of the peasants. But here again, variations are great. In Italy, Portugal, Spain, Austria, and France, agriculture is still the largest of eight standard categories of employment, whereas in Belgium and Holland it comes third, in Britain sixth (and, for comparison, in the United States, fourth).[35] Generally speaking, sociologists have not paid as much attention to these groups as to the elites, industrial workers and the "new middle class." In the more highly industrialized countries, such as Britain, Holland, Belgium, Germany, and to a lesser extent the Scandinavian countries, there is some evidence that the attitudes described there as characteristic of the service class have reached the countryside as well.[36] But for France, Italy, Austria, Spain, and countries with similar proportions of peasants and agricultural workers, our conclusions must be taken with more than one grain of salt, and point at best to possible trends of the future.[37]

As far as that larger part of the "new middle class" is concerned which we have left aside so far, our general conclusion can be adopted with much greater confidence. Despite the almost meaningless generality of the term "new middle class," most studies of the subject do not distinguish between its bureaucratic and its purely subordinate components, so that many of the results discussed above apply to both these groups. What we have called the political unreliability of the service class probably holds *a fortiori* for the non-bureaucratic sections of the "new middle class"; for here we find a clear contradiction between the work situation of subordination, the status of low income and prestige, and the de-

[35] For figures, I have used here the appendix "Internationale Übersichten" to *Statistisches Jahrbuch für die Bundesrepublik Deutschland 1958* (Stuttgart, 1958), T.C. 2. The eight standard categories are: agriculture and fishing; mining and quarrying; manufacturing industries; building; electricity, gas and water; commerce; communications and transport; service occupations.

[36] *Current Sociology:* "Rural Sociology," VI/1 (1957).

[37] At this point I have to confess ignorance. Evidently the shortlived Poujade movement, or the so dramatically abolished original electoral law of the French Fifth Republic with an electoral college consisting of the "70,000 mayors," document the importance of the old middle class in France. Similar observations have been made in other countries. To explain these and other relevant phenomena, one has to be more familiar with this problem than I can claim to be.

scription as *Angestellter, salarié,* white collar, and, therefore, middle class. If there is any reason to qualify this conclusion, it is in the fact that these are also the occupational groups among which the proportion of women is largest. The statistical data gathered by Bolte and Croner suggest that about one half of the people in the category in question here are women.[38] To the present day, however, the social status and the class position of women are not as "serious" as that of men. For the unmarried woman's social status, her father's occupation is as important as her own, and in the case of married women the same is true for their husbands.

Even today the largest section of the ruled groups of European societies consists of the industrial *working class.* Moreover, it is the changes in the position and in the outlook of industrial workers that has occupied European sociologists above all. In Europe, sociology grew up as the study of working-class life and as late as the 1920's there was an element of truth in the naive identification of "sociology" and "socialism." Insofar as this is true, the discovery of the "new working class," that is, of industrial workers who no longer conformed to the radical expectations of the intellectual socialists of the 1920's and 1930's, came as something of a shock to social scientists. There are numerous studies in the post-war period which may be understood as an attempt on the part of their authors to explain to themselves what they regarded as the sudden advance of the *embourgeoisement* of the working class.[39]

Our thesis in this essay is not that the economic miracle has by itself converted class-conscious workers into bourgeois conservatives. We have placed great emphasis on the social miracle and on changes in the structure of power which may be of much greater

---

[38] Bolte, *op. cit.;* and Croner, *op. cit.*

[39] European sociology after World War II started with a large number of studies in industrial sociology. Most of these were devoted to the working class and betray the disappointment on the part of their authors with this class. If M. Stein could write a highly perceptive history of American sociology under the title of *The Eclipse of Community,* "the eclipse of the working class" might be an appropriate analogue for Europe.

importance than a decade of prosperity. Above all, the crucial change in attitude seems to me to lie in the fact that feelings of solidarity and of the desirability of collective action have given way, for many workers, to the desire to advance their position individually. For the individual, this means piecework earnings and "moonlighting," but also evening courses and the wish to be promoted; for his family, mobility by education becomes increasingly important (although, in this respect, the North-South slope is once again unmistakable in Europe). But we cannot conclude this section without referring to Lockwood's rather skeptical analysis of the "new working class." [40] To aspire to the values of those "above," to display these values credibly, and to be accepted as one of "them" are certainly three very different things, of which the last at least is still a distant dream. Despite all changes in their social position and attitudes, the ruled groups remain such, and many of their members realize this fact and behave accordingly.

THE INTELLECTUALS

No discussion of class is complete without referring at least in passing to the intellectuals. The very fact that they are hard to place in the structure of power (to say nothing of an additional fact that the analyst himself is usually one of them) adds to their interest. When K. Mannheim and A. Weber described intellectuals as "free-floating," they had two features of their social position in mind.[41] One of these relates to their social biography: intellectuals have often undergone a series of breaks with the groups to which they belonged. The other aspect concerns their actual position: intellectuals are neither rulers nor ruled nor, of course, servants. At least, it is under these conditions that they display that mixture of belonging and estrangement which may be the prerequisite of the critical task often ascribed to them. All this would not be true for "intellectuals" or the "intelligentsia" in the com-

[40] D. Lockwood, "The 'New Working Class,'" *European Journal of Sociology* I/2 (1960).
[41] Th. Geiger, *Aufgaben und Stellung der Intelligenz in der Gesellschaft* (Stuttgart, 1949).

prehensive French or Russian sense, which makes this group almost coextensive with white collar, and certainly with professional people. But if we use some notion like Lipset's, according
to which intellectuals are those who "create, distribute, and apply
culture," the above description would apply.[42] The position and
attitude of intellectuals in this sense are indicative of the class
structure of a society in that they betray its rigidity or looseness,
its stability or explosiveness, and often its neuralgic points.

At the risk of seeming unduly insistent on one point, the first
observation to be stressed about the position of intellectuals in
Europe today is that they are often no longer as "free-floating" as
the celebrated model of their social existence would have it. With
the generalization of social mobility by education, specialist
knowledge is no longer the prerogative of any one group, and
breaking with one's primary group has become an almost normal
feature in the social biographies of rulers and their servants. As
far as occupational position is concerned, almost all intellectuals
in Europe are striving for a secure position in some organization
or other, and on the whole they are doing so successfully. If we
look at the positions they occupy, many of them resemble closely
those of the upper reaches of the service class: the university lec-
turer, the newspaper editor, the manager responsible for job-
training in an enterprise, the government-employed town plan-
ner, etc. In many organizations, the distinction between "staff"
and "line" may give the intellectual rather more independence
than those along the line can enjoy; but this distinction is not, in
reality, always as clear as organizational charts would have it.
Thus, many intellectuals all over Europe have not only come to
resemble the service class in their profession and general outlook,
but they have become members of this class (or, rather, non-
class), that is, individuals competing with others for a place in the
sun.[43]

[42] S. M. Lipset, "American Intellectuals: Their Politics and Status," *Political
Man* (Garden City, 1960).
[43] V. Deneke, *Die frien Berufe* (Stuttgart, 1956); and R. Lewis and A. Maude,
Professional People (London, 1952).

III TOWARD THE SERVICE-CLASS SOCIETY?

Sociologists have given many names to this new society: post-capitalist and managerial, leisure-time and consumer's, advanced industrial and mass society are but a small selection. It cannot do much harm therefore to add one further name and claim that Europe is well under way toward a service-class society. Although only a fraction of the population can be counted among the service class proper, the values of this category have spread to all other groups. Paramount among these values is the replacement of cohesive feelings and groupings by individual competition. In the past, progress was a matter of immense public interest; in the present, progress has become a private affair or, rather, a matter of the abstract sum of innumerable advances in individual happiness.

THE POLITICS OF SERVICE

Much has been and more should be said about the structure and climate of the service-class society. As a general proposition, it seems to me desirable that such analyses should lose some of the snobbish temper of *Kulturkritik* which they so often have today. But this essay is about class, and class is about power, and power is about politics. And it is in the sphere of politics that the service-class society displays its most problematic face.

Our image of the history of representative government is obviously too neat to be correct. Yet there remains an element of truth in it despite the somewhat unexpected figures about the development of suffrage mentioned at an earlier stage: representative government worked, for the first time, at a time at which the two conflicting parties were the Conservatives and the Liberals, representing an old society of social and economic privileges and a new society of free enterprise, respectively. Toward the end of the nineteenth century—that is, with the progress not only of industrialization, but also of universal suffrage—Conservatives and Liberals merged into a new conservative group which from now on was opposed by the new progressives, the Socialists. Ever since, representative government has meant in many countries, some

variant of the competition for power between the newly privileged and the newly underprivileged, or those who felt that they
belonged to either of these groups.

In the service-class society, however, this social basis of representative government is giving way .This does not, to be sure,
affect the strength of the traditional conservative position (although its platforms have undeniably changed as well). But
where there was the progressive party, the Liberals, and later the
Socialists, there tends to be a great vacuum today; and since representative government lives on the productive antagonism of in-
ertia and progress, its very foundations are in danger.

To be sure, all the countries of Europe still contain Socialist
parties. In some of them, these have been, or are government parties. But I think it is fair to say that most of these parties are
Socialist only in name—a generalization which is correct to the
extent to which the service society has come about. In terms of
their political platforms, the parties of the traditional Right and
Left in Germany, the Scandinavian countries, Holland, and Belgium have become virtually indistinguishable. In England and
France, this is not quite true as yet, but there are clear tendencies
in the same direction. All political parties are trying to become
"people's parties," that is, non-ideological election machines appealing to all sectors of the electorate alike. In this way, the
value of the individual competition is translated into politics. To
many voters, it is no longer the party that matters, but the individuals it offers for choice as ministers or members of parliament.
Studies of political behavior in many European countries show
an ever increasing volume of the floating vote: one no longer belongs to one party, but one supports the most appealing candidate.

Of course, there are still vested interests and pressures on governments and parliaments. In fact, the situation I have in mind
tends to favor even minor pressure groups. For the majority of
voters no longer seems to have any clear set of economic or social
interests which are translated into political decisions—with the
single exception of one overriding, if negative, desire, and that is,
not to be pushed about, not to strengthen authority, not to see

the sphere of individual enjoyment reduced in any way. Perhaps this is one of the reasons for the apparent revival of old-fashioned liberalism in several countries of Europe, the struggle of "Orpington man" *vs.* the State. With the exception of this concern, however, appeal seems to count for more than interest, personality for more than program.

The absence of a progressive political force is the result of the absence of a suppressed class in the classical meaning of this term. When the sense of solidarity gives way to individual competition there is little hope for radical political groups. This development has many an advantageous aspect both for the individual and for the political system. The individual can fill the horizon of chances, which is all that politics can ever bring about, with his own personality. The political system is no longer threatened by groups which intend to transform not only society but its constitutional foundations as well. At the same time, representative government becomes singularly ineffective in this pacific world. In the absence of a progressive force, the powers that be, and above all the inert force of bureaucracy, keep things running without ever changing them. This is the world in which Parkinson's laws become almost laws of nature immune to human intervention, even if it takes the form of control by elected parliaments. In the service-class society, representative government lies dormant, and a very uninspiring kind of bureaucratic conservatism dominates the scene. Whatever has been started, goes on and on and on.

Post-war elections in many European countries testify clearly to this new conservative mood. Three or four successive electoral victories by the same party, and possibly even victories with increasing majorities, are simply not permitted by the classical theory of representative government. Yet this conservatism is not the ugliest consequence of the pervasive influence of the service class. The mood in question also means that most people take but little interest in the world of politics, which is after all always to some extent a world of solidarities. Lack of political interest, however, is the historical concomitant of authoritarian rule. To be sure, in the past it was the authoritarian rulers who prevented the many from taking an interest in politics, whereas in the present it may be the indifference of the many that produces and supports authoritarian rulers. But the difference is not as great as it may seem. In the service-class societies of Europe, the political situation is often not unlike that described so brilliantly by Marx in his *Eighteenth Brumaire of Louis Bonaparte*:[44] there are large numbers of individuals who cannot form solid political groups and represent themselves. They have to be represented, and they love the man who pretends to do so without actually hurting what few concerns and interests they have. The inability to form cohesive organization was, in Marx's analysis, based on a lack of communication among the small peasants of France. Today, it is based on the diffusion of service-class values. But in either case, the social situation favors developments like Gaullism in France, or the "Chancellor democracy" of Germany.

The course of history is not predetermined. Nothing is further from my intention here than to suggest that the development of a new authoritarianism by way of a new conservatism is "historically inevitable," or that it will go on forever. It is equally uncertain whether the relations between classes will remain as relatively peaceful as they are today. The service-class society may be a passing phase of development, a brief interlude between clearer lines of class and political cleavage, or it may be here to stay. For the present, however, the theory of the prevalence of the service class and its values seems to me to provide a reasonably good explanation of such diverse phenomena as the success of the Liberals in British by-elections, the French Fifth Republic, and Adenauer's four electoral victories in Germany.

44 K. Marx, *Der achtzehnte Brumaire des Louis Bonaparte*, new ed. (Berlin, 1946).

6 / IS THERE AN AMERICAN POWER ELITE?

C. WRIGHT MILLS / The Power Elite*

The elite are those who occupy the command posts at the heads of the major institutions of the country. These institutions include the larger business corporations and the main sections of the federal government—in particular, the political directorate, the executive bureaucracy, and the military establishment. Accordingly, the elite—at first glance—is composed of the political outsiders who now occupy the political directorate, the admirals and the generals of the higher echelons, and the top executives and strategic owners of the larger corporations.

This straightforward conception of the elite has one practical and two theoretical advantages. The practical advantage is that it seems the easiest and the most concrete way into the whole problem—if only because a good deal of information is more or less readily available for sociological reflection about these individuals and their institutions.

But the theoretical advantages are much more important. The institutional or structural definition, first of all, does not force us to prejudge by definition what we ought properly to leave open for investigation. The elite conceived morally, for example, as people having a certain type of character, is not an ultimate definition, for apart from being rather morally arbitrary, it leads the

* From A. Kornhauser, ed., *Problems of Power in American Democracy* (Detroit, Wayne State University Press, 1937), pp. 145–168. Portions of the original article have been omitted.

sociologist immediately to ask why these people have this or that sort of character. Accordingly, we should leave open the type of characters which the members of the elite in fact turn out to have, rather than by definition to select them in terms of one type or another. And in similar manner, we do not want, by our definition, to prejudge whether the elite are conscious members of a set of cliques or of a social class.

The second theoretical advantage, of defining the elite in terms of the major institutions which they head, is even more important. This approach, as I have already intimated, allows us to fit the other three conceptions of the elite into place in a systematic way:

The institutional positions men occupy throughout their lifetime determine their chances to get and to hold selected values.

The kind of psychological beings they become is in large part determined by the values they thus experience and the institutional roles they play.

And whether or not they come to feel that they belong to a select social class, and whether or not they act according to what they hold to be its interests—these are also matters in large part determined by their institutional position, and in turn, the select values they possess and the characters they acquire.

I need now to make clear a simple and very much overlooked distinction which, to my mind, is the single most important distinction available in the sociological sciences. It is the distinction between personal milieu and social structure. And we may think of it in this way:

When a handful of men do not have work and do not seek jobs, we may look for the causes in their immediate situations and character. But when twelve million men are unemployed, then we cannot believe that all of them suddenly "got lazy" and turned out to be "no good." Economists call this "structural unemployment"—meaning, for one thing, that the men involved cannot personally control their job chances. Now, what individual men are usually aware of and what they usually try to do are limited by the horizon of their specific milieu. Most men do not transcend the boundaries of their jobs and families and local communities. In other milieux which they encounter they are and they remain visitors. That is why "great changes" are out of their control, for great changes, by definition, are those whose causes lie outside the ordinary milieu of ordinary men but which nevertheless affect their conduct and their outlook. And that is why in periods full of such changes many ordinary men feel that they are "powerless," which in all sober fact they are. Mass unemployment, for example, does not originate in one factory or in one town, nor is it due to anything that one factory or one town does or fails to do. Moreover, there is little or nothing that one man, one factory, or one town can do about it when it sweeps over their personal milieu.

But the great historical changes—do not their causes lie somewhere? And cannot we trace them? Yes they do, and yes we can. Simply to tag them, we call them structural changes, and we define them by realizing in our definition that they are changes which transcend the milieux of most men. They transcend these personal milieux not only because they effect a great range of milieux, but because, by their nature, the structural principles of change have to do with the unintended, hence, the unexpected, consequences of what men, seated in and limited by various milieux may be trying to do or trying to ward off.

But not all men are ordinary in the sense of being limited by narrow milieux. Some have access to many more milieux than do others, and some in addition are so placed in the social structure that they can look down, so to speak, upon the milieux of many ordinary men.

This is the most important general meaning that I wish to give the term, *elite*. This is *the* position of the elite.

The elite are those who command the leading institutions and whose commanding positions so place them in their social structure that they transcend, to a greater or to a lesser extent, the ordinary milieux of ordinary men and women.

From even the most superficial examination of the history of Western society, we learn that the power of any decision-maker is first of all limited by the level of technique, by the *means* of power and violence and organization that prevail in a given society. In this connection, we also learn that there is a rather straight line running upward through the history of the West; that the means of oppression and exploitation, of violence and destruction, as well as the means of production and reconstruction, have been progressively enlarged and increasingly centralized.

As the institutional means of power and the means of communications that tie them together have become steadily more efficient, those now in command of these enlarged and centralized structures have come into command of instruments of rule quite unsurpassed in the history of mankind. And we are not yet at the climax of their development. We can no longer lean upon nor take soft comfort from the historical ups and downs of ruling groups of previous epochs. In that sense, Hegel is correct: we learn from history that we cannot learn from it.

For every epoch and for every social structure, we must work out an answer to the question of the power of the elite. And the major questions about the American elite today—about its composition and its unity, and its power—must now be faced with due attention to the awesome means of power that are now available to them. Caesar could do less with Rome than Napoleon with France; Napoleon less with France than Lenin with Russia; and Lenin less with Russia than Hitler with Germany. But what was Caesar's power at its peak compared with the power of the changing inner circle of Soviet Russia or of Eisenhower's temporary administration? The men of either circle can cause great cities to be wiped out in a single night and in a few weeks turn continents into thermo-nuclear wastelands. That the facilities of power are enormously enlarged and decisively centralized means that the decisions of small groups are now more consequential.

Within the American society, major national power now resides in the economic, the political, and the military domains. Other institutions seem off to the side of modern history, and, on occasion, duly subordinated to these. No family is as directly powerful in national affairs as any major corporation; no church is as directly powerful in the external biographies of young men in America today as the U. S. Army; no college is as powerful in the shaping of international events as the National Security Council. Religious, educational, and family institutions are not autonomous centers of national power; on the contrary, these decentralized areas are increasingly shaped by the big three, in which developments of decisive and immediate consequence now occur.

Families and churches and schools adapt to modern life; governments and armies and corporations shape it; and, as they do so, they turn these lesser institutions into means for their ends. Religious institutions provide chaplains to the armed forces where they are used as a means of increasing the effectiveness of its morale. Schools select and train men for their jobs in corporations and their specialized tasks in the armed forces. The extended family has, of course, long been broken up by the industrial revolution, and now the son and the father are removed from the family, by compulsion if need be, whenever the army of the state sends out the call. And the symbols of all these lesser institutions are used to legitimate the power and the decisions of the big three.

The life fate of the modern individual depends not only upon the family into which he was born or which he enters by marriage, but increasingly upon the corporation in which he spends the most alert hours of his best years; not only upon the school where he is educated as a child and adolescent, but also upon the state which touches him throughout his life; not only upon the church in which on occasion he hears the word of God, but also upon the army in which he is disciplined.

If the centralized state could not rely upon the inculcation of nationalist loyalties in public and private schools, its leaders would promptly modify the decentralized educational system. If the bankruptcy rate among the top five hundred corporations were as high as the general divorce rate among the thirty-seven million married couples, there would be economic catastrophe on an international scale. If members of armies gave to them no more of their lives than do believers to the churches to which they belong, there would be a military crisis.

Within each of the big three, the typical institutional unit has become enlarged, has become administrative, and, in the power of its decisions, has become centralized. Behind these developments, within each of them, there is the giant and fabulous technology; for as institutions, they have incorporated this technology and guide it, even as it shapes and paces their developments.

The economy—once a great scatter of small productive units in autonomous balance—has become dominated by two or three hundred giant corporations, administratively and politically interrelated, which together hold the keys to economic decisions.

The political order, once a decentralized set of several dozen states with a weak spinal cord, has become a centralized, executive establishment which has taken up into itself many powers previously scattered and now enters into each and every cranny of the social structure.

The military order, once a slim establishment in a context of distrust fed by state militia, has become the largest and most expensive feature of government, and, although well-versed in smiling public relations, now has all the grim and clumsy efficiency of a sprawling bureaucratic domain.

In each of these institutional areas, the means of power at the disposal of centralized decision-making units have increased enormously, and their central executive powers enhanced, as, below each of their centers, modern administrative routines are elaborated and tightened up.

As each of these domains becomes enlarged and centralized, the consequences of its activities become greater, and its traffic with the others increases. The decisions of a handful of corporations bear upon military and political as well as upon economic developments around the world. The decisions of the military establishment rest upon and grievously affect political life as well as the very level of economic activity. The decisions made within the political domain determine economic activities and military programs. There is no longer, on the one hand, an economy, and, on the other, a political order containing a military establishment unimportant to politics and to money-making. There is a political economy linked, in a thousand ways, with military institutions and decisions. On each side of the world-split running through central Europe and around the Asiatic rimlands, there is ever increasing the interlocking of economic, military, and political structures. And if there is government intervention in the corporate economy, so is there corporate intervention in the governmental process. In the structural sense, this triangle of power is the source of the interlocking directorate that is most important for the historical structure of the present.

The fact of the interlocking is clearly revealed at each of the points of crisis of modern capitalist society—slump, war, and boom. In each, men of decision are led to an awareness of the interdependence of the major institutional orders. In the nineteenth century, when the scale of all institutions was smaller, their liberal integration was achieved in the automatic economy, by an autonomous balance of market forces, and in the automatic political domain, by bargaining and voting. It was then assumed that out of the oscillations and frictions that followed the circumscribed decisions then possible, a new equilibrium would in due course emerge. That can no longer be assumed, and it is not assumed by the men at the top of each of the three dominant hierarchies.

For given the scope of their consequences, decisions in any one of these ramify into the others, and hence top decisions become coordinated decisions. They become decisions with the total context of the nation, and indeed of the world, in mind. In their calculated risks, men of decision must anticipate long-range consequences, lest they be fatally overwhelmed by new and unforeseen problems.

At the pinnacle of each of the three enlarged and centralized domains, there have arisen the men of the higher circles, who make up the economic, the political, and the military elites. At the top of the economy, among the corporate rich, there are the corporation executives; at the top of the political order, above the middle levels of the Congress, there are the members of the political directorate; and at the top of the military establishment, the elite of soldier-statesmen cluster in and around the Joint Chiefs of Staff and the upper echelon. And as each of these domains has coincided with the others, and as decisions tend to become total in their consequence, the leading men in each of the three domains of power—the warlords, the corporation chieftains, the political directorate—tend to come together, to form the power elite of America.

If the power to decide such national issues as are decided were shared in an absolutely equal way, there would be no power elite; in fact, there would be no gradation of power, but only a radical homogeneity. At the opposite extreme as well, if the power to decide issues were absolutely monopolized by one small group, there would be no gradation of power; there would simply be this small group in command, and below it, the undifferentiated, dominated mass. American society today represents neither the one nor the other of these extremes, but a conception of them is none the less useful. It makes us realize more clearly the question of the structure of power in the United States and the position of the power elite within it.

To say that there are obviously gradations of power, and of opportunities to decide, within modern society is not to say that the powerful are united, that they fully know what they do, or that they are consciously joined in conspiracy. Such issues are best faced if we become, in the first instance, more concerned with the structural position of the high and mighty, and with the consequences of their decisions, than with the extent of their awareness or the purity of their motives.

The formation of the power elite, as we may now know it, occurred during World War II and its aftermath. In the course of the organization of the nation for that war, and the consequent stabilization of the war-like posture, certain types of man have been selected and formed, and, in the course of these institutional and psychological developments, new opportunities and intentions have arisen among them.

Like the tempo of American life in general, the long-term trends of the power structure have been speeded up since World War II, and certain newer trends within and between the dominant institutions have also set in to shape the power elite and give historically specific meaning to its fifth epoch:

(1) Insofar as the structural clue to the power elite today lies in the political order, that clue is the decline of politics as a genuine and public debate of alternative decisions—with nationally responsible and policy-coherent parties and with autonomous organizations connecting the lower and middle levels of power with the top levels of decision. America is now in considerable part more a formal political democracy than a democratic social structure, and even the formal political mechanics are weak.

The long-time trend of business and government to become more intricately and deeply involved with each other has, in this epoch, reached a point of explicitness not before evident. Now, in a hundred ways, they are difficult to see as two distinct worlds. And it is in terms of the executive agencies of the state that the rapprochement has proceeded most decisively. The growth of the executive branch of the government, with its agencies that patrol the complex economy, does not mean merely the "enlargement of government" as some sort of autonomous bureaucracy: it has meant the ascendancy of the corporation's man as a political outsider.

If, during the New Deal, the corporate chieftains joined the political directorate, as of World War II they have come to dominate it. Long interlocked with government, now they moved into quite full direction of the economy of the war effort and of the post-war era. And this shift of the corporation executives into the political directorate has accelerated the long-term relegation of the professional politicians in the Congress to the middle levels of power.

(2) Insofar as the structural clue to the power elite today lies in the enlarged and military state, that clue is that, with the military ascendancy, the warlords have, for the first time, become of decisive political relevance and have gained decisive political power. The military structure of America is now in considerable part a political structure. For, the seemingly permanent military threat places a premium on the military and upon their control of men, material, money, and power. Virtually all political and economic actions are now judged in terms of military definitions of reality: the higher warlords have ascended to a firm position within the power elite of the fifth epoch.

In some part at least this fact has come about by virtue of one simple historical fact, pivotal for the years since 1939: the focus of elite attention has been shifted from domestic problems, centered in the thirties around slump, to international problems, centered in the forties and fifties around war.

Since the governing apparatus of the United States has by long historic usage been adapted to and shaped by domestic clash and balance, it has not, from any angle, had suitable agencies and traditions for the handling of international problems. And such formal democratic mechanics as had arisen in the century and a half of national development prior to 1941 had not been extended to the United States handling of international affairs. It is, in considerable part, in this vacuum that the power elite has grown.

(3) Insofar as the structural clue to the power elite today lies in the economic order, that clue is the fact that the economy is at once a permanent war economy and a private corporation economy. American capitalism is now in considerable part a military capitalism, and the most important relation of the big corporation to the state rests on the coincidence of interests between military and corporate needs, as defined by warlords and corporate rich. Within the elite as a whole, this coincidence of interest between the high military and the corporate chieftains strengthens both of them and further subordinates the role of the merely political men. Not politicians, but corporate executives, sit with the military and plan the organization of war effort.

(4) The shape and meaning of the power elite today can be understood only when these three sets of structural trends are seen at the point of their coincidence: the military capitalism of private corporations exists in a weakened and formal democratic system containing an already quite politicized military order. Accordingly, at the top of this structure, the power elite has taken its shape from the coincidence of interest between those who control the major means of production and those who control the newly enlarged means of violence; from the decline of the professional politician and the rise to explicit political command of the corporate chieftains and the professional warlords; from the absence of

any genuine civil service of skill and integrity, independent of vested interests.

The power elite is composed of political, economic, and military men, but these instituted elites are frequently in some tension: they come together only on certain coinciding points and only on certain occasions of "crisis." In the long peace of the nineteenth century, the military were not in the high councils of state, not of the political directorate—and neither were the economic men; they made raids upon the state but they did not join its directorate. During the thirties, the political man was ascendant, and now the military and the corporate men are in top positions.

Of the three types of circles that compose the power elite today, it is the military that have benefited the most in their enhanced power, although the corporate have also become more explicitly and, in fact, more decisively intrenched in the more public decision-making circles. It is the professional politician that has lost the most, so much that in examining the events and decisions, one is tempted to speak of a political vacuum in which the corporate rich and the high warlord, in their coinciding interests, rule.

But we must always be historically specific and we must always be open to complexities: (1) the simple Marxian view makes the big economic man the real holder of power; (2) the simple liberal view makes the big political man the chief of the power system; and (3) there are some who would view the warlords as virtual dictators. These are each an over-simplified view. And it is to avoid them that we use the term "power elite" rather than, for example, "ruling class."

"Ruling class," we feel, is a badly loaded phrase. "Class" is an economic term; "rule," a political one. The phrase, "ruling class" thus contains the theory that an economic class rules politically. That short-cut theory may or may not at times be true, but we do not want to carry that one rather simple theory about in the terms that we use to define our problems; we wish to state the theories explicitly, using terms of more precise and unilateral meaning. More specifically, the phrase "ruling class," in its common political connotations, does not allow enough autonomy to the political order and its agents, and it says nothing about the military as such. It should be clear by now that we do not accept as adequate the simple view that high economic men unilaterally make all decisions of national consequence. We hold that such a simple view of "economic determinism" must be elaborated by "political determinism" and by "military determinism"; that the higher agents of each of these three domains now often have a noticeable degree of autonomy; and that only in the often intricate ways of coalition do they make up and carry through the most important decisions. Those are the major reasons we prefer "power elite" to "ruling class" as a characterizing phrase for the higher circles, when we consider them in terms of power.

Insofar as the power elite has come to wide public attention, it has done so in terms of the "military clique," and, in fact, the power elite does take its current shape from the entrance into it in a decisive way of the military. Their presence and their ideology are its major legitimations, whenever the power elite feels the need to provide any. But what is called the "Washington military clique" is not composed merely of military men, and it does not prevail merely in Washington. Its members exist all over the country, and it is a coalition of generals in the roles of corporation executives, of politicians masquerading as admirals, of corporation executives acting like politicians, of civil servants who become majors, of vice-admirals who are also the assistants to a Cabinet officer, who is himself, by the way, really a member of an important managerial clique.

Neither the idea of a "ruling class" nor of a simple monolithic rise of "bureaucratic politicians," nor of a "military clique" is the correct view. The power elite today involves the often uneasy coincidence of economic, military, and political power.

Now, even if our understanding were limited to these structural trends, we would have grounds for believing the power elite a useful, indeed, an indispensable, concept for the interpretation of what is going on at the topside of modern American society. But we are not, of course, so limited: our conception of the power elite does not need to rest only upon the correspondence of the institutional hierarchies involved, nor upon the many points at which their shifting interests coincide. The power elite, as we conceive it, also rests upon the similarity of its personnel, and their personal and official relations with one another, upon their social and psychological affinities.

The power elite is not an aristocracy, which is to say that it is not a political ruling group based upon nobility of origin. It has no compact basis in a small circle of great families, whose members can and do consistently occupy the top positions in the several higher circles which overlap as the power elite. But such nobility is only one possible basis of common origin; and, if it does not exist for the American elite, neither does this elite derive socially from the full range of strata composing American society. They derive, in substantial proportions, from the upper classes, both new and old, of local society and the metropolitan 400. The bulk of the very rich, of the corporate executives, of the political outsiders, and the high military derive from at most the upper third of the income and occupational pyramids. Their fathers were at least of the professional and business strata, and very frequently higher than that. They are native-born Americans of native parents, primarily from urban areas, and, with the exception of the politicians among them, overwhelmingly from the East. They are mainly Protestants, especially Episcopalian or Presbyterian.

The power elite is composed of men of similar origin and education; and their careers and their styles of life are remarkably similar. Accordingly, there are psychological and social bases for their unity, resting upon the fact that they are of similar social type and leading to the fact of their easy intermingling. This kind of unity reaches its frothier culmination in the sharing of that prestige that is to be had in the world of the celebrity; it reaches a more solid culmination in the fact of this interchangeability of positions within and between the three dominant institutional orders.

Today in America, there are several important structural coincidences of interest between these institutional domains, including the development of a permanent war establishment by a privately incorporate economy inside a political vacuum. But the unity of the power elite does not rest solely upon their psychological similarity and their social intermingling, nor entirely upon the structural coincidences of their commanding positions and interests. It is at times the unity of a more explicit coordination. To say that these three higher circles are increasingly coordinated, that this is one basis of their unity, and that at times—as during the wars—such coordination is quite decisive, is not to say that the coordination is total or continuous, or even that it is very sure-footed. Much less is it to say that willful coordination is the sole or the major basis of their unity or that the power elite has emerged as the realization of a plan. But it is to say that as the institutional mechanics of our time have opened up avenues to men pursuing their several interests, many of them have come to see that these several interests could be realized more easily if they worked together, in informal as well as in more formal ways, and that, accordingly, they have done so.

WILLIAM KORNHAUSER / Power Elite or Veto Groups*

I

In the 1950's two books appeared purporting to describe the structure of power in present-day America. They reached opposite conclusions: where C. Wright Mills found a "power elite," David Riesman found "veto groups." Both books have enjoyed a wide response, which has tended to divide along ideological lines. It would appear that *The Power Elite* has been most favorably received by radical intellectuals, and *The Lonely Crowd* has found its main response among liberals. Mills and Riesman have not been oblivious to their differences. Mills is quite explicit on the matter: Riesman is a "romantic pluralist" who refuses to see the forest of American power inequalities for the trees of short-run and discrete balances of power among diverse groups. [244]¹ Riesman has been less explicitly polemical, but he might have had Mills in mind when he spoke of those intellectuals "who feel themselves very much out of power and who are frightened of those who they think have the power," and who "prefer to be scared by the power structures they conjure up than to face the

* From Seymour Lipset and Leo Lowenthal, eds., *Culture and Social Character* (New York, Free Press of Glencoe, 1961), pp. 252–267.
¹ Page references in the text for remarks by C. Wright Mills refer to *The Power Elite* (New York: Oxford University Press, 1956).

possibility that the power structure they believe exists has largely evaporated." [257–258]²

I wish to intervene in the controversy just long enough to do two things: (1) locate as precisely as possible the items upon which Riesman and Mills disagree; and (2) formulate certain underlying issues in the analysis of power that have to be met before such specific disagreements as those between Riesman and Mills can profitably be resolved.

We may compare Mills and Riesman on power in America along five dimensions:

1. structure of power: how power is distributed among the major segments of present-day American society;
2. changes in the structure of power: how the distribution of power has changed in the course of American history;
3. operation of the structure of power: the means whereby power is exercised in American society;
4. bases of the structure of power: how social and psychological factors shape and sustain the existing distribution of power;
5. consequences of the structure of power: how the existing distribution of power affects American society.

1. STRUCTURE OF POWER

It is symptomatic of their underlying differences that Mills entitles his major consideration of power simply "the power elite," whereas Riesman has entitled one of his discussions "who has the power?" Mills is quite certain about the location of power, and so indicates by the assertive form of his title. Riesman perceives a much more amorphous and indeterminate power situation, and conveys this view in the interrogative form of his title. These contrasting images of American power may be diagrammed as two different pyramids of power. Mills's pyramid of power contains three levels:

2 Page references in the text for remarks by David Riesman refer to *The Lonely Crowd* (New York: Doubleday Anchor, 1953).

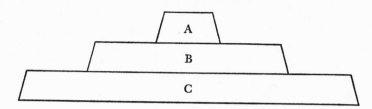

The apex of the pyramid (A) is the "power elite": a unified power group composed of the top government executives, military officials, and corporation directors. The second level (B) comprises the "middle levels of power": a diversified and balanced plurality of interest groups, perhaps most visibly at work in the the halls of Congress. The third level (C) is the "mass society": the powerless mass of unorganized and atomized people who are controlled from above.

Riesman's pyramid of power contains only two major levels:

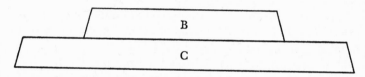

The two levels roughly correspond to Mills's second and third levels, and have been labeled accordingly. The obvious difference between the two pyramids is the presence of a peak in the one case and its absence in the other. Riesman sees no "power elite," in the sense of a single unified power group at the top of the structure, and this in the simplest terms contrasts his image of power in America with that of Mills. The upper level of Riesman's pyramid (B) consists of "veto groups": a diversified and balanced plurality of interest groups, each of which is primarily concerned with protecting its jurisdiction by blocking efforts of other groups that seem to threaten that jurisdiction. There is no decisive ruling group here, but rather an amorphous structure of power centering in the interplay among these interest groups. The lower level of the pyramid (C) comprises the more or less unorganized public, which is sought as an ally (rather than dominated) by the interest groups in their maneuvers against actual or threatened encroachments on the jurisdiction each claims for itself.

2. CHANGES IN THE STRUCTURE OF POWER

Riesman and Mills agree that the American power structure has gone through four major epochs. They disagree on the present and prospective future in the following historical terms: Mills judges the present to represent a fifth epoch, whereas Riesman judges it to be a continuation of the fourth.

The first period, according to Mills and Riesman, extended roughly from the founding of the republic to the Jacksonian era. During this period, Riesman believes America possessed a clearly demarcated ruling group, composed of a "landed-gentry and mercantilist-money leadership." [239] According to Mills, "the important fact about these early days is that social life, economic institutions, military establishment, and political order coincided, and men who were high politicians also played key roles in the economy and, with their families, were among those of the reputable who made up local society." [270]

The second period extended roughly from the decline of Federalist leadership to the Civil War. During this period power became more widely dispersed, and it was no longer possible to identify a sharply defined ruling group. "In this society," Mills writes, "the 'elite' became a plurality of top groups, each in turn quite loosely made up." [270] Riesman notes that farmer and artisan groups became influential, and "occasionally, as with Jackson, moved into a more positive command." [240]

The third period began after the Civil War and extended through McKinley's administration in Riesman's view [240] and until the New Deal according to Mills. [271] They agree that the era of McKinley marked the high point of the unilateral supremacy of corporate economic power. During this period, power once more became concentrated, but unlike the Federalist period and also unlike subsequent periods, the higher circles of economic institutions were dominant.

The fourth period took definite shape in the 1930's. In Ries man's view this period marked the ascendancy of the "veto groups," and rule by coalitions rather than by a unified power group. Mills judges it to have been so only in the early and middle Roosevelt administrations: "In these years, the New Deal as a system of power was essentially a balance of pressure groups and interest blocs." [273]

Up to World War II, then, Mills and Riesman view the historical development of power relations in America along strikingly similar lines. Their sharply contrasting portrayal of present-day American power relations begins with their diverging assessments of the period beginning about 1940. Mills envisions World War II and its aftermath as marking a new era in American power relations. With war as the major problem, there arises a new power group composed of corporate, governmental, and military directors.

> The formation of the power elite, as we may now know it, occurred during World War II and its aftermath. In the course of the organization of the nation for that war, and the consequent stabilization of the war-like posture, certain types of man have been selected and formed, and in the course of these institutional and psychological developments, new opportunities and intentions have arisen among them.[3]

Where Mills sees the ascendancy of a power elite, Riesman sees the opposite tendency toward the dispersal of power among a plurality of organized interests:

> There has been in the last fifty years a change in the configuration of power in America, in which a single hierarchy with a ruling class at its head has been replaced by a number of "veto groups" among which power is dispersed [239].
>
> The shifting nature of the lobby provides us with an important clue as to the difference between the present American political scene and that of the age of McKinley. The ruling class of businessmen could relatively easily (though perhaps mistakenly) decide where their interests lay and what editors, lawyers, and legislators might be paid to advance them. The lobby ministered to the clear

[3] C. Wright Mills, "The Power Elite," in A. Kornhauser, ed., *Problems of Power in American Society* (Detroit, Wayne University Press, 1957), p. 161.

leadership, privilege, and imperative of the business ruling class. Today we have substituted for that leadership a series of groups, each of which has struggled for and finally attained a power to stop things conceivably inimical to its interests and, within far narrower limits, to start things. [246–247]

In short, both Mills and Riesman view the current scene from an historical perspective; but where one finds a hitherto un-known *concentration* of power, the other finds an emerging *inde-terminacy* of power.

3. OPERATION OF THE STRUCTURE OF POWER

Mills believes the power elite sets all important public policies, especially foreign policy. Riesman, on the other hand, does not believe that the same group or coalition of groups sets all major policies, but rather that the question of who exercises power varies with the issue at stake: most groups are inoperative on most issues, and all groups are operative primarily on those issues that vitally impinge on their central interests. This is to say that there are as many power structures as there are distinctive spheres of policy. [256]

As to the modes of operation, both Mills and Riesman point to increasing *manipulation,* rather than command or persuasion, as the favored form of power play. Mills emphasizes the secrecy be-hind which important policy-determination occurs. Riesman stresses not so much manipulation under the guise of secrecy as manipulation under the guise of mutual tolerance for one an-other's interests and beliefs. Manipulation occurs, according to Riesman, because each group is trying to hide its concern with power in order not to antagonize other groups. Power relations tend to take the form of "monopolistic competition": "rules of fairness and fellowship [rather than the impersonal forces of competition] dictate how far one can go." [247] Thus both be-lieve the play of power takes place to a considerable extent back-stage; but Mills judges this power play to be under the direction of one group, while Reisman sees it as controlled by a mood and structure of accommodation among many groups.

Mills maintains that the mass media of communication are important instruments of manipulation: the media lull people to sleep, so to speak, by suppressing political topics and by emphasizing "entertainment." Riesman alleges that the mass media give more attention to politics and problems of public policy than their audiences actually want, and thereby convey the false impression that there is more interest in public affairs than really exists in America at the present time. Where Mills judges the mass media of communication to be powerful political instruments in American society [315–316], Riesman argues that they have relatively little significance in this respect. [228–231]

4. BASES OF THE STRUCTURE OF POWER

Power tends to be patterned according to the structure of interests in a society. Power is shared among those whose interests coincide, and divides along lines where interests diverge. To Mills, the power elite is a reflection and solidification of a *coincidence of interests* among the ascendant institutional orders. The power elite rests on the "many interconnections and points of coinciding interests" of the corporations, political institutions, and military services. [19] For Riesman, on the other hand, there is an amorphous power structure, which reflects a *diversity of interests* among the major organized groups. The power structure of veto groups rests on the divergent interests of political parties, business groups, labor organizations, farm blocs, and a myriad of other organized groups. [247]

But power is not a simple reflex of interests alone. It also rests on the capabilities and opportunities for cooperation among those who have similar interests, and for confrontation among those with opposing interests. Mills argues in some detail that the power elite rests not merely on the coincidence of interests among major institutions but also on the "psychological similarity and social intermingling" of their higher circles. [19] By virtue of similar social origins (old family, upper-class background), religious affiliations (Episcopalian and Presbyterian), education (Ivy League college or military academy), and the like, those who head up the major institutions share codes and values as well as material interests. This makes for easy communication, especially when many of these people already know one another, or at least know many people in common. They share a common way of life, and therefore possess both the will and the opportunity to integrate their lines of action as representatives of key institutions. At times this integration involves "explicit co-ordination," as during war. [19–20] So much for the bases of power at the apex of the structure.

At the middle and lower levels of power, Mills emphasizes the lack of independence and concerted purpose among those who occupy similar social positions. In his book on the middle classes,[4] Mills purports to show the weakness of white-collar people that results from their lack of economic independence and political direction. The white-collar worker simply follows the more powerful group of the moment. In his book on labor leaders,[5] Mills located the alleged political impotence of organized labor in its dependence on government. Finally, the public is conceived as composed of atomized and submissive individuals who are incapable of engaging in effective communication and political action. [302 ff.]

Riesman believes that power "is founded, in large measure, on interpersonal expectations and attitudes." [253] He asserts that in addition to the diversity of interest underlying the pattern of power in America there is the psycho-cultural fact of widespread feelings of weakness and dependence at the top as well as at the bottom of the power structure: "If businessmen feel weak and dependent they do in actuality become weaker and more dependent, no matter what material resources may be ascribed to them." [253] In other words the amorphousness of power in America rests in part on widespread feelings of weakness and dependence. These feelings are found among those whose position in the social structure provides resources that they could exploit, as well as among those whose position provides less access to the means of power. In fact, Riesman is concerned to show that people at all levels of the social structure tend to feel weaker than their objective position warrants.

The theory of types of conformity that provides the foundation of so much of Riesman's writings enters into his analysis of power

4 *White Collar* (New York, Oxford University Press, 1951).
5 *The New Men of Power* (New York, Harcourt, Brace and Company, 1948).

at this point. The "other-directed" orientation in culture and character helps to sustain the amorphousness of power. The other-directed person in politics is the "inside-dopester," the person who possesses political competence but avoids political commitment. This is the dominant type in the veto groups, since other-direction is prevalent in the strata from which their leaders are drawn. "Both within the [veto] groups and in the situation created by their presence, the political mood tends to become one of other-directed tolerance." [248] However, Riesman does not make the basis of power solely psychological:

> This does not mean, however, that the veto groups are formed along the lines of character structure. As in a business corporation there is room for extreme inner-directed and other-directed types, and all mixtures between, so in a veto group there can exist complex "symbiotic" relationships among people of different political styles. . . . Despite these complications I think it fair to say that the veto groups, even when they are set up to protect a clearcut moralizing interest, are generally forced to adopt the political manners of the other-directed. [249]

Riesman and Mills agree that there is widespread apathy in American society, but they disagree on the social distribution of political apathy. Mills locates the apathetic primarily among the lower social strata, whereas Riesman finds extensive apathy in higher as well as lower strata. Part of the difference may rest on what criteria of apathy are used. Mills conceives of apathy as the lack of political meaning in one's life, the failure to think of personal interests in political terms, so that what happens in politics does not appear to be related to personal troubles.[6] Riesman extends the notion of apathy to include the politically uninformed as well as the politically uncommitted.[7] Thus political indignation undisciplined by political understanding is not a genuine political orientation. Riesman judges political apathy to be an important *basis* for amorphous power relations. Mills, on the other hand, treats political apathy primarily as a *result* of the concentration of power.

[6] *White Collar*, p. 327.
[7] David Riesman and Nathan Glazer, "Criteria for Political Apathy," in Alvin W. Gouldner, ed., *Studies in Leadership* (New York, Harper & Brothers, 1950)

5. CONSEQUENCES OF THE STRUCTURE OF POWER

Four parallel sets of consequences of the structure of power for American society may be inferred from the writings of Mills and Riesman. The first concerns the impact of the power structure on the interests of certain groups or classes in American society. Mills asserts that the existing power arrangements enhance the interests of the major institutions whose directors constitute the power elite. [276 ff.] Riesman asserts the contrary: no one group or class is decisively favored over others by the culminated decisions on public issues. [257]

The second set of consequences concerns the impact of the structure of power on the quality of politics in American society. Here Mills and Riesman are in closer agreement. Mills maintains that the concentration of power in a small circle, and the use of manipulation as the favored manner of exercising power, lead to the decline of politics as public debate. People are decreasingly capable of grasping political issues, and of relating them to personal interests.[8] Riesman also believes that politics has declined in meaning for large numbers of people. This is not due simply to the ascendancy of "veto groups," although they do foster "the tolerant mood of other-direction and hasten the retreat of the inner-directed indignants." [251] More important, the increasing complexity and remoteness of politics make political self-interest obscure and aggravate feelings of impotence even when self-interest is clear.[9]

The third set of consequences of the American power structure concerns its impact on the quality of power relations themselves. Mills contends that the concentration of power has taken place without a corresponding shift in the bases of legitimacy of power: power is still supposed to reside in the public and its elected representatives, whereas in reality it resides in the hands of those who direct the key bureaucracies. As a consequence, men of power are neither responsible nor accountable for their power. [316–317] Riesman also implies that there is a growing discrepancy between the facts of power and the images of power, but for

8 *White Collar*, pp. 342–350.
9 "Criteria for Political Apathy," p. 520.

the opposite reason from Mills: power is more widely dispersed than is generally believed. [257–258]

Finally, a fourth set of consequences concerns the impact of the power structure on democratic leadership. If power tends to be lodged in a small group that is not accountable for its power, and if politics no longer involves genuine public debate, then there will be a *severe weakening of democratic institutions,* if not of leadership (the power elite exercises leadership in one sense of the term, in that it makes decisions on basic policy for the nation). Mills claims that power in America has become so concentrated that it increasingly resembles the Soviet system of power:

> Official commentators like to contrast the ascendancy in totalitarian countries of a tightly organized clique with the American system of power. Such comments, however, are easier to sustain if one compares mid-twentieth-century Russia with mid-nineteenth-century America, which is what is often done by Tocqueville-quoting Americans making the contrast. But that was an America of a century ago, and in the century that has passed, the American elite have not remained as patrioteer essayists have described them to us. The "loose cliques" now head institutions of a scale and power not then existing and, especially since World War I, the loose cliques have tightened up. [271]

If, on the other hand, power tends to be dispersed among groups that are primarily concerned to protect and defend their interests rather than to advance general policies and their own leadership, and if at the same time politics has declined as a sphere of duty and self-interest, then there will be a *severe weakening of leadership.* Thus Riesman believes that "power in America seems to [be] situational and mercurial; it resists attempts to locate it." [257] This "indeterminacy and amorphousness" of power inhibits the development of leadership: "Where the issue involves the country as a whole, no individual or group leadership is likely to be very effective, because the entrenched veto groups cannot be budged." [257] "Veto groups exist as defense groups, not as leadership groups." [248] Yet Riesman does not claim that the decline of leadership directly threatens American democracy, at least in the short run: the dispersion of power among a diversity of balancing "veto groups" operates to support

democratic institutions even as it inhibits effective leadership.
The long-run prospects of a leaderless democracy are of course less
promising.

TWO PORTRAITS OF THE AMERICAN POWER STRUCTURE

	Mills	Riesman
Levels	a. Unified power elite b. Diversified and balanced plurality of interest groups c. Mass of unorganized people who have practically no power over elite	a. No dominant power elite b. Diversified and balanced plurality of interest groups c. Mass of unorganized people who have some power over interest groups
Changes	a. Increasing concentration of power	a. increasing dispersion of power
Operation	a. One group determines all major policies b. Manipulation of people at the bottom by group at the top	a. Who determines policy shifts with the issue b. Monopolistic competition among organized groups
Bases	a. Coincidence of interests among major institutions (economic, military, governmental)	a. Diversity of interests among major organized groups b. Sense of weakness and dependence among those in higher as well as lower status
Consequences	a. Enhancement of interests of corporations, armed forces, and executive branch of government b. Decline of politics as public debate c. Decline of responsible and accountable power —loss of democracy	a. No one group or class is favored significantly over others b. Decline of politics as duty and self-interest c. Decline of capacity for effective leadership

II

In the second part of this paper, I wish to raise certain critical questions about Riesman's and Mills's images of power. One set of questions seeks to probe more deeply the basic area of disagreement in their views. A second set of questions concerns their major areas of agreement.

Power usually is analyzed according to its distribution among the several units of a system. Most power analysts construe the structure of power as a *hierarchy*—a rank-order of units according to their amount of power. The assumption often is made that there is only one such structure, and that all units may be ranked vis-à-vis one another. Units higher in the hierarchy have power over units lower in the structure, so there is a one-way flow of power. Mills tends to adopt this image of the structure of power.

Riesman rejects this conception of the power structure as mere hierarchy:

> The determination of who [has more power] has to be made all over again for our time: we cannot be satisfied with the answers given by Marx, Mosca, Michels, Pareto, Weber, Veblen, or Burnham. [255]
>
> The image of power in contemporary America presented [in *The Lonely Crowd*] departs from current discussions of power which are usually based on a search for a ruling class. [260]

Riesman is not just denying the existence of a power elite in contemporary American society; he is also affirming the need to consider other aspects of power than only its unequal distribution. He is especially concerned to analyze common responses to power:

> If the leaders have lost the power, why have the led not gained it? What is there about the other-directed man and his life situation which prevents the transfer? In terms of situation, it seems that the pattern of monopolistic competition of the veto groups resists individual attempts at power aggrandizement. In terms of character, the other-directed man simply does not seek power; perhaps, rather, he avoids and evades it. [275]

Whereas Mills emphasizes the *differences* between units according to their power, Riesman emphasizes their *similarities* in this respect. In the first view, some units are seen as dominated by other units, while in the second view, all units are seen as subject to constraints that shape and limit their use of power *in similar directions*.

The problem of power is not simply the differential capacity to make decisions, so that those who have power bind those who do not. Constraints also operate on those who are in decision-making positions, for if these are the places where acts of great consequence occur, so are they the targets for social pressures. These pressures become translated into restrictions on the alternatives among which decision-makers can choose. Power may be meaningfully measured by ascertaining the range of alternatives that decision-makers can realistically consider. To identify those who make decisions is not to say how many lines of action are open to them, or how much freedom of choice they enjoy.

A major advance in the study of power is made by going beyond a formal conception of power, in which those who have the authority to make decisions are assumed to possess the effective means of power and the will to use it. Nor can it be assumed that those not in authority lack the power to determine public policy. The identification of effective sources of power requires analysis of how *decision-makers are themselves subject to various kinds of constraint*. Major sources of constraint include (1) opposing elites and active publics; and (2) cultural values and associated psychological receptivities and resistances to power. A comparison of Mills and Riesman with respect to these categories of constraint reveals the major area of disagreement between them.

Mills implies that both sources of constraint are by and large inoperative on the highest levels of power. (1) There is little opposition among the top power-holders. Since they are not in opposition to one another, they do not constrain one another. Instead, there are unified and mutually supportive. Furthermore, there are few publics to constrain the elite. Groups capable of effective participation in broad policy determination have been replaced by atomized masses that are powerless to affect policy, since they lack the social bases for association and communication. Instead, people in large numbers are manipulated through organizations and media controlled by the elite. (2) Older values and codes no longer grip elites, nor have they been replaced by new values and codes that could regulate the exercise of power. Top men of power are not constrained either by an inner moral sense or by feelings of dependence on others. The widespread permissiveness toward the use of expedient means to achieve success produces "the higher immorality," that is to say, elites that are irresponsible in the use of power.

In sharp contrast to Mills, Riesman attaches great importance to both kinds of constraints on decision-makers. (1) There is a plethora of organized groups, "each of which has struggled for and finally attained a power to stop things conceivably inimical to its interests." [247] Furthermore, there is extensive opportunity for large numbers of people to influence decision-makers, because the latter are constrained by their competitive relations with one another to bid for support in the electoral arena and more diffusely in the realm of public relations. (2) The cultural emphasis on "mutual tolerance" and social conformity places a premium on "getting along" with others at the expense of taking strong stands. People are psychologically disposed to avoid long-term commitments as a result of their strong feelings of dependence on their immediate peers. "Other-directed" persons seek approval rather than power.

In general, the decisive consideration in respect to the restraint of power is the presence of multiple centers of power. Where there are many power groups, not only are they mutually constrained; they also are dependent on popular support, and therefore responsive to public demands. Now, there are many readily observable cases of institutionalized opposition among power groups in American society. In the economic sphere, collective bargaining between management and labor is conflict of this kind; and to the extent that "countervailing power" among a few large firms has been replacing competition among many small firms in the market place, there is a de facto situation of opposition among economic elites. In the political sphere, there is a strong two-party system and more or less stable factionalism within both parties, opposition among interest blocs in state and national legislatures, rivalry among executive agencies of government and the military services, and so forth.

Mills relegates these conflicting groups to the middle levels of power. Political parties and interest groups, both inside and outside of government, are not important units in the structure of power, according to Mills. It would seem that he takes this position primarily with an eye to the sphere of foreign policy, where only a few people finally make the big decisions. But he fails to put his argument to a decisive or meaningful test: he does not examine the pattern of decisions to show that foreign policy not only is made *by* a few people (this, after all, is a constitutional fact), but that it is made *for their particular interests*. Mills's major premise seems to be that all decisions are taken by and for special interests; there is no action oriented toward the general interests of the whole community. Furthermore, Mills seems to argue that because only a very few people occupy key decision-making *positions*, they are free to decide on whatever best suits their particular interests. But the degree of *autonomy* of decision-makers cannot be inferred from the *number* of decision-makers, nor from the *scope* of their decisions. It is determined by the character of decision-making, especially the dependence of decision-makers on certain kinds of *procedure* and *support*.

Just as Mills is presenting a distorted image of power in America when he fails to consider the pressures on those in high positions, so Riesman presents a biased picture by not giving sufficient attention to *power differentials* among the various groups in society. When Riesman implies that if power is dispersed, then it must be relatively equal among groups and interests, with no points of concentration, he is making an unwarranted inference. The following statement conjures up an image of power in America that is as misleading on its side as anything Mills has written in defense of his idea of a power elite.

> One might ask whether one would not find, over a long period of time, that decisions in America favored one group or class...

over others. Does not wealth exert its pull in the long run? In the past this has been so; for the future I doubt it. The future seems to be in the hands of the small business and professional men who control Congress, such as realtors, lawyers, car salesmen, undertakers, and so on; of the military men who control defense and, in part, foreign policy; of the big business managers and their lawyers, finance-committee men, and other counselors who decide on plant investment and influence the rate of technological change; of the labor leaders who control worker productivity and worker votes; of the black belt whites who have the greatest stake in southern politics; of the Poles, Italians, Jews, and Irishmen who have stakes in foreign policy, city jobs, and ethnic, religious and cultural organizations; of the editorializers and storytellers who help socialize the young, tease and train the adult, and amuse and annoy the aged; of the farmers—themselves a warring congeries of cattlemen, corn men, dairymen, cotton men, and so on—who control key departments and committees and who, as the living representatives of our inner-directed past, control many of our memories; of the Russians and, to a lesser degree, other foreign powers who control much of our agenda of attention; and so on. [257]

It appears that Riesman is asking us to believe that power differentials do not exist, but only differences in the spheres within which groups exercise control.

If Riesman greatly exaggerates the extent to which organized interests possess equal power, nevertheless he poses an important problem that Mills brushes aside. For Riesman goes beyond merely noting the existence of opposition among "veto groups" to suggest that they operate to smother one another's initiative and leadership. It is one thing for interest groups to constrain one another; it is something else again when they produce stalemate. Riesman has pointed to a critical problem for pluralist society: the danger that power may become fragmented among so many competing groups that effective general leadership cannot emerge.

On Mills's side, it is indisputable that American political institutions have undergone extensive centralization and bureaucratization. This is above all an *institutional* change wrought by the greatly expanded scale of events and decisions in the contemporary world. But centralization cannot be equated with a power elite. There can be highly centralized institutions and at the same time a fragmentation of power along a multiplicity of relatively independent public and private agencies. Thus Riesman would appear to be correct that the substance of power lies in the hands of many large organizations, and these organizations are not unified or coordinated in any firm fashion. If they were, surely Mills would have been able to identify the major mechanisms that could produce this result. That he has failed to do so is the most convincing evidence for their nonexistence.

To complete this analysis, we need only remind ourselves of the fundamental area of agreement between our two critics of American power relations. Both stress *the absence of effective political action* at all levels of the political order, in particular among the citizenry. For all of their differences, Mills and Riesman agree that there has been a decline in effective political participation, or at least a failure of political participation to measure up to the requirements of contemporary events and decisions. This failure has not been compensated by an increase in effective political action at the center: certainly Riesman's "veto groups" are not capable of defining and realizing the community's general aspirations; nor is Mills's "power elite" such a political agency. Both are asserting the inadequacy of political associations, including public opinion, party leadership, Congress, and the Presidency, even as they see the slippage of power in different directions. In consequence, neither is sanguine about the capacity of the American political system to provide responsible leadership, especially in international affairs.

If there is truth in this indictment, it also may have its sources in the very images of power that pervade Mills's and Riesman's thought. They are both inclined toward a negative response to power; and neither shows a willingness to confront the idea of a political system and the ends of power in it. Riesman reflects the liberal suspicion of power, as when he writes "we have come to realize that men who compete primarily for wealth are relatively harmless as compared with men who compete primarily for power." That such assertions as this may very well be true is beside the point. For certainly negative consequences of power can subsist alongside of positive ones. At times Riesman seems to recognize the need for people to seek and use power if they as individuals and the society as a whole are to develop to the fullest of their capacities. But his dominant orientation toward power remains highly individualistic and negative.

Mills is more extreme than Riesman on this matter, since he never asks what is socially required in the way of resources of power and uses of power, but instead is preoccupied with the magnitude of those resources and the (allegedly) destructive expropriation of them by and for the higher circles of major institutions. It is a very limited notion of power that construes it only in terms of coercion and conflict among particular interests. Societies require arrangements whereby resources of power can be effectively used and supplemented for public goals. This is a requirement for government, but the use of this term should not obscure that fact that government either commands power or lacks effectiveness. Mills does not concern himself with the *ends* of power, nor with the conditions for their attainment. He has no conception of the bases of political order, and no theory of the functions of government and politics. He suggests nothing that could prevent his "power elite" from developing into a full-blown totalitarianism. The logic of Mills's position finally reduces to a contest between anarchy and tyranny.

The problem of power seems to bring out the clinician in each of us. We quickly fasten on the pathology of power, whether we label the symptoms as "inside-dopesterism" (Riesman) or as "the higher immorality" (Mills). As a result, we often lose sight of the ends of power in the political system under review. It is important to understand that pivotal decisions increasingly are made at the national level, and that this poses genuine difficulties for the maintenance of democratic control. It is also important to understand that a multiplicity of public and private agencies increasingly pressure decision-makers, and that this poses genuine difficulties for the maintenance of effective political leadership. But the fact remains that there have been periods of centralized decision-making *and* democratic control, multiple constraints on power *and* effective leadership. There is no simple relationship between the extent to which power is equally distributed and the stability of democratic order. For a democratic order requires strong government as well as public consent by an informed citizenry. Unless current tendencies are measured against both sets of needs, there will be little progress in understanding how either one is frustrated or fulfilled. Finally, in the absence of more disciplined historical and comparative anaysis, we shall continue to lack a firm basis for evaluating such widely divergent diagnoses of political malaise as those given us by Mills and Riesman.

MARC PILISUK AND THOMAS HAYDEN / Is There a Military-Industrial Complex Which Prevents Peace?*

The question, "Does there exist a military-industrial complex which prevents peace?" at first seems debatable in straightforward yes-or-no terms. Indeed, it might have been answerable in the twenties or thirties but not in the post-war period. When there is permanent intermingling and coordination among military, industrial, and governmental elites, and whenever greater war-preparedness can be justified by reference to the communist movement, it becomes a much "stickier" question. Because it is sticky, the easiest conclusion to support is that a "complex" simply does not exist as an omnipresent obstacle to policy change. Indeed, this belief has become the accepted norm for "informed" discussion of interests vested in the perpetuation of military pre-paredness. The next most easily supported conclusion would be that we have become trapped in the hell-fires of militarism by a sinister but concealed elite of military-industrial leaders, which through its puppets, pulls the strings on every major policy decision. This latter theory is non-conformist, radical, and smacks too closely of classical conspiracy theory to be palatable to most

* From *The Journal of Social Issues* (July, 1963), pp. 70–113. Portions of the original article have been omitted. See also M. Pilisuk and R. Perrucci, eds., *The Triple Revolution: Social Problems in Depth* (Boston, Little, Brown and Company, 1968).

scholars. Indeed, the dominant attitude (explicit or tacit) in most
of the new literature is that there exists no military-industrial
complex capable of preventing peace. It is claimed that the military-industrial complex operates as a subgroup within the limits
of an essentially civilian society. In this view the complex is seen
as making an interest-conscious equation of its own interests with
those of the nation as a whole. But, it is argued, this tendency of
power aggrandizement is checked by countervailing interest blocks
in the society. Moreover, the "complex" is not seen as having a
corrosive effect on democratic processes; even if it is conceded that
military and technological expertise or well-financed public relations give the "complex" unusual privilege and visibility, this is
no different, in principle, from certain other influential groups,
all of which are limited by the web of constraints but comprise a
pluralist society. Usually, it is added that the internal differences
in the "complex" such as differences among the separate services
or between the military and the industrial procurement sectors,
tend to restrict further its ability to impose a policy "line" on the
United States. These points of view appear in scattered form
throughout the literature. A few examples are cited to demonstrate this.

Wise and Ross call their brilliantly rich study of the CIA *The
Invisible Government* without realizing the theoretical problems
immediately raised by such a title.[1] Does the CIA, and the
broader "intelligence community" actually have the tools and,
more importantly, the prerogatives of sovereignty (for its own
operations) associated with the concept of "government"? If this
is the case, then the conventional pluralist argument would be
perforated decisively, because it rests on the assumption that no
power centers are unaccountable to democratic review. The nature of the evidence used in the book, however, precludes an objective answer to this question. Using case studies primarily, although there also are chapters on the CIA structure, the authors
are concerned with such issues as: the contradictions between sinister CIA practices and professed U.S. policy objectives; the tendency of the CIA to support only conservative or reactionary gov-

[1] David Wise and Thomas Ross, *The Invisible Government* (New York,
Random House, 1964).

ernments; the danger that the CIA can influence specific policy objectives of the U.S. government, as in the case of the U-2 interference with the 1960 Paris summit meeting; the progressive acceptance in America of subversive techniques as part of a "necessary Cold War strategy." But it is explicitly maintained that the "invisible government" is subordinate, at least so far, to the visible one in general as well as in nearly every specific case. At worst, it has an undefined "quasi-independent" status which should be brought under somewhat greater congressional and executive review (p. 352). . . .

None of these denials of irresponsible military-industrial power marshal very significant evidence to support their views. There are examples given of specific conflicts between civilian and military groups which were lost by the military (e.g., the dropping of General Walker, the refusal to be first to break the moratorium on testing). There are examples given of heated divisions between the services over what military strategy should be pursued (the arguments over conventional warfare in the late fifties and the more recent RS 70 controversy). There are sociological studies which reveal underlying diversities within single corporations, between competing corporations, and within the demographic and institutional character of each branch of the armed services.[2] And, throughout, there are citations of American pluralism as an automatic check system against any elite group.[3]

At a more general level, these fragments of evidence point to-

[2] For a good sociological study of interservice differences, see Morris Janowitz, "Military Elites and the Study of War," *The Journal of Conflict Resolution,* I (1957), 1, pp. 9–18; also, *The Professional Soldier* (Glencoe, Ill., The Free Press, 1960).

[3] For the thesis that a "peacefare state" counterweighs the "warfare state," see Klaus Knorr's review of Fred J. Cook [*The Warfare State* (New York, Macmillan, 1962)] entitled "Warfare and Peacefare States and the Acts of Transition," *The Journal of Conflict Resolution,* VII (1963) 4, pp. 754–762. The "pluralist position," which usually is that the social system has semi-automatic checking mechanisms against tyranny, appears as basic in discussions not only of the military, but of economics and politics as well. See: Robert A. Dahl, *Who Governs?* (New Haven, Yale University Press, 1961); John K. Galbraith, *American Capitalism* (Boston, Houghton, 1956); Seymour M. Lipset, *Political Man* (Garden City, Doubleday, 1959); and Talcott Parsons, *The Social System* (Glencoe, Ill., The Free Press, 1951).

ward three grounds for denying that a military-industrial complex prevents peace:

1) it is held that the *scope* of decisions made by any interest group is quite narrow and cannot be said to govern anything so broad as foreign policy.

2) it is held that the "complex" is not *monolithic, not self-conscious,* and *not coordinated,* the presumed attributes of a ruling elite.

3) it is held that the military-industrial complex does not wield power if the term "power" is defined as the ability to realize its will even against the resistance of others and regardless of external conditions.

These formulations, to repeat, are made neither explicitly nor consistently in the new literature. But they crystallize the basic questions about definition which the new literature raises. Moreover, they are quite definitely the major contentions made by academic criticisms of power elite theory. The more widely read of these academic critics include Daniel Bell, Robert Dahl, and Talcott Parsons.[4] Since their critiques are mainly directed at the work of C. Wright Mills,[5] it is with Mills that we will begin to analyze the theories which claim there *is* a military-industrial complex blocking peace.

THE THESIS OF ELITE CONTROL

Mills is by far the most formidable exponent of the theory of a power elite. In his view, the period in America since World War II has been dominated by the ascendance of corporation and military elites to positions of institutional power. These "commanding heights" allow them to exercise control over the trends of the business cycle and international relations. The Cold War set the

[4] Daniel Bell, *The End of Ideology* (Glencoe, Ill., The Free Press, 1959); Robert A. Dahl, *op. cit.,* and see also *A Modern Political Analysis* (New York, Prentice Hall, 1963); Talcott Parsons, *op. cit.,* and also see *Structure and Process in Modern Societies* (Glencoe, Ill., The Free Press, 1959).

[5] C. Wright Mills, *The Power Elite* (New York, Oxford University Press, 1959). See also Mills's *The Causes of World War III* (New York, Simon and Schuster, 1958).

conditions which legitimize this ascendance, and the decline and incorporation of significant left-liberal movements, such as the CIO, symbolizes the end of opposition forces. The power elite monopolizes sovereignty, in that political initiative and control stem mainly from the top hierarchical levels of position and influence. Through the communications system the elite facilitates the growth of a politically indifferent mass society below the powerful institutions. This, according to the Mills argument, would explain why an observer finds widespread apathy. Only a small minority believes in actual participation in the larger decisions which affect their existence and only the ritual forms of "popular democracy" are practiced by the vast majority. Mills's argument addresses itself to the terms of the three basic issues we have designated, i.e., scope of decision power, awareness of common interest, and the definition of power exerted.

By *scope*, we are referring to the sphere of society over which an elite is presumed to exercise power. Mills argues that the scope of this elite is general, embracing all the decisions which in any way could be called vital (slump and boom, peace and war, etc.). He does not argue that *each* decision is directly determined, but rather that the political alternatives from which the "Deciders" choose are shaped and limited by the elite through its possession of all the large-scale institutions. By this kind of argument, Mills avoids the need to demonstrate how his elite is at work during each decision. He speaks instead in terms of institutions and resources. But the problem is that his basic evidence is of a rather negative kind. No major decisions have been made for twenty years contrary to the policies of anti-communism and corporate or military aggrandizement; *therefore* a power elite must be prevailing. Mills might have improved his claims about the scope of elite decisions by analyzing a series of actual decisions in terms of the premises which were *not* debated. This could point to the mechanisms (implicit or explicit) which led to the exclusion of these premises from debate. By this and other means he might have found more satisfying evidence of the common, though perhaps tacit, presuppositions of seemingly disparate institutions. He then might have developed a framework analyzing "scope" on different levels. The scope of the Joint Chiefs of Staff, for instance, could be seen as limited, while at the same time the Joint Chiefs could be placed in a larger elite context having larger scope. Whether this could be shown awaits research of this kind. Until it is done, however, Mills's theory of scope remains open to attack, but, conversely, is not subject to refutation.

Mills's theory also eludes the traditional requirements for inferring monolithic structure, i.e., consciousness of elite status, and coordination. The modern tradition of viewing elites in this way began with Mosca's *The Ruling Class* in a period when family units and inheritance systems were the basic means of conferring power. Mills departs from this influential tradition precisely because of his emphasis on institutions at the basic elements. If the military, political, and economic *institutional orders* involve a high coincidence of interest, then the groups composing the institutional orders need not be monolithic, conscious, and coordinated, yet still they can exercise elite power.[6] This means specifically that a military-industrial complex could exist as an expression of a certain fixed ideology (reflecting common institutional needs), yet be "composed" of an endless shuffle of specific groups. For instance, our tables show 82 companies have dropped out of the list of 100 top defense contractors, and only 36 "durables" have remained on the list in the years since 1940. In terms of industry, the percentage of contracts going to the automobile industry dropped from 25 percent in World War II to 4 percent in the missile age. At the same time, the aircraft companies went from 34 to 54 percent of all contracts, and the electronics industry from 9 to 28 percent.[7] Mills's most central argument is that this ebb-and-flow is not necessarily evidence for the pluralists. His stress is on the unities which underlie the procession of competition and change. The decision to change the technology of warfare was one which enabled one group to "overcome" another in an overall system to which both are fundamentally

[6] See James H. Meisel, *The Myth of the Ruling Class* (Ann Arbor, University of Michigan Press, 1958), for the best available discussion of this innovation in theorizing about elites.

[7] M. J. Peck and F. M. Scherer, *The Weapons Acquisition Process* (Cambridge, Harvard University Press, 1962).

committed. Moreover, the decision issued from the laboratories and planning boards of the defense establishment and only superficially involved any role for public opinion. The case studies of weapons development by Peck and Scherer, in which politics is described as a marginal ritual, would certainly buttress Mills's point of view.

Making this institution analysis enables Mills to make interesting comments on his human actors. The integration of institutions means that hundreds of individuals become familiar with several roles: General, politician, lobbyist, defense contractor. These men are the power elite, but they need not know it. They conspire, but conspiracy is not absolutely essential to their maintenance. They mix together easily, but can remain in power even if they are mostly anonymous to each other. They make decisions, big and small, sometimes with the knowledge of others and sometimes not, which ultimately control all the significant action and resources of society.

Where this approach tends to fall short, is in its unclarity about how discontinuities arise. Is the military-industrial complex a feature of American society which can disappear and still leave the general social structure intact? Horst Brand has suggested a tension between financial companies and the defense industries because of the relatively few investment markets created by defense.[8] Others are beginning to challenge the traditional view that defense spending stimulates high demand and employment. Their claim is that the concentration of contracts in a few states, the monopolization of defense and space industry by the largest 75 or 100 corporations, the low multiplier effect of the new weapons, the declining numbers of blue-collar workers required, and other factors, make the defense economy more of a drag than a stimulant.[9] Mills died before these trends became the subject of debate, but he might have pioneered in discussion of them if his

[8] Horst Brand, "Disarmament and American Capitalism," *Dissent* (Summer, 1962), pp. 236–251.
[9] See Seymour Melman, ed., *A Strategy for American Security* (New York, Lee Offset, Inc., 1963); see also Melman's *The Peace Race* (New York, Braziller, 1962); and Amital Etzioni, *The Hard Way to Peace* (New York, Collier, 1962), and *The Moon-Doggle* (Garden City, Doubleday, 1964).

analytic categories had differentiated more finely between various industries and interest groups in his power elite. His emphasis was almost entirely on the "need" for a "permanent war economy" just when that need was being questioned even among his elite.

However, this failure does not necessarily undermine the rest of Mills's analysis. His institutional anaysis is still the best means of identifying a complex without calling it monolithic, conscious, and coordinated. Had he differentiated more exactly he might have been able to describe various degrees of commitment to an arms race, a rightist ideology constricting the arena of meaningful debate, and other characteristics of a complex. This task remains to be done, and will be discussed at a later point.

Where Mills's theory is most awkward is in his assertions that the elite can, and does, make its decisions against the will of others and regardless of external conditions. This way of looking at power is inherited by Mills, and much of modern sociology, directly from Max Weber. What is attributed to the elite is a rather fantastic quality: liberal omnipotence. Conversely, any group that is *not* able to realize its will even against the resistance of others is only "influential" but not an elite. Mills attempts to defend this viewpoint but, in essence, modifies it. He says he is describing a tendency, not a finalized state of affairs. This is a helpful device in explaining cracks in the monolith—for instance, the inability of the elite to establish a full corporate state against the will of small businessmen. However, it does not change the ultimate argument—that the power elite cannot become more than a tendency, cannot realize its actual self, unless it takes on the quality of omnipotence.

When power is defined as this kind of dominance, it is easily open to critical dispute. The conception of power depicts a vital and complex social system as essentially static, as having within it a set of stable governing components, with pre-charted interests which infiltrate and control every outpost of decision-authority. Thereby, internal accommodation is made necessary and significant change, aside from growth, becomes impossible. This conception goes beyond the idea of social or economic determinism.

In fact, it defines a "closed social system." A "closed system" may be a dramatic image, but it is a forced one as well. Its defender sees events such as the rise of the labor movement essentially as a means of rationalizing modern capitalism. But true or false as this may be, did not the labor movement also constitute a "collective will" which the elite could not resist? An accommodation was reached, probably more on the side of capital than labor, but the very term "accommodation" implies the existence of more than one independent will. On a world scale, this becomes even more obvious. Certainly the rise of communism has not been through the will of capitalists, and Mills would be the first to agree. Nor does the elite fully control technological development; surely the process of invention has some independent, even if minor, place in the process of social change.

Mills's definition of power as dominance ironically serves the pluralist argument, rather than countering it. When power is defined so extremely, it becomes rather easy to claim that such power is curbed in the contemporary United States. The pluralists can say that Mills has conjured up a bogeyman to explain his own failure to realize his will. This is indeed what has been done in review after review of Mills's writings. A leading pluralist thinker, Edward Shils, says that Mills was too much influenced by Trotsky and Kafka:

> Power, although concentrated, is not so concentrated, so powerful, or so permeative as Professor Mills seem to believe.... There have been years in Western history, e.g., in Germany during the last years of the Weimar Republic and under the Nazis when reality approximated this picture more closely.... But as a picture of Western societies, and not just as an ideal type of extreme possibilities which might be realized if so much else that is vital were lacking, it will not do.[10]

But is Mills's definition the only suitable one here? If it is, then the pluralists have won the debate. But if there is a way to designate an irresponsible elite without giving it omnipotence, then the debate may be recast at least.

[10] Edward Shils, "Professor Mills on the Calling of Sociology," *World Politics*, XIII (1961), p. 4.

This fundamental question is not answered in the other major books which affirm the existence of a military-industrial complex. Cook's *The Warfare State* and Perlo's *Militarism and Industry*[11] are good examples of this literature which is theoretically inferior to Mills's perplexing account.

REVISING THE CRITERIA FOR INFERRING POWER

After finding fault with so many books and divergent viewpoints, the most obvious conclusion is that current social theory is currently deficient in its explanation of power. We concur with one of Mills's severest critics, Daniel Bell, who at least agrees with Mills that most current analysis concentrates on the "intermediate sectors," e.g., parties, interest groups, formal structures, without attempting to view the underlying system of "renewable power independent of any momentary group of actors." However, we have indicated that the only formidable analysis of the underlying system of renewable power, that of Mills, has profound shortcomings because of its definition of power. Therefore, before we can offer an answer of our own to the question, "Is there a military-industrial complex which blocks peace?" it is imperative to return to the question of power itself in American society.

We have agreed essentially with the pluralist claim that ruling-group models do not "fit" the American structure. We have classified Mills's model as that of a ruling group because of his Weberian definition of power, but we have noted also that Mills successfully went beyond two traps common to elite theories, *viz.*, that the elite is total in the scope of its decisions, and that the elite is a coordinated monolith.

But we perhaps have not stressed sufficiently that the alternative case for pluralism is inadequate in its claim to describe the historical dynamics of American society. The point of our dissent from pluralism is over the doctrine of "countervailing power." This is the modern version of Adam Smith's economics and of the

11 Victor Perlo, *Militarism and Industry* (New York, International Publishers, 1963).

Madisonian or Federalism theory of checks-and-balances, adapted to the new circumstances of large-scale organization. Its evidence is composed of self-serving incidents and a faith in semi-mystical resources. For instance, in the sphere of political economy, it is argued that oligopoly contains automatic checking mechanisms against undue corporate growth, and that additionally, the factors of "public opinion" and "corporate conscience" are built-in limiting forces.[12] We believe that evidence in the field, however, suggests that oligopoly is a means of stabilizing an industrial sphere either through tacit agreements to follow price leadership or rigged agreements in the case of custom-made goods; that "public opinion" tends much more to be manipulated and apathetic than independently critical; that "corporate conscience" is less suitable as a description than Reagan's terms, "corporate arrogance."

To take the more immediate example of the military sphere, the pluralist claim is that the military is subordinate to broader, civilian interests. The first problem with the statement is the ambiguity of "civilian." Is it clear that military men are more "militaristic" than civilian men? To say so would be to deny the increasing trend of "white-collar militarism." The top strategists in the Department of Defense, the Central Intelligence Agency, and the key advisory positions often are Ph.D.'s. In fact, "civilians" including McGeorge Bundy, Robert Kennedy, Walt Rostow, and Robert McNamara are mainly responsible for the development of the only remaining "heroic" form of combat: counter-insurgency operations in the jungles of the underdeveloped countries. If "militarism" [13] has permeated this deeply into the "civilian" sphere, then the distinction between the terms becomes largely nominal. Meisel's description is imaginative and alluring:

---

[12] For this argument, see A. A. Berle, *The Twentieth Century Capitalist Revolution* (New York, Harcourt, 1954) and J. K. Galbraith, *American Capitalism*. For sound criticisms, but without sound alternatives, see Mills's and Perlo's books. Also see Michael Reagan, *The Managed Economy* (New York, Oxford, 1963) and Berland Nossiter, *The Mythmakers* (Boston, Houghton, 1964) for other refutations of the countervailing power thesis.

[13] We are defining the term as "primary reliance on coercive means, particularly violence or the threat of violence, to deal with social problems."

What we still honor with the name of peace is only the domestic aspect of a world-wide industrial mobilization let up at intervals by the explosions of a shooting war. . . . The industrial revolution in its class-struggle aspect is becoming externalized, projected upon the industrial field, that it is being relegated, so to speak, from barricade to barracks. . . . The armies, navies, and air forces of our time [are] the embodiment of the industrial revolution in its aggressive form.[14]

While the more traditional military men have not taken kindly to the take-over of military planning by civilian professors, the take-over has, nonetheless, gone far. More than three hundred universities and non-profit research institutions supply civilian personnel to, and seek contracts from, the Department of Defense. Approximately half of these institutions were created specifically to do specialized strategic research. Probably the most influential of the lot of these civilian centers is the Rand Corporation.[15]

The main point here is that the pluralist argument relies on "countervailing forces" which are more mythical than real. The Wise and Ross book shows indisputably that at least during certain instances the Executive is not countervailing the CIA. Moreover, who is countervailing the "military-civilian" Executive centered in the Pentagon and the White House? What Knorr sees as a "peacefare state" countervailing the "warfare state" is merely its white-collar brother. The symbolic figure of the Arms Control and Disarmament Agency demonstrates this reality vividly. One side of the ACDA figure is a diplomat with tie and attaché case; the other side is a warrior dedicated to the pursuit of stabilizing control measures which might assure national advantages in a never-ending cold war.

ACDA's narrow conception of its own role is as much a function of its internal quest for respectability as it is a matter of the prerogatives given it by a reluctant Congress. It has sought re-

14 James H. Meisel, *The Fall of The Republic* (Ann Arbor, University of Michigan Press, 1962).
15 I. L. Horowitz, *The War Game: Studies of the New Civilian Militarists* (New York, Ballantine, 1963).

spectability not only in its apparent choice of essentially technical questions for study but also in its manner of study. One favored study technique is to collapse large socially significant questions into several questions answerable by short-term studies and suited for study by the grossly over-simplified techniques of policy appraisal employed by those same operations research corporations which serve, and live upon, defense contracts. These organizations have traditionally produced quick answers embedded in rationalistic models which ring with scientism and jargon. *Strategy and Conscience,* a powerfully written book by Anatol Rapoport,[16] documents the manner in which the rationalist models employed in such strategic studies frequently conceal (often unknowingly) gross assumptions of the nature of the cold war. The point here is that if these are the same assumptions which necessitate a high level of military preparedness, then it matters little whether the studies are commissioned by civilian or military authorities.

CONSENSUS

All that countervailing power refers to is the relationship between groups who fundamentally accept "the American system" but who compete for advantages within it. The corporate executive wants higher profits, the laborer a higher wage. The President wants the final word on military strategies, the Chairman of the Joint Chiefs does not trust him with it. Boeing wants the contract, but General Dynamics is closer at the time to the Navy Secretary and the President, and so on: what is prevented by countervailing forces is the dominance of society by a group or clique or a party. But this process suggests a profoundly important point; that *the constant pattern in American society is the rise and fall of temporarily irresponsible groups.* By temporary we mean that, outside of the largest industrial conglomerates,[17] the groups which wield significant power to influence policy decisions are not guaranteed stability. By irresponsible we mean that there

16 (New York, Harpers, 1964).
17 The term used in recent hearings by Senator Philip A. Hart refers to industrial organizations like Textron, which have holdings in every major sector of American industry.

are many activities within their scope which are essentially unaccountable in the democratic process. These groups are too uneven to be described with the shorthand term "class." Their personnel have many different characteristics (compare IBM executives and the Southern Dixiecrats) and their needs as groups are different enough to cause endless fights as, for example, small *vs.* big business. No one group or coalition of several groups can tyrannize the rest as is demonstrated, for example, in the changing status of the major financial groups, particularly the fast-rising Bank of America which has been built from the financial needs of the previously neglected small consumer.

However, it is clear that these groups exist within consensus relationships of a more general and durable kind than their conflict relationships. This is true, first of all, of their social characteristics. . . .

The second evidence of consensus relationships, besides attitude and background data indicating a pro-business sympathy, would come from an examination of the *practice* of decision-making. By analysis of such actual behavior we can understand which consensus attitudes are reflected in decision-making. Here, in retrospect, it is possible to discover the values and assumptions which are defended recurrently. This is at least a rough means of finding the boundaries of consensus relations. Often these boundaries are invisible because of the very infrequency with which they are tested. What are visible most of the time are the parameters of conflict relationships among different groups. These conflict relationships constitute the ingredients of experience which give individuals or groups their uniqueness and varieties, while the consensus relations constitute the common underpinnings of behavior. The tendency in social science has been to study decision-making in order to study group differences; we need to study decision-making also to understand group commonalities.

Were such studies done, our hypothesis would be that certain "core beliefs" are continuously unquestioned. One of these, undoubtedly, would be that efficacy is preferable to principle in foreign affairs. In practice, this means that violence is preferable to

non-violence as a means of defense. A second is that private property is preferable to collective property. A third assumption is
that the particular form of constitutional government, which is
practiced within the United States is preferable to any other system of government. We refer to the preferred mode as limited
parliamentary democracy, a system in which institutionalized
forms of direct representation are carefully retained but with
fundamental limitations placed upon the prerogatives of governing. Specifically included among the areas of limitation are many
matters encroaching upon corporation property and state hegemony. While adherence to this form of government is conceivably
the strongest of the domestic "core values," at least among business elites, it is probably the least strongly held of the three on
the international scene. American relations with, and assistance
for, authoritarian and semi-feudal regimes occurs exactly in those
areas where the recipient regime is evaluated primarily upon the
two former assumptions and given rather extensive leeway on the
latter one.

The implications of these "core beliefs" for the social system
are immense, for they justify the maintenance of our largest institutional structures: the military, the corporate economy, and a
system of partisan politics which protects the concept of limited
democracy. These institutions, in turn, may be seen as current
agencies of the more basic social structure. We use the term "social structure" as Robert S. Lynd does as the stratification of people identified according to kinship, sex, age, division of labor,
race, religion, or other factors which differentiate them in terms
of role, status, access to resources, and power. According to Lynd:

> This structure established durable relations that hold groups of
> people together for certain purposes and separate them for others.
> Such social structures may persist over many generations. Its con-
> tinuance depends upon its ability to cope with historical changes
> that involve absorption of new groupings and relations of men
> without fundamental change in the structure of the society of a
> kind that involves major transfer of power.[18]

[18] Robert S. Lynd and Helen Merrill Lynd, *Middletown* (New York, Harcourt,
1959).

The "renewable basis of power" in America at the present time underlies those institutional orders linked in consensus relationships: military defense of private property and parliamentary democracy. These institutional orders are not permanently secure, by definition. Their maintenance involves a continuous coping with new conditions, such as technological innovation and with the inherent instabilities of a social structure which arbitrarily classifies persons by role, status, access to resources, and power. The myriad groups composing these orders are even less secure because of their weak ability to command "coping resources," e.g., the service branches are less stable than the institution of the military, particular companies are less stable than the institutions of corporate property, political parties are less stable than the institution of parliamentary government.

In the United States there is no ruling group. Nor is there any easily discernible ruling institutional order, so meshed have the separate sources of elite power become. But there is a social structure which is organized to create and protect power centers with only partial accountability. In this definition of power we are avoiding the Weber-Mills meaning of *omnipotence* and the contrary pluralist definition of power as consistently *diffuse*. We are describing the current system as one of overall "minimal accountability" and "minimal consent." We mean that the role of democratic review, based on genuine popular consent, is made marginal and reactive. Elite groups are minimally accountable to publics and have a substantial, though by no means maximum, freedom to shape popular attitudes. The reverse of our system would be one in which democratic participation would be the orienting demand around which the social structure is organized.

Some will counter this case by saying that we are measuring "reality" against an "ideal," a technique which permits the conclusion that the social structure is undemocratic according to its distance from our utopian values. This is a convenient apology for the present system, of course. We think it possible, at least in theory, to develop measures of the undemocratic in democratic conditions, and place given social structures along a continuum. These measures, in rough form, might include such variables as economic security, education, legal guarantees, access to information, and participatory control over systems of economy, government, and jurisprudence.

The reasons for our concern with democratic process in an article questioning the power of a purported military-industrial complex are two-fold. First, just as scientific method both legitimizes and promotes change in the world of knowledge, democratic method legitimizes and promotes change in the world of social institutions. Every society, regardless of how democratic, protects its core institutions in a web of widely shared values. But if the core institutions should be dictated by the requisites of military preparedness, then restrictions on the democratic process, i.e., restrictions in either mass-opinion exchange (as by voluntary or imposed news management) or in decision-making bodies (as by selection of participants in a manner guaranteeing exclusion of certain positions), then such restrictions would be critical obstacles to peace.

Second, certain elements of democratic process are inimical to features of militarily oriented society, and the absence of these elements offers one type of evidence for a military-industrial complex even in the absence of a ruling elite. . . .

The absence of a countervailing force for peace cannot, we have claimed, be demonstrated by an absence of conflicting interests among powerful sectors of American society. Indeed, such conflicts are ever-present examples of American pluralism. Demonstrating the absence of a discussion of the shared premises, among the most potent sectors of society, would go far in highlighting the area of forced or acquiescent consensus. But even the absence of debate could not complete the case unless we can show how the accepted premises are inconsistent with requisites of a viable peace-time social system. It is to this question: of the compatibility of the unquestioned assumptions of American society with conditions of peace, that we now turn. The "core beliefs" which we listed as unchallenged by any potent locus of institutionalized power are:

a) Efficacy is preferable to principle in foreign affairs (thus military means are chosen over non-violent means);

b) Private property is preferable to public property; and

c) Limited parliamentary democracy is preferable to any other system of government.

What characteristics of a continuing world system devoid of military conflict fly in the face of these assumptions?

We identify three conditions for enduring peace which clash with one or more of the core beliefs. These are: 1) the requirements for programming an orderly transition and the subsequent maintenance of a non-defense economy within a highly automated and relatively affluent society; 2) the conditions for peaceful settlement of internal disputes within underdeveloped countries and between alien nations and commercial interests; and 3) the conditions under which disparities in living standards between have and have-not nations can be handled with minimum violence.[19], [20]

Is there, then, a military-industrial complex which prevents peace? The answer is inextricably imbedded into the mainstream of American institutions and mores. Our concept is not that American society contains a ruling military-industrial complex. Our concept is more nearly that American society *is* a military-industrial complex. It can accommodate a wide range of factional interests from those concerned with the production or utilization of a particular weapon to those enraptured with the mystique of optimal global strategies. It can accommodate those with rabid desires to advance toward the brink and into limitless intensifica-

[19] Briefly, the incongruities are that a peacetime economy, in this country, would require a level of long-term planning and control, which would in turn, require a degree of participatory involvement by effected people and firms that runs counter to the priorities on private property and governmental limitation. International order in peacetime would violate the priorities for efficacy and military solution in the protection of natural interests; and the needs of the have-not peoples for food and for local self-determination would and do clash violently with all three of the unchallenged domestic premises.

[20] David Horowitz, "World Economic Disparities: the Haves and the Have-Nots," Center for Study of Democratic Institutions (Santa Barbara, 1962). See also Quincy Wright, William Evans, and Morton Deutsch, eds., *Preventing World War III: Some Proposals* (New York, Simon and Schuster, 1962).

tion of the arms race. It can even accommodate those who wish either to prevent war or to limit the destructiveness of war through the gradual achievement of arms control and disarmament agreements. What it cannot accommodate is the type of radical departures needed to produce enduring peace.

The requirements of a social system geared to peace, as well as the requirements for making a transition to such a social system, share a pattern of resource distribution which is different from the one the world now has. Moreover, these requirements for peace are, in significant measure, inconsistent with constraints set by the more enduring convergencies among power structures in the United States. The same is true whether one speaks of allocation of material or of intellectual resources. Both are geared to the protection of the premises rather than to avenues of change. We are not saying that war is inevitable or that the changes cannot be made. We are saying that the American political, military, and industrial system operates with certain built-in stabilizers which resist a change in the system. If there is to be peace, as opposed to detente or temporary absence of war, marked changes will be needed. Whether this society can or will accommodate to such changes is a question which is fundamentally different from the questions posed by most studies conventionally grouped under the rubric of peace research. One difference which marks the question of capacity to accommodate is in the theoretical conception or model of the cold war which is assumed. And a second distinction lies in the manner in which the end product of the research may be suited to meet the social forces (as apart from the intellectual arguments) which promote long-term changes in policy.

ROLE OF THE PEACE SCHOLARS

In recent years, intellectual attention to the problem of peace has usually been directed to the problem of averting war. The context of this problem is that of the non-zero-sum game in which the players have both a joint common advantage (in averting nuclear war) and a bargaining problem in deciding upon the competitive distribution of other non-sharable advantages. Much of the intellectual attention from social scientists has been directed to problems of trust, controls, and assurances of good faith—problems relevant to protecting the common advantage. Meanwhile the strategists have tended to give relatively greater emphasis to the problem of competitive advantage. There have been clashes between these two groups of intellectuals but both share, and both assume that foreign adversaries also share, the assumption that nuclear war ought to be avoided. The question is one of means to that end and of risks to be taken.

In the question of permanent peace with its contingent institutions, there is no such fundamental agreement about the desirability of the end. In fact, we have argued that there exists a large area of consensus which precludes the very set of contingent institutions which may be needed for lasting peace. Without certain shared end values, research on the part of peace protagonists cannot be used as a rational wedge in policy debate. The clash is with a social system some of whose very bases of organization run counter to the requirements of stable peace. Under such circumstances, there are zero-sum components to the conflict. Some institutions and some status positions within the society must change and some may actually have to perish if certain newer ones are to thrive. Research in this area becomes what most researchers who are justly sensitive about their scientific objectivity dread—a part of a political struggle. . . .

Obviously, we have not answered our own question of whether there exists a military-industrial complex which can prevent peace. We have argued that the conditions of a stable peace will differ markedly from the conditions of temporary avoidance of war and that constellations of powerful and divergent interests coalesce on certain policies which work against social change. We have tried to show that the absence of monolithic decision-power among these groups, while essentially correct, is a weak argument in the absence of a countervailing force for peace. We have attempted to prejudge—on scant and early evidence—the rise of a politically viable force with a critical stake in the decisions which move us toward peace and in the particular national and local programs which will offset the nation's defense efforts. We have hinted at the nature of social science research which could prove helpful to such a countervailing force.[21]

21 This point is more fully developed in the original paper and in Marc Pilisuk, "The Poor and the War on Poverty," *The Correspondent* (Summer, 1965). See also Pilisuk's "Dominance of the Military," *Science* (January 18, 1963), pp. 247–248.

PART III

POLITICS AND SOCIAL CHANGE

EDITOR'S INTRODUCTION

The theme of this section of the Reader is political change. Chapter 7 deals with political movements; Chapter 8 with the internal analysis of political parties; and Chapter 9 with the process of revolution.

As Moore points out, political movements result from dissatisfaction with the status quo. One of the accompaniments of a political movement is ideology, what Moore calls its "charter myth." [1] Moore traces two recurring problems faced by political movements that are trying to achieve power: finding or constructing a body of supporters; entering into tactical alliances with other groups. If and when power is achieved, there is the problem of whether to share it with other groups (this is similar to the problem of whether to engage in tactical alliances); and whether to leave the old social structure intact or to smash it and build new revolutionary institutions.

Included in the chapter on political movements is a discussion by Kornhauser of the social conditions that facilitate the rise of totalitarian movements; and a discussion by Jacobs and Landau of one contemporary political movement—the so-called "New Left" in the United States.

One important problem that confronts political movements is the relationship between means and ends. As Michels points out, even political groups that desire to obtain a better social order, justice, and equality, tend in operation to be run as oligarchies. In a struggle with an entrenched opposition, how else could they get into power? Conspiratorial groups with the motto "the end

1 The functions and relevance of contemporary ideologies are discussed in Part 4 of this Reader.

justifies the means" are only carrying this to its logical conclusion.

The paradox of getting into power is also examined in the selection included by Paul Goodman. In his article, Goodman examines the chances of "radical" candidates in the 1962 elections. He concludes that there is no way to avoid compromising one's principles if one is truly trying to achieve power; and that the problem is not so much how to capture centralized power as how to abolish it.

The last chapter in this section deals with revolutions. Revolutions are sweeping political changes in which an oppressed social group takes over political power. They should be distinguished from *coups d'état,* which are merely changes in the personnel of the ruling elite. One of the key questions in the study of revolutions is why some oppressed people revolt, while others remain in subjugation for centuries without any apparent effort to throw off their yoke. Other questions touched upon by the selections on revolution included here are: What causes revolutions? Do revolutions really change anything? Is it possible to achieve revolutionary ends without using violent means?

The most optimistic note on revolutions is struck by Shridharani, who uses the model of Gandhi's successful non-violent resistance movement to point the way toward an alternative to armed revolution. But this model does not necessarily apply to all conditions. (How could Vietnamese peasants react non-violently to American bombers flying overhead? By letting themselves get killed?) Perhaps the most depressing note on revolutions is Brinton's remark that "the achievement of government efficiency is really the most striking uniformity we can note in estimating the political changes effected by our revolutions." [2]

One clue to the origins of revolutions is provided by Brinton who says that "revolutionary movements seem to originate in the discontents of not unprosperous people who feel restraint, cramp, annoyance rather than downright cursing oppression." And the

[2] Brinton's analysis is based on case studies of the English, French, Russian, and American revolutions. But I would not consider the latter in quite the same category as the others. For the success of the American breakaway from England merely provided a somewhat more favorable situation for American merchants, without changing much else.

lead is further amplified by Davies who maintains that the crucial social condition underlying a revolution is a sudden cutback in a previously expanding economy. Such a cutback, according to Davies, leads to an intolerable gap between expectations and reality. This is the social condition under which a spark could set off a revolution.

In an article not included in this anthology, Moore adds to the above a number of observations concerning the conditions under which peasant revolutions are more likely to take place. A primary factor seems to be the absence of a successful agricultural revolution led by the upper classes, which leaves the peasants to face all kinds of stresses and strains as their society is drawn into the modern world. Also, societies with centralized governments seem more likely to have revolutions than those which are more decentralized; and similarly those in which the link between lord and peasant is relatively weak. On the other hand, a weak state of solidarity among the peasants can impede concerted political action, and thus favor the status quo.[3]

THE NEW LEFT IN THE U.S.[4]

One way to clarify further the problems of political change is to examine in greater detail some of the dilemmas facing a particular historical social movement. For my purpose here, I have chosen to analyze the tension between reform and revolution in what has been termed "the New Left" in the U.S.

The New Left is in large part the revolt of pampered middle-class kids who have come to understand that the world they were being groomed to take over is not the kind of world they want at all. This movement is sparked by a reaction to the dehumanizing qualities of contemporary bureaucratized life, to its impersonality and its disregard for people's feelings. It has a strong moral flavor, and a concern with overcoming hypocrisy. The movement has an implicit vision of the good community in which men act as broth-

[3] See Barrington Moore, Jr., *Social Origins of Dictatorship and Democracy* (Boston, Beacon Press, 1966). On the last point, see also Edward Banfield, *The Moral Basis of a Backward Society* (New York, Free Press).
[4] This discussion is a slight revision of my article "If not now, when?" that appeared in *Manas* (January 25, 1967), pp. 6–8.

ers, and of the possibility of a more satisfying life in the here and now.

Certain main characteristics of those connected with the New Left stand out clearly:

1. They tend to be non-ideological, without a dogmatic adherence to a systematic world view;

2. They emphasize direct action, including civil disobedience, which grows out of their concern for building the good community *now*.

3. They emphasize participatory democracy—a goal of trying to make it possible for individuals to share in the social decisions that determine the quality and direction of their life.

The non-ideological nature of the New Left is in large part a reaction against the shortcomings of the old Left, in this country, and socialism in eastern Europe. Many of the students feel that a world run by communists might be as rotten a place as a world run by capitalists. Thus some of the people in the New Left lean toward socialism, some lean toward anarchism, some believe in the possibility of obtaining a humanized welfare state, but most are not sure. They are sure that there is a strong connection between means and ends, and that the world they want cannot be obtained by using morally unjustifiable means. This is part of the reason for the non-violent spirit which pervades much of the movement.[5] The people in it want men to stop hating each other one day, and know that you can't get much of a world through a movement filled with hate. But in spite of a general antipathy towards Stalinism, there is little red-baiting within the New Left, and there is an open-hearted tendency to work with anybody who is willing to work on a project, regardless of his other political beliefs. The New Left has a large amount of built-in immunity to manipulation. I think that the people in the movement sense this

[5] There is a potential split in the New Left between those who advocate non-violence and those who see the need for self defense, and if necessary armed revolution, sabotage, etc. Some Black militants feel they are more likely to attract a following nowadays by quoting Fanon rather than Gandhi. An article that illustrates the evolution that has been taking place among some of the leaders of the American civil-rights movement is Stokely Carmichael, "What We Want," *New York Review of Books* (September 22, 1966), pp. 5–8.

in spite of their lack of strong ideological commitment, and for this reason are not at all afraid to work with so-called Communists.

The direct-action emphasis grows out of the experiences of the civil-rights movement, in which it was found that a minority that is willing to face jail or death in its attempt to bring about social change will often be able to force an unwilling majority to grant concessions that could not otherwise be obtained. The tactics and flavor of the civil-rights movement have tended to pervade the whole of the New Left, so that organized mass civil disobedience is now accepted as one of the tactics for bringing about change.

The prior involvement of many of the Berkeley students in the civil-rights movement, for example, helped them to dare to stage a sit-in on campus, and to challenge campus authority with a direct confrontation. The emphasis on direct action reflects a desire to bring about immediate social change without waiting to go through established legal and political channels. This accounts for the flavor of distrust of conventional politics that can be found in the New Left. Perhaps most typical is the motto, "If not now, when?"

This impatience can be seen especially among students involved in the civil-rights movement. Most of those who lead or participate in sit-ins and other forms of direct action are not opposed to the existence of civil-rights laws. It is just that they know that to bring about a free society, you must do more than just lobby for better laws or better interpretation of laws, as the NAACP has tended to do. You have to live free. The essence of the direct-action philosophy is that it involves the insistence of a determined minority to act as though it had certain legal rights, instead of merely trying to change the laws by writing to their congressmen. These tactics of direct action were used in the Berkeley Free Speech Movement as an alternative to trying to work through student government for changes in the rules governing political expression on campus. Similarly, one possibility in a militant anti-war movement would be to organize mass draft refusals.

What is stressed by the people in this movement is that people should be able to have a say in decisions that determine the shape of the social institutions in which they are involved. The emphasis on participatory democracy is a direct reaction to the bureaucratic paternalism which pervades our society. This paternalism is part of the schools, jobs, and government programs that affect most people's lives deeply. Our school systems, for example, are viewed by many in the New Left as largely a set of prearranged hurdles and mazes over and through which students must pass to get educated. Students are processed in giant education factories, and sent along their way with cumulative record cards, gradepoint averages, and assorted IBM cards. And the structure of power is set up in such a way that the sham of democratic participation covers their real powerlessness.

The basic tension in the New Left is between reform and revolution. Some of the people in the student movements are willing to settle for some minor adjustments in the basic social institutions, while others are in favor of wholesale and sweeping changes. Some of the latter feel that revolution is so far in the future that they must try to obtain reforms now. In one way, those who favor reform might be said to be more realistic, for minor changes can certainly be brought about by student pressure. Likewise, in spite of its militant tone, much of the Negro civil-rights movement is basically reformist. Demands for jobs, money, and even "black power" (i.e., election of Negro leaders in Negro constituencies) are basically reform demands that can be satisfied *without changing the basic nature of the capitalist warfare state.* So far, only a small number of Black militants have openly favored such radical steps as ending U.S. intervention in foreign revolutions, abolishing the draft, or curbing the power of American corporations through some form of socialism.

Reform means getting more equal justice under the law, adding to the benefits to be received from the welfare state, getting some of the courses taught in college put on a pass-fail basis, voting for the lesser of the two evils, etc. Reform means going the road of coalition politics in the hope of obtaining political power. Most of the participants in the student-protest movements are reformers at heart; they may be turned into revolutionaries by the turn of events, i.e., when they see their attempts at reform re-buffed; or when they see them put into practice without curing the evils they sought to cure.

The revolutionary conception of the good community leads in at least two different directions. On the one hand are the social-ists who would like to see the abolition of private control of the means of production and distribution, and the substitution of public political control. On the other hand are individualist and communist anarchists. The latter are furthest removed from the reformers, although many of them share the socialist vision about the desirability of abolishing private ownership and control of industry.

The basic criticism voiced by the anarchists is that large-scale bureaucratic organizations tend to be dehumanizing and that the only way really to reform them is to abolish them and to substi-tute other things in their place. This leads to the demand to es-tablish various kinds of parallel institutions which could eventu-ally replace existing ones.

Participatory democracy, for example, works best when you have small decentralized social units rather than large ones. This means that there is a tendency among some of the people in the New Left to favor the break-up of large universities, large facto-ries, large hospitals, etc. Thus a central administration deciding policies that will affect 20,000 students may be replaced by 100 separate and semi-autonomous social units of 200 students, each of which will decide its own policies.

The romantic reaction to the dehumanization and depersonal-ization found in large social units is similar in some respects to some of the right-wing arguments against the growing power of the bureaucratic state. Parts of the student New Left movement thus tend to have a quaint old-fashioned right-wing air about them in their opposition to compulsory military conscription or compulsory education.

The tension between reform and revolution in the student movement can be seen in innumerable situations. Generally, this tension has not been resolved. Some of those who want to end the war in Vietnam think that this can be done by influencing one of the major parties. Others see such measures as involving too much compromise, and hope for the establishment of a social climate within which people cannot be persuaded to take any part in the war machine. Some of them would counsel refusal to cooperate with the draft, with taxation, or with any kind of work related to the military. They see the problem as not so much military intervention here and there as the fact that the concentration of military power in the hands of the state makes such intervention possible. Thus they seek to build a movement in which local areas become self-governing, in which communities organize themselves to solve their problems by local effort whenever possible.

So far as production and distribution are concerned, the reformer would add to the benefits of the welfare state perhaps by a bigger war on poverty, or perhaps even by socializing certain industries. Thus the guaranteed annual income can be seen as a type of social reform which would stabilize the capitalist system by putting a floor under the income of the poorer segments of the society and taking away some of their revolutionary potential. The alternative envisaged by some communist anarchists is the type of society within which work in the conventional sense is not necessary. Certain types of basic commodities could be made in mass quantities by automation, for example, and distributed free to all who wish them: while at the same time people would be free to make luxury items by hand and to trade them.

In education the reformer would make classes smaller, and would pay more attention to including in the curriculum such neglected aspects as Negro history. The revolutionary outlook questions the need for predetermined curricula, for required courses and degrees, for compulsory education in lower grades.

I am not sure whether the tension between reform and revolution can ever be entirely resolved. People in the Movement seem to want both, which is why their actions are sometimes so contradictory. At the present time, the balance seems to be in favor of reform; thus most of those who are against the Vietnam war would not go so far as to oppose all militarism; those who want greater social equality would not go so far as to espouse communist anarchism, etc.

In practice, this means that the students and others in the New Left are not quite sure where they are going. What to do in the next election, for example. Support a political candidate, or abstain? What if abstention means the election of the worse of two evils? The problems to be solved seem almost too great: On the one hand, the attainment of political power is not within the range of realistic possibilities within the near future, barring some major upheaval such as that caused by a war on American soil. On the other hand, the creation of alternative or parallel institutions is difficult work; and it is hard to imagine these being able to survive as islands in a generally hostile environment.

The natural tendency for young people is to become more revolutionary in philosophy as they find that the reforms they put their faith in don't really work because they leave the system-produced evils unchanged. But young people also marry as they grow older, and they take jobs in the system, which leads to the prediction that the tension between reform and revolution will continue within the New Left movement.

7 / POLITICAL MOVEMENTS

BARRINGTON MOORE, JR. / Notes on the Process of Acquiring Power*

Hundreds of books have been written to describe the ways in which particular groups or individuals have come to exercise domination over large numbers of their fellows. Despite this tempting wealth of factual material, or perhaps because of it, modern social science has very largely avoided any attempt to discover and explain, within a strictly empirical framework, what recurring patterns there may be in these myriads of events. The following pages represent a very modest effort in this direction.

If there is indeed a distinguishable process of acquiring power, or, as is more likely, a series of such processes, the attempt to distinguish them must be formulated in terms of a time sequence. It should indicate the conditions in the society as a whole that lead to a concentration of power. In addition, it should indicate the sequence of stages through which the concentration takes place.

There is of course no need to adopt *a priori* the view that all societies pass through absolutely identical or even closely similar stages whenever power becomes concentrated. A more fruitful approach may be to try to analyze the range of problems encountered by different types of social groups on the road to power, and the variety of solutions they have attempted at each stage of

* From Moore, *Political Power and Social Theory* (Cambridge, Harvard University, 1958), pp. 9–27.

the journey. Though what I have to say is concerned primarily with the acquisition of power and authority over an entire society, many of these observations apply also to the acquisitions of domination over smaller groupings. The establishment of a new and vigorous administration in a corporation, a university, or a labor union displays recognizable similarities to corresponding phenomena in society as a whole.

The first question that occurs rather naturally is how the power-seeking process begins. Are there, for example, any common features in the situations that start the Bolsheviks on the way to the Kremlin, the early Christians on the route that leads to Innocent III, the French kings on the road to Versailles, the Moguls on the way to the splendors of Shah Jahan's reign? Here we may limit our attention to some of the grosser structural features of the societies that nourish the seekers after power.

There are, I suggest, at least three main types of situations that serve to initiate an active search for political power and political centralization. The first and simplest is the case in which a society undertakes some new set of activities that by their very nature require a high degree of central coordination. A second and much more complex case occurs when either external shock or internal decay produces a movement for the forced reintegration of a society around new or partially new patterns of behavior. The third type, for which the somewhat unsatisfactory term "monarchical absolutism" may be offered, is found where the rulers of one segment of a loosely ordered system gradually expand their control over the whole system or a substantial part of it. Perhaps none of these generalized causal antecedents ever occur in a completely pure form. Certainly cases can be found where all of these factors are intertwined with one another. Yet each of the three is at least analytically distinguishable, and empirical approximations may be found in the record of history.

Among the new activities requiring a high degree of central coordination, the emergence of warfare on a large scale provides one of the clearest examples. The development of irrigation systems on a broad territorial base is another. Marx, and some who follow in his footsteps, have regarded this factor as the major one behind the growth of Oriental despotisms.[1] The growth of modern industry provides still another illustration. Though recent research has thrown some doubt upon the thesis that increasing monopoly characterizes industrial advance,[2] the expanding role of the central government over the past fifty years can scarcely be denied.

What is it about such new activities, which evidently are not limited to modern industrial society, that bring about great concentrations of power? In the illustrations that have been offered three general characteristics may be observed. In the first place, the activity in each case calls for the allocation of large amounts

---

[1] The main modern work to argue this thesis is of course Karl A. Wittfogel, *Oriental Despotism: A Comparative Study of Total Power* (New Haven, 1957). This work became available only at the time of revising this essay. Wittfogel's work has been received with extravagant claims. G. P. Murdock, writing in the *American Anthropologist*, LIX, No. 3 (June 1957), pp. 545–547, has the following to say: "This is a truly great book, one of the major contributions to the science of man in our time. . . . [It] may conceivably even outrank that of the entire corpus of theoretical literature in political science. . . . It provides for the first time a solid theoretical framework on which the 'free world' might base a direct positive assault on the foundations of Communism and Fascism to replace the unorganized rearguard defense which it has presented for some decades to the ideational attacks of its enemies. The political and social systems of Soviet Russia, Communist China, and recent Nazi Germany fall clearly into the pattern of bureaucratic Asiatic despotisms. Far from representing the emergence of new postcapitalistic configurations, they are obvious reversions to a common precapitalistic political typology. . . ." In the light of such claims, and similar ones (see Richard L. Walker in the *Yale Review*, Summer, 1957), I feel it necessary to make some points that would otherwise seem excruciatingly obvious. Wittfogel's central thesis, taken of course from Marx and Weber, is that under certain historical conditions (specified on p. 12) the imperatives of large-scale irrigation and flood control works produce bureaucratic despotism. Whether or not Wittfogel is right in the detailed application of this thesis to the societies he discusses I do not know. But the imperatives of water control simply won't do as an explanation of the central features of Nazi Germany and Stalinist Russia. Even if we put the best possible face on Wittfogel's argument and regard hydraulic despotism as some sort of an ancestor of modern totalitarianism, his argument throws very little light on why totalitarianism emerges in the era of advanced industrialism. Nor are matters helped much if we generalize from water control to the control of major resources. Wittfogel's work tells us practically nothing about why this centralized control appears under modern condition. And for that matter, as the case of Calvinist Geneva, discussed in the next essay, shows, major elements of totalitarianism can appear without centralized control of resources.

[2] See A. D. H. Kaplan, *Big Business in a Competitive System* (Washington, D.C., 1954), pp. 234–241.

of human and natural resources. The allocation is a continuous process that requires frequent changes of direction. This is particularly true of a military organization, in which large bodies of men and materials may have to be shifted rapidly from one place to another in accord with swiftly changing circumstances. Likewise, when industry fails to flow in the directions deemed socially desirable, the pressure for political control rises. In the second place, each activity is one in which large numbers of people have to be persuaded or compelled to act against their earlier habits and perhaps even their natural inclinations. One recalls the effort of disciplining the labor force that has accompanied modern industrialization, as well as its sterner counterparts in military organizations and the great public works of Oriental despotism. Finally, in each activity a competitive advantage accrues to that social unit which can mobilize or control the larger quantity of resources. Up to a limit in size that cannot be specified in general terms, this is true of both an industrial concern and a territorial state.

In the preceding cases the development of new activities required both centralized decision-making and the use of compulsion. In some circumstances the element of compulsion may be absent, or nearly so, from a system of centralized coordination. For example, a centralized dispatching arrangement in a taxi fleet deprives the individual cab driver of the opportunity to make certain decisions on his own. It represents one form of modern centralized decision-making, though no doubt a trivial one. The dispatching system supplies the driver with fares much more continuously than is possible without this device. In this case, since centralized decision-making assists the individuals in the group to achieve their individual purposes, i.e., making money by driving taxis, there is little or no objection to the system.

If we wished to be absolutely precise in our terminology, we might call such cases examples of the concentration of authority, as distinguished from the concentration of power. Since the distinction requires knowledge about the subjective feelings of those who obey, it is far from an easy one to apply in practice. Both elements are present in widely varying proportions in any concrete case. This essay will concentrate on the type of situation in which the element of compulsion plays a major part, though the element of accepted authority will also be observed in many of them.

The second type of situation suggested as the source of power-seeking movements is one of external shock or internal decay. To choose a remote example first, the forceful unification of China for the first time, in the third century B.C., by means that recall modern totalitarian movements, was preceded by the disintegration of an earlier form of agrarian society with some resemblances to European feudalism. Communications improved, the use of iron increased, and the rigid barriers between social classes began to dissolve. The time was also one of intellectual ferment about which Mencius exclaimed bitterly, "Sage kings cease to arise . . . and unemployed scholars indulge in unreasonable discussions." [3] The essence of such situations is that human institutions fail to satisfy the expectations put upon them by a significant portion of the people living under them. A period of widespread and prolonged unemployment produces exactly these consequences in modern industrial society. Then the family breadwinner literally cannot fulfill the expectations laid upon him by his own conscience, by the members of his family, his friends, and the rest of the community.

This type of institutional failure can come about either through damage from external and internal sources to the political and social structure, or through changes in the purely subjective factor of the level of expectations itself. Poverty can exist for centuries and be regarded as part of the nature of the cosmos until a different way of looking at the world becomes available, frequently through contact with another society. The importance of this element in contemporary Asian revolutions has often been pointed out. Though the subjective factor of a change in the level of expectations can be separated from the objective elements of the economic and political structure, the two ordinarily change together.[4]

[3] Derk Bodde, *China's First Unifier* (Leiden, 1938), pp. 1–2.
[4] Some sociologists might object to this formulation, since they regard a built-in set of expectations as an essential part of any institution. Unless we know what to expect from other people, there can be no regularity and predictability in human behavior, they assert. Granting this point, I still think that people may change their ideas before they change the structure of their insti-

One possible consequence of institutional failure may be an added flow of power to whatever central authority already exists. Toynbee regards empire-building as the symptom and consequence of social disintegration, and has collected a number of illustrations.[5] Examining crises or institutional failures within a shorter time period, Sorokin has collected a number of cases purporting to show that political centralization is the typical response.[6]

The characteristic course of events is that the central authority finds it necessary, and often also agreeable, to substitute decisions made by itself for those made by individuals in a more diffuse manner throughout the society. Where the diffuse system of decision-making breaks down, as in the collapse of price cues for producers' decisions in a depression, the central authority substitutes its own cues and decisions. In some cases power and responsibility may be thrust upon people against their will, while in others they may be actively sought by ambitious individuals.

Not always, however, does the failure of a social system lead to a strengthening of the position of those at its apex. On more or less *a priori* grounds, one might suspect that the opposite course of events occurs more frequently. As the supporting institutional framework is eroded, it may collapse under the rulers instead of providing greater opportunities and demands for intervention and revolution by administrative fiat. There may be a break-up of the larger system into smaller units warring with one another, as happened repeatedly in India and China, as well as in Europe with the disintegration of the Roman Empire. Modern technology may make this particular form of disintegration unlikely in the future, though it cannot be ruled out completely.

The partial failure of a set of institutions to live up to what

---

tutions, as well, of course, as afterward. Thus there were many changes in ideas and expectations before the collapse of the *ancien régime* in the French and Russian revolutions. Hence the two are separable, not only theoretically but also empirically.

[5] Arnold J. Toynbee, *A Study of History*, abridgment by D. C. Somervell (New York, 1947), pp. 190, 336–349.
[6] P. A. Sorokin, *Social and Cultural Dynamics* (New York, 1937), III, pp. 196–208. See also *ibid.*, pp. 185–196 for a more general analysis of political centralization.

is expected of them provides an atmosphere receptive to demands for a more or less extensive overhaul of the status quo. At this juncture the future course of events depends heavily upon the models of a better world that become available to various strategic groups in the population. In the meantime the rulers may increase their efforts to prevent the population from gaining access to any models except those of their own creation, whose virtues they may stress with an increasingly frantic tone.

As a third very general source and type of political consolidation and expansion I have suggested the term "monarchical absolutism." It may be distinguished from the preceding one partly on the ground that it does not necessarily derive from the disintegration of a previously existing social system, though in some cases, particularly the rise of the Romanoffs, and perhaps some Asiatic despotisms, this may play an important part.

The central feature of absolute monarchy is that the ruler of one segment of a large and loosely organized polity imposes himself upon and brings order to the larger group. Purely personal factors, such as the ambition of an able and energetic ruler, may under favorable circumstances be all that is required to start the process of acquiring power in the form of monarchical absolutism. Especially in its early stages, monarchical absolutism does not appear to be propelled forward by the deep tides of economic and social change. Once the process has begun, a tradition may be established that it is the duty of the monarch to expand and consolidate his authority through incorporating various classes and interest groupings in the service of the state.[7] Since the monarch who fails to do this runs the risk of losing his authority to vigorous domestic and foreign rivals, the process perpetuates itself. It is worth noting that monarchical absolutism usually takes a long time, as much as several hundred years, to run its course.

Roughly the sequence of events just described appears to have taken place in France with the rise of the Capetian dynasty in the tenth century and the extension of the monarch's role, with

[7] The development of such a doctrine played a notable part in the consolidation of Moscow's power in the second half of the fifteenth century. See V. Kliuchevskii, *Kurs Russkoi Istorii* (2nd ed.; Moscow, 1937), II, pp. 111–146.

occasional interruptions and retrogressions, up to the Revolution.[8] An approximately parallel growth took place in Prussia and Russia. In India the same phenomenon occurred several times, as vigorous indigenous or foreign dynasties managed to establish peace and order over a substantial part of the peninsula.

In the course of extending their power, the rulers of a developing absolutism are likely to produce their own distinctive rationalizations and doctrines, such as the divine right of kings, or the Confucian ethic of China. But, in contrast with totalitarian regimes, there remain considerable areas of social life with which the absolute monarch does not seek to interfere. In *The Age of Absolutism*, Max Beloff points out that in spite of their claims of absolute power these monarchs were "in a sense conservative, since legitimacy was of their essence." Power was limited by law and custom and compelled to respect large areas of the status quo. Existing privileges and vested interests were strong enough to resist central coordination.[9] Monarchical absolutism does not display the same intention or capacity to reconstruct the entire social order as do revolutionary movements arising out of a period of social decay.

II

All groups and individuals who seek power are discontented about some aspect of the society in which they live. In many cases the discontent merely reflects the fact that one person wants power when another person happens to have it. There is no demand for changing the structure of the system itself. For the rest of this discussion we may leave this form of personal ambition aside, with only occasional observations, in order to concentrate upon the growth patterns of movements that arise out of a failure of social institutions to match human expectations. Discontent in this setting is likely to express itself in the formulation of a doctrine.

The creation of a doctrine has often been one of the very first steps along the road to power. With widely varying degrees of

---

[8] Hedwig Hintze, *Staatseinheit und Föderalismus im alten Frankreich und in der Revolution* (Berlin and Leipzig, 1928).

[9] Max Beloff, *The Age of Absolutism, 1660–1815* (London, 1954), pp. 49–50.

elaboration, the doctrine provides an explanation of what is wrong with the current state of affairs and what should be done to correct this state. We may designate such a doctrine the charter myth of a power-seeking organization.

Probably no charter myth has ever been completely static. Instead it undergoes modification and elaboration in response to the vicissitudes of the organization's life. In this connection it is worth noticing that in the course of its growth a doctrine does not necessarily become milder and more tolerant as it becomes incorporated into a working institutional system. The Inquisition, as is well known, was a relatively late development in Christianity, organized partly to counter indiscriminate popular frenzy against those who professed unpopular opinions. In Islam one may point to the strenuous efforts of the seventeenth-century Mogul emperor Aurangzeb to uproot and destroy Hinduism, after an extended period of religious tolerance by his predecessors.[10] The emergence of a real or imaginary threat to rulers whose power has a strong theocratic tinge may bring about a compulsory orthodoxy which is more repressive than that found in the early and fanatical stages of a movement, because it has more powerful instruments at its command.

Any concrete charter myth, such as Christianity or Marxism, contains a mixture of truth and propaganda. A large portion of political theory concerns itself with the critical evaluation of such myths from a variety of ethical positions. No such attempt can be made here, and the discussion will be confined to a few empirical suggestions concerning the content and structure of such myths.

Among the enormous variety of charter myths that have arisen in the course of human history, one may distinguish two frequently recurring issues. One issue is that of nativism versus xenophilia. By nativism I mean an energetic and somewhat distorted reaffirmation of the indigenous way of life, a reaction often produced in a society that feels itself threatened by forces beyond its understanding and control. But social disturbances may also produce xenophilia, or a longing to copy the ways of another cul-

10 See H. G. Rawlinson, *India: A Short Cultural History,* 4th ed. (London, 1952), Chap. XIX.

ture. The other issue is that of hierarchy and discipline versus equality and freedom. A "time of troubles" may produce demands for either more or less equality, often in terms of some larger principle such as race or reason. Either hierarchy or equality may conceivably be combined with one of the remaining pair, nativism or xenophilia.

The combination of nativism with a stress on discipline and authority yields a result familiar in the modern world, called pseudo-conservatism in its more diffuse social manifestations, and fascism when it becomes an organized political movement.[11] The partial break-up of a society can result in a call for a return to some semi-imaginary past, and a reaffirmation of the sturdier virtues, in order to attain a hoped-for future. This result is, perhaps, especially likely to occur where the virtues of physical courage, self-control, and subordination to authority have been successful in the past. In its early stages, the pseudo-conservative movement can take the form of support for the existing rulers. In any case, those in power are likely to try to make use of it. The erosion of the status quo may produce a Cato before it brings forth a Catiline or a Hitler. Pseudo-conservatism, however, soon goes beyond the status quo to demand a thorough redistribution of privilege and authority. As in the Nazi movement, or even in extreme right-wing Republican statements in the United States, pseudo-conservatism calls for the overthrow of the existing regime on the grounds that it has grown "too soft" or has made its way to power through "treachery" to the ancient way of life.

Where nativism and egalitarianism are combined in a charter myth, the egalitarian aspect often falls short of universal application. Sparta, living under the permanent emergency of a Helot revolt, constitutes a well-known example. There the equality prevailing in the ruling caste did not of course extend to the suppressed Helots. In nationalist movements, too, the conception of equality is ambiguous. During the early stages, admiration for the oppressor may occur along with a demand for equality with the dominant group. Both themes are very noticeable in Indian na-

[11] See T. W. Adorno *et al., The Authoritarian Personality* (New York, 1950), pp. 675–685.

tionalism. Even the Nazis displayed some Anglophile sentiments, particularly admiration for the supposed cunning of the British aristocracy, regarded as the major reason for the German defeat in 1918. Later such admiration may turn to hate. One might summarize the characteristic stages of development in a series of slogans. First: "We ought to be equal to you, our oppressors!" Second: "We really are equal to you, our oppressors!" Third: "We are superior to you and everyone else, though in comparison to such unfortunates as you, we are equal among ourselves!" Thus for nativist movements the doctrine of equality serves two purposes. It furnishes the ground for denying the out-group's claim of superiority. And it emphasizes similarities within the in-group, in order to distinguish the in-group from the out-group.

Nativism represents a twisted or idealized affirmation of the existing order, so twisted as to be genuinely revolutionary. Nevertheless, in its more developed form of a fanatical religious or secular patriotism, nativism is always tied to a particular group. In Germany it may take the form of National Socialism, while in Japan it appears in the guise of a revival of the imperial cult. In India it becomes Hindu or Islamic communalism, and in the United States 200 percent Americanism.

Egalitarianism, on the other hand, generally represents a rejection and negation of the existing order. This fact may account for what appears to be its greater capacity for xenophilia. English egalitarianism once looked to the French Revolution, while the French revolutionists looked to republican Rome, the Greek tyrannicides, or to an imaginary state of nature. About equalitarian movements among American Negroes it has often been observed that their center of gravity lies outside the Negro caste, and that they take their standards of behavior from the American middle class.

In contrast to nativism, egalitarianism represents a universal, though utopian, principle for the ordering of social relationships. For this reason its appeal can readily transcend national and religious boundaries. During the initial stages of political upheaval, this universal quality may constitute one of the strategic advantages of Communism over nativist forms of authoritarian rule, especially in Asia. However, as the superpatriotism of latter-day Stalinism demonstrates, once an egalitarian revolution acquires a territorial base and a vested interest in a particular social order, it may acquire the traits we have noticed in nativism.

As a program in its own right, egalitarianism by definition calls for the replacement of the status quo by a society in which the prevailing inequalities will be leveled out or perhaps merely reserved. It may take either a secular or a religious form, an attempt at the active reconstruction of the world or a withdrawal from it. Even in the latter instance, as in monasticism in both its Asiatic and Western forms, it may achieve considerable secular power. However, since the acquisition of power requires the development of hierarchy and discipline at some point, an egalitarian movement starts off at an initial disadvantage in relation to its competitors. Sooner or later, if it is to be effective, it must compromise with its initial principles. Christianity required several centuries to reach this compromise, while Marxism, especially in its Leninist version, reached this stage very rapidly.[12]

Thus the quest for power is justified in terms of some larger scheme of values. For the early stages of a movement, therefore, it is probably always correct to assert that power is an instrumental value, something that is sought not in its own right, but to obtain something else. Very rapidly, however, power tends to become an ultimate value. The very fact that power is such a vital instrument in the pursuit of many other values tends to transform it, in the course of its acquisition, from a mere instrument to an end in itself. The process may be clearly observed in the rise of the Papacy and in Russian Marxism, as well as in many other movements.

In addition to providing a justification for the search for power, the charter myth usually contains at least rudimentary rules for the allocation of authority within the power-seekers'

---

[12] For these developments in Christianity, I have found the following sources to be the most helpful: F. Heiler, *Altkirchliche Autonomie und Päpstlicher Zentralismus* (Munich, 1941); Henry C. Lea, *Studies in Church History* (Philadelphia, 1869); J. Haller, *Das Papsttum: Idee und Wirklichkeit* 2nd rev. ed., 5 vols. (Basle, 1951–1953). All references to Haller, *Das Papsttum,* are to this edition unless otherwise noted.

own organization. As part of such rules there is also some explicit or implicit provision designating what persons may interpret the doctrine in the future. Still another very significant aspect of the charter myth is the definition of membership in the group.

Among these rules, the one defining membership may be the most important in giving the group its character. A sharp boundary line between those who belong and those who do not aids a movement in preserving its identity in the course of subsequent struggles. The necessity to preserve this boundary line becomes increasingly important the more a movement seeks to control the entire span of the individual member's behavior, personality, and inmost thoughts. Thus the early Christian communities were at first "bound together merely by the ties of spontaneous aggregation," though they could refuse membership to persons deemed unworthy of it. At an early period the test of membership became the act of partaking of the Lord's Supper. Out of this early symbolism there grew the dread power of excommunication.[13] Certain aspects of the definition of membership in the Christian community, particularly the treatment of those whose faith had temporarily lapsed under the stress of persecution, became a matter of acrid dispute among the early bishops.[14] In general, the struggle over doctrine and personnel may easily lead to serious splits in the early stages of a movement. This has been true not only of groups that begin with a rejection of the pursuit of secular power, such as Christianity and Buddhism, but also of movements with stronger political emphasis, such as Islam and of course Marxism.

In the course of such struggles, a marked strategic advantage accrues to the victorious faction if it can also establish that no rules governing the appointment of people to various posts and no element in the doctrine are immune to interpretation by whatever person stands at the apex of the organization.[15] The struggle

13 Lea, *Studies in Church History,* pp. 232–235.

14 *Ibid.,* pp. 240–243.

15 At the height of papal authority, its arbitrary nature reached the point where the "popes sometimes, in virtue of their supreme authority, granted as a special privilege the right not to be excommunicated without cause" (*ibid.,* p. 403).

of the Roman bishops to gain exclusive authority over doctrine and the appointment of subordinates constitutes the major theme of early church history. During these internal conflicts, the popes made use of forgeries that in scope and boldness of execution far surpass the Stalinist rewriting of history for similar purposes.[16]

Thus the main function of the charter myth lies in the establishment of legitimacy, or obedience that will occur without coercion. Through rules governing the allocation of authority within a power-seeking organization, it provides the basis of legitimacy within such a group. Through its public program and the doctrines used to justify this program, it attempts to establish a similar basis for obedience and acceptance within the larger society.

III

Now we may examine some of the alternatives facing the seekers after power in their subsequent efforts to master the internal environment of their own organization and the external environment of the larger society.[17] We may begin with the conception of a small group of men known personally to one another. It may be the ruler and his associates who have limited authority over a small area and wish to extend this authority much more widely. Or it may be a group that is out of power in a particular state or community. (In the latter case, the members of the group will probably be united around some program, which need not have secular power as its objective.) Such a group may be regarded as the primary cell, with the leader as its nucleus, out of which a larger and more differentiated social structure may grow.

One process that may occur, especially if the original nucleus

[16] The entry under "forgeries" in the index of Lea, *Studies in Church History*, occupies a full column of fine print. Concerning the most famous of these, known as the Pseudo-Isidore, which greatly strengthened the power of the pope, Haller remarks that they were "the biggest, the boldest, and the most fateful in their consequences, of any forgeries that have ever been attempted." See his discussion in *Das Papsttum* II, pp. 54–62. It seems likely that the development of printing may have made this type of deception less easy to perpetrate on a wide scale. On the other hand, it aids in the rapid and widespread dissemination of lies about contemporary events.

[17] I take the distinction between the internal and the external environment from George C. Homans, *The Human Group* (New York, 1950), p. 90.

is not committed to the pursuit of secular power, is growth by simple division and the formation of new cells. This is roughly what happened in the spread of the Christian communities around the Mediterranean basin in the first centuries of our era. However, if the group takes up the pursuit of secular power, simple cell division will probably turn out to be no more than a beginning stage and a transition to other more tightly knit and hierarchical structures. Indeed, because the early Christian communities were larger than the original body of apostles, they adopted a more hierarchical arrangement for settling their internal affairs. In turn, this hierarchical arrangement set the pattern for the efforts of one of the divisions, the Roman see, to take command of the entire Christian world.[18]

One way in which a hierarchical structure may emerge is through the extension of the personal relationships and personal loyalties that exist within the original nucleus to a wider circle of people. This process results in the spread of a diffuse obligation, covering a wide variety of activities. The outcome may be provisionally labeled "feudalism," a form that has arisen in many parts of the world. As is well known, feudalism may also grow from the bottom upward as inferiors commit themselves to superiors for protection. Repeated experience in both Europe and Asia demonstrates that feudal relationships are adequate to coordinate, at least loosely, the activities of a large number of people over a wide area of territory.

Though feudalism constitutes a much more distinctly hierarchical form of coordination and growth than cell division, it remains a very loose form of social organization. It will not serve to focus the energies and activities of a large number of people on a narrow social front or upon a single goal. Under feudalism the leader turns over to his subordinate a piece of territory to do with as he likes provided certain minimal obligations of loyalty, military support, or tribute are met. In the same way, the inferior may commit himself to the charge of a superior in return for protection. The relationship that arises is a personal one that in-

[18] Haller, *Das Papsttum*, I, pp. 47–136; Lea, *Studies in Church History*, pp. 104–153.

cludes within it a large variety of functions and obligations. Its diffuse nature makes it an inadequate instrument for a vigorous group with a definite policy in mind which the group wishes to impose on an extensive territory or a large number of people.[19]

A rational bureaucracy, with its firm allocation of rights and duties for each post in a well-defined chain of command, is a far superior instrument for the execution of a definite policy. In its classic form, made familiar through Weber's analysis, a bureaucracy controls very specifically a limited range of the activities of the subordinate members. One gives and receives orders only in one's official capacity. In a large corporation the vice-president in charge of sales can require his subordinates to drop one kind of selling technique and adopt another. But he cannot impose a *corvée* or the requirement of military service on the company salesmen. Their obligation is limited to selling the company products. Furthermore, the company is free to discharge inadequate salesmen and hire better ones, while the salesman becomes an interchangeable part, able to perform as effectively for one company as another—if he is lucky enough to get a job.

Under feudalism the system of interchangeable parts does not exist, or occurs on a very restricted scale. The serf is tied to the land and the vassal to his overlord. But feudal relationships may be transformed into bureaucratic ones in a variety of ways. An increase in the number of activities carried on within a society brings with it the specialization that modifies the diffuse feudal bond. An attempt to impose more precise coordination and greater economic burdens for military purposes has similar consequences. Both elements were significant in the rise of royal absolutism in Europe. The transformation required the destruction of the old order, sometimes peacefully and gradually but more often violently and painfully, as part of the birth pangs of the new.

Just as feudalism may be transformed into rationalist bureaucracy through the effort to achieve a closer control over the activi-

[19] See Otto Hintze, "Wesen und Verbreitung des Feudalismus," *Sitzungsberichte der Preussischen Akademie der Wissenschaften* (1929), p. 323. As the author puts it, feudalism is characterized by a division of state power according to its objects, that is, land and people, instead of according to its functions, as in the modern state.

ties of a group, so may the rationalist and legal bureaucracy be transformed into a totalitarian hierarchical structure. From the standpoint of the supreme authority, the chief defect of a bureaucracy is that it operates according to rules that are impersonal and not subject to ready change. These rules, necessary to give a bureaucracy its qualities of regularity and precision, also serve to inhibit the leader from exercising his power fully.

In the absence of rules, on the other hand, the supreme authority in a totalitarian system can alter policy and shift the personal instruments of his power with minimal hindrance from the organization. In this manner he can nip attachments to a particular locality or to a particular function, such as the military, economic, police, or propaganda, before they can consolidate themselves and become a threat. For this reason a totalitarian ruler makes strong efforts to be informed about every local quarrel and to act as the authority that settles these quarrels. At the same time he frequently jumps over intervening links in the chain of command to make his power felt at the lowest levels.[20] What I have elsewhere called the "vested interest in confusion" seems to be an essential element in the internal dynamics of totalitarianism.

Also in contrast to rational bureaucracy, totalitarian rule seeks a full commitment of the subordinate's personality to the dictator's objectives. In this way it represents an extension of the charismatic relationship that binds the original band of followers to the leader. Just as they are to devote their whole lives and feelings to the leader's mission, so also are the subsequent adherents. Naturally this commitment is never fully realized in practice. It rapidly becomes diluted, as the movement grows, and is replaced by other bonds, such as the bureaucratic and the feudal types. Nevertheless, the movement may retain, and even elaborate, some traits designed to prevent the followers from developing strong external attachments that would divert resources and energies away from the group goal. The practice of sacerdotal celibacy is a well-known example. It appears to have been demanded, in the Catholic Church, mainly to prevent the

---

[20] Such behavior was characteristic of the papacy at the height of its power. See Haller, *Das Papsttum,* 1st ed. (Stuttgart, 1939), II², pp. 6–7.

clergy from acquiring property interests in conflict with the Roman hierarchy.[21] Personal relationships with those outside the movement or hostile to it may be forbidden, as is the case with Communists. The round of internal activities and rituals may be increased so as to absorb the whole of the member's time and energy.

If we leave aside the simple process of cell division, the internal aspects of the growth of a power structure out of a single cell consist essentially in the allocation of human and material resources to subordinates, along with a corresponding allocation of tasks or functions, combined with devices to ensure loyalty and obedience to the guiding nucleus. Among such devices coercion plays a well-known role. Where the allocation of resources is emphasized, subsequent development takes the form of feudalism or tax farming. Where the allocation of functions is stressed, rational bureaucracy arises. Totalitarianism represents, in part, an attempt to allocate functions without granting control over the resources that the function requires, in order to prevent the growth of independent bases of power in the hands of subordinates.

To avoid possible misunderstanding, it is perhaps necessary to point out that there is no inevitable sequence of stages in the forms of feudalism, rational bureaucracy, and totalitarian hierarchy. Each of the three, as I have tried to indicate, contains within it disruptive forces that can transform it into either of the other two.[22] But it would be a mistake to regard these tendencies as merely disruptive. It is highly likely that none of the three types of hierarchical structure sketched in the last few paragraphs could ever exist in a pure form. Even the most cold-blooded and precision-minded rational bureaucracy expends considerable effort to build up organizational loyalty. It also demands certain standards of behavior outside the office as well as during working hours, often on pain of dismissal. In other words, it displays

---

[21] Henry C. Lea, *History of Sacerdotal Celibacy in the Christian Church,* 3rd ed., 2 vols. (New York, 1907).

[22] This point is argued much more fully and on the basis of a concrete case in my *Terror and Progress USSR* (Cambridge, Harvard University Press, 1954).

certain feudal and totalitarian traits. Likewise, no feudal system will work unless a superior can give at least some orders and expect them to be carried out in the manner of a rational bureaucracy. The same is true of a totalitarian dictator. Since no one system will operate successfully by itself, traits must be adopted from the others to supplement its internal deficiencies. In turn, the adoption of these traits may undermine the system. Any concrete and empirical system of power and authority is likely to contain an unstable mixture of the three. The situation recalls the Hegelian dialectic with emphasis on inevitable internal contradictions.[23]

As we turn from the internal aspects of growth to the external ones, i.e., the relationships between the power-seeking group and the surrounding society, it is possible to distinguish at least four recurring problems that are faced by any group as it tries to establish legitimacy and control in the larger arena. One problem is that of finding or constructing a body of supporters. Such a clientele may range from a small tightly knit body to a large and amorphous mass following. Another and closely related problem concerns the kinds of tactical alliances, if any, that are sought in the struggle for political victory. Some groups display a marked willingness to enter into tactical alliances at considerable cost to their program and organizational identity, while others try to maintain a position of splendid isolation and doctrinal purity. The third and fourth problems occur only when and if power is achieved. Then there is the problem either of sharing it, as in the form of a coalition or the toleration of organized opposition, or of rejecting political partnership. Finally, there is the choice between leaving the existing structure unchanged—as happens, for example, after a palace revolution—or using power to alter or pulverize the old structures, such as social classes and estates, religious bodies, economic corporations, guilds, trade unions, and even kinship structures and the family—all in order to create a new structure.

The way in which these problems are solved depends not only

[23] The most persuasive exposition known to me is Herbert Marcuse, *Reason and Revolution: Hegel and the Rise of Social Theory* (New York, 1941).

upon the structure of the group that seeks power, but also upon the structure of the society in which the search takes place. In some cases, the disturbance spreads to neighboring societies, and they too become part of the relevant environment of those who pursue power. Here the discussion will be limited to a few concluding observations on the influence of structural differences in the surrounding society upon these four choices.

Let us consider first a stable society, in which most of the population accepts most features of the status quo, and where authority is sufficiently diffused so that there is no readily identifiable and single set of levers of command sufficiently powerful to set the whole society in motion in a given direction. Around the turn of the century, after the first wave of industrialism had passed over it, American society still approximated this model. Then Bryce could write of American public opinion that political light and heat radiated from no single center. Instead, our basic consensus arose primarily out of myriad individual interchanges.[24]

Where these conditions prevail, a group that seeks a substantial share in power must be able to combine a large variety of minor contradictions to create a broad political base. This is the familiar pattern of a democratic political party. A group that has a wide range of severe grievances against the status quo and is organized around a comprehensive program cannot mobilize sufficient support to gain overwhelming power. Instead, there tends to be a large number of pressure groups with individual grievances. These do their best to reward their friends and punish their enemies. But they display little interest in gaining control of the society as a whole. The power-seekers in such a society are pushed toward the choice of creating a large clientele and of making numerous loose tactical alliances. When formally in power, they must share it through the toleration of organized opposition and confine themselves to moderately reformist programs meeting immediate grievances.

In a stable despotism, too, most of the people accept most features of the status quo. The various empires in India at the apogee of their power may serve as a satisfactory empirical ex-

24 James Bryce, *The American Commonwealth* (New York, 1910), pp. 325–328.

ample. Such a situation provides the most favorable background for a palace revolution. Under these conditions, a group that tries to carry out a coup does not require any mass clientele or any tactical alliances that spread deep into the society. All that is necessary is the benevolent neutrality of key elements among the higher élite, particularly the group that controls the instruments of violence. The new rulers can grasp the levers of command, after which life proceeds much as it did before. Instability at the top may not seriously damage the rest of the society for a long time, as the four centuries of the Roman Empire suggest. In such instances, then, the solution of these problems takes the form of minimal clientele and tactical alliances, and the monopoly of power by those who seize it. The rulers must of course be certain of at least the passive acceptance of their supremacy by the key elements in the society—the priesthood, the military, and the heads of major economic units. Should totalitarianism stabilize itself in the course of the twentieth century and lose the *élan* with which it rose to power, this ancient political pattern might reassert itself.

The transformation and decay of a society call for still other solutions. In the modern world, the sources of this transformation may be found partly in the structural difficulties inherent in modern industrialism, some of which were foreseen by Marxists around the turn of the century,[25] and partly in the erosion of traditional values and beliefs by modern secular rationalism. As Western industrialism and rationalism have spread eastward, into Russia and the Orient, they have speeded the decay of ancient social systems. As already noted, such periods of rapid change favor the rise of either nativist or egalitarian movements with comprehensive philosophies—or pseudo-philosophies, as they are termed by their opponents. Such movements are likely to develop totalitarian features.

A totalitarian movement tries to acquire a considerable mass clientele, especially from individuals turned loose upon the world

[25] See particularly Rudolf Hilferding, *Finanzkapital* (Vienna, 1910), Part V, for a penetrating analysis of the factors behind the transition from liberal society to a structure resembling modern totalitarianism.

by the destruction of prior social bonds. It is, on the other hand, chary of tactical alliances. It may enter into alliances, but where it does so, it seeks to dominate its partners, or else to isolate and destroy them one by one. The notion of mutual gains through mutual compromises is foreign to fanatical movements, though in time such behavior may be forced upon them by the sheer requirements of survival. Soon after it gains power, though not necessarily immediately afterward, the totalitarian movement does its best to pulverize and atomize those segments of society that have maintained some degree of corporate identity. Others it seeks to control by penetration both before and after the seizure of power. In so doing a totalitarian regime is aided by the process of atomization and the destruction of the traditional order that precedes its rise to power. Along with these destructive processes, a totalitarian movement seeks to create new institutions and new levers of command that will give it something approaching its ultimate goal of total control of all social activities.

IV

The preceding pages are not and do not purport to be a complete theory of power, even in sketchy outline form. They have stressed the acquisition of power and mentioned the growth of checks on power-holders only incidentally. Any adequate theory of power would have to take as much account of the latter as the former, as well as of many other elements that I have altogether failed to discuss. Yet, by way of conclusion, the suggestion may be offered that there are at least four discernible processes of acquiring power that take their essential pattern from the way in which the process begins. The totalitarian ones, in either its nativist or egalitarian forms, is perhaps the easiest to recognize. Its source lies in shock to a social system or the more gradual decay of existing institutions, and the rise of new demands on these institutions. Its charter myth soon develops a stress on hierarchy. Subsequently it develops its own characteristic internal structure and way of coping with the external social environment. Monarchical absolutism, the second pattern, may begin under conditions of greater fragmentation than totalitarianism. It advances more slowly and is perhaps more the consequence of individual ambition than deeper social causes. Despite some of the pretensions of its charter myth, it is strongly conservative and unable to free itself from dependence on strongly established vested interests. Though its internal structure may contain some elements prominent in totalitarianism, such as espionage within its hierarchical instruments, the element of rational bureaucracy, with its allocation of rights and duties to specific stations according to universal norms, is perhaps more important. Reluctant to share power with other groups in the society, it must necessarily do so. As a third pattern, the rise of new activities, for which I will refrain from coining any special term, can be expected to produce a charter myth with a strong emphasis on hierarchy if these activities are ones that go counter to long-established human wants. If, on the contrary, these activities are ones that a substantial number of people wish to pursue, the charter myth may take an egalitarian form or even deny the relevance of authority. For example, early industrialism in England was accompanied by the development of classical economic theory with its stress on the "invisible hand." Finally, feudalism appears to be a transition form that may emerge out of the decay of a more centralized regime or, perhaps less frequently, out of a highly fragmented polity that has never known centralization. Its charter myth places a high emphasis on loyalty to a person instead of to an office, which in turn limits the forms of subsequent growth.

Though each of these four types may go through its own distinctive process of growth and decay, there does not seem to be any inevitable sequence of stages in which one type, such as monarchical absolutism or feudalism, necessarily precedes or follows other types. The forms distinguished here appear to be recurring subpatterns within the overall process or irreversible historical development that characterizes human society as a whole. None of them occurs in an absolutely pure form. Instead significant variations are found in these subpatterns at each stage of human history. For example, in the preindustrial world the basic features of centralized totalitarian regimes have emerged in several countries, as pointed out in the next essay, while on the other hand the rise of modern industry has introduced significant new elements into the totalitarian complex. To trace the historical fate of each of these four types would be an enormous task far beyond the limits of this essay. If these tentative formulations are near the mark, one would expect to find during any given historical epoch an emphasis upon one of these forms combined with a subordinate utilization of the others.

WILLIAM KORNHAUSER / Political Vulnerability of Mass Society*

Aristocratic and democratic critics of mass society agree that individual freedom is threatened by the growth of mass relations even as they differ on the nature of these relations. Aristocratic theorists diagnose mass society as a state of decline in authority, with the lack of traditional restraints on the popular exercise of power that this implies. They generally believe that mass society invites dictatorship based on mass support.[1] Since popular democracy stirs large numbers of previously quiescent people into action, aristocratic critics judge it to be a cause of popular dictatorship. Therefore, they fear all equalitarian tendencies that thrust large numbers of formerly passive people into the public realm. Such participation, aristocratic critics allege, results in the loss of that exclusiveness of elites which is required for the creative and value-sustaining functions with which they are charged. This excess of participation results from doctrines and practices that replace pre-established status distinctions and prerogatives with universal criteria of participation. The transformation from minority rule to

* From Kornhauser, The Politics of Mass Society (Glencoe, Ill., The Free Press, 1959), pp. 119–128. Portions of the original chapter have been omitted.
[1] See Franz Neumann, The Democratic and the Authoritarian State (Glencoe, Ill., The Free Press, 1957), pp. 236–243, for a discussion of dictatorship based on mass support, which he terms "caesaristic dictatorship" to distinguish it from "simple dictatorship—whether it be military or bureaucratic, the rule of a junta, a caudillo, or even an absolute monarchy" (p. 236).

popular sovereignty undermines the hierarchical structure of society, and thereby leaves masses unrestrained. In short, aristocratic critics see equalitarianism as the primary factor both in undermining the insulation of elites, and in permitting the rise of mass movements destructive of individual liberty: "The democratising of Europe," Nietzsche wrote, "is at the same time an involuntary arrangement for the rearing of tyrants" (quoted by Peter Viereck.[2])

Democratic critics reject the idea that equalitarian tendencies *per se* result in a mass society: "The masses, contrary to prediction [of aristocratic critics], did not result from growing equality of condition . . ." [3] According to many of these theorists, mass society is produced by the growth of large cities and bureaucratic organization, rather than by equalitarianism. For, it is argued, these structural trends deprive people of the social bases of involvement and control in the social order. The growth of the metropolis atomizes community and the growth of bureaucracy thrusts decision-making centers beyond the effective range of understanding and influence, leaving only the isolated and exposed individual. Mills expresses this belief that "the mass society . . . is largely a metropolitan society":

> The growth of the metropolis, segregating men and women into narrowed routines and environments, causes them to lose any firm sense of their integrity as a public. The members of publics in smaller communities know each other more or less fully, because they meet in the several aspects of the total life routine. The members of masses in a metropolitan society know one another only as fractions in specialized milieux. . . . In every major area of life, the loss of a sense of structure and the submergence into powerless milieux is the cardinal fact. . . . This loss of any structural view or position is the decisive meaning of the lament over the loss of community. In the great city, the division of milieux and of segregating routines reaches the point of closest contact with the individual and the family, for, although the city is not

2 Peter Viereck, "The Revolt Against the Elite," in *The New American Right,* Daniel Bell, ed. (New York, Criterion Books, 1956), pp. 91–116.
3 Hannah Arendt, *The Origins of Totalitarianism* (New York, Harcourt, Brace, 1951) p. 310.

the unit of prime decision, even the city cannot be seen as a total structure by most of its citizens.[4]

In short, democratic critics generally believe that the specialization and centralization of urban-industrial society are the primary factors in undermining self-governing communities, and in encouraging the growth of elite-domination.

It is evident that these two views of mass society may be distinguished by their relative concern for the protection of authority, on the one hand, and community, on the other. Correspondingly, one view locates the major threat to freedom in equalitarianism, and the other in urbanism-industrialism. Now the difficulties of both these views are immediately apparent. Some relatively democratic societies exhibit pronounced mass movements (e.g., France); others do not (e.g., England). It also is clear that there are marked variations in the extent of mass tendencies displayed by urban-industrial societies; England, for example, is more highly urbanized than the United States but is prey to less mass behavior and fewer mass movements. Our problem, then, is to specify more accurately the conditions under which these processes are associated with the rise of mass movements, and the conditions under which they are not so related. But before turning to this task . . . it is necessary to clarify the relation between the rise of mass movements and the threat to freedom.

Aristocratic and democratic critics alike believe that mass society is *vulnerable to totalitarianism,* rather than to traditional forms of dictatorship. De Tocqueville suggested the distinctive vulnerability of mass society long before the rise of nazism and communism. He wrote:

> I think, then, that the species of oppression by which democratic nations are menaced is unlike anything that ever before existed in the world. . . . I seek in vain for an expression that will accurately convey the whole of the idea I have formed of it; the old words *despotism* and *tyranny* are inappropriate: the thing itself is new.[5]

[4] C. Wright Mills, *The Power Elite* (New York, Oxford University Press, 1956).
[5] Quoted by J. L. Talmon, in *The Rise of Totalitarian Democracy* (Boston, Beacon Press, 1952), p. v. (See the selection from de Tocqueville's *Democracy in America* in Chapter 4 of this Reader.)

A recent critic of mass society has written that modern totalitarianism is a "dictatorship resting on popular enthusiasm and is thus completely different from absolute power wielded by a divine-right King, or by a usurping tyrant." [6] Lederer[7] and Arendt[8] in particular have argued that mass society is threatened by totalitarianism. They imply that mass society prevents the development of genuinely authoritarian as well as libertarian forms of rule, since even authoritarianism as an institution involves *limited*, if concentrated, power.[9]

Mass movements against democracy must be sharply distinguished from traditional movements against democracy. Not all anti-democratic ideologies are mass-oriented. Monarchical parties —for example, the PNM in Italy—are not mass movements. Nor in general are the aristocratic parties of Europe, such as the pre-Nazi Conservatives in Germany. This kind of predominantly upper-class resistance to democracy is very different from mass movements against democracy, epitomized by fascism in Italy and nazism in Germany, as well as by communist movements wherever they develop. These mass movements are characteristically *populistic* attacks on democratic institutions and constitutional liberty. They are profoundly revolutionary since they seek to abrogate all institutional restraints on political power, rather than to reinstate some form of aristocratic or theocratic rule.

The decline of community and association creates the opportunity for mass movements to smash all institutional restraints on power and to transform the scope of power. Thus, while totalitarianism is a dictatorship based on mass support, and while it is also based on elite-domination of centralized organization, its dis-

---

[6] *Ibid.*, p. 6.

[7] Emil Lederer, *State of the Masses* (New York, W. W. Norton, 1940).

[8] *Op. cit.* See also Arendt, "Authority in the Twentieth Century," *The Review of Politics*, XVIII (1956), pp. 403–17.

[9] Arendt argues that many a liberal notes the decline of liberty and cries totalitarianism; and many a conservative measures the decline of authority and errs equally if he equates this with totalitarianism. She goes on to say that certainly liberty has been threatened, and certainly authority has declined, but totalitarianism may not be equated with either. Totalitarianism, unlike authoritarianism, is not bound to any laws or codes; and unlike ordinary dictatorships or tyrannies, rests not upon parties but *movements* which remain in power even after power has been obtained.

tinctive character lies in the fact that it is a permanently mobilized mass movement which seeks to control all aspects of life. Totalitarian dictatorships involve total domination, limited neither by received laws or codes (as in traditional authoritarianism) nor even by the boundaries of governmental functions (as in classical tyranny), since *they obliterate the distinction between state and society.* Totalitarianism is limited only by the need to keep large numbers of people in a state of constant activity controlled by the elite.

But mass society itself is *not* totalitarian.... It may be transformed into a totalitarian society, however. It is more likely to change in this direction than is either pluralist or communal society. In short, mass society is vulnerable to totalitarianism, even though it is not totalitarian and in any given case may never become so. For mass society possesses only weak defenses against mass-oriented elites who seek to abrogate all restraints on power and raise up new kinds of totalistic ideologies. "It is the mass-oriented elite, Fascist and Communist alike, which is the advocate and engineer of activism." [10] The mass-oriented elite above all distinguishes fascism from ordinary conservatism and communism from democratic socialism. Fascism and communism are extraordinary in this sense: they act outside of and in opposition to constitutional order of any kind.

Totalitarian elites strive to create masses as well as to mobilize existing masses. People cannot be mobilized against the established order until they first have been divorced from prevailing codes and relations. Only then are they available for "activist modes of intervention" in the political process. Thus it is that when large numbers of people are available, and when opportunities exist for the further creation of mass-consciousness (as when pre-existing elites are inadequate to protect their institutions), fascist and communist movements alike gain support at the expense of political parties committed to the social order. Conversely, when such conditions do not obtain, they both lose ground to constitutional forces, as an examination of changes in

[10] Phillip Selznick, *The Organizational Weapon* (New York, McGraw Hill, 1952), p. 294.

voting strength of Fascist and Communist parties in several countries shows.

We have been able to identify eight European countries (Austria, Belgium, Denmark, France, Germany, Italy, Norway, Sweden) in which the anti-democratic extremes (communism and fascism) ran candidates in at least two consecutive national elections since 1920. Comparing changes from one election to the next for each country, we find that the communist and fascist vote increased or decreased together 16 times out of a total of 24 pairs of elections. In other words, the two anti-democratic extremes changed in the same direction twice as often as they changed in opposite directions. In no country did the two extremes change in opposite directions more often than they changed in the same direction. This pattern gains further significance when we compare changes in the voting strength of each extreme with its democratic counterpart on a Left-Right continuum. Out of 54 pairs of elections the communist and socialist vote changed in *opposite* directions 34 times, or in 63 percent of the cases; and in only one country did the democratic Left and the anti-democratic Left increase or decrease together more often than not. The results for the Right are even more striking: out of 24 pairs of elections the fascist and the democratic Right[11] changed in opposite directions 17 times, or in 71 percent of the cases. We may infer that changes in conditions that favor one anti-democratic extreme also favor the other, that changes that weaken one extreme also weaken the other, and that changes in conditions affect the democratic parties in the opposite direction from their effect on the political extremes. This suggests that, in spite of important differences between them, anti-democratic mass movements spring from similar social conditions.

What are these conditions? The major set of circumstances associated with the emergence and development of mass movements must include those factors that weaken social arrangements intermediate between the individual and the state. This much is sug-

---

11 We have included in the "democratic Right" all parties standing between the democratic Left (especially socialist parties) and the extreme Right (especially Fascist parties), hence parties of the "center" as well as of the "Right."

gested by the structure of mass society. Such factors are those associated with *major discontinuities in social process* as measured by the rate, scope, and mode of social change. Thus, it is not democratization *per se* which produces extremist mass movements, but the discontinuities in political authority that may accompany the introduction of popular rule. Where the pre-established political authority is highly autocratic, rapid and violent displacement of that authority by a democratic regime is highly favorable to the emergence of extremist mass movements that tend to transform the new democracy in anti-democratic directions. Likewise, it is not the growth of urban-industrial organization *per se* that induces mass tendencies, but the discontinuities in community that may be associated with urbanization and industrialization. Where the pre-established community consists of small homogeneous units, rapid urbanization and industrialization are highly favorable to extremist mass movements.

All of these discontinuities are likely to involve major impairment of intermediate relations. Intermediate relations are especially fragile because participation in them often is *voluntary,* they generally lack control over the means of coercion possessed by the state, and they lack the bonds of intimacy possessed by the family. Depending on voluntary participation, and lacking the more permanent and organic qualities of family and state, intermediate relations are less adaptable to major discontinuities in social conditions.

A reconsideration of the two approaches to the genesis of mass tendencies may show that part of the difference between them is a product of different starting points (contexts) and, correspondingly, of different intermediate structures with which they are concerned. The aristocratic critics are committed to some version of a status society, and it is that which they are concerned to preserve against the encroachment of democracy, even when the latter is pluralist. That they nevertheless help to locate the sources of mass society is due to the fact that democratization sometimes is more a process of tearing down the old social order than it is a process of building up a new order.

A society having a traditional system of authority is greatly in need of social formations which can bridge the transition to a new (therefore as yet non-traditional) system of democratic power. Otherwise, no group is able to influence deeply the collective activity; and instead of new values being built into the social structure, there is merely a cultural vacuum and social atomization. Equalitarianism can mean the negation of authority and community, as de Tocqueville saw, even though it also can mean a new kind of authority and community. The aristocratic critics of mass society do not err when they insist on the potential tradition-eroding and fragmenting effects of democratization, so long as their context is held in view. A pluralist context is another matter.

Starting from a pluralist premise, democratic critics proceed to locate the emergence of mass tendencies, not in status-eroding processes, since pluralist society is not status-bound, but in group-eroding processes, since pluralist society rests on a rich and diversified group life. Their worry is that access to power will be closed off, since they begin with an open system and are committed to sustaining it. Therefore, democratic critics focus on the threat of growing specialization and centralization of organization to participation and control through the local community and association.

A difference related to that of context is the kind of intermediate structure which each view stresses. Not all intermediate structures are equally critical safeguards against mass tendencies. Those are critical which in the given context are, or have been, major bases of cohesion. It is only natural, therefore, that the aristocratic and democratic approaches, which took shape in different centuries, should identify the dissolution of different kinds of social formations as the major potential source of masses. In the nineteenth-century European context, given the feudal heritage, status groups were critical, such that the failure to develop new forms of association to replace them was potentially mass-producing. But in the twentieth century, and especially in America (since it never had a feudal past and hence no fixed hierarchy of status groups),[12] interest groups and other kinds of voluntary association have been more important, and the dissolu-

[12] See Louis Hartz, *The Liberal Tradition in America* (New York, Harcourt, Brace, 1955).

tion of this kind of group life a greater source of mass tendencies. Writing in the nineteenth century, de Tocqueville emphasized the indispensability of new forms of association where *aristocracies* are lost or absent.

> In aristocratic nations the body of the nobles and the wealthy are in themselves natural associations which check the abuses of power. In countries where such associations do not exist, if private individuals cannot create an artificial and temporary substitute for them I can see no permanent protection against the most galling tyranny; and a great people may be oppressed with impunity by a small fraction or by a single individual.[13]

Writing in the twentieth century, Mills also emphasized the importance of private asssociations for freedom. But now the problem is defined not as the threat to freedom arising from the failure to develop substitutes for status groups, but as the threat arising from the failure to *preserve* old forms of (private) association in the face of the growth of bureaucratic organization.

> The executive ascendancy in economic, military, and political institutions has lowered the effective use of all those voluntary associations which operate between the state and the economy on the one hand, and the family and the individual in the primary group on the other. . . . Such associations are replaced in virtually every sphere of life by centralized organizations.[14]

Finally, it should be clear that the kinds of discontinuities in intermediate relations which have been discussed are usually *not* productive of mass movements in totalitarian contexts. Totalitarian elites destroy independent groups and change intermediate relations which they control (for example, the organization and membership of the totalitarian party), without thereby creating opportunities for the rise of new mass movements. On the contrary, totalitarian elites seek to keep the population in an atomized state by means of perpetual and unpredictable change, such as forced migrations, terror, and purge, in order to prevent the

13 Alexis de Tocqueville, *Democracy in America*, 2 vols. (New York, Knopf, 1945), Vol. I, p. 195.
14 Mills, *op. cit.*, pp. 306, 310.

formation of independent movements.[15] Deliberate atomization is a technique of total domination. Thus, in the totalitarian society there are masses—created, nurtured, and mobilized by the elite—but there are no independent mass movements.

In summary, major discontinuities in social process produce mass movements by destroying pre-established intermediate relations and by preventing the formation of new associations aligned with the social order. . . .

[15] Zbigniew K. Brzezinski, *The Permanent Purge* (Cambridge, Harvard University Press, 1955).

PAUL JACOBS AND SAUL LANDAU / The New Radicals*

THE MOVEMENT'S THEMES

The Movement is a mélange of people, mostly young; organizations, mostly new; and ideals, mostly American. In 1960 and 1961 the Freedom Riders and Negro college students who sat-in in the South were acting in the spirit of The Movement. Most of those who protested against President Kennedy's Cuban policy in 1962 were responding to the impulse of The Movement. That same impulse took them south for the Student Nonviolent Coordinating Committee (SNCC) in 1963, got them arrested in Sproul Hall at the University of California in 1964, and marched them to Washington in 1965 to demonstrate their opposition to the war. Movement youth can be found today in the San Joaquin Valley of California, helping striking farm workers; some will become organizers in the slum communities of northern cities; others will try to change the university system in America.

These young people believe that they must make something happen, that they are part of a movement stirring just below the surface of life hitherto accepted all over the world. So they identify with the Zengakuren students whose snake-dance demonstrations prevented President Eisenhower from visiting Japan, and wince at the photos of the young rebel shot by a policeman in

* From Jacobs and Landau, *The New Radicals* (New York, Vintage Books, 1966), pp. 3–14. A portion of the original text has been omitted.

Santo Domingo. They empathize with the young Soviet poets who read their poetry at the statue of Mayakovsky in Moscow until the police break up the meeting.

How many people are in the American Movement? Certainly, it is possible to count those who are members of the organizations within The Movement, but that would be to misunderstand one of the basic facts of its nature: The Movement is organizations plus unaffiliated supporters, who outnumber by the thousands, and perhaps even hundreds of thousands, those committed to specific groups. The Movement's basic strength rests on those unaffiliated reserves, who are just as much a part of it as the organization youth.

The leitmotifs that dominate The Movement extend far beyond politics. The Movement is much more than anti-Vietnam marches, civil-rights demonstrations, and student sit-ins. To be in The Movement is to search for a psychic community, in which one's own identity can be defined, social and personal relationships based on love can be established and can grow, unfettered by the cramping pressures of the careers and life-styles so characteristic of America today.

The Movement rejects the careers and life-styles of the American liberal, too, for to The Movement it is the liberal way of life and frame of mind that represent the evil of America. Those in The Movement feel that modern American liberals have substituted empty rhetoric for significant content, obscured the principles of justice by administrative bureaucracy, sacrificed human values for efficiency, and hypocritically justified a brutal attempt to establish American hegemony over the world with sterile anti-communism. The Movement sees the liberals righteously proclaiming faith in American democracy from their comfortable suburban homes or offices, while the United States Air Force drops napalm on villages and poisons the rice paddies.

So, those in The Movement see not only the openly authoritarian or totalitarian society as an enemy but the administered, bureaucratic, dehumanized, rhetorical-liberal one as well. They reject liberal authority. They were stirred, momentarily, by President Kennedy's call for a commitment to freedom, but were so disappointed by his actions in Cuba and Vietnam that they turned on him with bitterness. And the Johnson Administration's foreign policy reinforces their view that America flouts, in action, the traditions of freedom and justifies the use of military instruments associated with the Nazis.

The new movement is also a revolt against the post-war "overdeveloped society," with its large bureaucracies in government, corporations, trade unions, and universities. To those in The Movement the new technologies of automation and cybernation, with their computers and memory-bank machines, are instruments of alienation, depersonalizing human relations to a frightening degree. The brain machines and the translation of human qualities into holes punched into a card are viewed as devices that break down communication and destroy community in the interests of efficiency. Technology's emphasis on routine efficiency has created a set of values, rationalized by its supporters as representing "the facts of modern life." But The Movement sees these values as false, imposed on the whole society without "the consent of the governed." Even worse, the decision-making over which the governed no longer have control extends far beyond politics: in the technological order every aspect of the people's lives is under the control of administrators far removed from responsibility to the governed. And the elders of those in The Movement have exchanged their decision-making right for the comforts of American affluence. All that remains is nineteenth-century rhetoric about democracy and freedom, and technology has drained the words of their content.

In their personal life-style, their aesthetic sense, many in The Movement reject affluence and its associated symbols. The ambition to escape from poverty is no spur to action in their lives, for many are children of America's post-Depression *nouveau* middle class. Their parents are the once-poor scholars who head rich academic institutes; the ex-union organizers who run their own large businesses; the former slum-dwellers who develop segregated real-estate tracts; the families once on the WPA who live in suburbia —all those who have made it. But their parents' desire to own, to accumulate, to achieve the status and prestige which go with material wealth, are meaningless goals to the children. To them tele-vision is not a wonder but a commonplace, and they see the $5,000 a year their parents spend on the analyst as too high a price to pay for the loss of human values.

The marvels of the space age are commonplace to them, too, and the voices to which they listen are not those of the orbiting astronauts exchanging banalities. They respond instead to the sense and sound of friendship and community, to the exultation they feel when thousands of people link hands and sing "We Shall Overcome." And to achieve that feeling of community, of life, they have been willing to sacrifice most middle-class comforts.

They are willing to do this, for until they enter The Movement their inability to affect the quality of their own lives disturbs them profoundly. Those of the upper middle class were trapped, protected to the point of coddling through their childhood and early teens, sated with *nouveau* affluence by the time they were twenty. They knew they could achieve a place in the society of their parents, but it was not a society in which they wanted a place; it offered little beyond physical comfort. They believed the ideals they were taught, and felt miserable when the ideals were exposed as empty words. Their awareness that Negroes and mil-lions of poor have been left out of the society moved them to act rather than depend on the persuasion techniques advocated by their elders.

Many of them were born in the year of The Bomb, and so their history begins with the history of nuclear destruction. The twen-ties and even the thirties are almost pre-history to them, and the burning issues which agitated the older generation's radicals and liberals are devoid of meaning. Some know of the mid-fifties' Mc-Carthyism and the House Un-American Activities Committee (HUAC), but the internecine wars of the thirties have little per-sonal significance for them.

In some measure, too, the modes of extreme personal behavior adopted by this group—their permissive view of marijuana or hallucinogenics like LSD, their matter-of-fact acceptance of sex-ual freedom and their habitual profanity—are part of their search for identity. That search assumes a rejection of everything connected with their old identity and of the technological, bureaucratic values they see as dominant in American life. It is also possible that their difficulties in finding personal meaning in the routine politics of the civil-rights struggle and their anguish in seeing the country carry out a foreign policy they believe to be totally bad force these young people into seeking meaning in experiences. They think the ivory-towered men of ideas have cheated them, lied to them, and that action and spontaneous experience will show them truth.

Above all, those in The Movement now restlessly seek to find a new politics and a new ideology that will permit them to link existential humanism with morally acceptable modes of achieving radical social change.

THE MOVEMENT'S ORIGINS

The Movement's origins are elusive and have many strands. In the 1930's and 1940's the radical movement encompassed a broad spectrum of organizations and political beliefs: the Communists and their front groups; the Socialists, Trotskyists, and other anti-Stalinist organizations; sections of the CIO and a few other unions. The communist groups, drawing world-wide support, dominated American radicalism, since their size and prestige were greater than any of the other political tendencies. And although the American Communist Party was shaken in 1939 by the Stalin-Hitler non-aggression pact, the Nazi attack on the Soviet Union returned them to political acceptability.

But by the mid-fifties the old movement was nearly dead. The Communist Party had declined badly in the post-war period, because of government persecution and its own internal weaknesses. The trade unions were no longer crusading, many once radical anti-Communists had become supporters of the Establishment, and the socialists were barely distinguishable from the liberal Democrats.

Then, when today's young radicals were still in junior-high school, the entire communist world was shaken by the revelations about Stalin made at the 20th Party Congress. The communist movement soon suffered further blows from the uprisings in

Hungary and Poland. The Labor Youth League (LYL), the Communist Party youth group, was disbanded shortly after the shock of 1956, but it would have declined from internal stress anyway. At the very time the American Marxists were being disillusioned by the actions of Soviet socialism, England, France, and Israel joined in an invasion of Egypt. A few intellectuals, faced with Western imperialism and brutal Soviet Marxism, began seeking a fresh way out of the crisis, developing what C. Wright Mills described as the New Left.

It started in England, where in 1957 a group of university intellectuals published two new journals, *Universities and Left Review* and *The New Reasoner*. In 1959 they merged into the *New Left Review*. Many of the editors had been members of or had been close to the Communist Party at Oxford. For them the failure of Marxism was more a failure of the vulgar Communist Marxists than of the theory. In the new journals the ideals of socialism were rediscovered, and the kind of humanist analysis that had been forgotten through purges, war, and Cold War was revived. Often, too, *New Left Review* debated ideas that could not comfortably be talked about within the framework of Soviet Marxism: alienation and humanism.

New Left political clubs of college and working-class youth followed the magazine's formation, and through 1959 this small group lit a new spark under dormant English radicalism—Aldermaston marches in support of peace and against nuclear testing grew larger each year, and the Labour Party swung to the New Left position on nuclear weapons, for one year.

By the end of the fifties concern for racial justice was developing among American students. A strong reaction to the indignities of fear and anxiety heaped on the country by McCarthy and a general rejection of the symbols of American affluence were growing. Some youth responded with the "beat" mood; others developed an interest in the new British intellectual radicalism; still others rejected the style of life practiced by J. D. Salinger's characters.

Simultaneously, a group in the American pacifist movement, strongly influenced by pacifist leader A. J. Muste, was developing a "third camp" position, which rejected both the American and Soviet Cold War positions, concentrating instead on attempting to create a third force to resist all militarism. Many "third camp" pacifists had been involved in the civil-rights struggle, to which they had brought the non-violent techniques that they had been studying and practicing since the outbreak of World War II. And although their original interest and commitment had an informal religious base, they moved over easily to politics.

As McCarthyism waned in the late fifties, a group of university intellectuals, much like the British New Left although less vigorous and certain, began to develop around the universities of Wisconsin, California at Berkeley, and Chicago. At Wisconsin the Socialist Club was formed by ex-LYLers and younger undergraduates who had never experienced Communist Party schooling; at Berkeley a similar group called SLATE formed a student political party; at Chicago a student political party founded in the early fifties was revived.

Another generation graduated from high school, and the colleges and universities became breeding grounds for campus political activity and the civil-rights drive. Some of the young people in The Movement began to exhibit an inclination for activism and a spirit of anti-intellectualism, in part a rejection of the very university system in which they were involved. "The University" came to be regarded as part of the Establishment, and as the point of immediate contact, the most oppressive part.

Unlike their immediate predecessors, who had published magazines like *Studies* and *New University Thought,* this new group of youth activists knew little about the debates of the thirties. They learned about Stalinism, Trotskyism, and Social Democracy only in an academic context. Outside the classroom they referred with a sneer to the "old days"—the thirties, forties, and now the fifties. Like the rest of American society, the old Left, they believed, had in some way "betrayed" them: they had "sold out" or else were "hung up" on old and dead battles. To most of these young people Marx, Lenin, and Trotsky had little relevance for what they understood to be America's problems. They simultaneously refused to identify with the Soviet Union or to be greatly concerned about injustice in any of the communist societies. Their enemy was the American society and its Establishment.

Many of the young people in the activist generation were the children of parents who had been the radicals and Left liberals of the thirties and the forties. At home they had heard the discussions about civil rights, and they knew of the political pall that hung over the country during the McCarthy era. They had learned a set of ideals from their parents and now, much to their parents' discomfiture, they were trying to put those ideals into practice.

And so by 1960 this new generation was throwing itself against American society, literally and figuratively. They found a new hero in Castro, the man of action, the man without an ideology, whose only interest seemed to be bettering the life of the Cuban people. They responded to the youthful Castro with enthusiasm and demanded "fair play" for the Cuban Revolution.

In May, 1960 they were ready for an action of their own, and the opportunity was provided by the House Un-American Activities Committee. Hundreds of students from the campuses of the University of California at Berkeley and San Francisco State College, joined by some of the people who were moving away from the inactivity of the "beat" coffee houses, demonstrated physically against the Committee's San Francisco hearing. And after the demonstration, which received enormous publicity, they scorned the allegation that they had been led or inspired by the Communists. That charge, which they knew to be untrue, only reinforced their feelings of distrust for the celebrants of American society.

They identified, too, with the Freedom Riders who went south in 1960 and 1961; for this again meant taking direct action with their own bodies against segregation. They were not interested in theory, and so the long historical articles even in such Left journals as *Studies* were not seen by them as being relevant.

This new activist Movement influenced even those who thought of themselves as being outside of society. As the apolitical "beats"—almost alone as symbols of protest in the fifties—

turned their concern to concrete issues of racial equality and peace, their style, dress, and decor affected the activists. Arguments about politics began to include discussions of sexual freedom and marijuana. The language of the Negro poet-hipster permeated analyses of the Cuban Revolution. Protests over the execution of Caryl Chessman ultimately brought together students and some Bohemians—the loose and overlapping segments of what was to become known as The Movement.

President Kennedy gauged accurately the need of many youth to participate in programs for justice, and a few of the new activists were attracted to the Peace Corps. The Peace Corps stressed, at least in its appeal, a non-paternalistic, activist program in which people would be helped to help themselves, but most activists rejected the Peace Corps or any other government program. They felt American society supported racism, oppressive institutions, capital punishment, and wars against popular movements in underdeveloped countries. "Alienation" was used to describe the society's effects on its citizens, and American society was seen as the source of injustice and suffering everywhere. While opposed to injustice and suppression of liberty in general, the activists did not feel the same outrage against Castro or Mao or Khrushchev that they could against their own rulers. It was "our" fault. Brought up and nurtured on the United Nations and liberal political values, hearing them articulated so well by President Kennedy and Adlai Stevenson, they demanded purity at home first, and when it was not forthcoming, quickly became convinced that it was impossible, that there was something rotten at the core of American society.

This dashing of hopes, the feeling that they had succumbed to what turned out to be only rhetoric on the part of Kennedy and Stevenson, was an important part of their turning so bitterly against the Establishment.

And while the older ones among them had been able to articulate their views in a speech or a pamphlet, some of the younger ones, those who came into The Movement later and rejected politics—a small but growing number of middle-class youth—made a virtue of their inability to articulate and analyze coherently.

They talked "from the gut," stumblingly, haltingly, using the language of the new folk-singers, deliberately adopting a style that was the antithesis of what they had heard from their professors.

In their revulsion against the liberal intellectuals who were celebrating America and the end of ideology, the young activists rejected all ideology and traditional party politics, turning instead to where the action was, to SNCC, formed in 1960 by Negroes and whites, southern and northern. SNCC wasn't political; it was concerned with right and wrong, with people. The SNCC ideal of morality in action also provided the spur for the Students for a Democratic Society (SDS) and its community and campus programs: the decision to act was reinforced by the role of the liberal intellectuals in the 1961 Bay of Pigs episode and the 1962 missile crisis.

What began perhaps as a rebellion against affluence and liberal hypocrisy grew in a few years into a radical activism that protested injustice at the very core of the society. But when even this was tolerated by the structures that were under attack, some of the young radicals began to think about something beyond rebellion or radical protest. The Movement now is struggling to develop an ideology that will guide them toward building an organization that can compete for political power.

8 / THE DILEMMA OF
POLITICAL PARTIES

ROBERT MICHELS / The Iron
Law of Oligarchy*

...Is it impossible for a democratic party to practice a democratic policy, for a revolutionary party to pursue a revolutionary
policy? Must we say that not *socialism* alone, but even a socialistic
policy, is utopian? The present chapter will attempt a brief answer to this inquiry.

Within certain narrow limits, the democratic party, even when
subjected to oligarchical control, can doubtless act upon the state
in the democratic sense.[1] The old political caste of society, and
above all the "state" itself, are forced to undertake the revaluation of a considerable number of values—a revaluation both
ideal and practical. The importance attributed to the masses increases, even when the leaders are demagogues. The legislature
and the executive become accustomed to yield, not only to claims
proceeding from above, but also to those proceeding from below.
This may give rise, in practice, to great inconveniences, such as
we recognize in the recent history of all the states under a parliamentary regime; in theory, however, this new order of things
signifies an incalculable progress in respect of public rights, which

* From Michels, *Political Parties* (New York, Dover Books, 1959), pp. 365–408.
First published in 1912. Some of the original footnotes and portions of the
original text have been omitted.
1 Especially where there exists universal, equal, and direct suffrage, and where
the working class is strongly organized and is awake to its own interests. (Cf.
Franco Savorgnan, *Soziologische Fragmente,* Wagner, Innsbruck, 1909, p. 105).
In this case the leaders have every interest in exercising upon the state all
the pressure they can to render it more democratic.

thus come to conform better with the principles of social justice. This evolution will, however, be arrested from the moment when the governing classes succeed in attracting within the governmental orbit their enemies of the extreme Left, in order to convert them into collaborators. Political organization leads to power. But power is always conservative. In any case, the influence exercised upon the governmental machine by an energetic opposition party is necessarily slow, is subject to frequent interruptions, and is always restricted by the nature of oligarchy.

The recognition of this consideration does not exhaust our problem, for we have further to examine whether the oligarchical nature of organization be not responsible for the creation of the external manifestations of oligarchical activity, whether it be not responsible for the production of an oligarchical policy. The analysis here made shows clearly that the internal policy of the party organizations is today absolutely conservative, or is on the way to become such. Yet it might happen that the external policy of these conservative organisms would be bold and revolutionary; that the anti-democratic centralization of power in the hands of a few leaders is no more than a tactical method adopted to effect the speedier overthrow of the adversary; that the oligarchs fulfill the purely provisional function of educating the masses for the revolution, and that organization is after all no more than a means employed in the service of an amplified Blanquist conception.

This development would conflict with the nature of party, with the endeavor to organize the masses upon the vastest scale imaginable. As the organization increases in size, the struggle for great principles becomes impossible. It may be noticed that in the democratic parties of today the great conflicts of view are fought out to an ever-diminishing extent in the field of ideas and with the weapons of pure theory, that they therefore degenerate more and more into personal struggles and invectives, to be settled finally upon considerations of a purely superficial character. The efforts made to cover internal dissensions with a pious veil are the inevitable outcome of organization based upon bureaucratic principles, for, since the chief aim of such an organization is to enroll the greatest possible number of members, every struggle on behalf of ideas within the limits of the organization is necessarily regarded as an obstacle to the realization of its ends, an obstacle, therefore, which must be avoided in every possible way. This tendency is reinforced by the parliamentary character of the political party. "Party organization" signifies the aspiration for the greatest number of members. "Parliamentarism" signifies the aspiration for the greatest number of votes. The principal fields of party activity are electoral agitation and direct agitation to secure new members. What, in fact, is the modern political party? It is the methodical organization of the electoral masses. The socialist party, as a political aggregate endeavoring simultaneously to recruit members and to recruit votes, finds here its vital interests, for every decline in membership and every loss in voting strength diminishes its political prestige. Consequently great respect must be paid, not only to new members, but also to possible adherents, to those who in Germany are termed *mitläufer*, in Italy *simpatizzanti*, in Holland *geestverwanten*, and in England *sympathizers*. To avoid alarming these individuals, who are still outside the ideal worlds of socialism or democracy, the pursuit of a policy based on strict principle is shunned, while the consideration is ignored whether the numerical increase of the organization thus effected is not likely to be gained at the expense of its quality.

The last link in the long chain of phenomena which confer a profoundly conservative character upon the intimate essence of the political party (even upon that party which boasts itself revolutionary) is found in the relationships between party and state. Generated to overthrow the centralized power of the state, starting from the idea that the working class need merely secure a sufficiently vast and solid organization in order to triumph over the organization of the state, the party of the workers has ended by acquiring a vigorous centralization of its own, based upon the same cardinal principles of authority and discipline which characterize the organization of the state.[2] It thus becomes a govern-

[2] Albert Schäffle believes that socialism needs merely to produce a great general at the right moment in order to inherit the power of the centralized military organization (Schäffle, *Quintessenz des Sozialismus*, Perthes, Gotha, 1879, 7th ed., p. 68).

mental party, that is to say, a party which, organized itself like a government on the small scale, hopes some day to assume the reins of government upon the large scale. The revolutionary political party is a state within the state, pursuing the avowed aim of destroying the existing state in order to substitute for it a social order of a fundamentally different character.[3] To attain this essentially political end, the party avails itself of the socialist organization, whose sole justification is found precisely in its patient but systematic preparation for the destruction of the organization of the state in its existing form. The subversive party organizes the *framework* of the social revolution. For this reason it continually endeavors to strengthen its positions, to extend its bureaucratic mechanism, to store up its energies and its funds.

Every new official, every new secretary, engaged by the party is in theory a new agent of the revolution; in the same way every new section is a new battalion; and every additional thousand francs furnished by the members' subscriptions, by the profits of the socialist press, or by the generous donations of sympathetic benefactors, constitute fresh additions to the war-chest for the struggle against the enemy. In the long run, however, the directors of this revolutionary body existing within the authoritarian state, sustained by the same means as that state and inspired by the like spirit of discipline, cannot fail to perceive that the party organization, whatever advances it may make in the future, will never succeed in becoming more than an ineffective and miniature copy of the state organization. For this reason, in all ordinary circumstances, and as far as prevision is humanly possible, every attempt of the party to measure its forces with those of its antagonists is foredoomed to disastrous failure. The logical consequence of these considerations is in direct conflict with the hopes entertained by the founders of the party. Instead of gaining revolutionary energy as the force and solidity of its structure has increased, the precise opposite has occurred; there has resulted, *pari*

---

[3] Devoting all its energies to the imitation of the outward apparatus of power characteristic of the "class-state," the socialist party allots no more than a secondary importance to psychological enfranchisement from the mentality which dominates this same class-state. This neglect of the psychical factor is disastrous to the democratic principle, especially insofar as it springs from psychological sources....

passu with its growth, a continued increase in the prudence, the timidity even, which inspires its policy. The party, continually threatened by the state upon which its existence depends, carefully avoids (once it has attained to maturity) everything which might irritate the state to excess. The party doctrines are, whenever requisite, attenuated and deformed in accordance with the external needs of the organization.[4] Organization becomes the vital essence of the party. During the first years of its existence, the party did not fail to make a parade of its revolutionary character, not only in respect of its ultimate ends, but also in respect of the means employed for their attainment—although not always in love with these means. But as soon as it attained to political maturity, the party did not hesitate to modify its original profession of faith and to affirm itself revolutionary only "in the best sense of the word," that is to say, no longer on lines which interest the

---

[4] A classical example of the extent to which the fear of injuring the socialist organization will lead even the finest intelligences of the party to play tricks with socialist theory is afforded by the history of that celebrated preface which in 1895 Frederick Engels wrote for a posthumous edition of Marx's book, *Die Klassenkämpfe in Frankreich, 1848-9.* This preface became the subject of great international discussions, and has been justly considered as the first vigorous manifestation of reformism in German socialism. For Engels here declares that socialist tactics will have more success through the use of legal than of illegal and revolutionary means, and thus expressly repudiates the Marxist conception of the socialist revolution. It was not till some years later that Kautsky published a letter from Engels in which the latter disavowed his preface, saying: "My text had to suffer from the timid legalism of our friends in Berlin, who dreaded a second edition of the anti-socialist laws— a dread to which I was forced to pay attention at the existing political juncture" (Karl Kautsky, *Der Weg zur Macht,* Buchhandlung "Vorwärts," 1909, p. 42). From this it would appear that the theory (at that time brand-new) that socialism could attain to its ends by parliamentary methods—and this was the quintessence of Engels' preface—came into existence from a fear lest the socialist party organization (which should be a means, and not an end in itself) might suffer at the hands of the state. Thus Engels was fêted, on the one hand, as a man of sound judgment and one willing to look facts in the face (cf. W. Sombart, *Friedrich Engels, Ein Blatt zur Entwicklungsgeschichte des Sozialismus,* Separat-Abdruck der "Zukunft," Berlin, 1895, p. 32), and was attacked, on the other hand, as a pacifist utopist (cf. Arturo Labriola, *Riforme e Rivoluzione sociale, ed. cit.,* pp. 181 and 224); whereas in reality Engels would seem to have been the victim of an opportunist sacrifice of principles to the needs of organization, a sacrifice made for love of the party and in opposition to his own theoretical convictions.

police, but only in theory and on paper.[5] This same party, which at one time did not hesitate, when the triumphant guns of the bourgeois governors of Paris were still smoking, to proclaim with enthusiasm its solidarity with the communards, now announces to the whole world that it repudiates anti-militarist propaganda in any form which may bring its adherents into conflict with the penal code, and that it will not assume any responsibility for the consequences that may result from such a conflict. A sense of responsibility is suddenly becoming active in the socialist party. Consequently it reacts with all the authority at its disposal against the revolutionary currents which exist within its own organization, and which it has hitherto regarded with an indulgent eye. In the name of the grave responsibilities attaching to its position it now disavows anti-militarism, repudiates the general strike, and denies all the logical audacities of its past.

The history of the international labor movement furnishes innumerable examples of the manner in which the party becomes increasingly inert as the strength of its organization grows; it loses its revolutionary impetus, becomes sluggish, not in respect of action alone, but also in the sphere of thought. More and more tenaciously does the party cling to what it calls the "ancient and glorious tactics," the tactics which have led to a continued increase in membership. More and more invincible becomes its aversion to all aggressive action.

The dread of the reaction by which the Socialist Party is haunted paralyzes all its activities, renders impossible all manifestation of force, and deprives it of all energy for the daily struggle. It attempts to justify its misoneism by the false pretence that it must reserve its strength for the final struggle. Thus we find that the conservative tendencies inherent in all forms of possession manifest themselves also in the socialist party. For half a century the socialists have been working in the sweat of their brow to create a model organization. Now, when three million workers

[5] Maximilian Harden is not far wrong when he compares the revolutionary parties in their attitude towards the state authorities to a cock which is as it were glued to its place because a chalk-line has been drawn in front of its beak, a line which to the bird represents an insuperable obstacle.

have been organized—a greater number than was supposed necessary to secure complete victory over the enemy[6]—the party is endowed with a bureaucracy which, in respect of its consciousness of its duties, its zeal, and its submission to the hierarchy, rivals that of the state itself; the treasuries are full; a complex ramification of financial and moral interests extends all over the country. A bold and enterprising tactic would endanger all this: the work of many decades, the social existence of thousands of leaders and subleaders, the entire party, would be compromised. For these reasons the idea of such a tactic becomes more and more distasteful. It conflicts equally with an unjustified sentimentalism and a justified egoism. It is opposed by the artist's love of the work he has created with so much labor, and also by the personal interest of thousands of honest bread-winners whose economic life is so intimately associated with the life of the party and who tremble at the thought of losing their employment and the consequences they would have to endure if the government should proceed to dissolve the party, as might readily happen in case of war.

Thus, from a means, organization becomes an end. To the institutions and qualities which at the outset were destined simply to ensure the good working of the party machine (subordination, the harmonious cooperation of individual members, hierarchical relationships, discretion, propriety of conduct), a greater importance comes ultimately to be attached than to the productivity of the machine. Henceforward the sole preoccupation is to avoid anything which may clog the machinery. Should the party be attacked, it will abandon valuable positions previously conquered, and will renounce ancient rights rather than reply to the enemy's offensive by methods which might "compromise" its position. Naumann writes sarcastically: "The war-cry 'Proletarians of all countries unite!' has had its due effect. The forces of the organized proletariat have gained a strength which no one believed possible when that war-cry was first sounded. There is money in

[6] ... Today, the German trade unionists are as numerous as the English, while in the intervening years the numerical strength of the socialist movement has more than doubled, but the conquest of power seems more remote than ever.

the treasuries. Is the signal for the final assault never to be given? ... Is the work of preliminary organization to go on for ever?" As the party's need for tranquillity increases, its revolutionary talons atrophy. We have now a finely conservative party which (since the effect survives the cause) continues to employ revolutionary terminology, but which in actual practice fulfills no other function than that of a constitutional opposition.

All this has deviated far from the ideas of Karl Marx, who, were he still alive, ought to be the first to revolt against such a degeneration of Marxism. Yet it is quite possible that, carried away by the spectacle of an army of three million men acting in his name, swearing on solemn occasions *in verba magistri,* he also would find nothing to say in reprobation of so grave a betrayal of his own principles. There were incidents in Marx's life which render such a view possible. He certainly know how to close his eyes, in public at any rate, to the serious faults committed by the German social democracy in 1876.[7]

The Marxist theory of the state, when conjoined with a faith in the revolutionary energy of the working class and in the democratic effects of the socialization of the means of production, leads logically to the idea of a new social order which to the school of Mosca appears utopian. According to the Marxists, the capitalist mode of production transforms the great majority of the population into proletarians, and thus digs its own grave. As soon as it has attained maturity, the proletariat will seize political power, and will immediately transform private property into state property. "In this way it will eliminate itself, for it will thus put an end to all social differences, and consequently to all class antagonisms. In other words, the proletariat will annul the state, *qua* state. Capitalist society, divided into classes, has need of the state as an organization of the ruling class, whose purpose it is to maintain the capitalist system of production in its own interest and in order to effect the continued exploitation of the proletariat. Thus to put an end to the state is synonymous with putting an end to

[7] Karl Kautsky, Preface to Karl Marx, *Randglossen zum Programm der deutschen Arbeiterpartei* (1875), "Neue Zeit," anno ix, Vol. 1, pp. 508 *et seq.*

the existence of the dominant class." [8] But the new collectivist
society, the society without classes, which is to be established
upon the ruins of the ancient state, will also need elective elements. It may be said that by the adoption of the preventive rules
formulated by Rousseau in the *Contrat Social,* and subsequently
reproduced by the French revolutionists in the *Déclaration des
Droits de l'Homme,* above all by the strict application of the
principle that all officers are to be held on a revocable tenure, the
activity of these representatives may be confined within rigid
limits. It is none the less true that social wealth cannot be satisfactorily administered in any other manner than by the creation
of an extensive bureaucracy. In this way we are led by an inevitable logic to the flat denial of the possibility of a state without
classes. The administration of an immeasurably large capital,
above all when this capital is collective property, confers upon
the administrator influence at least equal to that possessed by the
private owner of capital. Consequently the critics in advance of
the Marxist social order ask whether the instinct which today
leads the members of the possessing classes to transmit to their
children the wealth which they (the parents) have amassed, will
not exist also in the administrators of the public wealth of the
socialist state, and whether these administrators will not utilize
their immense influence in order to secure for their children the
succession to the offices which they themselves hold.

The constitution of a new dominant minority would, in addition, be especially facilitated by the manner in which, according
to the Marxist conception of the revolution, the social transformation is to be effected. Marx held that the period between the
destruction of capitalist society and the establishment of communist society would be bridged by a period of revolutionary transition in the economic field, to which would correspond a period of
political transition, "when the state could not be anything other
than the revolutionary dictatorship of the proletariat." [9] To put

---

8 Friedrich Engels, *Die Entwicklung des Sozialismus von der Utopie zur
Wissenschaft,* Buchhandlung "Vorwärts," 4th ed. (Berlin, 1891), p. 40.
9 Karl Marx, *Randglossen zum Programm der deutschen Arbeiterpartei,*
"Waffenkammer des Sozialismus," 10th semi-annual vol. (Frankfort-on-the
Main, 1908), p. 18.

the matter less euphemistically, there will then exist a dictatorship in the hands of those leaders who have been sufficiently astute and sufficiently powerful to grasp the scepter of dominion in the name of socialism, and to wrest it from the hands of the expiring bourgeois society.

There is little difference, as far as practical results are concerned, between individual dictatorship and the dictatorship of a group of oligarchs. Now it is manifest that the concept *dictatorship* is the direct antithesis of the concept *democracy*. The attempt to make dictatorship serve the ends of democracy is tantamount to the endeavor to utilize war as the most efficient means for the defense of peace, or to employ alcohol in the struggle against alcoholism. It is extremely probable that a social group which had secured control of the instruments of collective power would do all that was possible to retain that control. Theophrastus noted long ago that the strongest desire of men who have attained to leadership in a popularly governed state is not so much the acquirement of personal wealth as the gradual establishment of their own sovereignty at the expense of popular sovereignty. The danger is imminent lest the social revolution should replace the visible and tangible dominant classes which now exist and act openly, by a clandestine demagogic oligarchy, pursuing its ends under the cloak of equality.

Thus the social revolution would not effect any real modification of the internal structure of the mass. The socialists might conquer, but not socialism, which would perish in the moment of its adherents' triumph. We are tempted to speak of this process as a tragicomedy in which the masses are content to devote all their energies to effecting a change of masters. All that is left for the workers is the honor "de participer au recrutement gouvernemental." The result seems a poor one, especially if we take into account the psychological fact that even the purest of idealists who attains to power for a few years is unable to escape the corruption which the exercise of power carries in its train. In France, in working-class circles, the phrase is current, *homme élu, homme foutu.* The social revolution, like the political revolution, is equivalent to an operation by which, as the Italian proverb expresses it: "Si cambia il maestro di cappella, ma la musica è sempre quella." [10]

Fourier defined modern society as a mechanism in which the extremest individual licence prevailed, without affording any guarantee to the individual against the usurpations of the mass, or to the mass against the usurpations of the individual. History seems to teach us that no popular movement, however energetic and vigorous, is capable of producing profound and permanent changes in the social organism of the civilized world. The preponderant elements of the movement, the men who lead and nourish it, end by undergoing a gradual detachment from the masses, and are attracted within the orbit of the "political class." They perhaps contribute to this class a certain number of "new ideas," but they also endow it with more creative energy and enhanced practical intelligence, thus providing for the ruling class an ever-renewed youth. The "political class" (continuing to employ Mosca's convenient phrase) has unquestionably an extreme fine sense of its possibilities and its means of defense. It displays a remarkable force of attraction and a vigorous capacity for absorption which rarely fail to exercise an influence even upon the most embittered and uncompromising of its adversaries. From the historical point of view, the anti-romanticists are perfectly right when they sum up their skepticism in such caustic phraseology as this: "Qu'est ce qu'une révolution? Des gens qui se tirent des coups de fusil dans une rue: cela casse beaucoup de carreaux; il n'y a guère que les vitriers qui y trouvent du profit. Le vent emporte la fumée. Ceux qui restent dessus mettent les autres dessous. ... C'est bien la peine de remuer tant d'honnêtes pavés qui n'en pouvaient pas!" Or we may say, as the song runs in *Madame Angot:* "Ce n'est pas la peine de changer de gouvernement!" In France, the classic land of social theories and experiments, such pessimism has struck the deepest roots.

[10] There is a new conductor, but the music is just the same.

FINAL CONSIDERATIONS

"A prendre le terme dans la rigueur de l'acception il n'a jamais existé de véritable démocratie, et il n'en existera jamais. Il est contre l'ordre naturel que le grand nombre gouverne, et que le petit soit gouverné."—J. J. ROUSSEAU, *Contrat Social.*

Leadership is a necessary phenomenon in every form of social life. Consequently it is not the task of science to inquire whether this phenomenon is good or evil, or predominantly one or the other. But there is great scientific value in the demonstration that every system of leadership is incompatible with the most essential postulates of democracy. We are now aware that the law of the historic necessity of oligarchy is primarily based upon a series of facts of experience. Like all other scientific laws, sociological laws are derived from empirical observation. In order, however, to deprive our axiom of its purely descriptive character, and to confer upon it that status of analytical explanation which can alone transform a formula into a law, it does not suffice to contemplate from a unitary outlook those phenomena which may be empirically established; we must also study the determining causes of these phenomena. Such has been our task.

Now, if we leave out of consideration the tendency of the leaders to organize themselves and to consolidate their interests, and if we leave also out of consideration the gratitude of the led towards the leaders, and the general immobility and passivity of the masses, we are led to conclude that the principal cause of oligarchy in the democratic parties is to be found in the technical indispensability of leadership.

The process which has begun in consequence of the differentiation of functions in the party is completed by a complex of qualities which the leaders acquire through their detachment from the mass. At the outset, leaders arise *spontaneously;* their functions are *accessory* and *gratuitous.* Soon, however, they become *professional* leaders, and in this second stage of development they are *stable* and *irremovable.*

It follows that the explanation of the oligarchical phenomenon which thus results is partly *psychological;* oligarchy derives, that is to say, from the psychical transformations which the leading personalities in the parties undergo in the course of their lives. But also, and still more, oligarchy depends upon what we may term the *psychology of organization itself,* that is to say, upon the tactical and technical necessities which result from the consolidation of every disciplined political aggregate. Reduced to its most concise expression, the fundamental sociological law of political parties (the term "political" being here used in its most comprehensive significance) may be formulated in the following terms: "It is organization which gives birth to the dominion of the elected over the electors, of the mandataries over the mandators, of the delegates over the delegators. Who says organization, says oligarchy."

Every party organization represents an oligarchical power grounded upon a democratic basis. We find everywhere electors and elected. Also we find everywhere that the power of the elected leaders over the electing masses is almost unlimited. The oligarchical structure of the building suffocates the basic democratic principle. That which *is* oppresses *that which ought to be.* For the masses, this essential difference between the reality and the ideal remains a mystery. Socialists often cherish a sincere belief that a new elite of politicians will keep faith better than did the old. The notion of the representation of popular interests, a notion to which the great majority of democrats, and in especial the working-class masses of the German-speaking lands, cleave with so much tenacity and confidence, is an illusion engendered by a false illumination, is an effect of mirage. In one of the most delightful pages of his analysis of modern Don Quixotism, Alphonse Daudet shows us how the "brav' commandant" Bravida, who has never quitted Tarascon, gradually comes to persuade himself, influenced by the burning southern sun, that he has been to Shanghai and has had all kinds of heroic adventures. Similarly the modern proletariat, enduringly influenced by glib-tongued persons intellectually superior to the mass, ends by believing that by flocking to the poll and entrusting its social and economic cause to a delegate, its direct participation in power will be assured.

The formation of oligarchies within the various forms of democracy is the outcome of organic necessity, and consequently affects every organization, be it socialist or even anarchist. Haller long ago noted that in every form of social life relationships of dominion and of dependence are created by Nature herself. The supremacy of the leaders in the democratic and revolutionary parties has to be taken into account in every historic situation present and to come, even though only a few and exceptional minds will be fully conscious of its existence. The mass will never rule except *in abstracto*. Consequently the question we have to discuss is not whether ideal democracy is realizable, but rather to what point and in what degree democracy is desirable, possible, and realizable at a given moment. In the problem as thus stated we recognize the fundamental problem of politics as a science. Whoever fails to perceive this must, as Sombart says, either be so blind and fanatical as not to see that the democratic current daily makes undeniable advance, or else must be so inexperienced and devoid of critical faculty as to be unable to understand that all order and all civilization must exhibit aristocratic features. The great error of socialists, an error committed in consequence of their lack of adequate psychological knowledge, is to be found in their combination of pessimism regarding the present, with rosy optimism and immeasurable confidence regarding the future. A realistic view of the mental condition of the masses shows beyond question that even if we admit the possibility of moral improvement in mankind, the human materials with whose use politicians and philosophers cannot dispense in their plans of social reconstruction are not of a character to justify excessive optimism. Within the limits of time for which human provision is possible, optimism will remain the exclusive privilege of utopian thinkers.

The socialist parties, like the trade unions, are living forms of social life. As such they react with the utmost energy against any attempt to analyze their structure or their nature, as if it were a method of vivisection. When science attains to results which conflict with their apriorist ideology, they revolt with all their power. Yet their defense is extremely feeble. Those among the representatives of such organizations whose scientific earnestness and personal good faith make it impossible for them to deny outright the existence of oligarchical tendencies in every form of democracy, endeavor to explain these tendencies as the outcome of a kind of atavism in the mentality of the masses, characteristic of the youth of the movement. The masses, they assure us, are still infected by the oligarchic virus simply because they have been oppressed during long centuries of slavery, and have never yet enjoyed an autonomous existence. The socialist regime, however, will soon restore them to health, and will furnish them with all the capacity necessary for self-government. Nothing could be more anti-scientific than the supposition that as soon as socialists have gained possession of governmental power it will suffice for the masses to exercise a little control over their leaders to secure that the interests of these leaders shall coincide perfectly with the interests of the led. This idea may be compared with the view of Jules Guesde, no less anti-scientific than anti-Marxist (though Guesde proclaims himself a Marxist), that whereas Christianity has made God into a man, socialism will make man into a god.

The objective immaturity of the mass is not a mere transitory phenomenon which will disappear with the progress of democratization *au lendemain du socialisme*. On the contrary, it derives from the very nature of the mass as mass, for this, even when organized, suffers from an incurable incompetence for the solution of the diverse problems which present themselves for solution—because the mass *per se* is amorphous, and therefore needs division of labor, specialization, and guidance. "L'espèce humaine veut être gouvernée; elle le sera. J'ai honte de mon espèce," wrote Proudhon from his prison in 1850. Man as individual is by nature predestined to be guided, and to be guided all the more in proportion as the functions of life undergo division and subdivision. To an enormously greater degree is guidance necessary for the social group.

From this chain of reasoning and from these scientific convictions it would be erroneous to conclude that we should renounce all endeavors to ascertain the limits which may be imposed upon the powers exercised over the individual by oligarchies (state, dominant class, party, etc.). It would be an error to abandon the desperate enterprise of endeavoring to discover a social order which will render possible the complete realization of the idea of popular sovereignty. In the present work, as the writer said at the outset, it has not been his aim to indicate new paths. But it seemed necessary to lay considerable stress upon the pessimist aspect of democracy which is forced on us by historical study. We had to inquire whether, and within what limits, democracy must remain purely ideal, possessing no other value than that of a moral criterion which renders it possible to appreciate the varying degrees of that oligarchy which is immanent in every social regime. In other words, we have had to inquire if, and in what degree, democracy is an ideal which we can never hope to realize in practice. A further aim of this work was the demolition of some of the facile and superficial democratic illusions which trouble science and lead the masses astray. Finally, the author desired to throw light upon certain sociological tendencies which oppose the reign of democracy, and to a still greater extent oppose the reign of socialism.

The writer does not wish to deny that every revolutionary working-class movement, and every movement sincerely inspired by the democratic spirit, may have a certain value as contributing to the enfeeblement of oligarchic tendencies. The peasant in the fable, when on his deathbed, tells his sons that a treasure is buried in the field. After the old man's death the sons dig everywhere in order to discover the treasure. They do not find it. But their indefatigable labor improves the soil and secures for them a comparative well-being. The treasure in the fable may well symbolize democracy. Democracy is a treasure which no one will ever discover by deliberate search. But in continuing our search, in laboring indefatigably to discover the indiscoverable, we shall perform a work which will have fertile results in the democratic sense. We have seen, indeed, that within the bosom of the democratic working-class party are born the very tendencies to counteract which that party came into existence. Thanks to the diversity and to the unequal worth of the elements of the party, these tendencies often give rise to manifestations which border on tyranny. We have seen that the replacement of the traditional legitimism of the powers-that-be by the brutal plebiscitary rule of

Bonapartist parvenus does not furnish these tendencies with any moral or aesthetic superiority. Historical evolution mocks all the prophylactic measures that have been adopted for the prevention of oligarchy. If laws are passed to control the dominion of the leaders, it is the laws which gradually weaken, and not the leaders. Sometimes, however, the democratic principle carries with it, if not a cure, at least a palliative, for the disease of oligarchy. When Victor Considérant formulated his "democratico-pacificist" socialism, he declared that socialism signified, not the rule of society by the lower classes of the population, but the government and organization of society in the interest of all, through the intermediation of a group of citizens; and he added that the numerical importance of this group must increase *pari passu* with social development. This last observation draws attention to a point of capital importance. It is, in fact, a general characteristic of democracy, and hence also of the labor movement, to stimulate and to strengthen in the individual the intellectual aptitudes for criticism and control. We have seen how the progressive bureaucratization of the democratic organism tends to neutralize the beneficial effects of such criticism and such control. None the less it is true that the labor movement, in virtue of the theoretical postulates it proclaims, is apt to bring into existence (in opposition to the will of the leaders) a certain number of free spirits who, moved by principle, by instinct, or by both, desire to revise the base upon which authority is established. Urged on by conviction or by temperament, they are never weary of asking an eternal "Why?" about every human institution. Now this predisposition toward free inquiry, in which we cannot fail to recognize one of the most precious factors of civilization, will gradually increase in proportion as the economic status of the masses undergoes improvement and becomes more stable, and in proportion as they are admitted more effectively to the advantages of civilization. A wider education involves an increasing capacity for exercising control. Can we not observe every day that among the well-to-do the authority of the leaders over the led, extensive though it be, is never so unrestricted as in the case of the leaders of the poor? Taken in the mass, the poor are powerless and disarmed vis-à-vis their leaders. Their intellectual and cultural inferiority makes it impossible for them to see whither the leader is going, or to estimate in advance the significance of his actions. It is, consequently, the great task of social education to raise the intellectual level of the masses, so that they may be enabled, within the limits of what is possible, to counteract the oligarchical tendencies of the working-class movement.

In view of the perennial incompetence of the masses, we have to recognize the existence of two regulative principles:

1. The *ideological* tendency of democracy towards criticism and control;

2. The *effective* counter-tendency of democracy toward the creation of parties ever more complex and ever more differentiated —parties, that is to say, which are increasingly based upon the competence of the few.

To the idealist, the analysis of the forms of contemporary democracy cannot fail to be a source of bitter deceptions and profound discouragement. Those alone, perhaps, are in a position to pass a fair judgment upon democracy who, without lapsing into dilettantist sentimentalism, recognize that all scientific and human ideals have relative values. If we wish to estimate the value of democracy, we must do so in comparison with its converse, pure aristocracy. The defects inherent in democracy are obvious. It is none the less true that as a form of social life we must choose democracy as the least of evils. The ideal government would doubtless be that of an aristocracy of persons at once morally good and technically efficient. But where shall we discover such an aristocracy? We may find it sometimes, though very rarely, as the outcome of deliberate selection; but we shall never find it where the hereditary principle remains in operation. Thus monarchy in its pristine purity must be considered as imperfection incarnate, as the most incurable of ills; from the moral point of view it is inferior even to the most revolting of demagogic dictatorships, for the corrupt organism of the latter at least contains a healthy principle upon whose working we may continue to base hopes of social resanation. It may be said, therefore, that the more humanity comes to recognize the advantages which democracy, however imperfect, presents over aristocracy, even at its best, the less likely is it that a recognition of the defects of democracy will provoke a return to aristocracy. Apart from certain formal differences and from the qualities which can be acquired only by good education and inheritance (qualities in which aristocracy will always have the advantage over democracy—qualities which democracy either neglects altogether, or, attempting to imitate them, falsifies them to the point of caricature), the defects of democracy will be found to inhere in its inability to get rid of its aristocratic scoriæ. On the other hand, nothing but a serene and frank examination of the oligarchical dangers of democracy will enable us to minimize these dangers, even though they can never be entirely avoided.

The democratic currents of history resemble successive waves. They break ever on the same shoal. They are ever renewed. This enduring spectacle is simultaneously encouraging and depressing. When democracies have gained a certain stage of development, they undergo a gradual transformation, adopting the aristocratic spirit, and in many cases also the aristocratic forms, against which at the outset they struggled so fiercely. Now new accusers arise to denounce the traitors; after an era of glorious combats and of inglorious power, they end by fusing with the old dominant class; whereupon once more they are in their turn attacked by fresh opponents who appeal to the name of democracy. It is probable that this cruel game will continue without end.

PAUL GOODMAN / On
Getting into Power*

The spirited candidacy of Stuart Hughes for Senator—like an ac-
tualization of Leo Szilard's courageous plan to finance and organize a national party for peace—makes it useful to review the am-
biguities involved in this kind of politics.

"War is the health of the State"—modern history teaches no
other lesson, whether we think of the weird personal, fanatic, and
dynastic wars of the sixteenth and seventeenth centuries or the
economic and geo-political wars of recent generations. The sovereign national States have lived and grown by preparing for war
and waging war; and as the Powers have aggrandized themselves,
they have become more crashingly destructive. I do not mean that
men have not used also simpler social organizations, feudal,
tribal, free city, in order to kill one another *en masse,* but centralized sovereign power, radiating from baroque capitals, has proved
to be the ideal executive of murderous will. In our own nation at
present, it would be impossible to describe the economy without
regarding war-making as a crucial factor; the foreign relations of
the United States are carried on entirely in terms of bellicose
power-blocs, and either to expand "influence" or to hang onto it;
and to mention my own field where I can speak at first hand, our
primary education and heavily State-subsidized higher education
have become regimented to apprentice-training for war, more di-

* From *Liberation* (October, 1962), pp. 4–8. Footnotes have been omitted.

rectly if less sickeningly than the psychological national regimentation endemic in French and German schooling. (The Russians go in for both the technological and psychological aspects.)

This solidifying of national sovereign bellicosity is at present all the more irrational, and of course all the more necessary if the sovereigns are to maintain themselves, since the cultural, technological, economic, and communications relations of the world are now overwhelmingly supra-national. (What a pity that, partly to combat colonialism and partly out of the emulative stupidity and cupidity of their Western-trained leaders, peoples of Africa and Asia are adopting the same fatal and outmoded style.)

The only possible pacifist conclusion from these facts is the anarchist one, to get rid of the sovereignties and to diminish, among people, the motivations of power and grandiosity. This means, regionally, to decentralize or centralize directly in terms of life-functions, empirically examined. My own bias is to decentralize and localize wherever it is feasible, because this makes for alternatives and more vivid and intimate life. It multiplies initiative. And it is safer. On the basis of this weakening of the Powers, and of the substitution of function for power, it would be possible also to organize the world community, as by the functional agencies of the United Nations, UNICEF, WHO, somewhat UNESCO; and to provide *ad hoc* cooperation like the Geophysical Year, exploring space, or feeding the Chinese.

Rigidly applied, this logic would seem to make pacifist State politics absurd. It is not in the nature of sovereign power to decree itself out of existence. (Thus, it is absurd for picketers of the White House to petition Mr. Kennedy as the President, rather than to sermonize him as a man or lecture him as a boy.) Also, such politics confuses the basic issue, that *pacifism is necessarily revolutionary*. A moment's recollection of the defection of the French and German socialist deputies from their pacifism in 1914 will show that this confusion is not trivial. Nevertheless, the attitude of the General Strike for Peace is as follows: in November we shall urge people actively and explicitly to refuse to vote, to strike against voting, except for candidates who are unambiguously committed to immediate action to relax the Cold War, for instance, Stuart Hughes or Robert Kastenmeier. Our reasoning is that, in our increasingly monolithic society and economy, any anti-war activity is likely to exert a revolutionary influence willy-nilly. And secondly, as Professor Hughes himself has said, the machinery of an electoral campaign *can* be a powerful means of education, especially by compelling mention of what the mass-media ordinarily refuse to mention. We wish to cooperate with pacifist activity of *every* kind, whether SANE, Quaker, Third Party politics, or Committee for Nonviolent Action, because although "objectively" we are in a revolutionary situation in that the powers-that-be are certainly bent on destroying themselves and everything else, nevertheless people do not take this seriously and there is an almost total lack of practical will to make the necessary reorganization of society. To say it grimly, unlike 1914, people do not even have political representatives to betray them.

Personally, what I enjoy about Professor Hughes's campaign is that often, when the students were out getting signatures to put him on the ballot, people would say, "Do you mean he is *neither* a Democrat *nor* a Republican? Then give me the pen!" (It is said, by people from Massachusetts, that this response is peculiarly appropriate to the ordinary local politics of Massachusetts; but I take this as local boasting.) In the deadly routine that the Americans have sunk into, the mere possibility of an *alternative* is a glorious thing. Especially if there is the framework of a permanent organization. Also such a campaign must be a remarkable experience for Hughes himself, to confront many people who do not at all have the same assumptions. And it gives some concrete activity to his phalanx, the New England professors of the Council of Correspondence. The students of Brandeis, Harvard, etc. are also busy with it; but on them this *kind* of political involvement might be, in my opinion, more ambiguous, and that is why I am writing this essay.

For let me turn to an issue much deeper and more fateful for pacifism than these questions of strategy and tactics. This is the assumption, now appallingly unanimous among the ordinary electorate, professional politicians, most radicals, and even political scientists who should know better, that politics is essentially a matter of "getting into power," and then "deciding," directing, controlling, coercing, the activities of society. The model seems to be taken from corporations with top-management, and there is something prestigious about being a "decision-maker." (Even C. Wright Mills was mesmerized by this image; but, as I tried to show recently in *Commentary*, in such a set-up less and less of human value is really decided by any responsible person, though plenty of disvalue is ground out by the set-up itself.) It is taken for granted that a man wants "power" of this kind, and it is quite acceptable for people like Joseph Kennedy and his sons to work toward it, even though this is directly contrary to the political ideal that the office and its duties seek the man rather than the man the office. It is axiomatic that a party's primary purpose is to get into power, although this was not the original idea of "factions," in Madison's sense, which were functional but divisive interest groups. More dangerously still, it is taken for granted that a nation wants to be a Great Power, and maintain itself so at any cost, even though this may be disadvantageous to its culture and most of its citizens.

And following the popular Leviathan like a jolly-boat, the political-sociologists devote their researches to the analysis and simulation of power struggles, as if this were their only possible subject; and as advisers, they take part in the power struggles, rather than helping to solve problems. Unfortunately, the thinking of Hughes and Szilard seems to share some of this assumption about the paramountcy of "getting into power"—just as Dave Riesman is always hounding people who are in "power." And frankly, when I question such a universal consensus, I wonder if I am on the right planet. Nevertheless, these persons are deluded. They are taking a base and impractical, and indeed neurotic, state of affairs as if it were right and inevitable. The state of affairs is impractical because, finally, no good can come of it; though of course, since it *is* the state of affairs, it must be transiently coped with and changed. Unless we remember much more clearly than we seem to, what this "power" is, our behavior in the madhouse cannot be prudent and therapeutic. So with chagrin I

find myself forced to review elementary political theory and history.

Living functions, biological, psychosociological, or social, have
very little to do with abstract, preconceived "power" that manages and coerces from outside the specific functions themselves.
Indeed, it is a commonplace that abstract power—in the form of
"will power," "training," "discipline," "bureaucracy," "reform-
schooling," "scientific management," etc.—uniformly *thwarts*
normal functioning and debases the persons involved. (It has a
natural use, in emergencies, when not high-grade but minimal
low-grade behavior is required.) Normal activities do not need
extrinsic motivations, they have their own intrinsic energies and
ends-in-view; and decisions are continually made by the on-going
functions themselves, adjusting to the environment and one another.

We may then define the subject of normal politics. It is the
constitutional relations of functional interests and interest groups
in the community in which they transact. This is the bread-and-
butter of ancient political theory and obviously has nothing to do
with sovereignty or even power—for the ancients the existence of
power implies unconstitutionality, tyranny. But even modern authors who move in a theory of "sovereignty," like Spinoza, Locke,
Adam Smith, Jefferson, or Madison, understand that the commonwealth is strongest when the functional interests can seek
their own level and there is the weakest exercise of "power," e.g.,
Spinoza tries to play power like a fish, Jefferson to de-energize it,
Madison to balance it out.

Let us now quickly sketch the meaning of the recent transcend-
ent importance of "power" and "getting into power," as if otherwise communities could not function.

First, and least important, there is the innocuous, non-violent,
and rather natural development of a kind of abstract power in an
indigenous (non-invaded) society. The functions of civilization
include production, trade and travel, the bringing up of the
young in the mores; also subtle but essential polarities like experimentation and stability; also irrational and superstitious fantasies like exacting revenge for crime and protecting the taboos.

Different interests in the whole will continually conflict, as individuals or as interest-groups; yet, since all require the commonwealth, there is also a strong functional interest in adjudication and peace, in harmonizing social invention or at least compromise. It is plausible that, in the interests of armistice and adjudication, there should arise a kind of abstract institution above the conflicts, to settle them or to obviate them by plans and laws; this would certainly be power. (This derivation is plausible but I doubt that it is historical, for in fact it is just this kind of thing that lively primitive communities accomplish by quick intuition, tone of voice, exchange of a glance, and suddenly there is unanimity, to the anthropologist's astonishment.) Much more likely, and we know historically, abstract power is invented in simple societies in emergencies of danger, of enemy attack or divine wrath. But such "dictatorship" is *ad hoc* and surprisingly lapses. Surprisingly, considering that power corrupts; yet it makes psychological sense, for emergency is a negative function, to meet a threat to the pre-conditions of the interesting functions of life; once the danger is past, the "power" has no energy of function, no foreground interest, to maintain it. To give a very late example: it seemed remarkable to the Europeans, but not to the Americans, that Washington, like Cincinnatus, went home to his farm; and even the Continental Congress languished. There were no conditions for "power."

(Indeed—and this is why I have chosen the example—in the last decades of the eighteenth century, in many respects the Americans lived in a kind of peaceful community anarchy, spiced by mutinies that were hardly punished. The Constitution, as Richard Lee pointed out, was foisted on them by trickery, the work of very special interest groups; it would have been quite sufficient simply to amend the Articles.)

Altogether different from this idyl is the universal history of most of the world, civilized or barbarian. Everywhere is invasion, conquest, and domination, involving for the victors the necessity to keep and exercise power, and for the others the necessity to strive for power, in order to escape suffering and exploitation. This too is entirely functional. The conqueror is originally a pirate; he and his band do not share in the commonwealth, they have interests apart from the community preyed on. Subsequently, however, piracy becomes government, the process of getting people to perform by extrinsic motivations, of penalty and blackmail, and later bribery and training. But it is only the semblance of a commonwealth, for activity is directed. Necessarily, such directed and extrinsically motivated performance is not so strong, efficient, spontaneous, inventive, well-structured, or lovely as the normal functioning of a free community of interests. Very soon society becomes lifeless. The means of community action, initiative, decision, have been pre-empted by the powerful. But the slaveholders, exploiters, and governors share in that same society and are themselves vitiated. Yet they never learn to get down off the people's back and relinquish their power. So some are holding on to an increasingly empty power; others are striving to achieve it; and most are sunk in resignation. Inevitably, as people become stupider and more careless, administration increases in size and power; and conversely. By and large, the cultures that we study in the melancholy pages of history are pathetic mixtures, with the ingredients often still discernible: There is a certain amount of normal function surviving or reviving—bread is baked, arts and sciences are pursued by a few, etc.; mostly we see the abortions of lively social functioning saddled, exploited, prevented, perverted, drained dry, paternalized by an imposed system of power and management that pre-empts the means and makes decisions *ab extra*. And the damnable thing is that, of course, everybody believes that except in this pattern nothing could possibly be accomplished: if there were no marriage-license and no tax, none could properly mate and no children be born and raised; if there were no tolls there would be no bridges; if there were no university charters, there would be no higher learning; if there were no usury and no iron law of wages, there would be no capital; if there were no mark-up of drug prices, there would be no scientific research. Once a society has this style of thought, that every activity requires licensing, underwriting, deciding by abstract power, it becomes inevitably desirable for an ambitious man to seek power and for a vigorous nation to try to be a Great Power. The more that have the power-drive, the more it seems to be necessary to the others to compete, or submit, just in order to survive. (And importantly they are right.) Many are ruthless and most live in fear.

Even so, this is not the final development of the belief in "power." For that occurs when to get into power, to be prestigious and in a position to make decisions, is taken to be the social good itself, apart from any functions that it is thought to make possible. The pattern of dominance-and-submission has then been internalized and, by its clinch, fills up the whole of experience. If a man is not continually proving his potency, his mastery of others and of himself, he becomes prey to a panic of being defeated and victimized. Every vital function must therefore be used as a means of proving or it is felt as a symptom of weakness. Simply to enjoy, produce, learn, give or take, love or be angry (rather than cool), is to be vulnerable. This is different, and has different consequences, from the previous merely external domination and submission. A people that has life but thwarted functions will rebel when it can, against feudal dues, clogs to trade, suppression of thought and speech, taxation without representation, insulting privilege, the iron law of wages, colonialism. But our people do not rebel against poisoning, genetic deformation, imminent total destruction.

Rather, people aspire to be top-managers no matter what the goods or services produced. One is a promoter, period; or a celebrity, period. The Gross National Product must increase without consideration of the standard of life. There is no natural limit, so the only security is in deterrence. The environment is rife with projected enemies. There is a huddling together and conforming to avoid the vulnerability of any idiosyncrasy, at the same time as each one has to be one-up among his identical similars. Next, there is excitement in identifying with the "really" powerful, the leaders, the great nations, the decision-makers, dramatized on the front page. But these leaders, of course, feel equally powerless in the face of the great events. For it is characteristic of the syndrome that as soon as there is occasion for any practical activity, toward happiness, value, spirit, or even simple safety, everyone suffers from the feeling of utter powerlessness; the internalized submissiveness now has its innings. Modern technology is too complex; there is a population explosion; the computer will work out the proper war-game for us; they've got your number, don't stick your neck out; "fall-out is a physical fact of our nuclear age, it can be faced like any other fact" (*Manual of Civil Defense*); "I'm strong, I can take sex or leave it" (eighteen-year-old third-offender for felonious assault). In brief, the under-side of the psychology of power is that Nothing Can Be Done; and the resolution of the stalemate is to explode. This is the Cold War.

I have frequently explored this psychology of proving, resignation, and catastrophic explosion (Wilhelm Reich's "primary masochism"), and I shall not pursue it again. It is filling the void of vital function by identifying with the agent that has frustrated it; with, subsequently, a strongly defended conceit, but panic when any occasion calls for initiative, originality, or even animal response. Here I have simply tried to relate this psychology to the uncritical unanimous acceptance of the idea of "getting into power in order to . . ." or just "getting into power" as an end in itself. There is a vicious circle, for (except in emergencies) the very exercise of abstract power, managing and coercing, itself tends to stand in the way and alienate, to thwart function and diminish energy, and so to increase the psychology of power. But of course the consequence of the process is to put us in fact in a continual emergency, so power creates its own need. I have tried to show how, historically, the psychology has been exacerbated by the miserable system of extrinsic motivation by incentives and punishments (including profits, wages, unemployment), reducing people to low-grade organisms no different than Professor Skinner's pigeons; whereas normal function is intrinsically motivated toward specific ends in view, and leads to growth in inventiveness and freedom. Where people are now directly in feelingful contact with what is to be done, nothing is done well and on time; they are always behind and the emergency becomes chronic. Even with good intentions, a few managers do not have enough *mind* for the needs of society—not even if their computers gallop through the calculations like lightning. I conclude that the consensus of recent political scientists, that political theory is essentially the study of power-maneuvers, is itself a neurotic ideology. Normal politics has to do with the relations of specific functions in a community; and *such a study would often result in practical political inventions that would solve problems*—it would not merely predict elections and solve nothing, or play war-games and destroy mankind.

Let me sum up these remarks in one homely and not newsy proposition: Throughout the world, it is bad domestic politics that creates the deadly international politics. Conversely, pacifism is revolutionary: we will not have peace unless there is a profound change in social structure, including getting rid of national sovereign power.

After this pedantic excursion, let me return, for a paragraph, to Professor Hughes. He does not have the psychology that Nothing Can Be Done, for he is doing something with immense energy. Indeed, his most valuable service, in my opinion, is to show that even in the framework of routine politics, there is a possible alternative mode of proceeding. (Adlai Stevenson, by contrast, never seemed to believe this.) Also, he obviously has no wish to "get into power" except precisely to stop the arms race and relax the Cold War. His campaign is primarily educational; and even if he were elected, I think, he would not feel that he has "power" but a splendid public forum. (This is the line of Kastenmeier and the Liberal Project Congressmen.)

Yet we cannot overlook the deep contradiction between peace and "getting into power" at all. With the strong background support of the unusually courageous New England professors, the hard work of politically renascent youth, and the total disgust of many of the electorate in the face of our insane policies, Professor Hughes has been able to by-pass the demoralizing and stupefying demands of the political clubhouse, or the emasculating horse's-ass-making requirements of rising to an important nomination through respectable channels. Nevertheless, the program with which he now appears before the electorate—I presume he means it sincerely—is inadequate to the needs of the situation. In foreign affairs, it is the kind of compromising that has no future. As a domestic program it is valueless, as if he had not put his mind to this as immediately important; yet it is just in this, in my view, that he could shake and begin to revive our people. And suppose he (or Szilard's candidates) were elected: he could hardly take a Constitutional oath to proceed to ring down the flag. Of course he has no such purpose, but nothing less will serve.

Concretely, our system of government at present comprises the military-industrial complex, the secret para-military agencies, the scientific war-corporations, the blimps, the horse's asses, the police, the administrative bureaucracy, the career diplomats, the lobbies, the corporations that contribute party funds, the underwriters and real-estate promoters that batten on urban renewal, the official press and the official opposition press, the sounding-off and jockeying for the next election, the national unity, etc., etc. All this machine is grinding along by the momentum of the power and profit motives and style long since built into it; it *cannot* make decisions of a kind radically different than it does. Even if an excellent man happens to be elected to office, he will find that it is no longer a possible instrument for social change on any major issues of war and peace or the way of life of the Americans. Indeed, as the members of the Liberal Project have complained, office does not give even a good public forum, for the press does not report inconvenient speeches.

So we must look, finally, not to this kind of politics, but to direct functioning in what concerns us closely, in order to dispel the mesmerism of abstract power altogether. This has, of course, been the thinking of radical pacifism. The civil disobedience of the Committee for Nonviolent Action is the direct expression of each person's conscience of what it is impossible for him to live with. The studied withdrawal and boycotting advocated by the General Strike for Peace is a direct countering of the social drift toward catastrophe that occurs just because we cooperate with it. (The same holds for refusal in what is one's "private" important business, like the women's strike against poisoned milk, or young men's refusing the draft.) Best of all, in principle, is the policy that Dave Dellinger espouses and tries to live by, to live communally and without authority, to work usefully and feel friendly, and so *positively to replace an area of power with peaceful functioning*. Interestingly, even a critical and purgative group like *The Realist* is coming around to this point of view—with a hard row to hoe among urban poor people. Similar is to work in foreign lands as a citizen of humanity, trying to avoid the power blocs and their aims; e.g., the Friends Service. The merit of all these activities is that they produce a different kind of human relations and look to a different quality of life. This is a global and perhaps impossibly difficult task. But think. There is no history of mankind without these wars, which now have come to the maximum: can we have any hope except in a different kind of human relations?

It will be said that there is no time. Yes, probably. But let me cite a remark of de Tocqueville. In his last work, *L'Ancien Régime,* he notes "with terror," as he says, how throughout the eighteenth century writer after writer and expert after expert pointed out that this and that detail of the Old Régime was unviable and could not possibly survive; added up, they proved that the entire Old Régime was doomed and must soon collapse; and yet *there was not a single man who foretold that there would be a mighty revolution.*

9 / REVOLUTION: VIOLENT *vs.* NON-VIOLENT

JAMES C. DAVIES / Toward a Theory of Revolution*

In exhorting proletarians of all nations to unite in revolution, because they had nothing to lose but their chains, Marx and Engels most succinctly presented that theory of revolution which is recognized as their brain child. But this most famed thesis, that progressive degradation of the industrial working class would finally reach the point of despair and inevitable revolt, is not the only one that Marx fathered. In at least one essay he gave life to a quite antithetical idea. He described, as a precondition of widespread unrest, not progressive degradation of the proletariat but rather an improvement in workers' economic conditions which did not keep pace with the growing welfare of capitalists and therefore produced social tension.

A noticeable increase in wages presupposes a rapid growth of productive capital. The rapid growth of productive capital brings about an equally rapid growth of wealth, luxury, social wants, social enjoyments. Thus, although the enjoyments of the workers

* From *American Sociological Review* (February, 1962), pp. 5–19. Table and some original notes have been omitted.
† Several people have made perceptive suggestions and generous comments on an earlier version of this paper. I wish particularly to thank Seymour Martin Lipset, Lucian W. Pye, John H. Schaar, Paul Seabury, and Dwight Waldo.

have risen, the social satisfaction that they give has fallen in comparison with the increased enjoyments of the capitalist, which are inaccessible to the worker, in comparison with the state of development of society in general. Our desires and pleasures spring from society; we measure them, therefore, by society and not by the objects which serve for their satisfaction. Because they are of a social nature, they are of a relative nature.[1]

Marx's qualification here of his more frequent belief that degradation produces revolution is expressed as the main thesis by de Tocqueville in his study of the French Revolution. After a long review of economic and social decline in the seventeenth century and dynamic growth in the eighteenth, de Tocqueville concludes:

So it would appear that the French found their condition the more unsupportable in proportion to its improvement. . . . Revolutions are not always brought about by a gradual decline from bad to worse. Nations that have endured patiently and almost unconsciously the most overwhelming oppression often burst into rebellion against the yoke the moment it begins to grow lighter. The regime which is destroyed by a revolution is almost always an improvement on its immediate predecessor. . . . Evils which are patiently endured when they seem inevitable become intolerable when once the idea of escape from them is suggested.[2]

On the basis of de Tocqueville and Marx, we can choose one of these ideas or the other, which makes it hard to decide just when revolutions are more likely to occur—when there has been social

[1] The *Communist Manifesto* of 1848 evidently antedates the opposing idea by about a year. See Edmund Wilson, *To the Finland Station,* Anchor Books edition (New York, Doubleday & Co. [n.d.]), p. 157; Lewis S. Feuer, *Karl Marx and Friedrich Engels: Basic Writings on Politics and Philosophy* (New York, Doubleday & Co., Inc., 1959), p. 1. The above quotation is from Karl Marx and Frederick Engels, "Wage Labour and Capital," *Selected Works in Two Volumes* (Moscow: Foreign Languages Publishing House, 1955), Vol. 1, p. 94.
[2] A. de Tocqueville, *The Old Regime and the French Revolution,* trans. by John Bonner (New York, Harper & Bros., 1856), p. 214. The Stuart Gilbert translation (Garden City: Doubleday & Co., Inc., 1955), pp. 176–177, gives a somewhat less pungent version of the same comment. *L'Ancien régime* was first published in 1856.

and economic progress or when there has been regress. It appears that both ideas have explanatory and possibly predictive value, if they are juxtaposed and put in the proper time sequence.

Revolutions are most likely to occur when a prolonged period of objective economic and social development is followed by a short period of sharp reversal.[3] The all-important effect on the minds of people in a particular society is to produce, during the former period, an expectation of continued ability to satisfy needs—which continue to rise—and, during the latter, a mental state of anxiety and frustration when manifest reality breaks away from anticipated reality. The actual state of socio-economic development is less significant than the expectation that past progress, now blocked, can and must continue in the future.

Political stability and instability are ultimately dependent on a state of mind, a mood, in a society. Satisfied or apathetic people who are poor in goods, status, and power can remain politically quiet and their opposites can revolt, just as, correlatively and more probably, dissatisfied poor can revolt and satisfied rich oppose revolution. It is the dissatisfied state of mind rather than the tangible provision of "adequate" or "inadequate" supplies of food, equality, or liberty which produces the revolution. In actuality, there must be a joining of forces between dissatisfied, frustrated people who differ in their degree of objective, tangible welfare and status. Well-fed, well-educated, high-status individuals who rebel in the face of apathy among the objectively deprived can accomplish at most a *coup d'état*. The objectively deprived, when faced with solid opposition of people of wealth, status, and power, will be smashed in their rebellion as were peasants and Anabaptists by German noblemen in 1525 and East Germans by the Communist elite in 1953.

Before appraising this general notion in light of a series of revolutions, a word is in order as to why revolutions ordinarily do not occur when a society is generally impoverished—when, as de Tocqueville put it, evils that seem inevitable are patiently en-

---

[3] Revolutions are here defined as violent civil disturbances that cause the displacement of one ruling group by another that has a broader popular basis for support.

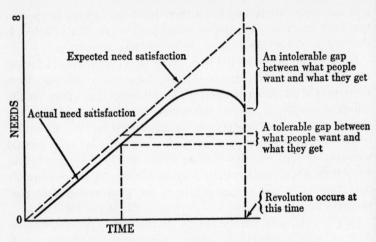

FIGURE 1. NEED SATISFACTION AND REVOLUTION

dured. They are endured in the extreme case because the physical and mental energies of people are totally employed in the process of merely staying alive. The Minnesota starvation studies conducted during World War II [4] indicate clearly the constant preoccupation of very hungry individuals with fantasies and thoughts of food. In extremis, as the Minnesota research poignantly demonstrates, the individual withdraws into a life of his own, withdraws from society, withdraws from any significant kind of activity unrelated to staying alive. Reports of behavior in Nazi concentration camps indicate the same preoccupation.[5] In less extreme and barbarous circumstances, where minimal survival is possible but little more, the preoccupation of individuals with staying alive is only mitigated. Social action takes place for the most part on a local, face-to-face basis. In such circumstances the family is a—perhaps the major—solidary unit[6] and even the local

[4] The full report is Ancel Keys, *et al., The Biology of Human Starvation* (Minneapolis, University of Minnesota Press, 1950). See J. Brozek, "Semi-starvation and Nutritional Rehabilitation," *Journal of Clinical Nutrition*, 1 (January, 1953), pp. 107–118 for a brief analysis.

[5] E. A. Cohen, *Human Behavior in the Concentration Camp* (New York: W. W. Norton & Co., 1953), pp. 123–125, 131–140.

[6] For community life in such poverty, in Mezzogiorno Italy, see E. C. Ban-

community exists primarily to the extent families need to act together to secure their separate survival. Such was life on the American frontier in the sixteenth through nineteenth centuries. In very much attenuated form, but with a substantial degree of social isolation persisting, such evidently is rural life even today. This is clearly related to a relatively low level of political participation in elections.[7] As Zawadzki and Lazarsfeld have indicated,[8] preoccupation with physical survival, even in industrial areas, is a force strongly militating against the establishment of the community-sense and consensus on joint political action which are necessary to induce a revolutionary state of mind. Far from making people into revolutionaries, enduring poverty makes for concern with one's solitary self or solitary family at best and resignation or mute despair at worst. When it is a choice between losing their chains or their lives, people will mostly choose to keep their chains, a fact which Marx seems to have overlooked.[9]

It is when the chains have been loosened somewhat, so that they can be cast off without a high probability of losing life, that people are put in a condition of proto-rebelliousness. I use the term proto-rebelliousness because the mood of discontent may be dissipated before a violent outbreak occurs. The causes for such dissipation may be natural or social (including economic and political). A bad crop year that threatens a return to chronic hunger may be succeeded by a year of natural abundance. Recovery from sharp economic dislocation may take the steam from the boiler of

---

field, *The Moral Basis of a Backward Society* (Glencoe, Ill., The Free Press, 1958). The author emphasizes that the nuclear family is a solidary, consensual, moral unit (see p. 85) but even within it, consensus appears to break down, in outbreaks of pure, individual amorality—notably between parents and children (see p. 117).

[7] See Angus Campbell, *et al.*, *The American Voter* (New York, John Wiley & Sons, 1960), Chap. 15, "Agrarian Political Behavior."

[8] B. Zawadzki and P. F. Lazarsfeld, "The Psychological Consequences of Unemployment," *Journal of Social Psychology*, 6 (May 1935), pp. 224–251.

[9] A remarkable and awesome exception to this phenomenon occurred occasionally in some Nazi concentration camps, e.g., in a Buchenwald revolt against capricious rule by criminal prisoners. During this revolt, one hundred criminal prisoners were killed by political prisoners. See Cohen, *op. cit.*, p. 200.

rebellion.[10] The slow, grudging grant of reforms, which has been the political history of England since at least the Industrial Revolution, may effectively and continuously prevent the degree of frustration that produces revolt.

A revolutionary state of mind requires the continued, even habitual but dynamic expectation of greater opportunity to satisfy basic needs, which may range from merely physical (food, clothing, shelter, health, and safety from bodily harm) to social (the affectional ties of family and friends) to the need for equal dignity and justice. But the necessary additional ingredient is a persistent, unrelenting threat to the satisfaction of these needs: not a threat which actually returns people to a state of sheer survival but which puts them in the mental state where they believe they will not be able to satisfy one or more basic needs. Although physical deprivation in some degree may be threatened on the eve of all revolutions, it need not be the prime factor, as it surely was not in the American Revolution of 1775. The crucial factor is the vague or specific fear that ground gained over a long period of time will be quickly lost. This fear does not generate if there is continued opportunity to satisfy continually emerging needs; it generates when the existing government suppresses or is blamed for suppressing such opportunity.

Three rebellions or revolutions are given considerable attention in the sections that follow: Dorr's Rebellion of 1842, the Russian Revolution of 1917, and the Egyptian Revolution of 1952. Brief mention is then made of several other major civil disturbances, all of which appear to fit the J-curve pattern.[11] After considering these specific disturbances, some general theoretical and research problems are discussed.

10 See W. W. Rostow, "Business Cycles, Harvests, and Politics: 1790–1850," *Journal of Economic History*, 1 (November, 1941), pp. 206–221 for the relation between economic fluctuation and the activities of the Chartists in the 1830s and 1840s.

11 This curve is of course not to be confused with its prior and altogether different use by Floyd Allport in his study of social conformity. See F. H. Allport, "The J-Curve Hypothesis of Conforming Behavior," *Journal of Social Psychology*, 5 (May, 1934), pp. 141–183, reprinted in T. H. Newcomb & E. L. Hartley, *Readings in Social Psychology* (New York, Henry Holt & Co., 1947), pp. 55–67.

No claim is made that all rebellions follow the pattern, but just that the ones here presented do. All of these are "progressive" revolutions in behalf of greater equality and liberty. The question is open whether the pattern occurs in such markedly retrogressive revolutions as Nazism in Germany or the 1861 Southern rebellion in the United States. It will surely be necessary to examine other progressive revolutions before one can judge how universal the J-curve is. And it will be necessary, in the interests of scientific validation, to examine cases of serious civil disturbance that fell short of producing profound revolution—such as the Sepoy Rebellion of 1857 in India, the Pullman Strike of 1894 in America, the Boxer Rebellion of 1900 in China, and the Great Depression of the 1920s and 1930s as it was experienced in Austria, France, Great Britain, and the United States. The explanation for such still-born rebellions—for revolutions that might have occurred—is inevitably more complicated than for those that come to term in the "normal" course of political gestation.

DORR'S REBELLION OF 1842

Dorr's Rebellion[12] in nineteenth-century America was perhaps the first of many civil disturbances to occur in America as a consequence, in part, of the Industrial Revolution. It followed by three years an outbreak in England that had similar roots and a similar program—the Chartist agitation. A machine-operated textile industry was first established in Rhode Island in 1790 and grew rapidly as a consequence of domestic and international demand, notably during the Napoleonic Wars. Jefferson's Embargo Act of 1807, the War of 1812, and a high tariff in 1816 further stimulated American industry.

Rapid industrial growth meant the movement of people from farms to cities. In Massachusetts the practice developed of hiring mainly the wives and daughters of farmers, whose income was thereby supplemented but not displaced by wages. In Rhode Island whole families moved to the cities and became committed to

---

[12] I am indebted to Beryl L. Crowe for his extensive research on Dorr's Rebellion while he was a participant in my political behavior seminar at the University of California, Berkeley, Spring, 1960.

the factory system. When times were good, industrialized families earned two or three times what they got from the soil; when the mills were idle, there was not enough money for bread.[13] From 1807 to 1815 textiles enjoyed great prosperity; from 1834 to 1842 they suffered depression, most severely from 1835 to 1840. Prosperity raised expectations and depression frustrated them, particularly when accompanied by stubborn resistance to suffrage demands that first stirred in 1790 and recurred in a wave-like pattern in 1811 and then in 1818 and 1820 following suffrage extension in Connecticut and Massachusetts. The final crest was reached in 1841, when suffrage associations met and called for a constitutional convention.[14]

Against the will of the government, the suffragists held an election in which all adult males were eligible to vote, held a constitutional convention composed of delegates so elected and in December 1841 submitted the People's Constitution to the same electorate, which approved it and the call for an election of state officers the following April, to form a new government under this unconstitutional constitution.[15]

These actions joined the conflict with the established government. When asked—by the dissidents—the state supreme court rendered its private judgment in March, 1842 that the new constitution was "of no binding force whatever" and any act "to carry it into effect by force will be treason against the state." The legislature passed what became known as the Algerian law, making it an offense punishable by a year in jail to vote in the April elec-

13 Joseph Brennan, *Social Conditions in Industrial Rhode Island: 1820–1860* (Washington, D.C., Catholic University of America, 1940), p. 33.
14 The persistent demand for suffrage may be understood in light of election data for 1828 and 1840. In the former year, only 3600 votes were cast in Rhode Island, whose total population was about 94,000. (Of these votes, 23 percent were cast for Jackson and 77 percent for Adams, in contrast to a total national division of 56 percent for Jackson and 44 percent for Adams.) All votes cast in the 1828 election amount to 4 percent of the total Rhode Island population and 11 percent of the total U.S. population excluding slaves. In 1840, with a total population of 109,000 only 8300 votes—8 percent —were cast in Rhode Island, in contrast to 17 percent of the national population excluding slaves.
15 A. M. Mowry, *The Dorr War* (Providence, R.I., Preston & Rounds Co., 1901), p. 114.

tion, and by life imprisonment to hold office under the People's Constitution.

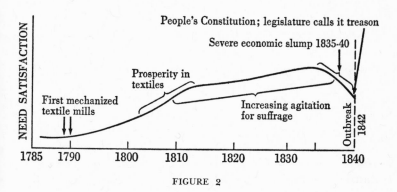

FIGURE 2

The rebels went stoutly ahead with the election, and on May 3, 1842 inaugurated the new government. The next day the People's legislature met and respectfully requested the sheriff to take possession of state buildings, which he failed to do. Violence broke out on the 17th of May in an attempt to take over a state arsenal with two British cannon left over from the Revolutionary War. When the cannon misfired, the People's government resigned. Sporadic violence continued for another month, resulting in the arrest of over 500 men, mostly textile workers, mechanics, and laborers. The official legislature called for a new constitutional convention, chosen by universal manhood suffrage, and a new constitution went into effect in January, 1843. Altogether only one person was killed in this little revolution, which experienced violence, failure, and then success within the space of nine months.

It is impossible altogether to separate the experience of rising expectations among people in Rhode Island from that among Americans generally. They all shared historically the struggle against a stubborn but ultimately rewarding frontier where their self-confidence gained strength not only in the daily process of tilling the soil and harvesting the crops but also by improving their skill at self-government. Winning their war of independence, Americans continued to press for more goods and more democracy. The pursuit of economic expectations was greatly facilitated by the growth of domestic and foreign trade and the gradual establishment of industry. Equalitarian expectations in politics were satisfied and without severe struggle—in most Northern states—by suffrage reforms.

In Rhode Island, these rising expectations—more goods, more equality, more self-rule—were countered by a series of containing forces which built up such a head of steam that the boiler cracked a little in 1842. The textile depression hit hard in 1835 and its consequences were aggravated by the Panic of 1837. In addition to the frustration of seeing their peers get the right to vote in other states, poor people in Rhode Island were now beset by industrial dislocation in which the machines that brought them prosperity they had never before enjoyed now were bringing economic disaster. The machines could not be converted to produce food and in Rhode Island the machine tenders could not go back to the farm.

When they had recovered from the preoccupation with staying alive, they turned in earnest to their demands for constitutional reform. But these were met first with indifference and then by a growing intransigence on the part of the government representing the propertied class. Hostile action by the state supreme court and then the legislature with its Algerian law proved just enough to break briefly the constitutional structure which in stable societies has the measure of power and resilience necessary to absorb social tension.

THE RUSSIAN REVOLUTION OF 1917

In Russia's tangled history it is hard to decide when began the final upsurge of expectations that, when frustrated, produced the cataclysmic events of 1917. One can truly say that the real beginning was the slow modernization process begun by Peter the Great over two hundred years before the revolution. And surely the rationalist currents from France that slowly penetrated Russian intellectual life during the reign of Catherine the Great a hundred years before the revolution were necessary, lineal antecedents of the 1917 revolution.

Without denying that there was an accumulation of forces over at least a 200-year period,[16] we may nonetheless date the final upsurge as beginning with the 1861 emancipation of serfs and reaching a crest in the 1905 revolution.

The chronic and growing unrest of serfs before their emancipation in 1861 is an ironic commentary on the Marxian notion that human beings are what social institutions make them. Although serfdom had been shaping their personality since 1647, peasants became increasingly restive in the second quarter of the nineteenth century.[17] The continued discontent of peasants after emancipation is an equally ironic commentary on the belief that relieving one profound frustration produces enduring contentment. Peasants rather quickly got over their joy at being untied from the soil after two hundred years. Instead of declining, rural violence increased.[18] Having gained freedom but not much free land, peasants now had to rent or buy land to survive: ritual personal slavery was exchanged for financial servitude. Land pressure grew, reflected in a doubling of land prices between 1868 and 1897.

It is hard thus to tell whether the economic plight of peasants was much lessened after emancipation. A 1903 government study indicated that even with a normal harvest, average food intake per peasant was 30 percent below the minimum for health. The only sure contrary item of evidence is that the peasant population grew, indicating at least increased ability of the land to support life, as the following table shows.

The land-population pressure pushed people into towns and cities, where the rapid growth of industry truly afforded the chance for economic betterment. One estimate of net annual in-

---

[16] There is an excellent summary in B. Brutzkus, "The Historical Peculiarities of the Social and Economic Development of Russia," in R. Bendix and S. M. Lipset, *Class, Status, and Power* (Glencoe, Ill., The Free Press, 1953), pp. 517–540.

[17] Jacqueries rose from an average of 8 per year in 1826–30 to 34 per year in 1845–49. T. G. Masaryk, *The Spirit of Russia* (London, Allen and Unwin, Ltd., 1919), Vol. 1, p. 130. This long, careful, and rather neglected analysis was first published in German in 1913 under the title *Zur Russischen Geschichts- und Religionsphilosophie.*

[18] Jacqueries averaged 350 per year for the first three years after emancipation. *Ibid.*, pp. 140–141

Table 1. POPULATION OF EUROPEAN RUSSIA
(1480–1895)

	Population in Millions	Increase in Millions	Average Annual Rate of Increase*
1480	2.1	—	—
1580	4.3	2.2	1.05%
1680	12.6	8.3	1.93%
1780	26.8	14.2	1.13%
1880	84.5	57.7	2.15%
1895	110.0	25.5	2.02%

* Computed as follows: dividing the increase by the number of years and then dividing this hypothetical annual increase by the population at the end of the preceding 100-year period.

Source for gross population data: *Entsiklopedicheskii Slovar,* St. Petersburg, 1897, Vol. 40, p. 631. Russia's population was about 97% rural in 1784, 91% in 1878, and 87% in 1897. See Masaryk, *op. cit.,* p. 162n.

come for a peasant family of five in the rich blackearth area in the late nineteenth century was 82 rubles. In contrast, a "good" wage for a male factory worker was about 168 rubles per year. It was this difference in the degree of poverty that produced almost a doubling of the urban population between 1878 and 1897. The number of industrial workers increased almost as rapidly. The city and the factory gave new hope. Strikes in the 1880's were met with brutal suppression but also with the beginning of factory legislation, including the requirement that wages be paid regularly and the abolition of child labor. The burgeoning proletariat remained comparatively contented until the eve of the 1905 revolution.[19]

There is additional, non-economic evidence to support the view that 1861 to 1905 was the period of rising expectations that preceded the 1917 revolution. The administration of justice be-

[19] The proportion of workers who struck from 1895 through 1902 varied between 1.7 percent and 4.0 percent per year. In 1903 the proportion rose to 5.1 percent but dropped a year later to 1.5 percent. In 1905 the proportion rose to 163.8 percent, indicating that the total working force struck, on the average, closer to twice than to once during that portentous year. In 1906 the proportion dropped to 65.8 percent; in 1907 to 41.9 percent; and by 1909 was down to a "normal" 3.5 percent. *Ibid.,* p. 175n.

fore the emancipation had largely been carried out by noblemen and landowners who embodied the law for their peasants. In 1864 justice was in principle no longer delegated to such private individuals. Trials became public, the jury system was introduced, and judges got tenure. Corporal punishment was alleviated by the elimination of running the gauntlet, lashing, and branding; caning persisted until 1904. Public joy at these reforms was widespread. For the intelligentsia, there was increased opportunity to think and write and to criticize established institutions, even sacrosanct absolutism itself.

But Tsarist autocracy had not quite abandoned the scene. Having inclined but not bowed, in granting the inevitable emancipation as an act not of justice but grace, it sought to maintain its absolutist principle by conceding reform without accepting anything like democratic authority. Radical political and economic criticism surged higher. Some strong efforts to raise the somewhat lowered floodgates began as early as 1866, after an unsuccessful atempt was made on the life of Alexander II, in whose name serfs had just gained emancipation. When the attempt succeeded fifteen years later, there was increasing state action under Alexander III to limit constantly rising expectations. By suppression and concession, the last Alexander succeeded in dying naturally in 1894.

When it became apparent that Nicholas II shared his father's ideas but not his forcefulness, opposition of the intelligentsia to absolutism joined with the demands of peasants and workers, who remained loyal to the Tsar but demanded economic reforms. Starting in 1904, there developed a "League of Deliverance" that coordinated efforts of at least seventeen other revolutionary, proletarian, or nationalist groups within the empire. Consensus on the need for drastic reform, both political and economic, established a many-ringed circus of groups sharing the same tent. These groups were geographically distributed from Finland to Armenia and ideologically from liberal constitutionalists to revolutionaries made prudent by the contrast between their own small forces and the power of Tsardom.

Events of 1904–05 mark the general downward turning point of expectations, which people increasingly saw as frustrated by the continuation of Tsardom. Two major and related occurrences made 1905 the point of no return. The first took place on the Bloody Sunday of January 22, 1905, when peaceful proletarian petitioners marched on the St. Petersburg palace and were killed by the hundreds. The myth that the Tsar was the gracious protector of his subjects, however surrounded he might be by malicious advisers, was quite shattered. The reaction was immediate, bitter, and prolonged and was not at all confined to the working class. Employers, merchants, and white-collar officials joined in the burgeoning of strikes which brought the economy to a virtual standstill in October. Some employers even continued to pay wages to strikers. University students and faculties joined the revolution. After the great October strike, the peasants ominously sided with the workers and engaged in riots and assaults on landowners. Until peasants became involved, even some landowners had sided with the revolution.

The other major occurrence was the disastrous defeat of the Russian army and navy in the 1904–05 war with Japan. Fundamentally an imperialist venture aspiring to hegemony over the people of Asia, the war was not regarded as a people's but as a Tsar's war, to save and spread absolutism. The military defeat itself probably had less portent than the return of shattered soldiers from a fight that was not for them. Hundreds of thousands, wounded or not, returned from the war as a visible, vocal, and ugly reminder to the entire populace of the weakness and selfishness of Tsarist absolutism.

The years from 1905 to 1917 formed an almost relentless procession of increasing misery and despair. Promising at last a constitutional government, the Tsar, in October, 1905, issued from on high a proclamation renouncing absolutism, granting lawmaking power to a duma, and guaranteeing freedom of speech, assembly, and association. The first two dumas, of 1906 and 1907, were dissolved for recalcitrance. The third was made pliant by reduced representation of workers and peasants and by the prosecution and conviction of protestants in the first two. The brief period of a free press was succeeded in 1907 by a reinstatement of censorship and confiscation of prohibited publications. Trial of offenders against the Tsar was now conducted by courts-martial. Whereas there had been only 26 executions of the death sentence, in the 13 years of Alexander II's firm rule (1881–94), there were 4,449 in the years 1905–10, in six years of Nicholas II's soft regimen.[20]

But this "white terror," which caused despair among the workers and intelligentsia in the cities, was not the only face of misery. For the peasants, there was a bad harvest in 1906 followed by continued crop failures in several areas in 1907. To forestall action by the dumas, Stolypin decreed a series of agrarian reforms designed to break up the power of the rural communes by individualizing land ownership. Between these acts of God and government, peasants were so preoccupied with hunger or self-aggrandizement as to be dulled in their sensitivity to the revolutionary appeals of radical organizers.

After more than five years of degrading terror and misery, in 1910 the country appeared to have reached a condition of exhaustion. Political strikes had fallen off to a new low. As the economy recovered, the insouciance of hopelessness set in. Amongst the intelligentsia the mood was hedonism, or despair that often ended in suicide. Industrialists aligned themselves with the government. Workers worked. But an upturn of expectations, inadequately quashed by the police, was evidenced by a recrudescence of political strikes which, in the first half of 1914—on the eve of war—approached the peak of 1905. They sharply diminished during 1915 but grew again in 1916 and became a general strike in February 1917.[21]

Figure 3 indicates the lesser waves in the tidal wave whose first trough is at the end of serfdom in 1861 and whose second is at the end of Tsardom in 1917. This fifty-six-year period appears to con-

[20] *Ibid.*, p. 189n.

[21] In his *History of the Russian Revolution,* Leon Trotsky presents data on political strikes from 1903 to 1917. In his *Spirit of Russia,* Masaryk presents comparable data from 1905 through 1912. The figures are not identical but the reported yearly trends are consistent. Masaryk's figures are somewhat lower, except for 1912. Cf. Trotsky, *op. cit.,* Doubleday Anchor Books ed., 1959, p. 32 and Masaryk, *op. cit. supra,* p. 197n.

stitute a single long phase in which popular gratification at the termination of one institution (serfdom) rather quickly was replaced with rising expectations which resulted from intensified industrialization and which were incompatible with the continuation of the inequitable and capricious power structure of Tsarist society. The small trough of frustration during the repression that followed the assassination of Alexander II seems to have only briefly interrupted the rise in popular demand for more goods and more power. The trough in 1904 indicates the consequences of war with Japan. The 1905–06 trough reflects the repression of

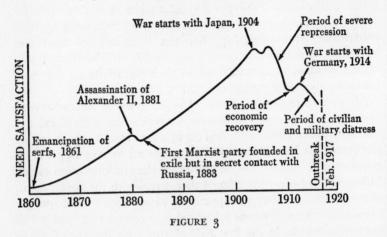

FIGURE 3

January 22, and after, and is followed by economic recovery. The final downturn, after the first year of war, was a consequence of the dislocations of the German attack on all kinds of concerted activities other than production for the prosecution of the war. Patriotism and governmental repression for a time smothered discontent. The inflation that developed in 1916 when goods, including food, became severely scarce began to make workers self-consciously discontented. The conduct of the war, including the growing brutality against reluctant, ill-provisioned troops, and the enormous loss of life, produced the same bitter frustration in the army.[22] When civilian discontent reached the breaking point

22 See Trotsky, *op. cit.*, pp. 18–21 for a vivid picture of rising discontent in the army.

in February, 1917, it did not take long for it to spread rapidly into the armed forces. Thus began the second phase of the revolution that really started in 1905 and ended in death to the Tsar and Tsardom—but not to absolutism—when the Bolsheviks gained ascendancy over the moderates in October. A centuries-long history of absolutism appears to have made this post-Tsarist phase of it tragically inevitable.

THE EGYPTIAN REVOLUTION OF 1952

The final slow upsurge of expectations in Egypt that culminated in the revolution began when that society became a nation in 1922, with the British grant of limited independence. British troops remained in Egypt to protect not only the Suez Canal but also, ostensibly, to prevent foreign aggression. The presence of foreign troops served only to heighten nationalist expectations, which were excited by the Wafd, the political organization that formed public opinion on national rather than religious grounds and helped establish a fairly unified community—in striking contrast to late-nineteenth-century Russia.

But nationalist aspirations were not the only rising expectations in Egypt of the 1920's and 1930's. World War I had spurred industrialization, which opened opportunities for peasants to improve, somewhat, their way of life by working for wages in the cities and also opened great opportunities for entrepreneurs to get rich. The moderately wealthy got immoderately so in commodity market speculation, finance, and manufacture, and the uprooted peasants who were now employed, or at any rate living, in cities were relieved of at least the notion that poverty and boredom must be the will of Allah. But the incongruity of a money-based modern semi-feudality that was like a chariot with a gasoline engine evidently escaped the attention of ordinary people. The generation of the 1930's could see more rapid progress, even for themselves, than their parents had even envisioned. If conditions remained poor, they could always be blamed on the British, whose economic and military power remained visible and strong.

Economic progress continued, though unevenly, during World

War II. Conventional exports, mostly cotton, actually declined, not even reaching depression levels until 1945, but direct employment by Allied military forces reached a peak of over 200,000 during the most intense part of the African war. Exports after the war rose steadily until 1948, dipped, and then rose sharply to a peak in 1951 as a consequence of the Korean war. But in 1945 over 250,000 wage earners[23]—probably over a third of the working force—became jobless. The cost of living by 1945 had risen to three times the index of 1937.[24] Manual laborers were hit by unemployment; white collar workers and professionals probably more by inflation than unemployment. Meanwhile the number of millionaires in pounds sterling had increased eight times during the war.[25]

Frustrations, exacerbated during the war by German and thereafter by Soviet propaganda, were at first deflected against the British[26] but gradually shifted closer to home. Egyptian agitators began quoting the Koran in favor of a just, equalitarian society and against great differences in individual wealth. There was an ominous series of strikes, mostly in the textile mills, from 1946–48.

At least two factors stand out in the postponement of revolution. The first was the insatiable post-war world demand for cotton and textiles and the second was the surge of solidarity with king and country that followed the 1948 invasion of the new state of Israel. Israel now supplemented England as an object of deflected frustration. The disastrous defeat a year later, by a new

[23] C. Issawi, *Egypt at Mid-Century: An Economic Survey* (London, Oxford University Press, 1954), p. 262. J. and S. Lacouture in their *Egypt in Transition* (New York, Criterion Books, 1958), p. 100, give a figure of over 300,000. Sir R. Bullard, editor, *The Middle East: A Political and Economic Survey* (London, Oxford University Press, 1958), p. 221 estimates total employment in industry, transport, and commerce in 1957 to have been about 750,000.

[24] International Monetary Fund, *International Financial Statistics,* Washington, D. C. See monthly issues of this report, 1950–53.

[25] J. and S. Lacouture, *op. cit.,* p. 99.

[26] England threatened to depose Farouk in February 1942, by force if necessary, if Egypt did not support the Allies. Capitulation by the government and the Wafd caused widespread popular disaffection. When Egypt finally declared war on the Axis in 1945, the prime minister was assassinated. See J. and S. Lacouture, *op. cit.,* pp. 97–98 and Issawi, *op. cit.,* p. 268.

nation with but a fifteenth of Egypt's population, was the beginning of the end. This little war had struck the peasant at his hearth, when a shortage of wheat and of oil for stoves provided a daily reminder of a weak and corrupt government. The defeat frustrated popular hopes for national glory and—with even more portent—humiliated the army and solidified it against the bureaucracy and the palace which had profiteered at the expense of national honor. In 1950 began for the first time a direct and open propaganda attack against the king himself. A series of peasant uprisings, even on the lands of the king, took place in 1951 along with some 49 strikes in the cities. The skyrocketing demand for cotton after the start of the Korean War in June, 1950 was followed by a collapse in March, 1952. The uncontrollable or uncontrolled riots in Cairo, on January 26, 1952, marked the fiery start of the revolution. The officers' coup in the early morning of July 23 only made it official.

OTHER CIVIL DISTURBANCES

The J-curve of rising expectations followed by their effective frustration is applicable to other revolutions and rebellions than just the three already considered. Leisler's Rebellion in the royal colony of New York in 1689 was a brief dress-rehearsal for the American Revolution eighty-six years later. In an effort to make the colony serve the crown better, duties had been raised and were being vigorously collected. The tanning of hides in the colony was forbidden, as was the distillation of liquor. An embargo was placed on unmilled grain, which hurt the farmers. After a long period of economic growth and substantial political autonomy, these new and burdensome regulations produced a popular rebellion that for a year displaced British sovereignty.[27]

The American Revolution itself fits the J-curve and deserves more than the brief mention here given. Again prolonged economic growth and political autonomy produced continually rising expectations. They became acutely frustrated when, following the French and Indian War (which had cost England so

[27] See J. R. Reich, *Leisler's Rebellion* (Chicago, University of Chicago Press, 1953).

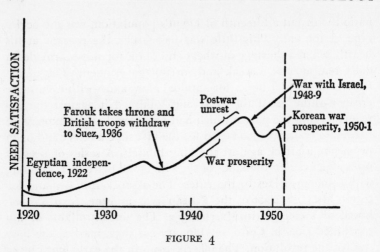

FIGURE 4

much and the colonies so little), England began a series of largely economic regulations having the same purpose as those directed against New York in the preceding century. From the 1763 Proclamation (closing to settlement land west of the Appalachians) to the Coercive Acts of April 1774 (which among other things, in response to the December 1773 Boston Tea Party, closed tight the port of Boston), Americans were beset with unaccustomed manifestations of British power and began to resist forcibly in 1775, on the Lexington-Concord road. A significant decline in trade with England in 1772[28] may have hastened the maturation of colonial rebelliousness.

The curve also fits the French Revolution, which again merits more mention than space here permits. Growing rural prosperity, marked by steadily rising land values in the eighteenth century, had progressed to the point where a third of French land was owned by peasant-proprietors. There were the beginnings of large-scale manufacture in the factory system. Constant pressure by the bourgeoisie against the state for reforms was met with considerable hospitality by a government already shifting from its old landed aristocratic and clerical base to the growing middle class. Counter

[28] See U. S. Bureau of the Census, *Historical Statistics of the United States, Colonial Times to 1957* (Washington, D.C., 1960), p. 757.

to these trends, which would *per se* avoid revolution, was the feudal reaction of the mid-eighteenth century, in which the dying nobility sought in numerous nagging ways to retain and reactivate its perquisites against a resentful peasantry and importunate bourgeoisie.

But expectations apparently continued rising until the growing opportunities and prosperity rather abruptly halted, about 1787. The fiscal crisis of the government is well known, much of it a consequence of a 1.5 billion livre deficit following intervention against Britain in the American war of independence. The threat to tax the nobility severely—after its virtual tax immunity—and the bourgeoisie more severely may indeed be said to have precipitated the revolution. But less well-known is the fact that 1787 was a bad harvest year and 1788 even worse; that by July, 1789 bread prices were higher than they had been in over 70 years; that an ill-timed trade treaty with England depressed the prices of French textiles; that a concurrent bumper grape crop depressed wine prices—all with the result of making desperate the plight of the large segment of the population now dependent on other producers for food. They had little money to buy even less bread. Nobles and bourgeoisie were alienated from the government by the threat of taxation; workers and some peasants by the threat of starvation. A long period of halting but real progress for virtually all segments of the population was now abruptly ended in consequence of the government's efforts to meet its deficit and of economic crisis resulting from poor crops and poor tariff policy.[29]

The draft riots that turned the city of New York upside down for five days in July, 1863 also follow the J-curve. This severe local disturbance began when conscription threatened the lives and fortunes of working men whose enjoyment of wartime prosperity was now frustrated not only by military service (which could be avoided by paying $300 or furnishing a substitute—neither means being available to poor people) but also by inflation.[30]

[29] See G. Lefebvre, *The Coming of the French Revolution* (Princeton University Press, 1947), pp. 101–109, 145–148, 196. G. Le Bon, *The Psychology of Revolution* (New York, G. Putnam's Sons, 1913), p. 143.

[30] The account by Irving Werstein, *July 1863* (New York, Julian Messner, Inc., 1957), is journalistic but to my knowledge the fullest yet available.

Even the riots in Nyasaland, in February and March, 1959, appear to follow the pattern of a period of frustration after expectations and satisfactions have risen. Nyasaland workers who had enjoyed the high wages they were paid during the construction of the Kariba dam in Rhodesia returned to their homes and to unemployment, or to jobs paying $5 per month at a time when $15 was considered a bare minimum wage.[31] One negative case—of a revolution that did not occur—is the depression of the 1930s in the United States. It was severe enough, at least on economic grounds, to have produced a revolution. Total national private production income in 1932 reverted to what it had been in 1916. Farm income in the same year was as low as in 1900; manufacturing as low as in 1913. Construction had not been as low since 1908. Mining and quarrying was back at the 1909 level.[32] For much of the population, two decades of economic progress had been wiped out. There were more than sporadic demonstrations of unemployed, hunger marchers, and veterans. In New York City, at least 29 people died of starvation. Poor people could vividly contrast their own past condition with the present—and their own present condition with that of those who were not seriously suffering. There were clearly audible rumbles of revolt. Why, then, no revolution?

Several forces worked strongly against it. Among the most depressed, the mood was one of apathy and despair, like that observed in Austria by Zawadzki and Lazarsfeld. It was not until the 1936 election that there was an increased turnout in the national election. The great majority of the public shared a set of values which since 1776 had been official dogma—not the dissident program of an alienated intelligentsia. People by and large were in agreement, whether or not they had succeeded economically, in a belief in individual hard work, self-reliance, and the promise of success. (Among workers, this non-class orientation had greatly impeded the establishment of trade unions, for exam-

---

[31] E. S. Munger, "The Tragedy of Nyasaland," American Universities Field Stac Reports Service, Vol. 7, no. 4 (August 1, 1959), p. 9.
[32] See U. S. Bureau of the Census, Historical Statistics of the United States: 1789–1945 (Washington, D.C., 1949), p. 14.

ple.) Those least hit by the depression—the upper-middle-class businessmen, clergymen, lawyers, and intellectuals—remained rather solidly committed not only to equalitarian values and to the established economic system but also to constitutional processes. There was no such widespread or profound alienation as that which had cracked the loyalty of the nobility, clergy, bourgeoisie, armed forces, and intelligentsia in Russia. And the national political leadership that emerged had constitutionalism almost bred in its bones. The major threat to constitutionalism came in Louisiana; this leadership was unable to capture a national party organization, in part because Huey Long's arbitrariness and demagogy were mistrusted.

The major reason that revolution did not nonetheless develop probably remains the vigor with which the national government attacked the depression in 1933, when it became no longer possible to blame the government. The ambivalent popular hostility to the business community was contained by both the action of government against the depression and the government's practice of publicly and successfully eliciting the cooperation of businessmen during the crucial months of 1933. A failure then of cooperation could have intensified rather than lessened popular hostility to business. There was no longer an economic or a political class that could be the object of widespread intense hatred because of its indifference or hostility to the downtrodden. Had Roosevelt adopted a demagogic stance in the 1932 campaign and gained the loyalty to himself personally of the Army and the FBI, there might have been a Nazi-type "revolution," with a potpourri of equalitarian reform, nationalism, imperialism, and domestic scapegoats. Because of a conservatism in America stemming from strong and long attachment to a value system shared by all classes, an anticapitalist, leftist revolution in the 1930s is very difficult to imagine.

SOME CONCLUSIONS

The notion that revolutions need both a period of rising expectations and a succeeding period in which they are frustrated qualifies substantially the main Marxian notion that revolutions occur after progressive degradation and the de Tocqueville notion that they occur when conditions are improving. By putting de Tocqueville before Marx but without abandoning either theory, we are better able to plot the antecedents of at least the disturbances here described.

Half of the general, if not common, sense of this revised notion lies in the utter improbability of a revolution occurring in a society where there is the continued, unimpeded opportunity to satisfy new needs, new hopes, new expectations. Would Dorr's rebellion have become such if the established electorate and government had readily acceded to the suffrage demands of the unpropertied? Would the Russian Revolution have taken place if the Tsarist autocracy had, quite out of character, truly granted the popular demands for constitutional democracy in 1905? Would the Cairo riots of January, 1952 and the subsequent coup actually have occurred if Britain had departed from Egypt and if the Egyptian monarchy had established an equitable tax system and in other ways alleviated the poverty of urban masses and the shame of the military?

The other half of the sense of the notion has to do with the improbability of revolution taking place where there has been no hope, no period in which expectations have risen. Such a stability of expectations presupposes a static state of human aspirations that sometimes exists but is rare. Stability of expectations is not a stable social condition. Such was the case of American Indians (at least from our perspective) and perhaps Africans before white men with Bibles, guns, and other goods interrupted the stability of African society. Egypt was in such a condition, vis-à-vis modern aspirations, before Europe became interested in building a canal. Such stasis was the case in Nazi concentration camps, where conformism reached the point of inmates cooperating with guards even when the inmates were told to lie down so that they could be shot.[33] But in the latter case there was a society with externally induced complete despair, and even in these camps there were occasional rebellions of sheer desperation. It is of course true that

[33] Eugen Kogon, *The Theory and Practice of Hell* (New York, Farrar, Straus & Co., 1950), pp. 284–286.

in a society less regimented than concentration camps, the rise of expectations can be frustrated successfully, thereby defeating rebellion just as the satisfaction of expectations does. This, however, requires the uninhibited exercise of brute force as it was used in suppressing the Hungarian rebellion of 1956. Failing the continued ability and persistent will of a ruling power to use such force, there appears to be no sure way to avoid revolution short of an effective, affirmative, and continuous response on the part of established governments to the almost continuously emerging needs of the governed.

To be predictive, my notion requires the assessment of the state of mind—or more precisely, the mood—of a people. This is always difficult, even by techniques of systematic public opinion analysis. Respondents interviewed in a country with a repressive government are not likely to be responsive. But there has been considerable progress in gathering first-hand data about the state of mind of peoples in politically unstable circumstances. One instance of this involved interviewing in West Berlin, during and after the 1948 blockade, as reported by Buchanan and Cantril. They were able to ascertain, however crudely, the sense of security that people in Berlin felt. There was a significant increase in security after the blockade.[34] Another instance comes out of the Middle Eastern study conducted by the Columbia University Bureau of Applied Social Research and reported by Lerner.[35] By directly asking respondents whether they were happy or unhappy with the way things had turned out in their life, the interviewers turned up data indicating marked differences in the frequency of a sense of unhappiness between countries and between "traditional," "transitional," and "modern" individuals in these countries.[36] There is no technical reason why such comparisons could

[34] W. Buchanan, "Mass Communication in Reverse," *International Social Science Bulletin*, 5 (1953), pp. 577–583, at p. 578. The full study is W. Buchanan and H. Cantril, *How Nations See Each Other* (Urbana, University of Illinois Press, 1953), esp. pp. 85–90.

[35] Daniel Lerner, *The Passing of Traditional Society* (Glencoe, Ill., The Free Press, 1958).

[36] *Ibid.*, pp. 101–103. See also F. P. Kilpatrick & H. Cantril, "Self-Anchoring Scaling, A Measure of Individuals' Unique Reality Words," *Journal of Individual Psychology*, 16 (November, 1960), pp. 158–173.

not be made chronologically as well as they have been geographically.

Other than interview data are available with which we can, from past experience, make reasonable inferences about the mood of a people. It was surely the sense for the relevance of such data that led Thomas Masaryk before the first World War to gather facts about peasant uprisings and industrial strikes and about the writings and actions of the intelligentsia in nineteenth-century Russia. In the present report, I have used not only such data—in the collection of which other social scientists have been less assiduous than Masaryk—but also such indexes as comparative size of vote as between Rhode Island and the United States, employment, exports, and cost of living. Some such indexes, like strikes and cost of living, may be rather closely related to the mood of a people; others, like value of exports, are much cruder indications. Lest we shy away from the gathering of crude data, we should bear in mind that Durkheim developed his remarkable insights into modern society in large part by his analysis of suicide rates. He was unable to rely on the interviewing technique. We need not always ask people whether they are grievously frustrated by their government; their actions can tell us as well and sometimes better.

In his *Anatomy of Revolution,* Crane Brinton describes "some tentative uniformities" that he discovered in the Puritan, American, French, and Russian revolutions.[37] The uniformities were: an economically advancing society, class antagonism, desertion of intellectuals, inefficient government, a ruling class that has lost self-confidence, financial failure of government, and the inept use of force against rebels. All but the last two of these are long-range phenomena that lend themselves to studies over extended time periods. The first two lend themselves to statistical analysis. If they serve the purpose, techniques of content analysis could be used to ascertain trends in alienation of intellectuals. Less rigorous methods would perhaps serve better to ascertain the effectiveness of government and the self-confidence of rulers. Because

[37] See the revised edition of 1952 as reprinted by Vintage Books, Inc., 1957, pp. 264–275. (See the next selection in this Reader.)

tensions and frustrations are present at all times in every society, what is most seriously needed are data that cover an extended time period in a particular society, so that one can say there is evidence that tension is greater or less than it was N years or months previously.

We need also to know how long is a long cycle of rising expectations and how long is a brief cycle of frustration. We noted a brief period of frustration in Russia after the 1881 assassination of Alexander II and a longer period after the 1904 beginning of the Russo-Japanese War. Why did not the revolution occur at either of these times rather than in 1917? Had expectations before these two times not risen high enough? Had the subsequent decline not been sufficiently sharp and deep? Measuring techniques have not yet been devised to answer these questions. But their unavailability now does not forecast their eternal inaccessibility. Physicists devised useful temperature scales long before they came as close to absolute zero as they have recently in laboratory condition. The far more complex problems of scaling in social science inescapably are harder to solve.

We therefore are still not at the point of being able to predict revolution, but the closer we can get to data indicating by inference the prevailing mood in a society, the closer we will be to understanding the change from gratification to frustration in people's minds. That is the part of the anatomy, we are forever being told with truth and futility, in which wars and revolutions always start. We should eventually be able to escape the embarrassment that may have come to Lenin six weeks after he made the statement in Switzerland, in January, 1917, that he doubted whether "we, the old [will] live to see the decisive battles of the coming revolution." [38]

[38] Quoted in E. H. Carr, *A History of Soviet Russia*, Vol. 1, *The Bolshevik Revolution: 1917–23* (London, Macmillan, 1950), p. 69.

CRANE BRINTON / Anatomy of Revolution*

Politically the revolution ends the worst abuses, the worst ineffi-
ciencies of the old regime. It settles for a time at least the kind of
internal conflict out of which the "dual sovereignty" arose. The
machinery of government works more smoothly after than immediately before the revolution. France is here a typical case. The
old overlapping jurisdictions, the confusions and the compromises inherited from the thousand-year struggle between the cen-
tripetal forces of the Crown and the centrifugal forces of the feudal nobility, the welter of accumulated precedents, were all
replaced by the work of the French Revolution. An able bureaucracy operating within neatly subordinated administrative areas, a
legal system efficiently codified, an excellent army well staffed and
well provided for, enabled Napoleon to do much that his Bour-
bon predecessors could not possibly have done. De Tocqueville
long ago pointed out that the French Revolution came to complete the work of a long line of French monarchs to make centralized power in France effective and complete.

Here is one detail among many. In the old France, weights and
measures varied from region to region, indeed from town to town.
A bushel at Toulouse might be much more than a bushel at

* From Brinton, *Anatomy of Revolution*, rev. ed. (Englewood Cliffs, N.J.,
Prentice-Hall, 1952), pp. 266–283. Portions of the original chapter have been
omitted.

neighboring Montauban. Worse yet, the very names of measures might be wholly different words. The coinage was, like the present English coinage, partly duodecimal, and very hard to handle by long division. What the revolution did about all this is familiar to every schoolboy. It substituted the uniform system of weights and measures known as the metric system, a system which has made its way without benefit of revolution through most of the world outside the British Empire and the United States.

This achievement of governmental efficiency is really the most striking uniformity we can note in estimating the political changes effected by our revolutions. With suitable allowances for local differences, for accidents, and for the inevitable residue of the unique with which all history and sociology must deal, England, America, and Russia also emerged from their revolutions with more efficient and more centralized governments. The process is less clear in England, partly because it took place before the full maturing of economic and cultural forces tending to promote such forms of efficiency as the metric system or the Code Napoléon. But, for all its complexities, the English government after 1660 was much better geared to the needs of the nation of shopkeepers than was the England of 1620, with knights' fees, ship money, benevolences, Star Chamber, Court of High Commission, and the other appurtenances of the immature Stuart despotism. Parliament after 1660 was more completely master of England than the first two Stuarts had been.

Russia is in this respect as in so many still a subject for dispute. Violent opponents of Stalin insist that the new bureaucrats are just as inefficient, pettily tyrannical, and stupid as they were said to have been under the Tsars. Some of the sentiments involved in statements of this sort would seem to be more or less a constant of Russian life, and to a certain extent of life under any government. Gogol's admirable comedy, *The Inspector-General,* deals as certainly with uniformities as any scientist could. Yet all in all, future historians will probably have to admit that as a piece of political machinery the Soviet system worked better than did that of the Tsars, that the Soviet bureaucracy was on the whole a more capable one than that of the Tsars. You may not like the Five

Year Plans, but you must admit that beneath their parade of statistics lies a concrete economic achievement greater than anything the old regime could show for a similar period. The Communists have, in short, brought the Industrial Revolution to Russia. Perhaps it was coming under Stolypin; perhaps the Communists brought it harshly, cruelly. But bring it they did.

These revolutions were all made in the name of freedom, were all directed against the tyranny of the few and toward the rule of the many. This whole phase of revolutions is peculiarly involved with the existence of certain sentiments in human beings which make it very hard to apply the methods of science to the study of men in society. Yet it would seem that the full importance of such matters as democracy, civil rights, written constitutions, and indeed the whole apparatus of popular government lies rather within that vague and important field the Marxists like to call ideology than in the field of concrete political agencies which we are now studying. Certainly one is struck by the fact that all our revolutions promoted the efficiency of the government rather than the "right" of the individual to a romantic freedom to be himself. Even the traditional apparatus of popular government can be analyzed as an instrument to get things done in a particular situation, however strange such an analysis might seem to conventionally minded contemporaries of Mussolini, Hitler, and Stalin. Bills of Rights, codes, and constitutions were in effect charters of the new ruling classes. Liberty as an ideal was one thing; liberty in politics, on the other hand, was another and less exalted matter.

These revolutions all saw much transfer of property by confiscation or forced sale. They saw the fall of one ruling class and its succession by another ruling class recruited in part, at least, from individuals who were before the revolution outside the ruling class. They were accompanied by a definite and concrete demand for the abolition of poverty, for the equal sharing of wealth; the men who guided the Russian Revolution continued long after its crisis period to insist that they were economic egalitarians, that Russia would not recognize private property in land and in capital goods. Marxist thought still separates our four revolutions into two different classes: the English, French, and American, all of which it considers to have been in their final results "bourgeois" revolutions, inevitable victories of business and industry over landed aristocracy; and the Russian Revolution, in its final phases, a true "proletarian" revolution. We may nevertheless be more impressed with the fact that in all four revolutions economic power changed hands, and that a newly amalgamated "ruling class" in the new Russia as in the new France directed the economic as well as the political life of the society.

In more detail, the English Revolution took land from the more devoted Cavaliers and ecclesiastical property from the more unyielding Episcopalians and Presbyterians and gave it to typical Puritans, businessmen and clergymen alike. The church livings came back at the Restoration of 1660 into Anglican hands, but save for the property of a few great lords very close to Charles II, confiscated Royalist lands remained in the possession of their new owner. Most of these owners made their peace with the Stuart government, and thus was laid the foundation for the ruling class under which England won an empire in the next two centuries, a ruling class in which landed wealth and industrial wealth were almost inextricably mixed, and which proved to be a very good ruling class.

The concrete economic changes in France follow a similar pattern. Lands confiscated from clergy and *émigré* nobles were acquired by revolutionists, and for the most part remained in the possession of the purchasers even after the Restoration of 1814. Much of this land no doubt finally ended up in the possession of small independent peasants, and helped to put the final touches on the establishment of that very French class universally regarded among writers and politicians as the core of modern France. But much of this transaction also benefited the middle class, and certainly the French ruling class *after* the revolution represents as striking a mixture of old wealth and new, of land and trade, as did the English.

In Russia the differences are not so great as they ought to be according to Marxist theory. There has been a transfer of economic power from one group to another rather than an equal sharing of economic power, an equal distribution of consumer goods, an end of struggle over economic goods or power—but you may put the Marxist formula as you like. The new Russian bureaucracy is, as we have seen, a privileged class which enjoys wealth in the form of consumer goods without yet possessing it in the forms we conventionally call "property." It is a class as yet notably unstable, as yet not sure of itself. But already the sons of the privileged show signs of inheriting their father's status, and it is not inconceivable that inheritance of property will come shortly. What seems to have taken place is a development of the lines of movement of Russian economic history. Just as the French Revolution put the finishing touches on the position of the peasantry, but by no means "gave" them the land suddenly, so the present status of Russian agriculture and industry seem to be a development of slavophile and other elements favoring collective farming over the *kulaks,* and of almost world-wide tendencies favoring large-scale bureaucratically managed industry over small independent competitive concerns. Here as in other countries the revolution certainly does not draw institutions out of a hat—nor out of a book, not even out of so impressive a book as *Das Kapital.*

None of these revolutions quite substituted a brand-new ruling class for the old one, at least not unless one thinks of a "class" without bothering about the human beings who make up the class, which is a favorite procedure of the Marxists. What happens is that by the end of the convalescent period there is well begun a kind of amalgamation, in which the enterprising, adaptable, or lucky individuals of the old privileged classes are for most practical purposes tied up with those individuals of the old suppressed classes who, probably through the same gifts, were able to rise. This *amalgame* is especially noticeable in the army and the civil service, but it is almost as conspicuous in business and industry, and higher politics. This analysis would be confirmed by a detailed study of the social origins of Bonaparte's officers, or the officers in the present Red Army, or of the men who actually ran the government of England in 1670, France in 1810, Russia today, though in the Russian case less conspicuously so, for more time has passed. Moreover, the new men in the post-revolutionary ruling classes have made distinct compromises with the older ones, with that old world from which the crisis period of the revolution is so extreme a revulsion. Your Downings, Fouchés, and Kalinins have no longer the fine freedom a Trotsky could enjoy. They are no longer revolutionaries, but rulers, and as such they are in some respects bound to "learn" from their predecessors. There are those who think Stalin has learned too well.

It is in the social arrangements that most intimately and immediately touch the average man that the actual changes effected by our revolutions seem slightest. The grand attempts at reform during the crisis period try to alter John Jones's relations with his wife, his children, try to give him a new religion, new personal habits. The Thermidoreans abandon most of this attempt, and in the end John Jones stands on certain matters about where he stood when the revolution began. Our study of revolutions should confirm something that sensible men have always known and that exasperated reformers have occasionally come to admit, at least to themselves—that in some very important ways the behavior of men changes with a slowness almost comparable to the kind of change the geologist studies.

When all necessary concessions are made to those who insist that events in history are unique, it remains true that the four revolutions we have studied do display some striking uniformities. Our conceptual scheme of the fever can be worked out so as to bring these uniformities clearly to mind. We shall find it worth while, in attempting to summarize the work of these revolutions, to recapitulate briefly the main points of comparison on which our uniformities are based.

We must be very tentative about the prodromal symptoms of revolution. Even retrospectively, diagnosis of the four societies we studied was very difficult, and there is little ground for belief that anyone today has enough knowledge and skill to apply formal methods of diagnosis to a contemporary society and say, in this case revolution will or will not occur shortly. But some uniformities do emerge from a study of the old regimes in England, America, France, and Russia.

First, these were all societies on the whole on the upgrade economically before the revolution came, and the revolutionary movements seem to originate in the discontents of not unprosperous people who feel restraint, cramp, annoyance, rather than downright crushing oppression. Certainly these revolutions are not started by down-and-outers, by starving, miserable people. These revolutionists are not worms turning, not children of despair. These revolutions are born of hope, and their philosophies are formally optimistic.

Second, we find in our pre-revolutionary society definite and indeed very bitter class antagonisms, though these antagonisms seem rather more complicated than the cruder Marxists will allow. It is not a case of feudal nobility against bourgeoisie in 1640, 1776, and 1789, or of bourgeoisie against proletariat in 1917. The strongest feelings seem generated in the bosoms of men —and women—who have made money, or at least who have enough to live on, and who contemplate bitterly the imperfections of a socially privileged aristocracy. Revolutions seem more likely when social classes are fairly close together than when they are far apart. "Untouchables" very rarely revolt against a God-given aristocracy, and Haiti gives one of the few examples of successful slave revolutions. But rich merchants whose daughters can marry aristocrats are likely to feel that God is at least as interested in merchants as in aristocrats. It is difficult to say why the bitterness of feeling between classes *almost* equal socially seems so much stronger in some societies than others—why, for instance, a Marie Antoinette should be so much more hated in eighteenth-century France than a rich, idle, much publicized heiress in contemporary America; but at any rate the existence of such bitterness can be observed in our pre-revolutionary societies, which is, clinically speaking, enough for the moment.

Third, there is what we have called the desertion of the intellectuals. This is in some respects the most reliable of the symptoms we are likely to meet. Here again we need not try to explain all the hows and whys, need not try to tie up the desertion of the intellectuals with a grand and complete sociology of revolutions. We need state simply that it can be observed in all four of our societies.

Fourth, the governmental machinery is clearly inefficient, partly through neglect, through a failure to make changes in old institutions, partly because new conditions—in the societies we have studied, pretty specifically conditions attendant on economic expansion and the growth of new monied classes, new ways of transportation, new business methods—these new conditions laid an intolerable strain on governmental machinery adapted to simpler, more primitive, conditions.

Fifth, the old ruling class—or rather, many individuals of the old ruling class—come to distrust themselves, or lose faith in the traditions and habits of their class, grow intellectual, humanitarian, or go over to the attacking groups. Perhaps a larger number of them than usual lead lives we shall have to call immoral, dissolute, though one cannot by any means be as sure about this as a symptom as about the loss of habits and traditions of command effective among a ruling class. At any rate, the ruling class becomes politically inept.

The dramatic events that start things moving, that bring on the fever of revolution, are in three of our four revolutions intimately connected with the financial administration of the state. In the fourth, Russia, the breakdown of administration under the burdens of an unsuccessful war is only in part financial. But in all our societies the inefficiency and inadequacy of the governmental structure of the society come out clearly in the very first stages of the revolution. There is a time—the first few weeks or months—when it looks as if a determined use of force on the part of the government might prevent the mounting excitement from culminating in an overthrow of the government. These governments attempted such a use of force in all four instances, and in all four their attempt was a failure. This failure indeed proved a turning point during the first stages, and set up the revolutionists in power.

Yet one is impressed in all four instances more with the ineptitude of the governments' use of force than with the skill of their opponents' use of force. We are here speaking of the situation wholly from a military and police point of view. It may be that the majority of the people are discontented, loathe the existing government, wish it overthrown. Nobody knows. They don't take plebiscites *before* revolutions. In the actual clash—even Bastille Day, Concord, or the February Days in Petrograd—only a minority of the people is actively engaged. But the government hold over its own troops is poor, its troops fight half-heartedly or desert, its commanders are stupid, its enemies acquire a nucleus of the deserting troops or of a previous militia, and the old gives place to the new. Yet, such is the conservative and routine-loving nature of the bulk of human beings, so strong are habits of obedience in most of them, that it is almost safe to say that no government is likely to be overthrown until it loses the ability to make adequate use of its military and police powers. That loss of ability may show itself in the actual desertion of soldiers and police to the revolutionists, or in the stupidity with which the government manages its soldiers and police, or in both ways.

The events we have grouped under the name of first stages do not of course unroll themselves in exactly the same order in time, or with exactly the same content, in all four of our revolutions. But we have listed the major elements—and they fall into a pattern of uniformities—financial breakdown, organization of the discontented to remedy this breakdown (or threatened breakdown), revolutionary demands on the part of these organized discontented, demands which, if granted, would mean the virtual abdication of those governing, attempted use of force by the government, its failure, and the attainment of power by the revolutionists. These revolutionists have hitherto been acting as an organized and nearly unanimous group, but with the attainment of power it is clear that they are not united. The group which dominates these first stages we call the moderates. They are not always in a numerical majority in this stage—indeed it is pretty clear that if you limit the moderates to the Kadets they were not in a majority in Russia in February, 1917. But they seem the natural heirs of the old government, and they have their chance. In three of our revolutions they are sooner or later driven from office to death or exile. Certainly there is to be seen in England, France, and Russia a process in which a series of crises—some involving violence, street fighting, and the like—deposes one set of men and puts in power another and more radical set. In these revolutions power passes by violent or at least extra-legal methods from Right to Left, until at the crisis period the extreme radicals, the complete revolutionists, are in power. There are, as a matter of fact, usually a few even wilder and more lunatic fringes of the triumphant extremists—but these are not numerous or strong and are usually suppressed or otherwise made harmless by the dominant radicals. It is therefore approximately true to say that power passes on from Right to Left until it reaches the extreme Left.

The rule of the extremists we have called the crisis period. This period was not reached in the American Revolution, though in the treatment of Loyalists, in the pressure to support the army, in some of the phases of social life, you can discern in America many of the phenomena of the Terror as it is seen in our three other societies. We cannot here attempt to go into the complicated question as to why the American Revolution stopped short of a true crisis period, why the moderates were never ousted in this country. We must repeat that we are simply trying to establish certain uniformities of description, and are not attempting a complete sociology of revolutions.

The extremists are helped to power no doubt by the existence of a powerful pressure toward centralized strong government, something which in general the moderates are not capable of providing, while the extremists, with their discipline, their contempt for half-measures, their willingness to make firm decisions, their freedom from libertarian qualms, are quite able and willing to centralize. Especially in France and Russia, where powerful foreign enemies threatened the very existence of the nation, the machinery of government during the crisis period was in part constructed to serve as a government of national defense. Yet though modern wars, as we know in this country, demand a centralization of authority, war alone does not seem to account for all that happened in the crisis period in those countries.

What does happen may be a bit over-simply summarized as follows: emergency centralization of power in an administration, usually a council or commission, and more or less dominated by a "strong man"—Cromwell, Robespierre, Lenin; government without any effective protection for the normal civil rights of the individual—or if this sounds unrealistic, especially for Russia, let us say the normal private life of the individual; setting up of extraordinary courts and a special revolutionary police to carry out the decrees of the government and to suppress all dissenting individuals or groups; all this machinery ultimately built up from a relatively small group—Independents, Jacobins, Bolsheviks—which has a monopoly on all governmental action. Finally, governmental action becomes a much greater part of all human action than in these societies in their normal condition: this apparatus of government is set to work indifferently on the mountains and molehills of human life—it is used to pry into and poke about corners normally reserved for priest or physician, or friend, and it is used to regulate, control, plan, the production and distribution of economic wealth on a national scale.

This pervasiveness of the Reign of Terror in the crisis period is partly explicable in terms of the pressure of war necessities and of economic struggles as well as of other variables: but it must probably also be explained as in part the manifestation of an effort to achieve intensely religious ends here on earth. The little band of violent revolutionists who form the nucleus of all action during the Terror behave as men have been observed to behave before when under the influence of active religious faith. Independents, Jacobins, Bolsheviks, all sought to make all human activity here on earth conform to an ideal pattern, which, like all such patterns, seems deeply rooted in their sentiments. A striking uniformity in all these patterns is their asceticism, or if you prefer, their condemnation of what we may call the minor as well as the major vices. Essentially, however, these patterns are a good deal alike, and all resemble closely what we may call conventional Christian ethics. Independents, Jacobins, and Bolsheviks, at least during the crisis period, really make an effort to enforce behavior in literal conformity with these codes or patterns. Such an effort means stern repression of much that many men have been used to regarding as normal; it means a kind of universal tension in which the ordinary individual can never feel protected by the humble routines to which he has been formed: it means that the intricate network of interactions among individuals—a network which is still to the few men devoted to its intelligent study almost a complete mystery—this network is temporarily all torn apart. John Jones, the man in the street, the ordinary man, is left floundering.

KRISHNALAL SHRIDHARANI / War Without Violence*

It is a revolution when the community rises against the state. The destruction of an undesirable established order is then the issue. Following upon the heels of its accomplishment comes the replacement of the crumbling administration by the people's government. Then it is that the revolution is consummated.

The community versus the state, which constitutes the final category of conflicts according to our classification, is a contest which has raged throughout the various histories of the civilized peoples. New nations have emerged in its aftermath, or the old ones have been assimilated by some other expanding states. It has claimed the undivided attention and painstaking analysis of many an outstanding philosopher and political economist. It has also left its indelible bloody streaks on the annals of many nations.

Violent overthrow of the government has been the only method popular with revolutionists irrespective of their creed, nationality or race. Almost to a single instance, all revolutions have resulted in carnage. What is even more significant, violence has never stopped at the conclusion of a revolution. It has had to be employed even during the aftermath, that is, when the replacement

* From Shridharani, *War Without Violence* (Bombay, Bharatiya Vidya Bharan, 1962), pp. 110–128. Portions of the original chapter have been omitted.

of the established order by the people's government has taken place. Born in a welter of blood, revolution also has to be consummated in blood.

In this carefully plotted and well-established pattern of revolution, the Gandhi struggle was perhaps the first and only variation. That a revolution could be accomplished without resorting to violence was the vast stake involved in the Indian movement. The Indian community was led by Gandhi in a "non-violent revolution" against the British government. The experiment was in this manner carried out on a national scale, almost an international scale, as the natives' fight against the British government of India at times reached the dimensions of a struggle against England and the Empire. For the mighty resources of the Empire could be, and sometimes were, summoned to suppress the insurrection in India.

1. THE POST-WORLD WAR I NON-COOPERATION MOVEMENT

Discontent grew by leaps and bounds. At this point, broken soldiers returned from the trenches with accounts of injustices and unequal treatment. In spite of unprecedented heroism and military acumen, no Indian received a commission—simply because he was an Indian. And all of them, they reported, were discriminated against by Europeans irrespective of rank and station. In India itself, the war boom was over and there was a general state of unemployment. Manufacturing tycoons, who had doubled and tripled their wealth overnight, forgot their abnormal profits of wartime and began to reduce wages and personnel. Consequently, the rumbling of discontent among the proletariat, audible in pre-war days, grew louder. The teeming farming population of upper India, especially inhabitants of the Punjab, were resentful of the ravages made on their male population by enforced enlistment in the British Army. Even the upper middle class, savoring the fast-fading taste of power and profit, was resentful of the turn of events. The inevitable disillusionment had come at last, and India was again a seething volcano.

As if to add fuel to the fire, the report of the Rowlatt Committee was published at this critical moment. This committee was appointed by the government to ascertain whether special emergency actions were necessary to stamp out the revolutionary spirit of the people. The commission, composed entirely of Englishmen with no Indians on it, recommended drastic measures to deal with the growing unrest. The Rowlatt Committee advised the government to curtail the people's right to gather in large assemblies. Freedom of speech and assembly as well as freedom of the press were to be greatly reduced and in many cases forfeited. Imprisonment without trial, a distinct breach of the *Habeas Corpus Act,* was to be a common practice with the police and civil authorities.[1] All India was aghast and aroused to the pitch of frenzy. Was that the reward of their services during the World War, they asked.

When this report reached Gandhi, he was still an invalid from overwork on behalf of the Allies. He felt himself and India betrayed by the Britons. He was mortally wounded. It was at his behest, according to his own self-condemnation, that India had made such tremendous sacrifices during the War. Gandhi realized that he had misled the people in his ignorance of British duplicity. Consequently, he felt it his duty to the Indian people to prevent the Rowlatt Report recommendations from becoming a law. First from his sickbed and subsequently from innumerable platforms he denounced the bill as a breach of the *Habeas Corpus Act* and urged the people to resist it at every step. The government, however, forced it through the council and appended it to the laws of the land.

Driven to desperation, Gandhi called upon the people to offer a Satyagraha. A day was appointed for complete *Hartal* as a sign of mourning. Each village and every city in the country was to stop all normal activity for twenty-four hours and every adult was to observe a fast. Streets were deserted and shop windows shrouded. Mass meetings were held in the evening to denounce

[1] For some of the leading features of the Rowlatt Act, and for its comparison to the Star Chamber in England under Judge Jeffreys, see J. T. Sunderland, *India in Bondage* (New York, 1932), pp. 450–451.

the act. Individuals were asked at these meetings to sign a Satyagraha pledge which bound them to disobey the act and such other
laws as would be recommended by the nationalist high command.
Finally huge processions marched through the "main streets" of
India shouting revolutionary slogans.

The government immediately struck back at the Satyagrahis in
order to nip their revolt in the bud. Processions were stopped by
the military at various places and large crowds were fired on at
Delhi, Calcutta, and Amritsar. Reports reached Gandhi that
there was serious trouble brewing in the Punjab. At the invita-
tion of the Punjab leaders, Gandhi started out for that province
on a peace mission. He was arrested en route and brought back to
Bombay. The Amritsar Punjabis, disappointed by the news of
Gandhi's arrest, called a meeting to voice their protest. Two
leading local leaders, consequently, were arrested and imprisoned. The undaunted populace, nevertheless, held a protest
meeting on the 18th of April, 1919. Some 20,000 unsuspecting
men, women, and children gathered together in the Jallianwalla
Baug, a walled-in garden with only one exit. All were peaceful
and pledged to non-violence, and none among them was armed
with even so much as a stick. Suddenly, General Dyer, a British
military officer, arrived on the scene with fifty picked soldiers
armed with machine guns. He posted his troops at the only exit
of the walled-in garden so that no one could escape. Without a
word of warning, he gave order to fire. About 1,650 rounds of
ammunition were leveled at the peaceful gathering of men,
women, and children at close range. The holocaust was over in a
few minutes. When Dyer[2] withdrew, some 1,200 dead and 3,600
wounded were lying in the garden.[3]

When this news broke, India was stunned. The leaders felt at a
loss to find words strong enough to denounce the barbarous brutality of the government, and the people were numbed and sick-

[2] Later, back in England, the people of General Dyer's province raised
20,000 pounds and honored him with a purse for his Empire-saving activities
in India. Of course, the House of Lords condemned him by a resolution for
his "punishment" of the Indians.
[3] For a detailed and dispassionate account, compare *The Hunter Commission
Report* with the *Congress Commission Report*.

ened by the tragic picture of carnage. When the first horror of the incident was over, sympathetic spokesmen of public opinion rallied around Gandhi to devise ways and means of "compelling repentance" on the part of the powers that be. The first few steps, suggested by Gandhi, included: huge processions singing national songs and shouting slogans; mass meetings codifying their protest to the government action; and picketing of government buildings by women. The authorities, as expected, tried to suppress the growing tension by such coercive measures as arrests of the Satyagrahis, *lathi*-charges (cracking heads open with bamboo sticks), firing on crowds, and wholesale massacres. The next move of the Satyagrahis, therefore, was to dramatize their suffering and sacrifices.

Then came Gandhi's call for non-cooperation. The people were asked to withdraw their aid and support which made the administration possible. Those who had been rewarded by the government with titles and honorary offices were to surrender their privileges. Rich people were to refrain from buying government loans and the poor were asked to refuse any petty service to the local authorities. Many lawyers suspended their practice and disputes began to be settled outside the courts. Government schools were deserted as the students decided either to go to "national institutions" or to the villages to carry on the *Swaraj* propaganda. Benches in legislative councils were unoccupied because the leaders were out among the people instigating non-violent revolution. A militant boycott of British goods was promulgated, coupled with a petition to the public to patronize indigenous products. Finally, Indians in government service, from high officials to petty tax-collectors, were asked to resign from their posts. Complete paralysis of the administration was the objective. This program was further bolstered by the nationalist propaganda at work in the Indian Army. Soldiers were persuaded to sever connections with the undesirable aliens.

Momentarily, everything seemed to be going on smoothly. There was panic in government quarters and many of the administrative departments were at a virtual standstill. The cable wire between Delhi and No. 10 Downing Street hummed frantically day and night. George Lloyd, then Governor of Bombay, confessed later on: "Gandhi's was the most colossal experiment in world history; and it came within an inch of succeeding."

True to the pattern of Satyagraha, more militant maneuvers were to follow. After non-cooperation had partly paralyzed the administration, the actual business of destroying the existing order was planned. This finesse was to be accomplished by non-payment of the government taxes and by civil disobedience of repressive laws. Bans on nationalist literature were to be disregarded, and the government monopoly of salt manufacture was to be broken by mass action. The Rowlatt Act, the immediate cause of all this friction, was to be completely shattered.

But this could not be. In spite of Gandhi's constant and eloquent appeals to his countrymen to refrain from hatred and violence, in spite of his own peerless example, violence broke out. The reports reached him that the mob was beyond control of his Satyagrahis in several places. Riots had occurred in Ahmedabad and Viramgam. At Cauri Chaura, especially, the crowds, unaccustomed to non-violence, went mad and committed atrocities. Gandhi was stunned by this news, and in deep agony of spirit, concluded that the time was not yet ripe for mass non-violence. Then he decided upon the drastic step of calling a halt! This decision produced the utmost consternation within the ranks of his colleagues. Many regarded it as a sacrifice of the people's cause on the altar of an individual's ideals. However, Gandhi's decision prevailed and the nation-wide Satyagraha was called off.

After a lapse of time, on March 18, 1922, Gandhi was arrested and tried on the charge of instigating the people to violence. He pleaded guilty in the following words: "The only course open to you, the Judge and the Assessors, is either to resign your posts and thus disassociate yourselves from evil if you feel that the law you are called upon to administer is an evil and that in reality I am innocent, or inflict upon me the severest penalty if you believe that the system and the law you are assisting to administer are good for the people of this country and that my activity is therefore injurious to the public weal." [4] The English judge imposed upon Gandhi the sentence of six years' rigorous imprisonment.

[4] Krishnadas, *Seven Months with Mahatma Gandhi* (Bihar, 1928), Vol. II, Appendix B, p. 18.

He, however, added: "If the course of events should make it possible for the government to reduce the period and release you, no one will be better pleased than I."

Thus the first experiment with non-violent direct action on a national scale suffered an abortive end. Although it failed to obtain its immediate objective, it was immensely successful in awakening India to the consciousness of her own potential power. Moreover, the experience gathered during this non-cooperation movement paved the way for India's next great movement of 1930.

2. CIVIL DISOBEDIENCE MOVEMENT. 1930-1934.

A lengthy period of reaction followed the apparent failure of the non-cooperation movement of 1920–1922. On one hand the people of India were brooding over the future of the Swaraj movement and on the other the British bureaucracy was tightening its grip over public affairs. It was indeed almost a clenched fist. What is more significant from our point of view, the efficacy of Satyagraha was seriously disputed. The radical youth groups and the labor organizations were not convinced of the "compelling power" of non-violent direct action. Leaders of public opinion and philosophers began to discover, one by one, many loopholes in the ideology of Satyagraha. It aroused widespread academic interest and discussion. Books were published either defending or denouncing Satyagraha and Gandhism in general. Gandhi contended that the failure was due to inadequate "preparedness" on the part of the people, but after his release from jail he kept silent and retired to his *Ashrama*. This period of reflection and uncertainty, however, brought to the people a greater realization of the implications of Satyagraha and of its various potentialities.

The period of demoralization over, new organizations and new trends began to revive the spirits of the people. Inspired by the Soviet Five-Year Plan, the urban workers were waiting for a Messiah from the steppes. The All-India Trade Union Congress, founded in 1921, was a powerful group by this time. On the farmers' front, the National Congress party was making a heroic effort to expand its activities and to seek recruits by the thousands from among agriculturists.

The labor movement came to a head in 1929. Strikes occurred all over India. The Bombay Textile Labour Union was the first. A general strike of the jute workers followed in Bengal. The Iron Works at Jamshedpur, one of the largest in the world, was the next to be threatened by a labor war. The Iron Plate Works in the same industrial town, connected with the Burma Oil Company, succeeded in suppressing the walk-out before it reached large proportions. The labor movement was becoming *class conscious* for the first time in India's short industrial history.

Meanwhile, the struggle on the nationalist front was reaching its climax. There were local Satyagrahas in the farming districts of Gujarat and Maharashtra. The conspicuous success of the Bardoli Satyagraha of 1928, already described in the previous chapter, infused new hope in the people and revived a general confidence in Gandhi's method. The absence of any Indian representative on the Simon Commission[5] drew the "Liberal" and the "Moderate" elements to the Congress fold. The nation was again all energy and enthusiasm.

About this time, a new element was gaining in importance in the Indian political mosaic. The youth of India was demanding a hearing. Their organizations spread like wildfire, and by 1928, there was hardly a town of any size in India without its unit of politically-minded young men. These societies were sincerely radical. Their guiding spirits were nationalists with overtones of socialism. They advocated that either Gandhi launch the nation once more in direct action or give up his leadership.

With the intuition of a born leader, Gandhi felt that the time was ripe for direct action against the British government of India. The situation called for a strong Congress president who could swing the youth leagues and the workers behind that body. Gandhi's choice was Pandit Jawaharlal Nehru.[6] One year previously,

[5] Composed of Englishmen only and presided over by Sir John Simon, this commission was appointed by the British Parliament to recommend constitutional changes in the Government of India.

[6] This was long before Gandhi decided to declare Jawaharlal Nehru as his "successor."

the Indian National Congress in its annual meeting at Calcutta
had given an ultimatum to the government to confer Dominion
Status in twelve months' time, or else! The government failed to
comply. Thereupon, in 1930, under the younger man's inspiration, India switched from dominion status to independence as her
goal on the memorable 26th of January. It was again a revolution, albeit non-violent; the community was rising against the
state.

To fulfill its new goal, *viz.,* complete independence, the Congress Executive authorized civil disobedience. It also appointed
Gandhi as the nation's "Dictator." Upon Gandhi's arrest, it was
decided that Pandit Nehru was to occupy the vacated position. A
list of Dictators was prepared but kept secret. The struggle, however, was not to start until Gandhi published his detailed plan of
attack and gave a signal.

When the plans were ready and the scene set, it was announced
to the waiting nation that civil disobedience would be inaugurated on March 12, 1930. Ten days prior to this scheduled date
Gandhi, conforming to the pattern of Satyagraha, had sent the
Ultimatum to the Viceroy and requested a prompt answer. The
people were advised accordingly to maintain a state of noncommittal "preparedness" pending the response of the government to Gandhi's final challenge. In this communication were
listed the minimum demands of the Congress to be fulfilled in a
maximum period of time.

The Viceroy's answer was unsatisfactory. Now it was incumbent upon the Satyagrahis to acquire by direct action what they
failed to secure through democratic procedure. Taking up the
challenge, Gandhi started on his famous "March to the Sea" with
a handful of his nearest and dearest. Upon arrival at Port
Dandi, Gandhi and his "first batch" violated the Salt Act by preparing salt from the sea water. That was the signal the country
awaited. The very next day witnessed India's transformation into
one vast battlefield. The community and the state at last openly
faced each other as enemies and in the following months, laws
were regularly broken by the citizenry and punishment was
meted out by the state.

The Satyagrahis attacked on many fronts and employed a variety of tactics. In big cities, they organized and led huge processions in defiance of police orders and prohibitory notices served by the warrant officers. In village and town alike, public meetings and conferences of local leaders were held in spite of the government ban. The usual boycott of British goods coupled with intensive picketing by women became general. Pickets were posted even at the gates of British banks, insurance companies, mints and bullion exchanges. As the press was now forbidden by the authorities to print campaign notices and news regarding government repression, the Satyagrahis issued their own bulletins and leaflets. Because these were regarded as illegal and revolutionary, they were freely distributed among the masses. Even more serious was the work of printing and selling proscribed literature. Stuccoed walls and sometimes the paved streets served as bulletin boards and blackboards. Foreign correspondents never failed to marvel at the spectacle of the sympathetic pedestrians carefully picking their way around the elaborate Congress announcements chalked on the sidewalks.

When the movement gathered momentum, certain more drastic stratagems were included in the general program. A boycott was called on all state-owned post offices, telegraph systems, trams and ship lines. Public saluting of the National Flag, instead of the Union Jack, and displaying the National Flag on public buildings as well as over civil and criminal courts was another maneuver employed by the civil resisters in order to provoke further government friction. Non-violent volunteers were wont to refuse to make parole rounds to the police, and others defied restraint orders served on them by the courts. Attempts were made to reoccupy Congress offices which had been seized by the police.

Civil disobedience of unjust laws was the principal feature of the strategy. The Salt Act was taken as the symbol of British exploitation of the masses and made a test case. The most formidable forces, therefore, were arrayed against the government monopoly of salt manufacture. In the wake of the violation of the Salt Act followed a redoubtable attack on the Forest Laws. And then came a general attack on as many obnoxious statutes of the state as were found vulnerable. Picketing of liquor and opium shops ate an alarming hole in the government earnings. Finally, the city-dwelling businessmen and manufacturers were called upon to withhold certain taxes, and village farmers were asked not to pay land revenue.

Meanwhile, the bureaucracy had set free all the repressive and coercive powers at its command. First, the ranking leaders were rounded up and imprisoned. All Congress offices were decreed illegal and confiscated. However, new leaders sprang from the people, and more offices were opened in outlying areas. Then followed wholesale arrests of groups and volunteer corps. When the jails and improvised "detention camps" were filled to capacity, baton charges on peaceful pickets and processions became the order of the day. Women Satyagrahis were insulted and ill-treated. Prisoners were subject to inhuman cruelties in the jails. Next on the program of suppression was the confiscation of the Satyagrahis' property. Finally, firing on unarmed crowds became a common spectacle.

The toll of suffering was tremendous. According to nationalist sources, during the one year of non-violent direct action (from March 12, 1930, when Satyagraha was inaugurated, to March 5, 1931, when the truce was signed), 10,000 Indians cheerfully forfeited their liberty to enter His Majesty's numerous prisons, detention camps, and improvised jails. A modest estimate shows that no less than 17,000 women also underwent various terms of imprisonment.[7] A score of them were expectant mothers when they found themselves behind prison bars. Consequently, a few "war babies" of India were born in prison.

The number of the *lathi* charges" mounted somewhere in the hundreds, and unarmed crowds were fired on without warning. Thousand were wounded and hundreds killed. Despite this "reign of terror," the people of India displayed a remarkable degree of restraint and non-violent discipline. What is more impor-

[7] Figures as quoted in *Condition of India, being a report of the Delegation sent by the India League in 1932* (London, 1934). The government has generally evaded stating exact figures concerning its repressive measures. Whenever stated, however, these figures fall far short of the nationalist estimates.

tant, slaughter and mutilation failed to repress the movement or intimidate the people. On the contrary, it exhausted the government itself. The coercive arms of the state were paralyzed by the Satyagrahic tactics of the opponents. After a full year of struggle, the government gave in and began negotiations with the Congress high command. Gandhi and the members of the Working Committee of the Congress were released from jail and the former was invited to Delhi.

For the first time in history, on March 5, 1931, the representative of His Majesty signed a truce treaty with Gandhi, the erstwhile "rebel." Satyagraha on a national scale had now come to a successful ending. The main demands of the people were granted in the treaty thereafter known as the "Gandhi-Irwin Pact," and the stage was set for further negotiations with a view to evolving a free India. Gandhi was invited to London for the Round Table Conference.

Now that Gandhi was in London and the other leaders inactive, with the "non-violent army" disbanded and agitation discontinued, now that people were rejoicing in their triumph and consequently were off guard—the government broke its promises. So when Gandhi landed in Bombay, he found his pact with Irwin, later Lord Halifax, violated by the government. He also discovered that the bureaucracy was in a belligerent mood and did not mean to carry out the terms of the treaty. Thereupon, Gandhi was forced to revive Satyagraha. The renewed movement, however, died a natural death in 1934. Meanwhile, the new constitution, a substantial if unsatisfactory result of the nationalist struggle, was completed. Later it became the law of the land.

In this manner the second nation-wide attempt at securing complete independence was, at best, a partial success. The movement, nevertheless, further prepared the country in the art of government and made the people confident of their strength and ability. According to all observers, foreign as well as domestic, it was a reborn India at the conclusion of the Civil Disobedience Movement. This angle has a great bearing on our special interest here, the fact that Satyagraha was proven to be an effective instrument of achieving political ends even when employed on a nation-wide scale. For the actual Satyagrahic engagement of the opponent culminated in the triumph of the nationalists as epitomized in the "Gandhi-Irwin Pact." The subsequent violation of the truce treaty by the Britons can in no way be regarded as weakness or a failure of Satyagraha as such. It might have, at the most, exposed a flagrant lack of statesmanship in the nationalist high command.[8]

Triumphant in a conflict between the community and the state, and between groups, Satyagraha has given evidence of being an effective mode of revolution or civil war. The Indian movement had even greater implications. It was not merely a struggle between the community on one hand and the state on the other, but it was also a conflict between a people and an alien government. To be sure, the British bureaucrats and the army in India had the might of England and her Dominions behind them. It cannot be denied that this power was utilized in the attempt to stamp out the nationalist uprising. Accordingly, the Indian struggle had many characteristics of a conflict between two nations; it was waged, in a way, on an international scale. When viewed in that light, the success of the 1930 Satyagraha indicated that non-violent direct action might prove to be an effective means of settling a conflict involving different states. . . .

[8] The magnitude of the success of the 1930–1934 Satyagraha became evident in 1937 when partial elections took place under the Government of India Act, 1935. The nationalists gained complete control over seven out of the eleven great Provinces of India, with partial control over two more Provinces under coalition ministries. In the remaining two Provinces, the National Congress party had single largest groups in the legislatures. The Satyagrahi "ex-convicts" became Premiers and Ministers in India's several Provinces.

PART IV

THE CONTEMPORARY
RELEVANCE
OF IDEOLOGY

EDITOR'S INTRODUCTION

Ideologies are world views propounded for the purpose of changing social reality and social relations, or of keeping them as they are. The former Mannheim termed "utopias," the latter "ideologies" proper,[1] but here I will use the term ideology to refer to both. Ideology can help to "support an elite and to justify the exercise of power," as Apter puts it in the selection included below, or it can be used by revolutionary groups to justify attempts to change the power distribution.

I would not distinguish between ideology and politics in the way that Haber does, because the key element of ideology is its emotional content, its lever to action. Thus it does not make sense to ask whether an ideology is true or false—the question is whether it is effective in maintaining the status quo, or in bringing into existence the social reforms seen as desirable.

Russell provides a good analysis of the factual inadequacies of Marxism.[2] But the inadequacy of Marxism as a description of the world is not important. What *is* important is the use of Marxist ideology as a lever to action. Various points of Marxist theory, such as the existence and sharpness of the class struggle, may be more or less true, according to the empirical evidence. But the more people who believe that there is class conflict and act on it, the more such conflict there will continue to be. In this sense, ideologies are myths or prophecies which are more or less self-fulfilling depending on how successful they are in accomplishing their aims.

The relevance of a given ideology for a society depends partly on its general level of development. Thus both nationalism and socialism are important ideologies in the "Third World" countries. These are countries in which groups of elites are trying to

---

1 Karl Mannheim, *Ideology and Utopia* (New York, Harvest Books, 1963).
2 For an excellent critique of the limits of Marxism, see Dwight Macdonald, *The Root is Man* (Los Angeles, Cunningham Press, 1953).

push for "modernization," and thus the theme of national unity is useful in promoting the necessary social cohesion and social effort. As Apter points out, the central function of ideology in the developing countries is to bolster the authority of the ruling elite. The low economic level of these countries makes some form of governmental economic intervention seem to be the only way of attaining more rapid economic growth. Thus the appeal and the relevance of socialist ideology for these countries.

In the more economically advanced countries, the dominant ideology favors some form of rationally administered and smoothly functioning welfare state. I have chosen to call this ideology "liberalism," although others may wish to use a different terminology. Implicit in the liberal ideology is that the world is getting better slowly, that we are gradually progressing toward a more perfect social order. This ideology minimizes the existence of conflict. Obviously, it is an ideology suitable for maintaining the status quo and the social advantages of what Dahrendorf calls the "service class." [3] It may not have any ideologue as profound or brilliant as Karl Marx, but it exists as a dominant political theme in the more affluent countries of the West.

What is wrong with liberalism as an ideology, according to Mills, is that several of the key assumptions made by eighteenth- and nineteenth-century liberals are no longer necessarily true. Liberalism assumes that the key values of freedom and security flourish in a world of small entrepreneurs, but this world is going out of existence with the ever-increasing size and scale of institutions in industrialized societies. Liberalism also assumes some autonomy of the different institutional orders, but these are coming to be increasingly interdependent. Liberalism assumes that the individual is the seat of rationality, but the dominant social trend is toward the shift of rationality to *institutions;* more and more the individual is forced to become a cog in a large machine, to follow the orders handed down by the very few at the top. Liberalism relies on the thinking individual, but life in the bureaucratized society is not necessarily conducive to independent political thought. Finally, liberalism assumes that authority is ex-

[3] See Chapter 5 of this Reader—Ed.

plicit, but the modern tendency is to deny that there is any locus of power that can be held responsible for what happens.

The "end of ideology" theme as expressed by such writers as Bell, is merely another way of asserting the correctness of the liberal ideology. Here I would agree with Haber's assertion that this is "a status quo ideological formulation designed to rationalize the incorporation of intellectuals into the American way of Life."

American workers, as Bell points out, are on the whole more satisfied than the intellectuals. The welfare state involves enough socialism and enough amelioration of living conditions to make the thought of revolution irrelevant—except perhaps among oppressed nationality groups such as the American Negroes. But it seems to me that the real danger of state socialism (as much as of the capitalistic welfare state) lies in the continuing ability of small groups of people to direct the lives of large numbers of others. Government control of the means of production may spell a more efficient welfare state, but it does not necessarily eliminate the warfare state.

VOLUNTARISM AS ALTERNATIVE IDEOLOGY [4]

One way to demonstrate that ideology is not dead is to sketch out some alternative to liberalism that would be relevant to the affluent societies of our contemporary epoch. Thus I offer the remarks on voluntarism below as a supplement to the two selections by anarchist writers included in this chapter.

I

Voluntarists want a society within which human beings are free to play—in which all activities become leisure activities and in which life consists in doing the things you want to do. Instead of jobs, work as play. Instead of state coercion, voluntary cooperation. Instead of families, voluntary unions of men, women, and children. Instead of schools to which children must go, schools to which children *may* go if it gives them joy.

Voluntarism means that people act for rewards intrinsically

[4] Adapted from the author's article "Voluntarism and Politics," that appeared in the November, 1966 issue of *Anarchy*.

connected with their action. Love provides its own justification. Voluntarism implies lives in which means and ends are joined, where nothing is merely a means to an end, but all activity comes to be undertaken as an end in itself. If there are things that "need doing," and nobody wants to do them, they just won't get done. Many aspects of life with which we are familiar might disappear, but then if they are dependent upon compulsion and coercion they are not worthwhile, and maybe we will invent alternative ways.

Applied to politics, the philosophy of voluntarism is anarchism. But voluntarism cannot be limited to the political sphere alone. Freeing men from political compulsion will not be possible without, at the same time, freeing them from economic compulsion. Ridding societies of economic compulsion, in turn, may be impossible without at the same time freeing men of certain habits of mind, which means that we must deal with the problems of education. Thus, to solve the problems in any one of the fields of politics, economics, education, and family life one will eventually end up dealing with all of them.

II

The historical roots of the philosophy of voluntarism go back to the traditions of anarchism, pacifism, communism, and non-authoritarian utopias. Important antecedents include the writings of such men as Godwin, William Morris, Kropotkin, Malatesta, Tolstoy, Thoreau, and Gandhi.

The anarchist theory is that government in the coercive sense is superfluous because man may be cooperative as well as aggressive. Social life can be carried out just as well on a voluntary as on a compulsory basis. The root of the anarchist analysis takes us close to some strands of modern sociological thought. Two examples may suffice. Concerning government and laws, the anarchists give us a picture of a ruling class or group, writing laws and otherwise manipulating the rest of the society largely for its own benefits. In education, the anarchists subject the very content of ideas taught by state-paid teachers to searing analysis: children learn from their teachers that the state is necessary because it is to the interests of those who run the state that they should believe this and be tractable.

The voluntarist approach draws upon both the utopian and communist traditions when it comes to ends. Only some of the utopians are congenial, however. A number of them, starting with Plato, have been in favor of forcing men to be free. This I cannot agree to; I much prefer the voluntaristic utopia of William Morris's *News From Nowhere* to the regimentation envisaged by Sir Thomas More. The real danger of the utopians lies in the belief held by most of them that *they* have found the truth, and that everybody else must be compelled to live according to the dictates of those who know best.

The root of the social problem is economic, for men can be coaxed to do evil to their brothers not only through physical coercion, but also through economic need. The ruling classes can have their orders obeyed because the others are dependent on them for a living. Thus, the ideal society should be based on the revolutionary communist slogan, "From each according to his ability, to each according to his needs." The various forms of social compulsion endorsed by state socialists do not provide a very attractive ideal, except to those living in "underdeveloped" economies and to those whose main objection to capitalism is that the profits are not widely enough shared. But living as I do in a wealthy society, neither capitalism nor state socialism appeal much to me: capitalism because it is based upon production for profit instead of need, and state socialism because it makes possible the substitution of new forms of coercion for the older ones.

From the pacifists, we can learn about means. The pacifist insight is crucial. Its root lies in an instinctive distaste for violence in social affairs. The pacifist knows that the chief evils of contemporary society are nationalism and organized warfare. They are evil in and of themselves, and also because they contribute to the strength of the state. The pacifist sees that ends and means mutually shape each other, and that it is a utopian folly to imagine that somehow a non-violent world can be brought about through the most violent means. I would be willing to grant that violent and bloody revolution may sometimes be the only way to bring about the end of dictatorial oppression. Still, I cannot conceive that a world of love could emerge from such a revolution because to kill people for "good" causes is still to brutalize yourself.

Connected with the pacifist ethic is an abhorrence of military conscription. Voluntarism is opposed to conscription and coercion in all forms. Under today's conditions, wars are never just and always immoral; but implicit in the voluntarist idea is the feeling that somehow wars are less evil if all of the soldiers are volunteers. That is why I admire the men of the International Brigades who volunteered to fight in Spain.

In a way, voluntarism is profoundly conservative, because if you are not willing to use coercion on behalf of bad causes, you are also not willing to use coercion on behalf of good ones. This means that even though I support the struggle of Southern Negroes in the United States for freedom, I do not favor sending government troops to Southern states to enforce integration; I know this will get me into trouble with my liberal friends, but once you accept the principle of armed intervention, you have given up your ability to criticize intervention against *your* cause. Southern Negroes will not be freed by external armed intervention; they will have to do this largely by themselves, and indeed they are beginning to have some limited success. On the other hand, I would see nothing wrong with volunteers going to help them if they want such help.

How to get from the less pleasant present to some more pleasant future is a key issue of voluntarism. The controversy over the role of violence cannot ever be entirely resolved, for it is in the nature of the human situation that we are continually faced with impossible dilemmas. However much my pacifist inclinations make me abhor bloodshed and violence, my sympathy with the plight of those who are exploited makes me able to understand why some men are driven to revolutions for national liberation and to military uprisings. Instead of absolute condemnation of all social violence, I would follow the stand taken by Gandhi, which counsels us to resist evil, and to try to use non-violent means because such means are morally preferable. Instead of the belief in force held by such anarchists as Bakunin and Stirner, or the belief in absolute non-violence as held by the religious anarchists like Tolstoy, I prefer the painful ambivalence of Malatesta. I am not so sure of what I would do if I were a Vietnamese today, or a black man in South Africa.

III

It would be nice if we could have an anarchist society, but this is a goal which is unlikely to be achieved in the near future. In a world in which most people are not ready for this, we have a choice of trying to work within existing institutions to make them better, of setting up "parallel" institutions, or doing both. Parallelism is attractive because it promises immediate results. It involves doing today in the here and now what you think should be done. You try to establish on a voluntary basis those social organizations that you think are good, and you do not wait until you have fifty-one percent of the ballots or the bullets.

Voluntarism is opposed to bringing about social change by capturing command of the centers of economic and political power. If over half of the people voluntarily agreed with us, we would still be reluctant to force our will upon a dissenting minority. Because voluntarism is directed towards the abolition of power instead of its capture, it leads to a tendency to withdraw from existing institutions and a parallel effort to establish new ones. The voluntarist propagandizes, but does not force anyone to join in the new institutions. He tries to live as he sees fit, while residing in the larger existing system.

In America, a number of the students involved in such groups as SDS and SNCC tend to lean in the direction of anarchism; but there is still a basic ambivalence among many of them whether they wish to do things that are "politically relevant" or not. They feel alienated in the face of big business, big government, big universities. They suffer from the dominance of bureaucratic institutions. They react violently to the dehumanization encouraged by the spread of giant organizations and to the establishment of bureaucratization as a dominant trend and style of life. But they are not sure whether the way to achieve the world they want lies through traditional political action, or through direct action.

In the present situation there is no necessary contradiction between direct action and traditional political action, such as voting and writing letters to representatives. The same person might reasonably do both, without accepting political party activities as any panacea. While agitating for a voluntaristic society, we can still support reform efforts such as the provision of a guaranteed minimum annual income for all persons regardless of whether they work. And if your government is pursuing an evil war it behooves you to do everything you can through conventional politics to get your government to stop. It is not necessary to limit your efforts to such action, but you should not ignore its possible effectiveness.[5] Thus, to stop a war, you may try to vote better men into office or write letters to those who are in, or you may take direct personal action such as destroying military equipment or avoiding payment of taxes. These take on a political significance in that they are designed to influence a government to change its foreign policy. If you want a world in which conscription does not exist, we may lobby and vote and try to get the legislature to change the law. But you can also take direct action which has political implications by burning draft cards or refusing to be conscripted.

The difference between direct and indirect action can be seen most clearly in the civil-rights movement in the United States. Most of the students involved in the sit-in and other forms of direct action are not opposed to the existence of civil-rights laws. It is just that they know that to bring about a free society, you must do more than just lobby for better laws or better interpretation of the laws, as the NAACP has tended to do. The essence of the direct-action philosophy is that it involves the insistence of a determined minority to act as though it had certain legal rights instead of trying to change the laws by writing to their congressmen. These tactics were used in the Berkeley Free Speech Movement. The same philosophy leads young people to assert their sexual freedom in their behavior instead of concentrating on changing outmoded sex laws.

[5] It is possible that in a number of situations there is *no* effective conventional political action that a minority can take.

IV

Voluntarism implies a diversity of social forms. Different groups of people would be free to choose between alternative forms of social organization and ways of life. The voluntarist does not want all men living the way he would like to live, with everybody forced into the same strait-jacket of utopia. The voluntarist wants to live as he likes with his friends, and let others live as they like, with their friends. Voluntarism means the freedom to choose a life of creativity and pleasure, or one of ignominy, wretchedness, and boredom.

So far as education is concerned, for example, there could be many different kinds of experiments, but on a voluntary basis. Without uniformity, there might be some educational institutions with very low standards, but then nobody would be forced to go to them, and perhaps there would be a process of natural selection. If students did not have to go to school, if we eliminated all of the compulsory aspects, perhaps after a while the really bad schools and bad teachers would have no students.

Likewise, when freed of economic compulsion, people would enter and remain within only those associations in which they felt comfortable. Women would be freer to leave their husbands if they did not like them. And if a "boss" insults an economically independent man, he will be free to quit and go it alone, or to join another association, or to do nothing.

Now, there are all kinds of problems involved in applied anarchy. It could work with saints, but could social systems based on voluntarism work with ordinary mortals? The answer is yes and no. It *could* work, but *it would never work without some radical reconstruction of the economic basis of social life.* Political voluntarism depends upon economic voluntarism, and vice versa. Once men are assured that they have enough to eat and keep them comfortable from the elements, they will be free to combine for innumerable social purposes.

Whether the economic problem can be solved within the context of a larger society that operates upon coercive principles is not at all clear. As Staughton Lynd has put it, "Employment appears to be the Achilles heel of parallelism." This is *the* major problem to which we must address our efforts if we are to put our ideas into practice.

There is also the problem of numbers. It may be that in a society in which there are very large numbers, and in which anonymity is possible, that some forms of compulsion (i.e., policemen) are necessary. This seems to me to be an argument for keeping social units relatively small. But once you remove economic compulsion, if you can have what you want by taking it, there is not much left of conventional notions of crime.

Another important question concerns the problems of coordination and cooperation. In the absence of government coercion how would we be able to coordinate our activities? Among the answers to this question is that some of the existing uniformity is superfluous. There is no reason why all the pupils in all the schools of a state should have the same curriculum. This would free us of many school administrators. For other tasks, where genuine co-operation of different social units is needed, it can take place naturally without any governmental coercion at all. It is likely that there will be occasions in which men do not voluntarily cooperate and in which parts of a voluntarist society would "break down" because one community, for example, puts its sewage into the drinking water of another. But I think that these risks are preferable to the continued risks of more world wars.

A viable social order must rest largely upon voluntary cooperation in any event. Most people have internalized certain social mores, and they do not commit crimes because they do not want to commit them. Would we really have more murders if we had no police? Would the men in one community wilfully ignore the fact that their sewage was getting into the drinking water of another community, and hurting people in that other community once it had been called to their attention?

It may not be possible or even desirable to eliminate all authority—I would propose eliminating only that kind of authority which is based on coercion. Authority based upon knowledge related to the task at hand is generally respected, because when men trust each other they are not afraid to follow each other's suggestions.

Thus if there is to be a bridge built across a river, obviously even in a free society, people will voluntarily submit to following the suggestions of an engineer who knows about building bridges. But that will be because they want a bridge and he knows how to help them build it, and not because he has some title.

What are the implications of the foregoing? Politics cannot be ignored, but should definitely be relegated to second place. If and when it becomes possible for a humanitarian political movement to gain power, at some time in the future, there will be ample time for voluntarists to figure out how they wish to relate to such a movement. In the meantime, it is more important to put our efforts into trying to put our ideas into practice in the here and now. The key to arriving at a decentralization and democratization of social institutions is to concentrate our efforts on: (a) education, and (b) creating living examples of the kinds of communities we would like to see in widespread existence.

DAVID E. APTER / Ideology and Discontent*

A FUNCTIONAL APPROACH

I am inclined to the view that ideology helps to perform two main functions: one directly social, binding the community together, and the other individual, organizing the role personalities of the maturing individual.

These functions combine to legitimize authority. It is the relation to authority that gives ideology its political significance. In "early-stage" development communities, authority becomes legitimized on the basis of those ideologies that lay claim to superior planning and rationality and that provide moral bases for social manipulation for development purposes. Such authority is supported by large bodies of technicians, economists, administrative specialists, and fiscal experts. In short, ideology helps to support an elite and to justify the exercise of power. This observation is no less true for highly developed societies, even though in them the position of ideology is shakier, with corresponding weaknesses in social solidarity and individual identity. It is the curious mood of our time that the rise of unlimited opportunities in the development sphere, through the applications of social science to modern problems, is accompanied by much ideological restlessness.

THE SOLIDARITY ASPECT

The solidarity aspect of ideology was first made explicit by Marx. His views can be briefly summarized as follows. Change in

---

* From Apter (ed.), *Ideology and Discontent* (New York, Free Press of Glencoe, 1964), pp. 18–26. Portions of the original chapter have been omitted.

the material conditions of life is expressed in two forms: the intensification of class struggle resulting in the emergence of different kinds of systems and the evolution of a higher form of consciousness that coincides with the evolutionary pattern of system growth.[1]

Less clear is the degree of determinism Marx attributed to productive relations. This vagueness in the Marxian theory has, of course, been the basis for a great deal of debate. If productive relations determined all, then it ought to be unnecessary to study ideology. Yet ideology is very much a concern of the Marxians.

Lenin, the ideologue of Marxism, reinforced his polemics with claims to superior wisdom. From analysis of "material conditions," the ideologue can lay down a "correct" political line for the public to follow. Superior wisdom is equated with ideological authority by means of which the public is converted to the political line.[2] Indeed, ideological purity becomes the rock against

[1] Lichtheim points out that there is a conflict here, which Marxists in their "objectivism" do not like to admit. Although it is "in accordance with Marx's own manner to take a historical view of his work, such an approach presupposes a vantage-point made available by developments beyond the stage reflected in the Marxian system. In other words, it assumes that the Marxian categories are no longer quite applicable to current history. For obvious reasons, this is an admission which orthodox Marxists find it hard to make, while others may wonder why this particular scruple should arise in the first place. Its emergence is due to the fact that Hegel and following him, Marx, took a view of history which is not the familiar positivist one. They saw history as a process whose meaning reveals itself by stages, the succession of the latter reflecting man's growing awareness of his role in creating the historical world. To comprehend its past, mankind must raise itself to a higher level; hence, our ability to understand our predecessors suggests that we have reached a new altitude." George Lichtheim, *Marxism: An Historical and Critical Study* (London, 1961), p. xv.

It was this problem that concerned Mannheim. Although Marxism supported the objectivist school of thought, the consequences of his theories were to produce the neo-Marxian subjectivist school of the sociology of knowledge. Mannheim and his followers, however, cannot avoid the same criticism to which Marx was subject.

[2] This view is nicely brought out in the conflict between the "Economists" and Lenin. Consider, for example, the criticisms leveled against *Iskra*, Lenin's newspaper, and Lenin's reply. The criticism: "*Iskra's* excessive predilection for controversy is due primarily to its exaggerated idea of the role of 'ideology' (programs, theories . . .) in the movement, and is partly an echo of the internecine squabbles that have flared up among Russian emigrants in West-

which waves of deviationism must be dashed unless they submerge the promontories of revolution.[3]

Lenin made ideology into a form of philosophical propaganda. He was both ideologue and ideologist. In his hand, communism became a revolutionary dogma. Not a philosophy, it contained one; not an epistemology, it prescribed one; not a system of values, it was a program for achieving one. But he did not transform ideology into much more than propaganda. It is Sorel, rather

---

ern Europe, of which they have hastened to inform the world in a number of polemical pamphlets and articles. In our opinion, these disagreements exercise almost no influence upon the actual progress of the Russian Social-Democratic movement except perhaps to damage it by introducing an undesirable schism among the comrades working in Russia. For that reason we cannot but express our disapproval of *Iskra's* polemical zeal, particularly when it exceeds the bounds of decency." Lenin's reply was characteristic. He flayed the "Economists" for not staying ahead of the revolutionary consciousness of the people. He charged that the authors of the attack "fail to understand that an 'ideologist' is worthy of that name only when he marches ahead of the 'spontaneous movement,' points out the road, and when he is able, ahead of all others, to solve all the theoretical, political, tactical and organizational questions which the 'material elements' of the movement spontaneously encounter. In order to give 'consideration to the material elements of the movement' it is necessary to be critical of it, to point out its dangers and defects, and aspire to elevate spontaneity to consciousness. To say, however, that ideologists (i.e., conscious leaders) cannot divert the movement created by the interaction of environment and elements from its path is to ignore the elementary truth that consciousness participates in this interaction and creation."

Lenin equates ideology with more than the simple manipulation of ideas. Rather, it is created by those who share a higher consciousness and a more informed intelligence about social matters. He calls ideological "elements" those "conscious elements [who] operate according to plan." Nicolai Lenin, "A Conversation with Defenders of Economism," in Alexander Trachtenberg, ed., *Collected Works of Lenin,* IV (New York, 1929), Book II: "The Iskra Period," pp. 66–67.

[3] This aspect of ideology, building solidarity within confusion and vulnerability without, is one of the reasons why Marxism as an ideology is attractive to many youthful leaders of new states. Marx considers ideology to be those ideas that represent a particular mode of social organization. "To consider ideology as a set of ruling ideas which have been separated from the ruling individuals and given an independent force, an element of creativity in social affairs," he considers nonsense. The real basis of ideology, he points out, is in the material conditions of life, particularly in social relationships, division of labor, and productive power. Ideology is thus a screen for reality, a cloak. Karl Marx, *The German Ideology* (New York, 1939), pp. 41, 42, 43; see also Karl Mannheim, *Ideology and Utopia* (New York, 1946), p. 110.

than Lenin, who spins out the implications of solidarity to the fullest and "completes" Marx "instead of making commentaries on his text as his unfortunate disciples have done for so long." [4]

The feature of Sorel's work that makes explicit the solidarity function of ideology is the role of myth—more particularly the myth of the general strike. Myth is the social equivalent of metaphor, or, to put it another way, myth is to solidarity what metaphor is to identity. It is a way of binding the individual and the social together. For such myths to be useful, Sorel argues, they must be in tune with the worthier moral tendencies. It is on a moral basis that ideologies must be evaluated rather than on vague belief in dialectical progress. He taxes Marxians for failing to recognize that old myths can be revived in order to modify the historical processes, thus leading to reactionary revolutions. "Marx does not seem to have asked himself what would happen if the economic system were on the downgrade; he never dreamt of the possibility of a revolution which would take a return to the past, or even social conservation as its ideal. . . .

"These are dreams which Marx looked upon as reactionary, and consequently negligible, because it seemed to him that capitalism was embarked on an irresistible progress; but nowadays we see considerable forces grouped together in the endeavor to reform the capitalist economic system by bringing it, with the aid of laws, nearer to the medieval ideal. Parliamentary Socialism would like to combine with the moralists, the Church, and the democracy, with the common aim of impeding the capitalist movement; and, in view of middle-class cowardice, that would not perhaps be impossible." [5]

The myths and the utopias provide each great event with its moral dimension. Sorel asks, "what remains of the Revolution when we have taken away the epic of the wars against the coalition, and of that of the victories of the populace? What remains is not very savory: police operations, proscriptions, and sittings of servile courts of law." [6]

[4] Georges Sorel, *Reflections on Violence* (New York, 1950), p. 59.
[5] *Ibid.*, p. 107.
[6] *Ibid.*, p. 119.

For Sorel it is the myth of the proletarian general strike that activates the class struggle and carries it forward. In this sense, we can say that he carries Marx to an ideological conclusion, for without the ideology of the general strike, regardless of the full weight of material development or the evolutionary emphasis in dialectical materialism, the revolution may fail or become reactionary. Ideology is a necessary ingredient of progress.[7]

What makes Sorel interesting to us, however, is not his doctrine of the proletarian general strike or his justification of violence. It is, rather, the claim he makes for ideology. Its role is to build solidarity, and solidarity is the moral basis of society. Solidarity is for Sorel a moral system based on class and held together by myths. It is the foundation of change. Solidarity-producing myths are "good" when they lead to a higher morality. His plea for solidarity is thus also a plea for a more moral social personality and a superior human community.

This connection between solidarity and morality is the essence of authority, a fact well recognized by leaders of new nations. Solidarity and myth as expressed in ideology are commonly manipulated in order to supply a moral dimension to political forms. In this sense, the creation of myth, the moral solidarity of the community, and its authority are intimately linked.

THE IDENTITY ASPECT

Sorel helped to clarify the function of ideology for society in building its bonds of affect, social commitment, and historical perspective. The natural outcome of his analysis centers attention less on the particular polemics of his own ideology than on the diverse but concrete manifestations of solidarity in ideological form. These manifestations include the use of historical myths, the rewriting of history, the search for a golden age—all ingredients that serve to promote the ends of a political community. So

[7] Sorel, although an admirer of Marx, is by no means dazzled by his doctrine. He quotes with relish a "learned exponent of Socialism" who said that "the art of reconciling opposites by means of nonsense is the most obvious result which he had got from the study of the works of Marx." *Ibid.,* p. 138. See also Ernst Cassirer, *The Myth of the State* (New Haven, 1946), Part 1.

far, ideology in society has been our point of reference. But ideology, like language and dreams, is related to morphologies of behavior by universal psychobiological variables. Balance, mastery, and control are the desired results of ideological behavior. Ideas help men to control and change their environment. Such ideas arise out of action rather than out of pure speculation. Such was Freud's view. He wrote, "It must not be assumed that mankind came to create its first world system through a purely speculative thirst for knowledge. The practical need of mastering the world must have contributed to this effort." [8] These views of Freud's would apply to all forms of belief, including animism, magic, taboos, and presumably political beliefs.[9]

For Freud, ideology is a form of personal *rationalization*. (In this view, he might have agreed with Marx.) Both he and Marx saw ideas as a cloak behind which "reality" hides, although, of course, each had a different idea of reality. For Freud ideologies are elaborate mental fictions, which the observer must penetrate in order to understand personality. Ideology in his view is uniquely personal. The scholar who seeks to understand ideology is the psychotherapist who unravels the mental rationalizations of his patients. It is hard to say whether or not this attitude defined ideology as a pathological condition for Freud. Certainly he would consider political extremists emotionally suspect. He did not have much taste for the bizarre, despite the novelty of his views.

Yet Erikson, who recently became concerned with such matters, does not do too great violence to the ideas of Freud when, in his

[8] A. A. Brill, ed., *The Basic Writings of Sigmund Freud* (New York, 1938), p. 867.
[9] Perhaps Freud's most direct concern with ideology is his analysis of the "chosen people" myth. Freud's transposition of the Moses legend is remarkable for its imaginative skill. More to the point, Freud argues that "the human intellect has not shown itself elsewhere to be endowed with a very good scent for truth, nor has the human mind displayed any readiness to accept truth. On the contrary, it is the general experience that the human intellect errs very easily without our suspecting it at all, and that nothing is more readily believed than what—regardless of the truth—meets our wishes and illusions half-way." Sigmund Freud, *Moses and Monotheism* (New York, 1939), p. 204.

study of Luther, he emphasizes the forbidding emotional complex that led to greatness. His concern with the conditions leading to the formation of creative personalities leads him to both the study of the ideology and its role in personality. In psycho-history more than in any other form of social analysis, the observer relies on unorthodox sensitivities as he sniffs for evidence, clues and data, much of which has barely been touched by previous analysts. He is more on his own in social analysis than either the ordinary historian or the social scientist. Erikson's point is that, since he observes ideology in the context of personality, the psychotherapist *cum* social-science observer can contribute a great deal to the understanding of why individuals are so receptive to ideology. Erikson establishes a theory of personality formation based on that aspect of maturation he calls the search for identity. Because identity search coincides with role search, youth (as well as others who have never quite "found" themselves, as the vernacular goes) is particularly vulnerable to ideologies. This point adds another aspect of the study of ideology to the one offered by the Marxians, motivation. None of the Marxians can explain why class interest ought to *be,* and they are confused enough to deny the universality of the proposition by showing how it is possible for some individuals to emancipate themselves from that class interest. This contradiction is an important weakness in Marxian theory, for, much as Marx would have liked to deny the independent validity of ideas for action, he had to leave some loopholes for the gratuitous entry of nonworking-class Marxian ideas. The link between material conditions and class behavior cannot therefore be axiomatic. The result is an incomplete and inconclusive treatment of ideology. Erikson defines ideology as "an unconscious tendency underlying religious and scientific as well as political thought: the tendency at a given time to make facts amenable to ideas, and ideas to facts, in order to create a world image convincing enough to support the collective and the individual sense of identity. Far from being arbitrary or consciously manageable (although it is as exploitable as all of man's unconscious strivings), the total perspective created by ideological simplification reveals its strength by the dominance it exerts on the seeming logic of historical events, and by its influence on the identity formation of individuals (and thus on their 'ego-strength')." [10]

This formulation helps us understand why individuals are receptive to ideology, by showing how ideology satisfies the identity function. It also helps us to realize how it is that the creative ideologist is formed. By relating identity to maturation—by defining it as a critical problem for youth—Erikson suggests why it is that ideology has a particular attractiveness to youth. The first point provides some insight into the conditions of personal conflict that lead to the acceptance or rejection of ideologies. The second helps to explain prophets, charismatic leaders, and manipulators of ideology. The third is of particular relevance to new-development communities, where the emphasis on youth raises it to a particularly high level of prominence in society at the precise time when the search for identity is at its most critical stage.[11]

IDEOLOGY IN THE DEVELOPING AREAS

So far we have been exploring the significance of solidarity and identity as laid down by social theorists who have had something appropriate to say about them.[12]

[10] Erik H. Erikson, *Young Man Luther: A Study in Psychoanalysis and History* (London, 1958), p. 20. He goes on to describe his book as a study of "identity and ideology."

[11] "Youth stands between the past and the future, both in individual life and in society. It also stands between alternate ways of life. . . . Ideologies offer to the members of this age-group overly simplified and yet determined answers to exactly those vague inner states and those urgent questions which arise in consequence of identity conflict. Ideologies serve to channel youth's forceful earnestness and sincere asceticism as well as its search for excitement and its eager indignation toward that social frontier where the struggle between conservatism and radicalism is most alive. On that frontier, fanatic ideologists do their busy work and psychopathic leaders their dirty work; but there, also, true leaders create significant solidarities." *Ibid.*, pp. 38–39.

[12] "Solidarity" is a highly abstract term for the bonds that hold individuals together through shared emotions about the same highly valued ideas and objects. Ideology cannot therefore be other than significant in solidarity. Identity is the self-definition of individuals with reference to their roles and the roles of others. Ideology cannot help but suggest guidelines to the self-definition process. It is also the case, however, that ideology responds differently to different demands made upon it in both the solidarity and identity spheres. In addition, the relationship between solidarity and identity deeply affects the appropriateness of particular ideologies.

In this section, we shall discuss these matters with respect to both new and old nations. Rightly or wrongly, I visualize developing communities as if they were strung on a continuum. The new developing communities are trying to sort out certain problems that the older ones have more or less resolved, although not in all cases. These problems involve the more "primordial" sentiments based on race, language, tribe, or other factors, which, although not relevant to the development process, may be relevant to the maintenance of solidarity or identity. What I call "nationalism" is the ideology that embodies these primordial sentiments. It is well to bear this special meaning in mind as we discuss the relationship between nationalism and socialism. In the highly developed communities, such primordial sentiments are less a problem than are confusion, irresponsibility, withdrawal, and cynicism. Here we can find conditions pointing to what Durkheim called *anomie*. More common is something like Scheler's *ressentiment*. Generally there is a feeling of a fear and disappointment in the consequences of development. Boundless confidence in the benefits it will bring (common in new nations) is not very widespread in the older nations.

Countries that are neither new nor old in this process include Japan and the U.S.S.R. We shall briefly mention the former because in Japan nationalism has played a crucial part in relating solidarity, identity, and development to one another. The Soviet system we shall not discuss—partly because there is insufficient data. We do not know the role of ideology there at the moment; nor is it clear what ideologies are prevalent. If we can consider the ideology of the Soviet Union conservative, embodying as it does principles that are to be realized through the Soviet state, it is also true that we cannot evaluate its role without comparing it to an ideology of rebellion. The only hints we have are in the poems, plays, and novels of the angry young Soviet men. As the U.S.S.R. moves toward the highly developed end of the continuum, we may expect that a new language and a new ideology will emerge. But such a time is in the rather distant future!

What we are suggesting then is that the role of ideology in the new developing communities is to promote authority. In the middle of the continuum it maintains authority. In the older societies, ideologies compete, weakening solidarity and identity with the resulting danger of alienation. Paradoxically, however, consensus varies in the opposite direction. In the new developing areas consensus is low, primordial loyalties high. Ideology blends them. In the old developing areas, consensus is high and primordial loyalties low. Ideology makes minor differences important. Correspondingly, the identity problem in the new development communities is to achieve a political consensus—the problem of political socialization and indoctrination—while in the older ones it is private, associated with a lengthy period of role search. Let us explore these propositions a bit further.

Almost all communities at the beginning stages of their development are seriously handicapped by various antipathetic cultural strains. Ideology, often consciously manipulated for the purpose of building authority, helps to minimize the consequences of such strain. That is how ideology performs its solidarity function. Similarly, in the case of identity, competing socialization processes, new and traditional, make the identity problem a complex one; ideology is employed to introduce greater coherence.

Two contrasting cases come to mind from Africa: Mali and Nigeria. In Mali, cultural discontinuities are being made to give way before new political arrangements in society represented in a Malian version of Marxism. In Nigeria, no single ideology defines political orthodoxy, and instead there is a host of competing traditions and ideas.[13] The young are enthusiastic supporters of the regime in Mali. In Nigeria, youth is estranged from the leadership, and no ideology has caught on. In Mali, solidarity is brought about by the conscious manipulation of ideology.

[13] These problems take a different form in highly developed societies. Where the society is extremely complex, piecemeal legislation never quite solves problems to anyone's satisfaction. The individual feels lost. He is made trivial in a system, the magnitude of which dwarfs him. The result is a frustrating and continuous search for identity by the members of the society and a lack of solidarity among them.

SOCIALISM AS AN IDEOLOGY

Most of the political leaders in the developing areas profess to be socialists. This ideology enables them to repudiate prevailing hierarchies of power and prestige associated with traditionalism or colonialism. Furthermore, socialism helps to define as "temporary" (as a phase in economic growth) the commercial "market place" or "bazaar" economy.[14] Socialism, while it accepts the secularism of the market place, rejects the form; that is, roles associated with the market place are minimized.

In this sense, socialism has a very special meaning. It becomes the ethic for a system of political discipline leading to an emphasis on "science"—science for its own sake as a symbol of progress and as a form of political wisdom. In keeping with this aim, it offers a set of unified developmental goals that stress roles functional to the achievement of a workmanlike, rational society in which people extend helping hands to one another because they value highly the process of industrialization through community effort.

Such forms of socialism have very little to say about property or religion. Indeed they are largely silent on the subject of class antagonism. They are vague about the role of property, a factor central in Western ideas of socialism. The African variety, for example, prefers at present to delineate core values appropriate to modernization rather than to limit itself prematurely to particular economic forms.

In this sense, African socialism, like its counterparts in other developing areas, tends to look backward and forward at the same time. Although they may speak in the name of "revolution," in most cases political leaders are forced to make changes slowly by opening up the system to modernized roles. The result is that quite often what is called "socialism" is merely another name for "nationalism." [15]

14 For a discussion of the "bazaar economy," see D. E. Apter, "Political Organization and Ideology," in Moore and Feldman, eds., *Labor Commitment and Social Change in Developing Areas* (New York, 1960), p. 337; see also D. E. Apter, *The Politics of Modernization* (Chicago, forthcoming).
15 Nationalism may be a revolutionary ideology vis-à-vis colonialism, but it

What the various forms of socialism have in common, irrespective of their other ingredients, is an emphasis on development goals, for which individuals must sacrifice. Government is seen as a main source of development. Unity, represented in national citizenship, is the critical form of allegiance, with no other loyalties taking precedence over the state itself. Behind unity is the concept of society as a natural and organic body in which all the parts have their appointed functions, especially those linked to the development process.

Socialism is viewed as more rational than capitalism because of its emphasis on planning—more scientific, more secular, and more in keeping with the need to fit together and develop functionally modern roles. Socialism then has two aspects. In the content of its ideology, it defines modernity. In the application of its ideology, it defines social discipline manifested in solidarity groupings whose *raison d'être* is functionally for development. This functionality in turn lays down the terms of individual identity and establishes a new system of motivation that emphasizes achievement.[16]

NATIONALISM AND IDEOLOGY—

THE JAPANESE ILLUSTRATION

Quite often socialism, no matter how vaguely defined, breaks down into a number of competing dogmas that have the effects of weakening solidarity and confusing identity. When this danger arises, political leaders may opt for nationalism as the dominant ideology in new development communities. Nationalism incorporates primordial loyalties in a readily understandable synthesis, taking up the "slack" in identity and solidarity where socialism

---

is not normally so with respect to other aspects of social life. It is largely silent on the forms of economic organization.

[16] See David C. McClelland, "The Achievement Motive in Economic Growth," Hoselitz and Moore, eds., *Industrialization anl Society* (Paris, 1963), p. 74. McClelland points out that such achievement motivation becomes linked with identity because it is a desire to do well not for the sake of social recognition or prestige but "to attain an inner feeling of personal accomplishment." Ultimately, socialism as an egalitarian system is an effort to induce such achievement motivation.

fails. Diffuse enough to encompass all specific forms of loyalty and tradition, it elevates them to a national inheritance. The value of nationalism lies in its functional flexibility.[17]

As Herskovits has pointed out, "African leaders faced with the challenge of economic growth and the need to establish higher living standards began to re-examine traditional communal patterns with the objective of shaping them to fit the requirements of a new economic order. This re-examination occurred both where patterns of individual effort had become established and where socialistically oriented plans sought to use traditional communalism as an instrument to make the new system function." In this process, certain older values had to give way—the emphasis on age, hereditary status, kinship, and chieftancy, for example. Once these values have given way, the remaining aspects of traditional life can be translated into more modern circumstances.[18]

Then nationalism takes on a more explicitly ideological complexion. Perhaps the best example, and certainly the best studied, is Japan. What made the Japanese case so interesting was the ability of the country to develop rapidly within the shell of traditional culture. Existing social beliefs, mainly of an instrumental nature, allowed a bending and shaping of well-understood institutions, which, despite their alteration, provided a public sense of continuity. Some of these beliefs were represented in an emphasis on education for instrumental ends. Bellah points out that, in Japan, learning for its own sake "tends to be despised. The merely erudite man is not worthy of respect. Rather, learning should eventuate in practice. A truly learned man will be a truly loyal and filial man." [19]

The same considerations held for Japanese religion. "It was seen almost as a system of training which aided in the self-abnegating performance of actions expressing loyalty to one's lord." [20]

Religion and education, community and family, found their

17 See, for example, Janheinz Jahn, *Muntu: An Outline of Neo-African Culture* (London, 1958), *passim*.
18 M. J. Herskovits, *The Human Factor in Changing Africa* (New York, 1962), p. 467.
19 Robert N. Bellah, *Tokugawa Religion* (New York, 1957), p. 16.
20 *Ibid.*, p. 17.

natural and practical expression in the state, which could therefore contemplate change while continuing to hold the loyalties of its members. (We have in mind the massive alterations occurring when Tokugawa evolved into Meiji Japan.) The primacy of political values and the emphasis on the polity allowed modification in social institutions, particularly economic ones, without dramatically rupturing the values and social beliefs of the Japanese.

It is not our concern, nor are we qualified, to discuss the many factors relevant to this process. Even in the Japanese case, however, the accumulated changes could not all be absorbed by the nationalist ideology and political framework. The result can be seen in the growth of Japanese militarism from 1900 onward. If the Meiji government represented a "logical fulfillment of a conception of the polity which already existed in the Tokugawa Period," as Bellah indicates, militarism was a natural outgrowth of both, to the extent that it combined instrumentalism in the economic sphere with nationalism in the political.[21] Militarism was the imperial answer to the rise of trade unions, liberal and left-wing political thought, and advocacy of genuine parliamentary government.

As a result, education, religion, and the polity were brought together in an explicit orthodoxy, perhaps most clearly stated in the Japanese document, *Kokutai No Hongi* or *Cardinal Principles of the National Entity of Japan*. This document illustrates the uses of ideology in building and maintaining solidarity and identity in Japan. (It also illustrates how ideology as an instrument of solidarity can be applied through education.) As the editor points out in his introduction to *Kokutai No Hongi*, it is "primarily an educational book written for educators." [22] Hardly a pamphlet or tract in the ordinary sense, it is rather a religious document, which links together mythical history ("The great august Will of the Emperor in the administration of the nation is constantly clearly reflected in our history"), the role of the emperor in religious ceremony ("The Emperor, venerating in per-

---

21 *Ibid.*, p. 20.
22 Robert King Hall, ed., *Kokutai No Hongi, Cardinal Principles of the National Entity of Japan* (Cambridge, Mass., 1949), p. 30.

son the divine spirits of the Imperial Ancestors, increasingly becomes one in essence with Imperial Ancestry"), loyalty ("Loyalty means to reverence the Emperor as our pivot and to follow him implicitly"), and familial and national harmony ("In order to bring national harmony to fruition there is no way but for every person in the nation to do his allotted duty and to exalt it"). The nation then is like the family, the emperor like the father, and in the cultivation of both, people venerate themselves and realize higher purposes.

What makes this document so interesting is its explicit rejection of occidental individualism and liberalism. War is regarded as an expression of development, leading to great harmony. The martial spirit is sacred.[23] Life and death are basically one. "The monistic truth is found where life and death are transcended. Through this is life, and through this is death. However, to treat life and death as two opposites and to hate death and to seek life is to be taken up with one's own interests, and is a thing of which warriors are ashamed. To fulfill the Way of loyalty, counting life and death as one, is Bushido." [24]

Here we have a striking emphasis on loyalty and filial bonds that extends the notion of sacrifice and service further than in any Western ideology. At the same time, the primacy of national solidarity is linked to specific institutions, which trace their lineage to antiquity. The most immediate effects of modernization and industrialization are thereby deflected without hindering the modernization process in its economic sphere. Rather, education, industrial employment, and the enlargement of urban life help to reinforce rather than destroy the organic conception of society. Individual identity is found in service to the state and the emperor. Solidarity is expressed through the network of familial obligations, which includes the royal house. What are thus normally, in other systems, sources of tension, dislocation, and cultural strain are in the Japanese case twisted the other way around. Theirs is an explicitly traditionalist ideology, embodying instrumental ends, that was deliberately employed to make the identity and solidarity

23 *Ibid.,* p. 94.
24 *Ibid.,* p. 145.

problems simpler. (Witness, for example, the unbelievable expansion of the educational system in the nineteenth century.) Nationalism in Japan was able to do what socialism in the developing areas could not do: to serve its functional purposes while transmitting a scientific temper.

FRANTZ FANON / The
Wretched of the Earth*

Strengthened by the unconditional support of the socialist countries, the colonized peoples fling themselves with whatever arms they have against the impregnable citadel of colonialism. If this citadel is invulnerable to knives and naked fists, it is no longer so when we decide to take into account the context of the Cold War.

In this fresh juncture, the Americans take their role of patron of international capitalism very seriously. Early on, they advise the European countries to decolonize in friendly fashion. Later on, they do not hesitate to proclaim first the respect for and then the support of the principle of "Africa for the Africans." The United States is not afraid today of stating officially that they are the defenders of the right of all peoples to self-determination. Mr. Mennen Williams' last journey is only the illustration of the consciousness which the Americans have that the Third World ought not to be sacrificed. From then on we understand why the violence of the native is only hopeless if we compare it in the abstract to the military machine of the oppressor. On the other hand, if we situate that violence in the dynamics of the international situation, we see at once that it constitutes a terrible menace for the oppressor. Persistent *jacqueries* and Mau-Mau dis-

* From Fanon, *The Wretched of the Earth* (New York, Grove Press, 1965), pp. 61–83. Some footnotes and a portion of the original text have been omitted.

turbances unbalance the colony's economic life but do not
endanger the mother-country. What is more important in the eyes
of imperialism is the opportunity for socialist propaganda to infiltrate among the masses and to contaminate them. This is already a serious danger in the Cold War; but what would happen
to that colony in case of real war, riddled as it is by murderous
guerillas?

Thus capitalism realizes that its military strategy has everything
to lose by the outbreak of nationalist wars. Again, within the
framework of peaceful coexistence, all colonies are destined to
disappear, and in the long run neutralism is destined to be respected by capitalism. What must at all costs be avoided is strategic insecurity: the breakthrough of enemy doctrine into the
masses and the deep-rooted hatred of millions of men. The colonized peoples are very well aware of these imperatives which rule
international political life; for this reason even those who thun-
der denunciations of violence take their decisions and act in
terms of this universal violence. Today, peaceful coexistence between the two blocs provokes and feeds violence in the colonial
countries. Tomorrow, perhaps we shall see the shifting of that
violence after the complete liberation of the colonial territories.
Perhaps we will see the question of minorities cropping up. Already certain minority groups do not hesitate to preach violent
methods for resolving their problems and it is not by chance (so
the story runs) that in consequence Negro extremists in the
United States organize a militia and arm themselves. It is not by
chance, either, that in the so-called free world there exist committees for the defense of Jewish minorities in the U.S.S.R., nor an
accident if General de Gaulle in one of his orations sheds tears
over the millions of Moslems oppressed by Communist dictatorship. Both capitalism and imperialism are convinced that the
struggle against racialism and the movements towards national
freedom are purely and simply directed by remote control, fo-
mented from outside. So they decide to use that very efficacious
tactic, the Radio Free Europe Station, voice of the Committee for
the aid of over-ruled minorities. They practice anti-colonialism,
as did the French colonels in Algeria when they carried on

subversive warfare with the S.A.S.[1] or the psychological services. They "use the people against the people." We have seen with what results.

This atmosphere of violence and menaces, these rockets brandished by both sides, do not frighten or deflect the colonized peoples. We have seen that all their recent history has prepared them to understand and grasp the situation. Between the violence of the colonies and that peaceful violence that the world is steeped in, there is a kind of complicit agreement, a sort of homogeneity. The colonized peoples are well adapted to this atmosphere; for once, they are up to date. Sometimes people wonder that the native, rather than give his wife a dress, buys instead a transistor radio. There is no reason to be astonished. The natives are convinced that their fate is in the balance, here and now. They live in the atmosphere of doomsday, and they consider that nothing ought to be let pass unnoticed. That is why they understand very well Phouma and Phoumi, Lumumba and Tshombe, Ahidjo and Moumie, Kenyatta, and the men that are pushed forward regularly to replace him. They understand all these figures very well, for they can unmask the forces working behind them. The native and the underdeveloped man are today political animals in the most universal sense of the word.

It is true to say that independence has brought moral compensation to colonized peoples, and has established their dignity. But they have not yet had time to elaborate a Society, or to build up and affirm values. The warming, light-giving center where man and citizen develop and enrich their experience in wider and still wider fields does not yet exist. Set in a kind of irresolution, such men persuade themselves fairly easily that everything is going to be decided elsewhere, for everybody, at the same time. As for the political leaders, when faced with this situation, they first hesitate and then choose neutralism.

There is plenty to be said on the subject of neutralism. Some equate it with a sort of tainted mercantilism which consists of taking what it can get from both sides. In fact, neutralism, a

[1] Section Administrative Spéciale. An officers' corps whose task was to strengthen contact with the Algerians in non-military matters.

state of affairs created by the Cold War, if it allows underdeveloped countries to receive economic help from both sides, does not allow either party to aid underdeveloped areas to the extent that is necessary. Those literally astronomical sums of money which are invested in military research, those engineers who are tranformed into technicians of nuclear war, could in the space of fifteen years raise the standard of living of underdeveloped countries by sixty percent. So we see that the true interests of underdeveloped countries do not lie in the protraction nor in the accentuation of this Cold War. But it so happens that no one asks their advice. Therefore, when they can, they cut loose from it. But can they really remain outside it? At this very moment, France is trying out her atomic bombs in Africa. Apart from the passing of motions, the holding of meetings and the shattering of diplomatic relations, we cannot say that the peoples of Africa have had much influence, in this particular sector, on France's attitude.

Neutralism produces in the citizen of the Third World a state of mind which is expressed in everyday life by a fearlessness and an ancestral pride strangely resembling defiance. The flagrant refusal to compromise and the tough will that sets itself against getting tied up is reminiscent of the behavior of proud, poverty-stricken adolescents, who are always ready to risk their necks in order to have the last word. All this leaves Western observers dumbfounded, for to tell the truth there is a glaring divergence between what these men claim to be and what they have behind them. These countries without tramways, without troops, and without money have no justification for the bravado that they display in broad daylight. Undoubtedly, they are imposters. The Third World often gives the impression that it rejoices in sensation and that it must have its weekly dose of crises. These men at the head of empty countries, who talk too loud, are most irritating. You'd like to shut them up. But, on the contrary, they are in great demand. They are given bouquets; they are invited to dinner. In fact, we quarrel over who shall have them. And this is neutralism. They are ninety-eight percent illiterate, but they are the subject of a huge body of literature. They travel a great deal: the governing classes and students of underdeveloped countries are gold mines for airline companies. African and Asian officials may in the same month follow a course on socialist planning in Moscow and one on the advantages of the liberal economy in London or at Columbia University. African trade-union leaders leap ahead at a great rate in their own field. Hardly have they been appointed to posts in managerial organizations when they decide to form themselves into autonomous bodies. They haven't the requisite fifty years experience of practical trade-unionism in the framework of an industrial country, but they already know that non-political trade-unionism doesn't make sense. They haven't come to grips with the bourgeois machine, nor developed their consciousness in the class struggle; but perhaps this isn't necessary. Perhaps. We shall see that this will to sum everything up, which caricatures itself often in facile internationalism, is one of the most fundamental characteristics of underdeveloped countries.

Let us return to considering the single combat between native and settler. We have seen that it takes the form of an armed and open struggle. There is no lack of historical examples: Indo-China, Indonesia, and of course North Africa. But what we must not lose sight of is that this struggle could have broken out anywhere, in Guinea as well as Somaliland, and moreover today it could break out in every place where colonialism means to stay on—in Angola, for example. The existence of an armed struggle shows that the people are decided to trust to violent methods only. He of whom *they* have never stopped saying that the only language he understands is that of force, decides to give utterance by force. In fact, as always, the settler has shown him the way he should take if he is to become free. The argument the native chooses has been furnished by the settler, and by an ironic turning of the tables it is the native who now affirms that the colonialist understands nothing but force. The colonial regime owes its legitimacy to force and at no time tries to hide this aspect of things. Every statue, whether of Faidherbe or of Lyautey, of Bugeaud or of Sergeant Blandan—all these *conquistador* perched on colonial soil do not cease from proclaiming one and the same thing: "We are here by the force of bayonets..."[2] The sentence is easily completed. During the phase of insurrection, each settler reasons on a basis of simple arithmetic. This logic does not surprise the other settlers, but it is important to point out that it does not surprise the natives either. To begin with, the affirmation of the principle: "It's them or us" does not constitute a paradox, since colonialism, as we have seen, is in fact the organization of a Manichean world, a world divided up into compartments. And when in laying down precise methods the settler asks each member of the oppressing minority to shoot down 30 or 100 or 200 natives, he sees that nobody shows any indignation and that the whole problem is to decide whether it can be done all at once or by stages.[3]

This chain of reasoning which presumes very arithmetically the disappearance of the colonized people does not leave the native overcome with moral indignation. He has always known that his duel with the settler would take place in the arena. The native loses no time in lamentations, and he hardly ever seeks for justice in the colonial framework. The fact is that if the settler's logic leaves the native unshaken, it is because the latter has practically stated the problem of his liberation in identical terms: "We must form ourselves into groups of two hundred or five hundred, and each group must deal with a settler." It is in this manner of thinking that each of the protagonists begins the struggle.

For the native, this violence represents the absolute line of action. The militant is also a man who works. The questions that the organization asks the militant bear the mark of this way of looking at things: "Where have you worked? With whom? What

[2] Refers to Mirabeau's famous saying: "I am here by the will of the People; I shall leave only by the force of bayonets." (Transl.)
[3] It is evident that this vacuum cleaning destroys the very thing that they want to preserve. Sartre points this out when he says:
  "In short by the very fact of repeating them (concerning racist ideas) it is revealed that the simultaneous union of all against the natives is unrealisable. Such union only recurs from time to time and moreover it can only come into being as an active groupment in order to massacre the natives—an absurd though perpetual temptation to the settlers, which even if it was feasible would only succeed in abolishing colonisation at one blow." (*Critique de la Raison Dialectique*, p. 346).

have you accomplished?" The group requires that each individual perform an irrevocable action. In Algeria, for example, where almost all the men who called on the people to join in the national struggle were condemned to death or searched for by the French police, confidence was proportional to the hopelessness of each case. You could be sure of a new recruit when he could no longer go back into the colonial system. This mechanism, it seems, had existed in Kenya among the Mau-Mau who required that each member of the group should strike a blow at the victim. Each one was thus personally responsible for the death of that victim. To work means to work for the death of the settler. This assumed responsibility for violence allows both strayed and outlawed members of the group to come back again and to find their place once more, to become integrated. Violence is thus seen as comparable to a royal pardon. The colonized man finds his freedom in and through violence. This rule of conduct enlightens the agent because it indicates to him the means and the end....

It is understandable that in this atmosphere, daily life becomes quite simply impossible. You can no longer be a *fellah,* a pimp, or an alcoholic as before. The violence of the colonial regime and the counter-violence of the native balance each other and respond to each other in an extraordinary reciprocal homogeneity. This reign of violence will be the more terrible in proportion to the size of the implantation from the mother country. The development of violence among the colonized people will be proportionate to the violence exercised by the threatened colonial regime. In the first phase of this insurrectional period, the home governments are the slaves of the settlers, and these settlers seek to intimidate the natives and their home governments at one and the same time. They use the same methods against both of them. The assassination of the Mayor of Evian, in its method and motivation, is identifiable with the assassination of Ali Boumendjel. For the settlers, the alternative is not between *Algérie algérienne* and *Algérie française* but between an independent Algeria and a colonial Algeria, and anything else is mere talk or attempts at treason. The settler's logic is implacable and one is only staggered by the counter-logic visible in the behavior of the native insofar as one has not clearly understood beforehand the mechanisms of the settler's ideas. From the moment that the native has chosen the methods of counter-violence, police reprisals automatically call forth reprisals on the side of the nationalists. However, the results are not equivalent, for machine-gunning from aeroplanes and bombardments from the fleet go far beyond in horror and magnitude any answer the natives can make. This recurring terror demystifies once and for all the most estranged members of the colonized race. They find out on the spot that all the piles of speeches on the equality of human beings do not hide the commonplace fact that the seven Frenchmen killed or wounded at the Col de Sakamody kindles the indignation of all civilized consciences, whereas the sack of the douars[4] of Guergour and of the dechras of Djerah and the massacre of whole populations—which had merely called forth the Sakamody ambush as a reprisal—all this is of not the slightest importance. Terror, counter-terror, violence, counter-violence: that is what observers bitterly record when they describe the circle of hate, which is so tenacious and so evident in Algeria.

In all armed struggles, there exists what we might call the point of no return. Almost always it is marked off by a huge and all-inclusive repression which engulfs all sectors of the colonized people. This point was reached in Algeria in 1955 with the 12,000 victims of Philippeville, and in 1956 with Lacoste's instituting of urban and rural militias.

Then it became clear to everybody, including even the settlers, that "things couldn't go on as before." Yet the colonized people do not chalk up the reckoning. They record the huge gaps made in their ranks as a sort of necessary evil. Since they have decided to reply by violence, they therefore are ready to take all its consequences. They only insist in return that no reckoning should be kept, either, for the others. To the saying "All natives are the same," the colonized person replies, "All settlers are the same." [5]

---

4 Temporary village for the use of shepherds. (Transl.)
5 This is why there are no prisoners when the fighting first starts. It is only through educating the local leaders politically that those at the head of the

When the native is tortured, when his wife is killed or raped, he complains to no one. The oppressor's government can set up commissions of inquiry and of information daily if it wants to; in the eyes of the native, these commissions do not exist. The fact is that soon we shall have had seven years of crimes in Algeria and there has not yet been a single Frenchman indicted before a French court of justice for the murder of an Algerian. In Indo-China, in Madagascar or in the colonies the native has always known that he need expect nothing from the other side. The settler's work is to make even dreams of liberty impossible for the native. The native's work is to imagine all possible methods for destroying the settler. On the logical plane, the Manicheism of the settler produces a Manicheism of the native. To the theory of the "absolute evil of the native" the theory of the "absolute evil of the settler" replies.

The appearance of the settler has meant in the terms of syncretism the death of the aboriginal society, cultural lethargy, and the petrification of individuals. For the native, life can only spring up again out of the rotting corpse of the settler. This, then, is the correspondence, term by term, between the two trains of reasoning.

But it so happens that for the colonized people this violence, because it constitutes their only work, invests their characters with positive and creative qualities. The practice of violence binds them together as a whole, since each individual forms a violent link in the great chain, a part of the great organism of violence which has surged upward in reaction to the settler's violence in the beginning. The groups recognize each other and the future nation is already indivisible. The armed struggle mobilizes

---

movement can make the masses accept 1) that people coming from the mother-country do not always act of their own free will and are sometimes even disgusted by the war; 2) that it is of immediate advantage to the movement that its supporters should show by their actions that they respect certain international conventions; 3) that an army which takes prisoners is an army, and ceases to be considered as a group of wayside bandits; 4) that whatever the circumstances, the possession of prisoners constitutes a means of exerting pressure which must not be overlooked in order to protect our men who are in enemy hands.

the people; that is to say, it throws them in one way and in one direction.

The mobilization of the masses, when it arises out of the war of liberation, introduces into each man's consciousness the ideas of a common cause, of a national destiny, and of a collective history. In the same way the second phase, that of the building-up of the nation, is helped on by the existence of this cement which has been mixed with blood and anger. Thus we come to a fuller appreciation of the originality of the words used in these underdeveloped countries. During the colonial period the people are called upon to fight against oppression; after national liberation, they are called upon to fight against poverty, illiteracy, and underdevelopment. The struggle, they say, goes on. The people realize that life is an unending contest.

We have said that the native's violence unifies the people. By its very structure, colonialism is separatist and regionalist. Colonialism does not simply state the existence of tribes; it also reinforces it and separates them. The colonial system encourages chieftaincies and keeps alive the old Marabout confraternities. Violence is in action all-inclusive and national. It follows that it is closely involved in the liquidation of regionalism and of tribalism. Thus the national parties show no pity at all towards the caids and the customary chiefs. Their destruction is the preliminary to the unification of the people.

At the level of individuals, violence is a cleansing force. It frees the native from his inferiority complex and from his despair and inaction; it makes him fearless and restores his self-respect. Even if the armed struggle has been symbolic and the nation is demobilized through a rapid movement of decolonization, the people have the time to see that the liberation has been the business of each and all and that the leader has no special merit. From thence comes that type of aggressive reticence with regard to the machinery of protocol which young governments quickly show. When the people have taken violent part in the national liberation they will allow no one to set themselves up as "liberators." They show themselves to be jealous of the results of their action and take good care not to place their future, their destiny or the fate of their country in the hands of a living god. Yesterday they were completely irresponsible; today they mean to understand everything and make all decisions. Illuminated by violence, the consciousness of the people rebels against any pacification. From now on the demagogues, the opportunists, and the magicians have a difficult task. The action which has thrown them into a hand-to-hand struggle confers upon the masses a voracious taste for the concrete. The attempt at mystification becomes, in the long run, practically impossible.

VIOLENCE IN THE INTERNATIONAL CONTEXT

We have pointed out many times in the preceding pages that in underdeveloped regions the political leader is forever calling on his people to fight: to fight against colonialism, to fight against poverty and underdevelopment, and to fight against sterile traditions. The vocabulary which he uses in his appeals is that of a chief of staff: "mass mobilization"; "agricultural front"; "fight against illiteracy"; "defeats we have undergone"; "victories won." The young independent nation evolves during the first years in an atmosphere of the battlefield, for the political leader of an underdeveloped country looks fearfully at the huge distance his country will have to cover. He calls to the people and says to them: "Let us gird up our loins and set to work," and the country, possessed by a kind of creative madness, throws itself into a gigantic and disproportionate effort. The program consists not only of climbing out of the morass but also of catching up with the other nations using the only means at hand. They reason that if the European nations have reached that stage of development, it is on account of their efforts: "Let us therefore," they seem to say, "prove to ourselves and to the whole world that we are capable of the same achievements." This manner of setting out the problem of the evolution of underdeveloped countries seems to us to be neither correct nor reasonable.

The European states achieved national unity at a moment when the national middle classes had concentrated most of the wealth in their hands. Shopkeepers and artisans, clerks and bankers monopolized finance, trade, and science in the national framework. The middle class was the most dynamic and prosperous of all classes. Its coming to power enabled it to undertake certain very important speculations: industrialization, the development of communications, and soon the search for outlets overseas.

In Europe, apart from certain slight differences (England, for example, was some way ahead) the various states were at a more or less uniform stage economically when they achieved national unity. There was no nation which by reason of the character of its development and evolution caused affront to the others.

Today, national independence and the growth of national feeling in underdeveloped regions take on totally new aspects. In these regions, with the exception of certain spectacular advances, the different countries show the same absence of infrastructure. The mass of the people struggle against the same poverty, flounder about making the same gestures, and with their shrunken bellies outline what has been called the geography of hunger. It is an underdeveloped world, a world inhuman in its poverty; but also it is a world without doctors, without engineers, and without administrators. Confronting this world, the European nations sprawl, ostentatiously opulent. This European opulence is literally scandalous, for it has been founded on slavery, it has been nourished with the blood of slaves, and it comes directly from the soil and from the subsoil of that underdeveloped world. The well-being and the progress of Europe have been built up with the sweat and the dead bodies of Negroes, Arabs, Indians, and the yellow races. We have decided not to overlook this any longer. When a colonialist country, embarrassed by the claims for independence made by a colony, proclaims to the nationalist leaders: "If you wish for independence, take it, and go back to the middle ages," the newly independent people tend to acquiesce and to accept the challenge; in fact you may see colonialism withdrawing its capital and its technicians and setting up around the young State the apparatus of economic pressure.[6] The apotheosis

In the present international context, capitalism does not merely operate an economic blockade against African or Asiatic colonies. The United States with its anti-Castro operations is opening a new chapter in the long story of independence is transformed into the curse of independence, and the colonial power through its immense resources of coercion condemns the young nation to regression. In plain words, the colonial power says: "Since you want independence, take it and starve." The nationalist leaders have no other choice but to turn to their people and ask from them a gigantic effort. A regime of austerity is imposed on these starving men; a disproportionate amount of work is required from their atrophied muscles. An autarkic regime is set up and each state, with the miserable resources it has in hand, tries to find an answer to the nation's great hunger and poverty. We see the mobilization of a people which toils to exhaustion in front of a suspicious and bloated Europe.

Other countries of the Third World refuse to undergo this ordeal and agree to get over it by accepting the conditions of the former guardian power. These countries use their strategic position—a position which accords them privileged treatment in the struggle between the two blocs—to conclude treaties and give un

---

of man's toiling advance towards freedom. Latin America, made up of new independent countries which sit at the United Nations and raise the wind there, ought to be an object lesson for Africa. These former colonies since their liberation have suffered the brazen-faced rule of Western capitalism in terror and destitution.

The liberation of Africa and the growth of consciousness among mankind have made it possible for the Latin American peoples to break with the old merry-go-round of dictatorships where each succeeding regime exactly resembled the preceding one. Castro took over power in Cuba, and gave it to the people. This heresy is felt to be a national scourge by the Yankees, and the United States is now organizing counter-revolutionary brigades, puts together a provisional government, burns the sugar-cane crops, and generally has decided to strangle the Cuban people mercilessly. But this will be difficult. The people of Cuba will suffer, but they will conquer. The Brazilian president Janio Quadros has just announced in a declaration of historic importance that his country will defend the Cuban Revolution by all means. Perhaps even the United States may draw back when faced with the declared will of the peoples. When that day comes, we'll hang out the flags, for it will be a decisive moment for the men and women of the whole world. The almighty dollar, which when all is said or done is only guaranteed by slaves scattered all over the globe, in the oil wells of the Middle East, the mines of Peru or of the Congo, and the United Fruit or Firestone plantations, will then cease to dominate with all its force these slaves which it has created and who continue, empty-headed and empty-bellied, to feed it from their substance.

dertakings. The former dominated country becomes an economically dependent country. The ex-colonial power, which has kept intact and sometimes even reinforced its colonialist trade channels, agrees to provision the budget of the independent nation by small injections. Thus we see that the accession to independence of the colonial countries places an important question before the world, for the national liberation of colonized countries unveils their true economic state and makes it seem more unendurable. The fundamental duel which seemed to be that between colonialism and anticolonialism, and indeed between capitalism and socialism, is already losing some of its importance. What counts today, the question which is looming on the horizon is the need for a redistribution of wealth. Humanity must reply to this question, or be shaken to pieces by it.

It might have been generally thought that the time had come for the world, and particularly for the Third World, to choose between the capitalist and socialist systems. The underdeveloped countries, which have used the fierce competition which exists between the two systems in order to assure the triumph of their struggle for national liberation, should however refuse to become a factor in that competition. The Third World ought not to be content to define itself in the terms of values which have preceded it. On the contrary, the underdeveloped countries ought to do their utmost to find their own particular values and methods and a style which shall be peculiar to them. The concrete problem we find ourselves up against is not that of a choice, cost what it may, between socialism and capitalism as they have been defined by men of other continents and of other ages. Of course we know that the capitalist regime, insofar as it is a way of life, cannot leave us free to perform our work at home, nor our duty in the world. Capitalist exploitation and cartels and monopolies are the enemies of underdeveloped countries. On the other hand the choice of a socialist regime, a regime which is completely orientated towards the people as a whole and based on the principle that man is the most precious of all possessions, will allow us to go forward more quickly and more harmoniously, and thus make impossible that caricature of society where all economic and political power is held in the hands of a few who regard the nation as a whole with scorn and contempt.

But in order that this regime may work to good effect so that we can in every instance respect those principles which were our inspiration, we need something more than human output. Certain underdeveloped countries expend a huge amount of energy in this way. Men and women, young and old, undertake enthusiastically what is in fact forced labor, and proclaim themselves the slaves of the nation. The gift of oneself, and the contempt for every preoccupation which is not in the common interest, bring into being a national *morale* which comforts the heart of man, gives him fresh confidence in the destiny of mankind and disarms the most reserved observers. But we cannot believe that such an effort can be kept up at the same frenzied pace for very long. These young countries have agreed to take up the challenge after the unconditional withdrawal of the ex-colonial countries. The country finds itself in the hands of new managers; but the fact is that everything needs to be reformed and everything thought out anew. In reality the colonial system was concerned with certain forms of wealth and certain resources only—precisely those which provisioned her own industries. Up to the present no serious effort had been made to estimate the riches of the soil or of mineral resources. Thus the young independent nation sees itself obliged to use the economic channels created by the colonial regime. It can, obviously, export to other countries and other currency areas, but the basis of its exports is not fundamentally modified. The colonial regime has carved out certain channels and they must be maintained or catastrophe will threaten. Perhaps it is necessary to begin everything all over again: to change the nature of the country's exports, and not simply their destination, to re examine the soil and mineral resources, the rivers, and—why not —the sun's productivity. Now, in order to do all this other things are needed over and above human output—capital of all kinds, technicians, engineers, skilled mechanics, and so on. Let's be frank: we do not believe that the colossal effort which the under developed peoples are called upon to make by their leaders will give the desired results. If conditions of work are not modified centuries will be needed to humanize this world which has been forced down to animal level by imperial powers.[7]

The truth is that we ought not to accept these conditions. We should flatly refuse the situation to which the western countries wish to condemn us. Colonialism and imperialism have not paid their score when they withdraw their flags and their police forces from our territories. For centuries the capitalists have behaved in the underdeveloped world like nothing more than war criminals. Deportations, massacres, forced labor, and slavery have been the main methods used by capitalism to increase its wealth, its gold or diamond reserves, and to establish its power. Not long ago Nazism transformed the whole of Europe into a veritable colony. The governments of the various European nations called for reparations and demanded the restitution in kind and money of the wealth which had been stolen from them: cultural treasures, pictures, sculptures, and stained glass have been given back to their owners. There was only one slogan in the mouths of Europeans on the morrow of the 1945 V-day: "Germany must pay." Herr Adenauer, it must be said, at the opening of the Eichmann trial, and in the name of the German people, asked once more for forgiveness from the Jewish people. Herr Adenauer has renewed the promise of his people to go on paying to the state of Israel the enormous sums which are supposed to be compensation for the crimes of the Nazis.[8]

---

[7] Certain countries who have benefitted by a large European settlement come to independence with houses and wide streets, and these tend to forget the poverty-stricken, starving hinterland. By the irony of fate, they give the impression by a kind of complicit silence that their towns are contemporaneous with independence.

[8] It is true that Germany has not paid all her reparations. The indemnities imposed on the vanquished nation have not been claimed in full, for the injured nations have included Germany in their anti-communist system of defense. This same preoccupation is the permanent motivation of the colonialist countries when they try to obtain from their former colonies, if not their inclusion in the Western system, at least military bases and enclaves. On the other hand they have decided unanimously to forget their demands for the sake of NATO strategy and to preserve the free world; and we have seen Germany receiving floods of dollars and machines. A Germany once more standing on its feet, strong and powerful, was a necessity for the Western camp. It was in the understood interests of so-called free Europe to have

In the same way we may say that the imperialist states would
make a great mistake and commit an unspeakable injustice if
they contented themselves with withdrawing from our soil the
military cohorts, and the administrative and managerial services
whose function it was to discover the wealth of the country, to
extract it and to send it off to the mother countries. We are not
blinded by the moral reparation of national independence; nor
are we fed by it. The wealth of the imperial countries is our
wealth too. On the universal plane this affirmation, you may be
sure, should on no account be taken to signify that we feel ourselves affected by the creations of Western arts or techniques. For
in a very concrete way Europe has stuffed herself inordinately
with the gold and raw materials of the colonial countries: Latin
America, China, and Africa. From all these continents, under
whose eyes Europe today raises up her tower of opulence, there has
flowed out for centuries toward that same Europe diamonds and
oil, silk and cotton, wood and exotic products. Europe is literally
the creation of the Third World. The wealth which smothers her
is that which was stolen from the underdeveloped peoples. The
ports of Holland, the docks of Bordeaux and Liverpool were specialized in the Negro slave-trade, and owe their renown to millions of deported slaves. So when we hear the head of a European
state declare with his hand on his heart that he must come to the
help of the poor underdeveloped peoples, we do not tremble with
gratitude. Quite the contrary; we say to ourselves: "It's a just
reparation which will be paid to us." Nor will we acquiesce in the
help for underdeveloped countries being a program of "sisters of
charity." This help should be the ratification of a double realization: the realization by the colonized peoples that *it is their due*,
and the realization by the capitalist powers that in fact *they must
pay*.[9] For if, through lack of intelligence (we won't speak of lack

a prosperous and reconstructed Germany which would be capable of serving
as a first rampart against the eventual Red hordes. Germany has made admirable use of the European crisis. At the same time the United States and
other European states feel a legitimate bitterness when confronted with this
Germany, yesterday at their feet, which today metes out to them cut-throat
competition in the economic field.

9 "To make a radical difference between the building up of socialism in Europe

of gratitude) the capitalist countries refuse to pay, then the relentless dialectic of their own system will smother them. It is a fact that young nations do not attract much private capital. There are many reasons which explain and render legitimate this reserve on the part of the monopolies. As soon as the capitalists know—and of course they are the first to know—that their government is getting ready to decolonize, they hasten to withdraw all their capital from the colony in question. The spectacular flight of capital is one of the most constant phenomena of decolonization.

Private companies, when asked to invest in independent countries, lay down conditions which are shown in practice to be inacceptable or unrealizable. Faithful to the principle of immediate returns which is theirs as soon as they go "over-seas," the capitalists are very chary concerning all long-term investments. They are unamenable and often openly hostile to the prospective program of planning laid down by the young teams who form the new government. At a pinch they willingly agree to lend money to the young states, but only on condition that this money is used to buy manufactured products and machines: in other words, that it serves to keep the factories in the mother country going.

In fact, the cautiousness of the Western financial groups may be explained by their fear of taking any risk. They also demand political stability and a calm social climate which are impossible to obtain when account is taken of the appalling state of the population as a whole immediately after independence. Therefore, vainly looking for some guarantee which the former colony cannot give, they insist on garrisons being maintained or the inclusion of the young state in military or economic pacts. The private

---

and our relations with the Third World (as if our only relations with it were external ones) is, whether we know it or not, to set the pace for the distribution of the colonial inheritance over and above the liberation of the underdeveloped countries. It is to wish to build up a luxury socialism upon the fruits of imperialist robbery—as if, inside the gang, the swag is more or less shared out equally, and even a little of it is given to the poor in the form of charity, since it's been forgotten that they were the people it was stolen from." Marcel Péju, "To die for De Gaulle?" Article appearing in *Temps Modernes*, Nos. 175–176 (October–November, 1960).

companies put pressure on their own governments to at least set up military bases in these countries for the purpose of assuring the protection of their interests. In the last resort these companies ask their government to guarantee the investments which they decide to make in such-and-such an underdeveloped region.

It happens that few countries fulfill the conditions demanded by the trusts and monopolies. Thus capital, failing to find a safe outlet, remains blocked in Europe, and is frozen. It is all the more frozen because the capitalists refuse to invest in their own countries. The returns in this case are in fact negligible and treasury control is the despair of even the boldest spirits.

In the long run the situation is catastrophic. Capital no longer circulates, or else its circulation is considerably diminished. In spite of the huge sums swallowed up by military budgets, international capitalism is in desperate straits.

But another danger threatens it as well. Insofar as the Third World is in fact abandoned and condemned to regression or at least to stagnation by the selfishness and wickedness of Western nations, the underdeveloped peoples will decide to continue their evolution inside a collective autarky. Thus the Western industries will quickly be deprived of their overseas markets. The machines will pile up their products in the warehouses and a merciless struggle will ensue on the European market between the trust and the financial groups. The closing of factories, the paying-off of workers, and unemployment will force the European working class to engage in an open struggle against the capitalist regime. Then the monopolies will realize that their true interests lie in giving aid to the underdeveloped countries—unstinted aid with not too many conditions. So we see that the young nations of the Third World are wrong in trying to make up to the capitalist countries. We are strong in our own right, and in the justice of our point of view. We ought on the contrary to emphasize and explain to the capitalist countries that the fundamental problem of our time is not the struggle between the socialist regime and them. The Cold War must be ended, for it leads nowhere. The plans for nuclearizing the world must stop, and large-scale investments and technical aid must be given to underdeveloped regions. The fate of the world depends on the answer that is given to this question.

Moreover, the capitalist regime must not try to enlist the aid of the socialist regime over "the fate of Europe" in face of the starving multitudes of colored peoples. The exploit of Colonel Gagarin doesn't seem to displease General de Gaulle, for is it not a triumph which brings honor to Europe? For some time past the statesmen of the capitalist countries have adopted an equivocal attitude towards the Soviet Union. After having united all their forces to abolish the socialist regime, they now realize that they'll have to reckon with it. So they look as pleasant as they can, they make all kinds of advances, and they remind the Soviet people the whole time that they "belong to Europe."

They will not manage to divide the progressive forces which mean to lead mankind towards happiness by brandishing the threat of a Third World which is rising like the tide to swallow up all Europe. The Third World does not mean to organize a great crusade of hunger against the whole of Europe. What it expects from those who for centuries have kept it in slavery is that they will help it to rehabilitate mankind, and make man victorious everywhere, once and for all. But it is clear that we are not so naive as to think that this will come about with the cooperation and the good will of the European governments. This huge task which consists of re-introducing mankind into the world, the whole of mankind, will be carried out with the indispensable help of the European peoples, who themselves must realize that in the past they have often joined the ranks of our common masters where colonial questions were concerned. To achieve this, the European peoples must first decide to wake up and shake themselves, use their brains, and stop playing the stupid game of the Sleeping Beauty.

11 / MARXISM AND SOCIALISM

KARL MARX AND FREDERICK ENGELS / The Communist Manifesto*

The history of all hitherto-existing society is the history of class struggles.

Freeman and slave, patrician and plebeian, lord and serf, guild-master[1] and journeyman, in a word, oppressor and oppressed, stood in constant opposition to one another, carried on an uninterrupted, now hidden, now open fight, a fight that each time ended, either in a revolutionary re-constitution of society at large, or in the common ruin of the contending classes.

In the earlier epochs of history, we find almost everywhere a complicated arrangement of society into various orders, a manifold gradation of social rank. In ancient Rome we have patricians, knights, plebeians, slaves; in the Middle Ages, feudal lords, vassals, guild-masters, journeymen, apprentices, serfs; in almost all of these classes, again, subordinate gradations.

The modern bourgeois[2] society that has sprouted from the ruins of feudal society has not done away with class antagonisms.

---

* From Marx and Engels, *The Communist Manifesto* (New York, International Publishers, 1948). Originally written in 1848. This is the manifesto's first section, entitled "Bourgeois and Proletarians."

[1] Guild-master, that is, a full member of a guild, a master within, not a head of a guild. [This and succeeding notes were written by Engels for the English edition of 1888.]

[2] By bourgeoisie is meant the class of modern capitalists, owners of the means of social production and employers of wage-labor. By proletariat, the class of modern wage laborers who, having no means of production of their own, are reduced to selling their labor-power in order to live.

It has but established new classes, new condition of oppression, new forms of struggle in place of the old ones.

Our epoch, the epoch of the bourgeoisie, possesses, however, this distinctive feature: it has simplified the class antagonisms. Society as a whole is more and more splitting up into two great hostile camps, into two great classes directly facing each other: Bourgeoisie and Proletariat.

From the serfs of the Middle Ages sprang the chartered burghers of the earliest towns. From these burgesses the first elements of the bourgeoisie were developed.

The discovery of America, the rounding of the Cape, opened up fresh ground for the rising bourgeoisie. The East-Indian and Chinese markets, the colonization of America, trade with the colonies, the increase in the means of exchange and in commodities generally, gave to commerce, to navigation, to industry, an impulse never before known, and thereby, to the revolutionary element in the tottering feudal society, a rapid development.

The feudal system of industry, under which industrial production was monopolized by closed guilds, now no longer sufficed for the growing wants of the new markets. The manufacturing system took its place. The guild-masters were pushed on one side by the manufacturing middle class; division of labor between the different corporate guilds vanished in the face of division of labor in each single workshop.

Meantime the markets kept ever growing, the demand ever rising. Even manufacture no longer sufficed. Thereupon, steam and machinery revolutionized industrial production. The place of manufacture was taken by the giant, Modern Industry; the place of the industrial middle class, by industrial millionaires, the leaders of whole industrial armies, the modern bourgeois.

Modern industry has established the world-market, for which the discovery of America paved the way. This market has given an immense development to commerce, to navigation, to communication by land. This development has, in its turn, reacted on the extension of industry; and in proportion as industry, commerce, navigation, railways extended, in the same proportion the bourgeoisie developed, increased its capital, and pushed into the background every class handed down from the Middle Ages.

We see, therefore, how the modern bourgeoisie is itself the product of a long course of development, of a series of revolutions in the modes of production and of exchange.

Each step in the development of the bourgeoisie was accompanied by a corresponding political advance of that class. An oppressed class under the sway of the feudal nobility, an armed and self-governing association in the medieval commune;[3] here independent urban republic (as in Italy and Germany), there taxable "third estate" of the monarchy (as in France), afterwards, in the period of manufacture proper, serving either the semi-feudal or the absolute monarchy as a counterpoise against the nobility, and, in fact, cornerstone of the great monarchies in general, the bourgeoisie has at last, since the establishment of Modern Industry and of the world-market, conquered for itself, in the modern representative State, exclusive political sway. The executive of the modern State is but a committee for managing the common affairs of the whole bourgeoisie.

The bourgeoisie, historically, has played a most revolutionary part.

The bourgeoisie, wherever it has got the upper hand, has put an end to all feudal, patriarchal, idyllic relations. It has pitilessly torn asunder the motley feudal ties that bound man to his "natural superiors," and has left remaining no other nexus between man and man than naked self-interest, than callous "cash payment." It has drowned the most heavenly ecstasies of religious fervor, of chivalrous enthusiasm, of philistine sentimentalism, in the icy water of egotistical calculation. It has resolved personal worth into exchange value, and in place of the numberless indefeasible chartered freedoms, has set up that single, unconscionable freedom—Free Trade. In one word, for exploitation, veiled by religious and political illusions, it has substituted naked, shameless, direct, brutal exploitation.

The bourgeoisie has stripped of its halo every occupation hith-

[3] "Commune" was the name taken, in France, by the nascent towns even before they had conquered from their feudal lords and masters local self-government and political rights as the "Third Estate." Generally speaking, for the economical development of the bourgeoisie, England is here taken as the typical country; for its political development, France.

erto honored and looked up to with reverent awe. It has converted the physician, the lawyer, the priest, the poet, the man of science, into its paid wage-laborers.

The bourgeoisie has torn away from the family its sentimental veil, and has reduced the family relation to a mere money relation.

The bourgeoisie has disclosed how it came to pass that the brutal display of vigor in the Middle Ages, which Reactionists so much admire, found its fitting complement in the most slothful indolence. It has been the first to show what man's activity can bring about. It has accomplished wonders far surpassing Egyptian pyramids, Roman aqueducts, and Gothic cathedrals; it has conducted expeditions that put in the shade all former Exoduses of nations and crusades.

The bourgeoisie cannot exist without constantly revolutionizing the instruments of production, and thereby the relations of production, and with them the whole relations of society. Conservation of the old modes of production in unaltered form, was, on the contrary, the first condition of existence for all earlier industrial classes. Constant revolutionizing of production, uninterrupted disturbance of all social conditions, everlasting uncertainty and agitation distinguish the bourgeois epoch from all earlier ones. All fixed, fast-frozen relations, with their train of ancient and venerable prejudices and opinions, are swept away, all new-formed ones become antiquated before they can ossify. All that is solid melts into air, all that is holy is profaned, and man is at least compelled to face with sober senses, his real conditions of life, and his relations with his kind.

The need of a constantly expanding market for its products chases the bourgeoisie over the whole surface of the globe. It must nestle everywhere, settle everywhere, establish connections everywhere.

The bourgeoisie has through its exploitation of the world-market given a cosmopolitan character to production and consumption in every country. To the great chagrin of Reactionists, it has drawn from under the feet of industry the national ground on which it stood. All old-established national industries have been destroyed or are daily being destroyed. They are dislodged by new industries, whose introduction becomes a life and death question for all civilized nations, by industries that no longer work up indigenous raw material, but raw material drawn from the remotest zones; industries whose products are consumed, not only at home, but in every quarter of the globe. In place of the old wants, satisfied by the productions of the country, we find new wants, requiring for their satisfaction the products of distant lands and climes. In place of the old local and national seclusion and self-sufficiency, we have intercourse in every direction, universal interdependence of nations. And as in material, so also in intellectual production. The intellectual creations of individual nations become common property. National one-sidedness and narrow-mindedness become more and more impossible, and from the numerous national and local literatures, there arises a world-literature.

The bourgeoisie, by the rapid improvement of all instruments of production, by the immensely facilitated means of communication, draws all, even the most barbarian, nations into civilization. The cheap prices of its commodities are the heavy artillery with which it batters down all Chinese walls, with which it forces the barbarians' intensely obstinate hatred of foreigners to capitulate. It compels all nations, on pain of extinction, to adopt the bourgeois mode of production; it compels them to introduce what it calls civilization into their midst, i.e., to become bourgeois themselves. In one word, it creates a world after its own image.

The bourgeoisie has subjected the country to the rule of the towns. It has created enormous cities, has greatly increased the urban population as compared with the rural, and has thus rescued a considerable part of the population from the idiocy of rural life. Just as it has made the country dependent on the towns, so it has made barbarian and semi-barbarian countries dependent on the civilized ones, nations of peasants on nations of bourgeois, the East on the West.

The bourgeoisie keeps more and more doing away with the scattered state of the population, of the means of production, and of property. It has agglomerated population, centralized means of production, and has concentrated property in a few hands. The necessary consequence of this was political centralization. Independent, or but loosely connected provinces, with separate interests, laws, governments, and systems of taxation, became lumped together into one nation, with one government, one code of laws, one national class-interest, one frontier, and one customs-tariff.

The bourgeoisie, during its rule of scarce one hundred years, has created more massive and more colossal productive forces than have all preceding generations together. Subjection of Nature's forces to man, machinery, application of chemistry to industry and agriculture, steam-navigation, railways, electric telegraphs, clearing of whole continents for cultivation, canalization of rivers, whole populations conjured out of the ground—what earlier century had even a presentiment that such productive forces slumbered in the lap of social labor?

We see then: the means of production and of exchange, on whose foundation the bourgeoisie built itself up, were generated in feudal society. At a certain stage in the development of these means of production and of exchange, the conditions under which feudal society produced and exchanged, the feudal organization of agriculture and manufacturing industry, in one word, the feudal relations of property, became no longer compatible with the already developed productive forces; they became so many fetters. They had to be burst asunder; they were burst asunder.

Into their place stepped free competition, accompanied by a social and political constitution adapted to it, and by the economical and political sway of the bourgeois class.

A similar movement is going on before our own eyes. Modern bourgeois society with its relations of production, of exchange and of property, a society that has conjured up such gigantic means of production and of exchange, is like the sorcerer, who is no longer able to control the powers of the nether world whom he has called up by his spells. For many a decade past the history of industry and commerce is but the history of the revolt of modern productive forces against modern conditions of production, against the property relations that are the conditions for the existence of the bourgeoisie and of its rule. It is enough to mention the commercial crises that by their periodical return put on its trial, each time more threateningly, the existence of the entire bourgeois society. In these crises a great part not only of the existing products, but also of the previously created productive forces, are periodically destroyed. In these crises there breaks out an epidemic that, in all earlier epochs would have seemed an absurdity —the epidemic of over-production. Society suddenly finds itself put back into a state of momentary barbarism; it appears as if a famine, a universal war of devastation had cut off the supply of every means of subsistence; industry and commerce seem to be destroyed; and why? Because there is too much civilization, too much means of subsistence, too much industry, too much commerce. The productive forces at the disposal of society no longer tend to further the development of the conditions of bourgeois property; on the contrary, they have become too powerful for these conditions, by which they are fettered, and so soon as they overcome these fetters, they bring disorder into the whole of bourgeois society, endanger the existence of bourgeois property. The conditions of bourgeois society are too narrow to comprise the wealth created by them. And how does the bourgeoisie get over these crises? On the one hand by enforced destruction of a mass of productive forces; on the other, by the conquest of new markets, and by the more thorough exploitation of the old ones. That is to say, by paving the way for more extensive and more destructive crises, and by diminishing the means whereby crises are prevented.

The weapons with which the bourgeoisie felled feudalism to the ground are now turned against the bourgeoisie itself.

But not only has the bourgeoisie forged the weapons that bring death to itself; it has also called into existence the men who are to wield those weapons—the modern working class—the proletarians.

In proportion as the bourgeoisie, i.e., capital, is developed, in the same proportion is the proletariat, the modern working class, developed—a class of laborers, who live only so long as they find work, and who find work only so long as their labor increases capital. These laborers, who must sell themselves piecemeal, are a commodity, like every other article of commerce, and are consequently exposed to all the vicissitudes of competition, to all the fluctuations of the market.

Owing to the extensive use of machinery and to division of labor, the work of the proletarians has lost all individual character, and, consequently, all charm for the workman. He becomes an appendage of the machine, and it is only the most simple, most monotonous, and most easily acquired knack, that is required of him. Hence, the cost of production of a workman is restricted, almost entirely, to the means of subsistence that he requires for his maintenance, and for the propagation of his race. But the price of a commodity, and therefore also of labor, is equal to its cost of production. In proportion, therefore, as the repulsiveness of the work increases, the wage decreases. Nay more, in proportion as the use of machinery and division of labor increases, in the same proportion the burden of toil also increases, whether by prolongation of the working hours, by increase of the work exacted in a given time, or by increased speed of the machinery, etc.

Modern industry has converted the little workshop of the patriarchal master into the great factory of the industrial capitalist. Masses of laborers, crowded into the factory, are organized like soldiers. As privates of the industrial army they are placed under the command of a perfect hierarchy of officers and sergeants. Not only are they slaves of the bourgeois class, and of the bourgeois State; they are daily and hourly enslaved by the machine, by the overlooker, and, above all, by the individual bourgeois manufacturer himself. The more openly this despotism proclaims gain to be its end and aim, the more petty, the more hateful, and the more embittering it is.

The less the skill and exertion of strength implied in manual labor, in other words, the more modern industry becomes developed, the more is the labor of men superseded by that of women. Differences of age and sex have no longer any distinctive social validity for the working class. All are instruments of labor, more or less expensive to use, according to their age and sex.

No sooner is the exploitation of the laborer by the manufacturer, so far, at an end, that he receives his wages in cash, than he is set upon by the other portions of the bourgeoisie, the landlord, the shopkeeper, the pawnbroker, etc.

The lower strata of the middle class—the small tradespeople, shopkeepers, and retired tradesmen generally, the handicraftsmen and peasants—all these sink gradually into the proletariat, partly because their diminutive capital does not suffice for the scale on which Modern Industry is carried on, and is swamped in the competition with the large capitalists, partly because their specialized skill is rendered worthless by new methods of production. Thus the proletariat is recruited from all classes of the population.

The proletariat goes through various stages of development. With its birth begins its struggle with the bourgeoisie. At first the contest is carried on by individual laborers, then by the workpeople of a factory, then by the operatives of one trade, in one locality, against the individual bourgeois who directly exploits them. They direct their attacks not against the bourgeois conditions of production, but against the instruments of production themselves; they destroy imported wares that compete with their labor, they smash to pieces machinery, they set factories ablaze, they seek to restore by force the vanished status of the workman of the Middle Ages.

At this stage the laborers still form an incoherent mass scattered over the whole country, and broken up by their mutual competition. If anywhere they unite to form more compact bodies, this is not yet the consequence of their own active union, but of the union of the bourgeoisie, which class, in order to attain its own political ends, is compelled to set the whole proletariat in motion, and is moreover yet, for a time, able to do so. At this stage, therefore, the proletarians do not fight their enemies, but the enemies of their enemies, the remnants of absolute monarchy, the landowners, the non-industrial bourgeois, the petty bourgeoisie. Thus the whole historical movement is concentrated in the hands of the bourgeoisie; every victory so obtained is a victory for the bourgeoisie.

But with the development of industry the proletariat not only increases in number; it becomes concentrated in greater masses, its strength grows, and it feels that strength more. The various interests and conditions of life within the ranks of the proletariat are more and more equalized, in proportion as machinery obliterates all distinctions of labor, and nearly everywhere reduces wages to the same low level. The growing competition among the bourgeois, and the resulting commercial crises, make the wages of the workers ever more fluctuating. The unceasing improvement of machinery, ever more rapidly developing, makes their livelihood more and more precarious; the collisions between individual workmen and individual bourgeois take more and more the character of collisions between two classes. Thereupon the workers begin to form combinations (Trades' Unions) against the bourgeois; they club together in order to keep up the rate of wages; they found permanent associations in order to make provision beforehand for these occasional revolts. Here and there the contest breaks out into riots.

Now and then the workers are victorious, but only for a time. The real fruit of their battle lies, not in the immediate result, but in the ever-expanding union of the workers. This union is helped on by the improved means of communication that are created by modern industry and that place the workers of different localities in contact with one another. It was just this contact that was needed to centralize the numerous local struggles, all of the same character, into one national struggle between classes. But every class struggle is a political struggle. And that union, to attain which the burghers of the Middle Ages, with their miserable highways, required centuries, the modern proletarians, thanks to railways, achieve in a few years.

This organization of the proletarians into a class, and consequently into a political party, is continually being upset again by the competition between the workers themselves. But it ever rises up again, stronger, firmer, mightier. It compels legislative recognition of particular interests of the workers, by taking advantage of the divisions among the bourgeoisie itself. Thus the ten-hours' bill in England was carried.

Altogether collisions between the classes of the old society further, in many ways, the course of development of the proletariat. The bourgeoisie finds itself involved in a constant battle. At first with the aristocracy; later on, with those portions of the bourgeoisie itself, whose interests have become antagonistic to the progress of industry; at all times, with the bourgeoisie of foreign countries. In all these battles it sees itself compelled to appeal to the proletariat, to ask for its help, and thus, to drag it into the political arena. The bourgeoisie itself, therefore, supplies the proletariat with its own elements of political and general education, in other words, it furnishes the proletariat with weapons for fighting the bourgeoisie.

Further, as we have already seen, entire sections of the ruling classes are, by the advance of industry, precipitated into the proletariat, or are at least threatened in their conditions of existence. These also supply the proletariat with fresh elements of enlightenment and progress.

Finally, in times when the class struggle nears the decisive hour, the process of dissolution going on within the ruling class, in fact within the whole range of old society, assumes such a violent, glaring character, that a small section of the ruling class cuts itself adrift, and joins the revolutionary class, the class that holds the future in its hands. Just as, therefore, at an earlier period, a section of the nobility went over to the bourgeoisie, so now a portion of the bourgeoisie goes over to the proletariat, and in particular, a portion of the bourgeois ideologists, who have raised themselves to the level of comprehending theoretically the historical movement as a whole.

Of all the classes that stand face to face with the bourgeoisie today, the proletariat alone is a really revolutionary class. The other classes decay and finally disappear in the face of modern industry; the proletariat is its special and essential product.

The lower-middle class, the small manufacturer, the shopkeeper, the artisan, the peasant, all these fight against the bourgeoisie, to save from extinction their existence as fractions of the middle class. They are therefore not revolutionary, but conservative. Nay more, they are reactionary, for they try to roll back the wheel of history. If by chance they are revolutionary, they are so only in view of their impending transfer into the proletariat, they thus defend not their present, but their future interests, they desert their own standpoint to place themselves at that of the proletariat.

The "dangerous class," the social scum, that passively rotting mass thrown off by the lowest layers of old society, may, here and there, be swept into the movement by a proletarian revolution; its conditions of life, however, prepare it far more for the part of a bribed tool of reactionary intrigue.

In the conditions of the proletariat, those of old society at large are already virtually swamped. The proletarian is without property; his relation to his wife and children has no longer anything in common with the bourgeois family-relations; modern industrial labor, modern subjection to capital, the same in England as in France, in America as in Germany, has stripped him of every trace of national character. Law, morality, religion, are to him so many bourgeois prejudices, behind which lurk in ambush just as many bourgeois interests.

All the preceding classes that got the upper hand, sought to fortify their already acquired status by subjecting society at large to their conditions of appropriation. The proletarians cannot become masters of the productive forces of society, except by abolishing their own previous mode of appropriation, and thereby also every other previous mode of appropriation. They have nothing of their own to secure and to fortify; their mission is to destroy all previous securities for, and insurances of, individual property.

All previous historical movements were movements of minorities, or in the interest of minorities. The proletarian movement is the self-conscious, independent movement of the immense majority, in the interest of the immense majority. The proletariat, the lowest stratum of our present society, cannot stir, cannot raise itself up, without the whole superincumbent strata of official society being sprung into the air.

Though not in substance, yet in form, the struggle of the proletariat with the bourgeoisie is at first a national struggle. The proletariat of each country must, of course, first of all settle matters with its own bourgeoisie.

In depicting the most general phases of the development of the proletariat, we traced the more or less veiled civil war, raging within existing society, up to the point where that war breaks out into open revolution, and where the violent overthrow of the bourgeoisie lays the foundation for the sway of the proletariat.

Hitherto, every form of society has been based, as we have already seen, on the antagonism of oppressing and oppressed classes. But in order to oppress a class, certain conditions must be assured to it under which it can, at least, continue its lavish existence. The serf, in the period of serfdom, raised himself to membership in the commune, just as the petty bourgeois, under the yoke of feudal absolutism, managed to develop into a bourgeois. The modern laborer, on the contrary, instead of rising with the process of industry, sinks deeper and deeper below the conditions of existence of his own class. He becomes a pauper, and pauperism develops more rapidly than population and wealth. And here it becomes evident, that the bourgeoisie is unfit any longer to be the ruling class in society, and to impose its conditions of existence upon society as an overriding law. It is unfit to rule because it is incompetent to assure an existence to its slave within his slavery, because it cannot help letting him sink into such a state, that it has to feed him, instead of being fed by him. Society can no longer live under this bourgeoisie, in other words, its existence is no longer compatible with society.

The essential condition for the existence, and for the sway of the bourgeois class, is the formation and augmentation of capital; the condition for capital is wage-labor. Wage-labor rests exclusively on competition between the laborers. The advance of industry, whose involuntary promoter is the bourgeoisie, replaces the isolation of the laborers, due to competition, by their revolutionary combination, due to association. The development of Modern Industry, therefore, cuts from under its feet the very foundation on which the bourgeoisie produces and appropriates products. What the bourgeoisie, therefore, produces, above all, are its own grave-diggers. Its fall and the victory of the proletariat are equally inevitable.

BERTRAND RUSSELL / Marx and Socialist Doctrine*

Socialism, like everything else that is vital, is rather a tendency than a strictly definable body of doctrine. A definition of social-ism is sure either to include some views which many would regard as not socialistic, or to exclude others which claim to be included. But I think we shall come nearest to the essence of socialism by defining it as the advocacy of communal ownership of land and capital. Communal ownership may mean ownership by a demo-cratic state, but cannot be held to include ownership by any state which is not democratic. Communal ownership may also be un-derstood, as anarchist communism understands it, in the sense of ownership by the free association of the men and women in a community without those compulsory powers which are necessary to constitute a state. Some socialists expect communal ownership to arrive suddenly and completely by a catastrophic revolution, while others expect it to come gradually, first in one industry, then in another. Some insist upon the necessity of completeness in the acquisition of land and capital by the public, while others would be content to see lingering islands of private ownership, provided they were not too extensive or powerful. What all forms have in common is democracy and the abolition, virtual or com-plete, of the present capitalistic system. The distinction between

* From Russell, *Roads to Freedom* (New York, Barnes and Noble, 1966), Chap. 1. First published in 1918. Portions of the original chapter omitted.

socialists, anarchists, and Syndicalists turns largely upon the kind
of democracy which they desire. Orthodox Socialists are content
with parliamentary democracy in the sphere of government, holding that the evils apparent in this form of constitution at present
would disappear with the disappearance of capitalism. Anarchists
and Syndicalists, on the other hand, object to the whole parliamentary machinery, and aim at a different method of regulating
the political affairs of the community. But all alike are democratic in the sense that they aim at abolishing every kind of privilege and every kind of artificial inequality: all alike are cham-
pions of the wage-earner in existing society. All three also have
much in common in their economic doctrine. All three regard
capital and the wages system as a means of exploiting the laborer
in the interests of the possessing classes, and hold that communal
ownership, in one form or another, is the only means of bringing
freedom to the producers. But within the framework of this common doctrine there are many divergencies, and, even among those
who are strictly to be called Socialists, there is a very considerable
diversity of schools.

Socialism as a power in Europe may be said to begin with
Marx. It is true that before this time there were socialist theories,
both in England and in France. It is also true that in France,
during the revolution of 1848, socialism for a brief period acquired considerable influence in the State. But the Socialists who
preceded Marx tended to indulge in Utopian dreams and failed
to found any strong or stable political party. To Marx, in collab-
oration with Engels, are due both the formulation of a coherent
body of socialist doctrine, sufficiently true or plausible to dominate the minds of vast numbers of men, and the formation of the
International Socialist movement, which has continued to grow
in all European countries throughout the last fifty years.

In order to understand Marx's doctrine, it is necessary to know
something of the influences which formed his outlook. He was
born in 1818, at Treves, in the Rhine Provinces, his father being
a legal official, a Jew who had nominally accepted Christianity.
Marx studied jurisprudence, philosophy, political economy, and
history at various German universities. In philosophy he imbibed

the doctrines of Hegel, who was then at the height of his fame, and something of these doctrines dominated his thought throughout his life. Like Hegel, he saw in history the development of an Idea. He conceived the changes in the world as forming a logical development, in which one phase passes by revolution into another, which is its antithesis—a conception which gave to his views a certain hard abstractness, and a belief in revolution rather than evolution. But of Hegel's more definite doctrines Marx retained nothing after his youth. He was recognized as a brilliant student, and might have had a prosperous career as a professor or an official but his interest in politics and his radical views led him into more arduous paths. Already in 1842 he became editor of a newspaper, which was suppressed by the Prussian Government early in the following year on account of its advanced opinions. This led Marx to go to Paris, where he became known as a Socialist and acquired a knowledge of his French predecessors.[1] Here in the year 1844 began his lifelong friendship with Engels, who had been hitherto in business in Manchester, where he had become acquainted with English Socialism and had in the main adopted its doctrines.[2] In 1845 Marx was expelled from Paris and went with Engels to live in Brussels. There he formed a German Working Men's Association and edited a paper which was their organ. Through his activities in Brussels he became known to the German Communist League in Paris, who, at the end of 1847, invited him and Engels to draw up for them a mani-

---

[1] Chief among these were Fourier and Saint-Simon, who constructed somewhat fantastic socialistic ideal commonwealths. Proudhon, with whom Marx had some not wholly friendly relations, is to be regarded as a forerunner of the anarchists rather than of orthodox socialism.

[2] Marx mentions the English Socialists with praise in *The Poverty of Philosophy* (1847). They, like him, tend to base their arguments upon a Ricardian theory of value, but they have not his scope or erudition or scientific breadth. Among them may be mentioned Thomas Hodgskin (1787–1869), originally an officer in the Navy, but dismissed for a pamphlet critical of the methods of naval discipline, author of *Labour Defended Against the Claims of Capital* (1825), and other works; William Thompson (1785–1833), author of *Inquiry into the Principles of Distribution of Wealth Most Conducive to Human Happiness* (1824), and *Labour Rewarded* (1825); and Piercy Ravenstone, from whom Hodgskin's ideas are largely derived. Perhaps more important than any of these was Robert Owen.

festo, which appeared in January, 1848. This is the famous *Communist Manifesto,* in which for the first time Marx's system is set forth. It appeared at a fortunate moment. In the following month, February, the revolution broke out in Paris, and in March it spread to Germany. Fear of the revolution led the Brussels Government to expel Marx from Belgium, but the German revolution made it possible for him to return to his own country. In Germany he again edited a paper, which again led him into a conflict with the authorities, increasing in severity as the reaction gathered force. In June, 1849, his paper was suppressed, and he was expelled from Prussia. He returned to Paris, but was expelled from there also. This led him to settle in England—at that time an asylum for friends of freedom—and in England, with only brief intervals for purposes of agitation, he continued to live until his death, in 1883. The bulk of his time was occupied in the composition of his great book *Capital.*[3] His other important work during his later years was the formation and spread of the International Working Men's Association. From 1849 onwards the greater part of his time was spent in the British Museum, accumulating, with German patience, the materials for his terrific indictment of capitalist society, but he retained his hold on the International Socialist movement. In several countries he had sons-in-law as lieutenants, like Napoleon's brothers, and in the various internal contests that arose his will generally prevailed.

The most essential of Marx's doctrines may be reduced to three: first, what is called the materialistic interpretation of history; second, the law of the concentration of capital; and, third, the class war.

1. *The Materialistic Interpretation of History.*—Marx holds that in the main all the phenomena of human society have their origin in material conditions, and these he takes to be embodied in economic systems. Political constitutions, laws, religions, philosophies—all these he regards as, in their broad outlines, expressions of the economic *régime* in the society that gives rise to them. It would be unfair to represent him as maintaining that the conscious economic motive is the only one of importance; it is rather

---

3 The first and most important volume appeared in 1867: the other two volumes were published posthumously (1885 and 1894).

that economics mold character and opinion, and are thus the prime source of much that appears in consciousness to have no connection with them. He applies his doctrine in particular to two revolutions, one in the past, the other in the future. The revolution in the past is that of the bourgeoisie against feudalism, which finds its expression, according to him, particularly in the French Revolution. The one in the future is the revolution of the wage-earners, or proletariat, against the bourgeoisie, which is to establish the Socialist Commonwealth. The whole movement of history is viewed by him as necessary, as the effect of material causes operating upon human beings. He does not so much advocate the socialist revolution as predict it. He holds, it is true, that it will be beneficent, but he is much more concerned to prove that it must inevitably come. The same sense of necessity is visible in his exposition of the evils of the capitalist system. He does not blame capitalists for the cruelties of which he shows them to have been guilty; he merely points out that they are under an inherent necessity to behave cruelly so long as private ownership of land and capital continues. But their tyranny will not last forever, for it generates the forces that must in the end overthrow it.

2. *The Law of the Concentration of Capital.*—Marx pointed out that capitalist undertakings tend to grow larger and larger. He foresaw the substitution of trusts for free competition, and predicted that the number of capitalist enterprises must diminish as the magnitude of single enterprises increased. He supposed that this process must involve a diminution, not only in the number of businesses, but also in the number of capitalists. Indeed, he usually spoke as though each business were owned by a single man. Accordingly, he expected that men would be continually driven from the ranks of the capitalists into those of the proletariat, and that the capitalists, in the course of time, would grow numerically weaker and weaker. He applied this principle not only to industry but also to agriculture. He expected to find the landowners growing fewer and fewer while their estates grew larger and larger. This process was to make more and more glaring the evils and injustices of the capitalist system, and to stimulate more and more the forces of opposition.

3. *The Class War.*—Marx conceives the wage-earner and the

capitalist in a sharp antithesis. He imagines that every man is, or must soon become, wholly the one or wholly the other. The wage-earner, who possesses nothing, is exploited by the capitalists, who possess everything. As the capitalist system works itself out and its nature becomes more clear, the opposition of bourgeoisie and proletariat becomes more and more marked. The two classes, since they have antagonistic interests, are forced into a class war which generates within the capitalist *régime* internal forces of disruption. The working men learn gradually to combine against their exploiters, first locally, then nationally, and at last internationally. When they have learned to combine internationally they must be victorious. They will then decree that all land and capital shall be owned in common; exploitation will cease; the tyranny of the owners of wealth will no longer be possible; there will no longer be any division of society into classes, and all men will be free.

All these ideas are already contained in the *Communist Manifesto,* a work of the most amazing vigor and force, setting forth with terse compression the titanic forces of the world, their epic battle, and the inevitable consummation. This work is of such importance in the development of socialism and gives such an admirable statement of the doctrines set forth at greater length and with more pedantry in *Capital,* that its salient passages must be known by anyone who wishes to understand the hold which Marxian socialism has acquired over the intellect and imagination of a large proportion of working-class leaders.

"A spectre is haunting Europe," it begins, "the spectre of Communism. All the Powers of old Europe have entered into a holy alliance to exorcise this spectre; Pope and Czar, Metternich and Guizot, French Radicals and German police-spies. Where is the party in opposition that has not been decried as communistic by its opponents in power? Where the Opposition that has not hurled back the branding reproach of Communism against the more advanced opposition parties, as well as against its reactionary adversaries?"

The existence of a class war is nothing new: "The history of all hitherto existing society is the history of class struggles." In these struggles the fight "each time ended, either in a revolutionary reconstitution of society at large, or in the common ruin of the contending classes."

"Our epoch, the epoch of the bourgeoisie ... has simplified the class antagonisms. Society as a whole is more and more splitting up into two great hostile camps, into two great classes directly facing each other: Bourgeoisie and Proletariat." *

The Communists, says Marx, stand for the proletariat as a whole. They are international. "The Communists are further reproached with desiring to abolish countries and nationality. The working men have no country. We cannot take from them what they have not got."

The immediate aim of the Communists is the conquest of political power by the proletariat. "The theory of the Communists may be summed up in the single sentence: Abolition of private property."

The materialistic interpretation of history is used to answer such charges as that communism is anti-Christian. "The charges against Communism made from a religious, a philosophical, and, generally, from an ideological standpoint, are not deserving of serious examination. Does it require deep intuition to comprehend that man's ideas, views, and conceptions, in one word, man's consciousness, changes with every change in the conditions of his material existence, in his social relations, and in his social life?"

The attitude of the Manifesto to the State is not altogether easy to grasp. "The executive of the modern State," we are told, "is but a Committee for managing the common affairs of the whole bourgeoisie." Nevertheless the first step for the proletariat must be to acquire control of the State. "We have seen above, that the first step in the revolution by the working class, is to raise the

* Russell here quotes extensively from sections of the Manifesto dealing with the history of the fall of feudalism; the growth of the bourgeoisie as a new force; the causes of the destitution of the proletariat; and the manner of growth of the class struggle. See the first part of the Manifesto, reprinted as the preceding selection in this Reader—Ed.

proletariat to the position of ruling class, to win the battle of democracy. The proletariat will use its political supremacy, to wrest, by degrees, all capital from the bourgeoisie, to centralize all instruments of production in the hands of the State, i.e., of the proletariat organized as the ruling class; and to increase the total of productive forces as rapidly as possible."

The Manifesto passes on to an immediate program of reforms, which would in the first instance much increase the power of the existing State, but it is contended that when the socialist revolution is accomplished, the State, as we know it, will have ceased to exist. As Engels says elsewhere, when the proletariat seizes the power of the State "it puts an end to all differences of class and antagonisms of class, and consequently also puts an end to the State as a State." Thus, although State Socialism might, in fact, be the outcome of the proposals of Marx and Engels, they cannot themselves be accused of any glorification of the State.

The Manifesto ends with an appeal to the wage-earners of the world to rise on behalf of communism. "The Communists disdain to conceal their views and aims. They openly declare that their ends can be attained only by the forcible overthrow of all existing social conditions. Let the ruling classes tremble at a Communistic revolution. The proletarians have nothing to lose but their chains. They have a world to win. Working men of all countries, unite!"

In all the great countries of the Continent, except Russia, a revolution followed quickly on the publication of the *Communist Manifesto,* but the revolution was not economic or international except at first in France. Everywhere else it was inspired by the ideas of nationalism. Accordingly, the rulers of the world, momentarily terrified, were able to recover power by fomenting the enmities inherent in the nationalist idea, and everywhere, after a very brief triumph, the revolution ended in war and reaction. The ideas of the *Communist Manifesto* appeared before the world was ready for them, but its authors lived to see the beginnings of the growth of that socialist movement in every country, which has pressed on with increasing force, influencing Governments more and more, dominating the Russian Revolution, and perhaps capable of achieving at no very distant date that international triumph to which the last sentences of the Manifesto summon the wage-earners of the world.

Marx's *magnum opus, Capital,* added bulk and substance to the theses of the *Communist Manifesto.* It contributed the theory of surplus value, which professed to explain the actual mechanism of capitalist exploitation. This doctrine is very complicated, and is scarcely tenable as a contribution to pure theory. It is rather to be viewed as a translation into abstract terms of the hatred with which Marx regarded the system that coins wealth out of human lives, and it is in this spirit, rather than in that of disinterested analysis, that it has been read by its admirers.... A critical examination of the theory of surplus value would require much difficult and abstract discussion of pure economic theory, without having much bearing upon the practical truth or falsehood of socialism; it has therefore seemed impossible within the limits of the present volume. To my mind the best parts of the book are those which deal with economic facts, of which Marx's knowledge was encyclopedic. It was by these facts that he hoped to instill into his disciples that firm and undying hatred that should make them soldiers to the death in the class war. The facts which he accumulates are such as are practically unknown to the vast majority of those who live comfortable lives. They are very terrible facts, and the economic system which generates them must be acknowledged to be a very terrible system. A few examples of his choice of facts will serve to explain the bitterness of many Socialists:

Mr. Broughton Charlton, county magistrate, declared, as chairman of a meeting held at the Assembly Rooms, Nottingham, on the 14th January, 1860, "that there was an amount of privation and suffering among that portion of the population connected with the lace trade, unknown in other parts of the kingdom, indeed, in the civilized world. . . . Children of nine or ten years are dragged from their squalid beds at two, three, or four o'clock in the morning and compelled to work for a bare subsistence until ten, eleven, or twelve at night, their limbs wearing away, their frames dwindling, their faces whitening, and their humanity absolutely sinking into a stone-like torpor, utterly horrible to contemplate." [4]

Three railway men are standing before a London coroner's jury—a guard, an engine-driver, a signalman. A tremendous railway accident has hurried hundreds of passengers into another world. The negligence of the employés is the cause of the misfortune. They declare with one voice before the jury that ten or twelve years before, their labor only lasted eight hours a day. During the past five or six years it has been screwed up to 14, 18, and 20 hours, and under a specially severe pressure of holiday-makers, at times of excursion trains, it often lasted for 40 or 50 hours without a break. They were ordinary men, not Cyclops. At a certain point their labor-power failed. Torpor seized them. Their brain ceased to think, their eyes to see. The thoroughly "respectable" British jurymen answered by a verdict that sent them to the next assizes on a charge of manslaughter, and, in a gentle "rider" to their verdict, expressed the pious hope that the capitalistic magnates of the railways would, in future, be more extravagant in the purchase of a sufficient quantity of labor-power, and more "abstemious," more "self-denying," more "thrifty," in the draining of paid labor-power. [5]

In the last week of June, 1863, all the London daily papers published a paragraph with the "sensational" heading, "Death from simple over-work." It dealt with the death of the milliner, Mary Anne Walkley, 20 years of age, employed in a highly respectable dressmaking establishment, exploited by a lady with the pleasant name of Elise. The old, often-told story, was once more recounted. This girl worked, on an average, 16½ hours, during the season often 30 hours, without a break, whilst her failing labor-power was revived by occasional supplies of sherry, port, or coffee. It was just now the height of the season. It was necessary to conjure up in the twinkling of an eye the gorgeous dresses for the noble ladies bidden to the ball in honor of the newly imported Princess of Wales. Mary Anne Walkley had worked without intermission for 26½ hours, with 60 other girls, 30 in one room, that only afforded ⅓ of the cubic feet of air required for them. At night, they slept in pairs in one of the stifling holes into which the bedroom was divided by partitions of board. And this was one of the

4 Vol. 1, p. 227.
5 Vol. 1, pp. 237–238.

best millinery establishments in London. Mary Anne Walkley fell ill on the Friday, died on Sunday, without, to the astonishment of Madame Elise, having previously completed the work in hand. The doctor, Mr. Keys, called too late to the deathbed, duly bore witness before the coroner's jury that "Mary Anne Walkley had died from long hours of work in an overcrowded workroom, and a too small and badly ventilated bedroom." In order to give the doctor a lesson in good manners, the coroner's jury thereupon brought in a verdict that "the deceased had died of apoplexy, but there was reason to fear that her death had been accelerated by over-work in an overcrowded workroom, &c." "Our white slaves," cried the *Morning Star,* the organ of the free-traders Cobden and Bright, "our white slaves, who are toiled into the grave, for the most part silently pine and die." [6]

Edward VI: A statute of the first year of his reign, 1547, ordains that if anyone refuses to work, he shall be condemned as a slave to the person who has denounced him as an idler. The master shall feed his slave on bread and water, weak broth and such refuse meat as he thinks fit. He has the right to force him to do any work, no matter how disgusting, with whip and chains. If the slave is absent a fortnight, he is condemned to slavery for life and is to be branded on forehead or back with the letter S; if he runs away thrice, he is to be executed as a felon. The master can sell him, bequeath him, let him out on hire as a slave, just as any other personal chattel or cattle. If the slaves attempt anything against the masters, they are also to be executed. Justices of the peace, on information, are to hunt the rascals down. If it happens that a vagabond has been idling about for three days, he is to be taken to his birthplace, branded with a redhot iron with the letter V on the breast and be set to work, in chains, in the streets or at some other labor. If the vagabond gives a false birthplace, he is then to become the slave for life of this place, of its inhabitants, or its corporation, and be branded with an S. All persons have the right to take away the children of the vagabonds and to keep them as apprentices, the young men until the 24th year, the girls until the 20th. If they run away, they are to become up to this age the slaves of their masters, who can put them in irons, whip them, &c., if they like. Every master may put an iron ring round the neck, arms or legs of his slave, by which to know him more easily and

3 Vol. 1, pp. 239–240.

to be more certain of him. The last part of this statute provides, that certain poor people may be employed by a place or by persons, who are willing to give them food and drink and to find them work. This kind of parish-slaves was kept up in England until far into the nineteenth century under the name of "roundsmen." [7]

Page after page and chapter after chapter of facts of this nature, each brought up to illustrate some fatalistic theory which Marx professes to have proved by exact reasoning, cannot but stir into fury any passionate working-class reader, and into unbearable shame any possessor of capital in whom generosity and justice are not wholly extinct.

Almost at the end of the volume, in a very brief chapter called "Historical Tendency of Capitalist Accumulation," Marx allows one moment's glimpse of the hope that lies beyond the present horror:

As soon as this process of transformation has sufficiently decomposed the old society from top to bottom, as soon as the laborers are turned into proletarians, their means of labor into capital, as soon as the capitalist mode of production stands on its own feet, then the further socialization of labor and further transformation of the land and other means of production into socially exploited and, therefore, common means of production, as well as the further expropriation of private proprietors, takes a new form. That which is now to be expropriated is no longer the laborer working for himself, but the capitalist exploiting many laborers. This expropriation is accomplished by the action of the immanent laws of capitalistic production itself, by the centralization of capital. One capitalist always kills many. Hand in hand with this centralization, or this expropriation of many capitalists by few, develop, on an ever extending scale, the cooperative form of the labor-process, the conscious technical application of science, the methodical cultivation of the soil, the transformation of the instruments of labor into instruments of labor only usable in common, the economizing of all means of production by their use as the means of production of combined, socialized labor, the entanglement of all peoples in the net of the world-market, and with

7 Vol. 1, pp. 758–759.

this, the international character of the capitalistic *régime*. Along with the constantly diminishing number of the magnates of capital, who usurp and monopolize all advantages of this process of transformation, grows the mass of misery, oppression, slavery, degradation, exploitation; but with this too grows the revolt of the working-class, a class always increasing in numbers, and disciplined, united, organized by the very mechanism of the process of capitalist production itself. The monopoly of capital becomes a fetter upon the mode of production, which has sprung up and flourished along with, and under it. Centralization of the means of production and socialization of labor at last reach a point where they become incompatible with their capitalist integument. This integument is burst asunder. The knell of capitalist private property sounds. The expropriators are expropriated.[8]

That is all. Hardly another word from beginning to end is allowed to relieve the gloom, and in this relentless pressure upon the mind of the reader lies a great part of the power which this book has acquired.

Two questions are raised by Marx's work. First, is his law of historical development true? Second, is socialism desirable? The second of these questions is quite independent of the first. Marx professes to prove that socialism *must* come, but scarcely concerns himself to argue that when it comes it will be a good thing. It may be, however, that if it comes, it will be a good thing, even though all Marx's arguments to prove that it must come should be at fault. In actual fact, time has shown many flaws in Marx's theories. The development of the world has been sufficiently like his prophecy to prove him a man of very unusual penetration, but has not been sufficiently like to make either political or economic history exactly such as he predicted that it would be. Nationalism, so far from diminishing, has increased, and has failed to be conquered by the cosmopolitan tendencies which Marx rightly discerned in finance. Although big businesses have grown bigger and have over a great area reached the stage of monopoly, yet the number of shareholders in such enterprises is so large that

the actual number of individuals interested in the capitalist system has continually increased. Moreover, though large firms have
grown larger, there has been a simultaneous increase in firms of
medium size. Meanwhile the wage-earners, who were, according to
Marx, to have remained at the bare level of subsistence at which
they were in the England of the first half of the nineteenth century, have instead profited by the general increase of wealth,
though in a lesser degree than the capitalists. The supposed iron
law of wages has been proved untrue, so far as labor in civilized
countries is concerned. If we wish now to find examples of capitalist cruelty analogous to those with which Marx's book is filled,
we shall have to go for most of our material to the Tropics, or at
any rate to regions where there are men of "inferior" races to exploit. Again: the skilled worker of the present day is an aristocrat
in the world of labor. It is a question with him whether he shall
ally himself with the unskilled worker against the capitalist, or
with the capitalist against the unskilled worker. Very often he is
himself a capitalist in a small way, and if he is not so individually, his trade union or his friendly society is pretty sure to be so.
Hence the sharpness of the class war has not been maintained.
There are gradations, intermediate ranks between rich and poor
instead of the clear-cut logical antithesis between the workers
who have nothing and the capitalists who have all. Even in Germany, which became the home of orthodox Marxianism and developed a powerful Social-Democratic party, nominally accepting
the doctrine of *Das Kapital* as all but verbally inspired, even
there the enormous increase of wealth in all classes in the years
preceding the war led Socialists to revise their beliefs and to
adopt an evolutionary rather than a revolutionary attitude.
Bernstein, a German Socialist who lived long in England, inaugurated the "Revisionist" movement which at last conquered the
bulk of the party. His criticisms of Marxian orthodoxy are set
forth in his "Evolutionary Socialism" [9] Bernstein's work, as is

[9] "Die Voraussetzungen des Sozialismus und die Aufgaben der Sozial-Demo-
kratie."

In March 1914 Bernstein delivered a lecture in Budapest, in which he withdrew from several of the positions he had taken up (vide Budapest *Volk-
stimne,* March 19, 1914.

common in Broad Church writers, consists largely in showing that the Founders did not hold their doctrines so rigidly as their followers have done. There is much in the writings of Marx and Engels that cannot be fitted into the rigid orthodoxy which grew up among their disciples. Bernstein's main criticisms of these disciples, apart from such as we have already mentioned, consist in a defence of piecemeal action as against revolution. He protests against the attitude of undue hostility to Liberalism which is common among Socialists, and he blunts the edge of the internationalism which undoubtedly is part of the teaching of Marx. The workers, he says, have a Fatherland as soon as they become citizens, and on this basis he defends that degree of nationalism which the war has since shown to be prevalent in the ranks of Socialists. He even goes so far as to maintain that European nations have a right to tropical territory owing to their higher civilization. Such doctrines diminish revolutionary ardor and tend to transform Socialists into a left wing of the Liberal Party. But the increasing prosperity of wage-earners before the war made these developments inevitable. Whether the war will have altered conditions in this respect, it is as yet impossible to know. Bernstein concludes with the wise remark that: "We have to take working men as they are. And they are neither so universally paupers as was set out in the *Communist Manifesto,* nor so free from prejudices and weaknesses as their courtiers wish to make us believe."

Bernstein represents the decay of Marxian orthodoxy from within; Syndicalism represents an attack against it from without, from the standpoint of a doctrine which professes to be even more radical and more revolutionary than that of Marx and Engels. The attitude of Syndicalists to Marx may be seen in Sorel's little book *La Décomposition du Marxisme,* and in his larger work, *Reflections on Violence,* authorized translation by T. E. Hulme (Allen & Unwin, 1915). After quoting Bernstein, with approval insofar as he criticizes Marx, Sorel proceeds to other criticisms of a different order. He points out (what is true) that Marx's theoretical economics remain very near to Manchesterism: the orthodox political economy of his youth was accepted by him on many points on which it is now known to be wrong. According to Sorel, the really essential thing in Marx's teaching is the class war. Whoever keeps this alive is keeping alive the spirit of socialism much more truly than those who adhere to the letter of Social Democratic orthodoxy. On the basis of the class war, French Syndicalists developed a criticism of Marx which goes much deeper than those that we have been hitherto considering. Marx's views on historical development may have been in a greater or less degree mistaken in fact, and yet the economic and political system which he sought to create might be just as desirable as his followers suppose. Syndicalism, however, criticizes, not only Marx's views of fact, but also the goal at which he aims and the general nature of the means which he recommends. Marx's ideas were formed at a time when democracy did not yet exist. It was in the very year in which *Das Kapital* appeared that urban working men first got the vote in England and universal suffrage was granted by Bismarck in Northern Germany. It was natural that great hopes should be entertained as to what democracy would achieve. Marx, like the orthodox economists, imagines that men's opinions are guided by a more or less enlightened view of economic self-interest, or rather of economic class interest. A long experience of the workings of political democracy has shown that in this respect Disraeli and Bismarck were shrewder judges of human nature than either Liberals or Socialists. It has become increasingly difficult to put trust in the State as a means to liberty, or in political parties as instruments sufficiently powerful to force the State into the service of the people. The modern State, says Sorel, "is a body of intellectuals, which is invested with privileges, and which possesses means of the kind called political for defending itself against the attacks made on it by other groups of intellectuals, eager to possess the profits of public employment. Parties are constituted in order to acquire the conquest of these employments, and they are analogous to the State." [10]

Syndicalists aim at organizing men, not by party, but by occupation. This, they say, alone represents the true conception and method of the class war. Accordingly they despise all *political* action through the medium of Parliament and elections: the kind

10 *La Décomposition du Marxisme,* p. 53.

of action that they recommend is direct action by the revolutionary syndicate or trade union. The battle cry of industrial *versus* political action has spread far beyond the ranks of French Syndicalism. It is to be found in the IWW in America, and among Industrial Unionists and Guild Socialists in Great Britain. Those who advocate it for the most part aim also at a different goal from that of Marx. They believe that there can be no adequate individual freedom where the State is all-powerful, even if the State be a socialist one. Some of them are out-and-out Anarchists, who wish to see the State wholly abolished; others only wish to curtail its authority. Owing to this movement, opposition to Marx, which from the Anarchist side existed from the first, has grown very strong.

12 / THE END OF IDEOLOGY OR OF LIBERALISM?

C. WRIGHT MILLS / Liberal Values in the Modern World*

Most of us now live as spectators in a world without political interlude: fear of total permanent war stops our kind of morally oriented politics. Our spectatorship means that personal, active experience often seems politically useless and even unreal. This is a time when frustration seems to be in direct ratio to understanding, a time of cultural mediocrity when the levels of public sensibility have sunk below sight. It is a time of irresponsibility, organized and unorganized; when common sense, anchored in fast-outmoded experience, has become myopic and irrelevant. Nobody feels secure in a simple place; nobody feels secure and there is no simple place.

It is a time when no terms of acceptance are available, but also no terms of rejection: those on top seem stunned, distracted, and bewildered, and don't know what to do. But what is much more damaging to us: those on the bottom are also without leaders, without counter-ideas, don't know what to do, do not have real demands to make of those in key positions of power.

Whatever the political promises of labor and leftward forces fifteen years ago, they have not been fulfilled; whatever leadership they have developed has hidden itself for illusory safety, or

* From Irving L. Horowitz, ed., *Power, Politics and People* (New York, Oxford University Press, 1963), pp. 187–195.

been buried by events it neither understands nor wishes to control. Organized labor in the forties and early fifties has been mainly another adaptive and adapting element. What goes on domestically may briefly be described in terms of the main drift toward a permanent war economy in a garrison state.

Internationally, of course, the world of nations has been polarized into two dead-locked powers, with no prospects of a structured peace, with a penumbra of variously graded and variously dependent satellites, puppets, and vacuums. For the first time in its easy history, the United States finds itself a nation in a military neighborhood, having common frontiers with a big rival. The United States is a sea and air power from an external position; wherever it turns, it faces a vast land power with an internal position. In the meantime, Europe has become a virtual colony, held by military force and economic dependence, and neither in the West nor in the East do U.S. spokesmen seem to have ideas and policies that have genuine appeal to the people residing there.

Internationally and domestically, the death of political ideas in the United States coincides with the general intellectual vacuum to underpin our malaise. Insofar as ideas are involved in our political impasse, these ideas center in the nature and present-day situation of liberalism. For liberalism is at once the main line of our intellectual heritage and our official political philosophy. I shall not here attempt a full analysis of liberalism's connection with the modern malaise. I only want to lay out some key themes, which I believe must be taken into account in any examination of liberalism today.

I

Like any social philosophy, liberalism can conveniently be understood and discussed: (1) as an articulation of *ideals* which, no matter what its level of generality, operates as a sort of moral optic and set of guidelines for judgments of men, movements and events; (2) as a *theory*, explicit or implied, of how a society works, of its important elements and how they are related, of its key conflicts and how they are resolved; (3) as a social phenomenon, that is, as an *ideology* or political rhetoric—justifying certain institutions and practices, demanding and expecting others. In these terms what is the situation of liberalism today?

As a set of articulated *ideals,* liberalism has been and is a major part of "the secular tradition of the west." As a political *rhetoric,* liberalism has been the ideology of the rising middle class. As a *theory* of society, liberalism is confined in relevance to the heroic epoch of the middle class. These points are connected, for as a carrier of ideals, liberalism has been detached from any tenable theory of modern society, and however engaging in its received condition, it is no longer a useful guideline to the future. For the eighteenth and part of the nineteenth centuries, liberal theory did clarify and offer insight; for the twentieth century, it just as often confuses.

II

Liberalism, as a set of ideals, is still viable, and even compelling to Western men. That is one reason why it has become a common denominator of American political rhetoric; but there is another reason. The ideals of liberalism have been divorced from any realities of modern social structure that might serve as the means of their realization. Everybody can easily agree on general ends; it is more difficult to agree on means and the relevance of various means to the ends articulated. The detachment of liberalism from the facts of a going society make it an excellent mask for those who do not, cannot, or will not do what would have to be done to realize its ideals.

As a kind of political rhetoric, liberalism has been banalized: now it is commonly used by everyone who talks in public for every divergent and contradictory purpose. Today we hear liberals say that one liberal can be "for," and another liberal "against," a vast range of contradictory political propositions. What this means is that liberalism as a common denominator of American political rhetoric, is without coherent content; that, in the process of its banalization, its goals have been so formalized as to provide no clear moral optic. The crisis of liberalism (and of American political reflection) is due to liberalism's success in becoming the official language for all public statement. To this fact was added its use in the New Deal Era when, in close contact with power, liberalism became administrative. Its crisis in lack of clarity is underpinned by its use by all interests, classes, and parties.

It is in this situation that professional liberals sometimes make a fetish of indecision, which they would call open-mindedness, as against inflexibility; of the absence of criteria, which they would call tolerance, as against dogmatism; of the formality and hence political irrelevance of criteria, which they would call "speaking broadly," as against "details."

We may not, of course, dismiss liberalism merely because it is a common denominator of political rhetoric. Its wide use as justification limits the choices and, to some extent, guides the decisions of those in authority. For if it is the common denominator, all powerful decisions made in the open must be justified in its terms, and this may restrain the deciders even if they do not "believe in it." For men are influenced in their use of authority by the rhetoric they feel they must employ. The leaders as well as the led, and even the mythmakers, are influenced by prevailing rhetorics of justification.

Liberals have repeatedly articulated a secular humanism, stressing the priceless value of the individual personality, and the right of each individual to be dealt with in accordance with rational and understandable laws, to which all power is also subject. They have been humanist in the sense that they see man as the measure of all things: policies and events are good or bad in terms of their effect on men; institutions and societies are to be judged in terms of what they mean to and for the individual human being. Liberals have assumed that men should control their own life-fates. It is in terms of this value that the entire concern with consent to authority and the opposition to violence should be understood. All loyalties to specific movements and organizations tend, for the liberal, to be conditional upon his own principles, rather than blindly to an organization. Liberals have assumed that there are rational ways to acquire knowledge, and that substantive reason, anchored in the individual, provides the way out.

As a set of such ideals, liberalism has very heavily contributed to the big tradition of the West, but it is not the sole carrier of this tradition; it is not to be identified with it. And it is a real question whether today it is the most whole-hearted carrier of it, for it is to be greatly doubted that, as a theory of society, liberalism is in a position to lead or help men carry these ideals into realization.

So, if as ideal, liberalism is the secular tradition of the West, as a theory of society, which enables these ideals, it is the ideology of one class inside one epoch. If the moral force of liberalism is still stimulating, its sociological content is weak; it has no theory of society adequate to its moral aims.

III

The assumptions of liberal theories about society have to do with how liberal values could be anchored, with how they could operate as a guide to policy. The liberal ideas of the eighteenth and nineteenth centuries were anchored in several basic assumptions about the condition of modern society that are no longer simple or clear:

(i) Liberalism has assumed that both freedom and security, its key values, flourish in a world of small entrepreneurs. But it is quite clear that one of the most decisive changes over the last hundred years is the enormous increase in the scale of property units. This has meant that the ideals of liberty and of security have changed: absolute liberty to control property has become tyranny. The meaning of freedom, positively put, has to be restated now, not as independence, but as control over that upon which the individual is dependent. Security, once resting on the small holding, has become, in the world of large property, anxiety —anxiety produced by the concentration of process and by the manner of living without expectation of owning. Positively, security must be group-guaranteed; individual men can no longer provide for their own futures.

If a particular ideal of freedom assumes for its realization the dominance of a scatter of small property, then, the social meaning of this ideal is quite different from a statement of freedom that assumes a situation of concentrated property. It is in its theory of society, tacit or explicit, that we find the political content of a social philosophy. If men assume the dominance of huge-scale property, and yet state eighteenth-century ideals, they are off-base. In the kindergarten of political philosophy one learns that the idea of freedom *in general* is more serviceable as politically irrelevant rhetoric than ideal. Twentieth-century problems cannot be solved by eighteenth-century phrases. Liberty is not an *a priori* individual fact, and it has been a social achievement only when liberal ideals have fortunately coincided with social realities.

Order can be reconciled with liberty by an underlying common sentiment, or by a balance of harmoniously competing groups. Common sentiment can grow from slowpaced tradition or be imposed from a powerful center. Competitive balance can be maintained only if each faction remains small enough and equal enough to compete freely. But now there is no common sentiment, and there is no balance, but a lopsided competition between and among dominant factions and midget interests.

Liberalism, in the nineteenth-century epoch of its triumph, never really took into account the changing economic foundations of the political ideals and forms it espoused. That simple fact goes far to explain the decline of liberalism in authoritative cogency. This is the fact upon which Marxism has been correctly focused and upon which it has capitalized.

(ii) Many classic liberals, perhaps especially of the Rousseauian and Jeffersonian persuasion, have assumed the predominance of rural or "small city states," in brief, of a small-scale community. Liberal discussion of the general will, and liberal notions of "public opinion" usually rest on such assumptions. We no longer live in this sort of small-scale world.

(iii) A third assumption about society, characteristic of classic liberalism, has been the stress upon the autonomy of different institutional orders. In the beginning, as with Locke, it would split off religious institutions from the political, so that the political justifications, whatever they may be, had to be secular. Later on, the economic order was split from the political order, in the classic case of *laissez-faire*, perhaps coming to a head in the early philosophical radicals in England. But that was not the end of making different institutional orders autonomous. The kinship order was also to be split from the other orders so that there was a free marriage market, just as there was a free commodity market.

Moreover, in each of these orders a similar principle was upheld: that of individual freedom of choice—as an economic agent; as a presumptuous political man, who had to be shown before he would obey; as a man on the marriage market making a free contract with his partner; and so on.

But what has happened is the fusion of several institutional orders; the coordination of the major orders has become the contemporary reality. We see in the United States today an increased coincidence and fusion of the economic, political, and military orders.

(iv) A fourth underlying sociological assumption, probably the most subtle and far-reaching, certainly the most philosophically relevant, is that the individual is the seat of rationality. When liberals speak of rationality and "the increase of enlightenment," they have assumed that the individual will be increased in stature and dignity because *his* power to reason and *his* knowledge will be increased. But the decisive fact here, as signified quite well by such writers as Max Weber and Karl Mannheim, is that the seat of rationality has shifted from the individual and is now in the big institution. The increase of enlightenment does not necessarily wise up the individual. This has to do with the distinction of substantive from formal rationality, in short, the growth of a bureaucratic organization of knowledge. The prevailing character as well as the distribution of rationality now leads to a whole set of questions to which we have no contemporary liberal answers. This modern weakness and irrationality of the individual, and especially his political apathy, is crucial for liberalism; for liberalism has classically relied on the reasoning individual as its lever for progressive change.

(v) Tied in with the belief in the growth of the individual's substantive rationality is the belief in the explicitness of authority. Men, as individuals or as groups of individuals, could learn to know who exercised power and so could debate it or obey. But today, one of the crucial political problems "for experts," as for laymen, is to locate exactly who has the power.

It is fashionable now, especially among those who have left what radical circles remain, to suppose that "there is no ruling class," just as it was fashionable in the thirties to suppose a set of class villains to be the source of all social injustice and public malaise. I should be as far from supposing that some enemy could be firmly located, that some one or two sets of men were responsible, as I should be from supposing that it is all merely impersonal, tragic drift. The view that all is blind drift is largely a fatalist projection of one's own feeling of impotence and perhaps a salve of guilt about it. The view that all is due to the conspiracy of an easily locatable enemy is also a hurried projection from the difficult effort to understand how structural shifts open opportunities to various elites and how various elites take advantage or fail to take advantage of them. To accept either view is to relax the effort rationally to understand in detail how it is.

There are obviously gradations of power and opportunities among modern populations, which is not to say that all ruling powers are united, or that they fully know what they do, or that they are consciously joined in conspiracy. One can, however, be more concerned with their structural position and the consequences of their decisive actions than with the extent of their awareness or the impurity of their motives. But such analysis has not been part of the liberal tradition, nor does this tradition provide decisive help in undertaking it.

IV

The root problem of any "democratic" or "liberal"—or even humanist—ideals is that they are in fact statements of hope or demands or preferences of an intellectual elite psychologically capable of individually fulfilling them, but they are projected for a population which in the twentieth century is not at present capable of fulfilling them.

What is inferred from this depends, in part, upon what is seen to be the causes of this mass incapability, and, in part, simply upon the degree of sanguinity. In nineteenth-century liberalism, the causes were seen largely as ignorance; so the answer was education. This was true of classic liberalism and, in part, of classic socialism, although the meaning and the further reasons for ignorance were more sophisticatedly worked out by socialist than by liberal writers. In the twentieth century, serious thinkers have further developed this socialist view, whether or not they know it as socialist, and have come to see that the whole structure of modern society, in particular its bureaucratic and communication systems virtually expropriate from all but a small intellectual elite the capacity for individual freedom in any adequate psychological meaning of the term.

The intellectual question for liberals, then, rests on the confrontation of the old individual ideals with new social and psychological facts. The old social anchors of individual freedom and individual security of small scattered properties and small-scale communities are gone; the roots of these values in autonomously operating institutions are dried up; the seat of rationality is no longer unambiguously the individual; the centers of power are as often hidden as explicit. And so the question becomes whether the ideals themselves must be given up or drastically revised, or whether there are ways of re-articulating them that retain their old moral force in a world that moral liberals never made.

DANIEL BELL / The End
of Ideology in the West*

Men commit the error of not knowing when to limit their hopes.
—Machiavelli

There have been few periods in history when man felt his world
to be durable, suspended surely, as in Christian allegory, between
chaos and heaven. In an Egyptian papyrus of more than four
thousand years ago, one finds: "... impudence is rife ... the
country is spinning round and round like a potter's wheel ... the
masses are like timid sheep without a shepherd ... one who yesterday was indigent is now wealthy and the sometime rich overwhelm him with adulation." The Hellenistic period as described
by Gilbert Murray was one of a "failure of nerve"; there was "the
rise of pessimism, a loss of self-confidence, of hope in this life and
of faith in normal human effort." And the old scoundrel Talleyrand claimed that only those who lived before 1789 could have
tasted life in all its sweetness.[1]

This age, too, can add appropriate citations—made all the
more wry and bitter by the long period of bright hope that pre-

---

* From Bell, *The End of Ideology* (New York, Free Press of Glencoe, 1960),
pp. 369–375.

[1] Karl Jaspers has assembled a fascinating collection of laments by philosophers of each age who see their own time as crisis and the past as a golden
age. These—and the quotations from the Egyptian papyri as well as the remark of Talleyrand—can be found in his *Man in the Modern Age,* rev. ed.
(London, 1951), Chap. II. The quotation from Gilbert Murray is from *Five
Stages of Greek Religion,* 2d ed. (New York, 1930), Chap. IV.

ceded it—for the two decades between 1930 and 1950 have an intensity peculiar in written history: world-wide economic depression and sharp class struggles; the rise of fascism and racial imperialism in a country that had stood at an advanced stage of human culture; the tragic self-immolation of a revolutionary generation that had proclaimed the finer ideals of man; destructive war of a breadth and scale hitherto unknown; the bureaucratized murder of millions in concentration camps and death chambers.

For the radical intellectual who had articulated the revolutionary impulses of the past century and a half, all this has meant an end to chiliastic hopes, to millenarianism, to apocalyptic thinking —and to ideology. For ideology, which once was a road to action, has come to be a dead end.

Whatever its origins among the French *philosophes,* ideology as a way of translating ideas into action was given its sharpest phrasing by the left Hegelians, by Feuerbach and by Marx. For them, the function of philosophy was to be critical, to rid the present of the past. ("The tradition of all the dead generations weighs like a nightmare on the brain of the living," wrote Marx.) Feuerbach, the most radical of all the left Hegelians, called himself Luther II. Man would be free, he said, if we could demythologize religion. The history of all thought was a history of progressive disenchantment, and if finally, in Christianity, God had been transformed from a parochial deity to a universal abstraction, the function of criticism—using the radical tool of alienation, or self-estrangement—was to replace theology by anthropology, to substitute Man for God. Philosophy was to be directed at life, man was to be liberated from the "specter of abstractions" and extricated from the bind of the supernatural. Religion was capable only of creating "false consciousness." Philosophy would reveal "true consciousness." And by placing Man, rather than God, at the center of consciousness, Feuerbach sought to bring the "infinite into the finite." [2]

2 The citation from Marx is from the celebrated opening passages of *The Eighteenth Brumaire of Louis Napoleon* which has a general discussion of alienation, but I have followed here with profit the discussion by Hans Speier in his *Social Order and the Risks of War* (New York, 1952), Chap. XI.

If Feuerbach "descended into the world," Marx sought to transform it. And where Feuerbach proclaimed anthropology, Marx, reclaiming a root insight of Hegel, emphasized History and historical contexts. The world was not generic Man, but men; and of men, classes of men. Men differed because of their class position. And truths were class truths. All truths, thus, were masks, or partial truths, but the real truth was the revolutionary truth. And this real truth was rational.

Thus a dynamic was introduced into the analysis of ideology, and into the creation of a new ideology. By demythologizing religion, one recovered (from God and sin) the potential in man. By the unfolding of history, rationality was revealed. In the struggle of classes, true consciousness, rather than false consciousness, could be achieved. But if truth lay in action, one must act. The left Hegelians, said Marx, were only *littérateurs*. (For them a magazine was "practice.") For Marx, the only real action was in politics. But action, revolutionary action as Marx conceived it, was not mere social change. It was, in its way, the resumption of all the old millenarian, chiliastic ideas of the Anabaptists. It was, in its new vision, a new ideology.

Ideology is the conversion of ideas into social levers. Without irony, Max Lerner once entitled a book *Ideas Are Weapons*. This is the language of ideology. It is more. It is the commitment to the consequences of ideas. When Vissarion Belinsky, the father of Russian criticism, first read Hegel and became convinced of the philosophical correctness of the formula "what is, is what ought to be," he became a supporter of the Russian autocracy. But when it was shown to him that Hegel's thought contained the contrary tendency, that dialectically the "is" evolves into a different form, he became a revolutionary overnight. "Belinsky's conversion," comments Rufus W. Mathewson, Jr., "illustrates an attitude toward ideas which is both passionate and myopic, which responds to them on the basis of their immediate relevances alone, and inevitably reduces them to tools." [3]

[3] Rufus W. Mathewson, Jr., *The Positive Hero in Russian Literature* (New York, 1958), p. 6.

What gives ideology its force is its passion. Abstract philosophical inquiry has always sought to eliminate passion, and the person, to rationalize all ideas. For the ideologue, truth arises in action, and meaning is given to experience by the "transforming moment." He comes alive not in contemplation, but in "the deed." One might say, in fact, that the most important, latent, function of ideology is to tap emotion. Other than religion (and war and nationalism), there have been few forms of channelizing emotional energy. Religion symbolized, drained away, dispersed emotional energy from the world onto the litany, the liturgy, the sacraments, the edifices, the arts. Ideology fuses these energies and channels them into politics.

But religion, at its most effective, was more. It was a way for people to cope with the problem of death. The fear of death—forceful and inevitable—and more, the fear of violent death, shatters the glittering, imposing, momentary dream of man's power. The fear of death, as Hobbes pointed out, is the source of conscience; the effort to avoid violent death is the source of law. When it was possible for people to believe, really believe, in heaven and hell, then some of the fear of death could be tempered or controlled; without such belief, there is only the total annihilation of the self.[4]

It may well be that with the decline in religious *faith* in the last century and more, this fear of death as total annihilation, unconsciously expressed, has probably increased. One may hypothesize, in fact, that here is a cause of the breakthrough of the irrational, which is such a marked feature of the changed moral temper of our time. Fanaticism, violence, and cruelty are not, of course, unique in human history. But there was a time when such frenzies and mass emotions could be displaced, symbolized, drained away, and dispersed through religious devotion and practice. Now there is only this life, and the assertion of self becomes possible—for some even necessary—in the domination over others.[5] One can challenge death by emphasizing the omnipo-

---

[4] See Leo Strauss, *The Political Philosophy of Hobbes* (Chicago, 1952), pp. 14–29.

[5] The Marquis de Sade, who, more than any man, explored the limits of

tence of a movement (as in the "inevitable" victory of communism), or overcome death (as did the "immortality" of Captain Ahab) by bending others to one's will. Both paths are taken, but politics, because it can institutionalize power, in the way that religion once did, becomes the ready avenue for domination. The modern effort to transform the world chiefly or solely through politics (as contrasted with the religious transformation of the self) has meant that all other institutional ways of mobilizing emotional energy would necessarily atrophy. In effect, sect and church became party and social movement.

A social movement can rouse people when it can do three things: simplify ideas, establish a claim to truth, and, in the union of the two, demand a commitment to action. Thus, not only does ideology transform ideas, it transforms people as well. The nineteenth-century ideologies, by emphasizing inevitability and by infusing passion into their followers, could compete with religion. By identifying inevitability with progress, they linked up with the positive values of science. But more important, these ideologies were linked, too, with the rising class of intellectuals, which was seeking to assert a place in society.

The differences between the intellectual and the scholar, without being invidious, are important to understand. The scholar has a bounded field of knowledge, a tradition, and seeks to find his place in it, adding to the accumulated, tested knowledge of the past as to a mosaic. The scholar, *qua* scholar, is less involved with his "self." The intellectual begins with *his* experience, *his* individual perceptions of the world, *his* privileges and deprivations, and judges the world by these sensibilities. Since his own status is of high value, his judgments of the society reflect the treatment accorded him. In a business civilization, the intellec-

---

self-assertion, once wrote: "There is not a single man who doesn't want to be a despot when he is excited . . . he would like to be alone in the world . . . any sort of equality would destroy the despotism he enjoys then." De Sade proposed, therefore, to canalize these impulses into sexual activity by opening universal brothels which could serve to drain away these emotions. De Sade, it should be pointed out, was a bitter enemy of religion, but he understood well the latent function of religion in mobilizing emotions.

tual felt that the wrong values were being honored, and rejected the society. Thus there was a "built-in" compulsion for the free-floating intellectual to become political. The ideologies, therefore, which emerged from the nineteenth century had the force of the intellectuals behind them. They embarked upon what William James called "the faith ladder," which in its vision of the future cannot distinguish possibilities from probabilities, and converts the latter into certainties.

Today, these ideologies are exhausted. The events behind this important sociological change are complex and varied. Such calamities as the Moscow Trials, the Nazi-Soviet pact, the concentration camps, the suppression of the Hungarian workers, form one chain; such social changes as the modification of capitalism, the rise of the welfare state, another. In philosophy, one can trace the decline of simplistic, rationalistic beliefs and the emergence of new stoic-theological images of a man, e.g. Freud, Tillich, Jaspers, etc. This is not to say that such ideologies as communism in France and Italy do not have a political weight, or a driving momentum from other sources. But out of all this history, one simple fact emerges: for the radical intelligentsia, the old ideologies have lost their "truth" and their power to persuade.

Few serious minds believe any longer that one can set down "blue-prints" and through "social engineering" bring about a new utopia of social harmony. At the same time, the older "counter-beliefs" have lost their intellectual force as well. Few "classic" liberals insist that the state should play no role in the economy, and few serious conservatives, at least in England and on the Continent, believe that the welfare state is "the road to serfdom." In the Western world, therefore, there is today a rough consensus among intellectuals on political issues: the acceptance of a welfare state; the desirability of decentralized power; a system of mixed economy and of political pluralism. In that sense, too, the ideological age has ended.

And yet, the extraordinary fact is that while the old nineteenth-century ideologies and intellectual debates have become exhausted, the rising states of Asia and Africa are fashioning new ideologies with a different appeal for their own people. These are the ideologies of industrialization, modernization, Pan-Arabism, color, and nationalism. In the distinctive difference between the two kinds of ideologies lie the great political and social problems of the second half of the twentieth century. The ideologies of the nineteenth century were universalistic, humanistic, and fashioned by intellectuals. The mass ideologies of Asia and Africa are parochial, instrumental, and created by political leaders. The driving forces of the old ideologies were social equality and, in the largest sense, freedom. The impulsions of the new ideologies are economic development and national power.

And in this appeal, Russia and China have become models. The fascination these countries exert is no longer the old idea of the free society, but the new one of economic growth. And if this involves the wholesale coercion of the population and the rise of new elites to drive the people, the new repressions are justified on the ground that without such coercions economic advance cannot take place rapidly enough. And even for some of the liberals of the West, "economic development" has become a new ideology that washes away the memory of old disillusionments.

It is hard to quarrel with an appeal for rapid economic growth and moc' rnization, and few can dispute the goal, as few could ever dispute an appeal for equality and freedom. But in this powerful surge—and its swiftness is amazing—any movement that instates such goals risks the sacrifice of the present generation for a future that may see only a new exploitation by a new elite. For the newly risen countries, the debate is not over the merits of communism—the content of that doctrine has long been forgotten by friends and foes alike. The question is an older one: whether new societies can grow by building democratic institutions and allowing people to make choices—and sacrifices—voluntarily, or whether the new elites, heady with power, will impose totalitarian means to transform their countries. Certainly in these traditional and old colonial societies where the masses are apathetic and easily manipulated, the answer lies with the intellectual classes and their conceptions of the future.

Thus one finds, at the end of the fifties, a disconcerting caesura. In the West, among the intellectuals, the old passions are spent.

The new generation, with no meaningful memory of these old debates, and no secure tradition to build upon, finds itself seeking new purposes within a framework of political society that has rejected, intellectually speaking, the old apocalyptic and chiliastic visions. In the search for a "cause," there is a deep, desperate, almost pathetic anger. The theme runs through a remarkable book, *Convictions*, by a dozen of the sharpest young left-wing intellectuals in Britain. They cannot define the content of the "cause" they seek, but the yearning is clear. In the United States too there is a restless search for a new intellectual radicalism. Richard Chase, in his thoughtful assessment of American society, *The Democratic Vista*, insists that the greatness of nineteenth-century America for the rest of the world consisted in its radical vision of man (such a vision as Whitman's), and calls for a new radical criticism today. But the problem is that the old politico-economic radicalism (preoccupied with such matters as the socialization of industry) has lost its meaning, while the stultifying aspects of contemporary culture (e.g., television) cannot be redressed in political terms. At the same time, American culture has almost completely accepted the avant-garde, particularly in art, and the older academic styles have been driven out completely. The irony, further, for those who seek "causes" is that the workers, whose grievances were once the driving energy for social change, are more satisfied with the society than the intellectuals. The workers have not achieved utopia, but their expectations were less than those of the intellectuals, and the gains correspondingly larger.

The young intellectual is unhappy because the "middle way" is for the middle-aged, not for him; it is without passion and is deadening.[6] Ideology, which by its nature is an all-or-none affair, and temperamentally the thing he wants, is intellectually devitalized, and few issues can be formulated any more, intellectually, in ideological terms. The emotional energies—and needs—exist,

[6] Raymond Aron, *The Opium of the Intellectuals* (New York, 1958); Edward Shils, "Ideology and Civility," *Sewanee Review*, Vol. LXVI, No. 3 (Summer, 1958), and "The Intellectuals and the Powers," in *Comparative Studies in Society and History*, Vol. I, No. 1 (October, 1958).

and the question of how one mobilizes these energies is a difficult one. Politics offers little excitement. Some of the younger intellectuals have found an outlet in science or university pursuits, but often at the expense of narrowing their talent into mere technique; others have sought self-expression in the arts, but in the wasteland the lack of content has meant, too, the lack of the necessary tension that creates new forms and styles.

Whether the intellectuals in the West can find passions outside of politics is moot. Unfortunately, social reform does not have any unifying appeal, nor does it give a younger generation the outlet for "self-expression" and "self-definition" that it wants. The trajectory of enthusiasm has curved East, where, in the new ecstasies for economic utopia, the "future" is all that counts.

And yet, if the intellectual history of the past hundred years has any meaning—and lesson—it is to reassert Jefferson's wisdom (aimed at removing the dead hand of the past, but which can serve as a warning against the heavy hand of the future as well), that "the present belongs to the living." This is the wisdom that revolutionists, old and new, who are sensitive to the fate of their fellow men, rediscover in every generation. "I will never believe," says a protagonist in a poignant dialogue written by the gallant Polish philosopher Leszek Kolakowski, "that the moral and intellectual life of mankind follows the law of economics, that is by saving today we can have more tomorrow; that we should use lives now so that truth will triumph or that we should profit by crime to pave the way for nobility."

And these words, written during the Polish "thaw," when the intellectuals had asserted, from their experience with the "future," the claims of humanism, echo the protest of the Russian writer Alexander Herzen, who, in a dialogue a hundred years ago, reproached an earlier revolutionist who would sacrifice the present mankind for a promised tomorrow: "Do you truly wish to condemn all human beings alive today to the sad role of caryatids ... supporting a floor for others some day to dance on? ... This alone should serve as a warning to people: an end that is infinitely remote is not an end, but, if you like, a trap; an end must be nearer—it ought to be, at the very least, the laborer's wage or pleasure in the work done. Each age, each generation, each life has its own fullness. . . ." [7]

[7] To see history as changes in sensibilities and style or, more, how different classes or people mobilized their emotional energies and adopted different moral postures is relatively novel; yet the history of moral temper is, I feel, one of the most important ways of understanding social change, and particularly the irrational forces at work in men. The great model for a cultural period is J. H. Huizinga's *The Warning of the Middle Ages,* with its discussion of changing attitudes toward death, cruelty, and love. Lucien Febvre, the great French historian, long ago urged the writing of history in terms of different sensibilities, and his study of Rabelais and the problem of covert belief (*Le problème de l'incroyance du XVIème siècle*) is one of the great landmarks of this approach. Most historians of social movements have been excessively "intellectualistic" in that the emphasis has been on doctrine or on organizational technique, and less on emotional styles. Nathan Leites's *A Study of Bolshevism* may be more important, ultimately, for its treatment of the changing moral temper of the Russian intelligentsia than for the formal study of Bolshevik behavior. Arthur Koestler's novels and autobiography are a brilliant mirror of the changes in belief of the European intellectual. Herbert Luethy's study of the playwright Bert Brecht (*Encounter,* July, 1956) is a jewel in its subtle analysis of the changes in moral judgment created by the acceptance of the image of "the Bolshevik." The career of Georg Lukacs, the Hungarian Marxist, is instructive regarding an intellectual who has accepted the soldierly discipline of the communist ethic; other than some penetrating but brief remarks by Franz Borkenau (see his *World Communism* [New York, 1939], pp. 172–175), and the articles by Morris Watnick (*Soviet Survey* [London, 1958], Nos. 23–25), very little has been written about this extraordinary man. Ignazio Silone's "The Choice of Comrades" (reprinted in *Voices of Dissent* [New York, 1959]) is a sensitive reflection of the positive experiences of radicalism. An interesting history of the millenarian and chiliastic movements is Norman Cohn's *The Pursuit of the Millennium.* From a Catholic viewpoint, Father Ronald Knox's study *Enthusiasm,* deals with the "ecstatic" movements in Christian history.

ROBERT A. HABER / The End of Ideology as Ideology*

INTRODUCTION

Since the mid-1930's, a sociological literature has developed analyzing or forecasting "the end of ideology" in the West. Major statements of this theory have been: Daniel Bell, *The End of Ideology;* Seymour Lipset, *Political Man;* and Edward Shils, "Ideology and Civility: on the Politics of the Intellectual."

While some left-wing intellectuals have taken issue with the theory, in general, its pronouncement was welcomed as an important air-clearing statement of the self-evident.

The "end of ideology" theory states that political theory and practice which aims at radical social transformation has ended, at least in the West. The reasons for this are: first, the disillusionment of the last forty years with mass movements, with revolution and with the socialist-classless utopia projected by Marxism. Second, Marxism-Leninism which has been the main carrier of ideology has been discredited as an intellectual-political system. Third, the class conflicts and system-wide problems which give rise to ideology have generally been solved, so no longer is there an objective base for such a social analysis. Further, the problems which are pressing for the society are of high complexity, do not have clear solutions, and political methods don't appear the most

* From *Our Generation* (November, 1966), pp. 51–68. A portion of the original article, which was written in 1962, has been omitted.

fruitful means of treatment. Finally, the social and economic theories, on which ideology has been based, have been disproved or brought into serious question, so the intellectual underpinnings for ideological politics is removed.

In addition to this contention about reality, the "end of ideology" theorists make a value assertion. They see the end of ideology as a desirable development. In its place they describe a different kind of politics—the politics of "civility," or as it will be called in this paper, reformism.

There are several key problems in analyzing this theory:

1. "Ideology" has passed through many meanings. The theorists use it vaguely. Can the concept be given a rigorous definition?
2. There is an empirical problem of verification. Has "it" ended? And, if so, are the causes those suggested by the theorists?
3. The theory is both descriptive and evaluative. It describes a change and holds that the change is *good*. Does the value judgment influence the empirical analysis?

This paper will attempt to give a precise statement of the theory and to subject it to critical analysis. It will give particular attention to the social conditions alleged to underlie the end of ideology, as contrasted with those leading to ideology.

WHAT IS MEANT BY THE "END OF IDEOLOGY"?

The writers give numerous examples of ideology. They include older views like Nazism, McCarthyism, Bolshevism, and contemporary passions like nationalism, Pan-Africanism and economic development. However, they are quite imprecise in defining ideology, in specifying the applicability of the theory, or in making clear the key variables responsible for the change they describe.

For instance, they attribute a number of characteristics to ideology: the discontinuity of good and evil, the secularization of religious fervor, the ease with which rhetoric replaces reason, passion substitutes for analysis, and double standards and distortion displace objective criteria of evaluation. But they do not include in their theory status quo ideology like the American Way of Life and Anti-Communism, even though these exhibit many of the same characteristics.

Also, they disclaim the applicability of the theory to the newly developed countries—where it is acknowledged, and lamented, that ideology *is* the basis of politics. However, they fail to specify the institutional or other characteristics which differentiate the "West" from the non-West for the purpose of indicating the decline or ascendence of ideology.

They do not analyze the radical right in America as a mass political movement having ideological bases, nor do they deal with the scope, social basis and ideological character of the "New Conservatism" such as represented by the *National Review,* the Chicago economists, and related intellectual centers. Nor do they deal with the neo-fascistic movements in western Europe and Japan. Often they seem to equate ideology with Marxism, and hence with a materialist analysis of society, a social dynamic built on class struggle, and a dialectic of history leading inevitably, though convulsively, to the "good society." Yet they do not identify the critical conditions which lead to the decline of the left while invigorating the right.

Several points can give specification of the object of their analysis:

First, the "end of ideology" is meant to be historically specific. It refers to the end since the last war of a kind of *idea system* held by intellectuals. It does not mean a rejection of the intellectual theory that ideas are socially determined or that they mask and rationalize economic or social relations.

Second, the theory concerns what Mannheim would call *utopian* thinking—ideas which transcend reality and themselves enter the dialectic as instruments of change. It is not referring to the relatively stable set of ideas with which a society justifies and mythologizes itself.

Third, the theory is almost wholly concerned with "*left*" ideology, that is, with utopian ideas oriented around equalitarian, democratic values, and critical of the existing order.

Fourth, their use of ideology refers to politics, the set of ideas underlying a political movement which seeks radical social transformation. The "end of ideology" theory is really an "end of ideological politics" theory.

IDEOLOGY AND IDEOLOGICAL POLITICS

The writers identify a number of values and attitudes alleged to define ideology. They stress its projection of a utopia, qualitatively different from present society, its belief in revolution or apocalyptic change, its willingness to sacrifice the present for the future, its rejection of the existing institutions of change and above all, its passionate, irrational, and millenarian conviction in the truth and ultimate triumph of its position.

This description fundamentally confuses the problem. In the first place, it is highly value-laden, reflecting the anti-ideology position of the theorists. A theorist's values should be clear in his writings, and research should have explicit policy motivation. But clarity of values does not excuse the requirement of scholarly rigor in defining independent and dependent variables.

More importantly, the theory fails to differentiate ideology—the set of ideas underlying a political movement—from the emotional bonds which fire and sustain the movement on a mass basis. The neglect of this crucial distinction derives from the failure to distinguish ideology from ideological politics.

Such a distinction is important. Ideology is an intellectual production describing the society. In understanding ideology, the social position of the intellectual is crucial. Politics is an attempt to influence the allocation of rewards in the society. In understanding politics, the institutional context of the political action is crucial.

Ideology as an intellectual production has several elements: 1) a set of moral values, taken as absolute, 2) an outline of the "good society" in which those values would be realized, 3) a systematic criticism (or, in the case of status quo ideology, affirmation) of the present social arrangements and an analysis of their dynamics, 4) a strategic plan of getting from the present to the future (or, in the case of status quo ideology, how continued progress is built into the existing system).

For ideology to be linked to a political movement and for that movement to develop a mass following certain requisites must be met: 1) the ideas must be easily communicated, which usually involves their simplification and sloganization, 2) they must establish a claim to truth, and 3) they must demand a commitment to action.

In this process the ideology as an intellectual production is altered. A basis of authority—divine, institutional or charismatic—is invoked to establish and maintain the claim to truth and the focus of the idea system is shifted to intermediate goals and instrumental actions.

Appeal may be pointed to the direct psychological experience of prospective recruits with society, rather than to the theoretical abstractions of that experience. The "passions of the mass" are attached to the movement by having it serve each individual as a vehicle for his own self-realization and as a release for his particular frustrations, aggressions and fears. The individual becomes psychologically dependent on the movement and sees society through its medium. Thus, many of the bonds on which the solidarity of the political movement is built may be quite irrelevant (and even contrary to) the ideals in the ideology behind that movement. As a consequence there is a wide range of both intellectual and psychological commitment to the movement.

The goal in this process for a left or opposition movement is to create a language and a common frame of reference which, on the one hand, separates the adherents of the movement from the dominant or status quo ideology of the society, and on the other, breaks the hold of that ideology on their thinking and unifies them behind a program of political opposition, leading ultimately to the overthrow of the dominant ideology and the interests it represents.

There is an implicit rejection of the socially sanctioned institutions of change, holding that they function to maintain social equilibrium within the fixed assumptions and power relations of the status quo.

An opposition movement based on ideology, however, need not be doctrinaire, it need not be demagogic; it need not be dehumanizing of either its members or its antagonists. It need not advocate violent revolution or sacrificing of the present for the future. Such conditions are historically specific, depending on the values of the movement, its leadership, the nature of the conflict it engages and the social experience of its adherents. For instance, none of these attributes apply to the non-violent civil-rights movements in the United States, yet they possess in varying degrees all the defining features of ideology and ideological politics.

Further, millenarian or chiliastic expectations are associated not with ideological movements in general, but with movements involving groups from the lowest social stratum whose possibilities for mobility within the existing system are substantially blocked. And when these tendencies exist, as they do in parts of the Negro movement, they are not necessarily associated with the doctrinaire and dehumanizing qualities which the "end of ideology" theorists ascribe to all ideology.

THE "END OF IDEOLOGY" HYPOTHESIS

In its most limited form, the theory states that the mass socialist movements of the 1930's have declined and that the vulgar Marxism which provided a base for those movements has been abandoned.

This is obvious, and hardly profound. One would expect political opposition to alter its form and its analysis on the basis of its own experience (and failures) and in response to the massive changes in the society as a whole. Even so, organizational remnants of the "old Left" continue to exist and to recruit new members. Furthermore, the hypothesis begs the question of how *mass* any of these old ideological movements were, even at their height.

However, the "end of ideology" theorists are making more general and serious assertions. They are saying:

1. Radical movements of all sorts have ceased to exist in the West, and
2. The ideas which intellectuals contribute to political movements have changed in quality. They are no longer ideological.

Both these hypotheses have an obvious range of truth; but also both have evident exceptions. The Communist Party has a mass base in Italy and France. The left wing of the Social Democratic Party is vigorous, if suppressed, in Germany and is even ascendent in England. In America, the civil-rights and peace movements, while not having explicit political structure, do have radical ideological currents.

And an intellectual community, loosely known in the United States, Canada, and Europe as the "New Left," is clearly ideological in its orientation. Outside of the United States materialism and various forms of economic determinism remain legitimate intellectual positions. The existence of exceptions suggests the hypotheses need closer examination.

WHAT HAS HAPPENED TO LEFT POLITICAL MOVEMENTS?

The lack of oppositional political movements from the Left is attributed to the ending of class conflict and the decline of the objective deprivations on which class conflict was based. It is undoubtedly correct that welfare capitalism has remedied many of the injustices of its *laissez-faire* predecessor. But it is highly oversimplified to see the decline of political opposition solely in these terms.

Conflict can decrease because there is increased harmony and real consensus among the various interests in the society. And it can decrease because it is suppressed, overtly through coercion and intimidation, or covertly through manipulation, the building of false consciousness and the structuring of the institutions and processes which are necessary for "conflict resolution." The "end of ideology" theorists put great emphasis on the decrease in conflict because of consensus; they virtually ignore the *more important* suppression of conflict.

There have been a number of major developments, particularly in the United States but having their parallels in the West generally, which have substantially altered the *context* in which political opposition can be expressed.

1. *Radical opposition is not possible within the political system.* An opposition (third) party cannot operate in the United

States because of election laws, lack of money and organizational resources necessary to operate in each state, anti-subversion laws, issue-raiding by the major parties, etc. And a radical faction cannot function within the two major parties, not only because they represent converging economic and social interests, but also because they are personality—rather than issue—oriented and there are no continuing deliberative bodies in which a factional (minority) caucus could operate. Consequently, it is not possible to organize and maintain a formal political constituency committed to a radical program.

2. *Revolutionary opposition has ceased to be possible.* The means of violence have reached a degree of sophistication and efficiency that their control by the state cannot be broken or challenged by extra-legal, private groups. To overthrow the government is no longer a realistic strategic goal; change must be in the context of an "evolutionary" process.

3. *The public is excluded from political responsibility.* A process of "concurrent consensus" maintains harmony among representatives of competing interests. This consensus is not necessarily static—but the decisions which lead to change are not made publicly nor publicly accountable. The information and alternatives of choice made directly available to the people are sharply limited. The press and mass media are virtually closed. An opposition must orient to the managerial elites rather than to constituents of those elites who have any functioning democratic control. Consequently, opposition organization is forced into an elite pattern and its primary strategic problem is gaining access to and influence in centers of power, rather than building a base of independent power through mass organization.

4. *Conflict is managed.* The state or the dominant institutions sharing in the status quo consensus have sufficient control of social resources to ameliorate any grievance which is used as a basis of generalized political opposition. The mechanism of "reform" is sensitive to the magnitude of the pressure for change. It operates to satisfy those whose psychological and intellectual commitment to the generalized movement is weakest. It thereby serves to divide the radical organization on short-run goals and to under-

mine the mass base of its leaders. The existence of a plurality of "intermediate groups" serves further as a cushion to absorb disruptive conflict, to divide its focus, and to siphon off the loyalties of dissidents by a variety of material and non-material enticements.

5. *The "foreign threat" is used to discredit any action which rests on generalized criticism of the domestic system.* "Anticommunism" is a basis to provide system integration as well as to specifically undermine any conceptual formulation which has Marxist or "pro-communist" implications. The post-war "red-purges" in the trade unions, in universities, in journalism and entertainment, in politics, the professions, and liberal voluntary organizations were the specific historical means by which dissent from the Left was isolated, destroyed or forced to conform to a non-ideological mold within the great American consensus.

These five aspects of the contemporary political system seem decisive in undercutting the generalization of social conflict and the limitation of mass political activity. Changes in the institutional context of politics have combined with direct and sustained attack on the individuals and organizations which were the vehicles of radical dissent. This suggests an end to politics, not an end to ideology.

The decisive factor in the decline of ideological politics is the end of a revolutionary alternate. Revolution has consistently been the basic framework of radical ideology. This is for good reason.

The defining characteristics of any social system is not the distribution of rewards—material, status, safety, etc.—but the *process* by which they are allocated. The "power structure" is not defined by its share of the wealth, but by the means through which it controls the allocation of wealth. (Of course, it also gets the lion's share.)

It is able to incorporate potentially disruptive movements by re-allocating resources, thus meeting material, immediate demands.

As already described, any political opposition movement consists of two (not discontinuous) types: 1) people with an integrated critique of society, ideologues committed to opposition of basic structural characteristics of the going social order, and 2) people with an immediate discontent who join and support the movement because it promises to relieve their grievances.

The second group is the larger, but in terms of radical goals it is politically impotent. If it becomes politically dangerous because a radical leadership gives it certain organization and articulated objectives, then it can be separated from the leadership (or the leadership bought off to forestall such separation) by the offer of concessions. These "reforms" meet immediate demands and they establish a constitutional (i.e., controlled) process of working for continued change.

The "power structure" thus neutralizes the radical potential of a movement through its control of the allocation decisions. This means 1) that the constituents of the opposition movement become beholden to established power interests for progress achieved, and 2) that the opposition leadership is pressured by the constituents to seek further benefits or concessions from the "power structure", that is to seek influence in the allocation process and consequently not to threaten the interests of any group presently dominant in that process.

The power structure has the advantage, because they have power: they are able to *deliver*. Leaders of the opposition are able only to motivate demands and promise rewards. A concession by the system solidifies an individual's commitment to the system. It weakens the vital "separating function" of radical ideology.

Radicals have recognized this situation. In its ideological formulation, they hold that the economic-political system functions as an integrated whole. Adjustments or reforms cannot fundamentally re-orient it to public, democratic values and away from exploitative, manipulative and anti-democratic ones. The magnitude of change does not determine its political quality. There can be tremendous changes in Gross National Product, standard of living, education, leisure, health, all without altering the exploitative character of the system. There may be incremental improvements in living standards, care of marginal people, security, social justice and equality before the law, etc., without there being any alteration in the political control of the society or change in the goals to which social resources are directed, or without there being any improvement in the non-material aspects of social existence.

In its political formulation, the revolutionary objective has generally been the response to this situation. This means the opposition seeks power rather than influence. Its goal is to replace the existing power structure: to overthrow it by killing or jailing its personnel, and by seizing the vital means of its functioning— the communication media, the police power, and the legislative authority. This means that they can organize on the basis of and build primary commitment to the utopia consequent on the social restructuring to be accomplished by the revolution. The promise of the utopia cannot be delivered, or even seriously challenged by the existing system. So there is no danger of the revolutionary organization being driven by minor reforms or concessions.

This revolutionary objective has *not* been adopted in the United States. The *political reasons* for this, as already noted, are that the established system is too decentralized, has too strong a control of the means of violence and facilities of organization for revolution either to be organized or to succeed. But there are also *ideological reasons* based on the political experience of this century: a revolutionary leadership won't give up elite power any more than the previous elite would. *If the central issue of the "revolution" is more democratic control, as it is for the contemporary radicals, then anti-democratic organization can hardly insure it. Furthermore, the idea of non-violence develops tremendous moral force for people horrified by the wars of our century and seeking freedom from the oppression of state or private power.*

The non-violent strategy involves several untested, and even unlikely assumptions:

1. That the political process is sufficiently disjunctive from the economic so that the former can be used to gain control of and to change the latter; i.e., it is possible to gain political power without having economic power.

2. That the economic system can be attacked directly and in a

way to highlight those points at which constitutionally superior political power must intervene.

3. That change can be made and sustained in terms of new values in small sections of social relations, while most relations are left intact and still reflect old values.

4. That successive demands for change in the allocation of resources can reach a point beyond which the system cannot adjust —that there are structural limitations on the ability of the system to satisfy the kind of immediate demands on which disadvantaged people can be organized—and when pushed to those limits, the system itself will be open to fundamental change.

5. That people can be organized in terms of a common interest beyond immediate gain, that they can see the enemy as those who profit from the status quo and not those who are in the same exploited position as themselves within the system, competing for its scarce resources: that reason can prevail over immediate perceived necessity.

Within a revolutionary strategy, none of these assumptions are necessary. But now, a political movement must build in terms of *all* of them. The ground is uncharted; since the organizational experience of previous movements has generally been within the revolutionary framework, it is not now directly applicable. If any of these assumptions prove false, that is, fail in practice, then the possibility for radical change in the organization and allocation of resources is highly unlikely.

HAS IDEOLOGY ENDED?

The existence of a "New Left" struggling with the intellectual and organizational problems of non-revolutionary radicalism indicates that ideology has not ended. That it has changed, and must necessarily have changed, should be obvious from what has already been said about the altered conditions in which ideology is transformed into political action. The major changes are:

1. *Values:* No longer is there a complete rejection of the system. Many of the equalitarian values mythologized (but barely realized) by contemporary society are embraced by New-Left intellectuals. The points of attack are more the processes by which

minority economic interests dominate formally democratic institutions and misallocate public resources for selfish ends.

2. *Utopia:* The oppositional emphasis is modified by a much greater uncertainty about the institutional structure of the good society. Concrete slogans such as nationalization, workers' control, state planning, and socialism are replaced by more complicated and speculative formulations of the market economy, decentralized planning and participatory democracy. The experiences and failures of the "socialist" countries have not yet been incorporated in a new utopian synthesis.

3. *Critique:* The aspects of contemporary society that are criticized include more than economic and political components. Increasing concern is given, for instance, to cultural and educational problems. How to extend the freeing potentiality of material abundance to the masses without losing the quality of high culture developed in the context of aristocratic or bohemian leisure.

4. *Strategy:* As noted, revolution and the crude Marxian dynamics of the class struggle are rejected or highly modified as a basis of historical analysis and as political strategy.

In spite of these changes in content and emphasis, the thinking of the "New Left" retains a basic ideological character. It begins from moral values which are held as absolute. It develops an image of utopia and a systematic critique of the present. While it doesn't see change as apocalyptic, it does hold a fundamental discontinuity: the good society will look and function very differently from this one.

The necessary conditions for ideological thinking must be analyzed in order to understand this change. By hypothesis these conditions are:

1. an independent intellectual class or group
2. the existence of real conflict
3. the existence of institutions which can develop and carry ideology
4. a language in which it can formulate its critique
5. the possibility of change.

That these conditions exist much less now than earlier in this century or in the nineteenth century suggests that ideological thinking should be decreased in amount and ideologists should be a rarer breed of intellectual. The way in which these conditions are realized, to the extent they are, suggests some of the particular aspects of contemporary ideology.

1. *An independent intellectual class.* If the intellectual is beholden to the system, he cannot separate himself from its values and assumptions, and hence, cannot create or embrace a total analysis of it. In part or whole he is committed to the ideology of the system, since his socially supported roles and rewards are rationalized and given importance in terms of that ideology.

The intellectual is not now independent. No longer is he denied status or material rewards; no longer is he limited in his location to the relatively segregated academic communities. He is employed as a consulting technician (where other people set the policy goals) by all the mainstream institutions—corporations, unions, government professional societies, foundations, churches, etc. He can get research money for work that is rationalized in terms of general social benefit. He can publish, and indeed, his advancement is largely conditional on publication that meets the scrutiny (i.e., conforms to the broad value framework) of his colleagues. The academic community is actively hostile to ideological formulations. In all these things, his advancement draws him into the thinking and values of the society. Whereas, intellectual independence requires either being cut off from or consciously rejecting the sanctioned or available social rewards.

Furthermore, ideological thinking is wholistic. To the degree that numerous opportunities and alternatives exist within the system, as they do for contemporary intellectuals, the approach to planning and conceptualization is more likely to be piecemeal than organic. This is reinforced by increasing professional specialization.

2. *The existence of real conflict.* Ideology is formulated in terms of conflicts of interests, the blocking of values by the holders of power. When conflict does not exist, or when contending interests are not directly laid bare, then there is no existential basis for ideology.

There is now very little visible conflict, except in the area of Negro rights. A plurality of governmental and voluntary institutions create bureaucratic channels of remedy which segregate issues. The most exploited groups are without the political facilities of self-expression. The ethic of service seeks to aid the welfare of the oppressed without providing trust or building their sovereignty. Lingering Social Darwinism combines with the conservative ethic of individual initiative to undermine the psychological basis of an assertion by the oppressed of a claim against society.

Expressed conflict is channeled into forms which obscure the underlying causes of the conflict and the real centers of power which govern the reward allocation and are responsible for the oppression complained of. Intermediate institutions are made visible and become targets of attack, while masking the decisive economic interests responsible both for the oppression and the maintenance of the intermediate buffer.

Not only is conflict suppressed, atomized and misdirected; but intellectuals are isolated from the places of conflict and its passion. The university is the place where the intellectual has the greatest freedom (compared with technical and consulting roles in government and other organizations) but it is an isolated institution providing a self-contained, highly artificial and modulated environment.

Furthermore, not only is freedom bought at the price of isolation, but it is anesthetized by a "professional standard" which prescribes that things be studied without reference to the observer's values—lest biasing commitment becloud "objectivity".

3. *The existence of institutions which can develop and carry the ideology*. An essential aspect of ideology is strategic. There must be the interplay between the experience of political action and the intellectual formulation. The action component of an ideological development must have organization form; it must be able to communicate and to organize people.

No institutions exist on a national scale which are sufficiently independent to be a vehicle for ideology. The labor unions to which leftists have traditionally looked, are legally, intellectually, and psychologically part of the system. Many universities are semi-independent, but as noted, the university is isolated from community power structure. In some areas, the church has the requisite independence, but it directs emotional energy to religious rather than political goals. There is no mass distribution opposition newspaper or opposition political party. The monopolization of financial and organizational resources by the status quo—supported by the direct coercive power of the state—prevents the creation of such an independent vehicle of mass communication and action.

4. *A language in which its critique can be formulated.* The main currents of left ideology have been broken by the discrediting of the Soviet translation of Marxist ideology and by the attack of social science methods and values. The old utopia has been shattered and not yet rebuilt.

The system has monopolized much of the language. Freedom, democracy, social justice, equality, and individualism are values which exist in the traditions of the society and are used to rationalize the institutions. It is difficult to use them also as points of appeal against the traditions.

5. *The possibility of change.* Another condition for ideology is a possibility of success. If intellectuals see no chance to alter the present they will retreat to apathy, privatism, and cynicism, and express their political energy within the established institutions for piecemeal reform. Passion will attach only to a cause that is real.

The degree to which these conditions do not now exist explains some of the features of contemporary ideological thinking.

1. The people who are doing it are often young. They are independent because they have yet to undertake family and social commitments. They are dissociated from the main academic currents of their discipline and they associate themselves with independent publications, institutes, or organizations.

2. They are likely to have some involvement in a non-traditional sort of political action. Where direct conflict does exist there is likely to be a greater degree of ideological thinking.

3. The lack of avowed institutions leads to a preoccupation with questions of "agents of social change." The labor movement,

the universities, the civil-rights movement, the Democratic Party, a third party are all exhaustively evaluated as to whether they can carry ideology and an ideological movement.

4. The monopolization of language has led to an elaborate rhetoric of participatory democracy, a shying from the traditional language of Marxism and socialism, and an overworking of some of the less tarnished ideas like alienation.

5. The realistic doubt that anything is possible leads to a preoccupation with strategy. Debates abound on realignment versus a labor party, university reform, violence *versus* non-violence.

THE "END OF IDEOLOGY" AS IDEOLOGY

A substantial number of those left intellectuals who, twenty or thirty years ago, were ideologists have since changed their position. They now represent a mode of political thought which might be called "reformist." In this group would fall the "end of ideology" theorists.

The "end of ideology" theorists present a fairly consistent set of values, which might be called "transitional values," in terms of which they justify a rejection of ideology as a basis for politics.

1. History is unknowable. The persecutions, manipulation, and suffering of people in the present cannot be morally justified as necessary conditions in the building of a future utopia.

2. The evils of the present are not so bad as the evils *inherent* in revolutionary or disruptive change.

3. The dangers inherent in mass action are greater than the evils of injustice more slowly ameliorated through parliamentary process.

4. No class or elite, once it gains privilege, will voluntarily give it up, hence no political strategy can "level" a present elite which is to serve as the vehicle for equalitarian transformation.

5. The values of free expression, association, and political organization are fundamental, both in the present and in any future. There is no conceivable ground on which they can be abrogated.

These values held in conjunction fairly well commit one's political energies to working within the system. Ideology is certainly a dangerous business and its end is much to be desired. The crucial elements however are Number 2 and Number 3. The others, particularly the civil-liberties emphasis, are all compatible with an ideological approach to politics (though they are certainly not characteristic of all ideologies). Numbers 2 and 3, however, disallow or at least treat with great suspicion, the value of social dislocation and of change which is not mediated through established parliamentary institutions. They are values which essentially ratify the present social order.

The origin of these values, according to the "end of ideology" theorists, is in the reflection on the horrors of Nazism, the atrocities and failures of Communists and the shattered hopes of the democratic left in the face of mass psychology and totalitarian attack.

It should be granted that catastrophic events can have a permanent effect on the ideas of a generation—independent of any shift in the social or economic position of the people involved. However, the reformist position reflects a fundamentally different perspective on the society, and, by hypothesis, a fundamentally altered social location of the reformist intellectual.

The essential points of the reformist position are:

1. A positive commitment to the values of the present, historically specific system of Welfare Capitalism. The system embraces his values—democracy, equality, and individual freedom. And the system is highly successful.

He celebrates the high level of material abundance, the progressive lessening of inequality and the progressive remedying of specific deprivations. He notes the wide degree of personal freedom from arbitrary authority: for production workers, guaranteed by trade unions; for the white-collar worker, afforded by the impersonalization of bureaucratic roles; for the political dissenter, guaranteed by civil liberties. He sees remarkable advance in education, science, and culture. And most important, he sees the general acceptance of welfare goals by all interests in the society and thereby the assurances of continued progress.

His perspective is on how far we have come. He has participated in the struggles for change and identifies himself with their successes. What was sound in the old ideologies has been realized, and what was unsound has been disproved and properly rejected.

He believes that the good society is defined by the *process* through which conflict is mediated and progress achieved, rather than by a new *structural* ordering of power, social relations, and resources. American democracy, of course, reflects (or closely approximates) that ideal process.

2. A belief that no issues of generalized conflict exist. There are limited situations of conflict—like the race issue, or poverty, or unemployment—but these are essentially discontinuous and the product of specialized anomalous conditions. They can be dealt with in isolation; they do not derive from fundamental contradictions or weakness in the system. Mechanisms within the system are fully adequate for their solution—such as constitutional legislation, public education, welfare programs, increased production, etc. There is no need to see solutions in the perspective of (or conditional on) total social reorganization.

3. The problems that do exist—like those of mass culture and mass education—are too complex to be conceptualized in solely political terms. And the value questions, as to what is desirable, are too indeterminant to allow coherent political solution. Issues must be dealt with in a pragmatic piecemeal way. Action should follow only when the goal is precise and its consequences understood and desirable. The interplay of differing interests and perspectives *over time,* within a libertarian constitutional framework, will yield the *best* solution, with the least danger of grave error.

4. The interests of all groups are to mediate and compose these conflicting interests. No group can be deprived of its rights or subjected to arbitrary authority in the name of some abstract value. Constitutional process is the only guarantee against the abuse of authority or extra-legal power. The side of justice is never so clean as to warrant an abridgement of the formal processes by which justice is publicly determined—for in that process the interests of all are assured a fair hearing and equitable treatment. This is essentially a position of moral relativism—that each group whatever its objective position contributes to the common

good and that every group is important in making up the composite.

5. The realities of world politics do not permit ideological nonalignment. Whatever one's views on domestic politics, the issues of the international scene must take precedence. It is necessary to oppose communist expansion and to provide democratic influence in the "Third World" and in non-communist revolutions. This requires an orientation to and support of national authority internationally.

These values—the acceptance of the present, discontinuity of conflict, complexity of issues, legitimacy of all interests, and separation of domestic and international issues are exactly opposite of the values inherent in ideology. They suggest a number of hypotheses about social position of those intellectuals who hold them. Again, exactly contrary hypotheses would be suggested for ideologists.

1. They do not have an independent perspective on the social system. They have a wide variety of alternatives and possibilities within the system.

2. Conflict is not salient to them, in terms either of being involved in social conflict, or of perceiving their own interests as directly at stake, or of a high identification and involvement with groups whose interests are so at stake.

3. Their approach to problems is in terms of specialization; formal criteria of method and validity, and scientific "objectivity," rather than speculation and wholistic or value-oriented analysis.

4. They are defensive of their status, every action must be defensive in the face of expected criticism.

5. They have experience with and are in relations of interdependency with a wide variety of groups in society.

6. They identify with national authority as an object of loyalty and patriotism.

A good deal of ideological thinking would come from youth and particularly students for several reasons. They have little established connection with the reward system of the society. They are often subsidized and enjoy a variety of immunities from social demands and obligations. Potentially, they have greater "independence" than any other group.

Their lack of responsibilities gives them greater possibility of geographical mobility and hence direct access to conflict situations. Their own incomplete socialization can give increased emotional saliency to conflict by transference of psychological and familial tensions.

They lack specialized skills and attachment to a professional discipline, so reflection on social issues is much more apt to take a wholistic form. And as students they are exposed to a variety of ideological and political positions as objects of study and as adjuncts to non-academic (extra-curricular) activities.

They have experienced little vertical mobility and have no recognized social status. Rather than being defensive, they are more apt to be assertive in an effort to define their own identity in the society.

CONCLUSION

One of the major problems in the sociology of knowledge is to demonstrate the linkage between "mental productions" and the existent base. The foregoing analysis of the "end of ideology" thesis has been developed with the view of providing the opportunity for an empirical test of some of these relationships.

The analysis has:

1. distinguished two types of political thinking, ideological and reformist, each characterized by a set of specific and mutually exclusive attributes;

2. hypothesized a number of social conditions necessary for ideological thinking;

3. hypothesized a number of values (called transitional values) held characteristically by those intellectuals who in the course of their lives have shifted from ideological to reformist thinking;

4. developed a number of hypotheses designed to differentiate ideological from reformist intellectuals on such dimensions as social position, past experience, status, self image, approach to work, and attitude to national authority.

It should be possible to test the relationships suggested in these hypotheses. A sample of intellectuals would be divided on the basis of ideological *versus* reformist (as determined by questionnaire, interview or content analysis of their writing). Correlations would then be sought with the social conditions.

The outcome of such an empirical study would, I believe, confirm that the "end of ideology" is a status quo ideological formulation designed to rationalize the incorporation of intellectuals into the American way of life.

13 / ANARCHISM

ERRICO MALATESTA / Anarchy*

We have said that Anarchy is society without government. But is the suppression of government possible, desirable, or wise? Let us see.

What is the government? There is a disease of the human mind called the metaphysical tendency, which causes man, after he has by a logical process abstracted the quality from an object, to be subject to a kind of hallucination which makes him take the abstraction for the real thing. This metaphysical tendency, in spite of the blows of positive science, has still strong root in the minds of the majority of our contemporary fellow-men. It has such influence that many consider government an actual entity, with certain given attributes of reason, justice, equity, independently of the people who compose the government.

For those who think in this way, government, or the State, is the abstract social power, and it represents, always in the abstract, the general interest. It is the expression of the rights of all, and is considered as limited by the rights of each. This way of understanding government is supported by those interested, to whom it is an urgent necessity that the principle of authority should be maintained, and should always survive the faults and errors of the persons who exercise power.

For us, the government is the aggregate of the governors, and the governors—kings, presidents, ministers, members of parliament, and what not—are those who have the power to make laws regulating the relations between men, and to force obedience to these laws. They are those who decide upon and claim the taxes,

* From Malatesta, *Anarchy* (London, Freedom Press, 1907). Portions of the original text have been omitted.

enforce military service, judge and punish transgressors of the laws. They subject men to regulations, and supervise and sanction private contracts. They monopolize certain branches of production and public services, or, if they wish, all production and public service. They promote or hinder the exchange of goods. They make war or peace with the governments of other countries. They concede or withhold free trade and many things else. In short, the governors are those who have the power, in a greater or lesser degree, to make use of the collective force of society, that is, of the physical, intellectual, and economic force of all, to oblige each to their (the governors') wish. And this power constitutes, in our opinion, the very principle of government and authority.

But what reason is there for the existence of government?

Why abdicate one's own liberty, one's own initiative in favor of other individuals? Why give them the power to be the masters, with or against the wish of each, to dispose of the forces of all in their own way? Are the governors such exceptionally gifted men as to enable them, with some show of reason, to represent the masses, and act in the interests of all men better than all men would be able to act for themselves? Are they so infallible and incorruptible that one can confide to them, with any semblance of prudence, the fate of each and all, trusting to their knowledge and goodness?

And even if there existed men of infinite goodness and knowledge, even if we assume what has never happened in history, and what we believe could never happen, namely, that the government might devolve upon the ablest and best, would the possession of governmental power add anything to their beneficent influence? Would it not rather paralyze or destroy it? For those who govern find it necessary to occupy themselves with things which they do not understand, and, above all, to waste the greater part of their energy in keeping themselves in power, striving to satisfy their friends, holding the discontented in check, and mastering the rebellious.

Again, be the governors good or bad, wise or ignorant, how do they gain power? Do they impose themselves by right of war, conquest, or revolution? If so, what guarantees have the public that their rules have the general good at heart? In this case it is simply a question of usurpation, and if the subjects are discontented nothing is left to them but to throw off the yoke, by an appeal to arms. Are the governors chosen from a certain class or party? Then inevitably the ideas and interests of that class or party will triumph, and the wishes and interests of the others will be sacrificed. Are they elected by universal suffrage? Now numbers are the sole criterion, and numbers are clearly no proof of reason, justice or capacity. Under universal suffrage the elected are those who know best how to take in the masses. The minority, which may happen to be the half minus one, is sacrificed. Moreover, experience has shown it is impossible to hit upon an electoral system which really ensures election by the actual majority.

Many and various are the theories by which men have sought to justify the existence of government. All, however, are founded, confessedly or not, on the assumption that the individuals of a society have contrary interests, and that an external superior power is necessary to oblige some to respect the interests of others, by prescribing and imposing a rule of conduct, according to which the interests at strife may be harmonized as much as possible, and according to which each may obtain the maximum of satisfaction with the minimum of sacrifice. If, say the theorists of the authoritarian school, the interests, tendencies, and desires of an individual are in opposition to those of another individual, or perhaps all society, who will have the right and the power to oblige the one to respect the interests of the other or others? Who will be able to prevent the individual citizen from offending the general will? The liberty of each, they say, has for its limit the liberty of others; but who will establish those limits, and who will cause them to be respected? The natural antagonism of interests and passions creates the necessity for government, and justifies authority. Authority intervenes as moderator of the social strife, and defines the limits of the rights and duties of each.

This is the theory; but to be sound the theory should be based upon an explanation of facts. We know well how in social economy theories are too often invented to justify facts, that is, to defend privilege and cause it to be accepted tranquilly by those who are its victims. Let us here look at the facts themselves.

In all the course of history, as in the present epoch, government is either brutal, violent, arbitrary domination of the few over the many, or it is an instrument devised to secure domination and privilege to those who, by force, or cunning, or inheritance, have taken to themselves all the means of life, and first and foremost the soil, whereby they hold the people in servitude, making them work for their advantage.

... Every time that, by military enterprise, physical brute force has taken the upper hand in society, the conquerors have shown the tendency to concentrate government and property in their own hands. In every case, however, because the government cannot attend to the production of wealth, and overlook and direct everything, it finds it necessary to conciliate a powerful class, and private property is again established. With it comes the division of the two sorts of power, that of the persons who control the collective force of society, and that of the proprietors, upon whom these governors become essentially dependent, because the proprietors command the sources of the said collective force.

Never has this state of affairs been so accentuated as in modern times. The development of production, the immense extension of commerce, the extensive power that money has acquired, and all the economic results flowing from the discovery of America, the invention of machinery, etc., have secured such supremacy to the capitalist class that it is no longer content to trust to the support of the government, and has come to wish that the government shall emanate from itself; a government composed of members from its own class, continually under its control and specially organized to defend it against the possible revenge of the disinherited. Hence the origin of the modern parliamentary system.

In many countries, the proletariat participates nominally in the election of the government. This is a concession which the bourgeois (i.e., proprietory) class have made, either to avail themselves of popular support in the strife against royal or aristocratic power, or to divert the attention of the people from their own emancipation by giving them an apparent share in political power. However, whether the bourgeoisie foresaw it or not, when first they conceded to the people the right to vote, the fact is that the right has proved in reality a mockery, serving only to consolidate the power of the bourgeoisie, while giving to the most energetic only of the proletariat the illusory hope of arriving at power.

So also with universal suffrage—we might say, especially with universal suffrage—the government has remained the servant and police of the bourgeois class. How could it be otherwise? If the government should reach the point of becoming hostile, if the hope of democracy should ever be more than a delusion deceiving the people, the proprietory class, menaced in its interests, would at once rebel, and would use all the force and influence which come from the possession of wealth, to reduce the government to the simple function of acting as policeman.

In all times and in all places, whatever may be the name that the government takes, whatever has been its origin, or its organization, its essential function is always that of oppressing and exploiting the masses, and of defending the oppressors and exploiters. Its principal characteristic and indispensable instrument are the policeman and the tax-collector, the soldier and the prison. And to these are necessarily added the time-serving priest or teacher, as the case may be, supported and protected by the government, to render the spirit of the people servile and make them docile under the yoke.

Certainly, in addition to this primary business, to this essential department of governmental action other departments have been added in the course of time. We even admit that never, or hardly ever, has a government been able to exist in a country that was at all civilized without adding to its oppressing and exploiting functions others useful and indispensable to social life. But this fact makes it none the less true that government is in its nature a means of exploitation, and that its origin and position doom it to be the defense of a dominant class, thus confirming and increasing the evils of domination.

With all this, the government does not change its nature. If it acts as regulator or guarantor of the rights and duties of each, it perverts the sentiment of justice. It justifies wrong and punishes every act which offends or menaces the privileges of the governors and proprietors. It declares just and *legal,* the most atrocious exploitation of the miserable, which means a slow and continuous material and moral murder, perpetrated by those who have on those who have not. Again, if it administers public services, it always considers the interests of the governors and proprietors, not occupying itself with the interests of the working masses, except insofar as is necessary to make the masses willing to endure their share of taxation. If it instructs, it fetters and curtails the truth, and tends to prepare the minds and hearts of the young to become either implacable tyrants or docile slaves, according to the class to which they belong. In the hands of the government everything becomes a means of exploitation, everything serves as a police measure, useful to hold the people in check. And it must be thus. If the life of mankind consists in strife between man and man, naturally there must be conquerors and conquered, and the government, which is the means of securing to the victors the results of their victory, and perpetuating those results, will certainly never fall to those who have lost, whether the battle be on the grounds of physical or intellectual strength, or in the field of economics. And those who have fought to secure to themselves better conditions than others can have, to win privilege and add dominion to power, and have attained the victory, will certainly not use it to defend the rights of the vanquished, and to place limits to their own power and to that of their friends and partisans.

The government—or the State, if you will—as judge, moderator of social strife, impartial administrator of the public interests, is a lie, an illusion, a Utopia, never realized and never realizable. If, in fact, the interests of men must always be contrary to one another, if, indeed, the strife between mankind had made laws necessary to human society, and the liberty of the individual must be limited by the liberty of other individuals, then each one would always seek to make his interests triumph over those of others. Each would strive to enlarge his own liberty at the cost of the liberty of others, and there would be government. Not simply because it was more or less useful to the totality of the members of society to have a government, but because the conquerors would wish to secure to themselves the fruits of victory. They would wish effectually to subject the vanquished, and relieve themselves of the trouble of being always on the defensive, and they would appoint men, specially adapted to the business, to act as police. Were this indeed actually the case, then humanity would be destined to perish amid periodical contests between the tyranny of the dominators and the rebellion of the conquered.

But fortunately the future of humanity is a happier one, because the law which governs it is milder.

In the present condition of society, the vast solidarity, which unites all men, is in a great degree unconscious, since it arises spontaneously from the friction of particular interests, while men occupy themselves little or not at all with general interests. And this is the most evident proof that solidarity is the natural law of human life, which imposes itself, in spite of all obstacles, even those artificially created by society as at present constituted.

On the other hand, the oppressed masses, who were never wholly resigned to oppression and misery, and who today more than ever show themselves ardent for justice, liberty, and well-being, are beginning to understand that they can emancipate themselves only by uniting in solidarity with all the oppressed and exploited over the whole world. And they understand also that the indispensable condition of their emancipation is the possession of the means of production, of the soil, and of the instruments of labor, which involves the abolition of private property. Science and the observation of social phenomena show that this abolition would, in the end, be of immense advantage even to the privileged classes, if only they could bring themselves to renounce the spirit of domination and concur with all their fellows in laboring for the common good.

Now, should the oppressed masses one day refuse to work for their oppressors; should they take possession of the soil and the instruments of labor, and apply them for the use and advantage of all who work; should they no longer submit to the domination, either of brute force or economic privilege; should the spirit of human fellowship and the sentiment of human solidarity, strengthened by common interests, grow among the people and put an end to strife between nations; what ground would then remain for the existence of a government?

When private property is abolished, government—which is its defender—must disappear. Should it survive, it would continually tend to reconstruct, under one form or another, a privileged and oppressing class.

But the abolition of government does not signify the doing away with human association. Far otherwise, for that cooperation which today is enforced, and directed to the advantage of the few, would be free and voluntary, directed to the advantage of all. Therefore it would become more intense and effective.

The social instinct and the sentiment of solidarity would develop to the highest degree; and every individual would do all in his power for the good of others, as much for the satisfaction of his own well-understood interests as for the gratification of his sympathetic sentiments.

By the free association of all, a social organization would arise through the spontaneous grouping of men according to their needs and sympathies, from the low to the high, from the simple to the complex, starting from the more immediate to arrive at the more distant and general interests. This organization would have for its aim the greatest good and fullest liberty of all; it would embrace all humanity in one common brotherhood, and would be modified and improved as circumstances were modified and changed, according to the teachings of experience.

This society of free men, this society of friends would be Anarchy.

We have hitherto considered government as it is, and as it must necessarily be in a society founded upon privilege, upon the exploitation and oppression of man by man, upon antagonism of interests and social strife, in a word, upon private property.

We have seen how this state of strife, far from being a necessary condition of human life, is contrary to the interests of the individual and of the species. We have observed how cooperation, solidarity of interest is the law of human progress, and we have concluded that, with the abolition of private property and the cessation of all domination of man over man, there would be no reason for government to exist—therefore it should be abolished.

But, it may be objected, if the principle on which social organization is now founded were to be changed, and solidarity substituted for strife, common property for private property, the government also would change its nature. Instead of being the protector and representative of the interests of one class, it would become, if there were no longer any classes, representative of all society. Its mission would be to secure and regulate social cooperation in the interests of all, and to fulfill public services of general utility. It would defend society against possible attempts to reestablish privilege, and prevent or repress all attacks, by whomsoever set on foot, against the life, well-being, or liberty of the individual.

There are in society certain matters too important, requiring too much constant, regular attention, for them to be left to the voluntary management of individuals, without danger of everything getting into disorder.

If there were no government, who would organize the supply and distribution of provisions? Who regulate matters pertaining to public hygiene, the postal, telegraph, and railway services, etc.? Who would direct public instruction? Who undertake those great works of exploration, improvement on a large scale, scientific enterprise, etc., which transform the face of the earth and augment a hundredfold the power of man?

Who would care for the preservation and increase of capital, that it might be transmitted to posterity enriched and improved?

Who would prevent the destruction of the forests, or the irrational exploitation and impoverishment of the soil?

Who would there be to prevent and repress crimes, that is, antisocial acts?

What of those who, disregarding the law of solidarity, would not work? Or of those who might spread infectious disease in a country by refusing to submit to the regulation of hygiene by science? Or what again could be done with those who, whether insane or not, might set fire to the harvest, injure children, or abuse and take advantage of the weak?

To destroy private property and abolish existing government without reconstituting a government that would organize collective life and secure social solidarity, would not be to abolish privilege and bring peace and prosperity upon earth. It would be to destroy every social bond, to leave humanity to fall back into barbarism, to begin again the reign of "each for himself," which would reestablish the triumph, firstly, of brute force, and, secondly, of economic privilege.

Such are the objections brought forward by authoritarians, even by socialists, who wish to abolish private property and class government founded upon the system of private property.

We reply:

In the first place, it is not true that with a change of social conditions the nature of the government and its functions would also change. Organs and functions are inseparable terms. Take from an organ its function, and either the organ will die, or the function will reinstate itself. Place an army in a country where there is no reason for or fear of foreign war, and this army will provoke war, or, if it did not succeed in doing that, it will disband. A police force, where there are no crimes to discover, and delinquents to arrest, will provoke or invent crimes, or will cease to exist.

For centuries there existed in France an institution, now included in the administration of the forests, for the extermination of the wolves and other noxious beasts. No one will be surprised to learn that, just on account of this institution, wolves still exist in France, and that, in rigorous seasons, they do great damage. The public take little heed of the wolves, because there are the appointed officials, whose duty it is to think about them. And the officials do hunt them, but in an intelligent manner, sparing their caves, and allowing time for reproduction, that they may not run the risk of entirely destroying such an interesting species. The

French peasants have indeed little confidence in these official wolf-hunters, and regard them rather as the wolf-preservers. And, of course, what would these officials do if there were no longer any wolves to exterminate?

A government, i.e., a number of persons deputed to make the laws, and entitled to utilize the collective forces of society to make every individual respect these laws, already constitutes a class privileged and separated from the rest of the community. Such a class, like every elected body, will seek instinctively to enlarge its power; to impose its tendencies, and to make its own interests predominate. Placed in a privileged position, the government always finds itself in antagonism to the masses, of whose force it disposes.

In order to understand how society could exist without a government, it is sufficient to turn our attention for a short space to what actually goes on in our present society. We shall see that in reality the most important social functions are fulfilled even nowadays outside the intervention of government. Also that government only interferes to exploit the masses, or defend the privileged, or, lastly, to sanction, most unnecessarily, all that has been done without its aid, often in spite of and in opposition to it. Men work, exchange, study, travel, follow as they choose the current rules of morality, or hygiene; they profit by the progress of science and art, have numberless mutual interests without ever feeling the need of any one to direct them how to conduct themselves in regard to these matters. On the contrary, it is just those things in which there is no governmental interference that prosper best and give rise to the least contention, being unconsciously adapted to the wish of all in the way found most useful and agreeable.

Nor is government more necessary for large undertakings, or for those public services which require the constant cooperation of many people of different conditions and countries. Thousands of these undertakings are even now the work of voluntarily formed associations. And these are, by the acknowledgement of every one, the undertakings which succeed the best. We do not refer to the associations of capitalists, organized by means of exploitation, although even they show capabilities and powers of free association, which may extend until it embraces all the peoples of all lands, and includes the widest and most varying interests. We speak rather of those associations inspired by the love of humanity, or by the passion for knowledge, or even simply by the desire for amusement and love of applause, as these represent better such groupings as will exist in a society where, private property and internal strife between men being abolished, each will find his interests compatible with the interests of everyone else, and his greatest satisfaction in doing good and pleasing others. Scientific societies and congresses, international life-boat and Red Cross associations, laborers' unions, peace societies, volunteers who hasten to the rescue at times of great public calamity, are all examples, among thousands, of that power of the spirit of association, which always shows itself when a need arises, or an enthusiasm takes hold, and the means do not fail. That voluntary associations do not cover the world, and do not embrace every branch of material and moral activity, is the fault of the obstacles placed in their way by governments, of the antagonisms created by the possession of private property, and of the impotence and degradation to which the monopolizing of wealth on the part of the few reduces the majority of mankind.

The government takes charge, for instance, of the postal and telegraph services. But in what way does it really assist them? When the people are in such a condition as to be able to enjoy and feel the need of such services they will think about organizing them, and the man with the necessary technical knowledge will not require a certificate from a government to enable him to set to work. The more general and urgent the need, the more volunteers will offer to satisfy it. Would the people have the ability necessary to provide and distribute provisions? Never fear, they will not die of hunger, waiting for a government to pass laws on the subject. Wherever a government exists, it must wait until the people have first organized everything, and then come with its laws to sanction and exploit what has already been done. It is evident that private interest is the great motive for all activity.

That being so, when the interest of every one becomes the interest of each (and it necessarily will become so as soon as private property is abolished) then all will be active. If they work now in the interest of the few, so much more and so much better will they work to satisfy the interests of all. It is hard to understand how anyone can believe that public services indispensable to social life can be better secured by order of a government than through the workers themselves who by their own choice or by agreement with others carry them out under the immediate control of all those interested.

Certainly in every collective undertaking on a large scale there is need for division of labor, for technical direction, administration, etc. But the authoritarians are merely playing with words, when they deduce a reason for the existence of government, from the very real necessity for organization of labor. The government, we must repeat, is the aggregate of the individuals who have received or have taken the right or the means to make laws, and force the people to obey them. The administrators, engineers, etc., on the other hand, are men who receive or assume the charge of doing a certain work. Government signifies delegation of power, that is, abdication of the initiative and sovereignty of everyone into the hands of the few. Administration signifies delegation of work, that is, the free exchange of services founded on free agreement.

A governor is a privileged person, because he has the right to command others, and to avail himself of the force of others to fulfil his own ideals and desires. An administrator or technical director is a worker like others, in a society where all have equal opportunities of development, and all can be at the same time intellectual and manual workers; when there are no other differences between men than those derived from diversity of talents, and all work and all social functions give an equal right to the enjoyment of social advantages. The functions of government are, in short, not to be confounded with administrative functions, as they are essentially different. That they are today so often confused is entirely on account of the existence of economic and political privilege.

But let us hasten to pass on to those functions for which government is thought indispensable by all who are not Anarchists. These are the internal and external defense of society, i.e., War, Police and Justice.

Government being abolished, and social wealth being at the disposal of the people, all antagonism between various nations would soon cease, and there would consequently be no more cause for war. But supposing that the rulers of countries not yet emancipated should attempt to reduce a free people to servitude, would these require a government to enable them to defend themselves? To make war we need men who have the necessary geographical and technical knowledge, and, above all, people willing to fight. A government has no means of augmenting the ability of the former, or the willingness or courage of the latter. And the experience of history teaches that a people really desirous of defending their own country are invincible. In Italy everyone knows how thrones tremble and regular armies of hired soldiers vanish before troops of volunteers, i.e., armies anarchically formed.

And as to the police and justice, many imagine that if it were not for the police and the judges, everybody would be free to kill, violate, or injure others as the humor took him; that Anarchists, if they are true to their principles, would like to see respected this strange kind of "liberty" that violates or destroys unrestrained the life and freedom of others. Such people believe that we, having overthrown the government and private property, then tranquilly allow the re-establishment of both, out of respect for the "liberty" of those who may feel the need of having a government and private property. A strange mode indeed of construing our ideas! . . .

The one essential is that a society be constituted in which the exploitation and domination of man by man are impossible. That the society, in other words, be such that the means of existence and development of labor may be free and open to everyone, and all may be able to cooperate, according to their wishes and their knowledge, in the organization of social life. Under such conditions everything will necessarily be performed in compliance with the needs of all, according to the knowledge and possibilities of the moment, and will improve with the increase of knowledge and power.

In fact, a program which would touch the basis of the new social constitution could not do more, after all, than indicate a method. And method, more than anything else, defines movements and determines their importance in history. Method apart, everyone says he wishes the good of mankind, and many truly wish it. As movements disappear, every organized action directed to a definite end disappears likewise. It is therefore necessary to consider Anarchy as, above all, a method.

There are two methods by which the different parties opposed to Anarchism expect, or say they expect, to bring about the greatest good of all. These are the authoritarian or State Socialist, and the individualist methods. The former entrusts the direction of social life to a few, and would result in the exploitation and oppression of the masses by that few. The second method trusts to the free initiative of individuals, and proclaims, if not the abolition, the reduction of government. However, as it respects private property, and is founded on the principle of each for himself, and therefore on competition, its liberty is only the liberty of the strong, the license of those who have to oppress and exploit the weak who have nothing. Far from producing harmony, it would tend always to augment the distance between the rich and the poor, and end also, through exploitation and domination, in authority. This second method, Individualism, is in theory a kind of Anarchy without cooperation. It is therefore no better than a lie, because liberty is not possible without equality, and true Anarchy cannot exist without solidarity, without cooperation. The criticism which Individualists pass on government is merely the wish to deprive it of certain functions, to hand them over virtually to the capitalist. But it cannot attack those repressive functions which form the essence of government, for without an armed force the proprietary system could not be upheld. Even more, under Individualism, the repressive power of government must always increase, in proportion to the increase, by means of free competition, want, inequality, and disharmony.

Anarchists present a new method: the free initiative and free agreement of all. Thus, after the revolutionary abolition of private property, everyone will have equal power to dispose of social wealth. This method, not admitting the re-establishment of private property, must lead, by means of free association, to the complete triumph of the principles of solidarity.

Thus we see that all the problems put forward to combat the Anarchist idea are on the contrary arguments in favor of Anarchy, because it alone indicates the way in which, by experience, those solutions which correspond to the dicta of science, and to the needs and wishes of all, can best be found.

How will children be educated? We do not know. What then? The parents, teachers, and all who are interested in the progress of the rising generation, will meet, discuss, agree, and differ, and then divide according to their various opinions, putting into practice the methods which they respectively hold to be best. That method which, when tried, produces the best results will triumph in the end.

And so for all the problems that may arise.

According to what we have said, it is evident that Anarchy, as the Anarchists conceive it, and as it can alone be comprehended, is based on socialism. Furthermore, were it not for that school of socialists who artificially divide the natural unity of the social question, considering only some detached points, and were it not also for the equivocations with which they strive to hinder the social revolution, we might say right away that anarchy is synonymous with socialism, for both signify the abolition of exploitation and of the domination of man over man, whether maintained by the force of arms or by the monopolization of the means of life.

Anarchy, like socialism, has for its basis and point of departure *equality of conditions*. Its aim is *solidarity*, and its method *liberty*. It is not perfect, nor is it the absolute ideal, which, like the horizon, always recedes as we advance towards it. But it is the open road to all progress and to all improvement made in the interest of all humanity.

With the abolition of this negative power constituting a government, society will become what it can be with the given forces and capabilities of the moment. If there are educationalists desirous of spreading education, they will organize the schools, and will be constrained to emphasize the use and enjoyment to be derived from education. And if there are no such men, or only a few of them, a government cannot create them. All it can do, as in fact it does nowadays, is to take these few away from practical, fruitful work in the sphere of education, and put them to direct from above what has to be imposed by the help of a police system. So they make out of intelligent and impassionate teachers mere politicians, who become useless parasites, entirely absorbed in imposing their own hobbies, and in maintaining themselves in power.

If there are doctors and teachers of hygiene, they will organize themselves for the service of health. And if there are none, a government cannot create them; all that it can do is to discredit them in the eyes of the people, who are inclined to entertain suspicions, sometimes only too well-founded, with regard to everything which is imposed upon them.

If there are engineers and mechanics, they will organize the railways, etc.; and if there are none, a government cannot create them.

The revolution, by abolishing government and private property, will not create energy which does not exist, but it will leave a free field for the exercise of all available energy, and of all existent capacity. While it will destroy every class interested in keeping the masses degraded, it will act in such a way that everyone will be free to work and make his influence felt, in proportion to his own capacity, and in conformity with his sentiments and interests. And it is only thus that the elevation of the masses is possible, for only with liberty can one learn to be free, as it is only by working that one can learn to work. A government, even had it no other disadvantages, must always have that of habituating the governed to subjection, and must also tend to become more oppressive and necessary, in proportion as its subjects are more obedient and docile.

But suppose government were the direction of affairs by the best people. Who are the best? And how shall we recognize their superiority? The majority are generally attached to old prejudices, and have ideas and instincts already outgrown by the more favored minority. But of the various minorities, who all believe themselves in the right, as no doubt many of them are in part, which shall be chosen to rule? And by whom? And by what criterion, seeing that the future alone can prove which party among them is the most superior? If you choose a hundred partisans of dictatorship, you will discover that each one of the hundred believes himself capable, if not of being sole dictator, at least of assisting very materially in the dictatorial government. The dictators would be those who, by one means or another, succeeded in imposing themselves on society. And, in course of time, all their energy would inevitably be employed in defending themselves against the attacks of their adversaries, totally oblivious of their desire, if ever they had had it, to be merely an educative power.

Should government be, on the other hand, elected by universal suffrage, and so be the emanation, more or less sincere, of the wish of the majority? But if you consider these worthy electors as incapable of providing for their own interests, how can they ever be capable of themselves choosing directors to guide them wisely? How solve this problem of social alchemy: to elect a government of geniuses by the votes of a mass of fools? And what will be the lot of the minority, who are the most intelligent, most active and most advanced in society?

To solve the social problem to the advantage of all, there is only one way. To expel the government by revolutionary means, to expropriate the holders of social wealth, putting everything at the disposal of all, and to leave all existing force, capacity and goodwill among men free to provide for the needs of all.

We fight for Anarchy and for socialism because we believe that Anarchy and socialism ought to be brought into operation as soon as possible. This means that the revolution must drive away the government, abolish private property, and entrust all public service, which will then embrace all social life, to the spontaneous, free, unofficial, and unauthorized operation of all those interested and of all willing volunteers.

There will certainly be difficulties and inconveniences, but the people will be resolute, and they alone can solve all difficulties anarchically, that is, by direct action and free agreement of those interested.

We cannot say whether Anarchy and socialism will triumph after the next revolutionary attempt, but this is certain, that if any of the so-called transition programs triumph, it will be because we have been beaten temporarily, and never because we have thought it wise to leave in existence any one part of that evil system under which humanity groans.

Whatever happens, we shall have some influence on events, by our numbers, our energy, our intelligence, and our steadfastness. Also, even if now we are conquered, our work will not have been in vain; for the more decided we shall have been in aiming at the realization of all our demands, the less will there be of government and of private property in the new society. And we shall have done a great work, for human progress is measured by the degree in which government and private property are diminished.

If today we fall without lowering our colors, our cause is certain of victory tomorrow.

PAUL GOODMAN / Drawing the Line*

A free society cannot be the substitution of a "new order" for the old order; it is the extension of spheres of free action until they make up most of the social life. (That such liberation is step by step does not mean that it can occur without revolutionary disruption, for in many spheres—e.g., war, economics, sexual education—any genuine liberation whatsoever involves a total change.)

In any present society, though much and even an increasing amount is coercive, nevertheless much is also free. If it were not so, it would be impossible for a conscientious libertarian to cooperate or live there at all; but in fact we are constantly drawing the line beyond which we refuse to cooperate. In creative work, in passion and sentiment, in spontaneous recreation, there are healthy spheres of nature and freedom: it is the spirit of these that we most often extrapolate to all acts of utopian free society, to making a living, to civil life, and law. But indeed, even the most corrupt and coercive functions of the present society draw on good natural power—the pity of it—otherwise the society could not survive for one moment; for free natural power is the only source of existence. Thus, people are fed, though the means, the cost, and the productive relations are coercive; and the total war would be the end of us all were it not for the bravery and endurance of mankind.

Free action is to live in present society as though it were a nat-

* From Goodman, *Drawing the Line* (New York, Random House, 1966). Originally written in 1944–1945. Portions of the original text have been omitted.

ural society. This maxim has three consequences, three moments:

(1) In the spheres which are in fact free and natural, we exercise personal excellence and give mutual aid.

(2) In many spheres which seem to be uncoerced, we have nevertheless been trapped into unnatural ways by the coercion that has formed us; for example, we have become habituated to the American timetable and the standard of living, though these are unnatural and coercive through and through. Here the maxim demands that we first correct ourselves.

(3) Finally, there are those natural acts or abstentions which clash openly with the coercive laws: these are the "crimes" which it is beholden on a free man to commit, as his reasonable desire demands and as the occasion arises.

The free spirit is rather millenarian than utopian. A man does not look forward to a future state of things which he tries to bring about by suspect means; but he draws now, so far as he can, on the natural force in him that is no different in kind from what it will be in a free society, except that there it will have more scope and be persistently reinforced by mutual aid and fraternal conflict. *Merely by continuing to exist and act in nature and freedom, a free man wins the victory, establishes the society;* it is not necessary for him to be the victor *over* any one. When he creates, he wins; when he corrects his prejudices and habits, he wins; when he resists and suffers, he wins. I say it this way in order to tell honest persons not to despond when it seems that their earnest and honest work is without "influence." The free man does not seek to influence groups but to act in the natural groups essential to him—for most human action is the action of groups. Consider if a million persons, quite apart from any "political" intention, did only natural work and did the best they could. The system of exploitation would disperse like fog in a hot wind. But of what use is the action, born of resentment, that is bent on correcting abuses yet never does a stroke of nature?

The action drawing on the most natural force will in fact establish itself. Might is right: but do not let the violent and the cowed imagine for a moment that their brutality is might. What great things have *they* accomplished, in practice, art, or theory?

Their violence is fear hidden from themselves by conceit, and nothing comes from it.

REVOLUTION, SOCIOLATRY, AND WAR
A MISCALCULATION IN THE MARXIAN DYNAMICS OF REVOLUTION

According to Marx and Engels, the dynamism of the people's revolution into socialism rises from the interaction of two psychological attitudes: (a) the spiritual alienation of the proletariat, because of extreme division of labor and capitalist productive relations, from man's original concern with production and from natural social cooperation; (b) the brute reaction to intolerable deprivation brought on by the falling rate of profit and the capitalist crisis. To expand these points somewhat:

(a) To Marx and Engels the specific properties of humanity are the ability to produce things and to give mutual aid in production. But the subdivision of labor and the capitalist use of machine technology dehumanize production: a man makes only a part of a commodity sold on a distant market, and performing an automatic operation he employs only a modicum of his powers. Further, the conditions of bourgeois competition and wage slavery isolate men from each other and destroy mutuality, family life, comradeship. There is therefore nothing in the capitalist institutions to engage the deep interest or keep the loyalty of the proletariat. They are made into fractional people and these fractions of men are indifferent to the bourgeois mores and society.

(b) On the other hand they are not indifferent to starvation, disease, sexual deprivation, infant mortality, and death in war; but these are the results of the wage cuts, imperialism, unemployment, and fluctuation inherent in the bourgeois need to counteract the falling rate of profit and to re-invest. At the level of resentment and frustration and animal reaction to pain, there is concern for a violent change, there is latent rebellion.

From these attitudes, the revolutionary idea emerges somewhat as follows: driven by need to consult their safety, and with understanding given by usually middle-class teachers who explain the causes of their hurt, and with their original human aspirations recalled from forgetfulness and already fulfilled somewhat by comradely unity, the proletariat turns toward a new order, new foundations, a socialism immeasurably improved yet in its main features not unlike original human nature. By contrast to this idea, the life of the bourgeoisie itself seems worthless. And being increased in numbers and with their hands on the productive machinery of all society, the proletarians know that they can make the idea a reality.

Psychologically—and even anthropologically and ethically— this Marxian formula has great power, if indeed all its elements exist as prescribed. But on the contrary, if any of the elements are missing the formula is disastrous and takes us as far from fraternal socialism as can be. Now there is no question that point (b) is missing: that by and large over the last century in the advanced industrial countries the real wages of the working class as a whole have not lingered at the margin of *physical* subsistence and reproduction; they have advanced to a point where even revolutionary writers agitate for a "sociological standard of living." (The reasons, of course, are the astounding increase in productivity, the high rate of technical improvement, the need for domestic markets, and such gross profits that the rate of profit has lost paramount importance.) What has been the result?

The spiritual alienation of point (a) has gone even further, I suppose, than Marx envisaged. He followed the dehumanization of production to the last subdivision of labor into an automatic gesture, but I doubt whether he (being sane) could have foreseen that thousands of adult persons could work day in and day out and not know what they were making. He did not foresee the dehumanization of consumption in the universal domestic use of streamlined conveniences whose operation the consumer does not begin to understand; the destruction of even the free choices in the market place by mass advertising and monopolistic controls; the segregation among experts in hospitals of all primary experience of birth, pain, and death, etc., etc.

Yet now these fractional persons, alienated from their natures, are not brought sharply to look out for themselves by intolerable deprivation. On the contrary, they are even tricked, by the increase in commodities, into finding an imitation satisfaction in their "standard of living"; and the kind of psychological drive that moves them is—emulation! The demand of the organized proletariat for a living wage and tolerable working conditions, a demand that in the beginning was necessarily political and revolutionary in its consequences, now becomes a demand for a standard of living and for leisure to enjoy the goods, *accepting the mores of the dominant class*. (What are we to say of "leisure" as a good for an animal whose specific humanity is to be productive?) Then if these persons have gone over to the ideals of another class, it is foolish to call them any longer "proletarians" ("producers of offspring," as Marx nobly and bitterly characterized the workers); but given the apparently satisfied alienation from concern in production—and where do we see anything else?—it is also unjust to call them workers.

Marx saw wonderfully the emptiness of life in the modern system; but he failed to utter the warning that this emptiness could proceed so far that, without the spur of starvation, it could make a man satisfied to be a traitor to his original nature. What he relied on to be a dynamic motor of revolution has become the cause of treason.

Lastly, the scientific teachers of the masses are no longer concerned to recall us to our original creative natures, to destroy the inhuman subdivision of labor, to look to the bands of comrades for the initiation of direct action. On the contrary, their interest has become the health and smooth functioning of the industrial machine itself: they are economists of full employment, sociologists of belonging, psychologists of vocational guidance, and politicians of administrative bureaus.

So far the psychology of the masses. But in the psychology of the bourgeoisie there is a correlated difference from what Marx envisaged. The Marxian bourgeois has the following characteristics: (a) Preoccupied with exchange value, with money which is featureless, he is alienated from all natural personal or social interests; this makes all the easier his ruthless career of accumulation, reinvestment, exploitation, and war. (b) On the other hand, he embodies a fierce lust, real even though manic, for wealth and power. The conditions of his role are given by the economy, but he plays the role with all his heart; he is an individual, if not quite a man. The spur of a falling rate of profit or of closed markets, therefore, drives him on to desperate adventures.

By and large I do not think that this type is now very evident. Partly, to be sure, it is that the owning classes adopt a democratic camouflage for their protection; but the fact that they are willing to do this already shows that they are different men. Other factors seem to be important: (1) In absentee ownership there is an emasculation of the drive for maximum exploitation of the labor and the machine; the owner does not have the inspiration of his daily supervision; he is not approached by inventors and foremen, etc.; but the salaried manager is usually concerned with stability rather than change. (2) But even if the drive to improve the exploitation is strong, the individual capitalist is disheartened by the corporate structure in which most vast enterprises are now imbedded; he is embarrassed by prudent or timid confrères. (Government regulation is the last stage of this corporative timidity.) (3) Not least, it now seems that even in peacetime there is a limit to the falling rate of profit; technical improvement alone guarantees an annual increment of more than two percent; by deficit spending the state can subsidize a low but stable rate of profit on all investment; there is apparently no limit to the amount of nonsense that people can be made to want to buy on the installment plan, mortgaging their future labor. And in fact we see, to our astonishment, that a large proportion, almost a majority, of the bourgeoisie are even now ready to settle for Plans that guarantee a low but stable profit. Or by collusion, a high and stable rate of profit. Shall we continue to call them bourgeois? They are *rentiers*.

The more dynamic wolf, on the other hand, is no longer a private enterpriser, but increasingly becomes a manager and administrator of the industrial machine as a whole: he is in the Government. He bares his teeth abroad.

SOCIOLATRY

With the conclusions so far reached, we can attempt a formal definition of the mass attitude that we call *Sociolatry* (after Comte).

Sociolatry is the concern felt by masses alienated from their deep natures for the smooth functioning of the industrial machine from which they believe they can get a higher standard of living and enjoy it in security. The revolutionary tension of the people is absorbed and sublimated by the interesting standard of living; but this standard is not physiological (which would be potentially revolutionary), nor is it principally economic, a standard of comfort and luxury (which would slow down the machine by breeding idleness, dilettantism, and eccentricity); it is a sociological standard energized by emulation and advertising, and cementing a sense of unanimity among the alienated. All men have—not the same human nature—but the same commodities. Thus, barring war, such an attitude of alienated concern could have a long duration. I say "barring war"—but we must ask below whether the war is not essentially related to the attitude.

On the part of the political elite: sociolatry is the agreement of the majority of the bourgeoisie to become *rentiers* of the industrial corporation in whose working they do not interfere; and the promotion of the more dynamic bourgeoisie to high-salaried, prestigious, and powerful places at the controls of the machine. Sociolatry is therefore the psychology of state capitalism and state socialism.

WHAT MUST BE THE REVOLUTIONARY PROGRAM?

Still barring from consideration the threat of war, we must now ask: what is a revolutionary program in the sociolatry? (By "revolutionary" I here refer to the heirs of Rousseau and the French Revolution: the conviction that man is born free and is in institutional chains; that fraternity is the deepest political force and the fountain of social invention; and that socialism implies the *absence* of state or other coercive power.)

For if indeed, with the steady expansion of technical productivity, the attitude of the masses has for a century moved toward sociolatry and the attitude of the bourgeoisie toward accepting a low but stable rate of profit, then the Marxian program is not only bankrupt but reactionary. The Marxian economic demands (for wages and conditions) cement the sociolatry; the Marxian political demands (for expropriation of the expropriators by seizing power) lead to state socialism.

It is with diffidence that I dissent from the social psychology of Karl Marx. When I was young, being possessed of an independent spirit, I refused to embrace the social science of Marx, but proceeded, as an artist and a human being, to make my own judgments of the social behavior I saw about. And then I found, again and again, that the conclusions I slowly and imperfectly arrived at were already fully and demonstrably (and I may say, beautifully) expressed by Karl Marx. So I too was a Marxist! I decided with pleasure, for it is excellent to belong to a tradition and have wise friends. This was Marx as a social psychologist. But as regards political action, on the other hand, I did not see, it never seemed to me, that the slogans of the Marxians, nor even of Marx, lead toward fraternal socialism; rather they lead away from it. Bakunin was better. Kropotkin I agree with.

Now (*still* barring the war!) there is a great advantage for the revolutionist in the existence of sociolatry and of even a tyrannical welfare state. The standard of living and the present use of the machinery of production may rouse our disgust, but it is an ethical disgust; it is not the fierce need to act roused by general biological misery. We may therefore act in a more piecemeal, educational, and thoroughgoing way. The results of such action will also be lasting and worth while if we have grown into our freedom rather than driven each other into it. Our attack on the industrial system can be many sided and often indirect, to make it crash of its own weight rather than by frontal attack.

Nor is it the case that the absence of tension and despair makes it impossible to awaken revolutionary feeling. For we know that the society we want is universally present in the heart, though now generally submerged: it can be brought into existence piecemeal, power by power, everywhere: and as soon as it appears in act, the sociolatry becomes worthless, ridiculous, disgusting by comparison. There is no doubt that, once awakened, the natural powers of men are immeasurably stronger than these alien institutions (which are indeed only the pale sublimations of natural powers).

On the one hand the kind of critique that my friends and I

express: a selective attitude toward the technology, not without peasant features, is itself a product of our surplus technology; on the other hand, we touch precisely the vulnerable point of the system, its failure to win human allegiance.

Then, as opposed to the radical programs that already presuppose the great state and corporative structure, and the present social institutions in the perfected form of the Sociolatry, we must —in small groups—draw the line and try action more directly satisfactory to our deep nature. (a) It is essential that our program can, with courage and mutual encouragement and mutual aid, be put into effect by our own effort, to a degree at once and progressively more and more, without recourse to distant party or union decisions. (b) The groups must be small, because mutual aid is our common human nature mainly with respect to those with whom we deal face to face. (c) Our action must be aimed not, as utopians, at a future establishment; but (as millenarians, so to speak) at fraternal arrangements today, progressively incorporating more and more of the social functions into our free society.

(1) It is treasonable to free society not to work at a job that realizes our human powers and transcends an unthinking and unchoosing subdivision of labor. It is a matter of guilt—this is a harsh saying—to exhaust our time of day in the usual work in office and factories, merely for wages. The aim of economy is not the efficient production of commodities, but cooperative jobs themselves worth doing, with the workers' full understanding of the machines and processes, releasing the industrial inventiveness that very many have. (Nor is it the case, *if we have regard to the whole output of social labor,* that modern technical efficiency requires, or is indeed compatible with, the huge present concentrations of machinery beyond the understanding and control of small groups of workers.[1])

(2) We must reassess our standard of living and see what parts are really useful for subsistence and humane well-being, and which are slavery to the emulation, emotional security, and infe-

[1] This point is argued at length in *Communitas* by Percival and Paul Goodman (Vintage, 1960).

riority roused by exploitative institutions and coercive advertising. The question is not one of the quantity of goods (the fact that we swamp ourselves with household furnishings is likely due to psychic causes too deep for us willfully to alter), but that the goods that make up the "standard of living" are stamped with alien values.

(3) We must allow, and encourage, the sexual satisfaction of the young, both adolescents and small children, in order to free them from anxious submissiveness to authority. It is probably impossible to prevent our own neurotic prejudices from influencing children, but we can at least make opportunity for the sexual gratification of adolescents. This is essential in order to prevent the patterns of coercion and authority from re-emerging no matter what the political change has been.

(4) In small groups we must exercise direct initiative in community problems of personal concern to ourselves (housing, community plan, schooling, etc.). The constructive decisions of intimate concern to us cannot be delegated to representative government and bureaucracy. Further, even if the government really represented the interests of the constituents, it is still the case that political initiative is itself the noble and integrating act of every man. In government, as in economic production, what is superficially efficient is not efficient in the long run.

(5) Living in the midst of an alienated way of life, we must mutually analyze and purge our souls until we no longer regard as guilty or conspiratorial such illegal acts as spring from common human nature. (Group psychotherapy is identical with contactful neighbor-love, that pays attention and comes across.) With regard to committing such "crimes" we must exercise prudence not of inhibitions but such prudence as a sane man exercises in a madhouse. On the other hand, we must see that many acts commonly regarded as legal and even meritorious are treason against our natural society, *if they involve us in situations where we cease to have personal responsibility and concern for the consequences.*

(6) We must progressively abstain from whatever is connected with the war.

I am sensible that this program seems to demand very great

initiative, courage, effort, and social invention; yet if once, looking about at our situation whatever it is, we *draw a line* (wherever we draw it!), can we not at once proceed? Those of us who have already been living in a more reasonable way do not find these minimal points too difficult; can those who have all their lives taken on the habits (if not the ideas) of the alienated society, expect not to make drastic changes? If we are to have peace, it is necessary to *wage* the peace. Otherwise, when their war comes, we also must hold ourselves responsible for it.

THE WAR

The emergency that faces sociolatry and state socialism is war, and we know that this catastrophe of theirs must overwhelm us all. Is it a necessity of their system? Must one not assume, and can one not observe, that beneath their acceptance and mechanical, unspontaneous pleasure in the current social satisfactions, there is a deep hatred for these satisfactions that makes men willing to rush off to armies and to toy with the idea of loosing explosive bombs?

UNANIMITY

In the mixed society of coercion and nature, positive political action is always dialectically good and evil. But nature underlies and coercion is imposed. Then we must act so as to avoid the isolation of a particular issue and the freezing of the coercive foreground, but always to submit the issue to the dynamism of the common natural powers that nobody disputes. The defining property of free political action is potential unanimity, drawing on common nature and undercutting the conflict of interests. Our political action is the emergence of unanimity from natural conflict. Many conflicts are wholly *theirs* and may profitably be disregarded. In others, such as the class struggle, where there is a direct attack on obvious goods such as sustenance or time of life, the issue is clearly enough drawn and we lend all force to freedom, justice, and nature. But where there is a natural conflict, between natural forces, the free man must not subscribe to a compromise but must invent a program, for natural conflict is solved only by invention, that introduces something new into the issue. If he cannot invent, it is likely that the conflict is internal in himself and inhibits his invention; then he must withdraw to the sure ground previous to the conflict where in fact he can invent.

DIALECTICS OF POSITIVE ACTION

It is unprofitable to strive, in coercive conditions, for a relative advantage in a situation that, even if the victory is won, is coercive. Thus, to demand a just trial when the law to be executed is unjust; or to exercise civil rights within the framework of the state. To demand higher pay when the standard of living that can be bought for money is unsatisfactory. To cry for military democracy when the war is unnatural violence. This is wasting one's strength and obscuring the true issues; it results in being frozen and trapped.

On the other hand, since the strength and the continuance of any society must depend on the naturalness of its conventions, it is profitable to defend the natural conventions even with scrupulosity—though scrupulosity is most often avoided by the wise. Thus, we appeal in the court as our court and enjoy the civil powers that were liberated by our own great men; we bargain because the market place has free choices; we demand a voice not for the soldier but the man. (Yes! and the next step is for the man to say "I quit.") This is essential to show that we are not alienated from society—if not this society, what society do we have?—but on the contrary, society is alienated from itself.

The ordinary man is baffled by social dilemmas. The free man must make social inventions that liberate strength. Nothing is more disheartening than to see an honest party or press, unwilling to lend itself to bad alternatives, that does not also continually produce a stream of good natural solutions. If a man cannot in fact invent a way out, what right has such a man to be libertarian on the issue at all? His negative criticism insults and disheartens the rest. Further, it is not sufficient to proffer as a solution a state of society and of institutions which is precisely not attainable by a man's present powers of action; he must invent an action which can be performed today. But indeed, *those who draw on natural powers find it easy to be inventive—on natural issues; a man who finds himself usually constrained merely to veto all the presented alternatives is almost surely coerced by unconscious resistance to some possible solution.*

In natural ethics there is no such principle as the choice of the lesser of two evils. Such a principle is self-contradictory, for any free action or abstention must draw on natural power and cannot depend on a negation. When a social issue has come to the pass of a choice between evils (as, conscripting an army to resist a tyrant), then we know that the citizens have long neglected their welfare; the free actions that we can then invent are all attended with great suffering. They must involve withdrawing utterly from the area of guilt, a painful sacrifice—and more and more painful till all the consequences work themselves out. The lesser evil is a sign that an interest has been allowed to develop in isolation until it now threatens even our lives. *It is the isolation of the issue from its causes that restricts the choice to the lesser evil.* Those who break the spell and again draw on all their forces will find other choices.

Thus, to resist the greater evil it is usual for well-intentioned men not to embrace the lesser evil but to form a "united front" with it; in the feeblest case, such a united front is called "critical support"; in the strongest case it is based on a program of "minimum demands," presumably relevant to the causes of the crisis. Now, in principle a united front is nothing but mutual aid itself; but in practice it is often the inhibition of precisely the natural force whose exercise would overcome the evil lesser and greater both. The formula of critical support usually comes to be simple acceptance. Therefore Gandhi said that by nature he was cooperative but he could not acquiesce to conditions that made it impossible to cooperate.

The formula of the "minimum program" is in principle the same as Drawing the Line: relax coercion at this point and we will cooperate, the presumption being that then the issue is no longer isolated and our action is not necessarily evil. But in practice this often comes to freezing the situation into a new coercive compromise and inhibiting the dynamism of the next step (but drawing the line is inseparable from the dynamism of the next step). The very granting of the minimum demands proves to be the form of the new coercion—otherwise it would not have been granted; as, social legislation prepares the corporate state. But social invention is impossible when the situation is frozen. Thus, with the aim of doing justice to the untouchables, Gandhi fasted against what seemed to be the reasonable minimum program of granting them a large number of sure constituencies in the Congress ("separate electorates"), because this would freeze their status as separate from the community.

In general, right action with regard to the lesser evil and the united front is part of what can be called "aggressive non-commitment" and "limited commitment":

Obviously a man cannot act rightly with regard to bad alternatives by simply not committing himself at all, for then he is in fact supporting whichever bad alternative happens to be the stronger. But the free man can often occupy an aggressive position outside either alternative, which undercuts the situation and draws on neglected forces; so that even after the issue has been decided between the alternatives, the issue is still alive: new forces have been marshaled that challenge the decision, except that now the challenger is not a bad alternative but an inventive solution. This is the right action when the presented alternatives are frozen fast in the coercive structure. On the other hand, when the situation is somewhat fluid or confused, the free man, "cooperative by nature," can make a limited commitment to a presented alternative, if (a) he can work to clarify the issue and (b) he can, if the issue crystallizes badly, withdraw still leaving the issue in doubt. He must retain considerable freedom of action; any free action, so long as it is exercised, will generate increasing power. The aggressively noncommittal man and the man who retains freedom of action when he commits himself to a limited extent will surely be effective and exert influence among those who are coerced, inhibited, and committed against their best nature.

But best of all is to act in situations where there is a natural unanimity and no need for either withdrawal or limitation, for such action inspires a man beyond his best judgment.

POSITIVE POLITICAL ACTION

We have been speaking of positive political action. Yet at least the word "politics" is anathema in anarchist writing. "Politics" is equated with coercion by the state apparatus and as the business of the group that is both the executive committee of the economic exploiters and practices exploitation on its own. This restriction of the term is unwise. For the fact is that throughout history, especially the best ages and many of the best men have spoken of themselves as political, and politics along with art and theory has been the noble activity of free men. Let us try to define politics as a free act, therefore belonging to free societies.

Anarchist writers often speak of "politics," the coercive functions of the state and the struggle for perquisites, as degenerating in free societies to mere "administrative functions." But in the first place, we can see today that it is precisely through administrative functions that the most poisonous features of state coercion come to express themselves. Secondly, it is false that such degeneration would occur or would be desirable. *Any measure of social initiation whatever, that is not routine and that faces initial opposition and must win its way to acceptance, is political.* Precisely a free man in a free society will often initiate new policies, enter into conflict with his fellows, and coerce them; but this is natural coercion.

It is best to define politics in the ancient way, as the constitutional relations among the functioning interests in a commonwealth. Then power springs from, and is limited by, function. The more modern notion of sovereignty, abstract power, is in principle illimitable, and in fact impedes function. It is imposed by pirates who are really outside the commonwealth; it is agreed to by neurotics who do not function of themselves and therefore have no counterforce.

A property of free political action is to be *positive*, in the legal sense of imposing a new convention. Here too the anarchists, true to their false intuition, condone only negative or abstaining political action, and they are justified by the centuries of unnatural coercive conventions. But it is not the case that out of day-today economic and domestic existence there arises any great thing without the imposition of a positive, yes even aggressive, idea. Consider the Zionist movement—to take an example from our coercive society: great cities have sprung up (some of them stupidly located), gardens have bloomed in deserts, and tribes of men have been set at rifle point; and all this is the effect of a mere idea in the mind of a journalist, working on prepared potentialities.

A free positive idea could be said naturally to coerce social forces into action—this is natural politics. A coercive positive idea will invariably inhibit or destroy natural forces—this is unnatural politics.

The alternative to natural politics is not no politics but coercive politics, for men will not cease to innovate positive social action. On the contrary, just the sentiment of routine and "administrative functions" invites bad innovations. Therefore we must speak of "waging the peace," just as we say "waging the war." The sense in which a free artist can speak of "arts of peace" —who knows what manner of peace one has with one's art!

Let me quote the great sentence of Michelet: "Initiation—education—government: these are three synonymous words."

To its initiator a positive idea seems at first coercive; then he recognizes it, perhaps only by acting it out, as the expression of his deeper powers, or sometimes of forces too deep to be properly called his own at all. If it is an idea that requires social cooperation, his fellows in turn will regard it as coercive. If then, as happens most often, the idea is erroneous—it is perhaps peculiar to his own nature or situation—their free judgment will safely resist him, especially since there are other positive ideas in the field. But if indeed he has a better reason, they must perforce again be naturally coerced; they are his pupils.

Civil liberty must mean the opportunity to initiate a policy, enterprise, or idea—this was how Milton or the early bourgeois meant it. It cannot mean merely freedom from restraint, as Mill seems to say, fighting a losing battle. Such liberty will not be preserved, except in form.